D0879653

ON
EXHIBIT ®

ART LOVER'S
TRAVEL GUIDE
TO
AMERICAN
MUSEUMS
2000

ART LOVER'S TRAVEL GUIDE TO AMERICAN MUSEUMS
2000

BY JUDITH SWIRSKY

ABBEVILLE PRESS PUBLISHERS
NEW YORK LONDON PARIS

ISBN 0-7892-0532-7

First Edition

10 9 8 7 6 5 4 3 2 1

Library of Congress Cataloging-in-Publication Data available upon request.

To Leo, ever supportive in every way.

CONTENTS

ACKNOWLEDGMENTS

Even in the somewhat solitary process of writing a book, the help, counsel, and encouragement of others is essential. I owe a debt of thanks to Marjorie and Larry Zelner, who have solved numerous technical problems for us with their expertise.

In the years to come, On Exhibit promises to continue providing the art-loving traveler — and art professional — with the most factual, timely, and comprehensive guide available to the hundreds of treasure houses that preserve America's artistic heritage. I thank the thousands of art lovers and hundreds of participating museums who have enthusiastically supported our effort

W O R L D W I D E

We at Acoustiguide Worldwide are especially pleased to be associated with *On Exhibit: The Art Lover's Travel Guide* because we share an important mission – to make the world's great works of art accessible to as many people as possible. For more than 40 years visitors to nearly every major museum and cultural institution around the globe have been accompanied by Accoustiguide audio tours.

As you flip though the pages of this book, you'll notice that you can find Acoustiguide audio programs at a host of museums across the United States – they're marked with a ⌒ symbol. We're proud to provide interpretation at so many of this country's finest institutions, among them the Museum of Modern Art, the National Gallery of Art, the Solomon R. Guggenheim Museum, the Detroit Institute of Art, the Fine Arts Museums of San Francisco, The Brooklyn Museum of Art, the Toledo Museum of Art, the Virginia Museum of Fine Arts, the Nelson-Atkins Museum, the Portland Art Museum, the San Diego Museum of Art, the Museum of the Pennsylvania Academy of Fine Arts, and the Museum of Contemporary Art, Chicago.

As Always we thank Judith Swirsky for her tireless efforts in making *On Exhibit* the comprehensive guide that art lovers have come to rely upon, and Robert Abrams and Abbeville Press for making this invaluable book a reality.

Wherever your travels take you, be sure to ask for an Acoustiguide. We look forward to exploring with you.

Barbara Roberts, President and CEO
Acoustiguide Worldwide

Acoustiguide Discount Coupon on Page 399

INTRODUCTION

Celebrating its seventh successful year of annual publication, On Exhibit's *Art Lover's Travel Guide to American Museums* is the comprehensive guide to art museums nationwide. Easy to use, up to date, and completely reliable, it is the ultimate museum reference.

Written for those who travel on business or for pleasure and love to explore interesting art museums, On Exhibit's annual travel guides allow you to "know before you go" with complete assurance. With this guide in hand, you will never again miss a "little gem" of a museum or an important exhibition for lack of information.

I encourage you to join the thousands of art lovers who are loyal fans of On Exhibit. Like them, you are certain to be completely delighted with this quick, yet comprehensive overview of the America's artistic riches.

IMPORTANT INFORMATION ON
HOW TO USE THIS GUIDE

- The On Exhibit *Art Lover's Travel Guide* has been designed to be reader-friendly.

- All museums are listed alphabetically by state, and then by city within each state.

- Most permanent collection and museum facility information is expressed in easily recognized standard abbreviations. These are explained in the front of the book – and, for your convenience, on the back of the enclosed bookmark.

- NOTE THE EXCLAMATION POINT ("!"). This is the symbol used to remind you to call or check for information or any other verification.

- All museums offering group tours require some advance notice. It is suggested that arrangements be made WELL in advance of your visit. When calling be sure to check on group size requirements and fee information. A group tour phone number is only included in cases where it is different from the regular museum number.

- As a reminder, it is recommended that students and seniors always present proper I.D.'s in order to qualify for museum fee discounts wherever they are offered (age requirements for both vary!).

- Admission and/or advance ticket requirements are included in the listings for certain special exhibitions.

- Please note that exhibitions at most college and university museums are only scheduled during the academic year. Due to the constraints of space student or faculty exhibits are rarely listed.

ON EXHIBIT

- Some museums that have no exhibition listings simply did not have the information available at press time, others did not respond to our request for information, and therefore have abbreviated listings.

- Every effort has been made to check the accuracy of all museum information, as well as exhibition schedules, at the time of publication. All hours, fees, days closed, and especially exhibitions, including those not already marked as tentative, are nonetheless subject to change at any time. We strongly suggest that you call to confirm any exhibition you wish to see.

- If you find any inaccuracies, please accept our apologies — but do let us know. Finally, if we have inadvertently omitted your favorite museum, a letter to us would be most appreciated, so we can include it in the 2001 edition.

EXPLANATION OF CODES

The coding system we have developed for this guide is made up primarily of standardized, easy to recognize abbreviations. All codes are listed under their appropriate categories.

MAIN CATEGORIES

AM	American	IND	Indian
AF	African	IMPR	Impressionist
AN/GRK	Ancient Greek	JAP	Japanese
AN/R	Ancient Roman	LAT/AM	Latin American
AS	Asian	MEX	Mexican
BRIT	British	MED	Medieval
BYZ	Byzantine	NAT/AM	Native American
CH	Chinese	OC	Oceanic
CONT	Contemporary	OM	Old Masters
DU	Dutch	OR	Oriental
EGT	Egyptian	P/COL	Pre-Columbian
EU	European	P/RAPH	Pre-Raphaelite
FL	Flemish	REG	Regional
FR	French	REN	Renaissance
GER	German	RUSS	Russian
IT	Italian	SP	Spanish

MEDIUM

CER	Ceramics	PHOT	Photography
DEC/ART	Decorative Arts	POST	Posters
DRGS	Drawings	PTGS	Paintings
GR	Graphics	SCULP	Sculpture
PER/RMS	Period Rooms	W/COL	Watercolors

17

ON EXHIBIT

SUBJECT MATTER

AB	Abstract	FIG	Figurative
ANT	Antiquities	FOLK	Folk Art
ARCH	Architectural	LDSCP	Landscape
CART	Cartoon	PRIM	Primitive
EXP	Expressionist	ST/LF	Still Life
ETH	Ethnic		

REGIONS

E	East	S	South
MID/E	Middle East	W	West
N	North		

PERM/COLL   Permanent Collection

The punctuation marks used for the permanent collection codes denote the following:

The colon (":") is used after a major category to indicate sub-listings with that category. For example, "AM: ptgs, sculp" indicates that the museum has a collection of American paintings and sculpture.

The semi-colon (";") indicates that one major category is ending and another major category listing is beginning. For example, "AM: ptgs; SP: sculp; DU; AF" indicates that the museum has collections that include American paintings, Spanish sculpture, and works of Dutch and African origin.

A number added to any of the above denotes century, i.e., "EU: ptgs 19, 20" means that the collection contains European painting of the nineteenth and twentieth centuries.

MUSEUM SERVICES

!	CALL TO CONFIRM OR FOR FURTHER INFORMATION
Y	Yes
☎	Telephone Number
ⓟ	Parking
♿	Handicapped Accessibility; "yes" means facility is completely accessible
🍴	Restaurant Facilities
ADM	Admission
SUGG/CONT	Suggested Contribution — Pay What You Wish, But You Must Pay Something
VOL/CONT	Voluntary Contribution — Free Admission, Contribution Requested.
F	Free
F/DAY	Free Day
SR CIT	Senior Citizen, with I.D. (Age may vary)
GT	Group Tours
DT	Drop in Tours
MUS/SH	Museum Shop
H/B	Historic Building
S/G	Sculpture Garden
TBA	To Be Announced
TENT!	Tentatively Scheduled
ATR!	Advance Tickets Required - Call
CAT	Catalog
WT	Exhibition Will Travel - see index of traveling exhibitions
☊	Acoustiguide Tour Available

HOLIDAYS

ACAD!	Academic Holidays — Call For Information		
LEG/HOL!	Legal Holidays — Call For Information		
THGV	Thanksgiving		
MEM/DAY	Memorial Day		
LAB/DAY	Labor Day		
Mo	Monday	Fr	Friday
Tu	Tuesday	Sa	Saturday
We	Wednesday	Su	Sunday
Th	Thursday		

19

MUSEUMS AND EXHIBITIONS BY STATE

ALABAMA

BIRMINGHAM

Birmingham Museum of Art
2000 8th Ave. North, Birmingham, AL 35203
📞: 205-254-2566 or 2565 ◉ www.artsBMA.org
Open: 10-5 Tu-Sa, 12-5 Su **Closed:** Mo, 1/1, THGV, 12/25
♿ ℗ **Museum Shop** ᵀᴵ: Terrace Café
Group Tours: 205-254-2318 **Drop-In Tours**: 11:30 & 12:30 Tu-Fr; 2:00 Sa, Su **Sculpture Garden**
Permanent Collection: AM: ptgs; EU: ptgs; OR; AF; P/COL; DEC/ART; PHOT; CONT; glass; REN: Kress Coll.

The Birmingham Museum of Art, with over 18,000 works in its permanent collection, is the largest municipal museum in the Southeast. In addition to the most extensive Asian art collection in the South, the museum houses the finest collection of Wedgewood china outside of England. "Art & Soul", an 8 minute video presentation, is available to familiarize visitors with the museum. **NOT TO BE MISSED:** Multi-level outdoor Sculpture Garden featuring a waterwall designed by sculptor Elyn Zimmerman and two mosaic lined pools designed by artist Valerie Jaudon; Hitt Collection of 18th C French paintings & decorative arts; Beeson collection of Wedgewood finest outside of England); Contemporary Glass; Kress Collection of Renaissance Art.

ON EXHIBIT 2000

05/09/1999 to Spring/2000   GALORE! THE CONTINUOUS PAINTING WALL
An ongoing exhibition which features new work by contemporary abstract painters. The exhibit is installed in a second floor passageway, thus inviting viewers to navigate a pathway through the Museum's collection and these installed works, while pondering formal and creative connections between the two.

10/03/1999 to 01/16/2000   SEARCHING FOR ANCIENT EGYPT
From the display of the interior wall of a 4,300-year-old funerary chapel to an exquisite gold-covered mummy mask, this exhibition features more than 130 extraordinary objects from every major period of ancient Egypt. Many of those included have not been on public view for 30 years. *Catalog Admission Fee*

10/18/1999 to 01/08/2000   WILLIAM WEGMAN: FASHION PHOTOGRAPHS
Large scale Polaroid photographs that take inspiration from the world of haute couture featuring designer clothes on dogs. *Catalog Will Travel*

03/05/2000 to 05/21/2000   SIGN AND GESTURE: CONTEMPORARY ABSTRACT ART FROM THE HASKELL COLLECTION
Various approaches to abstraction by artists including Francis, Frankenthaler. Held, Motherwell Richter and Stella. These are continued evidence of the vitality and power of abstract art. *Catalog*

03/05/2000 to 05/21/2000   RADCLIFFE BAILEY : THE MAGIC CITY
Bailey uses a mixed media style to merge aspects of African American cultural experience with emblematic components of expressionist painting. This is one artist's interpretation of the intersecting social and cultural histories of the city. *Catalog*

06/25/2000 to 09/24/2000   JONATHAN LASKER: SELECTIVE IDENTITY, PAINTINGS FROM THE 1990'S
The first exhibition to survey the work of this inventive painter who has made a defining contribution to American abstraction. *Catalog*

07/16/2000 to 09/10/2000   MATISSE MASTERPIECES FROM THE BALTIMORE MUSEUM OF ART
35 paintings and 15 bronzes from the Cone Collection will be shown. *Catalog Admission Fee*

09/24/2000 to 12/31/2000   GIRLFRIEND: THE BARBIE SESSIONS BY DAVID LEVINTHAL
Large format color saturated Polaroid photographs which blur the boundaries between fact and fiction. This series of 40 images, portraying Barbie dressed impeccably for a variety of occasions, continues Leventhal's on-going inquest into the realm where fantasies become plausible realities. *Catalog Will Travel*

American Sport Art Museum And Archives
Affiliate Institution: U.S. Sports Academy
One Academy Dr., Daphne, AL 36526
☎: 334-626-3303   ◙ www.asama.org
Open: 10-2 Mo-Fr   **Closed:** Sa, Su, LEG/HOL, ACAD!
♿ ℗ Free   **Museum Shop**   **Group Tours**: 334-626-3303   **Drop-In Tours**: Available upon request
Permanent Collection: :ptgs, sculp, gr all on the single theme of American sports heros

One of the largest collections of sports art in the world may be found at this museum which also features works highlighting an annual sport artist of the year. Of special interest is the two-story high mural on an outside wall of the Academy entitled "A Tribute to the Human Spirit". Created by world-renowned Spanish artist Cristobal Gabarron, the work pays tribute to Jackie Robinson on the 50th anniversary of his breaking the color barrier in major league baseball. Works by former "Sport Artists of the Year " are on display daily. **NOT TO BE MISSED:** "The Pathfinder", a large sculpture of a hammerthrower by John Robinson where the weight of the ball of the hammer is equal to the rest of entire weight of the body of the figure.

Wiregrass Museum of Art
126 Museum Ave., Dothan, AL 36302-1624
☎: 334-794-3871   ◙ www.snowhill.com/~wmuseuma
Open: 10-5 Tu-Sa, 1-5 Su   **Closed:** Mo, LEG/HOL!
Sugg/Cont: **ADM: Adult:** $1.00/visitor   ♿ ℗ At the Dothan Civic Center parking lot   **Museum Shop**
Group Tours   **Historic Building** Located in former 1912 electric plant
Permanent Collection: REG

Featured on the main floor galleries of this regional visual arts museum are a variety of works that reflect the ever changing world of art with emphasis on solo exhibits showcasing important emerging artists of the south. The museum, located in the South East corner of Alabama, approximately 100 miles from Montgomery, recently renovated four galleries for the display of decorative arts, African art and works on paper. **NOT TO BE MISSED:** ARTventures, a "hands on" gallery for children, schools, & families

ON EXHIBIT 2000
11/06/1999 to 01/09/2000	**OLD MASTER DRAWINGS FROM THE SHAFFER COLLECTION**
01/15/2000 to 03/26/2000	**HEART OF THE SOUTH: PAINTINGS OF KELLY FITZPATRICK**
04/01/2000 to 04/30/2000	**ALABAMA WATERCOLOR SOCIETY 2000**
05/06/2000 to 07/01/2000	**THE SCULPTURE OF FRANK FLEMING**

Fayette Art Museum
530 Temple Ave. N., Fayette, AL 35555
☎: 205-932-8727
Open: 9-Noon & 1-4 Mo & Tu, Th & Fr, and by appointment   **Closed:** W, Sa, Su, LEG/HOL!
Vol/Cont:
♿ ℗ Free   **Museum Shop**   **Group Tours**   **Drop-In Tours**: daily during museum hours   **Historic Building**
Permanent Collection: AM: ptgs 20; FOLK

Housed in a 1930's former school house, this collection consists mostly of 3,500 works of 20th century American art. Six folk galleries, opened in 1996., **NOT TO BE MISSED:** One of the largest collections of folk art in the Southeast.

ALABAMA

Gadsden Museum of Fine Arts

2829 W. Meighan Blvd., Gadsden, AL 35904
☎: 205-546-7365
Open: 10-4 Mo-We & Fr, 10am-8pm Th, 1-5 Su   **Closed:** Sa, LEG/HOL
Vol/Cont:
♿ Ⓟ Free   **Museum Shop**
Group Tours   Drop-In Tours
Permanent Collection: EU: Impr/ptgs; CONT; DEC/ART

Historical collections and works by local and regional artists are housed in this museum.

Huntsville Museum of Art

300 Church Street South, Huntsville, AL 35801
☎: 256-535-4350 ◉ www.hsv.tis.net/hma
Open: 10-5 Tu-Sa, 1-5 Su   **Closed:** LEG/HOL!
♿ Ⓟ Paid parking in garage across the street.
Museum Shop
Group Tours   Drop-In Tours: selected S afternoons
Permanent Collection: AM: ptgs, drgs, phot, sculp, folk, dec/art, reg 18-20; EU: works on paper; OR; AF

Focusing on American paintings and graphics from the 18th through the 20th century, as well as works by regional artists, the Huntsville Museum promotes the recognition and preservation of artistic heritage in its own and other Southeastern states, and serves as the leading visual arts center in North Alabama. Major touring exhibitions are scheduled each year.

ON EXHIBIT 2000

12/12/1999 to 03/12/2000   ENCOUNTERS: JAMES PITTS
The classic and elegant photographs of this Huntsville native, now living and working in New Mexico, are included in\collections throughout the world. Pitts' superbly crafted contact prints are painstakingly created with large format cameras, utilizing hand-coated platinum and palladium metals. This show is part of the Museum's highly-regarded Encounters series of solo exhibitions that highlight the work of noted, Southern contemporary artists.

12/19/1999 to 02/27/2000   THE CIRCLE UNBROKEN: CONTINUITY AND INNOVATION IN STUDIO FURNITURE
This juried showcase features contemporary American studio furniture of the highest craftsmanship and design. See work in all media, from the traditional to avant-garde.

01/16/2000 to 03/12/2000   A WOMAN'S WORK
This exhibition, the McDonnell Douglass Education Gallery, offers a variety of media by prominent women artists. Pieces were selected from the Museum's permanent collection.

02/27/2000 to 04/02/2000   YAM2000: YOUTH ART MONTH EXHIBITION
The annual exhibition gathers the exuberant artwork of nearly 200 North Alabama students, kindergarten through Grade 12, in observance of Youth Art Month. This show also features the Visual Arts Achievement Exhibition, presenting the blue ribbon finalists from middle and high school students in Alabama's 5th Congressional District.

03/12/2000 to 04/30/2000   CROSSING BOUNDARIES: CONTEMPORARY ART QUILTS
See a presentation of ground-breaking quilts produced by 38 members of the Art Quilt Network, a national organization of contemporary quilters, whose work crosses the boundary from tradition to innovation.

Huntsville Museum of Art - continued

02/02/2000 to 07/02/2000 WITNESS AND LEGACY: CONTEMPORARY ART ABOUT THE HOLOCAUST
This dramatic, thought-provoking show features works in various media and formats, created by 22 contemporary American artists in response to the Holocaust. Artists include Holocaust survivors, their children and others.

04/08/2000 to 06/18/2000 WATERCOLOR USA HONOR SOCIETY: 7TH BIENNIAL EXHIBITION
The invitational exhibition is comprised of works by award-winning members of the Watercolor USA Honor Society. The show is organized in conjunction with the Society's national conference and annual meeting, which will be held in Huntsville in 2000.

05/07/2000 to 06/04/2000 SOUTHERN EXPOSURE; REGIONAL ART FROM THE COLLECTION
A selection of outstanding art in all media from the Museum's permanent collection will celebrate the achievements of historical and contemporary artists with strong Southern ties.

06/18/2000 to 08/20/2000 ALLURE OF THE EAST
A fascinating survey of textiles, metalwork, furniture, weaponry and pottery demonstrates the brilliant mastery of design that blossomed under the penetrating influence of Islam in the Near East. Complementing these pieces are paintings in the "Orientalist" style by European artists, who were fascinated with the culture of these lands in the 19th century.

07/09/2000 to 09/10/2000 ENCOUNTERS: SHIELA HAGLER
This show marks the debut of a compelling series of photographs by this respected Alabama photographer. The works focus on the vanishing way of life in Cuba, a tiny agricultural and cattle-farming town in west-central Alabama.

07/19/2000 to 09/03/2000 RECENT ACQUISITIONS
Enjoy a selection of new works in various media, which the Museum has acquired through gifts and purchases within the past year.

07/23/2000 to 09/03/2000 VIEWS OF THE COLLECTION
See a selection of works from the Museum's own permanent collection.

MOBILE

Mobile Museum of Art

4850 Museum Dr., Langan Parkand 300 Dauphin Street (downtown), Mobile, AL 36608
☎: 334-343-2667 ◙ www.mobilemuseumofart.com
Open: 10-5 Tu-Sa, 1-5 Su **Closed:** THGV, 12/25
& ℗ Free at main Museum **Museum Shop**
Group Tours Drop-In Tours: unguided, guides by res. **Sculpture Garden**
Permanent Collection: AM: 19; AF; OR; EU; DEC/ART; CONT/CRAGTS

Beautifully situated on a lake in the middle of Langan Park, this museum offers the visitor an overview of 2,000 years of culture represented by more than 5500 pieces in its permanent collection. **NOT TO BE MISSED:** Boehm porcelain bird collection; 20th-century decorative arts collection

ON EXHIBIT 2000

11/05/1999 to 01/09/2000 TWENTIETH CENTURY AMERICAN DRAWINGS FROM THE ARKANSAS ARTS CENTER FOUNDATION COLLECTION
102 works by 100 artists such as Milton Avery, Thomas Hart Benton, Carolyn Brady, Charles Burchfield, Robert Cottingham, John Stuart Curry, Stuart Davis, Arthur Dove, Helen Frankenthaler, Sam Francis, Philip Guston, William Glakens, Edward Hopper, Lee Krasner, Roy Lichenstein, Reginald Marsh, Georgia O'Keefe, Jackson Pollock, Charles Sheeler and Mark Toby.

01/14/2000 to 03/05/2000 WATER: A CONTEMPORARY AMERICAN VIEW
Paintings and sculpture by contemporary American artists who use water as the subject for their works of art. Catalog

03/12/2000 to 05/07/2000 FROM SHIP TO SHORE : MARINE PAINTINGS
Organized by the Butler Institute of Art An exhibition of 43 oil paintings and 25 works on paper including drawings, pastels and watercolors.

ALABAMA

Mobile Museum of Art Downtown
300 Dauphin St., Mobile, AL 36602

☎: 334-343-2667
Open: 10-5 Tu-Sa, 1-5 Su
 ♿ © Metered and lot parking available. **Museum Shop**

A renovated early 1900's hardware store is home to this downtown art museum gallery.

ON EXHIBIT 2000
01/07/2000 to 01/26/2000 FIRST NIGHT MOBILE ART WORKS

01/31/2000 to 03/26/2000 STOP ASKING/WE EXIST: 25 AFRICAN AMERICAN CRAFT ARTISTS
Over 70 works by 25 contemporary African-American artists in a variety of craft media. Organized by The Society for Contemporary Crafts, Pittsburgh, PA.

MONTGOMERY

Montgomery Museum of Fine Arts
One Museum Dr., P.O. Box 230819, Montgomery, AL 36117

☎: 334-244-5700 ■ fineartsmuseum.com
Open: 10-5 Tu-Sa, till 9 Th, Noon-5 Su **Closed:** Mo, LEG/HOL!
 ♿ © Free **Museum Shop** 🍴: Tu-Sa 11-2
Group Tours Drop-In Tours: 1 Sa, Su; 6:30 Th
Permanent Collection: AM: ptgs, gr, drgs 18-20; EU: ptgs, gr, sculp, dec/art 19; CONT/REG; BLOUNT COLLECTION OF AM ART,

Set in a picturesque, English-style park, the Museum is noted for its holdings of 19th and 20th century American Paintings in the Blount Collection, its Southern regional art, and its Old Master prints. **NOT TO BE MISSED:** "A Peaceable Kingdom with Quakers Bearing Banners" by Edward Hicks, "New York Office" by Edward Hopper, interactive gallery for children

ON EXHIBIT 2000
11/20/1999 to 01/02/2000 CELEBRATING THE CREATIVE SPIRIT: CONTEMPORARY SOUTHEASTERN FURNITURE
The works shown here emphasize the whimsical side of personal artistic expression. It is as much about aesthetics as it is about function.

11/20/1999 to 01/02/2000 MARY ELLEN DOYLE: WATERCOLORS
Like so many artists before her, she finds her inspiration in the Long Island, New York landscape. Adding texture to her work, Doyle uses handmade paper.

11/20/1999 to 01/02/2000 THE 33RD MONTGOMERY ART GUILD MUSEUM EXHIBITION
The Museum strongly supports the local arts community.

01/08/2000 to 03/05/2000 FROM SHIP TO SHORE: MARINE PAINTING FROM THE BUTLER INSTITUTE OF AMERICAN ART
Over 60 paintings, ranging from ship portraiture to ocean views, highlight the general fascination with marine culture since colonial times. Included are works by William Bradford, Alfred Thompson Bricher, James Butterworth and William Trost Richards. *Will Travel*

01/29/2000 to 03/26/2000 EDWARD HOPPER: THE WATERCOLORS
The 60 Watercolors exhibited together for the first time in 40 years were observed works composed only through the choice of vantage point. Through a masterful light touch he captured the subtle and ephemeral shifts of light and air of a particular moment and place. *Catalog*

Montgomery Museum of Fine Arts - continued

06/17/2000 to 08/13/2000   PICASSO CERAMIC EDITION FROM THE EDWARD WESTON COLLECTION
A splendid representation of the limited edition ceramics created by Picasso at the Madoura workshop between 1947 and 1971.

08/26/2000 to 10/29/2000   THROUGH THESE EYES: THE PHOTOGRAPHS OF P.. H.. Polk
Polk taught photography at Tuskegee Institute from 1928-1938 and became head of the photography department in 1933. His portraits show the inherent dignity of the subjects regardless of race or social status, while also capturing a glimpse of Southern life.

08/26/2000 to 10/29/2000   CRAFTING A JEWISH STYLE: THE ART OF THE BEZALEL ACADEMY, 1906-1996
The major workshops of the School will include textiles, ceramics, manuscript illumination, and wood and metalwork. Ranging from Jewish Ceremonial Art to secular works the objects will demonstrate the talent and skill of one of the finest design academies in the world where artists address the question of how to define Jewish art.

11/11/2000 to 01/07/2001   ARTNOW: DAVID BIERK
Bierk's paintings are created as personal homage to the works of such historical painters as Albert Bierstadt, Henri Fantin, Caravaggio and Jusepe Ribera. Viewers will experience a fusion of past and present in Bierk's works.

ALASKA

Anchorage Museum of History and Art

121 W. Seventh Avenue, Anchorage, AK 99519-6650
📞: 907-343-4326
Open: 9-6 Mo-Su mid May-mid Sept; 10-5 Tu-Sa rest of year.   **Closed:** Mo, winter, 1/1 THGV, 12/25
ADM: Adult: $5.00   **Children:** Free under 18   **Seniors:** $4.50
Museum Shop   ⊺⊦ Café
Group Tours: 907-343-6187   **Drop-In Tours:** 10, 11, 1, 2, Alaska Gallery summer
Permanent Collection: ETH

The Anchorage Museum of History and Art is dedicated to the collection, preservation, and exhibition of Alaskan ethnology, history and art.

ON EXHIBIT 2000

06/1999 to 05/2000   ANIMALS AND ART

11/07/1999 to 01/02/2000   TRASHFORMATIONS: RECYCLED MATERIALS IN CONTEMPORARY AMERICAN ART AND DESIGN
Works in various media featuring the varied and inventive use of recycled materials in American art and design. *Will Travel*

11/11/1999 to 12/05/1999   MARY VER HOEF

11/26/1999 to 01/02/2000   DOLLS AND TOYS
Antique dolls and toys from the Museum's collection will be on view in this annual holiday exhibition.

12/05/1999 to 02/27/2000   LIGHT ART: NEW ART FORMS USING LIGHT AS A MEDIUM

11/19/2000 to 02/25/2001   WRAPPED IN PRIDE
Asanate strip-woven cloth, or kente, is the most popular and best known of all African textiles. This exhibition examines the history and use of traditional kente cloth and explores the impact contemporary kente production had in other African countries and the United States.

Totem Heritage Center

Affiliate Institution: Ketchikan Museums
601 Deermount, Ketchikan, AK 99901
📞: 907-225-5900   ◙   www.city.ketchikan.ak.us
Open: 8-5 Daily (5/1-9/30); 1-5 Tu-Fr (10/1-4/30 - no adm fee)   **Closed:** 1/1, EASTER, VETERAN'S DAY, THGV, 12/25
ADM: **Adult:** $4.00   **Children:** Free under 6
♿ Ⓟ   **Museum Shop**
Group Tours: 907-225-5900   **Drop-In Tours**
Permanent Collection: ETH

The Totem Heritage Center houses a world-renowned collection of original, unrestored totem poles, recovered from abandoned Tlingit and Haida villages near Ketchikan. These poles give silent testimony to the skill and artistry of 19th century Native carvers. The Center also features changing exhibits of Northwest Coast Native arts, imterpretive panels, classes in Northwest Coast Native Art traditions, and special cultural programs throughout the year. **NOT TO BE MISSED:** A new Pole, "Honoring Those who Give" carved by Tlingit carver Nathan Jackson to commemorate the founding of the Totem Heritage Center will be dedicated in August 1999 and visitors will see it at the entrance to the Center in 2000. There are two contemporary totem poles and five house posts located outside the Center. There is a Nature Trail around the Center.

MESA

Mesa Southwest Museum
53 N. Macdonald, Mesa, AZ 85201
☎: 480-644-2230 ◉ www.ci.mesa.azus/parkspec/msm/index.html
Open: 10-5 Tu-Sa, 1-5 Su   **Closed:** Mo, LEG/HOL!
Free Day: Varies   **ADM:** **Adult:** $4.00   **Children:** $2.00 (3-12)   **Students:** $3.50   **Seniors:** $3.50
& ⓟ Street parking in front of the museum & covered parking directly behind the museum on the first level of the parking garage. Handicapped spaces located in front of the museum.   **Museum Shop**
Group Tours: 480-644-3533 or 3071   **Drop-In Tours:** Reserved in Advance
Historic Building Sirrine House (1896)
Permanent Collection: ETH; P/COL; CER

Changing exhibitions of ancient to contemporary works based on Southwestern themes are featured in this multi-faceted museum. Undergoing a major expansion that will double its size, the new building of this 20 year old museum is scheduled to open in 2000. Please note that the museum will remain open during construction. **NOT TO BE MISSED:** "Superstitious Sunrise", full color wall mural by Jim Gukwa, "Hohokam Life" by Ka Graves, a series of watercolor interpretations of Hohokam Indian life (300 BC 1450 AD) Some pieces not on exhibit during the expansion. Mesoamerican Figurine Gallery

ON EXHIBIT 2000
09/25/1999 to 01/02/2000   MEXICAN MASKS OF THE 20TH CENTURY: A LIVING TRADITION
A wide variety of masks will be featured in an exhibition designed to introduce the viewer to the traditions of mask making in Mexican culture.

01/15/2000 to 03/27/2000   ARIZONA IMAGES OF ED MELL

04/16/2000 to 06/05/2000   THE BUFFALO SOLDIER: THE AFRICAN AMERICAN SOLDIER IN THE U.S. ARMY, 1866-1912
The exhibition recreates through a series of fascinating photographs from the collection of Anthony L Powell the role of black soldiers who served in Cavalry and Infantry Regiments on the Western Frontier.

PHOENIX

The Heard Museum
2301 North Central Avenue, Phoenix, AZ 85004
☎: 602-252-8840 ◉ www.heard.org
Open: 9:30-5 daily   **Closed:** LEG/HOL!
ADM: **Adult:** $7.00   **Children:** Free under 4, 4-12 $3.00   **Seniors:** $6.00
& ⓟ Free   **Museum Shop** ⅋
Group Tours: 602-251-0230   **Drop-In Tours:** Many times daily!   **Sculpture Garden**
Permanent Collection: NAT/AM; ETH; AF; OR; OC; SO/AM

The collection of the decorative and fine arts of the Heard Museum, which spans the history of Native American Art from the pre-historic to the contemporary, is considered the most comprehensive collection of its kind in the entire country. Named after the Heards who founded the museum based on their great interest in the culture of the native people of Arizona, the museum is housed in the original structure the Heards built in 1929 adjacent to their home called Casa Blanca. PLEASE NOTE: A new branch of the museum called Heard Museum North is now open at the Boulders Resort in Scottsdale (phone 602-488-9817 for information). **NOT TO BE MISSED:** Experience the cultures of 21 Native American tribes win the interactive exhibit "We are America's First People"

ARIZONA

The Heard Museum - continued

ON EXHIBIT 2000

to 01/2000   HORSE
The influence that the Horse has on indigenous cultures from its reintroduction by the Spanish to the 1500's to today. Horse tack and other gear are also shown.

11/13/1999 to 03/19/2000   POWERFUL IMAGES: PORTRAYALS OF NATIVE AMERICA
Pop and Native American cultures blend in the contemporary works on view.

Spring 2000   REMEMBERING OUR INDIAN SCHOOL DAYS: THE BOARDING SCHOOL EXPERIENCE
The controversial practice of removing Native American children from their homes and sending them to boarding school in order to facilitate education and assimilation is reflected in drawings reflecting their recollections and writings.

04/2000 to 07/2000   GIFTS OF PRIDE AND LOVE: THE CULTURAL SIGNIFICANCE OF KIOWA AND COMANCHE LATTICE CRADLES
A poignant display of familial relationships and women's artistic expression in Native American cultures.

04/2000 to 10/2000   QAMANITTUAQ: WHERE THE RIVER WIDENS-DRAWINGS BY BAKER LAKE ARTISTS
The first major survey of drawings from the Canadian Inuit Community of Baker Lake and is the first exhibition of Inuit art work to open in Arctic.

Phoenix Art Museum

1625 N. Central Ave., Phoenix, AZ 85004-1685
✆: 602-257-1880   ◙   http://www.phxart.org/
Open: 10-5 Tu-Su, till 9pm Th & Fr   **Closed:** Mo, I/1, 7/4, THGV, 12/25
Free Day: Th   ADM: **Adult:** $7.00   **Children:** $2.00 6-18   **Students:** $5.00 full time   **Seniors:** $5.00
& ⓟ   **Museum Shop**   ᵇ⌡: Eddie's Art Museum Cafe
Group Tours: 602-257-4356   **Drop-In Tours:** 2:00 daily & 6:00 on Th; Gallery Talks 12:00 daily
Permanent Collection: AM: Western, cont; AS; EU: 18-19;CONT Lat/Am; Fashion

The new 160,000 sq ft. Phoenix Art Museum is double its former size. The classically progressive design of the Museum integrates art and architecture with the southwestern landscape, accommodating large traveling exhibitions, a collection of over 13,000 works and a growing arts audience. Visitors enjoy an audiovisual orientation theater, an interactive gallery for children, a restaurant and Museum Store. **NOT TO BE MISSED:** "Attack Gallery" for children and their families; Thorne miniature rooms of historic interiors.

ON EXHIBIT 2000

09/18/1999 to 01/02/2000   MONET: LATE PAINTINGS OF GIVERNY FROM THE MUSEE MARMITON 22 paintings on loan from the distinguished Musée Marmiton in Paris offer an overview of Monet's late works, considered by the artist to be the finest of his career. *Catalog Will Travel*

09/25/1999 to 02/13/2000   FASHIONING THE TWENTIETH CENTURY
While a basic modernist vision has, with a few exceptions, held fast in the fashion designs of the 20th century, it has undergone regular "reformulation." Design evolution and the ever-faster cycling of styles through the last century is the subject of this exhibition. Focusing on typical examples from each distinctive period and featuring the work of many of the century's most prominent designers, the exhibition examines both the larger context in which each was produced and the creative impetus that gave it appearance and form.

10/12/1999 to 01/23/2000   JOHN SALVEST: TIME ON HIS HANDS
Phoenix Art Museum has invited art critic Kim Levin to select an artist from anywhere in the United States who has a distinguished track record, but is deserving of wider recognition. Levin, president of the International Association of Art Critics and a regular contributor to The Village Voice, has chosen John Salvest of Jonesboro, Arkansas. Salvest will exhibit recent sculptures and a wall installation made from mundane, everyday objects. Employing a method of repetition, Salvest arranges common objects into rows or columns, ultimately giving them new meaning as visual poetry. Over the past decade, his materials have included road maps, inserts, newspapers, cigarettes, and business cards.

Phoenix Art Museum - continued
11/0/1999 to 01/30/2000   ARIZONA HIGHWAYS: CELEBRATING THE TRADITION
Arizona Highways is an internationally acclaimed magazine and a leader in quality landscape photography. This exhibition celebrates its 75th anniversary by featuring the work of three generations of photographers: Ansel Adams, the most renowned among American landscape photographers; David Muench, who helped define the visual iconography of the American wilderness; and Pulitzer Prize-winning Jack Dykinga, who, with his own unique vision, is among the finest of the current generation of landscape photographers.

12/18/1999 to 03/05/2000   TAOS ARTISTS AND THEIR PATRONS: 1898-1950
As the 21st century dawns, this exhibition will explore the considerable achievements of the artists who worked in Taos, New Mexico during the first half of the 20th century, the individuals and institutions that supported their economic survival, and the forces that created such an art colony. Taos Artists commemorates the founding of the Taos art colony in 1898, but, more importantly, it examines the achievements of artists while celebrating their patrons. Although European art patronage has received substantial scholarly attention, Taos Artists is the first major study to place on firm, documentary footing the economic survival techniques exploited by American artists during the first half of the century. The exhibition will present nearly 100 works of art by such Taos artists as Walter Ufer, Victor Higgins, Ernest Blumenschein, Robert Henri and John Marin. Most of the works are major oil paintings, but also included are sculpture, drawings, watercolors and prints.

01/12/2000 to 06/18/2000   ROGER SHIMOMURA: AN AMERICAN DIARY
This is an exhibition of paintings by Roger Shimomura, based upon the diaries kept by his grandmother, Toku Shimomura, while interned in Camp Minidoka, Idaho, during World War II.

04/01/2000 to 07/02/2000   PAINTING REVOLUTION: KANDINSKY, MALEVICH AND THE RUSSIAN AVANT-GARDE
Phoenix Art Museum will be the first American venue for this extraordinary collection of abstract paintings, many of which have never been exhibited outside of Russia. The exhibition features approximately 85 works by the artists who pioneered abstract art in the early 20th century, creating the first "non-objective" art - that is, art that is purely about relationships among shapes, colors, textures, and other properties of form. Wassily Kandinsky and Kasimir Malevich, both of whom are recognized worldwide for their revolutionary paintings as well as for their theoretical writings, are represented with several works. Also included are works by Pavel Filonov, Natalya Goncharova, Mikhail Larionov, Lyubov Popova, Alexander Rodchenko, V.E. Tatlin, and a number of other pioneering artists who will be entirely new to American audiences.

07/01/2000 to 11/05/2000   WESTERN AMERICAN WORKS ON PAPER (WORKING TITLE)

10/21/2000 to 11/19/2000   35TH ANNUAL COWBOY ARTISTS OF AMERICA SALE & EXHIBITION
This unique major exhibition unveils more than 100 new works, never before viewed by the public, by the members of the Cowboy Artists of America. With some of the art works selling in the six figures, the sale has become the most prestigious in the country. The sale, which takes place on October 20, is a specially-ticketed event and a major fund raiser for the Museum. Following the sale, the artworks remain on exhibition at the Museum for viewing by the public.

PRESCOTT

Phippen Museum
Affiliate Institution: Art of the American West
4701 Hwy 89 N, Prescott, AZ 86301
☏: 520-778-1385 ◙ phippenmuseum.com (not yet in service)
Open: 10-4 Mo, & We-Sa, 1-4 Su   **Closed:** Tu, 1/1, THGV, 12/25
ADM: Adult: $3.00   **Children:** Free 12 & under   **Students:** $2.99   **Seniors:** $2.00
& Ⓟ Free   **Museum Shop   Group Tours   Drop-In Tours**
Permanent Collection: PTGS, SCULP

The Phippen is dedicated to excellence in exhibitions, and presents several stellar exhibits each calendar year featuring art of the American West. **NOT TO BE MISSED:** 3 foot high bronze of Father Kino by George Phippen; Spectacular view and historic wagons in front of the museum

ARIZONA

Phippen Museum - continued

ON EXHIBIT 2000
01/08/1999 to 04/16/2000   ARIZONA HISTORY THROUGH ART: THE LAST 100 YEARS

04/22/2000 to 07/16/2000   OUR LAND, OUR PEOPLE: ARIZONA HIGHWAYS PHOTOGRAPHY LEGACY

07/22/2000 to 11/05/2000   ON LOCATION IN MALIBU: PAINTINGS BY THE CALIFORNIA ART CLUB

11/11/2000 to 12/31/2000   14TH ANNUAL ARIZONA HOLIDAY SHOW AND SALE

SCOTTSDALE

Fleischer Museum
17207 N. Perimeter Dr., Scottsdale, AZ 85255
✆: 602-585-3108   ◉ www.fleischer.org
Open: 10-4 Daily   **Closed:** LEG/HOL!
&. ℗ Free   **Museum Shop**
Group Tours   Drop-In Tours: Mo-Fr; 10-4 by Reservation Only   **Sculpture Garden**
Permanent Collection: AM/IMPR; ptgs, sculp (California School)

Located in the 261 acre Perimeter Center, the Fleischer Museum was, the first museum to feature California Impressionist works. More than 80 highly recognized artists represented in this collection painted in "plein air" from the 1880's-1940's, imbuing their landscape subject matter with the special and abundant sunlight of the region. Russian & Soviet Impressionism from the Cold War era are represented in the permanent collection as well. **NOT TO BE MISSED:** "Mount Alice at Sunset" by Franz A. Bischoff, "Mist Over Point Lobos" by Guy Rose, "Spanish Boats" by Arthur G. Rider, "In the Orchard.c.1915-1917" by Joseph Raphael.

ON EXHIBIT 2000
10/20/1999 to 05/01/2000   MASTERWORKS OF AMERICAN SCULPTURE, SELECTIONS FROM THE MEMBERS OF THE NATIONAL SCULPTURE SOCIETY, 1875-1999
This comprehensive exhibit commemorates the dawn of a new millennium. The history of United States sculpture will be documented thru architecture, national monuments, and public art.   More than 110 works will be on display featuring fifty historical and fifty contemporary members.

Scottsdale Museum of Contemporary Arts
7380 E. Second St., Scottsdale, AZ 85251
✆: 602-994-2787   ◉ www.scottsdalearts.org
Open: 10-5 Tu-Sa; till 9 Th, 12-5 Su;   **Closed:** Mo, LEG/HOL!
Free Day: Tu   **ADM: Adult:** $5.00   **Children:** Free under 15   **Students:** $3.00
&. ℗ Free   **Museum Shop**
Group Tours: 602-874 4641   **Drop-In Tours**: 1:30 Su Oct-Apr, 3:00 Su (outdoor sculp) Nov-Apr   **Sculpture Garden**
Permanent Collection: CONT; REG

Four exhibition spaces and a beautiful outdoor sculpture garden are but a part of this community oriented multi-disciplinary cultural center. The opening of a new museum called Gerard L. Cafesjian Pavilion will open a new and exciting concept with walls extending to the very limits of the city under the auspices of Scottsdale Museum of Contemporary art. **NOT TO BE MISSED:** "The Dance" a bronze sculpture (1936) by Jacques Lipchitz; "Ambient Landscape" by Janet Taylor; "Time/Light Fusion" sculpture (1990) by Dale Eldred

ON EXHIBIT 2000
08/28/1999 to 02/13/2000   SELECTIONS FROM THE SCOTTSDALE MUSEUM OF CONTEMPORARY ART PRINT COLLECTION

Scottsdale Museum of Contemporary Arts - continued
09/24/1999 to 08/15/2000   KEITH HARING
Three large scale pieces which were included in the 1997 survey of his work.

11/06/1999 to 01/23/2000   LARRY KORNEGAY
Appealing assemblages with found and original elements illustrating the building blocks of our industrial existence.

11/20/1999 to 01/30/2000   AMERICA SEEN: PEOPLE AND PLACE
Paintings, prints and photographs which explore American pictorial art from the late 20's to the 1950's. Artists include Grant Wood, Norman Rockwell, Edward Hopper.

12/17/1999 to 02/27/2000   LOOKING FORWARD LOOKING BLACK
Examples of the way African-Americans have been represented in our culture

12/17/1999 to 03/19/2000   ART AT THE END OF THE CENTURY: CONTEMPORARY ART FROM THE MILWAUKEE MUSEUM
American and European artists using words, staged images, color and unorthodox media. Included are Johns, Richter, Salle, Ahearn and Holzer.

02/11/2000 to 03/09/2000   SELECTIONS FROM THE PERMANENT COLLECTION
The collection consists of 1500 objects in all media.

02/25/2000 to 05/07/2000   BARBARA RODGERS: DREAMING OF EDEN
Using the metaphor of a garden through paintings and photography, the artist addresses the issues of the life cycle, chaos and order, landscape and abstraction

03/17/2000 to 08/26/2000   DESIGN AT THE END OF THE CENTURY
Objects which provide the key to understanding the built environment and specific cultural climate

04/07/2000 to 06/11/2000   HOWARD BEN TRE: INTERIOR/EXTERIOR
An illustration of the artist's exploration of time and space between 1984 and 1998

05/19/2000 to 08/26/2000   XIAOZE XIE: THE SILENT FLOW OF DAILY LIFE
Photography of haunting images which explore the effects on society of cultural ideology and indoctrination and of censorship and the struggle for free expression.

06/30/2000 to 08/26/2000   DO IT
Works by artists around the world through written instructions and created by local participants Included are Marina Abramovic, Yolo Ono, and Nancy Spero.

Sylvia Plotkin Judaica Museum
10460 N. 56th St., Scottsdale, AZ 85253
☎: 480-951-0323 ◙ www.TempleBethIsrael.com
Open: 10-3 Tu-Th, Noon-3 (most)Su; OPEN AFTER FRI. EVENING SERVICES **Closed:** Mo, LEG/HOL!; JEWISH HOL! JUL & AUG
Sugg/Cont: **ADM: Adult:** $2.00
  ♿ Ⓟ In front & side of building   **Museum Shop**
Group Tours: 602-443-4150   **Drop-In Tours   Sculpture Garden**
Permanent Collection: JEWISH ART AND CEREMONIALS
TUNISIAN SYNAGOGUE PERIOD ROOM

Considered to be one of the most important centers of Jewish art and culture in the Southwest, the Sylvia Plotkin Judaica Museum has artifacts spanning 5000 years of Jewish history and heritage. The Museum hosts 3 special exhibitions a year, features guest speakers, Lecture Series, and interactive programs. It is advised to call ahead for summer hours. **NOT TO BE MISSED:** Reconstructed Tunisian Synagogue. To-scale replica of a portion of the Western Wall in Jerusalem

ARIZONA

ASU Art Museum

Affiliate Institution: Arizona State University
Nelson Fine Arts Center & Mathews Center, Tempe, AZ 85287-2911
☎: 602-965-2787 ◙ http://asuam.fa.asu.edu
Open: SEPT THRU MAY: 10-9 Tu, 10-5 We-Sa, 1-5 Su; SUMMER: 10-5 Tu-Sa, 1-5 Su   **Closed:** Mo, LEG/HOL!
Vol/Cont:
&. Ⓟ Metered parking or $3.00 lot weekdays unti 7; Free Tu after 7 and weekends; physically-challenged parking in front
of Nelson Center on Mill Ave.   **Museum Shop**
Group Tours: 602-965-2787
Historic Building Award winning new building by Antoine Predock
Permanent Collection: AM: ptgs, gr; EU: gr 15-20; AM: crafts 19-20; LAT/AM: ptgs, sculp; CONT; AF; FOLK

For more than 40 years the ASU Art Museum, founded to broaden the awareness of American visual arts in
Arizona, has been a vital resource within the valley's art community. The ASU Art Museum consists of both the
Nelson Center and the Matthews Center. **NOT TO BE MISSED:** Significant ceramics collection - new
acquisitions on exhibition Jan - May; important and challenging collections and exhibitions of contemporary art.

Center for Creative Photography

Affiliate Institution: University of Arizona
Tucson, AZ 85721-0103
☎: 520-621-7968 ◙ www.ccparizona.edu/ccp.html
Open: 9-5 Mo-Fr; 12-5 Sa, Su   **Closed:** Most LEG/HOL!
Vol/Cont: **Sugg/Cont:** $2.00
&. Ⓟ Pay parking in the Visitors' Section of the Park Avenue Garage on NE corner of Speedway & Park with direct
pedestrian access under Speedway to the Center's front door.   **Museum Shop   Group Tours:** education dept

With more than 60,000 fine prints in the permanent collection, the singular focus of this museum, located on
the campus of the University of Arizona, on is on the photographic image, its history, and its documentation.
NOT TO BE MISSED : Exhibitions in the Main Gallery, the Library and the second floor Print Viewing
reception area. Wall of Ansel Adams prints in the Lobby.

Tucson Museum of Art

140 N. Main Ave., Tucson, AZ 85701
☎: 520-624-2333 ◙ www.tucsonarts.com
Open: 10-4 Mo-Sa, 12-4 Su;   **Closed:** Mo,)Mem-Lab/Day, LEG/HOL!
Free Day: Su **ADM: Adult:** $2.00 (Members F)   **Children:** Free 12 & under **Students:** $1.00   **Seniors:** $1.00
&. Ⓟ Free lot on north side of building; pay lot on east side of building free with admission; commercial underground
parking garage under city hall across street   **Museum Shop**
Group Tours: 520-696-7450   **Drop-In Tours:** We, Th 11 am Historic Block
Historic Building Located on the site of the original Presidio - 5 historic properties   **Sculpture Garden**
Permanent Collection: P/COL; AM: Western; CONT/SW; SP: colonial; MEX

Past meets present in this museum and historic home complex set in the Plaza of the Pioneers. The
contemporary museum building itself, home to more than 5,000 works in its permanent collection, is a
wonderful contrast to five of Tucson's most prominent historic homes that are all situated in an inviting
parklike setting. One, the historic 1860's Edward Nye Fish House on Maine Ave., has recently opened as the
museum's John K. Goodman Pavilion of Western Art. PLEASE NOTE: 1. Tours of the Historic Block are
given at 11am We & Th. from 10/1 through 5/1. 2. Free art talks are offered at 1:30 on Mo & Th in the Art
Education Building. **NOT TO BE MISSED:** Modern & contemporary collection

Tucson Museum of Art - continued

ON EXHIBIT 2000

11/13/1999 to 01/09/2000   MEXICAN SILVER

11/20/1999 to 01/09/2000   GOTTLIEB IN ARIZONA
Paintings and works on paper created by Adolph Gottlieb during his 8 month residency in Tucson will be featured in an exhibition that examines their effect on his later works.

11/20/1999 to 01/30/2000   MOUNTAIN OYSTER CLUB COLLECTION

01/22/2000 to 02/05/2000   READY, SET, D'ART

02/12/2000 to 04/02/2000   IMAGES: TUCSON AT THE MILLENNIUM
The result of an invitation to all Tucsonians to create a visual record through photographs of what life is like there at the close of the century

02/19/2000 to 04/12/2000   SUNLIGHT AND SHADOW: AMERICAN IMPRESSIONISM, 1885-1945
78 works by American artists who have embraced and adapted the French style of Manet.

04/15/2000 to 06/18/2000   AFFINITIES OF FORM: ARTS OF AFRICA, OCEANIA, AND THE AMERICAS FROM THE RAYMOND AND LAURA WEILGUS COLLECTION
This exceptional collection has an unusual binding element–the collectors emphasis on aesthetic excellence as the primary criteria.

04/15/2000 to 06/18/2000   TUCSON ALL STARS

04/22/2000 to 06/21/2000   FIFTY FOR FIFTY: PHOTOGRAPHS BY JOSÉ GALVEZ
Galvez has been photographing the Latino experience for 25 years. In honor of his 50th birthday 50 0f his best images have been chosen for the show.

11/2000 to 12/2000   CONTEMPORARY SOUTHWEST IMAGES XV: THE STONEWALL FOUNDATION SERIES

University of Arizona Museum of Art
Olive And Speedway, Tucson, AZ 85721-0002

📞: 520-621-7567   ◉   http://artmuseumarizonaeru/art/arthtml
Open: MID AUG-MID MAY: 9-5 Mo-Fr & Noon-4 Su; MID MAY-MID AUG: 10-3:30 Mo-Fr & Noon-4   **Closed:** Sa, LEG/HOL!, ACAD
♿ ℗ $1.00 per hour in the UA garage at the NE corner of Park and Speadway (free parking Su only).   **Museum Shop**
Group Tours   Drop-In Tours: Upon request
Permanent Collection: IT: Kress Coll. 14-19; CONT/AM: ptgs, sculp; CONT/EU: ptgs, sculp; OR: gr; CONT: gr; AM: ptgs, gr

With one of the most complete and diverse university collections, the Tucson based University of Arizona Museum of Art features Renaissance, later European and American works in addition to outstanding contemporary creations by Lipchitz, O'Keeffe and Zuñiga. **NOT TO BE MISSED:** 61 plaster models & sketches by Jacques Lipchitz; 26 panel retablo of Ciudad Rodrigo by Gallego (late 15th C); Georgia O'Keeffe's "Red Canyon"; Audrey Flack's "Marilyn"

ON EXHIBIT 2000

10/03/1999 to 08/04/2000   INTERVALS
A decade by decade survey for the new millennium

11/07/1999 to 01/02/2000   THE PRIORITY OF COLOR: BARBARA KENNEDY, A RETROSPECTIVE EXHIBITION

12/12/1999 to 01/31/2000   WOMEN OF THE BOOK: JEWISH ARTISTS, JEWISH THEMES

01/09/2000 to 02/20/2000   GEORGE EHNAT

02/06/2000 to 04/12/2000   THE PEOPLE'S CHOICE

ARKANSAS

Fort Smith Art Center
423 North Sixth St., Fort Smith, AR 72901

☎: 501-784-2787
Open: 9:30-4:30 Tu-Sa   **Closed:** Su, Mo, EASTER, 7/4, THGV, 12/21 - 1/1
ADM: Adult: $1.00
♿ ⓟ Free   **Museum Shop   Group Tours   Historic Building** Pilot House for Belle Grove Historic District
Permanent Collection: CONT/AM: ptgs, gr, sculp, dec/arts; PHOT; BOEHM PORCELAINS

Located mid-state on the western border of Oklahoma, the Fort Smith Art Center, housed in a Victorian Second Empire home, features regional and nationally recognized artists in changing monthly exhibits **NOT TO BE MISSED:** Large Boehm Porcelain Collection

ON EXHIBIT 2000
01/2000   VICTOR KOULBAK: SILVERPOINT DRAWINGS
Traveling exhibit through Arts Center

03/2000 to 03/2000   50TH ANNUAL ART COMPETITION
A national art competition.

10/2000   AMERICAN WILDLIFE EXPEDITION SERIES: SUSAN MORRISON

11/2000   24TH ANNUAL PHOTOGRAPHY COMPETITION
Open to photographers nationwide

Arkansas Arts Center
9th & Commerce, MacArthur Park, Little Rock, AR 72203

☎: 501-372-4000   ◙ www.arartscenter.org
Open: 10-5 Mo-Sa, till 8:30 Fr, Noon-5 Su   **Closed:** 12/25
Vol/Cont: $2.00
♿ ⓟ Free   **Museum Shop** ⑪
Group Tours   Historic Building The Decorative Arts Museum is housed in a 1840 Greek Revival building **Sculpture Garden**
Permanent Collection: AM: drgs 19-20; EU: drgs; AM: all media; EU: all media; OR; CONT/CRAFTS

The state's oldest and largest cultural institution, features a permanent collection of over 10,000 objects that includes a nationally recognized collection of American and European drawings, contemporary American crafts and objects of decorative art. **NOT TO BE MISSED:** "Earth", a bronze sculpture by Anita Huffington

Arts & Science Center for Southeast Arkansas
701 Main St., Pine Bluff, AR 71601

☎: 870-536-3375
Open: 8-5 Mo-Fr, 1-4 Sa, Su   **Closed:** 1/1, EASTER, 7/4, THGV, 12/24, 12/25
♿ ⓟ   **Museum Shop**
Group Tours   Drop-In Tours
Permanent Collection: EU: ptgs 19; AM: ptgs, gr 20; OM: drgs; CONT/EU: drgs, DELTA ART; REG

The Museum, whose new building opened in Sept. '94, is home to a more than 1,000 piece collection of fine art that includes one of the country's most outstanding permanent collections of African American artworks. The museum also contains a noted collection of American drawings (1900 to the present) which are always on view. **NOT TO BE MISSED:** Collection of African/American art by Tanner, Lawrence, Bearden and others; Art Deco & Art Nouveau bronzes

---

Bakersfield Museum of Art

1930 "R" St., Bakersfield, CA 93301

☎: 661-323-7219
Open: 10-4 Tu-Sa, 12-4 Su **Closed:** Mo LEG/HOL!
Free Day: 3rd Fri each month, 12-4 **ADM: Adult:** $4.00 **Children:** Free under 12 **Students:** $1.00 **Seniors:** $2.00
& ℗ Free **Museum Shop**
Group Tours
Permanent Collection: PTGS; SCULP; GR; REG

Works by California regional artists are the main focus of the collection at this museum, a facility which is looking forward to the results of an expansion project due to start in early 1999. Besides the sculptures and flowers of the museum's gardens where, with 3 days notice, box lunches can be arranged for tour groups, visitors can enjoy the 7-9 traveling exhibitions and 1 local juried exhibitions presented annually.

ON EXHIBIT 2000

11/01/1999 to 03/28/2000 GEORGIA O'KEEFFE

09/2000 to 11/2000 EDGAR PAYNE/WILLIAM WENDT

Judah L. Magnes Memorial Museum

2911 Russell St., Berkeley, CA 94705

☎: 510-549-6950 ◙ www.jfed.org/magnes/magnes.htm
Open: 10-4 Su-Th **Closed:** Fr, Sa, JEWISH & FEDERAL/HOL!
Vol/Cont: Adult: $5.00
& ℗ Free **Museum Shop**
Group Tours: 510-549-6938 (by appt.) **Drop-In Tours:** 10-4 Su, We
Historic Building 1908 Berkeley landmark building (Burke Mansion) **Sculpture Garden**
Permanent Collection: FINE ARTS; JEWISH CEREMONIAL ART, RARE BOOKS & MANUSCRIPTS; ARCHIVES OF WESTERN U.S. JEWS

Founded in 1962, the Judah L. Magnes Memorial Museum is the third largest Jewish museum in the Western Hemisphere and the first Jewish museum to be accredited by the American Association of Museums. Literally thousands of prints, drawings and paintings by nearly every Jewish artist of the past two centuries are represented in the permanent collection, which also includes ceremonial and folk pieces and textiles from antiquity to the present, from around the world. **NOT TO BE MISSED:** "The Jewish Wedding" by Trankowsky; Menorahs 16-20th C.; changing exhibitions

University of California Berkeley Art Museum & Pacific Film Archive

Affiliate Institution: University of California
2626 Bancroft Way, Berkeley, CA 94720-2250

☎: 510-642-0808 ◙ www.bampfa.berkeley.edu
Open: 11-5 We-Su, 11-9 Th **Closed:** Mo, Tu, LEG/HOL!
Free Day: Th 11-noon, 5-9 **ADM: Adult:** $6.00 **Children:** Free under 12 **Students:** $4.00, 12-18 **Seniors:** $4.00
& ℗ Parking next to the museum on Bancroft Way, on Bowditch between Bancroft and Durant, and at Berkeley Public Parking, 2420 Durant Ave. **Museum Shop** ᵗ️: Cafe Grace 11-4 Tu-S
Group Tours: 510-642-5188 **Sculpture Garden**
Permanent Collection: AM: all media 20; VISUAL ART; AS; CH: cer, ptgs; EU: Ren-20

CALIFORNIA

University of California Berkeley Art Museum & Pacific Film Archive- continued

The UC Berkeley Art Museum is the principal visual arts center for the University of California at Berkeley. Since its founding in the 1960's with a bequest of 45 Hans Hoffmans paintings, the BAM has become one of the largest university art museums in the US. International in scope, the Museum's 10,000 work collection emphasizes twentieth-century painting, sculpture, photography and conceptual art, with especially significant holdings in Asian art. **NOT TO BE MISSED:** Contemporary collection including masterpieces by Calder, Cornell, Frankenthaler, Still, Rothko, and others

ON EXHIBIT 2000

10/30/1999 to 02/20/2000   BECOMING A BODHISATTVA
Includes previously unseen folk-style scrolls depicting the Ten Buddhist Hells, early Chinese Buddhist icons and Sino-Tibetan Taras and Mandalas.

12/08/1999 to 03/19/2000   ROMA/PACIFICA: THE PHOEBE HEARST INTERNATIONAL ARCHITECTURAL COMPETITION, 1898-99
This competition was the idea of Berard Maybeck Ultimately it was John Galern Howard who was hired to carry out the 4th prize entry.

12/15/1999 to 03/19/2000   EQUAL PARTNERS: MEN AND WOMEN PRINCIPALS IN CONTEMPORARY ARCHITECTURAL PRACTICE
Collaborative projects that are the result when male and female architects team together. Fifteen firms, each represented by two projects including an airport, a theatre, office buildings, museums and even a ferry terminal. The exhibition raises questions of the dynamics and their sociological implications..

02/2000   DRAMA FROM KABUKI: THE E.F. ROSENBLATT COLLECTION
Ukiyoe prints and paintings from a recent gift to the Museum.

CLAREMONT

Montgomery Gallery

Affiliate Institution: Pomona College
Montgomery Gallery-330 N. College Way, Claremont, CA 91711-6344
☎: 909-621-8283   ◙   www.pomona.edu/montgomery
Open: 12-5 Tu-Fr   **Closed:** Mo, ACAD!, LEG/HOL!, SUMMER
♿ ℗ Free   **Museum Shop**
Group Tours
Permanent Collection: KRESS REN: ptgs; GR; DRGS, PHOT; NAT/AM: basketry, cer, beadwork

---

Important holdings include the Kress Collection of 15th- and 16th-century Italian panel paintings; over 5,000 examples of Pre-Columbian to 20th-century American Indian art and artifacts, including basketry, ceramics, and beadwork; and a large collection of American and European prints, drawings, and photographs.

ON EXHIBIT 2000

01/18/2000 to 02/20/2000   PROJECT SERIES V: LYNNE BERMAN AND KATHY CHENOWETH
A new installation based on their current project, "Condo 2000"

01/18/2000 to 04/09/2000   BARBARA BENTSH: MODELS AND METHODS

02/2000 to 03/2000   PROJECT SERIES VI DUNH Q. LE
Photographic work and a video installation in conjunction with the Asian American resource center.

Richard L. Nelson Gallery & The Fine Arts Collection, UC Davis

Affiliate Institution: Univ. of California
Davis, CA 95616
☎: 916-752-8500
Open: Noon-5 Mo-Fr, 2-5 Su **Closed:** Sa, LEG/HOL! ACAD/HOL; SUMMER!
Vol/Cont:
  ♿ ℗ On campus lots 1, 2, 5, 6 (Handicapped), & 10; $4.00 fee charged weekdays **Museum Shop Group Tours**
Permanent Collection: DRGS, GR, PTGS 19; CONT; OR; EU; AM; CER

The gallery, which has a 2,500 piece permanent collection acquired primarily through gifts donated to the institution since the 1960's, presents an ongoing series of changing exhibitions. **NOT TO BE MISSED:** "Bookhead" and other sculptures by Robert Arneson; Deborah Butterfield's "Untitled" (horse)

Downey Museum of Art

10419 Rives Ave., Downey, CA 90241
☎: 562-861-0419
Open: Noon-5 We-Su **Closed:** LEG/HOL!
Vol/Cont:
  ♿ ℗ Ample free off-street parking **Museum Shop**
Permanent Collection: REG: ptgs, sculp, gr, phot 20; CONT

With over 400 20th century and contemporary works by Southern California artists, the Downey Museum has been the primary source of art in this area for over 35 years.

Fresno Art Museum

2233 N. First St., Fresno, CA 93703
☎: 209-441-4220
Open: 10-5 Tu-Fr; Noon-5 Sa, Su **Closed:** LEG/HOL!
ADM: Adult: $2.00 **Children:** Free 15 & under **Students:** $1.00 **Seniors:** $1.00
  ♿ ℗ Free **Museum Shop** 🍴 ! Th ONLY 12-2:00
Group Tours: 209-485-4810 **Sculpture Garden**
Permanent Collection: P/COL; MEX; CONT/REG; AM: gr, sculp

In addition to a wide variety of changing exhibitions, pre-Columbian Mexican ceramic sculpture, French Post-impressionist graphics, and American sculptures from the permanent collection are always on view. **NOT TO BE MISSED:** Hans Sumpfsumpf Gallery of Mexican Art containing pre-Columbian ceramics through Diego Rivera masterpieces.

Fresno Metropolitan Museum

1555 Van Ness Ave., Fresno, CA 93721
☎: 209-441-1444 ◉ www.fresnomet.org
Open: 11-5 Tu-Su (open Mo during some exhibits!) **Closed:** Mo, LEG/HOL
Free Day: 5-8 Th **ADM: Adult:** $5.00 **Children:** Free 2 & under **Students:** $4.00 **Seniors:** $4.00
  ♿ ℗ free lot adjacent to the museum **Museum Shop** 🍴: boxed lunches available during select exhibitions
Group Tours: 209-441-1444 **Drop-In Tours:** 9-4 daily during most exhibitions **Historic Building**
Permanent Collection: AM: st/lf 17-20; EU; st/lf 17-20; EU; ptgs 16-19; PHOT (Ansel Adams)

CALIFORNIA

Fresno Metropolitan Museum - continued
Located in the historic "Fresno Bee" building, the Fresno Metropolitan Museum is the largest cultural center in the central San Joaquin Valley. PLEASE NOTE: The museum offers $1.00 admission for all ages on the first Wednesday of the month. **NOT TO BE MISSED:** Oscar & Maria Salzar collection of American & European still-life paintings 17-early 20

HANFORD

Clark Center for Japanese Art
15770 Tenth Avenue, Hanford, CA 93230
☎: 209-582=4915. ◙ www.clarkjapaneseart.org
Open: by appt weekdays, and occasional weekends   **Closed:** July, Aug, Leg/Hols!
Museum Shop   Group Tours
Permanent Collection: Buddhist Paintings; sculp, Edo Paintings, folding screens (byohu)

In 1995 the Clark Center for Japanese Art, located about 45 miles south of Fresno in the town of Hanford, was founded by Elizabeth and Willard Clark to "collect, conserve, study, and exhibit" the paintings, sculpture, and decorative arts of Japan. The rapidly growing collection is comprised of many distinguished works representing artistic activity in Japan from the 12th to the 20th century. They present several special exhibitions per year

---
IRVINE

Irvine Museum
18881 Von Karman Ave. 12th Floor, Irvine, CA 92612
☎: 949-476-2565 ◙ www.ocartsnet.org/irvinemuseum
Open: 11-5 Tu-Sa **Closed:** S, Mo, LEG/HOL!
& ℗ Free parking with validation **Museum Shop**
Group Tours: 949-476-0294 **Drop-In Tours**: 11:15 Th
Permanent Collection: California Impressionist Art 1890-1930

Opened in Jan. 1993, this museum places its emphasis on the past by promoting the preservation and display of historical California art with particular emphasis on the school of California Impressionism (1890-1930).

LA JOLLA

Museum of Contemporary Art, San Diego
700 Prospect St., La Jolla, CA 92037-4291
☎: 858-454-3541; DT 858-234-1001 ◙ www.mcasandiego.org
Open: 10-5 Tu-Sa, 12-5 Su, till 8 We (La Jolla) **Closed:** Mo, 1/1, THGV, 12/25
Free Day: 1st Tu & Su of month **ADM: Adult:** $4.00 **Children:** Free under 12 **Students:** $2.00 **Seniors:** $2.00
& ℗ 2 hour free street parking at La Jolla; validated $2.00 2 hour parking at America Plaza garage for downtown location during the week plus some metered street parking and pay lots nearby.
Museum Shop
¶: Museum Cafe (at La Jolla location) 858–454-3945
Group Tours: ex 151 **Drop-In Tours**: LJ: 2pm Sa, Su, & 6pm We
Historic Building Former Ellen Scripps Browning Home - Irving Gill Architecture **Sculpture Garden**
Permanent Collection: CONT: ptgs, sculp, drgs, gr, phot ∩

Museum of Contemporary Art, San Diego - continued

Perched on a bluff overlooking the Pacific Ocean, this 50 year old museum recently underwent extensive renovation and expansion, the results of which *New York Times* architecture critic, Paul Goldberger, describes as an "exquisite project". Under the direction of noted architectural wizard, Robert Venturi, the original landmark Scripps house, built in 1916, was given added prominence by being cleverly integrated into the design of the new building. Additional exhibition space, landscaping that accommodates outdoor sculpture, a café and an expanded bookstore are but a few of the Museum's new features. Both this and the downtown branch at 1001 Kettner Blvd. at Broadway in downtown San Diego,(phone: 858-234-1001), operate as one museum with 2 locations where contemporary art (since the 1950's) by highly regarded national and international artists as well as works by emerging new talents may be seen. PLEASE NOTE: 1. Self-guided "Inform" audio tours of the Museum's permanent collection are available to visitors free of charge. 2. Downtown admission fees: $2.00 adults, $1.00 students & seniors, children free under 12 (a 3 day pass to both museums is available for $4.00.)

ON EXHIBIT 2000

09/26/1999 to 01/09/2000   THE MUSEUM AS MUSE: ARTISTS REFLECT

The Museum as Muse: Artists Reflect is an intellectually provocative and engaging exhibition that explores modern and contemporary artists' attitudes towards the museum. The exhibition, surveys the many ways in which artists have responded to the museum as an institution – examining its concepts and functions, commenting on its nature, exploring its relationship to the art it contains, and incorporating aspects of the museum into their own art.

LAGUNA BEACH

Laguna Art Museum

307 Cliff Drive at PCH, Laguna Beach, CA 92651-9990

☎: 949-494-8971   ◙   www.lagunaartmuseum.org
Open: 11-5 Tu-Su   **Closed:** Mo
Free Day: 1st Th 5-9 PM   **ADM: Adult:** $5.00   **Children:** Free under 12   **Students:** $4,00   **Seniors:** $4.00
♿   ℗ metered and non-metered street parking   **Museum Shop**
Group Tours   Drop-In Tours: 2 PM daily   **Historic Building** oldest museum in Orange County, built in 1918
Permanent Collection: Cont & Hist California art

Laguna Art Museum is an independent, 80-year-old non profit museum with an emphasis on American Art and particularly the art of California. Temporary exhibitions change quarterly.

LANCASTER

Lancaster Museum/Art Gallery

44801 North Sierra Hwy., Lancaster, CA 93534

☎: 805-723-6250
Open: 11-4 Tu-Sa, 1-4 Su   **Closed:** LEG/HOL! & 1-2 WEEKS BEFORE OPENING OF EACH NEW EXHIBIT!
♿   ℗ Ample and free   **Museum Shop   Group Tours**
Permanent Collection: REG; PHOT

About 75 miles north of Los Angeles, in the heart of America's Aerospace Valley, is the City of Lancaster Museum, a combined history and fine art facility that serves the needs of one of the fastest growing areas in southern California. The gallery offers 8 to 9 rotating exhibitions annually.

CALIFORNIA

University Art Museum
Affiliate Institution: California State University, Long Beach
1250 Bellflower Blvd., Long Beach, CA 90840
☎: 562-985-5761 ◙ www.csulb.edu/~uam
Open: 12-8 Tu-Th, 12-5 Fr-Su **Closed:** Mo, ACAD/HOL! LEG/HOL!
ADM: **Adult:** $3.00 **Students:** $1.00
& ℗ Free **Museum Shop** **Group Tours** **Drop-In Tours:** res req **Sculpture Garden**
Permanent Collection: CONT: drgs, gr; SCULP

Walking maps are available for finding and detailing the permanent site-specific Monumental Sculpture
Collection located throughout the 322 acre campus of this outstanding university art facility. **NOT TO BE
MISSED:** Extensive collection of contemporary works on paper

Autry Museum of Western Heritage
4700 Western Heritage Way, Los Angeles, CA 90027-1462
☎: 323-667-2000 ◙ www.autry-museum.org
Open: 10-5 Tu-Su and some Mo hols **Closed:** Mo, THGV, 12/25
ADM: **Adult:** $7.50 **Children:** $3.00 (2-12) **Students:** $5.00 **Seniors:** $5.00
& ℗ Free **Museum Shop** ⑪: Golden Spur Cafe for breakfast & lunch (9am-4:30pm) **Group Tours**
Permanent Collection: FINE & FOLK ART

Fine art is but one aspect of this multi-dimensional museum that acts as a showcase for the preservation and
understanding of both the real and mythical historical legacy of the American West. **NOT TO BE MISSED:**
Los Angeles Times Children's Discovery Gallery; Spirit of Imagination

ON EXHIBIT 2000
10/16/1999 to 01/30/2000 WESTERN AMERYKANSKI: POLISH POSTER ART AND THE WESTERN
The popularity and influence of American Western films in Europe will be shown in the museum's 115 works from the Polish-produced Western film posters. Many of Poland's most popular graphic artists are shown in a show that spans from the mid 1940's to the early 90's.

**02/26/2000 to 06/11/2000 ON GOLD MOUNTAIN - CHINESE INFLUENCE ON THE DISCOVERY OF GOLD
DISCOVERY OF GOLD IN CALIFORNIA**
The Chinese have been emigrating to America since the time of the California Gold Rush. Based on a book by Lisa See, this explores four generations of a Chinese American family from 1867 to the present. Sandy Lydon, an Asian scholar believes this may well be the most important exhibit ever mounted in the US focused specifically on the history of the Chinese in America

Summer/2000 WILD WEST SHOWS (working title)

California African-American Museum
600 State Drive, Exposition Park, Los Angeles, CA 90037
☎: 213-744-7432 ◙ www.caam.ca.gov
Open: 10-5 Tu-Su **Closed:** 1/1, THGV, 12/25
& ℗ Limited ($5.00 fee) next to museum **Museum Shop**
Group Tours
Permanent Collection: BENJAMIN BANNISTER: drgs; TURENNE des PRES: ptgs; GAFTON TAYLOR BROWN: gr;
AF: masks; AF/AM: cont NOTE: The permanent collection is not on permanent display!

California African-American Museum - continued
The primary goal of this museum is the collection and preservation of art and artifacts documenting the Afro-American experience in America. Exhibitions and programs focus on contributions made to the arts and various other facets of life including a vital forum for playwrights and filmmakers. The building itself features a 13,000 square foot sculpture court through which visitors pass into a spacious building topped by a ceiling of tinted bronze glass.

Gallery 825/Los Angeles Art Association
Affiliate Institution: Los Angeles Art Association
825 N. La Cienega Blvd., Los Angeles, CA 90069
✆: 310-652-8272
Open: Noon-5 Tu-Sa **Closed:** S, Mo, LEG/HOL!
Vol/Cont:
♿ Ⓟ Free rear of building **Museum Shop Group Tours**

For over 70 years Gallery 825/Los Angeles Art Association has been exhibiting and promoting some of the most important Southern California artists on the art scene today. Solo exhibitions are presented in the newly designed Helen Wurdemann Gallery.

Getty Center
1200 Getty Center Drive, Los Angeles, CA 90049-1681
✆: 310-440-3700 ⬛ www.getty.edu
Open: 11-7 Tu-We, 11-9 Th-Fr, 10-6 Sa-Su **Closed:** Mo, LEG/HOL!
♿ Ⓟ Advance Parking reservations at the new facility are a MUST! There is a $5.00 per car charge. Call 310-440-7300.
Museum Shop 🍴 **Group Tours Drop-In Tours**: On the hour
Permanent Collection: AN/GRK; AN/R; EU: ptgs, drgs, sculp; DEC/ART; AM: phot 20; EU: phot 20; Illuminated Manuscripts

The Museum Complex, situated on one of the great public viewpoints in Los Angeles, consists of 6 buildings, designed by Richard Meier. These are joined by a series of gardens, terraces, fountains, and courtyards. An electric tram transports visitors from the parking area up the hill to the central plaza where a grand staircase welcome their arrival. The collections span the history of art and will be amplified by special exhibitions. The Museum at the Villa in Malibu will open in 2001. It will be devoted to the display, study and conservation of classical antiquities. **NOT TO BE MISSED:** "Irises" by Vincent Van Gogh, 1889; Pontormo's "Portrait of Cosimo I de Medici" c1537; "Bullfight Suerte de Varas" by Goya, 1824 (recently acquired)

ON EXHIBIT 2000

ONGOING THE GETTY KOUROS
An exhibition that examines both sides of the ongoing controversy involving the authenticity of the Getty Kouros.

06/29/2000 to 09/01/2000 FOUNDRY TO FINISH: IN THE STUDIO OF ADRIAON DE VRIES
An explanation of the lost wax casting process of bronze through the work of one of the most skillful casters ever. Dutch sculptor de Vries used 13 working models of one of his masterpieces, "The Juggling Man" (about 1616) and provides a step by step demonstration of his sculpting and casting process. X-rays and photos will be displayed. Patination is also shown with the patinas of the period and how they were achieved

10/12/1999 to 01/09/2000 ADRIAEN DE VRIES, IMPERIAL SCULPTOR
A master of composition and technique, Adriaen de Vries (Dutch, 1556-1626) was a leading European sculptor around 1600 who created both small-scale and monumental bronzes for the most discerning princely patrons of the time, including Emperor Rudolph II of Prague. About 40 bronzes, many life-size and larger, as well as numerous prints and drawings, are brought together for the first time in this international loan exhibition revealing de Vries as one of the most progressive Northern European sculptors of his day. The works are drawn from collections in the United States and Europe, including the Louvre; the Nationalmuseum, Stockholm; the Rijksmuseum, Amsterdam; and the Kunsthistorisches Museum, Vienna.

CALIFORNIA

Laband Art Gallery

Affiliate Institution: Loyola Marymount University
7900 Loyola Blvd., Los Angeles, CA 90045

☎: 310-338-2880 ◙ www.lmu.edu/colleges/cfa/art/laband
Open: 11-4 We-Fr, Noon-4 Sa **Closed:** Mo, Tu, JUN - AUG.; LEG/HOL, ACAD/HOL, RELIGIOUS/HOL
Vol/Cont:
    ⴟ **Museum Shop** ‖: The Lair (cafeteria), Lion's Den (coffee bar) **Group Tours**
Permanent Collection: FL: om; IT: om; DRGS; GR

The Laband Art Gallery usually features exhibitions relating to Latin and Native American subjects, current social and political issues, Jewish & Christian spiritual traditions, and contemporary representational art.

Los Angeles County Museum of Art

5905 Wilshire Blvd., Los Angeles, CA 90036

☎: 323-857-6000 ◙ www.lacma.org
Open: 12-8 Mo, Tu, Th; 12-9 Fr; 11-8 Sa, Su **Closed:** W, 1/1, THGV, 12/25
ADM: Adult: $7.00 **Children:** $1.00 6-17, Free under 5 **Students:** $5.00 **Seniors:** $5.00
    ⴟ ℗ Paid parking available in lot at Spaulding and Wilshire directly across the street from the entrance to the museum (FREE after 6pm). **Museum Shop** ‖: Plaza Café and Pentimento
Group Tours: 323-857-6108 **Drop-In Tours:** Frequent & varied (call for information) **Sculpture Garden**
Permanent Collection: AN/EGT: sculp, ant; AN/GRK: sculp, ant; AN/R: sculp, ant; CH: ptgs, sculp, cer; JAP: ptgs, sculp, cer; AM/ART; EU/ART; DEC/ART

The diversity and excellence of the collections of the Los Angeles Museum offer the visitor to this institution centuries of art to enjoy from ancient Roman or pre-Columbian art to modern paintings, sculpture, and photography. Recently the Museum completed the first phase of the reorganization and reinstallation of major portions of its renowned American, Islamic, South & Southeast Asian and Far Eastern galleries, allowing for the display of many works previously relegated to storage. Always striving to become more user accessible, the Museum's hours of operation have been changed to create a better "business-and-family-friendly" schedule.
NOT TO BE MISSED: George de La Tour's "Magdelene with the Smoking Flame", 1636-1638; "Under the Trees" by Cézanne.

ON EXHIBIT 2000

10/10/1999 to 01/02/2000 LEE KRASNER
Consisting of approximately sixty works of art, this exhibition — the first retrospective of the Krasner's work since 1983 — will trace the development of the work of artist Lee Krasner (1908–84), from an early self-portrait (c. 1930), continuing with her geometric abstractions of the late 1930s and early 1940s (when she became an important member of New York's vanguard) to her mature works. The exhibition will include her Little Image paintings of the late 1940s; major collages of the early 1950s; works from the Earth Green series of the late 1950s; Umber Paintings or Night Journeys of the early 1960s; and great abstractions of the late 1960s and early 1970s. It will culminate with such late works as the magisterial series Eleven Ways to See (1976–77).

10/10 1999 to 01/02/2000 GESTURES: POSTWAR AMERICAN AND EUROPEAN ABSTRACTION FROM THE PERMANENT COLLECTION
An overview of post World War II abstract expressionism in the United States and the concurrent movement of European art informel, also known as lyrical abstraction. Forty-nine paintings, prints, drawings, and sculptures from the museum's permanent collection trace the ideological and formal parallels and differences between art produced in the United States and in Western Europe from the 1940s through the 1960s.

10/17/1999 to 01/09/2000 POMPEII: LIFE IN A ROMAN TOWN
This exhibition is based on the research of a consortium of scholars focusing on the sophisticated achievements of the people of ancient Pompeii. The Italian title, "Homo Faber, Natura, scienza e tecnica nell'antica Pompei," roughly translates as "Human Ingenuity: Nature, Science, and Technology in Ancient Pompeii." Objects from the exhibition are drawn from the regional museums of the area, archaeological collections of Pompeii, Naples, Oplonti, and Herculaneum. Some of the most spectacular objects in this group of over 390 objects are the highly detailed wall frescoes from private villas. Frescoes in the exhibition depict various subjects: elaborate gardens, marketplaces in Pompeii, and mythological scenes. The wide variety of objects of daily life included in the exhibition illustrate a keen interest in the observation of nature, and a sophisticated treatment of utilitarian objects such as delicate blown glass or masterfully crafted bronze instruments and vessels.

Los Angeles County Museum of Art - continued

10/24/1999 to 01/16/2000 "GHOST IN THE SHELL": PHOTOGRAPHY AND THE HUMAN SOUL, 1850–2000
The principal metaphor of this exhibition, "ghost in the shell," is the title of a Japanese graphic novel (and animated film) by Masamune Shirow, in which a character raises the question of what constitutes the distinction between human and machine. What is the elusive quality called the human soul? Since the invention of the camera a century and a half ago, artists, scientists, and philosophers have focused this machine on human faces, hoping to reveal, document, subvert, or deny the soul's existence. The exhibition documents the history of these efforts in more than 150 photographic portraits, from silver plates to video installations.

10/24/1999 to 06/19/2000 THE FINE ART OF AFRICAN MUSICAL INSTRUMENTS
An interactive exhibition of African musical instruments. This will be the second exhibition in a new educational space designed to accommodate yearlong exhibitions that are geared towards families and children and use cutting edge museum techniques. The exhibition at will focus on individual instruments as works of fine art, emphasizing both visual and aural aesthetics. The emphasis of the exhibition is on the active participation of the visitor. Each section will combine aesthetically beautiful instruments; didactics in the form of wall panels, case labels, interactive labels; hands-on instruments; listening stations; photo murals; computer games; and videos showing instructions on playing instruments and performances of the instruments in context. The exhibition will be divided into sections according to sound production: wind instruments, stringed instruments, instruments that make sound through a vibrating membrane (example: drums), and self-sounding instruments.

10/29/1999 to 01/02/2000 THE ART OF 20TH CENTURY ZEN: PAINTINGS AND CALLIGRAPHY BY JAPANESE MASTERS
This show examines modern examples of the traditional Zen artforms of painting and calligraphy. The works contain traditional visual motifs such as enso, a circle that symbolizes perfection, as well as new themes.

01/20/2000 to 04/02/2000 DRAWN TO PAINTING: LEON KOSSOFF'S DRAWINGS AND PRINTS AFTER NICOLAS POUSSIN
The act of drawing lies at the heart of Leon Kossoff's (b. 1926) creative enterprise and remains central to his approach to art. 'I think of everything I do as a form of drawing,' he once wrote. He has made drawings over five decades, using pencil, charcoal, ink, felt-tip pen and pastel on whatever surfaces come to hand.

02/13/2000 to 04/24/2000 ROBERT HEINECKEN: PHOTOGRAPHIST, A 35-YEAR RETROSPECTIVE
Photographic innovator and conceptual artists Robert Heinecken's role in the development of advanced contemporary art practice will be explored in this thirty-five-year retrospective. The exhibition will consist of approximately 120 pieces, favoring Heinecken's work of the 1980s and 1990s. This recent work, presented in depth, will be supported by carefully selected historical pieces to show the roots of the artist's concerns as well as his formal development.

02/17/2000 to 05/14/2000 THE AGE OF PIRANESI: PRINTMAKING IN ITALY IN THE EIGHTEENTH CENTURY
This exhibition will survey the museum's collection of eighteenth-century printmaking in Italy, with a selection of about 100 etchings, engravings, and woodcuts. Piranesi was arguably the greatest printmaker of the period, and his work is the most extensively represented in the museum's collection, as the show includes 31 prints by him, plus the Prima Parte album, spanning his career from the 1740s to the 1770s. The internationalism of the eighteenth century, as exemplified by the widespread popularity of "the grand tour", also is illustrated by the number of artists who traveled extensively.

02/20/2000 to 05/072000 ROBERT THERRIEN
At the age of 50, Robert Therrien is one of the most highly respected artists working in Southern California. Known predominantly as a sculptor, over the last 25 years he has produced a unique body of work in which forms and images that recur in his sculpture have been recycled and reinterpreted with the aid of painting, drawing, and photography. This exhibition will present eight major sculptures, most done within the last five years. It will also include a group of smaller reliefs and two-dimensional works in a variety of media that will help to explicate Therrien's very personal and unusual creative process.

02/24/2000 to 04/23/2000 TWO CENTURIES OF FRENCH MASTER DRAWINGS FROM THE COLLECTION OF JEFFREY E. HORVITZ
This exhibition of French master drawings from the seventeenth and eighteenth centuries will include 100 works. Among these are characteristic drawings by the most important artists of the time: Poussin, Claude Lorrain, Watteau, Boucher and Fragonard. These familiar names are seen here within the larger context of works of great importance by their contemporaries, often once highly esteemed artists whose reputations, for whatever reasons, have been eclipsed by the more celebrated masters. Among the latter group are superb drawings by Simon Vouet (a contemporary of Poussin), Claude Gillot (Watteau's teacher), Charles Natoire (Fragonard's teacher in Rome), and Pierre Peyron, who in his time was the rival of Jacques-Louis David. Thus, this selection of 100 drawings is a rich overview of the two centuries under survey emphasizing both the innovative work of surpassingly gifted artists and the extraordinary accomplishments of artists whose reputations merit reconsideration today. There has never been a comparable exhibit of French drawings held on the West Coast.

CALIFORNIA

Los Angeles County Museum of Art - continued

03/19/2000 to 06/04/2000   PHARAOHS OF THE SUN: AKHENATEN, NEFERTITI, AND TUTANKHAMEN
Pharaohs of the Sun: Akhenaten, Nefertiti, Tutankhamen, captures the revolutionary epoch known as the Amarna Age (1353 to 1336 B.C.) when the Pharaoh Akhenaten assumed the throne of Egypt at its peak of imperial glory. One of the most important international presentations of Egyptian art and culture in recent decades.   *Will Travel*

04/13/2000 to 07/31/2000   MODERN MASTERS OF KYOTO: TRANSFORMATION OF JAPANESE PAINTING TRADITION – NIHONGA FROM THE GRIFFITH AND PATRICIA WAY COLLECTION
This exhibition will present more than 80 examples of Kyoto Nihonga (hanging scrolls, screens, and an album) by over 40 artists. The paintings, dating from the 1860s to the 1940s, demonstrate the transition and transformation that occurred in Kyoto-school painting. Featuring two exceptional artists, Tsuji Kak (1870-1931) and his pupil Tomita Keisen (1879-1936), the exhibition will include works by their predecessors, their contemporaries, and their successors. Collectively they will demonstrate the evolution of Kyoto Nihonga in the late nineteenth century and its startling diversity of visions and styles after the turn of the century. With subject matter ranging from the moon and stars, landscape, seascape, birds and flowers, and figures, the exhibition offers visually dazzling material mostly unknown in the West.

05/28/2000 to 08/14/2000   MARTIN JOHNSON HEADE
The art of Martin Johnson Heade (1819–1904) is perhaps the most varied and inventive of any nineteenth-century American painter. This definitive exhibition of some seventy of Heade's finest paintings, drawn from public and private collections across the nation. This show examines Heade as a painter of remarkable originality, the only major artist to devote equal attention to landscape, marine, and still-life subjects. Included in the exhibition are the greatest of Heade's evocative Newburyport marsh scenes, his powerful thunderstorms-at-sea subjects, scintillating small studies of flowers in vases, and an outstanding group of orchid-and-hummingbird compositions, a dramatic combination invented by Heade. In addition, the important group of sixteen hummingbird studies called "The Gems of Brazil" has been lent from the distinguished private collection of Richard Manoogian. The show concludes with a series of five of Heade's most sensuous renderings of the magnolia blossom, a subject he came to specialize in after moving to Florida in 1883.   *Will Travel*

06/04/2000 to 08/27/2000 EDWARD RUSCHA: EDITIONS 1962-1999
For more than 35 years, Edward Ruscha has been not only an influential voice in post-war American painting, but also one of contemporary art's most significant graphic artists. From his first prints and artist's books made in the early 1960s to his latest projects, Ruscha has created a body of editioned work that is uniquely American in both subject and sensibility. Including work from a host of international graphics workshops with which the artist has collaborated, the exhibition will present a broad range of material that not only shows strong connections to Ruscha's now celebrated painting, but also evidence his fascination and experimentation with a myriad of printmaking media. A key feature of the exhibition will be a presentation of Ruscha's complete book projects, a body of work that is now considered pivotal in the history of contemporary "artist's books."

06/04/2000 to 09/11/2000   DEFINING MOMENTS IN CONTEMPORARY CERAMICS: STUDIO CERAMICS FROM THE LOS ANGELES COUNTY MUSEUM OF ART, THE SMITS COLLECTION AND RELATED WORKS
Defining Moments In Contemporary Ceramics surveys the major stylistic movements in ceramic history during the last half of the 20th century, and aims to illumine the great experiences of contemporary studio ceramics through exhibiting and publishing 200 works selected from the vast holdings of the Los Angeles County Museum of Art.

06/25/2000 to 09/11/2000   THE WORK OF CHARLES AND RAY EAMES: A LEGACY OF INVENTION
The exhibition will examine for the first time the extraordinary artistic and cultural impact of Charles and Ray Eames on twentieth-century life and design worldwide. Drawn primarily from the extensive Eames holdings of the Vitra Museum and Library of Congress collections, it will include a comprehensive selection of furniture, production material, paintings and sculptures, documentation and media. It will include over 300 objects and ephemera, two multi-media presentations, and 98 minutes of footage drawn from the Eames' vast production library.

07/02/2000 to 09/25/2000   SCYTHIAN GOLD FROM THE STEPPES OF UKRAINE
This exhibition of approximately 165 works of art will comprise the finest Scythian gold objects from the Treasures of Ukraine Museum and the Archaeological Institute in Kiev. Scythian graves and burial mounds continue to yield an astonishing wealth of gold and silver objects, many of which are in the so-called animal style associated with the central Asian steppes. Other objects reflect influence from ancient Near Eastern cultures, and still other pieces are either strongly in the Greek style or exhibit an intriguing blend of Greek and animal style elements. Many of the recently excavated objects in the exhibition constitute a new chapter, even a new book, on the interrelationships of the ancient Aegean world, the ancient Near East, and the steppes that extend from north of the Black Sea as far as the Altai Republic near Mongolia.

10/2000 to 02/2001   MADE IN CALIFORNIA, 1900–2000
This landmark exhibition that will address the relationship between the arts and California's evolving image over the past century. Through an unprecedented collaboration of nine programmatic departments, the exhibition will explore how the arts have contributed to the creation and dissemination of differing images of California, taking into consideration both "booster" images of the state and other coexisting and at times competing images.

Los Angeles Municipal Art Gallery
Affiliate Institution: Barnsdall Art Park
4800 Hollywood Blvd., Los Angeles, CA 90027
☎: 213-485-4581
Open: 12:30-5 We-Su, till 8:30 Fr **Closed:** Mo, Tu, 1/1, 12/25
ADM: **Adult:** $1.50
& ℗ Free, in Park **Museum Shop** **Drop-In Tours**: house only $2.00 adult:1.00 Sr; W-S Noon, 1, 2, 3
Historic Building 1921 Frank Lloyd Wright Hollyhock House
Permanent Collection: CONT: S/Ca art

The Los Angeles Municipal Art Gallery in the Barnsdall Art Park is but one of several separate but related arts facilities. **NOT TO BE MISSED:** Frank Lloyd Wright Hollyhock House

Museum of African American Art
4005 Crenshaw Blvd., 3rd Floor, Los Angeles, CA 90008
☎: 213-294-7071
Open: 11-6 Th-Sa, Noon-5 Su **Closed:** M-W, 1/1, EASTER, THGV, 12/25
& ℗ Free **Museum Shop** **Group Tours**
Permanent Collection: AF: sculp, ptgs, gr, cer; CONT/AM; sculp, ptgs, gr; HARLEM REN ART

Located on the third floor of the Robinsons May Department Store, this museum's permanent collection is enriched by the "John Henry Series" and other works by Palmer Hayden. Due to the constraints of space these works and others are not always on view. The museum requests that you call ahead for exhibition information. **NOT TO BE MISSED:** "John Henry Series" and other works by Palmer Hayden (not always on view).

Museum of Contemporary Art, Los Angeles
250 S. Grand Ave., Los Angeles, CA 90012
☎: 213-626-6222 ◘ www.MOCA-LA.org
Open: 11-5 Tu, We, Fr-Su; 11-8 Th **Closed:** Mo, 1/1, THGV, 12/25
ADM: **Adult:** $6.00 **Children:** Free under 12 **Students:** $4.00 **Seniors:** $4.00
& ℗ For California Plaza Parking Garage (enter from Lower Grand Ave): weekday parking fee of $2.75 every 20 minutes charged before 5pm & $4.40 flat rate after 5 PM weekdays and weekends; For The Music Center Garage (enter Grand Ave. between Temple & 1st. **Museum Shop** ⑪ Cafe 8:30-4 Tu-F; 11-4:30 Sa, Su
Group Tours: 213-621-1751 **Drop-In Tours:** 12, 1 & 2 daily; 6:00 Th
Historic Building First American building commission by Arata Isozaki
Permanent Collection: CONT: all media ♫

The Museum of Contemporary Art (MOCA) is the only institution in Los Angeles devoted exclusively to art created from 1940 to the present by modern-day artists of international reputation. The museum is located in two unique spaces: MOCA at California Plaza, the first building designed by Arata Isozaki; and The Geffen Contemporary at MOCA, (152 North Central Ave., L.A., CA 90013), a former warehouse redesigned into museum space by architect Frank Gehry.

ON EXHIBIT 2000
ONGOING TIMEPIECES: SELECTED HIGHLIGHTS FROM THE PERMANENT COLLECTION MOCA at California Plaza
Designed to increase family involvement, this exhibition of permanent collection works by artists of international reputation traces the development of contemporary art.

09/26/1999 to 01/02/2000 RAYMOND PETTIBON
This first major museum presentation of Petition's' drawings and books will include some 600 drawings chosen from the thousands he has made in the last two decades. These are done in a distinctive style and broad emotional spectrum, often elegiac, ironic or disturbing. Also on view will be a selection of his unique handmade books and watercolor drawings. *Will Travel*

CALIFORNIA

Museum of Contemporary Art, Los Angeles - continued

10/17/1999 to 02/13/2000 BARBARA KRUGER
A comprehensive survey of the work o this artist in the past three decades. It will "re-picture" her career through the pictures and words that have formed an ongoing lexicon in which she has continued to articulate a variety of Media and sites to raise issues of power, sexuality and representation. *Catalog Will Travel*

10/17/1999 to 1/23/2000   THE EXPERIMENTAL EXERCISE OF FREEDOM: LYGIA CLARK,, HELIA OITICICA, GEGO, MATTHIAS GOERITZ, AND MIRA SCHEINDEL
The exhibition will examine five artists who created innovative and highly individualistic work in Latin America from the late 50's to the 70's. The work embraces Minimalist, Kineticism Environmental Art, Conceptual Art, Body Art, Performance, Concrete and Poetry and goes in some cases beyond the current conventions of art history.

12/12/1999 to 03/06/2000   THE PANZA COLLECTION
The first comprehensive presentation of the two collections of Count and Countess Guiseppe Panza di Buomo at MOCA. Key works of abstract impressionism and pop art and works in a variety of media by Los Angeles artists. *Catalog*

03/12/2000 to 08/27/2000   THE SOCIAL DOCUMENT AS PHOTOGRAPHIC TRADITION
A selection of photographs made between the 30's and the 80's by major artists working in the documentary tradition. It is organized in thematically as Picturing California, The American Scene, Social Studies, Framing Nature. 250 photographs will be featured. *Catalog*

06/11/2000 to 10/01/2000   GABRIEL OROZCO
A sculptor by self definition, he moves among various disciplines–sculpture, photography, drawing and video. *Catalog*

08/20/2000 to 11/05/2000   JOHN GUTTMAN
Black & White photographs of American popular culture taken in the late 1930's at the height of the depression.

08/20/2000 to 11/05/2000 MEDI(T)ATIONS: ADRIAN PIPER"S VIDEOS, INSTALLATIONS, PERFORMANCES, AND SOUNDWORKS
A survey of Adrian Piper's works from the past twenty-five years. The first exhibition to bring together nearly all of Piper's video and audio works.

10/1/2000 to 02/04/2001   THE ART SCHOOL AND THE AVANT-GARDE IN THE 1990'S (WORKING TITLE)
The exhibition seeks to identify artists of the late 80's and 90's and trace relationships between them and the institutions at which they were formally educated.

10/29/2000 to 02/18/2001   ON THE EDGE (WORKING TITLE)
Contemporary artists living in the Pacific Rim whose work addresses the specific topographic conditions, experiences and the landscape of this geographic and geopolitical dynamic region. *Catalog*

12/10/2000 to 04/01/2001   STAN DOUGLAS
Videos, films, photographs by the Vancouver based artist whose multi-disciplinary works address historical narratives and explore the results of mass media, particularly television and film.

UCLA/at the Armand Hammer Museum of Art and Cultural Center
10899 Wilshire Blvd., Los Angeles, CA 90024-4201
☎: 310-443-7000
Open: 11-7 Tu, We, Fr, Sa; 11-9 Th; 11-5 Su   **Closed:** Mo, 1/1, 7/4, THGV, 12/25
Free Day: TH   **ADM: Adult:** $4.50   **Children:** Free under 17   **Students:** $3.00   **Seniors:** $3.00
&. Ⓟ Museum underground paid visitor parking available at $2.75 for the first three hours with a museum stamp, $1.50 for each additional 20 minutes, and a flat $3.00 rate after 6:30 T. Parking for the disabled is available on levels P1 & P3.
Museum Shop ⑪: Courtyard Cafe
Group Tours: 310-443-7041   **Drop-In Tours**: PERM/COLL: 1:00 S; CHANGING EXHS: 1pm Tu-S
Sculpture Garden
Permanent Collection: EU: 15-19

UCLA/at the Armand Hammer Museum of Art and Cultural Center - continued
With the largest collection of works by Honore Daumier in the country (more than 10,000) plus important collections of Impressionist and Post-Impressionist art, the Armand Hammer Museum is considered a major U.S. cultural resource. Opened in 1990, the museum is now part of UCLA. It houses the collections of the Wight Art Gallery and the Grunwald Center for the Graphic Arts (one of the finest university collections of graphic arts in the country with 35,000 works dating from the Renaissance to the present). **NOT TO BE MISSED:** Five centuries of Masterworks: over 100 works by Rembrandt, van Gogh, Cassatt, Monet, and others; The UCLA Franklin D. Murphy Sculpture Garden, one of the most distinguished outdoor sculpture collections in the country featuring 70 works by Arp, Calder, Hepworth, Lachaise, Lipchitz, Matisse, Moore, Noguchi, Rodin and others.

ON EXHIBIT 2000

ONGOING   THE ARMAND HAMMER COLLECTION

ONGOING   THE ARMAND HAMMER DAUMIER AND CONTEMPORARIES COLLECTION

ONGOING   THE UCLA GRUNWALD CENTER FOR THE GRAPHIC ARTS

ONGOING   THE UCLA FRANKLIN D. MURPHY SCULPTURE GARDEN
One of the most distinguished outdoor sculpture collections in the country.

USC Fisher Gallery
Affiliate Institution: University of Southern California
823 Exposition Blvd., Los Angeles, CA 90089-0292
☎: 213-740-4561   ◉ www.usc.edu/FisherGallery
Open: Noon-5 Tu-Fr, 11-3 Sa (closed during summer)   **Closed:** Mo, LEG/HOL! SUMMER
& ℗ Visitor parking on campus for $6.00 per vehicle   **Museum Shop**   �𝍢: on USC campus
Group Tours: 213-740-5537
Permanent Collection: EU: ptgs, gr, drgs; AM: ptgs, gr, drgs; PTGS 15-20,ARMAND HAMMER COLL; ELIZABETH HOLMES FISHER COLL.

Old master paintings from the Dutch and Flemish schools, as well as significant holdings of 19th century British and French, art are two of the strengths of USC Fisher Gallery. Implemented in 1997 was a program on Saturdays entitled "Families at Fisher", which includes art tours and a variety of hands-on activities. PLEASE NOTE: The permanent collection is available to museums, scholars, students, and the public by appointment.

ON EXHIBIT 2000

08/31/1999 to 05/12/2000   MAYNARD DIXON: THE "JINKS ROOM" MURAL
A room size mural painted in 1912 by this important California artist includes old English Yuletide scenes and whimsical processions of elves, friars, fairies and the like unlike anything Dixon ever painted.

CALIFORNIA

USC Fisher Gallery - continued

11/17/1999 to 02/12/2000 WHAT IS IT? THE 'BORDER' ART OF FOUR EMERGENT AMERICAN SCULPTORS (working title)
Four artists from diverse cultural backgrounds and areas of the US but translate traditional genres into new hybrid forms. Included are Einar and James de la Torre using hot glass and found objects, also the Wonder Boxes of Steve la Ponsie whose works invoke the pop street scene of Tijuana and downtown Los Angeles as well as the rag and bone installations of Ronald Gonzalez. *Catalog*

03/01/2000 to 04/21/2000 LUIDMILA IVANOVA: BETWEEN ST PETERSBURG AND LENINGRAD A REVISIT OF RUSSIAN MODERNISM 1920s-1930s (working title)
Ivanova was active toward the end of the Russian avant-garde period and worked under Petory Vodkin, Pavel Vilanov, and Matiushin. Featured are more than 150 ink, charcoal, and watercolor drawings, as well as oil and gouache paintings on paper and canvas. *Catalog*

Watts Towers Arts Center
1727 E. 107th St., Los Angeles, CA 90002
☎: 213-847-4646
Open: Art Center: 10-4 Tu-Sa, Noon-4 Su **Closed:** Mo, LEG/HOL!
 ᬓ ℗ Visitors parking lot outside of Arts center **Museum Shop**
Permanent Collection: AF; CONT; WATTS TOWER

Fantastic lacy towers spiking into the air are the result of a 33 year effort by the late Italian immigrant visionary sculptor Simon Rodia. His imaginative use of the "found object" resulted in the creation of one of the most unusual artistic structures in the world. PLEASE NOTE: Due to earthquake damage, the towers, though viewable, are enclosed in scaffolding for repairs that are scheduled to be completed by the April 2001. **NOT TO BE MISSED:** Watts Towers "Day of the Drum Festival" and Jazz Festival (last weekend in Sept.)

MALIBU

Frederick R. Weisman Museum of Art
Affiliate Institution: Pepperdine Center for the Arts, Pepperdine University
24255 Pacific Coast Highway, Mailbu, CA 90263
☎: 310-456-4851 ◙ www.pepperdine.edu
Open: 11-5 Tu-Su **Closed:** Mo, LEG/HOL!
 ᬓ ℗ Free **Museum Shop**
Group Tours Drop-In Tours: call for specifics!
Permanent Collection: PTGS, SCULP, GR, DRGS, PHOT 20

Opened in 1992, this museum's permanent collection and exhibitions focus primarily on 19th & 20th-century art. **NOT TO BE MISSED:** Selections from the Frederick R. Weisman Art Foundation

ON EXHIBIT 2000
ONGOING   SELECTIONS FROM THE FREDERICK R. WEISMAN COLLECTIONS

01/08/2000 to 04/02/2000   JOHN REGISTER
Regarded as one of America's most distinguished realist painters he is known for quiet small Los Angeles landscapes and moving depictions of empty public spaces/ *Catalog Will Travel*

05/27/2000 to 08/2000   VICTOR RAPHAEL: ENVISIONING SPACE
Using computerized digital imagery, Raphael makes art that explores the way we see and imagine space.

05/27/2000 to 08/2000   TIBOR JANKAY: CELEBRATING THE HUMAN SPIRIT
Jankay's art depicts people enjoying the simple joys of life. A holocaust survivor, this surveys the range of his talents and his love of life.

Monterey Museum of Art
559 Pacific St.   Location 2 -720 Via Miranda, Monterey, CA 93940
☎: 831-372-5477 Loc. 2 831-372-3689   ◙ www.montereyart.org
Open: 11-5 We-Sa, 1-4 Su, till 8pm 3rd Th of the month   **Closed:** Mo, Tu, LEG/HOL
Free Day: 1st Su of month   **ADM**: **Adult:** $3.00   **Children:** Free under 12
& ℗ Street parking and paid lots nearby to main museum   **Museum Shop**
Drop-In Tours: 2, Su; 1, Sa & Su for La Mirada   **Historic Building**
Permanent Collection: REG/ART; AS; PACIFIC RIM; FOLK; ETH; GR; PHOT

With a focus on its ever growing collection of California regional art, the Monterey Museum has added a modern addition to its original building, La Mirada, the adobe portion of which dates back to the late 1700's when California was still under Mexican rule. PLEASE NOTE: The admission fee for La Mirada, located at 720 Via Miranda, is $3.00.   **NOT TO BE MISSED:** Painting and etching collection of works by Armin Hansen

ON EXHIBIT 2000
ONGOING   BEHIND THE MASK: THE TEXTURES, SHAPES AND COLORS OF FOLK ART

ONGOING   SELECTIONS FROM THE RALPH K. DAVIES WESTERN COLLECTION

Hearst Art Gallery
Affiliate Institution: St. Mary's College
Box 5110, Moraga, CA 94575
☎: 510-631-4379   ◙ http://gaelnet.stmarys-ca.edu/gallery org
Open: 11-4:30 We-Su   **Closed:** Mo, TU, LEG/HOL!
Vol/Cont: **ADM**: **Adult:** $1.00
& ℗ Free   **Museum Shop**   ᵀᴵ: Café   **Group Tours:** 510-631-4069 (EXT 925)
Permanent Collection: AM: Calif. Ldscp ptgs 19-20; IT: Med/sculp; EU: gr; AN/CER; CHRISTIAN RELIGIOUS ART 15-20

Contra Costa County, not far from the Bay Area of San Francisco, is home to the Hearst Art Gallery, Located on the grounds of St. Mary's College, one of its most outstanding collections consists of many cultures and centuries. PLEASE NOTE: The museum is closed between exhibitions. **NOT TO BE MISSED:** 150 paintings by William Keith (1838 - 1911), noted California landscape painter

ON EXHIBIT 2000
01/12/2000 to 03/05/2000   TALKING WALLS DIALOGUE: INGRID AND PLATO, INTERACTIVE STILL LIVES, KNIT ONE SWIM TWO
Interactive installations by Ingrid Bachmann which explore the relationship between today's advancing technologies and the traditional sensory and intellectual richness of painting and other visual art practices.

Orange County Museum of Art, Newport Beach
850 San Clemente Dr., Newport Beach, CA 92660
☎: 949-759-1122   ◙ www.ocma.art
Open: 11-5 Tu-Su   **Closed:** Mo, 1/1, THGV, 12/25, 7/4, EASTER
ADM: **Adult:** $5.00   **Children:** Free under 16   **Students:** $4.00   **Seniors:** $4.00
& ℗ Free   **Museum Shop**   ᵀᴵ: 11:00-3:00 Tu-Fr
Group Tours: 949-759-1122, ext 204   **Drop-In Tours**: 1:00 Tu-Su,   **Sculpture Garden**
Permanent Collection: REG: Post War Ca. art

CALIFORNIA

Orange County Museum of Art, Newport Beach - continued

With an emphasis on historical and contemporary art, the Orange County Museum of Art, with its late 19th and 20th century collection of California art, is dedicated to the enrichment of cultural life of the Southern California community through a comprehensive visual arts program that includes a nonstop array of changing exhibitions and stimulating education programs. Additional exhibitions are on view at the Museum's South Coast Plaza Gallery, 3333 Bristol Street in Costa Mesa (open free of charge, 10-9 Mo-Fr, 10-7 Sa & 11-6:30 Su)

ON EXHIBIT 2000
07/03/1999 to 01/03/2000   MICHAEL BREWSTER

OAKLAND

Oakland Museum of California
1000 Oak St, Oakland, CA 94607-4892

\: 518-238-2200 or 888-625-6873   ◙   www.museumca.org
Open: 10-5 We-Su; 12-7 Su; 10-9 first Fr   **Closed:** Mo Tu, 1/1, 7/4, THGV, 12/25
Free Day: Second Su   **ADM: Adult:** $6.00   **Children:** Free 5 & under   **Students:** $4.00, 6-17   **Seniors:** $4,00
&   ℗ Entrance on Oak & 12th St. small fee charged   **Museum Shop** ||
Group Tours: 510-238-3514   **Drop-In Tours**: weekday afternoons on request; 12:30 weekends
Historic Building Arch by Kevin Roche   **Sculpture Garden**
Permanent Collection: REG/ART; PTGS; SCULP; GR; DEC/ART

The art gallery of the multi-purpose Oakland Museum of California features works by important regional artists that document the visual history and heritage of the state. Of special note is the Kevin Roche - John Dinkaloo designed building itself, a prime example of progressive museum architecture complete with terraced gardens. **NOT TO BE MISSED:** California art; Newly installed "On-line Museum" database for access to extensive information on the Museum's art, history and science collections (open for public use 1:00-4:30 T).

ON EXHIBIT 2000
01/23/1999 to 01/09/2000   CALIFORNIA UNDERGROUND: OUR CAVES AND SUBTERRANEAN HABITATS
A family oriented exhibition exploring the types of caves located in California Cave Photography, a complex form involving collaborative effort will be explained and represented by some of the world's most famous cave photographers

09/11/1999 to 01/30/2000   AMAZING BIKES: 2 CENTURIES ON WHEELS
The history, artful design and social and economic history of bicycles from the earliest pedal-less "running machines" to California's "mountain bike" of today. 60 examples dating from 1819 to present day.

10/14/1999 to 03/25/2000   MAIDU PAINTINGS BY DAL CASTRO: FROM THE AESSECHLIMAN COLLECTION OF THE OAKLAND MUSEUM OF CALIFORNIA
Castro's highly respected self taught Native American artist from Northern California depict Maidu creation myths, animal legends, ceremonies, historical events and portraits of tribal elders and ancestors. *Catalog Will Travel*

11/06/1999 to 03/12/2000   MEANING AND MESSAGE: CONTEMPORARY ART FROM THE MUSEUM COLLECTION
The exhibition showcasing the museum's holdings of contemporary design, often the most challenging for the visitor to understand. Northern California artists who have taken non-traditional approaches to their paintings, mixed media sculptures, photographs and wall installations. Included are works by Jonathan Borofsky, Bruce Conner, Terry Fox, David Ireland, Sono Osato, Marisa Hernandez and Baocchi Zhang.

12/15/1999 to 07/23/2000   CRAZY QUILTS

03/04/2000 to 07/23/2000   WOMEN OF TASTE: A COLLABORATION CELEBRATING QUILT ARTISTS AND CHEFS

50

Oakland Museum of California - continued

04/01/2000 to 06/25/2000   TREASURES OF THE TAR PITS

05/01/2000 to 09/30/2000   THE PHOTOREALISM OF ROBERT BECHTLE

09/09/2000 to 01/21/2001   PHOTOGRAPHY IN CALIFORNIA : GOLD RUSH TO MILLENNIUM *Catalog Will Travel*

09/30/2000 to 01/28/2001   CALIFORNIA SPECIES: BIOLOGICAL ART AND ILLUSTRATION

10/14/2000 to 11/26/2000   DAYS OF THE DEAD: (tentative title)

11/13/2000 to 05/13/2001   AREQUIPA POTTERY (tentative title)

OXNARD

Carnegie Art Museum

424 S. C St., Oxnard, CA 93030

☎: 805-385-8157
Open: 10-5 Th-Sa, 1-5 Su (Museum closed between exhibits)   **Closed:** MEM/DAY, LAB/DAY, THGV, 12/25
Sugg/Cont: ADM: **Adult:** $3.00   **Children:** Free under 6   **Students:** $2.00   **Seniors:** $2.00
  Free parking in the lot next to the museum   **Museum Shop**
Group Tours   **Historic Building**
Permanent Collection: CONT/REG; EASTWOOD COLL.

Originally built in 1906 in the neo-classic style, the Carnegie, located on the coast just south of Ventura, served as a library until 1980. Listed NRHP **NOT TO BE MISSED:** Collection of art focusing on California painters from the 1920's to the present.

ON EXHIBIT 2000

ONGOING   8-10 works from the Museum's permanent collection of 20th century California art

---

PALM SPRINGS

Palm Springs Desert Museum

101 Museum Drive, Palm Springs, CA 92262

☎: 760-325-7186   ◼ www.psmuseum.org
Open: 10-5 Tu-Sa, Noon-5 Su   **Closed:** Mo, LEG/HOL!
ADM: **Adult:** $7.50   **Children:** Free 5 & under   **Students:** $3,50   **Seniors:** $6.50
  Free parking in the north and south Museum lots, both with handicap parking; daily pay parking (free of charge in the evening) in the shopping center lot across the street from the museum.
Museum Shop   ⛾: Toor Gallery Cafe open 11-3 Tu-Sa & 12-3 Su
Group Tours   Drop-In Tours: 2 Tu-Su (Nov-May)
Historic Building Architectural landmark   **Sculpture Garden**
Permanent Collection: CONT/REG

Contemporary American art with special emphasis on the art of California and other Western states is the main focus of the 4,000 piece fine art and 2000 object Native American collection of the Palm Springs Desert Museum. The museum, housed in a splendid modern structure made of materials that blend harmoniously with the surrounding landscape, recently added 25,000 square feet of gallery space with the opening of the Steve Chase Art Wing and Education Center. **NOT TO BE MISSED:** William Holden and George Monntgomery Collections and Leo S. Singer Miniature Room Collection;

CALIFORNIA

Palm Springs Desert Museum - continued
ON EXHIBIT 2000
03/17/1999 to 01/23/2000   THE ROADRUNNER
Why does the Roadrunner run, rather than fly? The exhibition investigates this. *Catalog*

12/15/1999 to 03/12/2000   HOWARD BEN TRE: INTERIOR/EXTERIOR
The glass artist work works on paper, maquettes and photographs explore his concern with the poetics of time and space. The exhibition contains architectonic references such as "Cast Forms" and "Structures and Columns". *Catalog Will Travel*

02/16/2000 to 07/16/2000   IN SEARCH OF EL DORADO: SALTON SEE
California's largest inland body of water has received more publicity than any other. The evolution of the decades and loss of dreams is recorded here in a collection of black and white images.

03/29/2000 to 08/28/2000   THE AMERICAN LANDSCAPE: MERRILL MAHAFFEY AND KAREN KITCHEL
These two artists reveal different approaches to the American landscape. Mahaffey's monumental landscapes derive from 19th C. painting. Kitchel presents an intensely detailed and focused view of the western landscape.

09/02/2000 to 12/31/2000   DUANE HANSON: VIRTUAL REALITY
30 life size figurative sculptures created between 1970s and 1996. These portray American narratives and social types. These are shown with a brutal honesty that makes the viewer return for another look. *Catalog Will Travel*

PALO ALTO

Palo Alto Art Center
1313 Newell Rd., Palo Alto, CA 94303
✆: 650-329-2366   ◙   www.city.palo-alto.ca.us/palo/city/artsculture
Open: 10-5 Tu-Sa, 7-9 Th, 1-5 Su   **Closed:** Mo, 1/1, 7/4, 12/25
&   ℗   **Museum Shop**
Group Tours: 650-329-2370   **Drop-In Tours**: call for information
Sculpture Garden
Permanent Collection: CONT/ART; HIST/ART

Located in a building that served as the town hall from the 1950's to 1971, this active community art center's mission is to present the best contemporary fine art, craft, design, special exhibitions, and new art forms.

PASADENA

Norton Simon Museum
411 W. Colorado Blvd., Pasadena, CA 91105
✆: 626-449-6840   ◙   www.nortonsimon.org
Open: Noon-6 Th-Su   **Closed:** M-W, 1/1 THGV, 12/25
ADM: Adult: $4.00   **Children:** Free under 12   **Students:** $2.00   **Seniors:** $2.00
&   ℗ Free   **Museum Shop**
Group Tours: ex 245   **Sculpture Garden**
Permanent Collection: EU: ptgs 15-20; sculp 19-20; IND: sculp; OR: sculp; EU/ART 20; AM/ART 20   ∩

Thirty galleries with 1,000 works from the permanent collection that are always on display plus a beautiful sculpture garden make the internationally known Norton Simon Museum home to one of the most remarkable and renowned collections of art in the world. The seven centuries of European art on view from the collection contain remarkable examples of work by Old Master, Impressionist, and important modern 20th century artists. **NOT TO BE MISSED:** IMP & POST/IMP Collection including a unique set of 71 original master bronzes by Degas

52

Pacific Asia Museum
46 N. Los Robles Ave., Pasadena, CA 91101
☎: 626-449-2742   ◙ www.westmuse.org/Pacasiamuseum
Open: 10-5 We-Su   **Closed:** Mo, Tu, 1/1, MEM/DAY, 7/4, THGV, 12/25, 12/31
ADM: Adult: $5.00   **Children:** Free under 12   **Students:** $3.00   **Seniors:** $3.00
& ℗ Free parking at the Pasadena Mall southwest of the museum; $3.00 fee at lot north of museum   **Museum Shop**
Group Tours: 626-449-2742   **Drop-In Tours**
Historic Building California State Historical Landmark, National Register of Historic Places   **Sculpture Garden**
Permanent Collection: AS: cer, sculp; CH: cer, sculp; OR/FOLK; OR/ETH; OR/PHOT

The Pacific Asia Museum, which celebrated its 25th anniversary in '96, is the only institution in Southern California devoted exclusively to the arts of Asia. The collection, housed in the gorgeous Chinese Imperial Palace style Nicholson Treasure House built in 1925, features one of only two authentic Chinese style courtyard gardens in the U.S. open to the public. **NOT TO BE MISSED:** Chinese courtyard garden, Carved Jade, Ceramics, Japanese paintings

ON EXHIBIT 2000
12/15/1999 to 04/15/2000   CULTURAL PORTRAITS OF INDIA

01/22/2000 to 03/05/2000   OUTSTANDING STUDENTS OF BASHIR AHMAD (PAKISTAN MINIATURE PAINTING)

03/11/2000 to 04/23/2000   DAPHNE GILLEN (ASIAN THEMED SCULPTURE)

04/29/2000 to 06/11/2000   JULIE SMITH (JAPANESE KIMONO FABRICS)

05/2000 to 08/2000   MADE IN CALIFORNIA: CONTEMPORARY ASIAN AMERICAN ARTISTS BASED IN CALIFORNIA

08/05/2000 to 09/17/2000   LILY QUON (CHINESE PAINTING)

09/23/2000 to 11/12/2000   JOAN JUE-YEN (CHINA)

10/2000 to 03/2000   CHINESE CARPETS FROM SOUTHERN CALIFORNIA COLLECTIONS

11/18/2000 to 01/07/2001   NOBUYO OKUDA (JAPANESE SCULPTURE)

PENN VALLEY

Museum of Ancient & Modern Art
11392 Pleasant Valley Rd., Penn Valley, CA 95946
☎: 916-432-3080
Open: 10-5 Mo-Sa   **Closed:** 1/1, EASTER, 7/4, LAB/DAY, THGV, 12/25
& ℗ Free and plentiful   **Museum Shop**
Group Tours   Drop-In Tours: Upon request if available
Permanent Collection: AN/GRK; AN/R; ETRUSCAN; GR; CONT; DU; FR; GER; CONT/AM; DEC/ART; PHOT

Although the permanent collection has been assembled in little more than a 20 year period, the scope and extent of its holdings is truly mind-boggling. In addition to the outstanding collection of ancient Western Asiatic artworks, the museum features a group of historical art books containing woodcuts, etchings and engravings printed as early as 1529, a wonderful assemblage of African masks and sculptures from over 20 different tribes, and a superb group of Rembrandt etchings and other European masterpieces. The museum is located approximately 50 miles north east of Sacramento. **NOT TO BE MISSED:** One of the largest collections of 18th Dynasty Egypt in the U.S.; Theodora Van Runkel Collection of Ancient Gold; Hall of Miniatures; the TIME MACHINE

CALIFORNIA

Riverside Art Museum

3425 Mission Inn Ave., Riverside, CA 92501

☎: 909-684-7111
Open: 10-4 Mo-Sa **Closed:** S, Last 2 Weeks Aug; LEG/HOL!
Sugg/Cont: **ADM:** **Adult:** $2.00
&. ℗ Limited free parking at museum; metered street parking
Museum Shop ⚐: Open weekdays
Group Tours Drop-In Tours: daily upon request
Historic Building 1929 building designed by Julia Morgan, architect of Hearst Castle
Permanent Collection: PTGS, SCULP, GR

Julia Morgan, the architect of the Hearst Castle, also designed this handsome and completely updated museum building. Listed on the NRHP, the museum is located in the Los Angeles and Palm Springs area. Aside from its professionally curated exhibitions, the museum displays the work of area students during the month of May.

ON EXHIBIT 2000

01/2000 to 03/2000   IT'S ABOUT TIME

UCR/California Museum of Photography

Affiliate Institution: Univ. of California, Riverside
3824 Main St., Riverside, CA 92521

☎: 909-784-FOTO ◙ www.cmp.ucr.edu
Open: 11-5 Tu-Su **Closed:** Mo, 1/1, THGV, 12/25
Free Day: We **ADM:** **Adult:** $2.00 **Children:** Free under 12 **Students:** $1.00 **Seniors:** $1.00
&. ℗ Street parking and several commercial lots and garages nearby. **Museum Shop**
Group Tours: 909-787-4787 **Drop-In Tours:** 1, 3 Sa
Historic Building former Kress Dimestore, Art Deco
Permanent Collection: PHOT 19-20; CAMERA COLLECTION

Converted from a 1930's Kress dimestore into an award winning contemporary space, this is one of the finest photographic museums in the country. In addition to a vast number of photographic prints the museum features a 10,000 piece collection of photographic apparatus, an internet gallery, a community media lab, and digital studio. **NOT TO BE MISSED:** Junior League of Riverside Family Interactive Gallery; Internet Gallery, Permanent Collections room.

Crocker Art Museum

216 O St., Sacramento, CA 95814

☎: 916-264-5423 ◙ www.sacto.org/crocker
Open: 10-5 Tu-Su, till 9 Th **Closed:** Mo, 1/4, THGV 12/25
ADM: **Adult:** $4.50 **Children:** $2.00 (7-17) **Students:** $4.50 **Seniors:** $4.50
&. ℗ On-site metered parking **Museum Shop**
Group Tours: 916-264-5537 **Drop-In Tours:** 10-1 We-Fr, 5-8 Th, 12-4 Sa, 12-3 Su, on the hour
Historic Building Over 120 years old
Permanent Collection: PTGS: REN-20; OM/DRGS 15-20; CONT; OR; SCULP

Crocker Art Museum - continued

This inviting Victorian Italianate mansion, the oldest public art museum in the West, was built in the 1870's by Judge E. B. Crocker. It is filled with his collection of more than 700 European and American paintings displayed throughout the ballroom and other areas of the original building. Contemporary works by Northern California artists are on view in the light-filled, modern wing whose innovative facade is a re-creation of the Crocker home. Of special interest are two paintings, created by Charles Christian Nahl, that were commissioned for the spaces they still occupy. Both "Fandango" and "Sunday Morning in the Mines" are in their original frames (designed by I. Magnin of department store fame) and are so elaborate that one actually includes a high relief depiction of a pan of gold dust. **NOT TO BE MISSED:** Early California painting collection

ON EXHIBIT 2000

ONGOING   THE NEW EUROPEAN GALLERIES
A reinstallation of 15th to 19th century European paintings, sculpture and decorative arts that document the history of European art as it evolved over a 400-year period.

01/15/2000 to 03/21/2000   TREASURES OF THE STATE LIBRARY

SAN DIEGO

Mingei International Museum

1439 El Prado Balboa Park - Plaza de Panama, San Diego, CA 92122
☎: 619-239-0003   ◙   www.mingei.org
Open: 10-4 Tu-Su   **Closed:** Mo, LEG/HOL!
Free Day: 3rd Tu of each month   **ADM: Adult:** $5.00   **Children:** $2.00 (6-17)   **Students:** $2.00   **Seniors:** $5.00
& ℗ Parking a short distance from the museum in the Balboa Park lots   **Museum Shop**
Group Tours   Drop-In Tours: by appt
Permanent Collection: FOLK: Jap, India, Af, & over 80 other countries; international doll coll.   ◠

In Aug. 1996, this museum, dedicated to furthering the understanding of world folk art, moved its superb collection into a new 41,000 square foot facility on the Balboa Park Plaza which is also close to the site of San Diego Museum of Art, the Timken Museum of Art, and numerous other art related institutions. It is interesting to note that Mingei, the name of this museum, (founded in 1974 to further the understanding of arts of people from all cultures), is a combination of the Japanese words for people (min) and art (gei).

ON EXHIBIT 2000

06/06/1999 to 05/30/2000   ARTES DE MEXICO
This colorful delightful exhibition gives the opportunity for people to see the finest works representing living traditions in all media.

08/28/1999 to 01/2000   ARROWS OF THE SPIRIT-NORTH AMERICAN INDIAN ADORNMENT FROM PREHISTORY TO THE PRESENT
The relationship of great historical works to designs of contemporary adornment are shown here.

03/2000 to 08/2000   ETERNAL CROSSROADS-5000 YEARS OF GEORGIAN CULTURE   ◠

Museum of Photographic Arts

1649 El Prado, Balboa Park, San Diego, CA 92101
☎: 619-238-7559   ◙   www.mopa.org
Open: 10-5 Daily   **Closed:** LEG/HOL!
ADM: Adult: $3.50   **Children:** Free under 12
& ℗ Free in Balboa Park   **Museum Shop**
Group Tours   Drop-In Tours: 2:00 Su
Permanent Collection: PHOT

CALIFORNIA

Museum of Photographic Arts - continued

The Museum of Photographic Arts, dedicated exclusively to the care and collection of photographic works of art, is housed in Casa de Balbo, a structure built in 1915 for the Panama-California Exposition located in the heart of beautiful Balboa Park (designated as the number one urban park in America). Beginning Feb, 1, 1999 the Museum will be closed for renovation. The greatly expanded space is to open Spring 2000. During the renovation exhibitions will be presented at Museum of Contemporary Art Downtown, 1001 Kettner Blvd at Broadway.

San Diego Museum of Art

1450 El Prado, Balboa Park, San Diego, CA 92101
☎: 619-232-7931 ◙ www.sandiegomuseum.org
Open: 10-4:30 Tu-Su **Closed:** Mo, 1/1, THGV, 12/25
Free Day: 3rd Tu in month **ADM: Adult:** $8.00 **Children:** $3.00 (6-17) **Seniors:** $6.00
& ℗ Parking is available in Balboa Park and in the lot in front of the museum.
Museum Shop ‖: Sculpture Garden Cafe 10-3 Tu-F; 9-4:30 Sa, Su (619-696-1990) **Drop-In Tours**: Many times daily
Historic Building Built in 1926, the facade is similar to one at Univ. of Salamanca **Sculpture Garden**
Permanent Collection: IT/REN; SP/OM; DU; AM: 20 EU; ptgs, sculp 19; AS; AN/EGT; P/COL

Whether strolling through the treasures in the sculpture garden or viewing the masterpieces inside the Spanish Colonial style museum building, a visit to this institution, located in San Diego's beautiful Balboa Park, is a richly rewarding and worthwhile experience. In addition to family oriented self-led discovery guides of the collection, available in both English and Spanish, the museum recently installed the Image Gallery, interactive multimedia access to the permanent collection. PLEASE NOTE: There is a special admission fee of $4.00 for military with I.D. **NOT TO BE MISSED:** Frederick R. Weisman Gallery of Calif. art;, world-renowned collection of South Asian paintings

ON EXHIBIT 2000

09/25/1999 to 01/02/2000 STAR WARS: THE MAGIC OF MYTH
Original artwork, props, models, costumes, characters and other artifacts used to create the original STAR WARS TRILOGY.

10/30/1999 to 01/09/2000 PACIFIC ARCADIA: IMAGES OF CALIFORNIA 1600-1915

12/18/1999 to 02/27/2000 LAND OF THE WINGED HORSEMEN: ART IN POLAND, 1571-1764
In the first major display in America of works in all media from Poland during the 16th-18th c. Paintings, ceramics, glass, furniture, weaponry, metalworks, and textiles including a captured Turkish tent will be shown.

07/2000 to 09/2000 THE TOPKAPI PALACE: JEWELS AND TREASURES OF THE SULTANS ♫

Timken Museum of Art

1500 El Prado, Balboa Park, San Diego, CA 92101
☎: 619-239-5548 ◙ http://gort.ucsd.edu/sj/timken/
Open: 10-4:30 Tu-Sa, 1:30-4:30 Su **Closed:** LEG/HOL!; MONTH OF SEPT
Vol/Cont:
& **Museum Shop Group Tours Drop-In Tours**: 10-12 Tu-Th
Permanent Collection: EU: om/ptgs 13-19; AM: ptgs 19; RUSS/IC 15-19; GOBELIN TAPESTRIES

Superb examples of European and American paintings and Russian Icons are but a few of the highlights of the Timkin Museum of Art located in beautiful Balboa Park, site of the former 1915-16 Panama California Exposition. Treasures displayed within the six galleries and the rotunda of this museum make it a "must see".
NOT TO BE MISSED: "Portrait of a Man" by Frans Hals; "The Magnolia Flower" by Martin Johnson Heade

ON EXHIBIT 2000

10/15/1999 to 02/15/2000 VENETIAN VIEWS: LUCA CARLEVARIJS

10/15/1999 to 02/15/2000 THE ART OF CONSERVATION
15-20 important works from public collections in the western US that have been treated by the Balboa Art Conservation Center, a regional, non-profit art center during the last two decades.

Asian Art Museum of San Francisco

Affiliate Institution: The Avery Brundage Collection
Golden Gate Park, San Francisco, CA 94118
☎: 415-379-8801 ◙ www.asianart.org
Open: 9:30-5 We-Su, till 8:45pm 1st We each month   **Closed:** Sa, LEG/HOL!
ADM: Adult: $7.00   **Children:** $4.00 (12-17)   **Students:** $5.00   **Seniors:** $5.00
& ℗ Free parking in Golden Gate Park and all day $3.00 weekend parking in UCSF garage at corner of Irving St. & Second
Museum Shop ⫟ **Group Tours:** 415-379-8839   **Drop-In Tours:** frequent daily tours!
Permanent Collection: AS: arts; MID/E: arts; BRUNDAGE COLLECTION (80% of the holdings of the museum)

With a 12,000 piece collection that covers 40 countries and 6,000 years, the Asian Art Museum, opened in 1966 as a result of a gift to the city by industrialist Avery Brundage, is the largest of its kind outside of Asia. PLEASE NOTE: There are special hours during major exhibitions. Please call for specifics.

ON EXHIBIT 2000

09/22/1999 to 01/09/2000   THE ARTS OF THE SIKH KINGDOMS
This extraordinary exhibition that gives a view of the Punjab during the Sikh period. It is particularly significant showing how the Punjab was rooted in the interrelatedness of Sikh, Hindu and Islamic traditions. *Only Venue*

02/18/2000 to 05/30/2000   BAMBOO MASTERWORKS: JAPANESE BASKETS FROM THE LLOYD COTSEN COLLECTION

06/17/2000 to 09/11/2000   THE GOLDEN AGE OF CHINESE ARCHAEOLOGY: CELEBRATED DISCOVERIES FROM THE PEOPLE'S REPUBLIC OF CHINA ∩

10/25/2000 to 01/14/2001   BETWEEN THE THUNDER AND THE RAIN: CHINESE PAINTINGS FROM THE OPIUM WAR TO THE CULTURAL REVOLUTION (1840-1979)

Cartoon Art Museum

814 Mission St., San Francisco, CA 94103
☎: 415-CAR-TOON
Open: 11-5 We-Fr, 10-5 Sa, 1-5 Su   **Closed:** 1/1, 7/4, THGV, 12/25
ADM: Adult: $5.00   **Children:** $2.00 (6-12)   **Students:** $3.00   **Seniors:** $3.00
& ℗ Fifth & Mission Garage   **Museum Shop**
Group Tours: 415-227-8671   **Drop-In Tours:** Upon request if available
Permanent Collection: CARTOON ART; GRAPHIC ANIMATION

The Cartoon Art Museum, founded in 1984, is located in a new 6,000 square foot space that includes a childrens and an interactive gallery. With a permanent collection of 11,000 works of original cartoon art, newspaper strips, political cartoons, and animation cells, this is one of only 3 museums of its kind in the country and the only West Coast venue of its kind. PLEASE NOTE: Children under 5 are admitted free of charge.

Coit Tower

1 Telegraph Hill, San Francisco, CA
☎: 415-274-0203
Open: WINTER: 9-4:30 daily; SUMMER: 10-5:30 daily
℗ very limited timed parking   **Museum Shop   Group Tours**
Permanent Collection: murals

Though not a museum, art lovers should not miss the newly restored Depression-era murals that completely cover the interior of this famous San Francisco landmark. 25 social realist artists working under the auspices of the WPA participated in creating these frescoes that depict rural and urban life in California during the 1930's. Additional murals on the second floor may be seen only at 11:15 on Saturday mornings. The murals, considered one of the city's most important artistic treasures, and the spectacular view of San Francisco from this facility are a "must see" when visiting this city.

CALIFORNIA

Fine Arts Museums of San Francisco
Affiliate Institution: M. H. de Young Mem. Mus. & Calif. Palace of Legion of Hon.
Calif. Palace of the Legion of Honor, Lincoln Park, San Francisco, CA 94118-4501
☎: 415-863-3330 ◙ www.thinker.org
Open: See museum description **Closed:** Most holidays that fall on Mo, when the museum is regularly closed
Free Day: de Young, 1st We, Palace 2nd We
ADM: Adult: $7.00 **Children:** $3.00 (12-17) **Students:** $10 Annual Pass **Seniors:** $5.00
♿ ℗ Free parking in the park **Museum Shop** ‖: 2 Cafes open 10am-4pm
Group Tours: 425-750-3638 **Drop-In Tours:** We-Su (deYoung) & Tu-Su (Palace)!
Historic Building Calif. Palace of Legion of Honor modeled on Hotel de Salm in Paris
Permanent Collection: DeYoung: PTGS, DRGS, GR, SCULP; AM: dec/art; BRIT: dec/art; AN/EGT; AN/R; AN/GRK; AF;
OC. CA. PALACE OF LEGION OF HONOR: EU: 13-20; REN; IMPR: drgs, gr ◯

The de Young Museum: Situated in the heart of Golden Gate Park, the de Young features the largest collection of American art on the West Coast ranging from Native American traditional arts to contemporary Bay Area art.

The California Palace of the Legion of Honor: One of the most dramatic museum buildings in the country, the recently renovated and reopened Palace of the Legion of Honor houses the Museum's European art, the renowned Achenbach graphic art collection, and one of the world's finest collections of sculpture by Rodin. PLEASE NOTE: Children under 12 are admitted free at both facilities.

The hours for each museum are as follows:
de Young: hours 9:30-5 W-S, open till 8:45 with free adm. 1st W of the month

Palace of the Legion of Honor: hours 9:30-5:00 Tu-S with free adm. 2nd W of month. **NOT TO BE MISSED:** Rodin's "Thinker" & The Spanish Ceiling (Legion of Honor); Textile collection (deYoung); Gallery One, a permanent art education center for children & families (deYoung)

ON EXHIBIT 2000
ONGOING AT THE de YOUNG GALLERY ONE: AN EXHIBITION FOR CHILDREN

ONGOING AT THE de YOUNG ART OF OCEANIA GALLERY

09/18/1999 to 01/09/2000 SPIRIT COUNTRY: AUSTRALIAN ABORIGINAL ART FROM THE GANTNER MYER COLLECTION-LEGION
The last two centuries have seen a great awakening of appreciation of Australian aboriginal art . The 125 paintings shown here date from the 60's to the present including acrylic on canvas and works from the Kiberleys and North Western Australia. Aboriginal elders will make a sand painting of a sacred subject during the first week of the exhibition. *Catalog Will Travel*

10/02/1999 to 01/02/2000 WAYNE THIEBAUD: WORKS ON PAPER-DE YOUNG

10/30/1999 to 04/30/2000 THE WEIDERSPERG COLLECTION-DE YOUNG
Central Asian carpets and textiles were donated to the Museum in 1997. More than 20 0f the finest objects from the collection will be shown here. *Catalog*

11/20/1999 to 02/12/2000 NURTURING THE FUTURE: THE ART AND COLLECTION OF DAVID C. DRISKELL-DE YOUNG
A thematic journey documenting the strategies employed by 20th C. African American artists in creating artistic and racial identities. More than 100 paintings, sculpture and works on paper document the story of how this collection was assembled. *Catalog*

02/19/2000 to 05/14/2000 GEORGIA O'KEEFFE: THE POETRY OF THINGS-LEGION
The first exhibition to focus entirely on the artists painting of objects. The 68 works span the period from 1908-1963. It explores her spiritual, emotional and aesthetic relationships with the objects she choose to paint. *Catalog Will Travel*

Fine Arts Museums of San Francisco - continued

02/19/2000 to 05/14/2000   GEORGIA O'KEEFE–California Palace of the Legion of Honor
Georgia O'Keeffe: The Poetry of Things In 1915, Georgia O'Keeffe divided her early charcoal drawings into two categories: "landscapes" and "things." This exhibit focuses on the "things"–including flowers, crosses, and animal skulls–in 63 still-life paintings and drawings, dating between 1908 and 1963.

05/21/2000 to 07/30/2000   2000 BC: THE BRUCE CONNER STORY PART II-DE YOUNG
Famous for landmark nylon shrouded assemblages from the 50's and 60's and as a post war independent film maker, Connor has explored most media during his 40 year career. *Catalog*

06/10/2000 to 09/03/2000   WAYNE THIEBAUD: A PAINTINGS RETROSPECTIVE-LEGION
The first full retrospective in over 15 years of the work of this figurative painter and will celebrate the artist's 80th birthday. *Catalog Will Travel*

09/24/2000 to 01/07/2001   THE KINGDOMS OF EDWARD HICKS-DE YOUNG
The first major exhibition of Hicks life and work. More than 50 paintings ranging from his "Peaceable Kingdom" variants to other historical subjects showing the entire range of Hick's artistic interests.

Friends of Photography, Ansel Adams Center
250 Fourth St., San Francisco, CA 94103
☎: 415-495-7000
Open: 11-5 Tu-Su, 11-8 1st Th of the month   **Closed:** LEG/HOL!
ADM: Adult: $5.00   **Children:** $2.00 (12-17)   **Students:** $3.00   **Seniors:** $2.00
♿ Ⓟ Several commercial parking facilities located nearby   **Museum Shop**
Group Tours   Drop-In Tours: 1:15 & 2 Sa
Permanent Collection: PHOT; COLLECTION OF 125 VINTAGE PRINTS BY ANSEL ADAMS AVAILABLE FOR STUDY ONLY

Founded in 1967 by a group of noted photographers including Ansel Adams, Brett Weston, and Beaumont Newhall, the non-profit Friends of Photography is dedicated to expanding public awareness of photography and to exploring the creative development of the media.

ON EXHIBIT 2000

Special exhibits not available at time of printing

Mexican Museum
Affiliate Institution: Fort Mason Bldg.D.
Laguna & Marina Blvd., San Francisco, CA 94123
☎: 415-441-0404   ◉ www.mexicanmuseum.org
Open: 11-5 We-Su   **Closed:** Mo, Tu, LEG/HOL!
Free Day: 1st We of month   **ADM: Adult:** $4.00   **Children:** Free under 10   **Students:** $3.00   **Seniors:** $3.00
♿ Ⓟ Free   **Museum Shop**
Historic Building Fort Mason itself is a former military site in Golden Gate Rec. Area
Permanent Collection: MEX; MEX/AM; FOLK; ETH; MORE THAN 300 OBJECTS FROM THE NELSON ROCKERFELLER COLLECTION OF MEX/FOLK ART (over 9000 pieces in total)

With more than 9,000 objects in its collection, the Mexican Museum, founded in 1975, is the first institution of its kind devoted exclusively to the art and culture of Mexico and its people. Plans are underway to open in a new museum building in the Yerba Buena Gardens district in 2001. This 50,000 square foot facility will house the most extensive collection of Mexican and Mexican-American art in the U.S. **NOT TO BE MISSED:** "Family Sunday", a hands-on workshop for children offered once per exhibition (quarterly) (call 415-202-9721 to reserve).

CALIFORNIA

Museo Italoamericano

Ft. Mason Center, Bldg. C, San Francisco, CA 94123
📞: 415-673-2200   ◉ www.well.com/~museo
Open: Noon-5 We-Su, till 7pm 1st We of the month   **Closed:** Mo, Tu, LEG/HOL!
Free Day: 1st We of month   **ADM:** **Adult:** $2.00   **Children:** Free   **Students:** $1.00   **Seniors:** $1.00
♿ ⓟ Free   **Museum Shop   Group Tours**
Permanent Collection: IT & IT/AM: ptgs, sculp, phot 20

This unique museum, featuring the art of many contemporary Italian and Italian-American artists, was established in 1978 to promote public awareness and appreciation of Italian art and culture. Included in the collection are works by such modern masters as Francesco Clemente. Sandro Chia, and Luigi Lucioni. **NOT TO BE MISSED:** "Tavola della Memoria", a cast bronze sculpture from 1961 by Arnaldo Pomodoro

ON EXHIBIT 2000
10/07/1999 to 01/07/2000   GOTTARDO PIAZZONI

San Francisco Art Institute Galleries

800 Chestnut St,, San Francisco, CA 94133
📞: 415-771-7020   ◉ www.sfa.edu
Open: 10-5 Tu-Sa, till 8 Th, 12-5 Su   **Closed:** Mo. LEG/HOL
♿ ⓟ Street parking only   **Museum Shop**   🍴: Café, separate from Gallery

Founded in 1871, the Art Institute is the oldest cultural institution on the West Coast, and one of San Francisco's designated historical landmarks. The main building is a handsome Spanish colonial style structure designed in 1926 by architect Arthur Brown. Featured in the Walter/Bean Gallery are exhibitions by artists from the Bay Area and across the nation. The views of San Francisco and the Bay are among the best. **NOT TO BE MISSED:** Mural by Diego Rivera

ON EXHIBIT 2000
ONGOING   THE WALTER/MCBEAN GALLERY
A year round program is presented of innovative work by emerging and experimental artists from throughout the US and abroad.

San Francisco Craft & Folk Art Museum

Landmark Building A, Fort Mason, San Francisco, CA 94123-1382
📞: 415-775-0990
Open: 11-5 Tu-Sa, till 7pm 1st We of the month   **Closed:** Mo, 1/1, MEM/DAY, 7/4, LAB/DAY, THGV, 12/25
Free Day: 10-2 every Sa, 1st We of month   **ADM:** **Adult:** $3.00, fam $5.00   **Students:** $1.00   **Seniors:** $1.00
♿ ⓟ Free
Museum Shop   🍴: Right next door to famous Zen vegetarian restaurant, Greens
Group Tours: 415-775-0991   **Drop-In Tours:** 1:30 1st We 2nd Fr and 3rd Sa of month .
Historic Building Building served as disembarkation center during WW II & Viet Nam
Permanent Collection: No permanent collection

6 to 10 witty and elegant exhibitions of American and international contemporary craft and folk art are presented annually in this museum, part of a fascinating, cultural waterfront center in San Francisco. PLEASE NOTE: Group tours are free of charge to those who make advance reservations.

ON EXHIBIT 2000
10/23/1999 to 01/02/2000   BEYOND THE OBVIOUS: RETHINKING JEWELRY

01/2000 to 03/2000   RELIQUARIES FOR AMERICA-

01/2000 to 03/2000   IKAT EXHIBITION, CURATOR YOSHIKO WADA

San Francisco Museum of Modern Art
151 Third St., San Francisco, CA 94103-3159

☎: 415-357-4000 ◙ www.sfmoma.org

Open: 11-6 Th-Tu, till 9 Th, Summer Mem/Day to Lab/Day 10-6   **Closed:** W, 1/1, 7/4, THGV, 12/25

Free Day: 1st Tu of month, half price Th 6-9pm   **ADM:** **Adult:** $8.00   **Children:** Free 12 & under must be with adult **Students:** $4.00   **Seniors:** $5.00

& ℗ Pay garages at Fifth & Mission, the Moscone Center Garage(255 Third St.), and the Hearst Garage at 45 Third St.

Museum Shop ¶: Caffé Museo open 10-6 daily (except W), till 9pm Th

Group Tours: 415-357-4191

Drop-In Tours: daily (call 415-357-4096) or inquire in lobby

Permanent Collection: AM: ab/exp ptgs; GER: exp; MEX; REG; PHOT; FAUVIST: ptgs; S.F. BAY AREA ART; VIDEO ARTS

A trip to San Francisco, if only to visit the new home of this more than 60 year old museum, would be worthwhile for any art lover. Housed in a light filled architecturally brilliant and innovative building designed by Mario Botta, the museum features the most comprehensive collection of 20th century art on the West Coast. It is interesting to note that not only is this structure the largest new American art museum to be built in this decade, it is also the second largest single facility in the U.S. devoted to modern art. PLEASE NOTE THE FOLLOWING: 1. Admission is half price from 6-9 on Thursday evenings; 2. Spotlight tours are conducted every Thursday and live jazz in the galleries is provided on the 3rd Thursday of each month; 3. Special group tours called "Modern Art Adventures" can be arranged (415-357-4191) for visits to Bay Area private collections artists' studios, and a variety of museums and galleries in the area. **NOT TO BE MISSED:** "Woman in a Hat" by Matisse, one of 30 superb early 20th c. works from the recently donated Elise Hass Collection.

ON EXHIBIT 2000

ONGOING   FROM MATISSE TO DIEBENKORN: WORKS FROM THE PERMANENT COLLECTION OF PAINTING AND SCULPTURE

Works from the museum's permanent collection, displayed in the vastly expanded gallery space of the new museum building, include prime examples of European & American Modernism, Surrealism, Abstract Expressionism, and California Art. In addition to highlighting individual artists such as Matisse, Klee, Still and Guston, the exhibition also features a room-sized light installation by James Turrell.

ONGOING   PICTURING MODERNITY: PHOTOGRAPHS FROM THE PERMANENT COLLECTION

ONGOING   CONTEMPORARY ART 1960-1996: SELECTIONS FROM THE PERMANENT COLLECTION

08/20/1999 to 01/04/2000   FULL MOON: APOLLO MISSION PHOTOGRAPHS OF THE LUNAR LANDSCAPE

Extraordinary scientific photographic archives to the public with unprecedented fidelity and experimental immediacy.

10/02/1999 to 01/04/2000   DEGAS TO PICASSO: THE PAINTER, THE SCULPTOR AND THE CAMERA

The exhibition will explore the role of photography in the finished work and conceptual process of artists including Bonnard, Brancusi, Degas, Gauguin, Khnopff, Moreau, Mucha, Munch, Picasso, Rodin, Rosso, von Stuck, Valloton and Vuillard. *Catalog Will Travel*

10/15/1999 to 01/11/2000   SEEING TIME: SELECTIONS FROM THE PAMELA AND RICHARD KRAMLICH COLLECTION OF CONTEMPORARY ART (V/I/M)

Showcasing on of the largest private collections of media arts, included are works by historical figures such as Acconchi, Broodthaers, Graham and Naumann and leading contemporary artists including Barney, Douglass, McQueen, Mori, Tyson and Wall. *Catalog*

11/12/1999 to 02/20/2000   FAR OUT: DESIGN FROM THE SIXTIES (I/D)

An exploration of the way that Bay Area designers tuned in, dropped out, and made posters, clothes, objects and structures that merged with technology, nature, craft and commerce. It will be centered around the SFMOMA collection of the "Numbered Series "of Rock and Roll Posters and a simultaneous exhibition of a private collection of Japanese transistor radios of the early '60s. *Catalog*

CALIFORNIA

Yerba Buena Center for the Arts
701 Mission St., San Francisco, CA 94103-3138

☎: 415-978-ARTS (2787) ◙ www.YerbaBuenaArts.org
Open: 11-6 Tu-Su, till 8pm 1st Th of the month **Closed:** LEG/HOL!
Free Day: first Th of month **ADM: Adult:** $5.00 **Children:** $3.00 **Students:** $3.00 **Seniors:** $3.00
& ℗ There is a public parking garage at 5th and Mission Sts., one block away from the Center.
Museum Shop
❢ ex 114 **Sculpture Garden**

Opened in 1993 as part of a still evolving arts complex that includes the newly relocated San Francisco Museum of Modern Art, the Cartoon Art Museum, and the Ansel Adams Center for Photography, this fine arts and performance center features theme-oriented and solo exhibitions by a culturally diverse cross section of Bay Area artists. PLEASE NOTE: Admission for seniors is free from 11-3 on Thursdays. **NOT TO BE MISSED:** The building itself designed by prize-winning architect Fumihiko Maki to resemble a sleek ocean liner complete with porthole windows.

ON EXHIBIT 2000

11/20/1999 to 02/2000 BAY AREA NOW

03/2000 to 06/2000 UNDER EIGHTEEN

SAN JOSE

Rosicrucian Egyptian Museum and Planetarium
Rosicrucian Park, 1342 Naglee Ave., San Jose, CA 95191

☎: 408-947-3636 ◙ www.rosicrucian.org
Open: 10-5 Mo-Su **Closed:** 1/1, THGV, 12/25
ADM: Adult: $7.00 **Children:** $3.50 (7-15) **Students:** $5.00 **Seniors:** $5.00
℗ Free **Museum Shop**
Group Tours: 408-947-3633 **Drop-In Tours:** rock tomb only periodically during day
Permanent Collection: ANT: ptgs, sculp, gr

Without question the largest Egyptian collection in the West, the Rosicrucian is a treasure house full of thousands of objects and artifacts from ancient Egypt. Even the building itself is styled after Egyptian temples and, once inside, the visitor can experience the rare opportunity of actually walking through a reproduction of the rock tombs cut into the cliffs at Beni Hasan 4,000 years ago. **NOT TO BE MISSED:** A tour through the rock tomb, a reproduction of the ones cut into the cliffs at Beni Hasan 4,000 years ago; Egyptian gilded ibis statue in Gallery B

San Jose Museum of Art
110 S. Market St., San Jose, CA 95113

☎: 408-294-2787 ◙ www.sjmusart.org
Open: 10-5 Tu-Su, till 8pm Th **Closed:** Mo, LEG/HOL
Free Day: 1st Th; seniors 1st Tu; half price 5-8 PM T
ADM: Adult: $7.00 **Children:** Free 5 & under **Students:** $4.00 **Seniors:** $4.00
& ℗ Paid public parking is available underground at the Museum and at several locations within 3 blocks of the museum.
Museum Shop ❢: Caffe La Pastaia al Museo
Group Tours: 408-291-6840, 408-291-5393 school tours
Drop-In Tours: 12:30 & 2:30 Tu-S & 6:30 T
Historic Building 1892 Richardsonian Romanesque. Historic Wing; 1991 New Wing designed by Skidmore, Owings, & Merrill
Sculpture Garden
Permanent Collection: AM: 19-20; NAT/AM; CONT

62

San Jose Museum of Art - continued

Contemporary art is the main focus of this vital museum. Housed in a landmark building that once served as a post office/library, the museum added 45,000 square feet of exhibition space in 1991 to accommodate the needs of the cultural renaissance now underway in San Jose. Beginning in 1992, the Whitney Museum of American Art in New York agreed to send the San Jose Museum of Art four large exhibitions drawn from the Whitney's permanent collection. Each exhibition will be installed for a period of 12 months. PLEASE NOTE: Signed tours for the deaf are given at 12:30 on the 2nd Sa of the month.

ON EXHIBIT 2000

04/16/1999 to 06/25/2000   INNUENDO NON TROPPO: THE WORK OF GREGORY BARSAMIAN
Spinning constructions and strobe lights are employed in the creation of Barsamian's works of optical illusion some of which produce the appearance of vertical motion.

05/04/1999 to 06/11/2000   A CENTURY OF LANDSCAPE: SELECTIONS FROM THE PERMANENT COLLECTION OF THE WHITNEY MUSEUM OF AMERICAN ART

09/25/1999 to 01/10/2000   CATHERINE MCCARTHY

09/25/1999 to 01/10/2000   PIECING IT TOGETHER: PERSONAL NARRATIVE IN CONTEMPORARY ART

10/24/1999 to 01/09/2000   CARIOCA: A YEAR AMONG THE NATIVES OF RIO DE JANEIRO, NEW WORK BY SANDOW BIRK

05/20/2000 to 08/13/2000   BLURRING THE BOUNDARIES: INSTALLATION ART FROM THE SAN DIEGO MUSEUM OF CONTEMPORARY ART
Encompassing media as diverse as painting, sculpture, video and performance, installation art challenges viewers by asking them to participate in ways other than the purely visual. *Catalog Will Travel*

Fall/2000   AN AMERICAN DIARY: A SERIES OF PAINTINGS BY ROGER SHIMOMURA

01/23/2000 to 04/02/2000   BILL OWENS: THE SUBURBAN SEVENTIES

02/06/2000 to 04/16/2000   JOSEPH BEUYS MULTIPLES
300 multiples created by Beuys from 1965-1985 will be on view in their first public presentation. Organized in thematic sections, the works reveal key concepts in his work of nature, communication, and teaching & learning.

SAN MARINO

Huntington Library, Art Collections and Botanical Gardens
1151 Oxford Rd., San Marino, CA 91108
☎: 626-405-2141   ◉ www.huntington.org
Open: 12-4:30 Tu-Fr, 10:30-4:30 Sa, Su; JUNE-AUG: 10:30-4:30 Tu-Su   **Closed:** Mo, LEG/HOL!
Free Day: 1st Th of each month   **ADM: Adult:** $8.50   **Children:** Free under 12   **Students:** $6.00 (12-18)   **Seniors:** $8.00
& ℗ behind Pavilion   **Museum Shop**
️🍽: 1-4 Tu-F; 11:30-4:00 Sa, Su; ENG.TEA 1-3:45 Tu-Fr; 12-3: Sa, Su
Group Tours: 626-405-2126
Drop-In Tours: Introductory slide show given during day
Historic Building 1910 estate of railroad magnate, Henry E. Huntington
Sculpture Garden
Permanent Collection: BRIT: ptgs, drgs, sculp, cer 18-19; EU: ptgs, drgs, sculp, cer 18; FR: ptgs, dec/art, sculp 18; REN: ptgs; AM: ptgs, sculp, dec/art 18-20

CALIFORNIA

Huntington Library, Art Collections and Botanical Gardens - continued

The multi-faceted Huntington Library, Art Collection & Botanical Gardens makes a special stop at this complex a must! Known for containing the most comprehensive collections of British 18th & 19th century art outside of London, the museum also houses an outstanding American collection as well as one of the greatest research libraries in the world. A new installation of furniture and decorative arts, designed by California architects Charles & Henry Greene, opened recently in the Dorothy Collins Brown Wing which had been closed for refurbishing for the past 3 years. The Christopher Isherwood Archive is now at the Huntington. **NOT TO BE MISSED:** "Blue Boy" by Gainsborough; "Pinkie" by Lawrence; Gutenberg Bible; 12 acre desert garden; Japanese garden

ON EXHIBIT 2000

07/02/1999 to 08/20/2000   WORLDS OF PROFIT AND DELIGHT: POPULAR READING IN REAISSANCE ENGLAND
The exhibition takes its name from a quote from Christopher Marlow's "Dr. Faustus" . It Also deals with issues of popular literacy , how and when people learned to read in the Renaissance, etc.

09/25/1999 to 09/10/2000   THE LAND OF GOLDEN DREAMS: CALIFORNIA AND THE GOLD RUSH DECADE, 1848-1858
A major exhibition of original material from the Museum's collection. The four major themes of the exhibition will be the initial discovery of gold at Sutter's Mill on January 24, 1848 the early stages of migration to the gold fields, the epic days of the "49ers" in the mining camps and boom towns that sprung up in the wake of fortune seekers.

Summer/2000   RELIGION AND THE FOUNDING OF THE AMERICAN REPUBLIC
A traveling exhibition organized by the Library of Congress. *Will Travel*

03/04/2000 to 04/30/2000   THE ART OF BLOOMSBURY
The first major exhibition in America dealing with the "Bloomsbury Group". The circle included Roger Fry, Vanessa Bell, and Duncan Grant. *Will Travel*

09/2000 to 01/2001   CHAUCER EXHIBITION
The 600th anniversary of Geoffrey Chaucer's death will be commemorated in this exhibition. The centerpiece will be the Huntington's ,magnificent illuminated manuscript of the "Canturbury Tales".

SAN SIMEON

Hearst Castle
750 Hearst Castle Rd., San Simeon, CA 93452-9741

☎: 800-444-4445   ◙ www.hearstcastle.org
Open: 8:20-3:20 (to reserve a tour call toll free 1-800-444-4445)   **Closed:** 1/1, THGV, 12/25
ADM: **Adult:** $14.00   **Children:** $8.00 (6-12)
♿ ℗ Free   **Museum Shop** ⑪
Group Tours: 1-800-401-4775   **Historic Building**
Permanent Collection: IT/REN: sculp, ptgs; MED: sculp, ptgs; DU; FL; SP; AN/GRK: sculp; AN/R: sculp; AN/EGT: sculp

One of the prize house museums in the state of California is Hearst Castle, the enormous (165 rooms) and elaborate former estate of American millionaire William Randolph Hearst. The sculptures and paintings displayed throughout the estate, a mixture of religious, secular art and antiquities, stand as testament to the keen eye Mr. Hearst had for collecting. PLEASE NOTE: a 10% discount for groups of 12 or more (when ordered in advance for any daytime tour) has recently been implemented. Evening Tours are available for a fee of $25 adults and $13 for children ages 6-12 (hours vary according to the sunset). There are 4 different daytime tours offered. All last approximately 1 hour & 50 minutes, include a walk of 1/2 mile, and require the climbing of 150 to 400 stairs. All tickets are sold for specific tour times. Be sure to call 1-800-444-4445 to reserve individual tours. For foreign language tours call 805-927-2020 for interpreters when available. Hours of operation may vary according to the season! **NOT TO BE MISSED:** Antique Spanish ceilings; a collection of 155 Greek vases; New IWERKS Theater presentation at the Visitor Center shows the 40 minute film "Hearst Castle: Building the Dream" on a 5-story high screen.

CALIFORNIA

Bowers Museum of Cultural Art
2002 N. Main (New Address Jan 2000 655 Mission St SF, CA 94105.), Santa Ana, CA 92706
☎: 714-567-3600 ◙ www.friendsofphotography.org
Open: 10-4 daily, 11-8 first Th of month   **Closed:** Mo, LEG/HOL!
ADM: Adult: $6.00   **Children:** Free under 13, $2.00 13-adult   **Students:** $4.00   **Seniors:** $4.00
♿ ℗ Pay nearby
Museum Shop ⋔: Topaz Cafe
Group Tours   Drop-In Tours: 1:15 & 2 Sa
Permanent Collection: Phot; Collection of 125 vintage prints by Ansel Adams on tour thru 2001

This museum was founded to contain a record of Orange County and California history. Although the museum was erected in 1932 with funds established by Charles W. Bowers in 1924, it was not opened to the public until 1936. The Spanish Colonial-style buildings, and spacious grounds retain their flavor of the county's early heritage. The patio's entrance contains a life-size statue of Juan Rodriguez Cabrillo.

ON EXHIBIT 2000
10/29/1999 to 01/09/2000   NEW AND FORTHCOMING: African, Oceanic and New World Cultures

10/29/1999 to 01/09/2000   SHAMANS, GODS AND MYTHIC BEASTS: COLUMBIAN GOLD AND CERAMICS IN ANTIQUITY
Presented for the first time to the American public new finds from the southwest and north coastal regions of Columbia/
Catalog Will Travel

Santa Barbara Museum of Art
1130 State St., Santa Barbara, CA 93101-2746
☎: 805-963-4364 ◙ www.sbmuseart.org
Open: 11-5 Tu–Sa, 11-9 Fr, Noon-5 Su   **Closed:** Mo, 1/1, THGV, 12/25
Free Day: Th & 1st Su of month   **ADM: Adult:** $5.00   **Children:** Free under 6   **Students:** $2.00   **Seniors:** $3.00
♿ ℗ 2 city parking lots each one block away from the museum
Museum Shop ⋔
Group Tours: 805-884-6489   **Drop-In Tours**: 1:00 daily, overview of collection ; daily at noon special exhibitions
Permanent Collection: AN/GRK; AN/R; AN/EGP; AM; AS; EU: ptgs 19-20; CONT; PHOT; CA:reg ◠

With 20,000 works of art, a considerable number for a community of its size, the Santa Barbara Museum, completing a major expansion project in 1/98, offers a variety of collections that range from antiquities of past centuries to contemporary creations of today. PLEASE NOTE: In addition to a rich variety of special programs such as free Family Days, the museum offers a monthly bilingual Spanish/English tour. **NOT TO BE MISSED:** Fine collection of representative works of American Art

ON EXHIBIT 2000
NEW PERMANENT COLLECTION INSTALLATIONS
Installations of works in virtually every area of the permanent collection in the Museum's new gallery and in relocated and remodeled spaces, will allow for each specific discipline to be featured independently. Many fine works, previously in storage, will now be able to be on display.

11/06/1999 to 01/16/2000   COPY WORK: THE DICTIONARY PAGES AND OTHER DIVERSIONS BY GILLES BARBIER
Hand copied pages from a 1965 "Petit Larousse" dictionary

11/06/1999 to 01/31/2000   ANCIENT GOLD JEWELRY FROM THE DALLAS MUSEUM OF ART
One of the finest collections of Greek, Roman and Etruscan jewelry in the US

CALIFORNIA

University Art Museum, Santa Barbara
Affiliate Institution: University of California
Santa Barbara, CA 93106

✆: 805-893-2951
Open: 10-4 Tu-Sa, 1-5 Su & HOL   **Closed:** 1/1, EASTER, 7/4, THGV, 12/25
 ♿ **Museum Shop   Group Tours   Drop-In Tours**: acad year only: 2:00 Sa & 12:15 alternate Tu
Permanent Collection: IT: ptgs; GER: ptgs; FL: ptgs; DU: ptgs; P/COL; ARCH/DRGS; GR; OM: ptgs; AF

Outstanding among the many thousands of treasures in the permanent collection is one of the world's finest groups of early Renaissance medals and plaquettes. PLEASE NOTE: The museum will be closed for renovation during most of 1998. **NOT TO BE MISSED:** 15th through 17th century paintings from the Sedgwick Collection; Architectural drawing collection; Morgenroth Collection of Renaissance medals and plaquettes

SANTA CLARA

deSaisset Museum
Affiliate Institution: Santa Clara University
500 El Camino Real, Santa Clara, CA 95053-0550

✆: 408-554-4528   ▣   www.scu.edu/SCU/Departments/deSaisset
Open: 11-4 Tu-Su   **Closed:** Mo, LEG/HOL!
 ♿ Ⓟ Free in front of museum parking permit available at front gate   **Museum Shop**
Group Tours   Historic Building Adjacent to Mission Santa Clara
Permanent Collection: AM: ptgs, sculp, gr; EU: ptgs, sculp, gr 16-20; AS: dec/art; AF; CONT: gr, phot, IT/REN: gr

Serving Santa Clara University and the surrounding community, the de Saisset, since its inception in 1955, has been an important Bay Area cultural resource. PLEASE NOTE: It is wise to call ahead as the museum may have limited hours between rotating exhibitions. **NOT TO BE MISSED:** California history collection

ON EXHIBIT 2000
ONGOING   CALIFORNIA HISTORY EXHIBIT

09/25/1999 to 01/2000   ECO-TECH (working title)
This large scale interactive installation illustrates the "yarn ball theory of environmental complexity" which gives visitors the opportunity to experience the nature of systems theory first hand. These create a new way of thinking about technology etc.

04/2000 to 08/2000   IMAGENES/HISTORIAS: CHICANA ALTAR-INSPIRED ART
Home based sacred spaces fell within the creative realm of women. In the past decade several have focused on altar-inspired art. These emphasize the works as sites of cultural memory and reclamation.

09/2000 to 12/2000   THE ONE CHOSEN: IMAGES OF CHRIST IN RECENT NEW YORK ART
Included are images by 20 New York artists. Each asks the question "Whom is the one chosen? Is it self or another?"

01/2001 to 06/2001   ALASKA GOLD: LIFE ON THE NEW FRONTIER, 1898-1906
The story of two brothers who left their ranch at the turn of the century and lived for six years as gold minors on a Bering Sea beach near Nome, Alaska.

Triton Museum of Art
1505 Warburton Ave., Santa Clara, CA 95050

✆: 408-247-3754   ▣   www.TritonMuseum.org
Open: 10-5 We-Su, till 9pm Tu   **Closed:** Mo, LEG/HOL
Vol/Cont: $2.00
 ♿ Ⓟ Free   **Museum Shop   Group Tours**: ext 14   **Sculpture Garden**
Permanent Collection: AM: 19-20; REG; NAT/AM; CONT/GR

Triton Museum of Art - continued

Located in a seven acre park adjacent to the City of Santa Clara, the Triton has grown by leaps and bounds to keep up with the cultural needs of its rapidly expanding "Silicon Valley" community. The museum is housed in a visually stunning building that opened its doors to the public in 1987. **NOT TO BE MISSED:** The largest collection in the country of paintings by American Impressionist Theodore Wores; "on permanent display); Austen D. Warburton Collection of American Indian Art and Artifacts.

ON EXHIBIT 2000

10/05/1999 to 02/10/2000 ELAINE BADGLEY ARNOUX: BACK TO THE GARDEN

10/31/1999 to 01/02/2000 TRITON MUSEUM OF ART BIENNIAL STATEWIDE COMPETITION AND EXHIBITION: PASTELS

01/07/2000 to 02/06/2000 NEW WORKS BY CALIFORNIA ARTISTS: TOBY LURIE

03/12/2000 to 06/15/2000 THEODORE WORES

11/17/2000 to 01/07/2001 RUTH TUNSTALL GRANT

SANTA CRUZ

Museum of Art and History at the McPherson Center

705 Front St., Santa Cruz, CA 95060

☎: 831-429-1964 ◙ www.santacruzmah.org
Open: 12-5 Tu-Su, till 7 Fr **Closed:** Mo, LEG/HOL!
Free Day: 1st Fr of month **ADM:** **Adult:** $3.00 ($2 for county residents) **Children:** Free **Seniors:** $3.00
♿ Ⓟ Adjacent parking lot
Museum Shop ⑪: Indoor courtyard/cafe
Group Tours: 831-429-1964, ext 10 **Drop-In Tours:** Noon usually 1st Fr
Historic Building Museum store is housed in historic Octagon Building
Permanent Collection: CONT

Presenting visual and cultural experiences focused on regional history and modern art; art and history exhibitions from the permanent collection; changing exhibitions from the permanent collection; changing exhibitions of nationally and internationally renowned artists; group exhibitions that demonstrate various art techniques, mediums, crafts, and historic periods.

ON EXHIBIT 2000

11/13/1999 to 01/30/2000 WATERMARKS: NATIONAL WATERCOLOR SOCIETY PERMANENT COLLECTION

12/12/1999 to 01/09/2000 MATRIX 1

01/2000 to 04/2000 HISTORY EXHIBIT CELEBRATING SANTA CRUZ'S 100TH BIRTHDAY

01/15/2000 to 04/16/2000 JOEL LEIVICK AND KAREN MASSARO: SURVEYING TWO ARTISTS AT MID-CAREER

04/30/2000 to 06/25/2000 PERSONAL EDENS: THE GARDENS AND FILM SETS OF FLORENCE YOCH

05/2000 to 08/27/2000 MEDITATIONS ON METAL: SUSAN KINGSLEY

CALIFORNIA

Santa Monica Museum of Art Bergamot Arts Center

2525 Michigan Ave. Building G1, Santa Monica, CA 90404

☎: 310-586-6488 ◙ www.netvip.com/smmoa

Open: 11-6 Tu-Sa, Salons 7:30 when scheduled **Closed:** Mo, Su, 1/1, 7/4, THGV, 12/25

ADM: Adult: $3.00 **Students:** $2.00 **Seniors:** $2.00

♿ Ⓟ Free at Bergamot Arts Center; on-site parking for the disabled **Museum Shop**
⃛: "Gallery Cafe" at Bergamot Station

Group Tours

Historic Building Located in a renovated trolley station

Permanent Collection: NO PERMANENT COLLECTION

Located in a renovated trolley station in the historic Bergamont Arts Center Station area, this museum, devoted to the display of art by living artists, is the only art museum in the area dedicated to making contemporary art more accessible to a culturally and economically diverse audience.

ON EXHIBIT 2000

03/17/2000 to 05/13/2000 EAST OF THE RIVER: CHICANO ART COLLECTORS ANONYMOUS

06/02/2000 to 08/12/2000 THE ARTIST PROJECT SERIES –THREE COMMISSIONED OR COLLABORATIVE WORKS BY EMERGING CONTEMPORARY ARTISTS

12/17/2002 to 02/27/2000 KERRY JAMES MARSHALL *Will Travel*

Sonoma County Museum

425 Seventh St., Santa Rosa, CA 95401

☎: 707-579-1500

Open: 11-4 We-Su **Closed:** Mo, Tu, LEG/HOL!

ADM: Adult: $2.00 **Children:** Free under 12 **Students:** $1.00 **Seniors:** $1.00

♿ Ⓟ Free **Museum Shop Group Tours Historic Building** 1910 Federal Post Office

Permanent Collection: AM: ptgs 19 ; REG

The museum is housed in a 1909 Post Office & Federal Building that was restored and moved to its present downtown location. It is one of the few examples of Classical Federal Architecture in Sonoma County. **NOT TO BE MISSED:** Collection of works by 19th century California landscape painters

Iris and B. Gerald Cantor Center for the Visual Arts at Stanford University

Affiliate Institution: Stanford University

Stanford, CA 94305

☎: 650-723-4177 ◙ www.stanford.edu/dept/ccva/

Open: OPENING 1/99 **Closed:** 1/1, 7/4, THGV, 12/25

Vol/Cont:

♿ Ⓟ Metered parking at the Museum

Museum Shop

Group Tours Drop-In Tours: Rodin Garden: 2pm We, Sa, Su; Outdoor sculp: 2pm 1st S

Sculpture Garden

Permanent Collection: PHOT; PTGS; SCULP (RODIN COLLECTION); DEC/ART; GR; DRGS; OR; CONT/EU

Iris and B. Gerald Cantor Center for the Visual Arts at Stanford University - continued

Designed by the distinguished architects Polshek and Partners of New York, the Iris & B. Gerald Cantor Center for Visual Arts at Stanford University is now open. The Center encompasses the historic Museum building, which has been seismically strengthened and completely renovated; an enhanced B. Gerald Cantor Rodin Sculpture Garden; new sculpture garden areas; and a new wing. The latter includes galleries for the display of special exhibitions and the permanent collection of contemporary art, storage areas for large works, a conservation studio, a café, a bookshop, and an auditorium. All spaces, totaling approximately 120,000 square feet, have modern security, lighting, and climate control. NOT TO BE MISSED: Largest Rodin sculpture collection outside the Musée Rodin in Paris.

ON EXHIBIT 2000

10/13/1999 to 01/02/2000   A RENAISSANCE TREASURY: THE FLAGG COLLECTION OF EUROPEAN DECORATIVE ARTS AND SCULPTURE

An exhibition of seventy-five objects of luxurious materials and intricate design made for the elite of western Europe from the fourteenth through the early eighteenth century. Highlights include small elaborately painted altars for personal use, clocks with craftily engineered works, meticulously carved small-scale sculpture, and finely wrought works in silver, gold, and enamel.

STOCKTON

Haggin Museum

1201 N. Pershing Ave., Stockton, CA 95203

☎: 209-462-1566

Open: 1:30-5 Tu-Su; Open to groups by advance appt!   **Closed:** 1/1, THGV, 12/25
Sugg/Cont: **ADM: Adult:** $2.00   **Children:** $1.00   **Students:** $1.00   **Seniors:** $1.00
& ℗ Free street parking where available   **Museum Shop**
Group Tours   Drop-In Tours: 1:45 Sa, Su
Permanent Collection: AM: ptgs 19; FR: ptgs 19; AM: dec/art; EU: dec/art

Wonderful examples of 19th century French and American paintings from the Barbizon, French Salon, Rocky Mountain, and Hudson River Schools are displayed in a setting accented by a charming array of decorative art objects. **NOT TO BE MISSED:** "Lake in Yosemite Valley" by Bierstadt; "Gathering for the Hunt" by Rosa Bonheur

---

VENTURA

Ventura County Museum of History & Art

100 E. Main St., Ventura, CA 93001

☎: 805-653-0323

Open: 10-5 Tu-Su, till 8pm Th   **Closed:** 1/1, THGV, 12/25
ADM: Adult: $3.00   **Children:** Free under 16   **Students:** $3.00   **Seniors:** $3.00
& ℗ No charge at adjacent city lot   **Museum Shop**
Group Tours   Drop-In Tours: 1:30 Su; "ask me" docents often on duty
Permanent Collection: PHOT; CONT/REG; REG

Art is but a single aspect of this museum that also features historical exhibitions relating to the history of the region. **NOT TO BE MISSED:** 3-D portraits of figures throughout history by George Stuart. Mr. Stuart has created nearly 200 figures which are rotated for viewing every 4 months. He occasionally lectures on his works (call for information)!

ON EXHIBIT 2000

ONGOING   VENTURA COUNTY IN THE NEW WEST

An exhibit that traces the county's history from before European contact to World War II.

COLORADO

Aspen Art Museum
590 N. Mill St., Aspen, CO 81611
☎: 970-925-8050 ◙ www.aspen.com/art &destinationaspen.com/art
Open: 10-6 Tu-Sa, 12-6 Su, till 7pm Th   **Closed:** Mo, 1/1, THGV, 12/25, !
Free Day: Fr reception and gallery tour each Th 5-7   **ADM: Adult:** $3.00   **Children:** Free under 12   **Students:** $2.00
Seniors: $2.00
& ℗   **Museum Shop**
Group Tours   Drop-In Tours
Historic Building The museum is housed in a former hydroelectric plant (c.1855)
Sculpture Garden
Permanent Collection: SCULP

Located in an area noted for its natural beauty and access to numerous recreational activities, this museum, with its emphasis on contemporary art, offers the visitor a chance to explore the cultural side of life in the community. A free reception is offered every Thursday evening from 5-7pm for refreshments and gallery tours. PLEASE NOTE: The galleries may occasionally be closed between exhibits.

ON EXHIBIT 2000

12/09/1999 to 01/30/2000   MICHAEL KENNA: PHOTOGRAPHS

02/10/2000 to 04/16/2000   NATIVE AMERICAN EXHIBITION FROM LOCAL COLLECTIONS

10/12/2000 to 11/26/2000   ROARING FORK OPEN: LOCAL ARTISTS

CU Art Galleries
Affiliate Institution: University of Colorado/Boulder
Campus Box 318, Boulder, CO 80309
☎: 303-492-8300
Open: 8-5 Mo-Fr, till 8 Tu, 11–4 Sa; ; SUMMER:10–4:30 Mo-Fr, 12-7 We, 12-9 Sa   **Closed:** Su,1/1, 7/4, CHRISTMAS VACATION
Vol/Cont: **Sugg/Cont:** $3.00
& ℗ Paid parking in Euclid Auto Park directly south of the building
Museum Shop   Group Tours
Permanent Collection: PTGS 19-20; GR 19-20; PHOT 20; DRGS 15-20; SCULP 15-20

ON EXHIBIT 2000

Summer/2000   ARTISTS AND TECHNOLOGY COLLABORATIONS : REGIONAL REQUESTS FOR PROPOSALS

01/21/2000 to 03/18/2000   SUKOTHAI CERAMICS FROM THE COLORADO COLLECTION (working title)
To be held in conjunction with National Convention of Ceramic Educators in Denver.

01/21/2000 to 03/18/2000   RECENT ACQUISITIONS TO THE COLORADO COLLECTION

01/21/2000 to 03/18/2000   OLD MASTER'S REVISITED: MORALITY T ALES FROM THE COLORADO COLLECTION (working title)

09/01/2000 to 11/04/2000   SYSTEMS (working title)
Works by Peter Halley, Guillermo Kuitka, ME Carroll , Toba Khedoori, Andreas Gursky, Inigo Mongliano-Ovalie, Kathy Prendergast, Eduardo Kak, Annette Lawrence *Will Travel*

01/2001 to 03/2001   AFRO

70

Leanin' Tree Museum of Western Art

6055 Longbow Dr., Boulder, CO 80301

☎: 1-800-777-8716   ◙ www.leanintree.com
Open: 8-4:30 Mo-Fr, 10-4 Sa, Su   **Closed:** LEG/HOL!
Vol/Cont:
ᕷ ℗ Free
Museum Shop
Group Tours: 303-530-1442   **Drop-In Tours**: 8-4:30 Mo-Fr, 10-4 Sa, Su
Permanent Collection: WESTERN: sculp, ptgs, reg; CONT/REG; Largest collection of ptgs by actualist Bill Hughes (1932-1993) in the country.

This unusual fine art museum, just 40 minutes from downtown Denver, is housed in the corporate offices of Leanin' Tree, producers of greeting cards. With 200 original oil paintings and 75 bronze sculptures by over 90 artists Leanin' Tree is home to the largest privately owned collection of contemporary cowboy and western art on public view in America.

Colorado Springs Fine Arts Center

Affiliate Institution: Taylor Museum For Southwestern Studies
30 W. Dale St., Colorado Springs, CO 80903

☎: 719-634-5581
Open: 9-5 Tu-Fr, 10-5 Sa, 1-5 Su   **Closed:** LEG/HOL!
Free Day: Sa 10-5   **ADM: Adult:** $3.00   **Children:** $1.00 (6-12)   **Students:** $1.50   **Seniors:** $1.50
ᕷ ℗   **Museum Shop**
⟦ 11:30-3:00 Tu-F (summer only)
Group Tours: 719-475-2444   **Drop-In Tours:** by arrangement
Historic Building   Sculpture Garden
Permanent Collection: AM: ptgs, sculp, gr 19-20; REG; NAT/AM: sculp; CONT: sculp

Located in an innovative 1930's building that incorporates Art Deco styling with a Southwestern Indian motif, this multi-faceted museum is a major center for cultural activities in the Pikes Peak region. **NOT TO BE MISSED:** Collection of Charles Russell sculpture and memorabilia; hands-on tactile gallery called "Eyes of the Mind"; New sculpture acquisitions: "The Family", by William Zorach, "Hopi Basket Dancers", by Doug Hyde, "Resting at the Spring", by Allan Houser, "Prometheus" by Edgar Britton

ON EXHIBIT 2000

ONGOING   SACRED LAND: INDIAN AND HISPANIC CULTURES OF THE SOUTHWEST AND THE TALPA CHAPEL

ONGOING   CHARLES M. RUSSELL: ART OF THE AMERICAN WEST

ONGOING   EYES OF THE MIND, AN ADDED DIMENSION: SELECTIONS FROM THE TACTILE GALLERY COLLECTION

06/24/2000 to 09/27/2000   FOUR OBJECTS; FOUR ARTISTS; TEN YEARS
In 1986 four American still-life painters–Janet Fish, Sondra Freckelton, Nancy Hagin, and Harriet Shorr–agreed that each would select an object that they would all include in a painting. Ten years later they decided to repeat the project. The results of their efforts reveal the wide spectrum of choices which artists make during the creative process.

COLORADO

Gallery of Contemporary Art
Affiliate Institution: University of Colorado Springs
1420 Austin Bluffs Pkwy., Colorado Springs, CO 80933-7150
☎: 719-262-3567 ◙ harpy.uccs.edu/gallery/framesgallery.html
Open: 10-4 Mo-Fr, 1-4 Sa **Closed:** Su, LEG/HOL!
ADM: Adult: $1.00 **Children:** Free under 12 **Students:** $0.50 **Seniors:** $0.50
♿ ⓟ pay parking in adjacent lot **Museum Shop** ⑪: adjacent plaza
Group Tours Drop-In Tours

This non-collecting university art gallery, one of the most outstanding contemporary art centers in the nation, concentrates on cutting edge exhibitions of contemporary art with approximately 6 exhibitions throughout the year. Located on the second floor of the University science building, this is the only gallery in the Colorado Springs (Pikes Peak) region to feature contemporary art.

DENVER

Denver Art Museum
100 West 14th Ave. Pkwy., Denver, CO 80204
☎: 303-640-4433 ◙ www.denverartmuseum.org
Open: 10-5 Tu-Sa, 10-9 We, 12-5 Su **Closed:** Mo, LEG/HOL!
Free Day: Sa (Colorado residents only) **ADM: Adult:** $4.50 **Children:** Free under 5 **Students:** $2.50 **Seniors:** $2.50
♿ ⓟ Public pay lot located south of the museum on 13th St.; 2 hour metered street parking in front of the museum
Museum Shop ⑪: Palettes Tu-Sa 10-5; We 10-9, 12-5 Su
Group Tours: 303-640-7591 **Drop-In Tours**: 1:30 Tu-Su, 11 Sa, 12-12:30 We & Fr
Historic Building Designed by Gio Ponti in 1971 **Sculpture Garden**
Group Tours Drop-In Tours
Permanent Collection: AM: ptgs, sculp, dec/art 19; IT/REN: ptgs; FR: ptgs 19-20; AS; P/COL; SP; AM: cont; NAT/AM; ARCH: gr

With over 40,000 works featuring 19th century American art, a fine Asian and Native American collection, and works from the early 20th century Taos group, in addition two newly renovated floors house the European, American and Western Paintings, sculpture, design and textiles. PLEASE NOTE: The Museum offers many free family related art activities on Saturday. Call 303-640-7577 for specifics! Some special exhibitions have ticketed and timed entry.

ON EXHIBIT 2000
to 01/09/2000   TREASURES FROM THE DR. S.Y. YIP COLLECTION: CLASSIC CHINESE FURNITURE, PAINTING & CALLIGRAPHY
On a rotating basis this exceptional collection is on long term loan to the Museum.

02/06/1999 to 02/06/2000   ANCIENT CHINESE BRONZES FROM THE SZE HONG COLLECTION
The Chinese believed that bronze not gold was the ultimate status symbol. The exhibition showcases the technical and artistic achievements of the Chinese metalworkers from the Shang thru Tang dynasties (about 1200 BC-AD 907)

09/04/1999 to 08/27/2000   CERAMICS AND GLASS: SELECTIONS FROM THE NORWEST COLLECTION, 1890-1940 *working title)
The third and last of the exhibitions showcasing the exceptional modern design collections of the Norwest collection. Included are artistic styles from Arts and Crafts, Art Nouveau, Jugendstil, and Art Deco.

10/17/1999 to 03/26/2000   CHARLES SIMONDS
Miniature clay landscapes and buildings reminiscent of Rocky Mountain geology and the cave dwellings of Mesa Verde

11/20/1999 to 10/01/2000   TAKASHI NAKAZATO: CONTEMPORARY POTTERY FROM AN ANCIENT JAPANESE TRADITION
Three centuries of traditions are now applied to contemporary forms and designs.

Denver Art Museum - continued

02/12/2000 to 04/30/2000   THE KINGDOMS OF EDWARD HICKS
The first retrospective devoted to the life and work of Bucks County, Pennsylvania artist Edward Hicks. Included are paintings, decorated objects and important manuscripts which illustrate his deep spirituality and talent as an artist and his involvement in the doctrinal controversies that divided the Quakers in the early 19th C. *Will Travel*

03/12/2000 to 06/25/2000   HENRI MATISSE (working title)
Paintings, sculpture, prints and watercolors by Matisse who used color and a means of expression rather than description.

04/10/2000 to 07/30/2000   THE LEGACY OF ISADORA DUNCAN
A celebration of the contributions of this dance innovator

05/04/2000 to 10/01/2000   MARTHA DANIELS
A ceramicist primarily, she uses clay and glazes with a unique artistic voice . She is creating a grotto like structure of lashed bamboo enclosing a assemblage of towering ceramic figures.

06/03/2000 to 10/29/2000   COLORADO MASTERS OF PHOTOGRAPHY
Several important photographers in their 70's or older who lived and worked in the state.

09/09/2000 to 03/04/2001   THE ANCHUTZ COLLECTION: THE ART AND HISTORY OF THE AMERICAN WEST
This exceptional collection has been assembled with a consciousness of the history and an eye for the aesthetic beauty and quality of the works. Included are Russel, Bierstadt, and Remington as well as Moran, O'Keeffe, Catlin, Pollock and Ramsey.

Museo de las Americas

861 Santa Fe Drive, Denver, CO 80204

☎: 303-571-4401
Open: 10-5 Tu-Sa   **Closed:** Mo, 1/1, 7/4, THGV, 12/25
ADM: **Adult:** $3.00   **Children:** Free under 10   **Students:** $1.00   **Seniors:** $2.00
ᕒ ℗   **Museum Shop**
: Call to arrange for certain exhibitions   **Historic Building** Housed in a former J.C. Penny store built in 1924
Permanent Collection: SPANISH COLONIAL ART; CONT LAT/AM

The Museo de las Americas, opened in 7/94, is the first Latino museum in the Rocky Mountain region dedicated to showcasing the art, history, and culture of the people of the Americas from ancient times to the present. PLEASE NOTE: Bilingual tours are available with admission price - call ahead to reserve.

ON EXHIBIT 2000

12/17/1999 to 02/26/2000   VOODOO FLAGS OF HAITI
Sequined and beaded flags of satin, felt and other cloth are ritual objects in the practice of voodoo religion.

03/10/2000 to 05/20/2000   REVIVING THE SPIRIT OF CASAS GRANDES: THE POTTERY OF MATA ORTIZ
Comparing the beautiful work of Casas Grandes (1175-1400) -)to the contemporary potters from the small farming community near the pre-historic pueblo.

06/02/2000 to 08/12/2000   KEEPERS OF CULTURE: THE 100TH ANNIVERSARY OF MUTUAL PROTECTION SOCIETY OF UNITED WORKERS
Photographer Daniel Salazar portrays the spirit of the oldest, most active Hispanic organization founded on 1900.

08/25/2000 to 12/02/2000   DIEGO RIVERA: THE MURAL DRAWINGS
Rivera's Murals were the result of hundreds of preparatory drawings . The exhibition features a selection of these drawings.

12/15/2000 to 03/10/2001   TALES IN TEXTILES: MOLAS FROM PANAMA:
Decorative panels which comprise the front and back of Kuna women's blouses. These have gained world renown in textile art.

COLORADO

Museum of Outdoor Arts

7600 E. Orchard Rd. #160 N., Englewood, CO 80111
☎: 303-741-3609
Open: 8:30-5:30 Mo-Fr; some Sa from JAN-MAR & SEPT-DEC! **Closed:** LEG/HOL!
Sugg/Cont: $3.00 adults, guided tour $2.00
 ♿ Ⓜ **Museum Shop**
Group Tours: 303-741-3609, ext 290 **Sculpture Garden**
Permanent Collection: SCULP

Fifty five major pieces of sculpture ranging from contemporary works by Colorado artists to pieces by those with international reputations are placed throughout the 400 acre Greenwood Plaza business park, located just south of Denver, creating a "museum without walls". A color brochure with a map is provided to lead visitors through the collection.

Sangre deCristo Arts & Conference Center & Children's Center

210 N. Santa Fe Ave., Pueblo, CO 81003
☎: 719-543-0130
Open: 11-4 Mo-Sa **Closed:** LEG/HOL!
♿ Ⓜ 2 free lots **Museum Shop**
Group Tours
Permanent Collection: AM: Regional Western 19-20; REG: ldscp, cont

The broad range of Western Art represented in the collection covers works from the 19th and early 20th century through contemporary Southwest and modern regionalist pieces. **NOT TO BE MISSED:** Francis King collection of Western Art; Art of the "Taos Ten"

A. R. Mitchell Memorial Museum of Western Art

150 E. Main St., P.O. Box 95, Trinidad, CO 81082
☎: 719-846-4224
Open: early APR-through SEPT: 10-4 Mo-Sa; OCT-MAR by appt. **Closed:** 7/4
Vol/Cont:
♿ Ⓜ Street parking on Main St.; parking in back of building **Museum Shop**
Group Tours **Drop-In Tours**: often available upon request **Historic Building**
Permanent Collection: AM: ptgs; HISP: folk; AM: Western

Housed in a charming turn of the century building that features its original tin ceiling and wood floors, the Mitchell contains a unique collection of early Hispanic religious folk art and artifacts from the old west, all of which is displayed in a replica of an early Penitente Morada. The museum is located in southeast Colorado just above the New Mexico border. **NOT TO BE MISSED:** 250 works by Western artist/illustrator Arthur Roy Mitchell

---
BRIDGEPORT

Discovery Museum
4450 Park Ave., Bridgeport, CT 06604
☎: 203-372-3521 ◉ www.discoverymuseum.org
Open: 10-5 Tu-Sa, 12-5 Su, (Open 10-5 Mo during JUL & AUG)   **Closed:** LEG/HOL!
ADM: Adult: $7.00   **Children:** $5.50   **Students:** $5.50   **Seniors:** $5.50
⧖ ℗ Free on-site parking **Museum Shop** ⑪ Cafeteria **Group Tours**
Permanent Collection: AM: ptgs, sculp, phot, furniture 18-20; IT/REN & BAROQUE: ptgs (Kress Coll)

18th to 20th century American works provide the art focus in this interactive art and science museum. **NOT TO BE MISSED:** 14 unique hands-on exhibits that deal with color, line, and perspective in a studio-like setting.

Housatonic Museum of Art
900 Lafayette Blvd., Bridgeport, CT 06608-4704
☎: 203-332-5000 ◉ www.hctc.commnet.edu
Open: Mo-Fr 8:30 - 5:30 Th til 7; 9-3 Sa   **Closed:** Su, LEG/HOL! ACAD!
Vol/Cont:
⧖ ℗ Free parking in student lot; call ahead to arrange for handicapped parking.   **Museum Shop** ⑪ college cafeteria
Group Tours: 203-332-5062   : self-guided tours   **Sculpture Garden**
Permanent Collection: AM 19-20; EU: 19-20; AF; CONT: Lat/Am; CONT: reg; ASIAN; CONT: Hispanic

With a strong emphasis on contemporary and ethnographic art, the Housatonic Museum displays works from the permanent collection and from changing exhibitions.

BROOKLYN

New England Center for Contemporary Art, Inc.
Route 169, Brooklyn, CT 06234
☎: 860-774-8899
Open: (Open from 4/15-12/15 only) 10-5 Tu-Fr; Noon-5 Sa, Su   **Closed:** THGV
⧖ ℗ Free and ample **Museum Shop** **Sculpture Garden**
Permanent Collection: AM: cont/ptgs; CONT/SCULP; OR: cont/art

In addition to its sculpture garden, great emphasis is placed on the display of the contemporary arts of China in this art center which is located on the mid-east border of the state near Rhode Island. **NOT TO BE MISSED:** Collection of contemporary Chinese art; Collection of artifacts from Papua, New Guinea

---
FARMINGTON

Hill-Stead Museum
35 Mountain Rd., Farmington, CT 06032
☎: 860-677-9064
Open: MAY-OCT: 10-5 Tu-Su NOV-APR: 11-4, Tu-Su   **Closed:** Mo, LEG/HOL!
ADM: Adult: $7.00   **Children:** $4.00 (6-12)   **Students:** $6.00   **Seniors:** $6.00
⧖ ℗   **Museum Shop** **Group Tours**: 860-677-2940   **Drop-In Tours**: hour long tours on the hour & half hour
Historic Building National Historical Landmark
Permanent Collection: FR: Impr/ptgs; GR:19; OR: cer; DEC/ART

CONNECTICUT

Hill-Stead Museum - continued

Hill-Stead, located in a suburb just outside of Hartford, is a Colonial Revival home that was originally a "gentleman's farm." Designed by Theodale Pope at the turn of the century, the museum still houses her father's magnificent collection of French and American Impressionist paintings, Chinese porcelains, Japanese woodblock prints, and original furnishings. PLEASE NOTE: Guided tours begin every half hour, the last one being 1 hour before closing. **NOT TO BE MISSED:** Period furnishings; French Impressionist paintings, Sunken garden

---

GREENWICH

Bruce Museum

Museum Drive, Greenwich, CT 06830-7100

☎: 203-869-0376 ◙ www.brucemuseum.com
Open: 10-5 Tu-Sa, 1-4 Su   **Closed:** LEG/HOL! MONDAYS EXCEPT DURING SCHOOL VACATIONS
ADM: Adult: $3.50   **Children:** Free under 5   **Students:** $2.50   **Seniors:** $2.50
& ℗   **Museum Shop**
Group Tours
Historic Building original 1909 Victorian manor is part of the museum
Permanent Collection: AM: ptgs, gr, sculp 19; AM: cer, banks; NAT/AM; P/COL; CH: robes   ◯

In addition to wonderful 19th century American works of art, the recently restored and renovated Bruce Museum also features a unique collection of mechanical and still banks, North American and pre-Columbian artifacts, and an outstanding department of natural history. Housed partially in its original 1909 Victorian manor, the museum is just a short stroll from the fine shops and restaurants in the charming center of historic Greenwich. **NOT TO BE MISSED:** Two new acquisitions: namely, "The Kiss", a 23 1/2" bronze sculpture by Auguste Rodin, and an oil painting entitled "The Mill Pond, Cos Cob, CT., by Childe Hassam.

ON EXHIBIT 2000

10/30/1999 to 03/19/2000   WEAVING FOR THE GODS: TEXTILES OF THE ANCIENT ANDES

Bush-Holly Historic Museum

Affiliate Institution: The Historical Society of the Town of Greenwich
39 Strickland Rd., Greenwich, CT 06807

☎: 203-869-6899
Open: 12-4 We-Fr, 11-4 Sa, 1-4 Su (April-Dec) 11-4 Sa, 1-4Su (Jan-March)   **Closed:** Mo, Tu, 1/1 THGV, 12/25 April-Dec), **Free Day:** Visitor's Center is always free   **ADM: Adult:** $6.00   **Children:** Free under 12   **Students:** $4.00   **Seniors:** $4.00
& ℗   **Museum Shop**
Group Tours   Drop-In Tours
Historic Building Located in 18th century Bush-Holley House, Home of CT. first art colony
Permanent Collection: DEC/ART 18-19; AM: Impr/ptgs

American Impressionist paintings and sculpture groups by John Rogers are the important fine art offerings of the 1732 Bush-Holley House. It was in this historical house museum, location of the first Impressionist art colony, that many of the artists in the collection resided while painting throughout the surrounding countryside. **NOT TO BE MISSED:** "Clarissa", by Childe Hassam

ON EXHIBIT 2000

Changing exhibitions of local history may be seen in addition to the permanent collection of paintings and sculptures.

CONNECTICUT

HARTFORD

Wadsworth Atheneum

600 Main Street, Hartford, CT 06103-2990
☎: 860-278-2670 ◉ www.wadsworthatheneum.org
Open: 11-5 Tu-Su, till 8 on some 1st Th of month **Closed:** Mo, 1/1, 7/4, THGV, 12/25
Free Day: Th all day, Sa 11-12
ADM: Adult: $7.00 **Children:** $3.00 6-17, Free under 6 **Students:** $5.00 **Seniors:** $5.00
♿ Ⓟ limited metered street parking, Free Parking Travelers outdoor lot #7, Sa and Su only. Commercial lots nearby
Museum Shop 🍴: Lunch Tu-Sa, Brunch Su, dinner till 8 1st Th, (860-728-5989 to reserve) Coffee wine bar daily till 4:30
Group Tours: ext 3046 **Drop-In Tours:** Tu-Fr 12:30, Sa, Su 1, 2:30
Historic Building Sculpture Garden
Permanent Collection: AM: ptgs, sculp, drgs, dec/art; FR: Impr/ ptgs SP, IT; DU;: 17; REN, CER, EU: OM 16-17: EU: dec/art

Founded in 1842, the Wadsworth Atheneum is the oldest museum in continuous operation in the country. In addition to the many wonderful and diverse facets of the permanent collection, a gift in 1994 of two important oil paintings by Picasso; namely, "The Women of Algiers" and "The Artist" makes the collection of works by Picasso one of the fullest in New England museums. The museum is also noted for its collection of Hudson River School landscape paintings, collection of Thomas Cole, Caravaggio, Salvador Dali, Joan Miro, Piet Mondrian and many others. The Wadsworrth has just acquired six important paintings including Marsden Hartley's "Down East Young Blades" and Vallerio Castello "St Genevieve of Brabant Discovered by her Husband" **NOT TO BE MISSED:** Caravaggio's "Ecstasy of St. Francis", Wallace Nutting collection of pilgrim furniture, Colonial Period rooms: African-American art (Fleet Gallery) Elizabeth B. Miles English Silver Collection, Hudson River School collection, 4 Sol Lewitt Wall drawings

ON EXHIBIT 2000

09/24/1999 to 01/30/2000 ABOUT FACE: ANDY WARHOL PORTRAITS
Warhol (1928-1987) was fascinated by the face. His 1960's paintings of Marilyn, Liz, Jackie and others brought the portrait back into focus as a subject for post-war art. This exhibit shows how his interest in the portrait and the cult of celebrity was constant throughout his career.

10/03/1999 to 02/27/2000 IMAGES OF CHILDHOOD 1800-1900
This exhibition represents a wide range of children's dress along with schoolgirl samplers, antique toys and dolls, pint sized furniture and embroidered children's mourning pictures.

01/2000 to 03/2000 JOSEPH GRIGELY MATRIX
"Conversations with the Hearing" is the title is the title of an ongoing series of recent installations by Grigely who has been deaf since childhood. When he cannot decipher a word by lip reading, he has the speaker write it out. These papers are juxtaposed with his notes. During the exhibition Grigely transforms a gallery into his studio to meet people and make his work.

01/21/2000 to 03/26/2000 SALVADOR DALI'S OPTICAL ILLUSIONS
This major survey of Dali's Trompe l'oiel or illusionistic work features many of the artist's most provocative, dreamlike pictures in which double and triple images layer meaning upon mystery. *Will Travel*

04/28/2000 to 08/06/2000 CALDER IN CONNECTICUT
Calder settled in Roxbury and lived and worked there for the rest of his life. His revolutionary "mobile" and "stabile" sculptures were first shown at the Wadsworth Athenaeum 1935. This exhibition features paintings, jewelry, and prints as well as sculpture made at his home and local foundries. Displays of photographs films, drawings and letters will illuminate the life of this artist.

09/08/2000 to 12/03/2000 THE IMPRESSIONISTS AT ARGENTEUIL
More than fifty impressionist paintings by six influential artists--Eugène Boudin, Gustave Caillebotte, Edouard Manet, Claude Monet, Auguste Renoir, and Alfred Sisley – will explore the fascination with the small town of Argenteuil just outside Paris, which became the inspiration for, and the subject of, many of the most lyrical, dazzling, and progressive paintings of the day. The exhibition will show the richness of the artists' individual responses to the site, as well as the complex dialogue that developed among them as they studied similar motifs and subjects. *Will Travel*

CONNECTICUT

Davison Art Center

Affiliate Institution: Weslyan University
301 High St., Middletown, CT 06459-044nm
☏: 860-685-2500 ◉ www.wesleyan.edu/dac/home.html
Open: Noon-4 Tu-Fr; 2-5 Sa, Su (SEPT-early JUNE); closed June - August **Closed:** Mo, ACAD! LEG/HOL!
Vol/Cont:
ⓟ On street **Museum Shop**
Group Tours: 860-685-2500
Historic Building Historic 1830'S Alsop House
Permanent Collection: GR 15-20; PHOT 19-20; DRGS

Historic Alsop House (1830), on the grounds of Wesleyan University, is home to a fine permanent collection of prints, photographs and drawings.

New Britain Museum of American Art

56 Lexington St., New Britain, CT 06052
☏: 860-229-0257
Open: 1-5 Tu-Fr, 10-5 Sa, Noon-5 Su **Closed:** 1/1, EASTER, 7/4, THGV, 12/25
ADM: Adult: $3.00 **Children:** Free under 12 **Students:** $2.00 **Seniors:** $2.00
♿ ⓟ Free on street parking **Museum Shop**
Group Tours
Permanent Collection: AM: ptgs, sculp, gr 18-20

The New Britain Museum, only minutes from downtown Hartford, and housed in a turn of the century mansion, is one of only five museums in the country devoted exclusively to American art. The collection covers 250 years of artistic accomplishment including the nation's first public collection of illustrative art. A recent bequest by Olga Knoepke added 26 works by Edward Hopper, George Tooker and other early 20th century Realist artworks to the collection. PLEASE NOTE: Tours for the visually impaired are available with advance notice. **NOT TO BE MISSED:** Thomas Hart Benton murals; Paintings by Child Hassam and other important American Impressionist masters.

Silvermine Guild Art Center

1037 Silvermine Rd., New Canaan, CT 06840
☏: 203-966-5617
Open: 11-5 Tu-Sa, 1-5 Su **Closed:** 1/1, 7/4, 12/25 & HOL. falling on Mondays
ADM: Adult: $2.00
♿ ⓟ Ample and free **Museum Shop**
Group Tours
Historic Building The Silvermine Guild was established in 1922 in a barn setting **Sculpture Garden**
Permanent Collection: PRTS: 1959-present

Housed in an 1890 barn, and established as one of the first art colonies in the country, the vital Silvermine Guild exhibits works by well known and emerging artists. Nearly 30 exhibitions are presented yearly.

CONNECTICUT

Yale Center for British Art
Affiliate Institution: Yale University
1080 Chapel St, New Haven, CT 06520-8280
☎: 203-432-2800 ◙ www.yale.edu/ycba
Open: 10-5 Tu-Sa, Noon-5 Su **Closed:** Mo, LEG/HOL!
& ℗ Parking lot behind the Center and garage directly across York St. **Museum Shop**
Group Tours: 203-432-2858 **Drop-In Tours**: Introductory & Architectural tours one Sa per mo.
Historic Building Last building designed by noted American architect, Louis Kahn
Permanent Collection: BRIT: ptgs, drgs, gr 16-20

With the most comprehensive collection of English paintings, prints, drawings, rare books and sculpture outside of Great Britain, the Center's permanent works depict British life and culture from the 16th century to the present. The museum, celebrating its 20th anniversary in 1998, is housed in the last building designed by the late great American architect, Louis Kahn. **NOT TO BE MISSED:** "Golden Age" British paintings by Turner, Constable, Hogarth, Gainsborough, Reynolds

ON EXHIBIT 2000
10/15/1999 to 01/09/2000 A TREASURE HOUSE IN FARMINGTON: THE LEWIS WALPOLE LIBRARY
The library commemorates its 20th anniversary with this exhibition of its most treasured possessions. It is con sidered to be one of Yale's foremost resources for British studies.

10/27/1999 to 01/09/2000 PATRICK CAULFIED RETROSPECTIVE
Caulfiield is the most distinctive voices of the swinging sixties in London. He is considered the most widely admired and respected British artists of the 20th century. *Only Venue Catalog*

Yale University Art Gallery
Affiliate Institution: Yale University
1111 Chapel St., New Haven, CT 06520
☎: 203-432-0600 ◙ www.yale.edu/artgallery
Open: 10-5 Tu-Sa, 2-5 Su **Closed:** 1/1, 7/4, MONTH OF AUGUST, THGV, 12/25
& ℗ Metered street parking plus parking at Chapel York Garage, 201 York St. **Museum Shop**
Group Tours: 203-432-0620 education dept. **Drop-In Tours**: Noon We & other! **Sculpture Garden**
Permanent Collection: AM: ptgs, sculp, dec/art; EU: ptgs, sculp; FR: Impr, Post/Impr; OM: drgs, gr; CONT: drgs, gr; IT/REN: ptgs; P/COL; AF: sculp; CH; AN/GRK; AN/EGT

Founded in 1832 with an original bequest of 100 works from the John Trumbull Collection, the Yale University Gallery has the distinction of being the oldest museum in North America. Today over 100,000 works from virtually every major period of art history are represented in the outstanding collection of this highly regarded university museum. **NOT TO BE MISSED:** "Night Cafe" by van Gogh

ON EXHIBIT 2000
10/29/1999 to 01/02/2000 FROM JOHN TRUMBULL TO EDWARD HOPPER: THE MAKING OF AMERICAN MASTERPIECES
A group of paintings by Hopper, Abbey, Eakins and Bellows with studies the artists made for these works.

11/09/1999 to 02/19/2000 FOUR CENTURIES OF AMERICAN DESIGN
The artworks include a late 17th C. chest of drawers and a silver and gold water tower created in 1993. Included are glass, silver, furniture and textiles from the past 4 C.

12/14/1999 to 02/13/2000 CHANGING IMPRESSIONS: MARC ANTONIO RAIMONDI AND 16TH CENTURY PRINT CONNOISSEURSHIP
20 works highlighting an unusual aspect of 16th C printmaking and collecting. Impressions of Mars, Cupid and Venus have all been altered. Were these an experiment, or done to deceive collectors.

01/25/2000 to 04/08/2000 JASPER JOHN: NEW PAINTINGS AND WORKS ON PAPER

CONNECTICUT

Lyman Allyn Museum at Connecticut College
625 Williams St., New London, CT 06320

✆: 860-443-2545
Open: 10-5 Tu-Sa, 1-5 Su   **Closed:** Mo, LEG/HOL!
ADM: **Adult:** $4.00   **Children:** Free 6 & under   **Students:** $3.00   **Seniors:** $3.00
& Ⓟ Free   **Museum Shop** ‖: Bookstore Cafe
Group Tours: 860-443-2545 x112   **Drop-In Tours**: 2 weekly   **Sculpture Garden**
Permanent Collection: AM: ptgs, drgs, furn, Impr/ptgs; HUDSON RIVER SCHOOL: ptgs; 19th c. landscape, AM/CT DEC ART.

Founded in 1926 by Harriet U. Allyn as a memorial to her whaling merchant father, Lyman Allyn, Lyman Allyn Art Museum was established for the community of southeastern Connecticut to use, enjoy, and learn about art and culture. The Museum is housed in a handsome Neo-Classical building designed by Charles A. Platt, architect of The Freer Gallery of Art in Washington DC, the Lyme Art Association Building, and several buildings on the campus of Connecticut College, with whom the Museum has recently affiliated. **Outdoors on the Museum Grounds Sculpture by Sol Lewitt, Carol Kreeger Davidson, Niki Ketchman, David Smalley, Gavriel Warren, Jim Visconti and Robert Taplin NOT TO BE MISSED:** 19th century Deshon Allyn House open by appointment only, Toy and Doll Museum at 165 State Street, New London

ON EXHIBIT 2000
01/08/2000 to 03/12/2000   DRAWING IS ANOTHER KIND OF LANGUAGE: AMERICAN DRAWINGS
From Jasper Johns, Ellsworth Kelly and Sol LeWitt to Donald Judd, Brice Marden, Joel Shapiro (and many, many others!), the 100 drawings by renowned contemporary American artists featured in this major exhibition will be seen in the first public showing of works from one of the most important and distinguished private collections of its kind in America.

01/08/2000 to 03/19/2000   DENISE GREEN: RESONATING

·**01/16/2000 to 02/26/2000   CATHERINE LEE: ALPHABET SERIES**

09/2000 to 10/2000   PAT STEIR: PAINTINGS

09/29/2000 to 11/26/2000   KENNETH TYLER: THIRTY YEARS OF PAINTING
Tyler and his workshop transformed American printmaking into areas once considered the sole domain of painting and sculpture. Artists include Rauschenburg, Motherwell and Hockney.

Slater Memorial Museum
Affiliate Institution: The Norwich Free Academy
108 Crescent St., Norwich, CT 06360

✆: 860-887-2506
Open: SEPT-JUNE: 9-4 Tu-Fr & 1-4 Sa-Su; JULY-AUG: 1-4 Tu-Su   **Closed:** Mo, LEG/HOL! STATE/HOL!
ADM: **Adult:** $2.00
Ⓟ Free along side museum. However parking is not permitted between 1:30 - 2:30 during the week to allow for school buses to operate.   **Museum Shop**
Group Tours: ex 218   **Historic Building** 1888 Romanesque building designed by architect Stephen Earle
Permanent Collection: AM: ptgs, sculp, gr; DEC/ART; OR; AF; POLY; AN/GRK; NAT/AM

Dedicated in 1888, the original three story Romanesque structure has expanded from its original core collection of antique sculpture castings to include a broad range of 17th through 20th century American art. This museum has the distinction of being one of only two fine arts museums in the U.S. located on the campus of a secondary school. **NOT TO BE MISSED:** Classical casts of Greek, Roman and Renaissance sculpture

Florence Griswold Museum

96 Lyme St., Old Lyme, CT 06371

☎: 860-434-5542 ◙ www.flogris.org
Open: April thru Dec: 10-5 Tu-Sa, 1-5 Su; FEB through March : 1-5 We-Su **Closed:** Mo, LEG/HOL!
ADM: Adult: $5.00 **Children:** Free under 12 **Students:** $4.00 **Seniors:** $4.00
&. ℗ Ample and free **Museum Shop**
Group Tours Drop-In Tours: daily upon request
Historic Building
Permanent Collection: AM: Impr/ptgs; DEC/ART

The beauty of the Old Lyme, Connecticut countryside in the early part of the 20th century attracted dozens of artists to the area. Many of the now famous American Impressionists worked here during the summer and lived in the Florence Griswold boarding house, which is now a museum that stands as a tribute to the art and artists of that era. The site includes 11 landscaped acres, gardens, river frontage, and the Hartman education center. **NOT TO BE MISSED:** The Chadwick Studio: restored early 20th century artists' studio workplace of American Impressionist, William Chadwick. Free with admission, the Studio is open in the summer only.

ON EXHIBIT 2000
Temporary exhibitions usually from the permanent collection.

DECEMBER   CELEBRATION OF HOLIDAY TREES
A month long display of trees throughout the house is presented annually. Every year a new theme is chosen and each tree is decorated accordingly.

Aldrich Museum of Contemporary Art

258 Main St., Ridgefield, CT 06877

☎: 203-438-4519
Open: 12-5 Tu-Su, Fr 12-8 **Closed:** Mo, LEG/HOL!
Free Day: Tu **ADM: Adult:** $5.00 **Children:** Free under 12 **Students:** $2.00 **Seniors:** $2.00
&. ℗ Free **Museum Shop**
Group Tours Drop-In Tours: 2:00 Su
Historic Building Sculpture Garden
Group Tours Drop-In Tours

The Aldrich Museum of Contemporary Art, one of the foremost contemporary art museums in the Northeast, offers the visitor a unique blend of modern art housed within the walls of a landmark building dating back to the American Revolution. One of the first museums in the country dedicated solely to contemporary art, the Aldrich exhibits the best of the new art being produced. **NOT TO BE MISSED:** Outdoor Sculpture Garden

ON EXHIBIT 2000
Changing quarterly exhibitions of contemporary art featuring works from the permanent collection, collectors works, regional artists, and installations of technological artistic trends.

CONNECTICUT

Whitney Museum of American Art at Champion
Atlantic St. & Tresser Blvd., Stamford, CT 06921
☎: 203-358-7630
Open: 11-5 Tu-Sa **Closed:** 1/1, THGV, 7/4, 12/25
 ♿ Ⓟ Free parking in the Champion garage on Tresser Blvd. **Museum Shop**
Group Tours: 203-358-7641 **Drop-In Tours**: 12:30 Tu, Th, Sa
Group Tours Drop-In Tours

The Whitney Museum of American Art at Champion, the only branch of the renowned Whitney Museum outside of New York City, features changing exhibitions of American Art primarily of the 20th century. Many of the works are drawn from the Whitney's extensive permanent collection and exhibitions are supplemented by lectures, workshops, films and concerts.

ON EXHIBIT 2000
Call for current exhibition and special events information.

William Benton Museum of Art, Connecticut State Art Museum
Affiliate Institution: University of Connecticut
245 Glenbrook Rd. U-140, Storrs, CT 06269-2140
☎: 860-486-4520 ◉ www.benton.uconn.edu
Open: 10-4:30 Tu-Fr; 1-4:30 Sa, Su **Closed:** Mo, LEG/HOL
 ♿ Ⓟ Weekdays visitor's may park in the campus parking garage or metered lot on Grenbrook Road; Weekends or evenings park in metered or unmetered spaces of in any campus lot. Handicapped spaces in visitor's lot behind the Museum.
Museum Shop
Group Tours: 860-486-1711 or 486-4520
Permanent Collection: EU: 16-20; AM: 17-20; KATHE KOLLWITZ: gr; REGINALD MARSH: gr

One of New England's finest small museums. Its Collegiate Gothic building, on the national register of Historic Places, is the setting for a wide variety of culturally diverse changing exhibitions. Call ahead for exhibition information and programs.

ON EXHIBIT 2000
01/2000 to 03/2000 ERIN VALENTINO EXHIBIT

82

DELAWARE

DOVER

Sewell C. Biggs Museum of American Art
406 Federal Street P. O. Box 711, Dover, DE 19903
☎: 302-674-2111 ● www.biggsmuseum.org
Open: 10-4 We-Sa; 1:30-4:30 Su **Closed:** Mo, Tu, LEG/HOL!
Vol/Cont:
& ℗ Free **Museum Shop Group Tours Drop-In Tours**: time Varies **Historic Building**
Permanent Collection: AM; pntgs, sculp, Dec/Arts

A collection of about 500 objects assembled by one man. The focus is on the arts of Delaware and the Delaware Valley.

ON EXHIBIT 2000
to 01/09/2000 IMAGES OF KENT COUNTY

01/12/2000 to 03/05/2000 THE COTTAGE COLLECTION: OBJECTS FROM THE HOUSE OF SEWELL C. BIGGS

03/08/2000 to 05/07/2000 TOM WILSON: SUPER REALIST

06/28/2000 to 08/27/2000 BEYOND ILLUSTRATION: FRANK SCHOONOVER'S LANDSCAPES

09/06/2000 to 11/05/2000 CHARLES PARKS: SMALL WORKS

WILMINGTON

Broughton Masterpiece Presentations-First USA Riverfront Arts Center
800 South Madison Street, Wilmington, DE
☎: 888-395-0005, 302-777-7767 ● www.broughtonmasterpiece.com
Open: 9 am-8 PM (last tour at 6 PM daily
ADM & ℗ Free **Museum Shop** ¶: Coffee shop & restaurant

The Broughton Masterpiece Presentation international cultural exchange program features major, grand-scale international art exhibitions from the world's leading art, scientific historic and cultural institutions, and private collections. Call for current exhibition information. Past internationally-acclaimed exhibitions have included "Nicholas and Alexandra: The last Imperial Family of Tsarist Russia" (1998/1999) and "Splendors of Meiji: Treasures of Imperial Japan (1999).

Delaware Art Museum
2301 Kentmere Pkwy., Wilmington, DE 19806
☎: 302-571-9590 ● www.delart.mus.de.us/
Open: 9-4 Tu & Th-Sa, 10-4 Su, 9-9 We **Closed:** Mo, 1/1, THGV, 12/25
Free Day: 4-9 W; 9-12 Sa **ADM: Adult:** $5.00 **Children:** Free 6 & under **Students:** $2.50
& ℗ Free behind museum **Museum Shop** ¶: The Museum Cafe
Group Tours Drop-In Tours: 11 am 3rd Tu & Sa of the month
Permanent Collection: AM: ptgs 19-20; BRIT: P/Raph; GR; SCULP; PHOT

Begun as a repository for the works of noted Brandywine Valley painter/illustrator Howard Pyle, the Delaware Art Museum has grown to include other collections of note especially in the areas of Pre-Raphaelite painting and contemporary art. **NOT TO BE MISSED:** "Summertime" by Edward Hopper; "Milking Time" by Winslow Homer

DELAWARE

Delaware Art Museum - continued

ON EXHIBIT 2000

10/08/1999 to 01/02/2000   ELLSWORTH KELLY: FIVE DECADES OF LINE, FORM AND COLOR
The only East Coast venue for this major exhibition. View twenty-two unique works from the artist's collection before they become part of the San Francisco Museum of Modern Art's Permanent collection.

10/8/1999 to 03/05/2000   THE LAMPS OF TIFFANY: HIGHLIGHTS FROM THE EGON AND HILDEGARD NEUSTADT COLLECTION.
More than 40 lamps and two leaded-glass windows produced by the Corona, New York, workshops of Louis Comfort Tiffany, America's premier Aesthetic Movement decorators.

11/23/1999 to 01/10/2000   FANTASIES, FAIRY TALES AND MORE: ILLUSTRATIONS BY BEATRIX POTTER
A delightful group of 30 drawings show the varied talents and imaginations of three beloved British illustrators. Among the featured works are Beatrix Potter's pen and ink drawings for "Little Red Riding Hood" and "Sleeping Beauty"; Arthur Rackham's illustrations for The Fairy Tales of the Brothers Grimm and Fairy Tales by Hans Andersen; and Kate Greenaway's charming watercolors for Victorian keepsakes such as almanacs and her illustrations for Bret Harte's The Queen of Pirate Isle.

01/20/2000 to 03/19/2000   STUART DAVIS IN GLOUCESTER
38 paintings and works on paper survey his stylistic development from 'Ashcan' School realism through French Impressionism and Post-Impressionism to Cubism in his treatment of the Cape Ann land and seascapes.

04/06/2000 to 06/04/2000   BIENNIAL 2000: ART AT THE NEW MILLENNIUM
Diverse works by 40 innovative and outstanding regional artists invited to present their work. Painting, sculpture, installation, photography, computer and video art.

06/21/2000 to 08/13/2000   YOUNG AMERICA: TREASURES FROM THE SMITHSONIAN NATIONAL MUSEUM OF AMERICAN ART
54 works by the era's most famous artists, trace the transformation of the colonies into nationhood from the 1760s to the Civil War. Includes portraits by Gilbert Stuart, Charles Willson Peale; paintings by Benjamin West, Washington Allston; landscapes by Thomas Cole, Alvan Fisher; genre paintings by John Quidor, Lily Martin Spencer. Hudson River School landscapes by Asher B. Durand, Frederic E. Church. Sculptures by Horatio Greenough, Hiram Powers. Civil War era paintings by Samuel Colman, Homer Dodge Martin.   *Catalog   Will Travel*

06/22/2000 to 09/04/2000   CENTENNIAL CELEBRATION OF ARDEN: DELAWARE'S ARTS AND CRAFTS COMMUNITY
The first exhibition to examine the Arts and Crafts community of Arden, Delaware, from its founding in 1900 to the 1935 death of its visionary leader Frank Stephens. Started as a single-tax community, residents produced art, crafts, literary, musical and theatrical works for the community and to market to a broad audience. Painting, sculpture, ceramics, prints and drawings, plus metal, furniture, textiles, stained glass and book arts.

06/22/2000 to 09/04/2000   THE DU PONT FAMILY LEGACY AT THE DELAWARE ART MUSEUM
To celebrate the du Pont family's 200th anniversary in America, the museum will highlight its role and enormous contribution to the growth and development of the museum and its collections.

10/06/2000 to 01/03/2001   THE DEFINING MOMENT: VICTORIAN NARRATIVE PAINTINGS FROM THE FORBES MAGAZINE COLLECTION
Fifty paintings from the Forbes Magazine collection, assembled by Christopher Forbes in the landmark Old Battersea House in London, explore the 19th Century British predilection for narrative paintings. This skilled group of Victorian artists includes Pre-Raphaelite John Everett Millais and Royal Academicians William Powell Frith and James J. Tiss.

Art Museum of the Americas
201 18th St., N.W., Washington, DC 20006
☎: 202-458-6016
Open: 10-5 Tu-Su   **Closed:** LEG/HOL!
Vol/Cont:
Ⓟ Metered street parking   **Museum Shop**
Group Tours: 202-458-6301
Permanent Collection: 20th C LATIN AMERICAN & CARIBBEAN ART

Established in 1976, and housed in a Spanish colonial style building completed in 1912, this museum contains the most comprehensive collection of 20th century Latin American art in the country. **NOT TO BE MISSED:** The loggia behind the museum opening onto the Aztec Gardens

Arthur M. Sackler Gallery
1050 Independence Ave., SW, Washington, DC 20560
☎: 202-357-2700   ◙   www.si.edu/asia
Open: 10-5:30 Daily   **Closed:** 12/25
♿ Ⓟ Free 3 hour parking on Jefferson Dr; some metered street parking
Museum Shop
Group Tours: 202-357-4880 ex 245   **Drop-In Tours**: 11:30 daily
Permanent Collection: CH: jade sculp; JAP: cont/cer; PERSIAN: ptgs; NEAR/E: an/silver

Opened in 1987 under the auspices of the Smithsonian Institution, the Sackler Gallery, named for its benefactor, houses some of the most magnificent objects of Asian art in America.

ON EXHIBIT 2000
CONTINUING INDEFINITELY   PUJA: EXPRESSIONS OF HINDU DEVOTION
Approximately 180 bronze, stone and wooden objects made in India as offerings in an essential element of Hindu worship known as "puja" will be seen in an exhibition focusing mainly on their functional use rather than their aesthetic beauty.

CONTINUING INDEFINITELY   THE ARTS OF CHINA
Exquisite furniture, paintings, porcelain and jade from China's last two Imperial dynasties - the Ming (1368-1664) and Qing (1644-1911) will be on exhibit.

10/17/1999 to 01/17/2000   TREASURES FROM THE ROYAL TOMBS OF UR
Mid-third millennium BC gold & silver jewels, cups, bowls and other ancient objects excavated from the royal burial tombs of Ur will be on exhibit. *Catalog Will Travel*

11/08/1999 to 02/07/2000   ROY LICHTENSTEIN: LANDSCAPES IN THE CHINESE STYLE
Lichtenstein, a leading practitioner of "Pop Art" adapted his technique to capture the effect of classic Sung dynasty (960-1279) paintings. 26 examples with the 6 examples of the Chinese paintings which inspired them are shown.

11/17/1999 to 05/07/2000   IMAGING THE WORLD: NEW SELECTIONS OF CALLIGRAPHY FROM THE ISLAMIC WORLD
These works on paper are shown with inscribed textiles, coins, architectural fragments and other objects to show the art of writing and its spiritual and aesthetic dimensions.

11/17/1999 to 05/07/2000   ANTOIN SEVRUGUIN AND THE PERSIAN IMAGE
Sevruguin operated a successful studio in Tehran from 1850's-1934. These come from the Freer Gallery Collection and the Arthur M. Sackler Gallery Archives Collection and offer an important pictorial record of the social history and visual culture in Iran.

11/21/1999 to 02/28/2000   CONSTRUCTING IDENTITIES: RECENT WORKS BY JANNANE AL-ANI
Two pairs of large-format (4 x 6 Foot) photographs and a related video addressing a topical issue- Orientalism-and in particular the representation of women.

Arthur M. Sackler Gallery - continued
05/28/2000 to 11/05/2000   SHAHNAMA
The first exhibition to look at the historical figures made legendary in the epic "Book of Kings" composed in 1010 by the poet Findawski. It will include coins, paintings, metalwork and ceramics drawn from the permanent collections of the Sackler Gallery.

06/11/2000 to 11/26/2000   RUSSO/JAPANESE PRINTS
Recently acquired prints and prints on loan most in triptych format surveying the traditional medium to reportage of Japan's war with Imperial Russia.

Corcoran Gallery of Art
17th St. & New York Ave., NW, Washington, DC 20006-4804

☎: 202-639-1700
Open: 10-5 Mo & We-Su, till 9pm Th   **Closed:** 1/1, 12/25
ADM: Adult: $3.00   **Children:** Free under 12   **Students:** $1.00   **Seniors:** $1.00
 ⚐ ℗ Limited metered parking on street; commercial parking lots nearby   **Museum Shop**
🍴: Cafe 11-3 daily & till 8:30 Th; Gospel Brunch 11-2 Su (202-639-1786)
Group Tours: 202-786-2374   **Drop-In Tours**: Noon daily; 7:30 Th; 10:30, 12 & 2:30 Sa, Su
Permanent Collection: AM & EU: ptgs, sculp, works on paper 18-20

The beautiful Beaux Art building built to house the collection of its founder, William Corcoran, contains works that span the entire history of American art from the earliest limners to the cutting edge works of today's contemporary artists. In addition to being the oldest art museum in Washington, the Corcoran has the distinction of being one of the three oldest art museums in the country. Recently the Corcoran became the recipient of the Evans-Tibbs Collection of African-American art, one of the largest and most important groups of historic American art to come to the museum in nearly 50 years.   PLEASE NOTE: There is a special suggested contribution fee of $5.00 for families.   **NOT TO BE MISSED:** "Mt. Corcoran" by Bierstadt; "Niagra" by Church; Restored 18th century French room Salon Doré

ON EXHIBIT 2000
ONGOING   TREASURES OF THE CORCORAN: THE PERMANENT COLLECTION ON VIEW

10/01/1999 to 01/02/2000   EVAN SUMMER

10/27/1999 to 02/28/2000   WOMEN BY ANNIE LEIBOVITZ

11/20/1999 to 01/31/2000   TO CONSERVE A LEGACY: AMERICAN ART FROM HISTORICALLY BLACK COLLEGES AND UNIVERSITIES
The collections of 6 historically Black colleges will be showcased in a exhibition of over 150 artworks. *Will Travel*

12/4/1999 to 02/06/2000   THE WAY HOME: ENDING HOMELESSNESS IN AMERICA

03/01/2000 to 06/23/2000   THE TOPKAPI PALACE: JEWELS AND TREASURES OF THE SULTANS
Included in the treasures of jewels are art and artifacts from the Ottoman Sultan   Many objects have never before left the Palace including a emerald and diamond adorned Topkapi dagger and a magnificently crafted imperial throne. *Catalog Will Travel*

03/2000 to 06/2000   ARNOLD NEWMAN: SIXTY YEARS

03/2000 to 05/2000   JACK BOUL

05/07/2000 to 07/17/2000   DONALD SULTAN: IN THE STILL LIFE TRADITION

06/17/2000 to 09/10/2000   NORMAN ROCKWELL: PICTURES FOR THE AMERICAN PEOPLE
Seventy of his oil paintings and all 322 'Saturday Evening Post' covers are featured in this always popular show. *Will Travel*

12/2000 to 02/2001   BIENNIAL 2000

Dumbarton Oaks Research Library & Collection

1703 32nd St., NW, Washington, DC 20007-2961

☎: 202-339-6401   ◙   www.doaks.org
Open: 2-6 Tu-Su, Apr-Oct; 2-5 Nov-MarHearst   **Closed:** Mo, LEG/HOL
ADM: Adult: $4.00   **Children:** $3.00   **Seniors:** $3.00
 ♿ ℗ On-street parking only   **Museum Shop**
Group Tours: 202-339-6409
Permanent Collection: BYZ; P/COL; AM: ptgs, sculp, dec/art; EU: ptgs, sculp, dec/art

This 19th century mansion, site of the international conference of 1944 where discussions leading to the formation of the United Nations were held, is best known for its rare collection of Byzantine and Pre-Columbian art. Beautifully maintained and now owned by Harvard University, Dumbarton Oaks is also home to a magnificent French Music Room and to 16 manicured acres that contain formally planted perennial beds, fountains and a profusion of seasonal flower gardens. PLEASE NOTE: 1. Although there is no admission fee to the museum, a donation of $1.00 is appreciated. 2. With the exception of national holidays and inclement weather, the museum's gardens are open daily. Hours and admission from Apr to Oct. are 2-6pm, $3.00 adults, $2.00 children & seniors. From Nov. to Mar. the gardens are open from 2-5pm with free admission. **NOT TO BE MISSED:** Music Room; Gardens (open daily Apr - Oct, 2-6 PM, $3.00 adult, $2.00 children/seniors; 2-5 PM daily Nov-Mar, Free)

ON EXHIBIT 2000

ONGOING   PRE-COLUMBIAN COLLECTION
Prime works from Mesoamerica, lower Central America and the Andes collected by Robert Woods Bliss.

ONGOING   BYZANTINE COLLECTION
The recently re-installed and expanded collection of early Byzantine silver joins the on-going textile exhibit from the permanent collection.

Federal Reserve Board Art Gallery

2001 C St., Washington, DC 20551

☎: 202-452-3686
Open: 11-2 Mo-Fr or by reservation   **Closed:** LEG/HOL! WEEKENDS
 ♿ ℗ Street parking only   **Museum Shop**
Group Tours   Historic Building Designed in 1937 by Paul Cret
Permanent Collection: PTGS, GR, DRGS 19-20 (with emphasis on late 19th C works by Amer. expatriates); ARCH: drgs of Paul Cret PLEASE NOTE: The permanent collection may be seen by appointment only.

Founded in 1975, the collection, consisting of both gifts and loans of American and European works of art, acquaints visitors with American artistic and cultural values. **NOT TO BE MISSED:** The atrium of this beautiful building is considered one of the most magnificent public spaces in Washington, DC.

Freer Gallery of Art

Jefferson Dr. at 12th St., SW, Washington, DC 20560

☎: 202-357-2700   ◙   www.si.edu/asia
Open: 10-5:50 Daily   **Closed:** 12/25
 ♿ ℗ Free 3 hour parking on the Mall   **Museum Shop**
Group Tours: 202-357-4880 ext. 245   **Drop-In Tours:** 11:30 Daily   **Historic Building** Member NRHP
Permanent Collection: OR: sculp, ptgs, cer; AM/ART 20; (FEATURING WORKS OF JAMES McNEILL WHISTLER; PTGS

One of the many museums in the nation's capitol that represent the results of a single collector, the 75 year old Freer Gallery, renowned for its stellar collection of the arts of all of Asia, is also home to one of the world's most important collections of works by James McNeill Whistler. **NOT TO BE MISSED:** "Harmony in Blue and Gold", The Peacock Room by James McNeill Whistler

Freer Gallery of Art - continued

ON EXHIBIT 2000

ONGOING ANCIENT EGYPTIAN GLASS
15 rare and brilliantly colored glass vessels created during the reigns of Amenhotep III (1391-1353 B.C.) and Akhenaten (1391-1353 B.C.) are highlighted in this small but notable exhibition.

ONGOING KOREAN CERAMICS

ONGOING ANCIENT CHINESE POTTERY AND BRONZE

ONGOING SETO AND MINO CERAMICS

ONGOING SHADES OF GREEN AND BLUE: CHINESE CELADON CERAMICS
Featured will be 44 celadon glazed Chinese ceramics presented with examples from Thailand, Korea, Japan and Vietnam.

ONGOING ARMENIAN GOSPELS

ONGOING ART FOR ART'S SAKE
Lacking a moral message, the 31 works on view by Whistler, Dewing, Thayer, and others working in the late 1880's, were created to be beautiful for beauty's sake alone.

05/05/1999 to 02/19/2000 WINGED FIGURES
Abbott Thayer , a leading American artist is an opportunity to show a group of paintings which his patron purchased to give to the gallery he had promised to the Smithsonian Institution.

05/17/1999 to 01/09/2000 A BREATH OF SPRING
The masterpiece 14th C painting "A Breath of Spring" and a new poem by Ondaatje author of "The English Patient" This is considered one of the earliest and greatest examples of pure ink painting on the subject of the flowering plum.

05/29/1999 to 01/30/2000 MASTERPIECES OF CHINESE PAINTING
10th to early 18th C. painting and calligraphy from the Freer collection. Major formats of handscrolls, traditional books, hanging scrolls which evolved from Buddhist temple banners, became fashionable during the Song dynasty (960-1279) are on view.

06/29/1999 to 04/02/2000 WHISTLER PRINTS I: THE HADENS
The second in a series of small exhibitions focused on James McNeill Whistler's printmaking career. These, mostly drypoints and etchings, were done in the period when Whistler worked in London and portrayed members of his half-sister' Deborah and her husband. *Will Travel*

Spring/2000 ARRANGEMENT IN WHITE AND YELLOW

Hillwood Museum

4155 Linnean Ave., NW, Washington, DC 20008
☎: 202-686-8500
Open: BY RESERVATION ONLY: 9, 10:45, 12:30, 1:45, 3:00 Tu-Sa **Closed:** FEB. & LEG/HOL!
ADM: **Adult:** $10.00 **Children:** $5.00 **Students:** $5.00 **Seniors:** $10.00
♿ Ⓟ Free **Museum Shop** 🍴: Reservations accepted (202) 686-8893)
Group Tours: 202-686-5807
Sculpture Garden
Permanent Collection: RUSS: ptgs, cer, dec/art; FR: cer, dec/art, glass 18-19

The former home of Marjorie Merriweather Post, heir to the Post cereal fortune, is filled primarily with the art and decorative treasures of Imperial Russia which she collected in depth over a period of more than 40 years. NOTE: children under 12 are not permitted in the house. There are no changing exhibitions. PLEASE NOTE: Due to extensive renovation, the home will be closed to the public for the next several years. **NOT TO BE MISSED:** Carl Faberge's Imperial Easter Eggs and other of his works; glorious gardens surrounding the mansion

Hirshhorn Museum and Sculpture Garden
Affiliate Institution: Smithsonian Institution
Independence Ave. at Seventh St., NW, Washington, DC 20560
☎: 202-357-2700 ◙ www.si.edu/hirshhorn
Open: Museum: 10-5:30 Daily; Plaza: 7:30am - 5:30 PM, S/G: 7:30am - dusk **Closed:** 12/25
& ℗ metered parking nearby, commercial lots nearby **Museum Shop**
❚❘: Plaza Café MEM/DAY to LAB/DAY only
Group Tours: 202-357-3235 **Drop-In Tours:** 10:30 - 12 Mo-Fr; 12 -2 Sa, Su **Sculpture Garden**
Permanent Collection: CONT: sculp, art; AM: early 20th; EU: early 20th; AM: realism since Eakins

Endowed by the entire collection of its founder, Joseph Hirshhorn, this museum focuses primarily on modern and contemporary art of all kinds and cultures in addition to newly acquired works. One of its most outstanding features is its extensive sculpture garden. PLEASE NOTE: No tours are given on holidays. **NOT TO BE MISSED:** Rodin's "Burghers of Calais"; works by Henry Moore and Willem deKooning, third floor

ON EXHIBIT 2000
10/07/1999 to 01/17/2000 REGARDING BEAUTY: A VIEW OF THE LATE 20TH CENTURY
To celebrate the 25th anniversary of the Hirshhorn the exhibition represents a spectrum of 20th C art which questions, comments on or reconsiders beauty. 80 paintings, sculpture, multi-media, drawings and installations by 35 artists active since 1950 will be included. Included are Jannine Antoni, John Baldesarri, Matthew Barney, Louise Bourgeois William de Kooning, Marlene Dumas, Lucien Freud, Yves Klein, Roy Lichtenstein, Richter, Risk, Ruschka, etc. *Catalog Will Travel*

02/17/2000 to 04/23/2000 ROBERT GOBER: SCULPTURE AND DRAWING
Winner of the 1996 Larry Aldrich Foundation Award, this presentation features Gober's installations, drawings, and a new major sculpture created specifically for this exhibition. *Catalog Will Travel*

04/20/2000 to 06/25/2000 SALVADOR DALI'S OPTICAL ILLUSIONS
This major survey of Dali's Trompe l'oiel or illusionistic work features many of the artist's most provocative, dreamlike pictures in which double and triple images layer meaning upon mystery. *Catalog Will Travel*

06/15/2000 to 09/10/2000 EDWARD RUSCHA *Catalog Will Travel*

Howard University Gallery of Art
2455 6th St., NW, Washington, DC 20059
☎: 202-806-7070
Open: 9:30-4:30 Mo-Fr; 1-4 Su (may be closed some Sundays in summer!) **Closed:** LEG/HOL!
& ℗ Metered parking; Free parking in the rear of the College of Fine Arts evenings and weekends **Museum Shop**
Group Tours
Permanent Collection: AF/AM: ptgs, sculp, gr; EU: gr; IT: ptgs, sculp (Kress Collection); AF

In addition to an encyclopedic collection of African and African-American art and artists there are 20 cases of African artifacts on permanent display in the east corridor of the College of Fine Arts. PLEASE NOTE: It is advisable to call ahead in the summer as the gallery might be closed for inventory work. **NOT TO BE MISSED:** The Robert B. Mayer Collection of African Art

Kreeger Museum
2401 Foxhall Rd., NW, Washington, DC 20007
☎: 202-338-3552 ◙ www.kreegermuseum.com
Open: Tours only at 10:30 & 1:30 Tu-Sa **Closed:** Mo, LEG/HOL! & AUG; call for information on some additional closures
ADM: Adult: $5.00
& ℗ Free parking for 40 cars on the grounds of the museum. **Museum Shop**
Group Tours: 202-338-3552 **Drop-In Tours:** 10:30 & 1:30 Tu-Sa
Sculpture Garden
Permanent Collection: EU: ptgs, sculp 19,20; AM: ptgs, sculp 19,20; AF; P/COL

DISTRICT OF COLUMBIA

Kreeger Museum - continued
Designed by noted American architect Philip Johnson as a stunning private residence for David Lloyd and Carmen Kreeger, this home has now become a museum that holds the remarkable art collection of its former owners. With a main floor filled with Impressionist and post-Impressionist paintings and sculpture, and fine collections of African, contemporary, and Washington Color School art on the bottom level, this museum is a "must see" for art lovers traveling to the D.C. area. PLEASE NOTE: Only 35 people for each designated time slot are allowed on each 90 minute tour of this museum at the hours specified and only by reservation. Children under 12 are not permitted. **NOT TO BE MISSED:** Collection of 9 Monet Paintings; Robert Kapilow to create symphony about Washington Monuments which will be the culmination of a 3 part Millenium presented by the Kreeger Museum, Kennedy Center, National Public Radio and the National Symphony Orchestra.

National Gallery of Art
4th & Constitution Ave., N.W., Washington, DC 20565
☎: 202-737-4215 ◉ www.nga.gov
Open: 10-5 Mo-Sa, 11-6 Su **Closed:** 1/1, 12/25
&. ℗ Limited metered street parking; free 3 hour mall parking as available.
Museum Shop ❱❚: 3 restaurants plus Espresso bar
Group Tours: 202-842-6247 **Drop-In Tours:** daily!
Permanent Collection: EU: ptgs, sculp, dec/art 12-20; OM; AM: ptgs, sculp, gr 18-20; REN: sculp; OR: cer ♡

The two buildings that make up the National Gallery, one classical and the other ultra modern, are as extraordinary and diverse and the collection itself. Considered one of the premier museums in the world, more people pass through the portals of the National Gallery annually than almost any other museum in the country. Self-guided family tour brochures of the permanent collection as well as walking tour brochures for adults are available for use in the museum. In addition, advance reservations may be made for tours given in a wide variety of foreign languages. **NOT TO BE MISSED:** The only Leonardo Da Vinci oil painting in an American museum collection

ON EXHIBIT 2000

ONGOING MICRO GALLERY
Available for public use, the recently opened Micro Gallery consists of 13 computer terminals that make it possible for visitors to access detailed images of, and in-depth information to, nearly every one of the 1700 works on display in the National Gallery's permanent collection.

09/26/1999 to 01/09/2000 THE DRAWINGS OF ANNIBALE CARRACCI
The first monographic exhibition of Annibale Carracci (1560-1609), one of the greatest draftsmen of all time, celebrates his naturalism, imagination, and wide range of subjects. Among ninety-five of the master's best drawings will be grand compositions, quick jottings, individual figure studies, landscapes, and genre scenes.

10/03/1999 to 01/09/2000 TILMAN RIEMENSCHNEIDER: MASTER SCULPTOR OF THE LATE MIDDLE AGES
The first major survey of master sculptor Tilman Riemenschneider (active in Würzburg, Germany, from 1483 to 1531) in almost seventy years presents more than fifty of his finest works in a variety of media, including fragments of altarpieces, independent figures, objects for private devotion, and models he created for assistants. The exhibition will bring together five of his exquisite yet little known alabaster sculptures. Reimenschneider struck a balance between elegance and expressive strength. He was solidly anchored in the late Gothic tradition while expressing humanist concerns. Will Travel

10/17/1999 to 01/16/2000 BRASSEI: THE EYE OF PARIS
This retrospective celebrates the centenary of the artist's birth (born Gyula Halász on 9 September 1899 in Brasso, Transylvania) with approximately 125 works, including the artist's best-known photographs of Paris at night in the late 1920s and early 1930s. The first exhibition since Brassaï's death in 1984 to fully examine his career, this show also investigates many of his other projects, among them his studies of high society, and portraits of friends and colleagues, such as Jean Genet and Alberto Giacometti, as well as haunting studies of children's graffiti made after World War II. *Catalog Will Travel*

National Gallery of Art - continued

10/24/1999 to 01/09/2000   FROM SCHONGAUER TO HOLBEIN: MASTER DRAWINGS FROM BASEL AND BERLIN
This unprecedented exhibition of masterworks by many of the finest Renaissance artists in Germany and Switzerland is drawn from two of the foremost collections of these drawings in the world, the great art museums in Basel and Berlin. Dating from 1465 to 1545, approximately 190 drawings in a rich variety of color, style, and subject matter will focus on major groups by the greatest artists, providing mini-surveys of such masters as Martin Schongauer, Hans Holbein the Elder, Matthias Grünewald, Hans Baldung, Albrecht Altdorfer, Urs Graf, and Hans Holbein the Younger, as well as a rich selection of works by the towering artistic figure, Albrecht Dürer.

11/07/1999 to 02/27/2000   AN ENDURING LEGACY: MASTERPIECES FROM THE COLLECTION OF MR. AND MRS. PAUL MELLON
Highlights from the gifts and bequests of Paul Mellon (1907-1999), one of the Gallery's founding benefactors, will celebrate the legacy of his generosity to the National Gallery of Art. Approximately one hundred works including French, British, and American paintings, sculpture, drawings, watercolors, and prints will be on view. A section of the exhibition will be devoted to the work of Edgar Degas, and will include such masterpieces as Little Dancer Fourteen Years Old (in both wax and plaster models) and a selection of the master's unique small sculptures in wax of bathers, dancers, horses and riders, along with the monumental painting Scene from the Steeplechase: The Fallen Jockey.

02/13/2000 to 05/07/2000   MARTIN JOHNSON HEADE
The art of Martin Johnson Heade (1819–1904) is perhaps the most varied and inventive of any nineteenth-century American painter. This definitive exhibition of some seventy of Heade's finest paintings, drawn from public and private collections across the nation. This show examines Heade as a painter of remarkable originality, the only major artist to devote equal attention to landscape, marine, and still-life subjects. Included in the exhibition are the greatest of Heade's evocative Newburyport marsh scenes, his powerful thunderstorms-at-sea subjects, scintillating small studies of flowers in vases, and an outstanding group of orchid-and-hummingbird compositions, a dramatic combination invented by Heade. In addition, the important group of sixteen hummingbird studies called "The Gems of Brazil" has been lent from the distinguished private collection of Richard Manoogian. The show concludes with a series of five of Heade's most sensuous renderings of the magnolia blossom, a subject he came to specialize in after moving to Florida in 1883.   *Will Travel*

02/20/2000 to 05/07/2000   CARLETON WATKINS: THE ART OF PERCEPTION
Approximately 125 works by the celebrated nineteenth-century American photographer Carleton Watkins (1829-1916) represent the first major showing of his work in almost twenty years. The exhibition presents the artist's magnificent mammoth-plate prints, as well as panoramic and stereo format photographs, including his best-known studies of Yosemite and other celebrated works from California, Washington, and Oregon from the late 1850s through the early 1890s.

03/05/2000 to 06/11/2000   THE EBSWORTH COLLECTION: TWENTIETH-CENTURY AMERICAN ART
This exhibition of more than seventy works from the collection of Mr. and Mrs. Barney A. Ebsworth will explore one of the premier private holdings of American modernist art, comprised primarily of paintings, along with a small number of exceptional sculptures and works on paper. The exhibition will include masterpieces by Patrick Henry Bruce, Alexander Calder, Willem de Kooning, Arthur Dove, Arshile Gorky, Marsden Hartley, David Hockney, Edward Hopper, Jasper Johns, Georgia O'Keeffe, Jackson Pollock, Charles Sheeler, Joseph Stella, Wayne Thiebaud, and Andy Warhol.

04/09/2000 to 07/09/2000   O'KEEFFE ON PAPER
Some of Georgia O'Keeffe's most innovative creations are works on paper. The exhibition will present approximately fifty of her most stunning watercolors, charcoals, and pastels, drawn from public institutions, and rarely seen works from private collections. It also commemorates the publication of the Georgia O'Keeffe catalogue raisonné, a scholarly project of the National Gallery of Art in collaboration with The Georgia O'Keeffe Foundation, which will be published in the year 2000.

04/16/2000 to 08/06/2000   GERRIT DOU
This exhibition will bring together nearly forty of the finest paintings representing the full career of Gerrit Dou (1613-1675). Dou, Rembrandt's first pupil, was one of the most highly esteemed Dutch artists of the seventeenth century, acclaimed for the extraordinary refinement and detail of his paintings. The exhibition will present many of his best portraits and still lifes, as well as scenes of daily life, including images of mothers with children, painters in their studios, scholars, shopkeepers, schoolmasters, musicians, and astronomers.

05/14/2000 to 07/23/2000   RAPHAEL AND HIS CIRCLE: DRAWINGS FROM WINDSOR CASTLE
From the collection of the Royal Library, more than sixty drawings by Raphael (1483-1520) and his circle will provide an overview of the brief career of one of Western art's greatest painters. He developed the principles of composition, types of figure drawing, and systems of workshop collaboration that set the standards for much of the next four centuries. Also included are works by artists who helped form his style, and by his assistants, who disseminated interpretations of his style throughout Italy.

91

National Gallery of Art - continued

05/21/2000 to 10/09/2000   THE TRIUMPH OF THE BAROQUE: ARCHITECTURE IN EUROPE 1600-1750
A panorama of architecture in Europe from 1600 to 1750--including palaces, private residences, public buildings, and churches--will be presented. More than twenty-five architectural models and fifty related paintings, drawings, prints, and medals explore the unparalleled unification of the arts of painting, sculpture, architecture, landscape, and urban planning during the baroque era.

05/28/2000 to 08/20/2000   THE IMPRESSIONISTS AT ARGENTEUIL
More than fifty impressionist paintings by six influential artists--Eugène Boudin, Gustave Caillebotte, Edouard Manet, Claude Monet, Auguste Renoir, and Alfred Sisley – will explore the fascination with the small town of Argenteuil just outside Paris, which became the inspiration for, and the subject of, many of the most lyrical, dazzling, and progressive paintings of the day. The exhibition will show the richness of the artists' individual responses to the site, as well as the complex dialogue that developed among them as they studied similar motifs and subjects.

10/1/2000 to 01/28/2001   ART NOUVEAU: SOURCES AND CITIES, 1890-1914
This exhibition of approximately 350 works will explore one of the most exuberant and visually appealing styles in modern art, which flourished throughout Europe and in major American cities from about 1890 to the First World War. Opening with a selection of about thirty international art nouveau masterpieces that were displayed at the 1900 Paris Exposition Universelle, the exhibition will explore the sources of art nouveau and examine its interpretations in eight European and American cities.

10/01/2000 to 02/04/2001   COLLECTING FOR THE NATION: A DECADE OF ACQUISITIONS
This exhibition presents the greatest masterpieces acquired by the Gallery since 1991, when the fiftieth anniversary of its founding was celebrated with the exhibition Art for the Nation. Approximately seventy paintings and sixty works on paper will be on view, spanning five centuries, from about 1480 to 1980. There will be substantial representation of Renaissance, seventeenth-century Dutch, and nineteenth-century American and French works, including paintings by Peter Paul Rubens, Edgar Degas, Edouard Manet, Vincent van Gogh, Henri de Toulouse-Lautrec, Claude Monet, Henri Matisse, Thomas Cole, and Winslow Homer. Among the works on paper will be drawings by Botticelli, Albrecht Dürer, Raphael, Sir Anthony van Dyck, Rembrandt, Giovanni Battista Piranesi, Jean Honoré Fragonard, Jean-Auguste-Dominique Ingres, and Caspar David Friedrich.

10/22/2000 to 02/25/2001   PRINTS ABOUND: PARIS IN THE 1890S FROM THE COLLECTIONS OF VIRGINIA AND IRA JACKSON AND THE NATIONAL GALLERY OF ART (working title)
This exhibition of more than 150 prints, drawings, periodicals, illustrated books, music primers, and song sheets will explore the phenomenal outpouring of print publications in late nineteenth-century France. Primarily selected from the Virginia and Ira Jackson collection, the exhibition will feature works by some thirty artists, including Pierre Bonnard, Edouard Vuillard, Henri de Toulouse-Lautrec, Paul Gauguin, and Odilon Redon. Bonnard's achievement will be highlighted, and his work will be represented in depth by spirited posters, contributions to single- and multiple-artist portfolios, designs for music primers and illustrated books, and an outstanding four-panel folding screen of a fashionable street scene in fin-de-siècle Paris.

01/28/2000 to 04/22/2001   ALFRED STIEGLITZ AND MODERN ART IN AMERICA
This is the first exhibition to fully explore Alfred Stieglitz's seminal role in the development of modern art in America, and includes more than 150 paintings, sculptures, photographs, and works on paper. The first section focuses on Stieglitz's support of European modernism at his "291" gallery in New York and presents the first works shown in America by such key figures of modern art as Constantin Brancusi, Paul Cézanne, Henri Matisse, and Pablo Picasso. The second section examines Stieglitz's support of American modernism and concludes with the great mature works of the Stieglitz circle, including Charles Demuth, Arthur Dove, Marsden Hartley, John Marin, Georgia O'Keeffe, Paul Strand, and Stieglitz himself.

National Museum of African Art
Affiliate Institution: Smithsonian Institution
950 Independence Ave., S.W., Washington, DC 20560
☎: 202-357-4600   ◉   www.si.edu/nmafa
Open: 10-5:30 Daily   **Closed:** 12/25
♿ ℗ Free 3 hour parking along the Mall
Museum Shop   Drop-In Tours
Permanent Collection: AF/ART

Opened in 1987, The National Museum of African Art is dedicated to the collection, exhibition, conservation and study of the arts of Africa.

National Museum of African Art - continued
ON EXHIBIT 2000

ONGOING   IMAGES OF POWER AND IDENTITY
More than 100 objects both from the permanent collection and on loan to the museum are grouped according to major geographical & cultural regions of sub-Saharan Africa.

ONGOING   THE ANCIENT WEST AFRICAN CITY OF BENIN, A.D. 1300-1897
A presentation of cast-metal heads, figures and architectural plaques from the Museum's permanent collection of art from the royal court of the capital of the Kingdom of Benin as it existed before British colonial rule.

ONGOING   THE ART OF THE PERSONAL OBJECT
Aesthetically important and interesting utilitarian objects reflect the artistic culture of various African societies.

ONGOING   THE ANCIENT NUBIAN CITY OF KERMA, 2500-1500 B.C.
A semi-permanent installation of 40 works from the Museum of Fine Arts in Boston celebrates Kerma, also known as Kush, the oldest city in Africa outside of Egypt that has been excavated.

ONGOING   CERAMIC ARTS AT THE NATIONAL MUSEUM OF AFRICAN ART

ONGOING   SOKARI DOUGLAS CAMP: THREE SCULPTURES

09/12/1999 to 01/02/2000   WRAPPED IN PRIDE: GHANIAN KENTE AND AFRICAN AMERICAN IDENTITY
Asante strip woven cloth called "kente" is the ,most popular and best known of all African textiles. The exhibition examines its history and use.

National Museum of American Art
Affiliate Institution: Smithsonian Institution
8th & G Sts., N.W., Washington, DC 20560
☎: 202-357-2700   ◉ www.nmaa.si.edu
Open: 10-5:30 Daily   **Closed:** 12/25
♿ Ⓟ Metered street parking with commercial lot nearby   **Museum Shop**   ‖: Patent Pending Cafe 11-3 Daily
Group Tours: 202-357-3095   **Drop-In Tours**: weekdays at Noon & 2
Historic Building Housed in Old Patent Office (Greek Revival architecture) mid 1800'S
Permanent Collection: AM: ptgs, sculp, gr, cont/phot, drgs, folk, Impr; AF/AM

The National Museum of American Art of the Smithsonian Institution, the first federal art collection, represents all regions, cultures and traditions in the United States. Today the collection contains over 37,500 works in all media, spanning more than 300 years of artistic achievement. The Old Patent Office Building, which houses the National Museum of American Art and the National Portrait Gallery, was built in the Greek Revival Style between 1836 and 1867 and is considered one of the finest neoclassical structures in the world. **NOT TO BE MISSED:** George Catlin's 19th C American-Indian paintings; Thomas Moran's Western Landscape paintings; James Hampton's "The Throne of the Third Heaven of the Nation's Millennium General Assembly"

ON EXHIBIT 2000
The Old Patent Office Building will be closed in January 2000. Public programs will be moved to the Renwick Gallery as will an exhibition program. During the renovation the collection will be called "Treasures to Go" and will tour the foremost American Art Collections in cities across the country. The breadth shows the determination to bring the finest works directly to the American people. PLEASE NOTE: DUE TO PLANNED CONSTRUCTION, CALL TO CONFIRM EXHIBITIONS.

09/24/1999 to 01/03/2000   MODERN AMERICAN REALISM: The Sara Roby Foundation Collection of the National Museum of American Art
This exhibition, held in conjunction with the special exhibition : Edward Hopper: The Watercolors, features 34 major examples of 20th century American realistic painting and sculpture.

09/24/1999 to 01/30/2000   GLASS! GLORIOUS GLASS!
The pieces explore the use of this ancient and common medium as a material for a modern artistic expression.

10/22/1999 to 01/03/2000   EDWARD HOPPER: THE WATERCOLORS
Painted primarily during his trips away from NY during the 1920's and 30's, these early watercolors brought Hopper his original success. He continued to return to the New England landscape for inspiration. *Catalog Will Travel*

DISTRICT OF COLUMBIA

National Museum of Women in the Arts
1250 New York Ave., N.W., Washington, DC 20005
☎: 202-783-5000 ◙ www.nmna.org
Open: 10-5 Mo-Sa, 12-5 Su **Closed:** 1/1, THGV, 12/25
ADM: Adult: $3.00 **Children:** Free **Students:** $2.00 **Seniors:** $2.00
& ℗ Paid parking lots nearby
Museum Shop ¶: Cafe 11:30-2:30 M-Fr
Group Tours: 202-783-7370 **Drop-In Tours:** during open hours
Historic Building 1907 Classical Revival building by Waddy Wood
Permanent Collection: PTGS, SCULP, GR, DRGS, 15-20; PHOT

National Museum of Women in the Arts - continued
Unique is the word for this museum established in 1987 and located in a splendidly restored 1907 Classical Revival building. The approximately 2600 works in the permanent collection are the result of the personal vision and passion of its founder, Wilhelmina Holladay, to elevate and validate the works of women artists throughout the history of art. **NOT TO BE MISSED:** 18th C botanical Dr by Maria Sybilla Merian; Lavinia Fontana "Portrait of a Noblewoman" c 1580; Frida Kahlo's "Self Portrait dedicated to Leon Trotsky" 1937

ON EXHIBIT 2000
ONGOING   ESTABLISHING THE LEGACY: FROM THE RENAISSANCE TO MODERNISM
A presentation of works from the permanent collection tracing the history of women artists from the Renaissance to the present.

10/07/1999 to 01/09/2000   DEFINING EYE: WOMEN PHOTOGRAPHERS OF THE 20TH CENTURY
80 legendary artists including Arbus, Goldin, Lange, Leibowitz, Sherman, Simpson, Modotti and Weems portraying women's experiences in and of the world. *Catalog Will Travel*

12/21/1999 to 05/07/2000   ELLEN LANYON: TRANSFORMATIONS, SELECTED WORKS FROM 1971-1999
The first retrospective in ten years shows how she has incorporated science and fantasy into her socially concerned artwork. *Catalog Will Travel*

01/24/2000 to 07/01/2000   BOOK AS ART XII: BOOKS FROM THE PERMANENT COLLECTION
Rare examples from the collection which have never before been exhibited

06/01/2000 to 09/24/2000   IMAGES OF THE SPIRIT: PHOTOGRAPHS BY GRAZIELLA ITURBIDE

National Portrait Gallery
Affiliate Institution: Smithsonian Institution
F St. at 8th, N.W., Washington, DC 20560-0213
☎: 202-357-2700 ◙ www.npg.si.edu
Open: 10-5:30 Daily **Closed:** 12/25
& ℗ Metered street parking; some commercial lots nearby **Museum Shop** ¶: 11-3:30
Group Tours: 202-357-2920 ex 1 **Drop-In Tours:** inquire at information desk
Historic Building This 1836 Building served as a hospital during the Civil War
Sculpture Garden
Permanent Collection: AM: ptgs, sculp, drgs, photo

Housed in the Old Patent Office built in 1836, and used as a hospital during the Civil War, this museum allows the visitor to explore U.S. history as told through portraiture. **NOT TO BE MISSED:** Gilbert Stuart's portraits of George and Martha Washington; Self Portrait by John Singleton Copley

ON EXHIBIT 2000
NATIONAL PORTRAIT GALLERY SET TO CLOSE FOR RENOVATION, JANUARY 9, 2000.

10/29/1999 to 01/02/2000   HENRI CARTIER-BRESSON

Phillips Collection

1600 21st St., N.W., Washington, DC 20009-1090

📞: 202-387-2151 ● www.phillipscollection.org
Open: 10-5 Tu-Sa, 12-7 Su, 5-8:30 Th for "Artful Evenings", (12-5 Su Summer) **Closed:** Mo,1/1, 7/4, THGV, 12/25
ADM: Adult: $6.50 **Children:** Free 18 & under **Students:** $3.25 **Seniors:** $3.25
♿ ℗ Limited metered parking on street; commercial lots nearby **Museum Shop**
🍴: Cafe 10:45-4:30 Mo-Sa; 12-4:30 Su **Group Tours:** ext 247 **Drop-In Tours:** 2:00 We & Sa
Historic Building
Permanent Collection: AM: ptgs, sculp 19-20; EU: ptgs, sculp, 19-20

Housed in the 1897 former residence of the Duncan Phillips family, the core collection represents the successful culmination of one man's magnificent obsession with collecting the art of his time. PLEASE NOTE: The museum fee applies to weekends only. Admission on weekdays is by contribution. Some special exhibitions may require an additional fee **NOT TO BE MISSED:** Renoir's "Luncheon of the Boating Party"; Sunday afternoon concerts that are free with the price of museum admission and are held Sept. through May at 5pm.; "Artful Evenings" ($5.00 pp) for socializing, art appreciation, entertainment, drinks and refreshments.

ON EXHIBIT 2000
ONGOING SMALL PAINTINGS AND WORKS ON PAPER

09/25/1999 to 01/23/2000 RENOIR TO ROTHKO: THE EYE OF DUNCAN PHILIPS
A museum-wide installation of some 300 works from the permanent collection along with archival materials correspondence, journals, manuscripts, ledgers, and historical photographs the exhibition will show how Duncan Phillips evolved as a collector and champion of modern art in America from the 1920s until his death in the 1960s.

02/19/2000 to 05/14/2000 HONORE DAUMIER
In spite of Daumier's stature as one of the greatest artists of the nineteenth century, there has never been a complete retrospective of his work in this country. This groundbreaking exhibition will include at least 67 paintings, 61 drawings and watercolors, 38 sculptures, and 70 lithographs that illustrate Daumier's extraordinary achievement.

06/10/2000 to 08/27/2000 BEN SHAHN'S NEW YORK: THE PHOTOGRAPHY OF MODERN TIMES
A pivotal, but heretofore little examined body of photographic work from the 1930s by Ben Shahn (1898-1969), a celebrated American social realist of the twentieth century. The exhibition will consider the function and meaning of his experimental work in photography within the larger social and political climate of the 1930s. *Catalog Will Travel*

09/23/2000 to 01/28/2001 DEGAS TO MATISSE: MASTERWORKS FROM THE DETROIT INSTITUTE OF ARTS
Fifty-seven paintings, sculptures and works on paper by such artists as Cézanne, van Gogh, Seurat, Brancusi, Matisse, Renoir, Degas, Picasso, and Gauguin from the collection of modern art assembled by Robert Tannahill and left to the Detroit Institute of Arts. This exhibition of select works from the Tannahill Collection offers Washington the chance to compare and contrast the taste and selections of its preeminent collector of modern art, Duncan Phillips, with those of Detroit's Robert Tannahill.

Renwick Gallery of the National Museum of American Art

Affiliate Institution: Smithsonian Institution
Pennsylvania Ave. at 17th St., N.W., Washington, DC 20560

📞: 202-357-2700 ● www.nmaa.si.edu
Open: 10-5:30 Daily **Closed:** 12/25
♿ ℗ limited street parking, commercial lots and garages nearby **Museum Shop**
Group Tours: 202-357-2531 **Drop-In Tours:** 12:00 weekdays special exh only
Historic Building French Second Empire style designed in 1859 by James Renwick, Jr.
Permanent Collection: CONT/AM: crafts; AM: ptgs

The Renwick Gallery of the National Museum of American Art, Smithsonian Institution, is dedicated to exhibiting American crafts of all historic periods and to collecting 20th century American crafts. The museum, which celebrated its 25th anniversary in 1997, rotates the display of objects from its permanent collection on a quarterly basis. It is housed in a charming French Second Empire style building across Pennsylvania Avenue from the White House that was designed in 1859 and named not for its founder, William Corcoran, but for its architect, James Renwick, Jr. **NOT TO BE MISSED:** Grand Salon furnished in styles of 1860'S & 1870'S

DISTRICT OF COLUMBIA

Renwick Gallery of the National Museum of American Art - continued
ON EXHIBIT 2000

09/24/1999 to 01/30/2000   GLASS! GLORIOUS GLASS!
The first in a projected series that will explore the Gallery's expanding permanent collection medium by medium.

10/24/1999 to 01/03/2000   MODERN AMERICAN REALISM: THE SARA ROBY COLLECTION OF THE NATIONAL MUSEUM OF AMERICAN ART
Held in conjunction with "Edward Hopper: The Watercolors" featuring 34 examples of major American Realist Painting and sculpture.20th C.

03/31/2000 to 08/20/2000   THE RENWICK INVITATIONAL: FIVE WOMEN IN CRAFT
The first in a series of biennial invitational exhibits showcasing mid-career craft artists, These five women are from diverse regions and backgrounds.

10/06/2000 to 01/21/2000   SPIRITED OBJECTS: TRADITIONAL CRAFT FOR THE 21ST CENTURY
The finest contemporary examples of traditional American crafts, featured are interpretations of materials across geographical regions and cultures.

11/17/2000 to 04/15/2001   GEORGE CATLIN'S INDIAN GALLERY
Included are Catlin's archival papers, artifacts and the collection of 445 paintings from his original Indian Gallery. In exchange for payment of his debt, Joseph Harrison purchased the paintings which his widow later donated to the Smithsonian in 1879.

Sewall-Belmont House
144 Constitution Ave., N.W., Washington, DC 20002

☎: 202-546-3989
Open: 10-3 Tu-Fr; Noon-4 Sa, Su   **Closed:** 1/1, THGV, 12/25
Vol/Cont:
Ⓟ Limited street parking only   **Museum Shop**
Drop-In Tours: 10-3 Tu-Fr; Noon-4 Sa, Su   **Historic Building**
Permanent Collection: SCULP, PTGS

Paintings and sculpture depicting heroines of the women's rights movement line the halls of the historic Sewall-Belmont House. One of the oldest houses on Capitol Hill, this unusual museum is a dedicated to the theme of women's suffrage.

BOCA RATON

Boca Raton Museum of Art
801 W. Palmetto Park Rd., Boca Raton, FL 33486
📞: 561-392-2500
Open: 10-4 Tu, Th, Fr; 12-4 Sa, Su; till 9pm We   **Closed:** LEG/HOL!
Sugg/Cont: ADM: Adult: $3.00   **Children:** Free under 12   **Students:** $1.00   **Seniors:** $2.00
&. Ⓟ Free   **Museum Shop   Group Tours**: 561-392-2500   **Drop-In Tours**: daily!
Historic Building In Old Floresta Historic District   **Sculpture Garden**
Permanent Collection: PHOT; PTGS 20

An AAM accredited institution, the Museum boasts over 3000 works of art of the highest quality and distinction, including a superb assembly of modern masters Braque, Demuth, Glackens, Matisse and Picasso, to name but a few. Recent donations include superb photography from the 19th century to present, African and Pre-Columbian art and a broad range of contemporary sculpture portraying a variety of styles and media.

ON EXHIBIT 2000
01/13/2000 to 05/05/2000   PARIS: 1860-1930: BIRTHPLACE OF EUROPEAN MODERNISM

International Museum of Cartoon Art
201 Plaza Real, Boca Raton, FL 33432
📞: 561-391-2200   ◙ www.cartoonart.org
Open: 10-6 Tu-Sa, 12-6 Su   **Closed:** Mo
ADM: Adult: $6.00   **Children:** 6-12 $3; Free under 5   **Students:** $4.00   **Seniors:** $5.00
&. Ⓟ Parking throughout Mizner Park in which the museum is located.   **Museum Shop**   ᴵᶠ Café
Group Tours: ext 118   **Sculpture Garden**
Permanent Collection: CARTOON ART

Started by Mort Walker, creator of the "Beetle Bailey" cartoon comic, and relocated to Florida after 20 years of operation in metropolitan NY, this museum, with over 160,000 works on paper, 10,000 books, 1,000 hours of animated film, and numerous collectibles & memorabilia, is dedicated to the collection, preservation, exhibition and interpretation of an international collection of original works of cartoon art. PLEASE NOTE: On the many family weekends planned by the museum, event hours are 10-5 Sa, and 12-5 Su with admission at $4.00 per person Call for information and schedule of programs.

ON EXHIBIT 2000
10/02/1999 to 01/30/2000   50 YEARS OF PEANUTS: THE ART OF CHARLES M. SCHULZ

11/1999 to 02/2000   PEPPER. AND SALT: WALL STREET JOURNAL'S CELEBRATION OF BUSINESS HUMOR

02/11/2000 to 05/14/2000   OSCARS AND ANIMATION

CORAL GABLES

Lowe Art Museum
Affiliate Institution: University of Miami
1301 Stanford Dr., Coral Gables, FL 33124-6310
📞: 305-284-3535   ◙ www.lowemuseum.org
Open: 10-5 Tu, We, Fr, Sa; 12-7 Th; 12-5 Su   **Closed:** Mo, 1/1, THGV, 12/25
Free Day: 1st Tu of the month   **ADM: Adult:** $5.00   **Children:** Free under 12   **Students:** $3.00   **Seniors:** $3.00
&. Ⓟ   **Museum Shop**
Group Tours: 305-284-3621   **Drop-In Tours**: by appt   **Sculpture Garden**
Permanent Collection: REN & BAROQUE: ptgs, sculp (Kress Collection); AN/R; SP/OM; P/COL; EU: art; AS: ptgs, sculp, gr, cer; AM: ptgs, gr; LAT/AM; NAT/AM; AF

FLORIDA

Lowe Art Museum - continued

Established in 1950, the Lowe recently underwent a multi-million dollar expansion and renovation. Its superb and diverse permanent collection is recognized as one of the major fine art resources in Florida. More than 10,000 works from a wide array of historical styles and periods including the Kress Collection of Italian Renaissance and Baroque Art, 17th - 20th century European and American art, Greco-Roman antiquities, Asian, African, pre-Columbian and Native American art. **NOT TO BE MISSED:** Kress Collection of Italian Renaissance and Baroque art

ON EXHIBIT 2000

11/02/1999 to 01/30/2000   TREASURES OF CHINESE GLASS WORKSHOPS: PEKING GLASS FROM THE GADIENT COLLECTION

11/02/1999 to 01/30/2000   QUEBEC SILVER FROM THE NATIONAL GALLERY OF CANADA
A rare opportunity to examine various phases of the silversmith's art in the Canadian context from the richest and most varied collection in existence.

02/10/2000 to 04/02/2000   THE GREAT AMERICAN POP ART STORE: MULTIPLES OF THE SIXTIES
From a ray gun and cast baked potato by Claes Oldenburg and shopping bags by Roy Lichtenstein to Robert Indiana's LOVE ring and Andy Warhol's Brillo boxes, the 100 items featured in this exhibition document the popularity of the Pop movement in the art and culture of the 1960's. *Catalog Will Travel*

06/08/2000 to 07/23/2000   CHRIS MANGIARACINA PAINTING
Large scale, richly painted canvases , juxtaposed imagery from an artist who often uses imagery from classical sources.

09/13/2000 to 11/25/2000   SPLENDOR IN THE GLASS: CONTEMPORARY GLASS FROM THE PALLEY COLLECTION

09/13/2000 to 11/25/2000   AMERICAN GLASS: MASTERS OF THE ART
Unique and innovative works in glass by 13 contemporary American artists.

12/2000 to 02/11/2001   JULIAN STANCZAK RETROSPECTIVE
The exhibition examines the artist's contribution to the development of post-war American painting as it relates to the "Op " movement.

DAYTONA BEACH

Museum of Arts and Sciences
1040 Museum Blvd., Daytona Beach, FL 32014
☏: 904-255-0285   ◙   www.moas.org
Open: 9-4 Tu-Fr, 12–5 Sa, Su   **Closed:** Mo, LEG/HOL!
ADM: **Adult:** $5.00   **Children:** $2.00   **Students:** $1.00
&   Ⓟ Free   **Museum Shop**
Group Tours: 904-255-0285 ext.16   **Drop-In Tours:** daily 904-255-0285 ext. 22   **Sculpture Garden**
Permanent Collection: REG: ptgs, gr, phot; AF; P/COL; EU: 19; AM: 18-20; FOLK; CUBAN: ptgs 18-20; OR; AM: dec/art, ptgs, sculp 17-20

The Museum of Arts and Sciences recently added a wing designed to add thousands of square feet of new gallery space. A plus for visitors is the lovely nature drive through Tuscawill Park leading up to the museum, and interpreted nature trails. **NOT TO BE MISSED:** The Dow Gallery of American Art, a collection of more than 200 paintings, sculptures, furniture, and decorative arts (1640-1910).

ON EXHIBIT 2000
09/18/1999 to 01/09/2000   TREASURES FROM THE COLLECTION OF A LA VIEILLE RUSSIE

01/22/2000 to 04/16/2000   KARSH PORTRAITS: THE SEARCHING EYE *Catalog Will Travel*

Museum of Arts and Sciences - continued
04/22/2000 to 08/20/2000   ON THE ROAD: ART AND THE AUTOMOBILE
From realist and photo-realist to semi-abstract, this exhibition of over 40 prints, drawings and photos examines the impact of the revolution of the car in modern culture and artistic expression. *Catalog   Will Travel*

04/22/2000 to 08/20/2000   JADE AND BRONZE: TREASURES OF ANCIENT CHINA *Catalog   Will Travel*

09/22/2000 to 11/19/2000   IMAGINATIONS AND OBJECTS OF THE FUTURE BY SALVADOR DALI *Catalog Will Travel*

09/22/2000 to 11/19/2000   ANIMALS IN BRONZE: THE MICHAEL AND MARY ERLANGER COLLECTION OF ANIMALIER BRONZES *Catalog   Will Travel*

12/02/2000 to 02/2001   YOUNG AMERICA: THE VIEW FROM THE EAST
54 works by the era's most famous artists, trace the transformation of the colonies into nationhood from the 1760s to the Civil War. Includes portraits by Gilbert Stuart, Charles Willson Peale; paintings by Benjamin West, Washington Allston; landscapes by Thomas Cole, Alvan Fisher; genre paintings by John Quidor, Lily Martin Spencer. Hudson River School landscapes by Asher B. Durand, Frederic E. Church. Sculptures by Horatio Greenough, Hiram Powers. Civil War era paintings by Samuel Colman, Homer Dodge Martin. *Catalog   Will Travel*

Southeast Museum of Photography
Affiliate Institution: Daytona Beach Community College
1200 West International Speedway Blvd., Daytona Beach, FL 32120-2811
☏: 904-254-5475   ▣ www.dbcc.cc.fl.us/dbcc/smp/welcome.htm
Open: Mo, We-Fr 9:30-4:30, Tu 9:30-7, Sa & Su 12-4   **Closed:** LEG/HOL!
⛪ Ⓟ On college campus   **Museum Shop**
Group Tours: 904-947-5469   **Drop-In Tours:** 20 minute "Art for Lunch" tours!

Thousands of photographs from the earliest daguerreotypes to the latest experiments in computer assisted manipulation are housed in this modern 2 floor gallery space opened in 1992. Examples of nearly every photographic process in the medium's 150 year old history are represented in this collection. Changing exhibitions of contemporary and historical photographs. **NOT TO BE MISSED:** Kidsdays, a Sunday afternoon program for children and parents where many aspects of the photographic process can be experienced.

ON EXHIBIT 2000

10/13/1999 to 01/19/2000   CITY
Lucien Perkins: Runway Madness; Andre Kertecz: Budapest, Paris, New York; Catherine Gfeller: Urban Friezes; Urban Images From the Permanent Collection; Orville Robertson: Night Walks With a Camera

Summer/2000   FRESH WORK III

Spring/2000   VOYAGES (PER)FORMED: EARLY PHOTOGRAPHY OF TRAVEL

02/08/2000 to 05/03/2000   PHOTOGRAPHS-MEMORY-KNOWLEDGE
1968: a Year in the World; The Magnum Photographs; Daytona Beach Self-Portrait: 1968; Selections from the Permanent Collection ; Ben Fernandez: A Funeral in Atlanta

05/23/2000 to 09/27/2000   PHOTOGRAPHY = ART
Fresh Work III: A curated biennial of new Photographic Art; Innovation/Imagination: Fifty years of Polaroid Photography Eieen Cowin: Still (and All); Evon Streetman

10/24/2000 to 01/24/2001   WORLD VIEWS: THREE PHOTOGRAPHERS OF TRAVEL, BETTY PRESS, SAM SWEEZY, REGIE LOUIE
Also Nancy Goldring: Travels in Sri Lanka; Tseng Kwong Chi: Citizen of the World; Voyages Performed: Early Photography and Travel: Historical Photograph albums with contemporary interpretive installations by Carol Flax, Peter GoinLorie Novak, and Abelardo Morrelll; See America: Susan Evans

FLORIDA

DeLand Museum of Art

600 N. Woodland Blvd., DeLand, FL 32720-3447

☎: 904-734-4371
Open: 10-4 Tu-Sa, 1-4 Su, till 8pm Tu   **Closed:** LEG/HOL!
ADM: Adult: $2.00   **Children:** $1.00 (4-12)   **Students:** $1.00   **Seniors:** $2.00
Ⅎ ℗ Free and ample   **Museum Shop**
Drop-In Tours: !
Permanent Collection: AM: 19-20; CONT: reg; DEC/ART; NAT/AM

The DeLand, opened in the New Cultural Arts Center in 1991, is located between Daytona Beach and Orlando. It is a fast growing, vital institution that offers a wide range of art and art-related activities to the community and its visitors. PLEASE NOTE: The permanent collection is not usually on display.

Museum of Art, Fort Lauderdale

1 E. Las Olas Blvd., Ft. Lauderdale, FL 33301-1807

☎: 954-525-5500
Open: 10-5 Tu-Sa, till 8pm Fr, Noon-5 Su   **Closed:** LEG/HOL!
ADM: Adult: $6.00   **Children:** 5-18 $1.00, Free under 4   **Students:** $3.00   **Seniors:** $5.00
Ⅎ
℗ Metered parking ($.75 per hour) at the Municipal Parking facility on S.E. 1st Ave. bordering the museum on the East side.
  Museum Shop
Group Tours: ex 239/241   **Drop-In Tours**: 1:00 Tu, Th, Fr (Free with admission)
Historic Building Built by renowned architect Edward Larrabee Barnes
Sculpture Garden
Permanent Collection: AM: gr, ptgs, sculp 19-20; EU: gr, ptgs, sculp 19-20; P/COL; AF; OC; NAT/AM

Aside from an impressive permanent collection of 20th-century European and American art, this museum is home to the William Glackens collection, the most comprehensive collection of works by the artist and others of his contemporaries who, as a group, are best known as "The Eight" and/or the Ashcan School. It also is home to the largest collection of CoBrA art in the U.S. **NOT TO BE MISSED:** The William Glackens Collection

ON EXHIBIT 2000

12/05/1999 to 01/19/2000   MATERIAL CULTURE AND EVERYDAY LIFE: SELECTIONS FROM THE PERMANENT COLLECTION
As artists rejected the abstract styles which dominated the art scene of the 50's they turned to depictions of the object. The impact and influence of art that is representative of popular culture and everyday life. Included are Rauschenberg, Warhol, Rosenquist, Lichtenstein and Haring.

12/10/1999 to 01/02/2000   HORTT ANNUAL MEMORIAL COMPETITION AND EXHIBITION

Summer/2000   JULIE TAYMOR: PLAYING WITH FIRE

Summer/2000   MINGWEI LEE: MONEY FOR ART AND THE LETTER WRITING PROJECT

Spring/2000   GARY HILL: LUMINAL OBJECTS

01/14/2000 to 04/30/2000   DO IT
Works by artists around the world through written instructions and created by local participants Included are Marina Abramovic, Yolo Ono, and Nancy Spero.

Museum of Art, Fort Lauderdale - continued
01/29/2000 to 04/30/2000   CAMILLE PISSARO AND THE PISSARO FAMILY
This exhibition kicks off a dialogue about artistic legacy It spans almost 100 years and includes about 100 works by the master and his family.

02/29/2000 to 05/30/2000   WILLEM DE KOOMING: TRANSFERS
The exhibition provides the opportunity to study the methods of one of America's most well known Abstract Expressionists. Some never before seen paintings are accompanied by sketches, drawings, and studies. *Catalog Will Travel*

10/15/2000 to 01/14/2001   PALACE OF GOLD AND LIGHT: TREASURES FROM THE TOPKAPI PALACE, ISTANBUL
Included in the treasures of jewels are art and artifacts from the Ottoman Sultan Many objects have never before left the Palace including a emerald and diamond adorned Topkapi dagger and a magnificently crafted imperial throne. *Catalog Will Travel*

GAINESVILLE

Samuel P. Harn Museum of Art
Affiliate Institution: Univ. of Florida
SW 34th St. & Hull Rd., Gainesville, FL 32611-2700
☎: 352-392-9826 ◙ www.arts.ufl.edu/harn
Open: 11-5 Tu-Fr, 10-5 Sa, 1-5 Su   **Closed:** Mo, LEG/HOL
Vol/Cont:
& ℗   **Museum Shop**
Group Tours   Drop-In Tours: 2:00 Sa, Su; 12:30 We; Family tours 2nd S of mo.
Permanent Collection: AM: ptgs, gr, sculp; EU: ptgs, gr, sculp; P/COL; AF; OC; IND: ptgs, sculp; JAP: gr ; CONT

The Samuel P. Harn Museum of Art provides the most advanced facilities for the exhibition, study and preservation of works of art. The Harn offers approximately 15 changing exhibitions per year. The museum's collection includes the arts of the Americas, Africa, Asia as well as contemporary international works of art. Exciting performance art, lectures and films are also featured. **NOT TO BE MISSED:** Approximately 15 changing exhibitions per year: the new art Bishop study center and library & related video, & CD-ROM resource center of the permanent collection.

ON EXHIBIT 2000
10/10/1999 to 01/02/2000   THE KARNOFF COLLECTION: ETRUSCAN AND SOUTH ITALIAN VASES

11/28/1999 to 03/26/2000   THE PROPHETIC PHOTOGRAPHS OF ROMAN VISHNIAC: JEWISH LIFE IN EASTERN EUROPE BEFORE THE HOLOCAUST

12/12/1999 to 04/09/2000   THE PERPETUAL WELL: CONTEMPORARY ART FROM THE COLLECTION OF THE JEWISH MUSEUM

04/08/2000 to 06/18/2000   DEFINING MODERNISM: GROUP F.64

04/23/2000 to 02/25/2001   TEN YEAR ANNIVERSARY EXHIBITION

07/16/2000 to 07/14/2001   INTIMATE RITUALS AND PERSONAL DEVOTIONS: SPIRITUAL ART THROUGH THE AGES

FLORIDA

Cummer Museum of Art & Gardens
829 Riverside Ave., Jacksonville, FL 32204
☎: 904-356-6857   ◙ www.cummer.org
Open: 10-9 Tu & T; 10-5 We, Fr, Sa; 12-5 Su   Closed: 1/1, EASTER, 7/4, THGV, 12/25
ADM: Adult: $5.00   Children: $1.00 (5 & under)   Students: $3.00   Seniors: $3.00
&   ℗ Opposite museum at 829 Riverside Ave.   Museum Shop
Group Tours: 904-355-0630   Drop-In Tours: 10-3 Tu-F(by appt); 3 S (w/o appt); 7 T
Historic Building Gardens founded in 1901 and 1931   Sculpture Garden
Permanent Collection: AM: ptgs; EU: ptgs; OR; sculp; CER; DEC/ART; AN/GRK; AN/R; P/COL; IT/REN

The Cummer Museum of Art & Gardens is located on the picturesque bank of the St. Johns River. Adjacent to the river are two-and-one-half acres of formal gardens. The museum's permanent collection ranges in date from 2,000 BC to the present, with particular strength in 18th and 19th-century American and European paintings. The Wark collection of 18th-century Meissen porcelain is one of the two finest collections in the world. Art Connections, a nationally-acclaimed interactive education center, also schedules an impressive array of activities for children through adults. **NOT TO BE MISSED:** One of the earliest and rarest collections of Early Meissen Porcelain in the world

ON EXHIBIT 2000
11/26/1999 to 01/23/2000   INTERACTION OF CULTURES: INDIAN AND WESTERN PAINTING (1710-1910) FROM THE EHRENFELD COLLECTION *Catalog Will Travel*

Jacksonville Museum of Contemporary Art
4160 Boulevard Center Dr., Jacksonville, FL 32207
☎: 904-398-8336
Open: 10-4 Tu, We, Fr; 10-10 Th; 1-5 Sa, Su   Closed: LEG/HOL!
ADM:
&   ℗ Free and ample   Museum Shop   Group Tours   Sculpture Garden
Permanent Collection: CONT; P/COL

The finest art from classic to contemporary is offered in the Jacksonville Museum, the oldest museum in the city. PLEASE NOTE: There is a nominal admission fee for non-museum member visitors. **NOT TO BE MISSED:** Collection of Pre-Columbian art on permanent display

Polk Museum of Art
800 E. Palmetto St., Lakeland, FL 33801-5529
☎: 941-688-7743
Open: 9-5 Tu-Fr, 10-5 Sa, 1-5 Su   Closed: Mo, LEG/HOL!
Vol/Cont: Sugg/Cont: $3.00
&   ℗   Museum Shop
Group Tours   Sculpture Garden
Permanent Collection: P/COL; REG; AS: cer, gr; EU: cer, glass, silver 15-19: AM: 20; PHOT

Located in central Florida about 35 miles east of Tampa, the 37,000 square foot Polk Museum of Art, built in 1988, offers a complete visual and educational experience to visitors and residents alike. The Pre-Columbian Gallery, with its slide presentation and hands-on display for the visually handicapped, is but one of the innovative aspects of this vital community museum and cultural center. **NOT TO BE MISSED:** "El Encuentro" by Gilberto Ruiz; Jaguar Effigy Vessel from the Nicoya Region of Costa Rica (middle polychrome period, circa A.D. 800-1200)

Polk Museum of Art - continued

ON EXHIBIT 2000

12/11/1999 to 03/05/2000   MIRIAM SHAPIRO: A RETROSPECTIVE
Shapiro has helped to establish the Pattern and Decoration Movement and has created a prominent position for women in the contemporary art world.

12/18/1999 to 02/20/2000   THE PASSIONATE OBSERVER: PHOTOGRAPHS BY CARL VAN VECHTEN
Van Vechten became a champion of the Harlem Renaissance and turned his attention to photography.

01/08/2000 to 04/02/2000   GLASS ART BY SUSAN B. GOTT
Susan Gott works out of the Phoenix Glass Studio in Tampa. She employs various glass casting techniques and surface treatments to create works that embody her interest in mythological imagery, symbolism and traditions from ancient cultures.

02/26/2000 to 04/30/2000   PAINTINGS BY MAGGIE DAVIS
Davis's work focuses on metaphysical concepts of renewal, rebirth and transformation.

11/11/2000 to 01/21/2001   CROSSING BOUNDARIES: CONTEMPORARY ART QUILTS
The Art Quilt Network is made up of American and Canadian quiltmakers. Membership is limited to 60. *Will Travel*

LARGO

Gulf Coast Museum of Art

12211 Waisingham Road, Largo, FL 33744
☎: 727-584-8634
Open: 10-4 Tu-Sa, 12-4 Su   **Closed:** Mo, LEG/HOL!
& ℗ Free   **Museum Shop   Group Tours**: by res   **Drop-In Tours**: call for information   **Sculpture Garden**
Permanent Collection: AM: ptgs 1940-1950'S; CONT FLORIDA ART: 1960 - present; CONT/CRAFTS

In operation for over 50 years, this museum just south of Clearwater, near Tampa, features a permanent collection of over 700 works of art (late 19th - 20th c) with a focus on American artists including I. Bishop, Breckenridge, Bricher, and Inness, also Florida Art from 1960 forward and American Fine Crafts, especially from the 12 Southeastern states.

ON EXHIBIT 2000

12/03/1999 to 01/30/2000   TRIALS AND TRIBUTES: A JUDY CHICAGO RETROSPECTIVE
This exhibition traces Chicago's career and concerns from the 60's to the present. It reveals her major projects Included will be works from her early California years, the dinner party period , the birth project , the power play series and the recent Holocaust project. *Will Travel*

12/03/1999 to 07/30/2000   FROM THE COLLECTION: LANDSCAPES
Traditional landscape genre and contemporary interpretations.

12/03/1999 to 07/30/2000   FROM THE COLLECTION: SOUTHEASTERN FINE CRAFTS

12/03/1999 to 07/30/2000   FROM THE COLLECTION: CONTEMPORARY FLORIDA ART

02/18/2000 to 04/16/2000   FLORIDA VISUAL ARTS FELLOWSHIP AWARDS
This is a state-wide competitive endeavor to award fifteen Florida fellowships.

02/18/2000 to 04/16/2000   BARON WOLLMAN: I SAW THE MUSIC
Wolman is one of the nation's premier documentary photographers. This exhibition is focused on the work he did around San Francisco during the 60's. He was a photographer for "Rolling Stones" and documented the political, social and cultural upheaval of the period.

05/05/2000 to 06/25/2000   ALEXA KLEINBARD: TALKING LEAVES
For the past 15 years Kleinbard's work has been influenced by environmental issues= and the changing natural environment. The Talking Leaves Series (Indian for Book) consists of 54 paintings and inspired by both environmental issues and carefully painted cut-out forms if leaves of specific plants

07/09/2000 to 07/30/2000   STUDIOWORKS 2000
A juried all media exhibition which presents the work of the Museum's instructors and students.

FLORIDA

Maitland Art Center
231 W. Packwood Ave., Maitland, FL 32751-5596
☎: 407-539-2181   ◙ www.maitartcenter.org
Open: 9-4:30 Mo-Fr; 12-4:30 Sa, Su   **Closed:** LEG/HOL!
Vol/Cont:
  ♿ ℗ Across the street from the Art Center with additional parking just west of the Center   **Museum Shop**
Group Tours   **Drop-In Tours**: Upon request if available   **Historic Building** State of Florida Historic Site
Permanent Collection: REG: past & present

The stucco buildings of the Maitland Center are so highly decorated with murals, bas reliefs, and carvings done in the Aztec-Mayan motif, that they are a "must-see" work of art in themselves. One of the few surviving examples of "Fantastic" Architecture remaining in the southeastern U.S., the Center is listed in the N.R.H.P. **NOT TO BE MISSED:** Works of Jules Andre Smith, (1890 - 1959), artist and founder of the art center

ON EXHIBIT 2000
01/07/2000 to 02/27/2000   SEXTET, SEPARATED AT BIRTH
Recent works by Susan Bach, Richard Calvin, Calvert LaFollette, Breton Morse, Sa Sisaleumsak whose unique style relates and compliments one another.

03/10/2000 to 04/31/2000   LEGENDS FROM THE OPERA
Costume and set designs by Charles Caine, from his collection.

05/05/2000 to Summer/2000   ALL IN THE FAMILY
The art of Edward Faust, his daughter Virginia Bettinghaus, her son Duncan McCleilan , and daughter Melissa McCleleilan. Paintings, photographs, prints, woodcuts, glass woodcuts and sculpture, porcelain and stoneware.

07/17/2000 to 09/02/2000   IN APPRECIATION
Works purchased for the collection in honor of service to the center and memory of special friends.

Museum of Art and Science/Brevard
1463 Highland Ave., Melbourne, FL 32935
☎: 407-242-0737   ◙ www.artandscience.org
Open: 10-5 Tu-Sa; 1-5 Su   **Closed:** Mo, LEG/HOL!
Free Day: 1-5 Th   **ADM: Adult:** $5.00   **Children:** $2.00   **Students:** $2.00   **Seniors:** $3.00
  ♿ ℗ Free in front of the museum   **Museum Shop**
Group Tours: 407-254-7782   **Drop-In Tours**: 2-4 Tu-Fr; 12:30-2:30 Sa; 1-5 Su
Permanent Collection: OR; REG: works on paper

Serving as an actively expanding artistic cultural center, the 20 year old Brevard Museum of Art and Science is located in the historic Old Eau Gallie district of Melbourne near the center of the state. The Children's Science Center features more than 35 hands on exhibits teaching concepts of physical science.

ON EXHIBIT 2000
12/11/1999 to 01/30/2000   SUNLIGHT AND SHADOW: AMERICAN IMPRESSIONISM
Impressionist still life and portraiture will be shown with landscape painting.

03/11/2000 to 05/07/2000   MIRIAM SHAPIRO
The first retrospective exhibition of the artist's works on paper.

FLORIDA

MIAMI

Lilia Fontana Miami-Dade Community College Kendall Campus Art Gallery
11011 Southwest 104th St., Miami, FL 33176-3393
☎: 305-237-2322   ◙   www.mdcc.edu
Open: 8-4 Mo, Th, Fr; 12-7:30 Tu, We   **Closed:** Sa, S, LEG/HOL!, ACAD!, first 3 weeks of Aug
♿ ℗ Free in student lots
Museum Shop   ⫯⫰ **Drop-In Tours**
Permanent Collection: CONT: ptgs, gr, sculp, phot; GR: 15-19

With nearly 600 works in its collection, the South Campus Art Gallery is home to original prints by such renowned artists of the past as Whistler, Tissot, Ensor, Corot, Goya, in addition to those of a more contemporary ilk by Hockney, Dine, Lichtenstein, Warhol and others. **NOT TO BE MISSED:** "The Four Angels Holding The Wings", woodcut by Albrecht Dürer, 1511

Miami Art Museum
101 W. Flagler St., Miami, FL 33130
☎: 305-375-3000
Open: 10-5 Tu-Fr; till 9 third Th; 12-5 Sa, Su   **Closed:** Mo, 1/1, THGV, 12/25
Free Day: 5-9 3rd Th; by contrib Tu   **ADM: Adult:** $5.00   **Children:** Free under 12   **Students:** $2.50   **Seniors:** $2.50
♿ ℗ Discounted rate of $2.00 with validated ticket at Cultural Center Garage, 50 NW 2nd Ave.   **Museum Shop**
Group Tours: 305-375-4073   **Drop-In Tours:** by res
Historic Building Designed by Philip Johnson 1983
Sculpture Garden
Permanent Collection: The acquisition of a permanent collection is now under way, with the first gifts of works including those by Adolph Gottlieb, Robert Rauschenberg, Helen Frankenthaler and Jean Dubuffet.

MAM exhibits and collects, preserves and interprets international art, with a focus on art of the western hemisphere, The focus is on works from the 1940's to the present complemented by art from other eras for historical perspective. **NOT TO BE MISSED:** The Dream Collection, featuring the first gifts to the permanent collection.

MIAMI BEACH

Bass Museum of Art
2121 Park Ave., Miami Beach, FL 33139
☎: 305-673-7530   ◙   ttp://ci.miami-beach.fl.us/culture/bass/bass/html
Open: 10-5 Tu-Sa, 1-5 Su, 1-9 2nd & 4th W of the month   **Closed:** LEG/HOL!
ADM: Adult: $5.00   **Children:** Free under 6   **Students:** $3.00   **Seniors:** $3.00
♿ ℗ On-site metered parking and street metered parking   **Museum Shop**
Group Tours   Sculpture Garden
Permanent Collection: PTGS, SCULP, GR 19-20; REN: ptgs, sculp; MED; sculp, ptgs; PHOT; OR: bronzes

Just one block from the beach in Miami, in the middle of a 9 acre park, is one of the great cultural treasures of Florida. Located in a stunning 1930 Art Deco building, the Museum is home to more than 6 centuries of artworks including a superb 500 piece collection of European art donated by the Bass family for whom the museum is named. Expansion and renovation plans are underway which will result in the addition of state-of-the-art gallery space, a cafe and new museum shop. PLEASE NOTE: On occasion there are additional admission fees for some special exhibitions. **NOT TO BE MISSED:** "Samson Fighting the Lion", woodcut by Albrecht Dürer

FLORIDA

Wolfsonian/Florida International University
1001 Washington Ave., Miami Beach, FL 33139
☎: 305-531-1001
Open: 10-6 Tu-Sa, till 9 T, Noon-5 Su
ADM: Adult: $5.00   **Children:** Free under 6   **Students:** $3.50   **Seniors:** $3.50
ⓅMetered street parking, valet parking at the Hotel Astor (opposite the museum at 956 Washington Ave), and 3 near-by Municipal lots
Museum Shop
Permanent Collection: AM & EU: furn, glass, cer, metalwork, books, ptgs, sculp, works on paper, & industrial design 1885-1945

Recently opened, The Wolfsonian, which contains the 70,000 object Mitchell Wolfson, Jr. collection of American and European art and design dating from 1885-1945, was established to demonstrate how art and design are used in cultural, social and political contexts. It is interesting to note that the museum is located in the heart of the lively newly redeveloped South Beach area.

NAPLES

Philharmonic Center for the Arts
5833 Pelican Bay Blvd., Naples, FL 34108
☎: 941-597-1900   ◉ www.naplesphilcenter.org
Open: OCT-MAY: 10-4 Mo-Fr, (10-4 Sa theater schedule permitting)   **Closed:** Sa, LEG/HOL!
Free Day: call for schedule   **ADM: Adult:** $4.00   **Children:** $2.00   **Students:** $2.00
& Ⓟ Free   **Museum Shop**
Group Tours: ex 279
Drop-In Tours: OCT & MAY: 11am Th & Sa; NOV-APR: 11 am Mo thru Sa
Sculpture Garden

Four art galleries, two sculpture gardens, and spacious lobbies where sculpture is displayed are located within the confines of the beautiful Philharmonic Center. Museum quality temporary exhibitions are presented from October through May of each year. PLEASE NOTE: Free Family Days where gallery admissions and the 11am docent tour are offered free of charge are scheduled for the following Saturdays: 1/3, 2/7, 3/7, 4/4, 5/2, 6/16.

ON EXHIBIT 2000

12/1999 to 01/2000   JULES OLITSKY
A survey of paintings, prints and sculpture by one of the countries leading abstract artists.

12/1999 to 01/2000   LUCIEN CLERQUE
Images of the famed French photographer, a friend and mentor Pablo Picasso.

02/2000 to 03/2000   HENRY MOORE
Sculpture, drawings and prints by one of the 20th centuries great artists.

02/2000 to 03/2000   THE HUMAN FACTOR: FIGURATION IN American art, 1850-1995
Paintings, sculpture, prints and drawings celebrating the human form.   Artists include Diebenkorn, Haring, Segal and Rothenberg.

04/2000 to 05/2000   CONFRONTATIONAL CLAY: THE ARTIST AS SOCIAL CRITIC
Devices used by famous names to convey thoughts on a variety of contemporary issues.

04/2000 to 05/2000   AMERICAN LANDSCAPES
Over a century of works p.n. paper, Realist, Tonalist, and Impressionist works including the Hudson River School.

Joan Lehman Museum of Contemporary Art
770 NE 125th St., North Miami, FL 33161
☎: 305-893-6211
Open: 11-5 Tu-Sa; 12-5 Su **Closed:** 1/1, THGV, 12/25
Free Day: Mem Day, Tu **ADM: Adult:** $5.00 **Children:** Free under 12 **Students:** $3.00 **Seniors:** $3.00
& ℗ Free parking to the east, south and west of the museum. **Museum Shop**
Group Tours: by appt **Drop-In Tours:** 2pm Sa & Su
Permanent Collection: CONT

In operation since 1981, the museum was, until now, a small but vital center for the contemporary arts. Recently the museum opened a new state-of-the-art building renamed The Joan Lehman Museum of Contemporary Art in honor if its great benefactor. Part of a new civic complex for North Miami, the museum provides an exciting and innovative facility for exhibitions, lectures, films and performances. PLEASE NOTE: Special language tours in Creole, French, German, Italian, Portuguese and Spanish are available by advance reservation. Among the artists in the permanent collection are John Baldesarri, Dan Flavin, Dennis Oppenheim. Alex Katz, Uta Barth, Teresita Fernandez, Garry Simmons, and Jose Bedia.,

ON EXHIBIT 2000
03/31/1999 to 05/28/2000 SWEET DREAMS AND NIGHTMARES
Surrealist imagery by Man Ray, Dorothea Tanning and Yves Tanguy will be combined with more recent works in an exhibition that explores the topics of dreams and the subconscious.

11/17/1999 to 03/12/2000 FRANK STELLA: CHANGING THE RULES
Pivotal paintings, reliefs and sculptural works, explore how Stella established rules and parameters that would change from series to series. Also included are his commission for the American Airlines Arena featuring his drawings and models for this enormous sculptural sculpture.

11/26/1999 to 01/01/2000 PABLO CANO: MARIONETTES
Performances and exhibition of play exploring the underwater mythical civilization of Atlantis.

01/20/2000 to 03/26/2000 MATTHEW RITCHIE
This British artists living in New York presents recent work which he describes as all about information . He says that his work is about the idea of time- part of an ever expanding universe-collapsed onto a flat surface.

03/31/2000 to 05/28/2000 INVERTED ODYSSEYS: CLAUDE CAHUN, MAYA DEREN, CINDY SHERMAN
Organized in collaboration with Grey Art Gallery at NYU. These photographers shed new light on the history of photography. *Catalog Will Travel*

06/08/2000 to 09/03/2000 MYTHIC PROPORTIONS : PAINTING IN THE NINETIES
Since the 1970's the art world has foretold the death of painting. During the past few years the medium has made a comeback. The exhibition seeks to explore paintings renewed relevance.

06/08/2000 to 09/10/2000 SEYDOU KEITA, PHOTOGRAPHER: PORTRAITS FROM BAMAKO, MALI (1950-1960)
40 photographs from Mali, West Africa capturing the cultural changes in his country through his subjects dress and props.

Appleton Museum of Art
4333 NE Silver Springs Blvd., Ocala, FL 34470-5000
☎: 352-236-7100 ▣ www.fsu.edu/~svad/Appleton/AppletonMuseum.html
Open: 10-4:30 Tu-Sa, 1-5 Su **Closed:** Mo, 1/1, LEG/HOL!
ADM: Adult: $5.00 **Children:** Free under 18 **Students:** $2.00
& ℗ Free **Museum Shop Group Tours:** 352-236-7100 x109 **Drop-In Tours:** 1:15 Tu-Fr
Permanent Collection: EU; PR/COL; AF; OR; DEC/ART; ISLAMIC CERAMICS; ANTIQUITIES

FLORIDA

Appleton Museum of Art - continued

The Appleton Museum of Art in central Florida, home to one of the finest art collections in the Southeast, recently opened the Edith-Marie Appleton wing which allows for the display. Situated among acres of tall pines and magnolias, the dramatic building sets the tone for the many treasures that await the visitor within its walls. With the addition of The Edith-Marie Appleton Wing in 1/97, the museum became one of the largest art institutions in Florida. **NOT TO BE MISSED:** Rodin's "Thinker", Bouguereau's "The Young Shepherdess" and "The Knitter"; 8th-century Chinese Tang Horse

ON EXHIBIT 2000
09/29/2000 to 11/12/2000   THE FLORIDA WATERCOLOR SOCIETY ANNUAL EXHIBITION

ORLANDO

Orlando Museum of Art
2416 North Mills Ave., Orlando, FL 32803-1483
📞: 407-896-4231 📧 www.OMArt.org
Open: 9-5 Mo-Sa, 12-5 Su   **Closed:** Mo, LEG/HOL!
Free Day: Orange, Osceola and Seminole county residents are admitted free 12-5 Th
ADM: **Adult:** $4.00   **Children:** $3.00 (4-11)   **Students:** $4.00   **Seniors:** $4.00
  ♿ © Free on-site parking on campus in front of Museum. Overflow lot 1/8 mile away.
Museum Shop
Group Tours: ex 248   **Drop-In Tours:** 2:00, Th, Su
Permanent Collection: P/COL; AM; 19-20; AM gr 20; AF

Designated by the state of Florida as a "Major Cultural Institution" the Orlando Museum, established in 1924, recently completed its major expansion and construction project making it the only museum in the nine county area of central Florida capable of providing residents and tourists with world class exhibits. **NOT TO BE MISSED:** Permanent Collection of Art of the Ancient Americas (1200 BC to 1500 AD)complete with hands on exhibit.

ON EXHIBIT 2000
12/18/1999 to 02/27/2000   A TASTE FOR SPLENDOR: TREASURES FROM THE HILLWOOD MUSEUM
About 200 objects from the extraordinary collection of Marjorie Merriweather Post ranging from 19th century French furniture to porcelains and gold boxes commissioned by Catherine The Great and treasures by Faberge including two of the Imperial Easter Eggs. *Will Travel*

03/11/2000 to 05/21/2000   TWENTIETH CENTURY STILL-LIFE PAINTINGS FROM THE PHILLIPS COLLECTION *Will Travel*

06/02/2000 to 08/11/2000   IN PRAISE OF NATURE: ANSEL ADAMS AND PHOTOGRAPHERS OF THE AMERICAN WEST
An eclectic and varied photographic record of the American West during the first century of photography (1850-1950). In addition to Adams, the 150 works will include images by Jackson, Watkins, Muybridge and Fiske as well as Lange, Evans, Rothstein and Cunningham. ADM: Adults, $6.00; SR, STU $4.00; under 12 F *Will Travel*

08/19/2000 to 10/15/2000   FLORIDA INVITATIONAL EXHIBITION
A juried exhibition of emerging and id-career artists from all over the state.

12/23/2000 to 02/25/2001   LATINO ART: TREASURES FROM THE SMITHSONIAN'S MUSEUM OF AMERICAN ART
The goal of the exhibition is to convey the wide range of artists of Latin Heritage living in the US from the 17th-20th C and their ability to convey the vitality of Latino artistic traditions and innovations. *Will Travel*

Hibel Museum of Art

150 Royal Poinciana Plaza, Palm Beach, FL 33480
📞: 561-833-6870 ◙ www.hibel.com
Open: 10-5 Tu-Sa, 1-5 Su **Closed:** Mo, 1/1, 7/4, THGV, 12/25
♿ Ⓟ Free **Museum Shop Group Tours Drop-In Tours**: Upon request if available
Permanent Collection: EDNA HIBEL: all media

The 22 year old Hibel Museum is the world's only publicly owned non profit museum dedicated to the art of a single living American woman.

Society of the Four Arts

Four Arts Plaza, Palm Beach, FL 33480
📞: 561-655-7226
Open: 12/2-4/24: 10-5 Mo-Sa, 2-5 Su **Closed:** Museum closed May-Oct
Sugg/Cont: ADM: Adult: $3.00
♿ Ⓟ Free **Museum Shop Group Tours Sculpture Garden**
Permanent Collection: SCULP

Rain or shine, this museum provides welcome relief from the elements for all vacationing art fanciers by presenting monthly exhibitions of paintings or decorative arts. **NOT TO BE MISSED:** Philip Hulitar Sculpture Garden

Pensacola Museum of Art

407 S. Jefferson St., Pensacola, FL 32501
📞: 850-432-6247 ◙ www.artsnwfl.org/pma
Open: 10-5 Tu-Fr, 10-4 Sa **Closed:** Su, Mo, LEG/HOL!
Free Day: Tu **ADM: Adult:** $2.00 **Students:** $1.00 **Seniors:** $2.00
♿ Ⓟ Free **Museum Shop**
Group Tours Drop-In Tours: check for availability **Historic Building**
Permanent Collection: CONT/AM: ptgs, gr, works on paper; Glass:19,20

Now renovated and occupied by the Pensacola Museum of Art, this building was in active use as the city jail from 1906 - 1954.

John and Mable Ringling Museum of Art

5401 Bay Shore Rd., Sarasota, FL 34243
📞: 941-359-5700
Open: 10-5:30 Daily **Closed:** 1/1,THGV, 12/25
ADM: Adult: $9.50 **Children:** Free 12 & under **Seniors:** $8.50
♿ Ⓟ Free **Museum Shop** ⑪: Banyan Café 11-4 daily
Group Tours Drop-In Tours: call 813-351-1660 (recorded message)
Historic Building Ca'D'Zan was the winter mansion of John & Mable Ringling
Sculpture Garden
Permanent Collection: AM: ptgs, scupl; EU: ptgs, sculp 15-20; DRGS; GR; DEC/ART; CIRCUS MEMORABILIA

FLORIDA

John and Mable Ringling Museum of Art - continued

Sharing the grounds of the museum is Ca'd'Zan, the winter mansion of circus impresario John Ringling and his wife Mable. Their personal collection of fine art in the museum features one of the country's premier collections of European, Old Master, and 17th century Italian Baroque paintings. **NOT TO BE MISSED:** The Rubens Gallery - a splendid group of paintings by Peter Paul Rubens.

ON EXHIBIT 2000

ONGOING "A BOLT FROM THE SKY": SPLENDORS OF EUROPEAN ART IN THE RINGLING MUSEUM

A historical journey through five centuries awaits visitors to the 21 galleries of the Art Museum. The galleries will be transformed into settings where visitors can figuratively voyage through time. They will evoke environments such as a German castle from the Renaissance, an Italian palace, an English country house, a French salon, or a Fifth Avenue ballroom. Paintings, sculpture and furnishings from the collection, some not seen in decades, will be arranged in imaginative, decorative configurations that will recall their original settings in European style galleries.

ONGOING   BOYS FROM BARABOO TO BIG TOP BOSSES: HISTORY OF THE RINGLING CIRCUS 1884-1964

The exhibition will trace the history of this American success from its early beginnings, to the heyday of the tented show, to its evolution as an arena circus.

01/14/2000 to 03/19/2000   GREEN WOODS AND CRYSTAL WATERS: THE AMERICAN LANDSCAPE TRADITION SINCE 1950

This important exhibition features 80 works drawn from public and private collections, that demonstrate the vitality and variety of the American landscape in the second half of the 20th century. Exhibition includes works by some of the most influential artists of the period, including Amenoff, Avery, Beal, Chaet, Downes, Gornik, Hopper, Jacquette, Katz, Kent, Leslie, Milton, Neel, O'Keeffe, Porter, Thiebaud and Welliver.

02/2000 to 05/2000   RESTORATION AND REDISCOVERY: CRAFT AND MATERIALS IN THE CA' D'ZAN RESTORATION

04/14/2000 to 06/04/2000   THE PEOPLE'S CHOICE

This intriguing show seeks to answer the question: What is a democratic and populist painting? The exhibition serves as a global analysis of what people, defined by their nationality, look for in art.

07/28/2000 to 11/05/2000   SARASOTA BIENNIAL

The exhibition series, Featuring Florida, is a tradition that began at The John and Mable Ringling Museum 50 years ago. Now, at the end of the 20th century, the Ringling Museum is looking to the future as it replaces Featuring Florida with the first Sarasota Biennial. While the Featuring Florida series selected finished work by artists chosen by a jury process, the Sarasota Biennial will search out the state's most significant and current artists through studio visits and by nurturing artist networks and direct, sustained collaborations.

12/15/2000 to 12/18/2001   THE GILDED AGE: PAINTINGS FROM THE SMITHSONIAN'S NATIONAL MUSEUM OF AMERICAN ART

This major exhibition features artists who brought a new sophistication and elegance into American art in the three decades before World War I. Wealthy industrialists (including John Ringling), eager to acquire culture began to patronize native artists who had achieved international recognition. This exhibition will include works by artists such as Louis Comfort Tiffany, John Singer Sargent, Winslow Homer, Childe Hassam, Mary Cassatt, and others that made an impact during this time of contending social and industrial forces.

ST. PETERSBURG

Florida International Museum
100 Second St. North, St. Petersburg, FL 33701
☎: 727-822-3693   ▣ www.floridamuseum.org
Open: 9am - 8pm daily (last tour starts at 6pm)   **Closed:** 1/1, THGV, 12/25
ADM: Adult: $13.95   **Children:** $5.95   **Students:** College Stud $7.95   **Seniors:** $12.95
&.   ℗ An abundance of nearby garage, street, and surface car parks
Museum Shop
Group Tours: Call for reservations and information   **Drop-In Tours**
Group Tours   Drop-In Tours

Florida International Museum - continued
The Florida International Museum is centered in the cultural heart of Tampa Bay-Downtown St. Petersburg. Opened in January 1995, it has been visited by over two million people in just five exhibitions, making it Florida's premier museum for blockbuster exhibitions. The museum was organized in 1992 for the purpose of creating a major international cultural center within a 300,000 square foot former department store building that has undergone a multi-million dollar renovation.

ON EXHIBIT 2000
11/12/1999 to 05/29/2000   A THOUSAND DAYS THAT CHANGED THE WORLD
The largest collection of Kennedy artifacts including ,many items of a personal nature relating to the President and First Lady. Call 1-800-JFK-Show or go to www.floridamuseum.org

Museum of Fine Arts-St. Petersburg Florida
255 Beach Dr., N.E., St. Petersburg, FL 33701-3498
✆: 727-896-2667   ◉ www.fine-arts.org
Open: 10-5 Tu-Sa, 1-5 Su, till 9pm 3rd Th   **Closed:** Mo, THGV,12/25, 1/1
ADM: Adult: $6.00 ($4 for groups of 10 or more)   **Children:** Free 6 & under   **Students:** $2.00   **Seniors:** $5.00
ⓗ ⓟ Free parking also available on Beach Dr. & Bayshore Dr.   **Museum Shop**
Group Tours   Drop-In Tours: 10, 11, 1, 2, 3 Tu-Fr; 11 to 2 hourly Sa; 1 & 2 Su   **Sculpture Garden**
Permanent Collection: AM: ptgs, sculp, drgs, gr; EU: ptgs, sculp, drgs, gr; P/COL; DEC/ART; P/COL; OR; STEUBEN GLASS; NAT/AM; AS: art; AF/ART

With the addition in 1989 of 10 new galleries, the Museum of Fine Arts, considered one of the premier museums in the southeast, is truly an elegant showcase for its many treasures that run the gamut from Dutch and Old Master paintings to one of the finest collections of photography in the state. The museum is home to the William Glackens 's Collection . The most comprehensive of his contemporaries known as the "Eight" or the " Ashcan School" . It is also home to the largest collection of CoBrA art in the western hemisphere. PLEASE NOTE: Spanish language tours are available by advance appointment. **NOT TO BE MISSED:** Paintings by Monet, Gauguin, Cézanne, Morisot, Renoir, and O'Keeffe

ON EXHIBIT 2000
ONGOING   RODIN BRONZES: FROM THE IRIS AND B. GERALD CANTOR FOUNDATION

11/07/1999 to 01/30/2000   WINSLOW HOMER GRAPHICS
The exhibition celebrates Homer as a printmaker and documentor of daily life in America between 1857 and 1880.

01/16/2000 to 01/30/2000   MINIATURE ART SOCIETY OF FLORIDA'S 25TH ANNIVERSARY CELEBRATION
Approximately 800 works of scrimshaw, sculpture and calligraphy will be shown.

02/13/2000 to 05/28/2000   THE FANTASTICAL WORLD OF CROATIAN NAIVE ART
Croatian Naïve art has rarely been seen in the US and such a large grouping has never been presented in an American Museum.

10/29/2000 to 01/07/2001   ABRAHAM BLOEMAERT AND HIS TIME

Salvador Dali Museum
100 Third St. South, St. Petersburg, FL 33701
✆: 813-823-3767   ◉ www.daliweb.com
Open: 9:30-5:30 Mo-Sa, 12-5:30 Su: 9:30-8:00 Th   **Closed:** THGV, 12/25
ADM: Adult: $9.00   **Children:** Free 10 & under   **Students:** $5.00   **Seniors:** $7.00
ⓗ ⓟ Free   **Museum Shop   Group Tours**: tours 9:30-3:30 Mo-Sa   **Drop-In Tours**: ! Call for daily schedule
Permanent Collection: SALVADOR DALI: ptgs, sculp, drgs, gr

Unquestionably the largest and most comprehensive collection of Dali's works in the world, the museum holdings amassed by Dali's friends A. Reynolds and Eleanor Morse include 95 original oils, 100 watercolors and drawings, 1,300 graphics, sculpture, and other objects d'art that span his entire career. **NOT TO BE MISSED:** Outstanding docent tours that are offered many times daily.

FLORIDA

Florida State University Museum of Fine Arts

Fine Arts Bldg., Copeland & W. Tenn. Sts., Tallahassee, FL 32306-1140
☎: 850-644-6836 ◙ www.fsu.edu/~svad/FSUMuseum/FSU-Museum.html
Open: 10-4 Mo-Fr; 1-4 Sa, Su (closed weekends during Summer Semester) **Closed:** LEG/HOL! Acad!
& Ⓟ Metered parking in front of the building with weekend parking available in the lot next to the museum.
Museum Shop Group Tours: 850-644-1299 **Drop-In Tours**: Upon request if available
Permanent Collection: EU; OR; CONT; PHOT; GR; P/COL: Peruvian artifacts; JAP: gr

With 7 gallery spaces, this is the largest art museum within 2 hours driving distance of Tallahassee. **NOT TO BE MISSED:** Works by Judy Chicago

ON EXHIBIT 2000
01/03/2000 to 02/06/2000 Ewing Galloway: Scenes of New York in the 20's and 30's
Works from a collection of 200 photographs that have not yet been shown to the public.

02/2000 to 04/2000 ABSTRACT VISIONS

10/01/2000 to 11/19/2000 30TH ANNIVERSARY OF ANTHROPOLOGY: SELECTIONS FROM THE LEWIS COLLECTION

10/06/2000 to 11/19/2000 FLORIDA PHOTOGENESIS: THE WORLD OF EXPERIMENTAL PHOTOGRAPHERS IN FLORIDA

Lemoyne Art Foundation, Inc.

125 N. Gadsden, Tallahassee, FL 32301
☎: 850-222-8800
Open: 10-5 Tu-Sa, 1-5 Su **Closed:** 1/1, 7/4, 12/25 (may be closed during parts of Aug!)
ADM: Adult: $1.00 **Children:** Free 12 & under **Students:** $1.00 **Seniors:** $1.00
& Ⓟ parking lot adjacent to the Helen Lind Garden and Sculptures; also, large lot across street available weekends and evenings **Museum Shop Drop-In Tours**: daily when requested **Historic Building Sculpture Garden**
Permanent Collection: CONT/ART; sculp

Located in an 1852 structure in the heart of Tallahassee's historic district, the Lemoyne is named for the first artist known to have visited North America. Aside from offering a wide range of changing exhibitions annually, the museum provides the visitor with a sculpture garden that serves as a setting for beauty and quiet contemplation. **NOT TO BE MISSED:** Three recently acquired copper sculptures by George Frederick Holschuh

Tampa Museum of Art

600 North Ashley Dr., Tampa, FL 33602
☎: 813-274-8130
Open: 10-5 Mo-Sa, 10-9 We, 1-5 Su **Closed:** 1/1, 7/4, 12/25
Vol/Cont: ADM: Adult: $5.00 **Children:** 6-18 $3.00; Free under 6 **Students:** $4.00 **Seniors:** $4.00
& Ⓟ Covered parking under the museum for a nominal hourly fee. Enter the garage from Ashley Dr. & Twiggs St.
Museum Shop Drop-In Tours: 1:00 We & Sa, 2:00 S **Sculpture Garden**
Permanent Collection: PTGS: 19-20; GR: 19-20; AN/GRK; AN/R; PHOT

A superb 400 piece collection of Greek and Roman antiquities dating from 3,000 BC to the 3rd century A.D. is one of the highlights of this comprehensive and vital art museum. The Tampa Museum has recently installed a vast new sculpture garden, part of an exterior expansion program completed in 1995. **NOT TO BE MISSED:** Joseph V. Noble Collection of Greek & Southern Italian antiquities on view in the new Barbara & Costas Lemonopoulos Gallery.

USF Contemporary Art Museum
Affiliate Institution: College of Fine Arts
4202 E. Fowler Ave., Tampa, FL 33620
☎: 813-974-4133
Open: 10-5 Mo-Fr, 1-4 Sa   **Closed:** STATE & LEG/HOL!
 ♿ Ⓟ Free parking in front of museum (parking pass available from museum security guard)   **Museum Shop**
Group Tours   Drop-In Tours
Permanent Collection: CONT: phot, gr

Located in a new building on the Tampa campus, the USF Contemporary Art Museum houses one of the largest selections of contemporary prints in the Southeast. PLEASE NOTE: The museum is occasionally closed between exhibitions!

VERO BEACH

Center for the Arts, Inc.
3001 Riverside Park Dr., Vero Beach, FL 32963-1807
☎: 561-231-0707   ■ vero=beach.fl.us/cita/index.html
Open: 10-4:30 Mo-Sa; 10-8 Th ; 1-4:30 Su   **Closed:** LEG/HOL
Sugg/Cont:
♿ Ⓟ Free   **Museum Shop**
Group Tours: ex 25   **Drop-In Tours:** 1:30-3:30 Sa, Su/ July-Oct; Wed-Su Nov-June   **Sculpture Garden**
Permanent Collection: AM/ART 20

Considered the premier visual arts facility within a 160 mile radius on Florida's east coast, The Center, which offers national, international and regional art exhibitions throughout the year, maintains a leadership role in nurturing the cultural life of the region. **NOT TO BE MISSED:** "Watson and the Shark" by Sharron Quasius; "Transpassage T.L.S.", 20 ft. aluminum sculpture by Ralph F. Buckley

ON EXHIBIT 2000

01/22/2000 to 02/27/2000   CHERYL TALL/RAINEY DIMMITT
Ceramic beads and torsos which are influenced by medieval folk art and mythology. The artists investigate the shared symbolism of human body and house.

01/29/2000 to 03/05/2000   ISLAND ANCESTORS : OCEANIC ART FROM THE MASCO COLLECTION
This exceptional collection contains ancestor and fertility figures, eating utensils, containers, masks, drums, ornaments and other objects from intriguingly remote parts of the world. *Catalog Will Travel*

03/04/2000 to 04/16/2000   Ken Falana
Falana's current series of large scale collages which rival the colors of sea coral are augmented by his smaller earlier work.

03/17/2000 to 05/16/2000   PAUL JENKINS: THE COLLAGES
Color abstractions on canvas have won Jenkins international acclaim .

03/18/2000 to 05/07/2000   MEXICAN ART FROM THE BRYNA COLLECTION: THREE DECADES: 1954-1982
Over 100 works in cast bronze, welded steel and stone sculpture as well as paintings, drawings and prints from this extensive collection.

05/20/2000 to 07/09/2000   THE GRONLUND COLLECTION: ABSTRACT PRINTS OF THE 20TH CENTURY
63 American prints from the 1920's through the 1980's by American masters of the medium. Included are Stuart Davis, Marsden Hartley, John Marin, Dorothy Dehner, Boris Margo, Robert Indiana, Robert Motherwell, Robert Rauschenburg, Larry Rivers, Amenoff, Dine, Graves, Mitchell, and Sultan with many others.

06/03/2000 to 07/16/2000   THREE GENERATIONS
Sun filled scenes and panoramas of people at leisure.

FLORIDA

Center for the Arts, Inc. - continued
07/22/2000 to 08/27/2000   JEAN CLAUDE RIGALAUD: SCULPTURE
A sculptor who works in geometric forms, he is always playfully engaging.

07/22/2000 to 09/10/2000   GRANT WOOD AND MARVIN COHN: THE ORIGINS OF REGIONALISM
Paintings that highlight the work of Grant Wood and a lesser known fellow artist. It reveals the origins of Regionalism in the 1930's *Will Travel*

09/02/2000 to 10/15/2000   PIECE BY PIECE: ARCHER, SKILES, TANENBAUM
Three collage artists . The processes of time, decay and memory are prominent themes in the work of all three artists.

09/16/2000 to 11/12/2000   MASTERPIECES OF PHOTOGRAPHY: THE RICHARD M. ROSS COLLECTION
Ross pursued the medium as an artist and collector. Included are masterpieces from the mid-19th C. to the 1980's. Included are Nadar, Cameron, Emerson, Robinson, Stieglitz, Curtis, Cunningham, Evans, Walker. Bresson and Karsh.

WEST PALM BEACH

Norton Museum of Art
1451 S. Olive Ave., West Palm Beach, FL 33401
\: 561-832-5196 ◉ www.norton.org
Open: 10-5 Tu-Sa, 1-5 Su   **Closed:** Mo, 1/1, MEM/DAY, 7/4, THGV, 12/25
Free Day: We 1:30-5   **ADM: Adult:** $6.00   **Children:** Free 12 & under   **Students:** $2.00 (13-21)
& ℗ Free   **Museum Shop** ⓘ: Open 11:30-2:30 Mo-Sa & 1-3 Su
Group Tours   Drop-In Tours: 12:30-1:30 weekdays, 2-3pm daily   **Sculpture Garden**
Permanent Collection: AM: ptgs, sculp 19-20; FR: ptgs, sculp 19-20; OR: sculp, cer

Started in 1940 with a core collection of French Impressionist and modern masterpieces, as well as fine works of American painting, the newly-renovated and expanded Norton's holdings also include major pieces of contemporary sculpture, and a noteworthy collection of Asian art. It is no wonder that the Norton enjoys the reputation of being one of the finest small museums in the United States. Free tours of permanent collection-ARTventure-daily 2-3pm PLEASE NOTE: An admission fee may be charged for certain exhibitions. **NOT TO BE MISSED:** Paul Manship's frieze across the main facade of the museum flanked by his sculptures of Diana and Actaeon

ON EXHIBIT 2000
10/28/1999 to 01/02/2000   HALF PAST AUTUMN: THE ART OF GORDON PARKS
A retrospective of Park's extraordinary career as a photojournalist, filmmaker, novelist poet and musician. *Catalog Will Travel*

11/13/1999 to 01/16/2000   GIRLFRIEND! THE BARBIE SESSIONS-PHOTOGRAPHS BY DAVID LEVANTHAL
Large format color saturated Polaroid photographs which blur the boundaries between fact and fiction. This series of 40 images, portraying Barbie dressed impeccably for a variety of occasions, continues Leventhal's on-going inquest into the realm where fantasies become plausible realities. *Will Travel*

11/20/1999 to 01/30/2000   AMERICAN MODERNISM FROM THE STIEGLITZ GROUP
Steiglitz' Gallery 291 in New York helped launch the careers of Marsden Hartley, Arthur P. Dove, John Marin, and Georgia O'Keeffe.

12/11/1999 to 02/27/2000   MARSDEN HARTLEY: AMERICAN MODERN
Superb examples of Harley's work from each period of his output: early post-impressionist Maine mountain scenes, Pre WWI abstractions made in Paris and Berlin, Provincetown landscapes and abstracts, New Mexican landscapes, still-lifes from the 1920's and 1930's, Bavarian mountain pastels, 1930's portraits and late Maine landscapes. *Will Travel*

01/15/2000 to 03/12/2000   THE ROYAL ACADEMY IN THE AGE OF QUEEN VICTORIA (1837-1901): 19TH CENTURY PAINTINGS FROM THE PERMANENT COLLECTION
London's Royal Academy contributed major works throughout the 19th c. Included are Alma-Tadema, Blake, Millais, etc who are just now beginning to attract more attention from the art world.

Norton Museum of Art - continued

02/05/2000 to 04/02/2000   THE ARRESTED IMAGE: 19TH CENTURY PHOTOGRAPHS
40 images from the collection including daguerreotypes by artists unknown, Nadar's modern views of Paris, Civil War photos, and Cameron's portraiture, it promises to reshape the conventional perception of Victorian photographic images.

04/01/2000 to 06/11/2000   BERLIN METROPOLIS: JEWS AND THE NEW CULTURE, 1890-1918
The contribution of Jews to the development of sophisticated avant-garde culture in a show which will experience the sights and sounds in 250 objects including paintings, sculpture, prints, posters and theater memorabilia from this period of extraordinary transformation for Berlin. *Catalog Will Travel*

04/08/2000 to 06/21/2000   MY FRIEND PICASSO: PHOTOGRAPHS BY LUCIEN CLERTUC *Will Travel*

07/01/2000 to 09/03/2000   ROAD WARRIORS: KNIGHT RIDERS
A exhibition which compares and contrasts the worlds of motorcycle rider and the medieval knight. Included will be three complex armors from the 15th and 16TH c along with armor components. Also included will be three distinctive bikes, built for road touring and off road racing. Clothing will also be shown

---

WINTER PARK

Charles Hosmer Morse Museum of American Art

445 Park Avenue North, Winter Park, FL 32789
☎: 407-645-5311   ◙ www.morsemus.org
Open: 9:30-4 Tu-Sa, 1-4 Su   **Closed:** Mo, 1/1, MEM/DAY, LAB/DAY, THGV, 12/25
Free Day: Open House Easter weekend, 7/4, Christmas Eve
ADM: Adult: $3.00   **Children:** Free under 12   **Students:** $1.00
& ℗   **Museum Shop**
Group Tours
Drop-In Tours: available during regular hours
Permanent Collection: Tiffany Glass; AM: ptgs (19 and early 20); AM: art pottery 19-20

Late 19th and early 20th century works of Louis Comfort Tiffany glass were rescued in 1957 from the ruins of Laurelton Hall, Tiffany's Long Island home, by Hugh and Jeannette McKean. These form the basis of the collection at this most unique little-known gem of a museum which has recently moved into new and larger quarters. Along with the Tiffany collection, the Museum houses a major collection of American art pottery, superb works by late 19th and early 20th century artists, including Martin Johnson Heade, Robert Henri, Maxfield Parrish, George Innis, and others. **NOT TO BE MISSED:** Tiffany chapel for the 1893 Chicago World's Columbian Exposition, opening in March 1999; the "Electrolier", elaborate 10' high chandelier, centerpiece of the Chapel; the Baptismal Font, also from the Chapel, which paved the way for Tiffany's leaded glass lamps; 2 marble, concrete and Favrile glass columns designed over 100 years ago by Tiffany for his Long Island Mansion.

Cornell Fine Arts Museum

Affiliate Institution: Rollins College
1000 Holt Ave., Winter Park, FL 32789-4499
☎: 407-646-2526   ◙   www.rollins.edu/cfam
Open: 10-5 Tu-Fr; 1-5 Sa, Su   **Closed:** Mo, 1/1, THGV, 7/4, LAB/DAY, 12/25
Vol/Cont:
&   ℗ parking in the adjacent lot
Museum Shop   ⅂: Café Cornell nearby in Social Science Bldg
Group Tours: 407-646-1536
Historic Building Case Bldg built in 1941 in continuous use as an art museum
Permanent Collection: EU: ptgs, Ren-20; SCULP; DEC/ART; AM: ptgs, sculp 19-20; PHOT; SP: Ren/sculp, pr Eu & AMo, dr; watch key coll

FLORIDA

Cornell Fine Arts Museum - continued

Considered one of the most outstanding museums in Florida, the Cornell, located on the campus of Rollins College, houses fine examples in many areas of art including American 19th C landscape painting, French portraiture, works of Renaissance and Baroque masters, and contemporary prints. **NOT TO BE MISSED:** Paintings from the Kress Collection; Cosimo Roselli, etc. "Christ with the Symbols of the Passion", by Lavinia Fontana, 1581

ON EXHIBIT 2000

11/05/1999 to 01/09/2000   KENNETH TYLER: 30 YEARS OF AMERICAN PRINTS
Tyler and his workshop transformed American printmaking into areas once considered the sole domain of painting and sculpture. Artists include Rauschenburg, Motherwell and Hockney.

01/21/2000 to 03/05/2000   BREAKING BOUNDARIES: 20 YEARS OF THE ATLANTIC CENTER FOR THE ARTS
The creative cross pollination of the Atlantic Center at New Smyrna Beach, Florida . The work of writers, dancers, composers and painters demonstrates the magic of the creative process.

01/21/2000 to 03/05/2000   PICASSO'S VOLLARD SUITE
Created for Picasso's dealer, these 100 works include his "Minotour " series and prints on "The Sculptors Studio".

03/17/2000 to 05/07/2000   BIZARRO WORLD! THE PARALLEL UNIVERSES OF COMICS AND ART
Exploring the influences that comic book illustrators have had on one another. The work of Crumb, Spiegelman and Lichtenstein, Guston and Brown are included.

06/2000 to 09/2000   ART OF THE TWENTIETH CENTURY
A review of art as seen through the works in the Cornell Collection

Albany Museum of Art
311 Meadowlark Dr., Albany, GA 31707

📞: 912-439-8400   📷 www.albanymuseum.com
Open: 10-5 Tu-Sa, till 7pm We; 1-4 Su   **Closed:** Mo, LEG/HOL!
Sugg/Cont:
♿ ℗ **Museum Shop**
Group Tours   Drop-In Tours
Permanent Collection: AM: all media 19- 20; EU: all media 19-20; AF: 19-20

With one of the largest museum collections in the south of Sub-Saharan African art, the Albany Museum, started in 1964, is dedicated to serving the people of the region by providing exposure to the visual arts through a focused collection, diversified programs and other activities. **NOT TO BE MISSED:** A 1500 piece collection of African art that includes works from 18 different cultures.

ON EXHIBIT 2000

to 02/27/2000   AUDUBON'S QUADRUPEDS
16 hand colored prints from the series "The Viviparous Quadrupeds of North America" *Will Travel*

11/12/1998 to 12/31/2000   THE WORLD AND THE NEXT: ART FROM AFRICA
Explore African culture through the Museum's ceremonial and everyday objects in its sub-Saharan African Art Collection. Many never before displayed objects will be shown.

01/07/2000 to 12/31/2000   HIGHLIGHTS FROM THE PERMANENT COLLECTION
Premier works including new acquisitions "Conversations" by Romare Bearden and "Street Girl" by Reginald Marsh.

01/14/2000 to 03/12/2000   PRIDE IN PLACE: LANDSCAPES BY THE EIGHT IN SOUTHERN COLLECTIONS
Landscape paintings, drawings and watercolors by this important group of artists. *Will Travel*

01/28/2000 to 03/26/2000   STUDIO GLASS FROM THE SCHUMAN COLLECTION
Harvey Littleton and Dominick Lubino are included in this collection.

03/16/2000 to 08/31/2000   LOCAL COLOR: DAVID LANIER
Lanier uses color and habitat for wildlife to merge in works which create powerful images of the natural world.

04/06/2000 to 06/11/2000   ALL THE SYMPTOMS OF AN ARTIST
An interdisciplinary show which explores the links with health care, healing and art.

06/29/2000 to 09/03/2000   JUDITH GODWIN: STYLE AND GRACE
A survey of the career of a most exuberant and original abstract painter. *Will Travel*

06/29/2000 to 09/03/2000   THE BEAUTIFUL AND THE BOLD: SCULPTURES BY PAM SOLDWEDEL
Organic shapes in stone and metal incorporate the mystery and passion central to human experience.

12/03/2000 to 02/04/2001   THE HUMAN FACTOR: FIGURATION IN AMERICAN ART, 1950-1995
Paintings, sculpture, prints and drawings from the collection of the Sheldon Memorial Art Gallery provides a mini survey of the of the aesthetics, issues and ideas in figurative works   Included are Alice Neal, George Segal and Robert Longo.. *Will Travel*

03/01/2001 to 05/30/2001   THE WALTER O. EVANS COLLECTION OF AFRICAN AMERICAN ART
On display from this major Detroit collection will be important works from 19th century artists Edward Bannister and Henry Tanner through such modern masters as Elizabeth Catlett and Romare Bearden

GEORGIA

Georgia Museum of Art
Affiliate Institution: The University of Georgia
90 Carlton St., Athens, GA 30602-1719
☎: 706-542-4662 ◉ www.uga.edu/gamuseum
Open: 10-5 Tu-Th & Sa, 10-9 Fr, 1-5 Su **Closed:** Mo, LEG/HOL!
Sugg/Cont: $1.00
   Ⓟ **Museum Shop**
‖: On Display Cafe open 10-2:30 Mo-Fr
Group Tours: 706-462-4642 **Drop-In Tours:** by appt.
Permanent Collection: AM: sculp, gr; EU: gr; JAP: gr; IT/REN: ptgs (Kress Collection); AM: ptgs 19-20

The Georgia Museum of art, which moved to a new facility on Carlton St., on the east campus of the University of Georgia in September of '96, has grown from its modest beginnings, in 1945, of a 100 piece collection donated by Alfred Holbrook, to more than 7,000 works now included in its permanent holdings. PLEASE NOTE: Public tours are often offered on Sundays (call for information). **NOT TO BE MISSED:** Paintings from the permanent collection on view continually in the C.L. Moorhead Jr. Wing.

ON EXHIBIT 2000
11/23/1999 to 01/09/2000 SUSAN HAUPTMAN

11/27/1999 to 01/09/2000 WILL BARNET AND BOB BLACKBURN: AN ARTISTIC FRIENDSHIP IN RELIEF

12/18/1999 to 03/26/2000 COLONIAL POWDER HORNS FROM THE JAMES ROUTH COLLECTION

01/15/2000 to 03/05/2000 VISION IN HAND

01/22/2000 to 03/19/2000 MASTERWORKS FROM THE SAN CARLOS NATIONAL MUSEUM, MEXICO CITY

Atlanta International Museum at Peachtree Center
285 Peachtree Center Avenue, Atlanta, GA 30303
☎: 404-688-2467
Open: 11-5 Tu-Sa **Closed:** Su, Mo, LEG/HOL!
Free Day: 1-5 We **ADM: Adult:** $3.00 **Children:** $3.00 **Students:** $3.00 **Seniors:** $3.00
   Ⓟ pay in Baker Street Garage **Museum Shop** ‖: In Marriott Hotel
Group Tours
Permanent Collection: International Focus of Art and Design

The Atlanta International Museum celebrates cultural diversity and minority pride.

Hammonds House Galleries and Resource Center
503 Peoples St., Atlanta, GA 31310-1815
☎: 404-752-8730
Open: 10-6 Tu-Fr; 1-5 Sa, Su **Closed:** LEG/HOL!
ADM: Adult: $2.00 **Children:** $1.00 **Students:** $1.00 **Seniors:** $1.00
   Ⓟ Free **Museum Shop**
Group Tours Drop-In Tours: Upon request
Historic Building 1857 East Lake Victorian House restored in 1984 by Dr. Otis T. Hammonds
Permanent Collection: AF/AM: mid 19-20; HAITIAN: ptgs; AF: sculp

Hammonds House Galleries and Resource Center - continued
As the only fine art museum in the Southeast dedicated to the promotion of art by peoples of African descent, Hammonds House features changing exhibitions of nationally known African-American artists. Works by Romare Bearden, Sam Gilliam, Benny Andrews, James Van Der Zee and others are included in the 125 piece collection. **NOT TO BE MISSED:** Romare Bearden Collection of post 60's serigraphs; Collection of Premiero Contemporary Haitian Artists

High Museum of Art
1280 Peachtree St., N.E., Atlanta, GA 30309
☎: 404-733-HIGH ◙ www.high.org
Open: 10-5 Tu-Th, 10-5 Sa; 12-5 Su; Fr extended hours, 10-9 **Closed:** Mo, 1/1, THGV, 12/25
ADM: Adult: $6.00 **Children:** $2.00 6-17; Free under 6 **Students:** $4.00 **Seniors:** $4.00
♿ Ⓟ Parking on deck of Woodruff Art Center Building on the side of the museum and neighborhood lots; some limited street parking **Museum Shop** ⅈ: Mo 8:30-3; Tu-Fr 8:30-5, weekends 10-5
Group Tours: 404-733-4550 **Drop-In Tours**: ! by appt
Historic Building Building designed by Richard Meier, 1983
Permanent Collection: AM: dec/art 18-20; EU: cer 18; AM: ptgs, sculp 19; EU: ptgs, sculp, cer, gr, REN-20; PHOT 19-20 ; AM; cont (since 1970); self taught and folk

The beauty of the building, designed in 1987 by architect Richard Meier, is a perfect foil for the outstanding collection of art within the walls of the High Museum of Art itself. Part of the Robert W. Woodruff Art Center, this museum is a "must see" for every art lover who visits Atlanta. PLEASE NOTE: Admission, hours and Cafe hours vary with timed and dated tickets. **NOT TO BE MISSED:** The Virginia Carroll Crawford Collection of American Decorative Arts; The Frances and Emory Cocke Collection of English Ceramics: T. Marshall Hahn collection of Folk Art

ON EXHIBIT 2000
ONGOING MULTIPLE CHOICES: THEMES & VARIATIONS IN OUR COLLECTION
Reinstalled on the 2nd and 3rd floor, these works from the permanent collection will be grouped in themes vital to the study and enjoyment of art and art history.

ONGOING SEE FOR YOURSELF
For viewers of all ages, this exhibition of works from the permanent collection promotes a basic understanding of art by explaining such fundamental ingredients as line, color, light and composition.

02/26/1999 to 05/21/2000 JOHN TWACHTMAN: AN AMERICAN IMPRESSIONIST
A major retrospective of Twactman's work will be arranged chronologically. The early Venice and New York works; His time in France and Holland; the Connecticut years; and late Glouster works. *Catalog Will Travel*

11/06/1999 to 01/30/2000 NORMAN ROCKWELL: PICTURES FOR THE AMERICAN PEOPLE
Seventy of his oil paintings and all 322 'Saturday Evening Post' covers are featured in this always popular show. *Will Travel*

11/20/1999 to 02/26/2000 THE ART OF NELLIE MAE ROWE: NINETY NINE AND A HALF WON'T DO
A self-taught artist from Georgia, filled her home with drawings, sculpture, photocollages, and dolls that she made from such everyday items as cardboard, paper, cloth, felt-tip pens, and even chewing gum.

11/20/1999 to 02/26/2000 THE ART OF NELLIE MAE ROWE: NINETY NINE AND A HALF WON'T DO
A self-taught artist from Georgia, filled her home with drawings, sculpture, photocollages, and dolls that she made from such everyday items as cardboard, paper, cloth, felt-tip pens, and even chewing gum.

01/08/2000 to 06/18/2000 FRANK LLOYD WRIGHT FURNITURE

02/26/2000 to 05/21/2000 ART ON THE EDGE: TODD MURPHY

04/11/2000 to 06/26/2000 RECENT PHOTOGRAPHY ACQUISITIONS

GEORGIA

High Museum of Art - continued

06/19/2000 to 04/16/2000   AFRICAN-AMERICAN SELF-TAUGHT ART FROM THE HIGH MUSEUM OF ART COLLECTION

06/20/2000 to 09/24/2000   THE DAVID DRISKELL COLLECTION: NARRATIVES OF AFRICAN-AMERICAN ART OF THE 20TH CENTURY

06/29/2000 to 09/24/2000   TO CONSERVE A LEGACY: AMERICAN ART FROM HISTORICALLY BLACK COLLEGES AND UNIVERSITIES
100 to 140 works showing the University's collections and the range of works in the African diaspora and identity seeking. Artists include Artis, Bearden, Lawrence, Catlett, deCarava , Douglas, etc. *Catalog Will Travel*

07/08/2000 to 10/14/2000   SAM DOYLE

High Museum of Folk Art & Photography Galleries at Georgia-Pacific Center
133 Peachtree Street, Atlanta, GA 30303
☎: 404-577-6940 ◉ www.high.org
Open: 10-5 Mo-Sa **Closed:** Su, LEG/HOL!
♿ ℗ Paid parking lot in the center itself with a bridge from the parking deck to the lobby; other paid parking lots nearby
Museum Shop
Group Tours: 404-733-4550   **Drop-In Tours**: call 404-733-4468
Permanent Collection: Occassional exhibits along with traveling exhibitions are drawn from permanent collection.

Folk art and photography are the main focus in the 4,5000 square foot exhibition space of this Atlanta facility formally called The High Museum of Art at Georgia-Pacific Center.

Michael C. Carlos Museum
Affiliate Institution: Emory University
571 South Kilgo St., Atlanta, GA 30322
☎: 404-727-4282 ◉ www.cc.emory.edu/CARLOS/carlos.html
Open: 10-5 Mo-Sa, Noon-5 Su **Closed:** 1/1, THGV, 12/25
Sugg/Cont: ADM: Adult: $3.00
♿ ℗ Visitor parking for a small fee at the Boisfeuillet Jones Building; free parking on campus except in restricted areas. Handicapped parking Plaza level entrance on So. Kilgo St.
Museum Shop   ‖: Caffé Antico
Group Tours: 404-727-0519   **Drop-In Tours**: 2:30 Sa, Su
Historic Building
Permanent Collection: AN/EGT; AN/GRK; AN/R; P/COL; AS; AF; OC; WORKS ON PAPER 14-20

Founded on the campus of Emory University in 1919 (making it the oldest art museum in Atlanta), this distinguished institution changed its name in 1991 to the Michael C. Carlos Museum in honor of its long time benefactor. Its dramatic 35,000 square foot building, opened in the spring of 1993, is a masterful addition to the original Beaux-Arts edifice. The museum recently acquired one of the largest (1,000 pieces) collections of Sub-Saharan African art in America. **NOT TO BE MISSED:** Carlos Collection of Ancient Greek Art; Thibadeau Collection of pre-Columbian Art; recent acquisition of rare 4th c Volute-Krater by the Underworld painter of Apulia

ON EXHIBIT 2000

ONGOING   TEARS OF THE MOON: ANCIENT AMERICAN PRECIOUS METALS FROM THE PERMANENT COLLECTION

ONGOING   DISCOVERING THE HISTORICAL AIDA

07/19/1999 to Summer 2001   MYSTERIES OF THE MUMMIES: ROTATING PREVIEW

GEORGIA

Michael C. Carlos Museum - continued
09/171999 to 01/09/2000   SO MANY BRILLIANT TALENTS: ART AND CRAFT IN THE AGE OF RUBENS

10/1999 to 10/2001   NOGUCHI'S BEGINNINGS (1985)
Sculptor Isamu Noguchi (1904-1988), son of a Japanese poet and an American writer, was born in the United States, but spent his childhood in Japan. His work draws from both Eastern and Western cultural traditions. On loan to Emory from the Isamu Noguchi Foundation in New York, Beginnings features five separate elements in adesite granite. The sculpture, evocative of Japanese rock gardens, was created in the artist's studio in Japan and was first exhibited in 1986 at the Venice Biennale, representing the United States.

10/15/1999 to 02/20/2000   USES OF PHOTOGRAPHY IN CONTEMPORARY ART
In collaboration with the citywide event, Atlanta Celebrates Photography, the Museum will present a contemporary exhibition which will include approximately 10 examples of contemporary art that uses photography as a medium of expression. Included in the exhibition is Joseph Beuys' Sand Drawings; Chris Burden's I Flew Back to L.A.-X; and Rauschenberg's Visitation I.

Ogelthorpe University Museum
Affiliate Institution: Ogelthorpe University
4484 Peachtree Road, NE, Atlanta, GA 30319
☎: 404-364-8555   ◉ www.museum.oglethorpe.edu
Open: 12-5 We-Su   **Closed:** Mo, Tu, LEG/HOL!
♿ ℗ Free   **Museum Shop   Group Tours:** 404-364-8552   **Drop-In Tours   Historic Building**
Permanent Collection: Realsitic figurative art, historical, metaphysical and international art

Established in 1993 just recently, this museum, dedicated to showing realistic art, has already instituted many "firsts" for this area including the opening of each new exhibition with a free public lecture, the creation of an artist-in-residence program, and a regular series of chamber music concerts. In addition, the museum is devoted to creating and sponsoring its own series of original and innovative special exhibitions instead of relying on traveling exhibitions from other sources. **NOT TO BE MISSED:** 14th century Kamakura Buddha from Japan

ON EXHIBIT 2000
02/2000 to 05/2000   FOUR OBJECTS; FOUR ARTISTS; TEN YEARS
In 1986 four American still-life painters–Janet Fish, Sondra Freckelton, Nancy Hagin, and Harriet Shorr–agreed that each would select an object that they would all include in a painting. Ten years later they decided to repeat the project. The results of their efforts reveal the wide spectrum of choices which artists make during the creative process. *Catalog Will Travel*

AUGUSTA

Morris Museum of Art
One 10th Street, Augusta, GA 30901-1134
☎: 706-724-7501   ◉ www.csra.net/mormuse
Open: 10-5:30 Tu-Sa, 12:30-5:30 Su   **Closed:** M, 1/1, THGV, 12/25
ADM: Adult: $2.00   **Children:** Free under 12   **Students:** $1.00   **Seniors:** $1.00
♿ ℗ Free marked spaces in West Lot; paid parking in city lot at adjacent hotel.   **Museum Shop   Group Tours**
Permanent Collection: REG: portraiture (antebellum to contemporary), still lifes, Impr, cont; AF/AM

Rich Southern architecture and decorative appointments installed in a contemporary office building present a delightful surprise to the first time visitor. Included in this setting are masterworks from antebellum portraiture to vivid contemporary creations that represent a broad-based survey of 250 years of panting in the South. **NOT TO BE MISSED:** The Southern Landscape Gallery

ON EXHIBIT 2000
11/18/1999 to 01/30/2000   SUBDUED HUES: LANDSCAPE PAINTING IN THE SOUTH 1865-1925
Southern expression of the totalist style inspired by the Barbizon School. Included are works by Brenner, Dangerfield, Inness, Jefferson, Meeker and Tanner.

11/26/2000 to 02/04/2001   THE PEOPLE'S CHOICE

121

GEORGIA

COLUMBUS

Columbus Museum
1251 Wynnton Rd., Columbus, GA 31906
☎: 614-221-6801 ◉ www.columbusart.museum.oh.us
Open: 10-5:30Tu, We, Fr, Sa; 10-8:30 Th   **Closed:** Mo, LEG/HOL!
Free Day: Th 5:30-8:30   **Sugg/Cont:**   **ADM:** **Adult:** $4.00   **Children:** 6 and older $2.00   **Seniors:** $2.00
&   ℗ $2.00   **Museum Shop**   ❢❢ Colette Café 11:30-1:30 Tu-Fr, 3rd Th 5:30-7:30
Group Tours: 614-629-0359   **Drop-In Tours:** Fr, 12, Su 2   **Sculpture Garden**
Permanent Collection: PTGS; SCULP; GR 19-20; DEC/ART; REG; FOLK

The Columbus Museum is unique in the Southeast for its dual presentation of American art and regional history. The Museum features changing art exhibitions and two permanent galleries, Chattahoochee Legacy (the history of the Chattahoochee Valley) and Transformations (a hands-on children's discovery gallery). **NOT TO BE MISSED:** "Fergus, Boy in Blue" by Robert Henri; A hands-on discovery gallery for children.

ON EXHIBIT 2000
06/1999 to 06/2000   AFTER THE TRAIL OF TEARS: OBJECTS FROM THE YUCHI COLLECTION

10/17/1999 to 01/09/2000   ALMA THOMAS: A RETROSPECTIVE OF THE PAINTINGS
Spanning the artistic career of D.C. based Thomas (1891-1978), this exhibition of 60 paintings and studies ranges from examples of her early representational works of the 50's, through the development of her signature vibrant mosaic-like abstractions.

10/23/1999 to 01/02/2000   THIS LAND IS YOUR LAND: PHOTOGRAPHS BY MARILYN BRIDGES
An aerial photographer now focuses her attention on America's backyards. It provides a fresh perspective on our land.

10/31/1999 to 01/23/2000   THE FINE ARTS IN ANTEBELLUM SOUTH
The artistic environment available to citizens of Columbus, 1828-1860 will be surveyed including paintings, prints, panoramas, sculpture and architectural decoration.

11/19/1999 to 01/30/2000   SPECTACULAR ST. PETERSBURG: 100 YEARS OF RUSSIAN THEATRE DESIGN
The tumultuous changes in Russia are reflected in these theatrical designs.

12/04/1999 to 03/12/2000   SELECTIONS FROM THE ROBERT J. SHIFFLER COLLECTION
This collection includes the most cutting edge paintings, photographs and sculptures dating from the last two decades.

01/08/2000 to 04/30/2000   ARTIFICIAL REALITY: SOVIET PHOTOGRAPHY, 1930-1987
The change from the brightly colored experimental period following the Revolution to the artistic subversion of the collapse of Communism.

01/15/2000 to 07/23/2000   CRAFTING A JEWISH STYLE : THE ART OF BEZALEL
The school was founded in Jerusalem in 1906 to instruct the first generation of Jewish artists in Israel *Will Travel*

01/23/2000 to 04/02/2000   SELDOM SEEN: A SELECTION OF WORKS ON PAPER FROM THE PERMANENT COLLECTION

02/06/2000 to 04/09/2000   35 YEARS LATER: BRUNO ZUPAN AND THE COLUMBUS MUSEUM

02/18/2000 to 04/30/2000   ILLUSIONS OF EDEN: VISIONS OF THE AMERICAN HEARTLAND
The character and values of the American Midwest have a profound influence on the way the nation views itself. Four installations look at the cultural identity of the region.

02/27/2000 to 05/05/2000   DIGGING HISTORY: THE ARCHEOLOGY OF COLUMBUS

04/01/2000 to 05/28/2000   FACING DEATH: PORTRAITS FROM CAMBODIA'S KILLING FIELDS
Nearly 14,000 people were killed between 1975-79. These prints were found in the archives in 1993. *Will Travel*

04/10/2000 to 07/23/2000   CONTEMPORARY PRINTS AND PHOTOGRAPHS FROM THE PERMANENT COLLECTION

Columbus Museum - continued

05/19/2000 to 08/13/2000   PARIS 1900: THE "AMERICAN SCHOOL" AT THE UNIVERSAL EXPOSITION
The Pennsylvania Academy was a major lender to the Paris Exposition of 1900 which played a critical role in defining "American" artistic influences at the time. It featured all the major artists of the late 19th century. Approximately 50 of the paintings and sculpture will be featured here.

05/28/2000 to 08/20/2000   CELEBRATING THE CREATIVE SPIRIT: CONTEMPORARY SOUTHEASTERN FURNITURE-AN EXHIBITION OF ARTIST MADE FURNITURE
The works shown here emphasize the whimsical side of personal artistic expression. It is as much about aesthetics as it is about function.

06/11/2000 to 08/13/2000   POP! AN AMERICAN SENSATION *Will Travel*

08/20/2000 to 11/05/2000   EIGHTEENTH AND NINETEENTH CENTURY WORKS ON PAPER FROM THE PERMANENT COLLECTION

09/10/2000 to 11/05/2000   YOUNG AMERICA: PAINTING AND SCULPTURE FROM THE NATIONAL MUSEUM OF AMERICAN ART
54 works by the era's most famous artists, trace the transformation of the colonies into nationhood from the 1760s to the Civil War. Includes portraits by Gilbert Stuart, Charles Willson Peale; paintings by Benjamin West, Washington Allston; landscapes by Thomas Cole, Alvan Fisher; genre paintings by John Quidor, Lily Martin Spencer. Hudson River School landscapes by Asher B. Durand, Frederic E. Church. Sculptures by Horatio Greenough, Hiram Powers. Civil War era paintings by Samuel Colman, Homer Dodge Martin. *Catalog   Will Travel*

10/08/2000 to 12/31/2000   NO ORDINARY LAND: ENCOUNTERS IN A CHANGING ENVIRONMENT
Large format photographs showing how people interact with the landscape in places as diverse as Sri Lanka, Iceland, Costa Rica and New York. *Will Travel*

11/03/2000 to 12/31/2000   A BOUNTIFUL PLENTY: FOLK ART FROM THE SHELBURNE MUSEUM

SAVANNAH

Telfair Museum of Art
121 Barnard St., Savannah, GA 31401

📞: 912-232-1177
Open: 10-5 Tu-Sa, 1-5 Su   **Closed:** Mo, LEG/HOL!
Free Day: Su   **ADM: Adult:** $6.00   **Children:** $1.00 (6-12)   **Students:** $2.00   **Seniors:** $5.00
♿ ℗ Metered street parking and 7 visitor spots
Museum Shop
Group Tours   Drop-In Tours: 2 PM daily
Historic Building 1819 Regency Mansion designed by William Jay (National Historic Landmark)
Permanent Collection: AM: Impr & Ashcan ptgs; AM: dec/art; BRIT: dec/art; FR: dec/art

Named for its founding family, and housed in a Regency mansion designed in 1818 by architect William Jay, this museum features traveling exhibitions from all over the world. The Telfair, which is the oldest public art museum in the Southeast, also has major works by many of the artists who have contributed so brilliantly to the history of American art. The Telfair will break ground in late 1999 for a new building on Telfair Square. **NOT TO BE MISSED:** American Impressionist collection Original Duncan Phyfe furniture; casts of the Elgin Marbles

ON EXHIBIT 2000

to 02/2000   OLD MASTER PRINTS

to 02/2000   ROTUNDA PAINTINGS / PERMANENT COLLECTION

12/07/1999 to 02/2000   VOJTECH BLAU TAPESTRIES

GEORGIA

Telfair Museum of Art - continued

03/12/2000 to 05/28/2000   ROBERT GWATHMEY

Approximately 60 paintings and graphics surveying the life and career of this noted social realist. There is special emphasis on images of African-American life and the Southern Scene.

03/12/2000 to 05/28/2000   WILLIAM CHRISTENBERRY PHOTOS

03/12/2000 to 05/28/2000   MOSHE SAFDIE

05/2000 to 07/2000   JAPANESE PRINTS

08/2000 to 08/2000   RECENT ACQUISITIONS

09/12/2000 to 11/12/2000   SCENES FROM AMERICAN LIFE: TREASURES FROM THE SMITHSONIAN'S MUSEUM OF AMERICAN ART

65 realist works from the National Museum of American Art including Hopper, Benton, Sloan, Wyeth and others.

11/2000 to 01/2001   GEORGIA TRIENNIAL

Contemporary Museum
2411 Makiki Heights Drive, Honolulu, HI 96822
☎: 808-526-1322 ◉ www.tcmhi.org
Open: 10-4 Tu-Sa, Noon-4 Su **Closed:** M, LEG/HOL!
ADM: Adult: $5.00 **Children:** Free under 12 **Students:** $3.00 **Seniors:** $3.00
♿ ℗ Free but very limited parking **Museum Shop** ‖: Cafe
Group Tours Drop-In Tours: 1:30 Tu-Su **Sculpture Garden**
Permanent Collection: AM: cont; REG

Terraced gardens with stone benches overlooking exquisite vistas compliment this museum's structure which is situated in a perfect hillside setting. Inside are modernized galleries in which the permanent collection of art since 1940 is displayed.   PLEASE NOTE: The museum's other gallery location where exhibitions are presented is: The Contemporary Museum at First Hawaiian Center, 999 Bishop St., Honolulu, HI 96813 (open 8:30-3 M-T, 8:30-6 F), which mainly features works by artists of Hawaii. **NOT TO BE MISSED:** David Hockney's permanent environmental installation "L'Enfant et les Sortileges" built for a Ravel opera stage set.

Honolulu Academy of Arts
900 S. Beretania St., Honolulu, HI 96814-1495
☎: 808-532-8700 ◉ www.honoluluacademy.org
Open: 10-4:30 Tu-Sa, 1-5 Su **Closed:** Mo., LEG/HOL!
Free Day: 1st We **Vol/Cont:**   **ADM: Adult:** $7.00 **Children:** Free under 12 **Students:** $4.00 **Seniors:** $4.00
♿ ℗ Lot parking at the Academy Art Center for $1.00 with validation; some street parking also available
Museum Shop ‖: 11:30-2:00 Tu-Sa; (808-532-8734)
Group Tours: 808-532-3876 **Drop-In Tours:** 11:00 Tu-Sa; 1:15 Su
Historic Building 1927 Building Designed By Bertram G. Goodhue Assoc. **Sculpture Garden**
Permanent Collection: OR: all media; AM: all media; EU: all media; HAWAIIANA COLLECTION

Thirty galleries grouped around a series of garden courts form the basis of Hawaii's only general art museum. This internationally respected institution, 70 years old in '97, features extensive notable collections that span the history of art and come from nearly every corner of the world. PLEASE NOTE: Exhibitions may be seen in the main museum and in the Museum's Academy Art Center, 1111 Victoria St. (808-532-8741). **NOT TO BE MISSED:** James A. Michener collection of Japanese Ukiyo-e Woodblock prints; Kress Collection of Italian Renaissance Paintings

ON EXHIBIT 2000
ONGOING   TAISHO CHIC: 1912-1926 IN JAPAN
A display of Japanese works of art and everyday items whose design qualities reflect the inclusion of such early 20th century western art movements as Impressionism, Art Nouveau and Art Deco.

12/02/1999 to 06/252000   ART FOR, OF AND BY CHILDREN

01/2000   MICHAEL TOM: PAINTINGS
Tom will be exploring the medium of painting in a solo exhibition of his recent works..

01/20/2000 to 03/19/2000   MARCIA MORSE

. 03/2000   HONOLULU PRINTMAKER'S JURIED EXHIBITION

03/02/2000 to 05/07/2000   JAPANESE HAIR ORNAMENTS FROM THE NORA AND ALLEN ZEKKA COLLECTION

HAWAII

Honolulu Academy of Arts - continued

03/16/2000 to 07/30/2000 SEARCHING FOR ANCIENT EGYPT : ART, ARCHITECTURE, AND ARTIFACTS FROM THE UNIVERSITY OF PENNSYLVANIA MUSEUM OF ARCHEOLOGY AND ANTHROPOLOGY
From the display of the interior wall of a 4,300-year-old funerary chapel to an exquisite gold-covered mummy mask, this exhibition features more than 130 extraordinary objects from every major period of ancient Egypt. Many of those included have not been on public view for 30 years.

05/08/2000 to 05/14/2000 HAWAII QUILT GUILD EXHIBITION

05/15/2000 to 05/31/2000 HAWAII HANDWEAVER'S HUI BIENNIAL EXHIBITION

05/18/2000 to 07/16/2000 RECENT ACQUISITIONS: PRINTS AND PHOTOGRAPHS05

07/20/2000 to 01/2001 HAWAII AND ITS PEOPLE

09/2000 to 10/2000 ARTISTS OF HAWAII 2000 (50TH ANNIVERSARY

Boise Art Museum

670 S. Julia Davis Dr., Boise, ID 83702

☏: 208-345-8330 ☉ www.boiseartrmuseum.org
Open: 10-5 Tu-Fr; 12-5 Sa, Su; Open 10-5 Mo JUNE & AUG   **Closed:** Mo LEG/HOL!
ADM: Adult: $4.00   **Children:** $1.00 (grades 1-12)   **Students:** $2.00   **Seniors:** $2.00
&. ℗ Free   **Museum Shop**
Group Tours   Drop-In Tours: 12:15 Tu, 1:00 Sa   **Sculpture Garden**
Permanent Collection: REG; GR; OR; AM: (

The Boise Art Museum, in its parkland setting, is considered the only art museum in the state of Idaho. New Permanent Collection galleries and an atrium sculpture court have recently been added to the museum. **NOT TO BE MISSED:** "Art in the Park", held every September, is one of the largest art and crafts festivals in the region.

ON EXHIBIT 2000

12/02/1999 to 03/19/2000   GARDEN: AN INSTALLATION BY CHRIS BINION
A dramatic large scale installation the centerpiece of which is 1000 amaryllis which will emerge, bloom and die during the exhibition. .

12/04/1999 to 02/13/2000   JACK DOLLHAUSEN: DATE FOR A MILLENNIUM
Electrical and computer technology creates lively sculptures that engage the viewer through light, sound, and sensory perception. *Will Travel*

12/10/1999 to 02/13/2000   INNUENDO NON TROPPO: THE WORK OF GREGORY BARSAMIAN
Spinning constructions and strobe lights are employed in the creation of Barsamian's works of optical illusion some of which produce the appearance of vertical motion.

12/22/1999 to 02/27/2000   ANNE APPLEBY
Her suddenly toned non-representational paintings are based on her observations of nature

02/26/2000 to 05/07/2000   SENSE OF WONDER: AFRICAN ART FROM THE FALETTI FAMILY COLLECTION
Sub-Saharan African and Ethiopian art dating from the 15th to the early 20th C. The issues of sublime and the fantastic in African art are examined here with African cultures and European and American traditions particularly noted. *Will Travel*

03/04/2000 to 05/21/2000   JUDY HILL
Glazed ceramics which explore the fragility and contradiction inherent in the human psyche.

05/20/2000 to 07/30/2000   KERRY JAMES MARSHALL: MEMENTOS
The leaders of the Civil Rights Movement includes painting, photographs, prints, sculptural objects and a video installation. A poignant meditation on a tumultuous era .

08/25/2000 to 10/28/2001   A CERAMIC CONTINUUM: FIFTY YEARS OF THE ARCHIE BRAY INFLUENCE
The contribution of the Archie Bray Foundation for Ceramic Art to its residency program and ceramic art showing 85 works. *Will Travel*

ILLINOIS

CARBONDALE

University Museum

Affiliate Institution: Southern Illinois University at Carbondale
Carbondale, IL 62901-4508

☎: 618-453-5388 ◙ www.museum@siu.edu
Open: 9-3 Tu-Sa, 1:30-4:30 Su **Closed:** Mo, ACAD & LEG/HOL!
♿ ℗ Metered lot just East of the Student Center (next to the football stadium) **Museum Shop**
Group Tours Drop-In Tours: Upon request if available **Sculpture Garden**
Permanent Collection: AM: ptgs, drgs, gr; EU: ptgs, drgs, gr, 13-20; PHOT 20; SCULP 20; CER; OC; DEC/ART

Continually rotating exhibitions feature the fine and decorative arts as well as those based on science related themes of anthropology, geology, natural history, and archaeology. Also history exhibits. **NOT TO BE MISSED:** In the sculpture garden, two works by Ernest Trova, "AV-A-7 and AV-YELLOW LOZENGER", and a sculpture entitled "Starwalk" by Richard Hunt. New: Formal Japanese Garden

ON EXHIBIT 2000

ONGOING WPA ART EXHIBIT FROM PERMANENT COLLECTION

ONGOING DR. GEORGE FRAUNFELTER GEOLOGICAL EXHIBITION

01/2000 to 02/2000 MARTIN DESHT: PHOTOS

01/2000 to 03/2000 COMBINED FACULTY EXHIBIT

03/2000 to 05/2000 SHOUTS FROM THE WALL
Photographs and posters from the Spanish Civil War will be on loan from the Abraham Lincoln Brigade archive at Brandies University.

03/2000 to 05/2000 HIGHWIRE ARTISTS

08/2000 to 10/2000 JOEL FELDMAN & CHEONAE

08/2000 to 10/2000 ROBERT PAULSON: PAINTINGS08

11/2000 to 12/2000 LAILA-FARCAS-IONESCO : PAINTINGS

CHAMPAIGN

Krannert Art Museum

Affiliate Institution: University of Illinois
500 E. Peabody Dr., Champaign, IL 61820

☎: 217-333-1860 ◙ http://www.art.uiuc.edu/kam/
Open: 9-5 Tu-Fr, till 8pm We (SEPT-MAY), 10-5 Sa, 2-5 Su **Closed:** LEG/HOL!
Vol/Cont:
♿ ℗ On-street metered parking **Museum Shop** ⊪: Cafe/bookstore
Group Tours: 217-333-8642 Dorothy Fuller, Ed. Coord. **Drop-In Tours:** !
Permanent Collection: P/COL; AM: ptgs; DEC/ART; OR; GR; PHOT; EU: ptgs; AS; AF; P/COL; ANT

Located on the campus of the University of Illinois, Krannert Art Museum is the second largest public art museum in the state. Among its 8,000, works ranging in date from the 4th millennium B.C. to the present, is the highly acclaimed Krannert collection of Old Master paintings. **NOT TO BE MISSED:** "Christ After the Flagellation" by Murillo; "Portrait of Cornelius Guldewagen, Mayor of Haarlem" by Frans Hals; Reinstalled Gallery of Asian Art

---

Art Institute of Chicago
111 So. Michigan Ave., Chicago, IL 60603-6110

☎: 312-443-3600 ◉ www.artic.edu
Open: 10:30-4:30 Mo & We-Fr; 10:30-8 Tu; 10-5 Sa; Noon-5 Su **Closed:** 12/25, THGV
Sugg/Cont: **ADM: Adult:** $8.00 **Children:** $5.00 **Students:** $5.00 **Seniors:** $5.00
♿ ℗ Limited metered street parking; several paid parking lots nearby
Museum Shop ❙❙: Cafeteria & The Restaurant on the Park
Group Tours: 312-443-3933 **Drop-In Tours:** !
Historic Building
Sculpture Garden
Permanent Collection: AM: all media; EU: all media; CH; Korean; JAP; IND; EU: MED; AF; PHOT; architecture + textiles; South American

---

Spend "Sunday in the park with George" while standing before Seurat's "Sunday Afternoon on the Island of La Grande Jatte", or any of the other magnificent examples of the school of French Impressionism, just one of the many superb collections housed in this world-class museum. Renowned for its collection of post-World War II art, the museum also features the Galleries of Contemporary Art, featuring 50 of the strongest works of American and European art (1950's-1980). **NOT TO BE MISSED:** "American Gothic" by Grant Wood; "Paris Street; Rainy Day" by Gustave Caillebotte

ON EXHIBIT 2000
ONGOING   EIGHTEENTH-CENTURY FRENCH VINCENNES-SEVRES PORCELAIN

ONGOING   AYALA ALTARPIECE
One of the oldest and grandest Spanish medieval altarpieces in the U.S.

ONGOING   ALSDORF GALLERY OF RENAISSANCE JEWELRY
One of the most significant collections of its type ever given to an American museum.

ONGOING   WITH EYES OPEN: A MULTIMEDIA EXPLORATION OF ART

ONGOING   ART INSIDE OUT: EXPLORING ART AND CULTURE THROUGH TIME

09/25/1999 to 01/16/2000   KENNETH JOSEPHSON: A RETROSPECTIVE
Kenneth Josephson (born 1932) studied photography with Minor White at the Rochester Institute of Technology and was among the first generation of photographers to graduate with a degree in photography from the Illinois Institute of Design, where he studied with Aaron Siskind and Harry Callahan. As a teacher at the School of the Art Institute of Chicago for over 35 years (he retired in 1997), Josephson has spawned two generations of photographic artists.

09/30/1999 to 01/09/2000   IKAT: SPLENDID SILKS FROM CENTRAL ASIA
Examples of Ikat textiles, created by a method of weaving in which warp threads are tie-dyed before being set up on a loom, will be on loan from one of the most significant private collections of its kind. Traditionally woven and used by nomadic Uzbek peoples, the manufacture of these textiles has influenced contemporary fashion designer Oscar de la Renta , textile manufacturer Brunschwig et Fils and others. *Catalog Will Travel*

10/16/1999 to 01/16/2000   BILL VIOLA
More than a dozen major highly theatrical installations from the 1970's to the present are included in this exhibition of works by video art pioneer Viola. Considered one of the most important and influential figures in contemporary art, Viola's emotional, powerful and visually challenging images stem from his ongoing fascination with digital computer and other modern-day technological advances. *Catalog Will Travel*

11/06/1999 to 01/02/2000   CONTEMPORARY AMERICAN REALIST DRAWINGS: THE JALANE AND RICHARD DAVIDSON COLLECTION

ILLINOIS

Art Institute of Chicago - continued

12/15/1999 to 03/19/2000   RAPHAEL AND TITIAN: THE RENAISSANCE PORTRAIT
Two of the greatest and most celebrated portraits of the Italian renaissance form the centerpiece of this focused small-scale exhibition highlighting the remarkable innovations made in the art of portraiture during the 16th century. Raphael Sanzio's magnificent Donna Velata (Veiled Lady), c. 1516 had a profound influence on his contemporaries and also on later artists not only because of its beauty but because of the myth that the sitter was the artist's mistress. Responding to Leonardo's Mona Lisa, Raphael developed in the picture his own ideal of female beauty and deportment. Titian Vecellio's Portrait of a Man with Blue-Green Eyes (also called Young Englishman), 1540/45 was no less acclaimed and influential. The subject's suave, informal stance and psychological directness inspired countless other portraits by such artists as Peter Paul Rubens, Anthony Van Dyck, and Rembrandt.

02/19/2000 to 04/30/2000   TO CONSERVE A LEGACY: AMERICAN ART FROM HISTORICALLY BLACK COLLEGES AND UNIVERSITIES
The collections of 6 historically Black colleges will be showcased in a exhibition of over 150 artworks. *Will Travel*

03/2000 to 05/2000   MONET TO MOORE: THE MILLENNIUM GIFT OF THE SARA LEE CORPORATION
One of the finest corporate art collections in America, the Sara Lee Corporation collection feature masterworks of Impressionists and modern European art.

The Arts Club of Chicago
201 East Ontario St., Chicago, IL 60611
☎: 312-787-8664
Open: 11-6 Mo-Fr; 11-4 Sa   **Closed:** Su

ON EXHIBIT 2000

01/21/2000 to 03/17/2000   AT THE EDGE: A PORTUGESE FUTURIST – AMADEO DE SOUZA CARDOSO
Cardoso, who lived in Paris from 1906 to 1915, was friends with Modigliani, Gris, the Delauneys, Bracusi, Archipenko, Rivera, Boccioni, and Severini, and exhibited his creative, gorgeously colored variants on fauvism, cubism, and futurism in the contemporary galleries and salons in Paris, Lisbon, Berlin, and London. He was included in the 1913 Armory Show held in New York, Chicago, and Boston.

04/2000 to 05/2000   ALEX KATZ
Drawn largely from Katz's own collection and the collection of Colby College Museum of Art, this exhibition will concentrate on early collages from the 50s, drawings spanning his career, cutouts, and landscape paintings which give another view of the Internationally known realist portrait and landscape painter.

Chicago Cultural Center
78 East Washington St., Chicago, IL 60602
☎: 312-742-2783   ◉   www.ci.chi.il.us/Tour/CulturalCenter/
Open: 10-7 Mo-We, 10-9 Th, 10-6 Fr, 10-5 Sa, 11-5 Su   **Closed:** LEG/HOL!
♿ ℗ Commercial facilities in area
Museum Shop   ⏏️: corner bakery
Group Tours: 312-744-8032   **Drop-In Tours**: 2pm Tu-Sa
Historic Building

Located in the renovated 1897 historic landmark building originally built to serve as the city's central library, this vital cultural center, affectionately called the "People's Place", consists of 8 exhibition spaces, two concert halls, two theaters and a dance studio. The facility, which serves as Chicago's architectural showplace for the lively and visual arts, There are architectural tours of the building at 2pm Tu-Sa. **NOT TO BE MISSED:** The world's largest Tiffany stained glass dome in Preston Hall on the third floor

ON EXHIBIT 2000

0/11/1999 to 02/13/2000   YVETTE KAISER SMITH: SCULPTURE (working title0
Processes such as crocheting fiberglass and applying resin over rosin paper and paper bags to create sculptural bodies that are metaphors for physical and psychological states.

Chicago Cultural Center - continued

12/11/1999 to 02/13/2000   TIM LOWLY: PAINTINGS (working title)
The realist style focuses mostly on disabled children . He avoids any maudlin pull on our emotions and presents spiritual qualities.

12/17/1999 to 01/23/2000   DOIN' DEVON: PAINTINGS BY SALLIE RONIS
The rich cultural diversity of Chicago's Devon Avenue is reflected in these on-site paintings in abstract and figurative styles.

01/22/2000 to 04/02/2000   JUMPIN' BACKFLASH: ORIGINAL IMAGIST ARTWORK, 1966-1969
A new movement in Chicago in the late sixties of 13 artists who portrayed the figure and narrative worlds became a unique style for the city. This exhibition explores the lasting impact of that movement.

02/19/2000 to 04/30/2000   MARCOS REEYA: MIXED MEDIA WORKS (working title)
A street muralist, painter and assemblage maker, Raya creates a surreal world of jarring images that reflect his Mexican roots and life in Chicago.

04/22/2000 to 06/25/2000   POST-HYPNOTIC
Testing the blurry boundaries between transient society, titillation and the transforming experience of ecstasy, this looks at the resurgence of pronounced optical effects in the work of 28 painters.

David and Alfred Smart Museum of Art

Affiliate Institution: The University of Chicago
5550 S. Greenwood Ave., Chicago, IL 60637
☎: 773-702-0200   ◉ www.smartmuseum,uchicago.edu
Open: 10-4 Tu-Fr; 12-6 Sa, Su; till 9pm Th   **Closed:** Mo, LEG/HOL!
♿ ⓟ Free parking on lot on the corner of 55th St. & Greenwood Ave. after 4:00 weekdays, and all day on weekends.
Museum Shop ⑪: Museum Café
Group Tours: 773-702-4540   **Drop-In Tours**: 1:30 Su during special exhibitions   **Sculpture Garden**
Permanent Collection: AN/GRK: Vases (Tarbell Coll); MED/SCULP; O/M: ptgs, sculp (Kress Coll); OM: gr (Epstein Coll); SCULP:20

Among the holdings of the Smart Museum of Art are Medieval sculpture from the French Romanesque church of Cluny III, outstanding Old Master prints by Dürer, Rembrandt, and Delacroix from the Kress Collection, sculpture by such greats as Degas, Matisse, Moore and Rodin, and furniture by Frank Lloyd Wright from the world famous Robie House.

ON EXHIBIT 2000

11/19/1999 to 02/29/2000   THE PLACE OF THE ANTIQUE IN EARLY MODERN EUROPE
Italian Renaissance Portrait medallions and bronze sculptures, paintings with tales from Ovid's Metamorphoses, and a wide range of classisizing motives are featured here. Antiquarians and impact of collecting antiques on 16th to 118th C European culture will be studied.

11/19/1999 to 03/12/2000 SURREALISM IN AMERICA DURING THE 1930'S AND 1940's: SELECTIONS FROM THE PENNY AND ELTON YASUMA COLLECTION
Joseph Cornell, Man Ray, Alexander Calder, Dorathea Tanning played an important role in defining new movements in American art. Their work along with 50 other artists is featured in this unique exhibition which explores American Surrealism and the consequent development of Abstract Expressionism.

03/14/2000 to 09/11/2000   PIOUS JOURNEYS: CHRISTIAN DEVOTIONAL ART AND PRACTICE IN THE LATER MIDDLE AGES AND RENAISSANCE
Objects from the permanent collection in a unique thematic context. Included are liturgical pieces, architectural fragments, painted altarpieces, illuminated manuscripts, reliquaries and sacred jewelry.

04/13/2000 to 06/11/2000   TRANSFORMING IMAGES: THE ART OF SILVER HORN
The ledger book drawings ands hide paintings of the Kiowa artist Silver Horn whose life spanned the shift in traditional Plains Indian life from pre-reservation to post reservation periods at the turn of the century. In addition to loans from other collections, it will show the four complete drawing books in the collection of the Field Museum of Natural History which have never been shown publicly before.

ILLINOIS

Martin D'Arcy Museum of Art
Affiliate Institution: The Loyola Univ. Museum of Medieval, Renaissance and Baroque Art
6525 N. Sheridan Rd., Chicago, IL 60626
☎: 773-508-2679 ◉ www.luc.edu/depts/darcy
Open: 12-4 Tu-Fr during the school year; Summer hours 12-4 We & Fr **Closed:** Sa, Su, ACAD!, LEG/HOL!
♿ ℗ $3.00 visitor parking on Loyola Campus **Museum Shop Group Tours Drop-In Tours:** by request only
Permanent Collection: MED & REN; ptgs, sculp, dec/art

Sometimes called the "Cloisters of the Midwest", The Martin D'Arcy Gallery of Art is the only museum in the Chicago area focusing on Medieval: Renaissance and Baroque art. Fine examples of Medieval, Renaissance, and Baroque ivories, liturgical vessels, textiles, sculpture, paintings and secular decorative art of these periods are included in the collection. **NOT TO BE MISSED:** A pair of octagonal paintings on verona marble by Bassano; A German Renaissance Collectors Chest by Wenzel Jamitzer; A silver lapis lazuli & ebony tableau of the Flagellation of Christ that once belonged to Queen Christina of Sweden

ON EXHIBIT 2000
ONGOING   PERMANENT COLLECTION OF MEDIEVAL, RENAISSANCE, AND BAROQUE ART

Mexican Fine Arts Center Museum
1852 W. 19th St., Chicago, IL 60608-2706
☎: 312-738-1503 ◉ www.mfacmchicago.org
Open: 10-5 Tu-Su **Closed:** Mo, LEG/HOL!
♿ **Museum Shop Group Tours:** ex 16
Permanent Collection: MEX: folk; PHOT; GR; CONT

Mexican art is the central focus of this museum, the first of its kind in the Midwest, and the largest in the nation. Founded in 1982, the center seeks to promote the works of local Mexican artists and acts as a cultural focus for the entire Mexican community residing in Chicago. A new expansion project is underway that will triple the size of the museum. **NOT TO BE MISSED:** Nation's largest Day of the Dead exhibit and 2 annual performing arts festivals.

ON EXHIBIT 2000
There are many other special shows throughout the year. Please call for specific details on solo exhibitions and on "Dia de los Muertos", which are exhibitions held annually from the beginning of October through the end of November.

09/24/1999 to 01/15/2000   CAMINO A MICTLAN

10/08/1999 to 01/15/2000   ESPERANZA GAMA

01/14/2000 to 05/25/2000   LUIS JIMINEZ: WORKING CLASS HEROES, IMAGES FROM THE POPULAR CULTURE
In the first major traveling exhibition of his work, powerful figures by Jiminez, a highly recognized Mexican American artist, reflect his interest in the contemporary culture of the Mexican, U.S. border. Jiminez's brilliant signature fiberglass sculptures will be on view with many of his well-modeled figurative drawings.

Museum of Contemporary Art
220 East Chicago Ave., Chicago, IL 60611-2604
☎: 312-280-2660 ◉ www.mcachicago.org
Open: Tu, Th, Fr, Sa, Su 10-5; W 10-8 **Closed:** Mo, 1/1, THGV, 12/25
Free Day: Tu **ADM: Adult:** $7.00 **Children:** Free 12 & under **Students:** $4.50 **Seniors:** $4.50
♿ ℗ On-street and pay lot parking available nearby
Museum Shop ⫙ M-Café 11-5 Tu, Th, Fr; 11-8 W; 10-5 Sa, Su
Group Tours: 312-397-3898 **Drop-In Tours:** several times daily!
Historic Building Josef Paul Kleihues building opened July 1996. **Sculpture Garden**
Permanent Collection: CONTINUALLY CHANGING EXHIBITIONS OF CONTEMPORARY ART ⌢

Museum of Contemporary Art - continued
Some of the finest and most provocative cutting-edge art by both established and emerging talents may be seen in the building and sculpture garden, located on a prime 2 acre site overlooking Lake Michigan. Brilliantly designed, the building is the first American project for noted Berlin architect Josef Paul Kleihues. Among its many features is the restaurant on the second floor where visitors can enjoy a spectacular view of the sculpture garden and lakefront while dining on contemporary fusion cuisine. **NOT TO BE MISSED:** An entire room devoted to sculptures by Alexander Calder,

ON EXHIBIT 2000
Ongoing   JACOB HASHIMOTO: AN INFINITE EXPANSE OF SKY (10,000 KITES)
An installation in the M Café which hang in a cloudlike formation from the ceiling.

10/14/1999 to 03/19/2000   BEAT STREULI
Swiss photographer Beat Streuli documents the image of people in urban spaces. He captures people when they are at their most natural state, when they are not posing for the camera. Streuli uses a telephoto lens at a distance to catch his unknowing subjects appearing naturally, without artifice. For Streuli's first commission at a United States museum, the MCA's front lobby windows will be covered with transparent, large-scale colored photographs, so people from the outside will be able to see in reverse what those in the inside see.

12/11/1999 to 03/05/2000   MATERIAL EVIDENCE: CHICAGO ARCHITECTURE AT 2000
This forward-looking exhibition will investigate the idea of material as a defining component of architecture today. Focusing on current practice in Chicago, it will complement the exhibition At the End of the Century: 100 Years of Architecture.

12/19/1999 to 03/12/2000   AT THE END OF THE CENTURY: 100 YEARS OF ARCHITECTURE
This exhibition surveys the architecture of the 20th Century through drawings, scale models, new and archival photographs, artifacts, film, and video. Organized into 21 thematic sections that range from "Grand Planning at the Turn of the Century" and "Politics of Monumentality in 1930s Architecture" to "The House as an Aesthetic Laboratory" and "The Skyscraper: A 20th Century Building Type," the exhibition presents a sequence of episodes, movements and thematic developments that are of compelling significance from our vantage point at the end of this century.

04/01/2000 to 07/01/2000   YOSHITOMO NARA
Japanese artist Yoshitomo Nara will create a site-specific sculptural installation for the MCA's front lobby walls. Fifty brightly-painted fiberglass sculptures of stylized, cartoon-like kids clad in one-piece night-costumes will be installed perpendicular to the wall in a scattered formation. Culled from his menagerie of imaginary characters, these three-foot-high "sleepwalking characters" called The Little Pilgrims have gauzelike cloth hoods that conjure associations with growth, childhood, and violence. Visitors entering the MCA will encounter a dreamlike mass of seemingly half-conscious, three-dimensional, identical characters facing in all directions. A series of recent drawings by Nara will also be presented.

05/2000 to 09/2000   TONY FITZPATRICK: MAX AND GABY'S ALPHABET
The extraordinary four-color etchings of draftsman and printmaker Tony Fitzpatrick will be the starting point for a project designed to benefit Chicago school children. Fitzpatrick's latest series of prints is a delightful children's alphabet that will appeal to audiences of all ages with such images as "'A' is for 'Atomic,'" "'C' for 'Caterpillar,'" and "'R' is for 'Robot.'" Drawn in his characteristic style that is informed by sources such as children's books, field guides, circus posters, tattoo designs, and folk art.

07/01/2000 to 09/10/2000   TOBIAS REHBERGER
Tobias Rehberger will create an installation for the MCA consisting of numerous trays filled with various plants assembled across the front plaza space, up the stairway to the building, through the Museum Atrium, and into the sculpture garden. This project will be one of the first and most ambitious presentations of this emerging German artist, who lives and works in both Berlin and Frankfurt. Rehberger is best known for creating installations and sculptures that blur the boundaries between fine art and design. The artist often imbues his work with personal references to his friends, and joins a number of other design-oriented artists working today such as Jorge Pardo, Andrea Zittel, and Pae White.

07/2000 to 10/2000   SOL LEWITT: A RETROSPECTIVE
This exhibition will feature the work of one of the most important American artists of this century. The exhibition will include a full range of works that represent the artist's four-decade career, including his classic three-dimensional structures and wall drawings as well as artists' books, drawings, and photographs. This exhibition will be the first comprehensive examination of LeWitt's work since 1978.

11/21/2000 to 02/04/2001   EDWARD RUSCHA
This exhibition will survey Ruscha's paintings, drawings, and books from 1960 to the present. One of the most consistently inventive artists of the contemporary period, Ruscha has been a pioneer in the use of language and imagery drawn from the popular media. The show will consist of approximately sixty paintings, twenty-five drawings, and several books.

ILLINOIS

Museum of Contemporary Photography of Columbia College Chicago
600 South Michigan Ave., Chicago, IL 60605-1996

☎: 312-663-5554 **◙** www. Mocp.org
Open: 10-5 Mo-We Fr, 10-8 Th; 12-5 Sa   **Closed:** Su, LEG/HOL! AUG
Free Day: Mo eve   **Vol/Cont:**
& **Ⓟ** Pay nearby
Museum Shop
Group Tours   Drop-In Tours: !
Permanent Collection: CONT/PHOT

The basis of the permanent collection of this college museum facility is a stimulating and innovative forum for the collection, creation and examination of photographically related images, objects and ideas.

Oriental Institute Museum
Affiliate Institution: University of Chicago
1155 E. 58th St., Chicago, IL 60637-1569

☎: 773-702-9520 **◙** www-oi.uchicago.edu/01/MUS
Open: 10-4 Tu-Sa, 12-4 Su, till 8:30pm We   **Closed:** Mo, 1/1, 7/4, THGV, 12/25
Vol/Cont:
& **Ⓟ** On-street or coin operated street level parking on Woodlawn Ave. between 58th & 59th Sts. (1/2 block east of the institute)
Museum Shop
Group Tours: 773-702-9507   **Drop-In Tours**: 2:30 Su
Historic Building
Permanent Collection: AN: Mid/East

Hundreds of ancient objects are included in the impressive comprehensive collection of the Oriental Institute. Artifacts from the ancient Near East, dating from earliest times to the birth of Christ, provide the visitor with a detailed glimpse into the ritual ceremonies and daily lives of ancient civilized man. **NOT TO BE MISSED:** Ancient Assyrian 40 ton winged bull; 17' tall statue of King Tut; Colossal Ancient Persian winged bulls

ON EXHIBIT 2000
The Egyptian Gallery of the Oriental Institute Museum reopened Dec. 12, 1998 after 2 years of renovation. Other galleries featuring artifacts from other regions will open over the next three years.

Polish Museum of America
984 North Milwaukee Ave., Chicago, IL 60622

☎: 773-384-3352
Open: 11-4 Mo-Su
Sugg/Cont: **ADM: Adult:** $2.00   **Children:** $1.00
& **Ⓟ** Freeree parking with entrance from Augusta Blvd.
Museum Shop
Group Tours
Permanent Collection: ETH: ptgs, sculp, drgs, gr

The promotion of Polish heritage is the primary goal of this museum founded in 1935. One of the oldest and largest ethnic museums in the U.S., their holdings range from the fine arts to costumes, jewelry, and a broad ranging scholarly library featuring resource information on all areas of Polish life and culture. **NOT TO BE MISSED:** Polonia stained glass by Mieczyslaw Jurgielewicz

Terra Museum of American Art
664 N. Michigan Ave., Chicago, IL 60611
☎: 312-664-3939
Open: 10-8 Tu, 10-6 We–Sa, 12-5 Su   **Closed:** Mo, 1/1, 7/4, THGV, 12/25
Free Day: Tu & 1st Su
ADM: Adult: $5.00   For special exhibitions $7, Seniors $3.50   **Children:** Free under 14   **Students:** $1.00   **Seniors:** $2.50
 ♿   **Museum Shop   Group Tours:** 312-654-2255   **Drop-In Tours:** 12 weekdays; 12 & 2 weekends
Permanent Collection: AM: 17-20

With over 800 plus examples of some of the finest American art ever created, the Terra, located in the heart of Chicago's "Magnificent Mile", reigns supreme as an important repository of a glorious artistic heritage. **NOT TO BE MISSED:** "Gallery at the Louvre" by Samuel Morse; Maurice Prendergast paintings and monotypes

ON EXHIBIT 2000
10/09/1999 to 01/02/2000   ARTHUR WESLEY DOW AND AMERICAN ARTS AND CRAFTS
Dow's works influenced fine and decorative arts with works that reflect Japonisme, synthesis and impressionism. Also included are photographs by Edward Steichen and watercolors by Georgia O'Keeffe as well as woodblock prints, furniture, tiles and pottery *Will Travel*

EDWARDSVILLE

University Museum, Southern Illinois University
Affiliate Institution: So. Illinois Univ. at Edwardsville
Box 1150, Edwardsville, IL 62026-1150
☎: 618-650-2996
Open: 9-3 Tu-Sa, 1:30-4:30 Su   **Closed:** Mo, LEG/HOL
 ♿ ℗ Metered lot just East of the Student Center (next to the football stadium)
Museum Shop   Group Tours   Sculpture Garden
Permanent Collection: DRGS; FOLK; CER; NAT/AM

Works in many media from old masters to young contemporary artists are included in the permanent collection and available on a rotating basis for public viewing. The museum is located in the western part of the state not far from St. Louis, Missouri. **NOT TO BE MISSED:** Louis Sullivan Architectural Ornament Collection located in the Lovejoy Library

---

EVANSTON

Mary and Leigh Block Gallery
Affiliate Institution: Northwestern University
1967 South Campus Drive, On the Arts Circle, Evanston, IL 60208-2410
☎: 847-491-4000   ◙ www.nwu.edu/museum
Open: Noon-5 Tu-We, Noon-8pm Th-Su (Sculp. Garden open year round)   **Closed:** Mo, LEG/HOL! SUMMER (Gallery only)
 ♿   **Museum Shop   Group Tours:** 847-491-4852   **Sculpture Garden**
Permanent Collection: EU: gr, drgs 15-19; CONT: gr, phot; architectural drgs (Griffin Collection)

In addition to its collection of works on paper, this fine university museum features an outdoor sculpture garden (open free of charge year round) which includes outstanding examples of 20th-century works by such artistic luminaries as Joan Miro, Barbara Hepworth, Henry Moore, Jean Arp and others. **NOT TO BE MISSED:** The sculpture garden with works by Henry Moore, Jean Arp, Barbara Hepworth, and Jean Miro (to name but a few) is one of the major sculpture collections in the region.

ILLINOIS

Freeport Arts Center

121 No. Harlem Ave, Freeport, IL 61032

☎: 815-235-9755

Open: 10-6 Tu, 10-5 We-Su   **Closed:** Mo, 1/1, EASTER. 7/4, THGV, 12/25

Free Day: We   **ADM: Adult:** $1.00   **Students:** $0.50   **Seniors:** $0.50

& ℗ behind museum   **Museum Shop**

Group Tours   Drop-In Tours: any time, if scheduled 2 weeks in advance

Permanent Collection: EU: 15-20; AM: 19-20; CONT: ptgs, sculp; P/COL; AN/R; NAT/AM; AN/EGT; AS; AF; OC

The Freeport Arts, located in north western Illinois, has six permanent galleries of paintings, sculpture, prints, and ancient artifacts, as well as temporary exhibitions featuring the work of noted regional artists. It houses one of the largest Florentine mosaic collections in the world. **NOT TO BE MISSED:** Especially popular with children of all ages are the museum's antiquities and the Native American galleries.

ON EXHIBIT 2000

11/21/1999 to 01/09/2000   CHRIS FUSCO:-RUCH: COLORED PENCIL DRAWINGS
Fantastical pencil drawings on black paper inspired by underwater life

11/21/1999 to 01/09/2000   RAY CANTY: TEMPERA PAINTINGS

01/16/2000 to 02/27/2000   ART IN BLOOM
An array of paintings, photographs, drawings and sculpture representing flowers.

04/07/2000 to 05/28/2000   JANET CHECKER: PATTERNS AND PORTRAITS
Archeological designs and symbols from ancient textiles are incorporated here.

04/07/2000 to 05/28/2000   JOAN LIFFRING ZUG-BOURRET: MY LIFE WITH MY CAMERA
Works from Iowa's premiere woman photographer of the 20th C including Amana colonies, famous people and everyday life.

06/02/2000 to 07/23/2000   PALISADES ART LEAGUE

Mitchell Museum

Richview Rd., Mount Vernon, IL 62864-0923

☎: 618-242-1236

Open: 10-5 Tu-Sa, 1-5 Su   **Closed:** Mo, LEG/HOL!

Vol/Cont:

& ℗   **Museum Shop**

Group Tours   Sculpture Garden

Permanent Collection: AM: ptgs, sculp (late 19-early 20)

Works from the "Ashcan School", with paintings by Davies, Glackens, Henri, Luks, and Maurice Prenderghast, comprise one of the highlights of the Mitchell, a museum, located in south central Illinois, which also features significant holdings of late 19th and early 20th century American art. **NOT TO BE MISSED:** Sculpture park

ON EXHIBIT 2000

02/19/2000 to 04/19/2000   COSIMO CAVALLARO & HENRY GROSSMAN: NYC PORTRAITS

04/15/2000 to 06/18/2000   SING ME A RAINBOW: TRINIDAD AND TOBAGO

Mitchell Museum - continued

04/15/2000 to 06/25/2000   CARL HILEMAN PHOTOGRAPHS

06/24/2000 to 08/27/2000   ART & PHOTOGRAPH

06/24/2000 to 09/17/2000   RAY MARKLIN: ADVENTURES IN TIBET

09/23/2000 to 11/05/2000   CHONAE KIM : RECENT WORKS

09/23/2000 to 11/05/2000   PAUL SIERRA: THE NATURE OF MAN

11/21/2000 to 12/31/2000   BEADWORKS

PEORIA

Lakeview Museum of Arts and Sciences

1125 West Lake Ave., Peoria, IL 61614

☎: 309-686-7000   ◙   www.lakeview-museum.org
Open: 10-5 Tu-Sa, 1-5 Su,   **Closed:** Mo, LEG/HOL!
Free Day: Tu   **ADM:** **Adult:** $2.50   **Children:** $1.50   **Students:** $1,50   **Seniors:** $1.50
& ℗ Free   **Museum Shop**
Group Tours   Sculpture Garden
Permanent Collection: DEC/ART; AM: 19-20; EU:19

A multi-faceted museum that combines the arts and sciences, the Lakeview offers approximately 6 changing exhibitions per year. PLEASE NOTE: Prices of admission may change during special exhibitions! **NOT TO BE MISSED:** Discovery Center and Planetarium, a particular favorite with children.

ON EXHIBIT 2000

01/15/2000 to 03/19/2000   ILLINOIS WOMEN ARTISTS: THE NEW MILLENNIUM
Paintings and sculptures celebrating the creativity of 20 contemporary Illinois women.

03/31/2000 to 05/26/2000   FACES OF DIVERSITY: MASKS FROM AROUND THE WORLD
Theatre, ritual and social; masks .

06/10/2000 to 07/03/2000   TAKE ANOTHER LOOK: BRAIN TEASERS; ARTFUL ILLUSIONS; CRYPTIC CRITTERS; LVM COLLECTION;   THE FOURTH DIMENSIONS
The exhibit explores how we see, how the brain plays tricks on the eye, etc. Viewers learn the art of seeing by observing ordinary everyday objects from unexpected viewpoints.

09/15/2000 to 10/22/2000   TREASURES FROM THE HEARTLAND: CONTEMPORARY ART IN LOCAL COLLECTIONS

09/15/2000 to 10/22/2000   CONTEMPORARY FURNITURE
Furniture designed by artists looking more like sculpture than furniture.

11/04/2000 to 01/07/2001   THE POTTERS OF MATA ORTIZ: TRANSFORMING A TRADITION
Innovative ceramic vessels by contemporary Mexican potters inspired by traditional Casas Grandes ceramics. Also shown will be rugs, kachina dolls and Illinois Native American materials.

ILLINOIS

Quincy Art Center
1515 Jersey St., Quincy, IL 62301
☎: 217-223-5900
Open: 1-4 Tu-Su **Closed:** Mo, LEG/HOL!
Vol/Cont:
&. Ⓟ Free **Museum Shop Group Tours**: 217-223-6900 **Drop-In Tours**: Often available upon request
Historic Building 1887 building known as the Lorenzo Bull Carriage House
Permanent Collection: PTGS; SCULP; GR

The Quincy Art Center is housed in an 1887 carriage house designed by architect Joseph Silsbee who was a mentor and great inspiration to Frank Lloyd Wright. A modern wing added in 1990 features gallery, studio, and gift shop space. The museum and its historic district with architecture ranging from Greek Revival to Prairie Style, Located in the middle of the state, the museum is not far from the Missouri border. **NOT TO BE MISSED:** The Quincy Art Center, located in an historic district that 'Newsweek' magazine called one of the most architecturally significant corners in the country, is composed of various buildings that run the gamut from Greek Revival to Prairie Style architecture.

ON EXHIBIT 2000
12/15/1999 to 02/21/2000   HMONG ARTISTRY: PRESERVING A CULTURE ON CLOTH

Augustana College Gallery of Art
7th Ave. & 38th St., Art & Art History Dept., Rock Island, IL 61201-2296
☎: 309-794-7469
Open: Noon-4 Tu-Sa (SEPT-MAY) **Closed:** ACAD! & SUMMER
&. Ⓟ Parking available next to Centennial Hall at the northwest corner of Seventh Ave. & 38th St. **Museum Shop**
Group Tours
Permanent Collection: SWEDISH AM: all media

Swedish American art is the primary focus of this college art gallery.

Rockford Art Museum
711 N. Main St., Rockford, IL 61103
☎: 815-968-2787 ◙ RAM-artmuseum.rockford.org
Open: 11-5 Tu-Fr, 10-5 Sa, 12-5 Su **Closed:** Mo, LEG/HOL!
Vol/Cont:
&. Ⓟ Free **Museum Shop**
Group Tours Drop-In Tours: by res **Sculpture Garden**
Permanent Collection: AM: ptgs, sculp, gr, dec/art 19-20; EU: ptgs, sculp, gr, dec/art 19-20; AM/IMPR; TAOS ART, GILBERT COLL: phot; AF/AM; self-taught; contemporary glass

With 17,000 square feet of exhibition space, this is one of the largest arts institutions in the state of Illinois. Up to 12 exhibitions are presented annually, as are works from the over 1,200 piece permanent collection of 20th century American art. **NOT TO BE MISSED:** "The Morning Sun" by Pauline Palmer, 1920; ink drawings and watercolors by Reginald Marsh (available for viewing only upon request); plaster casts by Lorado Taft, c. 1900

Rockford Art Museum - continued

ON EXHIBIT 2000

11/05/1999 to 01/16/2000   THIRTY ONE SHOPPING DAYS 'TIL ARMAGEDDON: AMERICAN POP CULTURE IN ART AT THE END OF THE MILLENNIUM
Works from artists who have brought issues and images of popular culture into the realm of visual arts. The path of our culture from the 1960's to the end of the 20th c. as witnessed through painting, print, sculpture and video.

11/05/1999 to 01/16/2000   BELLE EMERSON KEITH

12/29/1999 to 01/05/2000   TIME PIECES: WORKS FROM THE PERMANENT COLLECTION
Objects in the permanent collection that celebrate or use moments in history as subject matter.

12/29/1999 to 03/05/2000   LL PERMANENT COLLECTION EXHIBITION: KLAWANS GIFT
This gift has two prominent focus groups: French graphics including Dubuffet, Arp, Lasanskoy, Derain and others, and Prints from Chicago and regional artists including Brown, Paschke, Florsheim, Colescott and others.

02/11/2000 to 04/23/2000   CEREMONIAL MASKS FROM AFRICA
Ethnographical material/African masks

02/11/2000 to 04/23/2000   GASTRO-AESTHETICS
Contemporary artists who use food both as theme and media.

05/12/2000 to 07/30/2000   THE PRODIGAL: ARTWORK FROM THE COLLECTION OF JERRY EVINRUD
This 200 piece thematic collection spans a diversity of artists , media. Continents, and time with works from the 17th C Rembrandt van Rijn etchings and 19th C. works by Rowlandson and Gillray to modern and contemporary works by Benton, He Qui, Golub and Mesple.

05/12/2000 to 07/30/2000   SOLO SERIES: JOE SIEGENTHALER
Ceramic artist: will;; concentrate on the recent ceramic heads created by this artist.

06/02/2000 to 11/26/2000   RAM PERMANENT COLLECTION:
Historic and contemporary art, regional art, photography, outsider art, American Impressionist paintings, and Taos School works.

Rockford College Art Gallery / Clark Arts Center
5050 E. State, Rockford, IL 61108
☎: 815-226-4034
Open: ACAD: 2-5 Daily   **Closed:** ACAD! & SUMMER
♿ ℗ Free; near Clark Arts Center   **Museum Shop**
Permanent Collection: PTGS, GR, PHOT, CER 20; ETH; REG

Located on a beautiful wooded site in a contemporary building, this museum presents a stimulating array of exhibitions that look at historic as well as contemporary artwork from around the country.

SPRINGFIELD

Springfield Art Association
700 North Fourth St., Springfield, IL 62702
☎: 937-325-4673   ▣ www.spfldmus-of-art.org
Open: 9-5 Tu-Th, Fr, 9-9 We, 9-3 Sa, 2-4 Su   **Closed:** Mo, LEG/HOL! (including Lincoln's birthday; 12/25-1/1)
♿ ℗ Free   **Museum Shop**
Group Tours: 937-324-3729   **Drop-In Tours**: by appt
Permanent Collection: AM: ptgs, gr, cer, dec/art; EU: ptgs; CH; JAP

ILLINOIS

Springfield Art Association - continued
Fanciful is the proper word to describe the architecture of the Italianate structure that houses the Springfield Art Association, a fine arts facility that has been important to the cultural life of the city for nearly a century.

ON EXHIBIT 2000

01/15/2000 to 02/27/2000   FUNDAMENTAL SOUL
100 self taught artists addressing many questions about creativity and art in society.

03/04/2000 to 04/16/2000   THE BERENICE ABBOTT INTERNATIONAL COMPETITION: A COMMEMORATIVE EXHIBITION BY CONTEMPORARY WOMEN WORKING IN DOCUMENTARY PHOTOGRAPHY

03/13/2000 to 04/15/2000   NANCY FLETCHER CASSELL
Organic, environmental and sensual drawings

04/21/2000 to 05/27/2000   TOMOKO PARRY: RECENT WORK
Expressive, lush, lavish floral watercolors.

04/21/2000 to 05/27/2000   GEORGE HAGEMAN
Formally derived from Oriental prototypes and decorated with American salt glaze.

04/22/2000 to 05/28/2000   PATRICIA BRUTCHIN: RECENT WORK
Figural works in cast bronze and terracotta.

04/22/2000 to 05/28/2000   JON BARLOW HUDSON: RECENT WORK
Symbology, mythology and spirituality as expressed in massive and contrasting materials.

140

ANDERSON

Anderson Fine Arts Center
32 West 10th Street, Anderson, IN 46016
📞: 765-649-1248 ◙ www.andersonart.org
Open: 10-5 Tu-Sa, till 8:30 Th, 12-5 Su **Closed:** Mo, LEG/HOL!
Free Day: Tu, 1st Su **ADM: Adult:** $2.50, fam $6.50 **Children:** $1.25 **Students:** $1.25 **Seniors:** $2.00
& ℗ **Museum Shop** ᵼᵼ: Garden on the Green; Caffé Pietro
Group Tours: 765-649-1248 **Historic Building**
Permanent Collection: REG: all media; AM: all media 20

With an emphasis on education, this museum presents 1 children's exhibitions annually; from May to the end of June.

BLOOMINGTON

Indiana University Art Museum
Affiliate Institution: Indiana University
Bloomington, IN 47405
📞: 812-855-IUAM ◙ www.indiana.edu/~iuam
Open: 10-5 We-Sa, 12-5 Su **Closed:** Mo Tu, LEG/HOL!
Vol/Cont:
& ℗ Indiana Memorial Union pay parking lot one block west of the museum **Museum Shop** ᵼᵼ: Coffee Shop
Group Tours: 812-855-1045 **Drop-In Tours**: 2:00 Sa **Historic Building** Designed by I.M. Pei **Sculpture Garden**
Permanent Collection: AF; AN/EGT; AN/R; AN/GRK; AM: all media; EU: all media 14-20; OC; P/COL; JAP; CH; OR

Masterpieces in every category of its collection, from ancient to modern, make this one of the finest university museums to be found anywhere. Among its many treasures is the best university collection of African art in the United States. **NOT TO BE MISSED:** The stunning museum building itself designed in 1982 by noted architect I.M. Pei.

COLUMBUS

Indianapolis Museum of Art - Columbus Gallery
390 The Commons, Columbus, IN 47201-6764
📞: 812-376-2597
Open: 10-5 Tu-Th & Sa, 10-8 Fr, 12-4 Su **Closed:** Mo, LEG/HOL!
Vol/Cont:
& ℗ Free **Museum Shop**
Group Tours

In an unusual arrangement with its parent museum in Indianapolis, four exhibitions are presented annually in this satellite gallery, the oldest continuously operating satellite gallery in the country. The Gallery is uniquely situated inside a shopping mall in an area designated by the city as an "indoor park".

ON EXHIBIT 2000
10/10/1999 to 01/02/2000 DALE CHIHULY: SEAFORMS
Exceptional examples of American master Chihuly's glass sculptures resembling brilliant undulating marine life will be on exhibit with a number of his working drawings. *Will Travel*

INDIANA

ELKHART

Midwest Museum of American Art
429 S. Main St., Elkhart, IN 46515
☎: 219-293-6660
Open: 11-5 Tu-Fr 1-4 Sa, Su **Closed:** Mo, LEG/HOL!
Free Day: Su **ADM:** Adult: $3.00 **Children:** Free under 5 **Students:** $1.00 **Seniors:** $4.00
♿ ℗ Free city lot just north of the museum **Museum Shop**
Group Tours Drop-In Tours: 12:20-12:40 Th Noontime talks-free
Permanent Collection: AM/IMPR; CONT; REG; SCULP; PHOT

Chronologically arranged, the permanent collection of 19th and 20th century paintings, sculptures, photographs, and works on paper, traces 150 years of American art history with outstanding examples ranging from American Primitives to contemporary works by Chicago Imagists. The museum is located in the heart of the mid-west Amish country. **NOT TO BE MISSED:** Original paintings by Grandma Moses, Norman Rockwell, and Grant Wood; The Vault Gallery (gallery in the vault of this former bank building.)

ON EXHIBIT 2000

12/03/1999 to 02/27/2000	THE ART OF ANTIQUE TOYS
03/31/2000 to 04/30/2000	CONTEMPORARY QUILTS
05/01/2000 to 06/04/2000	A SOCIAL ORDER: THE PAINTINGS OF TERRY RODGERS
06/09/2000 to 07/23/2000	DIANNE TESSLER : PAINTINGS FROM THE HEARTLAND
07/28/2000 to 10/15/2000	ROADWORKS: PHOTOGRAPHS BY LINDA MCCARTNEY
10/20/2000 to 11/26/2000	THE 22ND ELKHARDT REGIONAL

EVANSVILLE

Evansville Museum of Arts & Science
411 S.E Riverside Dr., Evansville, IN 47713
☎: 812-425-2406
Open: 10-5 Tu-Sa, Noon-5 Su **Closed:** 1/1, 7/4, LAB/DAY, THGV, 12/25
♿ ℗ Free and ample parking **Museum Shop Group Tours Sculpture Garden**
Permanent Collection: PTGS; SCULP; GR; DRGS; DEC/ART

Broad ranging in every aspect of its varied collections, the Evansville Museum will open its newly renovated permanent collection galleries and two changing exhibition galleries in the winter of '98. **NOT TO BE MISSED:** "Madonna and Child" by Murillo

FORT WAYNE

Fort Wayne Museum of Art
311 E. Main St., Fort Wayne, IN 46802-1997
☎: 219-422-6467 ◉ www.fwmoa.org
Open: 10-5 Tu-Sa, 12-5 Su **Closed:** Mo, 1/1, 7/4, THGV, 12/25
Free Day: 1st Su **ADM:** Adult: $3.00 **Children:** $2.00 (K-college) **Students:** $2.00 **Seniors:** $3.00
♿ ℗ Parking lot adjacent to building with entrance off Main St.
Museum Shop
Group Tours: 219-422-6467 x319 **Sculpture Garden**
Permanent Collection: AM: ptgs, sculp, gr 19-20; EU: ptgs, sculp, gr 19-20; CONT

Fort Wayne Museum of Art - continued

Since the dedication of the new state-of-the-art building in its downtown location in 1984, the Fort Wayne Museum, established more than 75 years ago, has enhanced its reputation as a major vital community and nationwide asset for the fine arts. Important masterworks from Dürer to de Kooning are included in this institution's 1,300 piece collection. **NOT TO BE MISSED:** Etchings by Albrecht Dürer on the theme of Adam and Eve.

ON EXHIBIT 2000

11/13/1999 to 01/16/2000   FOCUS EXHIBITION: JANE CALVIN
An exhibition of contemporary art featuring color photographs by Chicago artist Jane Calvin.

11/20/1999 to 02/20/2000   LASTING IMPRESSIONS: AMERICAN WOMEN ARTISTS FROM THE SELLARS COLLECTION
Alan and Louise Sellars have built a little known, but splendid collection of paintings by American women artists with works from 1850-1930. These women studied in prestigious academies, exhibited widely, received honors and awards in step with their male counterparts, and created magnificent works of art. Yet they remain largely unrecognized. This is a rare opportunity to view this private Indianapolis based collection.

12/11/1999 to 02/20/2000   POP(ular)/OP(tical): ART OF THE 60S AND 70S FROM THE PERMANENT COLLECTION
Pop artists Andy Warhol and Roy Lichtenstein and Op artists Victor Vasarely and Julian Stanczak are joined by fellow artists who defined art in the late 60s and 70s—an exciting period when everyday culture invaded "high" art.

12/11/1999 to 03/05/2000   INDIANA AMISH QUILTS
"Honeycomb," "Bow Tie," and "Nine Patch" are popular patterns in the subtle yet splendid quilts made by the Indiana Amish. On view will be a selection from our collection of 56 traditional quilts.

INDIANAPOLIS

Eiteljorg Museum of American Indians and Western Art

500 W. Washington St., White River State Park, Indianapolis, IN 46204
📞: 317-636-9378   🔘 www.eiteljorg.org
Open: 10-5 Tu-Sa, 12-5 Su; (Open 10-5 Mo JUNE-AUG)   **Closed:** Mo, 1/1, THGV, 12/25
Free Day: about 5 per year !   **ADM: Adult:** $5.00   **Children:** Free 4 & under   **Students:** $2.00   **Seniors:** $4.00
♿ Ⓟ Free   **Museum Shop   Group Tours**: ext 150   **Drop-In Tours**: 1 PM daily
Historic Building Landmark building featuring interior and exterior SW motif design
Permanent Collection: NAT/AM & REG artifacts : ptgs, sculp, drgs, gr, dec/art

The Eiteljorg, one of only two museums east of the Mississippi to combine the fine arts of the American West with Native American artifacts, is housed in a Southwestern style building faced with 8,000 individually cut pieces of honey-colored Minnesota stone. **NOT TO BE MISSED:** Works by members of the original Taos Artists Colony; 4 major outdoor sculptures including a 38' totem pole by 5th generation Heida carver Lee Wallace and George Carlson's 12-foot bronze entitled "The Greeting".

ON EXHIBIT 2000

10/02/1999 to 01/02/2000   GARY SMITH LANDSCAPES
Ploughed and unplowed, burnt and wet, golden and snow white fields became meaningful symbols to this well known artist. They prompted him to break from his successful and well known approach to painting.

11/13/1999 to 01/23/2000   EITELJORG FELLOWSHIP FOR NATIVE AMERICAN FINE ART

01/22/2000 to 04/16/2000   AMERICANOS: PORTRAIT OF THE LATINO COMMUNITY IN THE UNITED STATES

05/08/2000   NEW ART OF THE WEST 7
Artists who are influenced by the West. Twenty artists display work in this juried exhibition,

INDIANA

Indianapolis Museum of Art
1200 W. 38th St., Indianapolis, IN 46208-4196
📞: 317-923-1331   ◙   WWW.IMA-ART.ORG
Open: 10-5 Tu-Sa, till 8:30pm Th, 12-5 Su   **Closed:** Mo, LEG/HOL!
Vol/Cont:
&. ℗ Outdoor parking lots and parking garage of Krannert Pavilion   **Museum Shop**
🍴: 11am-1:45pm Tu-Sa; (Brunch Su by reservation 926-2628)   **Drop-In Tours**: 12 & 2 Tu-Su; 7pm Th
Permanent Collection: AM: ptgs; EU/OM; ptgs EU/REN:ptgs; CONT; OR; AF; DEC/ART; TEXTILES

Situated in a 152 acre park as part of a cultural complex, the Indianapolis Museum is home to many outstanding collections including a large group of works on paper by Turner, and world class collections of Post Impressionist, Chinese, and African art. PLEASE NOTE: 1. There is an admission fee for most special exhibitions. 2. The museum IS OPEN on 7/4.

ON EXHIBIT 2000
05/01/1999 to 04/30/2000   URSULA VON RYDINGSVARD
On the grounds! *Will Travel*

02/2000 to 04/2000   EUROPEAN MASTERWORKS: PAINTING AND SCULPTURE FROM THE SMITH COLLEGE MUSEUM OF ART
The 52 paintings and 7 sculptures include works by Picasso, Bonnard, Cézanne, Courbet, Degas, Gris, Monet, and Renoir as well as sculpture by Rodin and Rousseau. *Will Travel*

06/2000 to 08/2000   SELECTIONS FROM THE ASIAN COLLECTION
Selections from the Museum's outstanding collection will be featured.

10/14/2000 to 01/28/2001   CROSSROADS OF AMERICAN SCULPTURE
Will bring together David Smith, George Rickey, John Chamberlain, Robert Indiana, William Wiley and Bruce Nauman. These 6 Indian sculptors provide a glimpse into the sculptural ideas developed by American sculptors during the past 50 years.

LAFAYETTE

Greater Lafayette Museum of Art
101 South Ninth St., Lafayette, IN 47901
📞: 765-742-1128   ◙   www.glymart.org
Open: 11-4 Tu-Su   **Closed:** Mo, LEG/HOL!
&. ℗ Free 10th St. entrance   **Museum Shop**
Group Tours: ask for Paige@glymart.org   **Drop-In Tours**: 11-4 Tu-Su
Permanent Collection: AM: ptgs, gr, drgs, art pottery 19-20; REG: ptgs, works on paper; LAT/AM: gr

Art by regional Indiana artists, contemporary works by national artists of note, and a fine collection of art pottery are but three of several important collections to be found at the Greater Lafayette Museum of Art. **NOT TO BE MISSED:** Arts and craft items by Hoosier artists at museum store; Baber Collection of contemporary art

ON EXHIBIT 2000
10/30/1999 to 01/02/2000   MATTER MIND SPIRIT: THIRTEEN CONTEMPORARY WOMEN ARTISTS
Indiana's best contemporary women artists are featured here. *Will Travel*

01/14/2000 to 02/13/2000   JAMES VIEWEGH

01/14/2000 to 02/13/2000   THE ARTISTS OF ELI LILLY & COMPANY

01/15/2000 to 02/20/2000   HARLAN HUBBARD

144

Greater Lafayette Museum of Art - continued

02/25/2000 to 04/09/2000   100 AT THE CENTURY: PHOTOGRAPHS OF TIPPECANOE COUNTY AT THE MILLENNIUM

02/25/2000 to 04/16/2000   ELLIE DERHALL

02/25/2000 to 04/16/2000   COLORS OF THE WILD

04/22/2000 to 05/28/2000   NEW ARTISTS 2000

04/22/2000 to 06/04/2000   PAUL NEUFELDER

04/22/2000 to 06/11/2000   CHILDREN'S PLAY ILLUSTRATIONS

06/10/2000 to 07/23/2000   THE ART OF THE INUITS

06/10/2000 to 07/23/2000   THE VEVERS

08/05/2000 to 09/03/2000   ARTISTS OF WESTMINSTER

08/05/2000 to 09/10/2000   TEENAGERS IN THEIR BEDROOMS
From outlandish and rebellious to studious and serious, this revealing and provocative photographic essay of 30 American teens in their most personal environment, accompanied by their insightful commentary, allows for a glimpse into the contemporary teenage world.

09/22/2000 to 11/12/2000   GREG HORNBACK

11/18/2000 to 01/07/2001   GILBERT WILSON'S "MOBY DICK"

MUNCIE

Ball State University Museum of Art
2000 University Ave., Muncie, IN 47306
☎: 765-285-5242
Open: 9-4:30 Mo-Fr; 1:30-4:30 Sa, Su   **Closed:** !, LEG/HOL
 ♿ ℗ Metered street parking and metered paid garages nearby   **Museum Shop**
Group Tours: 765-285-3242   **Drop-In Tours**
Permanent Collection: IT/REN; EU: ptgs 17-19; AM: ptgs, gr, drgs 19-20; DEC/ART; AS; AF; OC; P/COL

5000 years of art history are represented in the 9,500 piece collection of the Ball State University Museum of Art. In addition to wonderful explanatory wall plaques, there is a fully cataloged Art Reference Terminal of the permanent collection.

NOTRE DAME

Snite Museum of Art
Affiliate Institution: University of Notre Dame
Notre Dame, IN 46556
☎: 219-631-5466 ◉ www.nd.edu/~sniteart
Open: 10-4 Tu, We 10-5 Th-Sa, 1-5 Su   **Closed:** Mo, LEG/HOL!
Vol/Cont:
 ♿ ℗ Available southeast of the museum in the visitor lot   **Museum Shop**
Group Tours: 219-631-4435
Sculpture Garden
Permanent Collection: IT/REN; FR: ptgs 19; EU: phot 19; AM: ptgs, phot; P/COL: sculp; DU: ptgs 17-18

INDIANA

Snite Museum of Art - continued

With 17,000 objects in its permanent collection spanning the history of art from antiquity to the present, this premier university museum is a "must see" for all serious art lovers. **NOT TO BE MISSED:** AF; PR/COL & NAT/AM Collections

ON EXHIBIT 2000

Fall/2000   PERCEPTION OF NATIVE AMERICANS

Fall/2000   ERIC GILL: SCULPTURE, WORKS ON PAPER AND GRAPHIC DESIGN

01/2000 to 03/2000   BREAKING BARRIERS
Selections from the Cuban collection

01/02/2000 to 02/28/2000   FACING DEATH: PORTRAITS FROM CAMBODIA'S KILLING FIELDS
Nearly 14,000 people were killed between 1975-79. These prints were found in the archives in 1993. *Will Travel*

09/2000 to 05/2000   JEFFREY BEACOM: PHOTOGRAPHS

09/2000 to 10/2000   UNIVERSITY OF NOTRE DAME FACULTY EXHIBITION

RICHMOND

Richmond Art Museum

350 Hub Etchison Pkwy, Richmond, IN 47374
☎: 765-966-0256
Open: 10-4 Tu-Fr 1-4 Sa, Su   **Closed:** Mo, LEG/HOL!
 ♿ Ⓟ Free   **Museum Shop**
Group Tours   Drop-In Tours: !
Permanent Collection: AM: Impr/ptgs; REG

Aside from its outstanding collection of American Impressionist works, the Richmond Art Museum, celebrating its 100th birthday on June 14, 1998, has the unique distinction of being housed in an operating high school. **NOT TO BE MISSED:** Self portrait by William Merritt Chase, considered to be his most famous work

ON EXHIBIT 2000

Summer/2000   MARCUS MOTE: A QUAKER ARTIST

Fall/2000   THE OVERBECKS: HANNAH AND HER SISTERS

01/15/2000 to 02/29/2000   LOIS MAIN TRMPLETON
Paintings, prints and collage with themes of jazz and poetry

03/04/2000 to 04/09/2000   ESTHER NUSSBAUM: A RETROSPECTIVE
A comprehensive look at the popular local artist's work

03/04/2000 to 04/09/2000   BRAD BOWDEN: ART AS ENVIRONMENT
Fine art boxes, painted interior environments,, hand painted furniture

South Bend Regional Museum of Art

120 S. St. Joseph St., South Bend, IN 46601
☎: 219-235-9102   ◙ www.sbt.infi.net/-sbrma
Open: 11-5 Tu-Fr; 12-5 Sa, Su   **Closed:** Mo, LEG/HOL!
Sugg/Cont: **ADM: Adult:** $3.00
 ♿ ℗ Free street parking, downtown parking garages.
Museum Shop   ⁕: Café   **Group Tours**
Permanent Collection: AM: ptgs 19-20; EU: ptgs 19-20; CONT: reg

Since 1947, the South Bend Regional Museum of Art has been serving the artistic needs of its community by providing a wide variety of regional and national exhibitions year-round. This growing institution recently completed a reconstruction and expansion project adding, among other things, a Permanent Collections Gallery and a cafe. **NOT TO BE MISSED:** Permanent site-specific sculptures are situated on the grounds of Century Center of which the museum is a part.

ON EXHIBIT 2000

12/11/1999 to 01/23/2000   THE PRACTICED HAND: CONSTRUCTIONS & SCULPTURAL FIBER
The museum will host 2 fiber exhibitions featuring 18 of the finest established and emerging artists of the Midwest. *Catalog*

Sheldon Swope Art Museum

25 S. 7th St., Terre Haute, IN 47807
☎: 812-238-1676   ◙ www.swope.org
Open: 10-5 Tu-Fr; 12-5 Sa, Su; till 8pm Th   **Closed:** Mo, LEG/HOL
Vol/Cont:
 ♿ ℗ Pay lot on Ohio Blvd.   **Museum Shop**
Group Tours   **Historic Building**
Permanent Collection: AM: ptgs, sculp, drgs 19-20;

The Sheldon Swope, opened in 1942 as a museum devoted to contemporary American art, and has expanded from the original core collection to Wabash Valley artists past and present. **NOT TO BE MISSED:** Painting by Grant Wood, Thomas Hart Benton, Edward Hopper

ON EXHIBIT 2000

Early/2000   PERMANENT INSTALLATION AND REOPENING OF THE 19TH AND EARLY 20TH c. GALLERIES

04/2000   PERMANENT INSTALLATION AND REOPENING OF THE NEWLY RENOVATED UPSTAIRS GALLERIES
Lobby: American Art of the 1940's; Gallery 4: Art of the American West; Gallery 5: Art of Post World-War II America; Temporary exhibition space

07/15/2000 to 08/14/2000   56TH ANNUAL WABASH VALLEY EXHIBITION

09/28/2000 to 11/05/2000   JOHN E. COSTIGAN EXHIBITION

11/30/2000 to 01/11/2001   MANIERRE DAWSION EXHIBITION

INDIANA

Purdue University Galleries
Affiliate Institution: Creative Arts Bldg., #1
West Lafayette, IN 47907

☎: 765-494-3061

Open: STEWART CENTER:10-5 & 7-9 Tu-T, 10-5 Fr, 1-4 Su; UNION GALLERY:10-5 Tu-Fr,1-4 Su   **Closed:** ACAD!
  ♿ &#9физ; Visitor parking in designated areas (a $3.00 daily parking permit for campus garages may be purchased at the Visitors Information Services Center); some metered street parking as well; Free parking on campus after 5 and on weekends.
Museum Shop
Group Tours
Permanent Collection: AM: ptgs, drgs, gr; EU: ptgs, gr, drgs; AM: cont/cer

In addition to a regular schedule of special exhibitions, this facility presents many student and faculty shows.

CEDAR FALLS

James & Meryl Hearst Center for the Arts
304 W. Seerly Blvd., Cedar Falls, IA 50613

☎: 319-273-8641 ◉ www.ci.cedar-fallsici.us/human-lersure/hearst-center
Open: 10-9 Tu, Th; 10-5 We, Fr; 1-4 Sa, Su **Closed:** Mo, 1/1, 7/4, THGV, 12/25
♿ ℗ Free **Museum Shop**
Group Tours: 319-268-5504
Historic Building Located in the former home of well-known farmer poet James Hearst **Sculpture Garden**
Permanent Collection: REG

Besides showcasing works by the region's best current artists, the Hearst Center's permanent holdings include examples of works by such well knowns as Grant Wood, Mauricio Lasansky, and Gary Kelly. **NOT TO BE MISSED:** "Man is a Shaper, a Maker", pastel by Gary Kelly; "Honorary Degree", lithograph by Grant Wood

ON EXHIBIT 2000

07/30/1999 to 09/17/2000   ART SHOW 12
A juried competition in all media with an exciting look at contemporary work.

12/05/1999 to 01/21/2000   FRIENDS OF THE CENTER ON EXHIBIT
The membership presents selections from their private collections or their own works of art.

12/15/1999 to 03/26/2000   THE GOOD EARTH: CHINESE FOLK ART & ARTIFACTS
A collection of Chinese peasant paintings and artifacts from Huxian. One of the ancient capitols of China, and the cradle of the revolution with a distinct culture, the works have a vigor and simplicity.

01/29/2000 to 03/26/2000   THE WOOD CARVERS OF CEDAR VALLEY
A showcase of the work of these dedicated artisans.

06/04/2000 to 07/16/2000   THE PAINTINGS OF SHAN-SHAN CUI
Born in China and educated in China and the US, Shan-Shan Cui brings her broad experience in art and design to her paintings.

06/04/2000 to 07/16/2000   ART SHOW II FOCUS
Additional works of the winner of the Art Show 11, 1999.

10/05/2000 to 11/22/2000   THE LEGEND OF SLEEPY HOLLOW
Chalk drawings by Gary Kelley for the book.

10/05/2000 to 11/22/2000   THREE ON PAPER
Margaret Whiting, Karla Oler, and Julie McLaughlin use handmade paper in constructed books, tribal themes and sculptural articles of clothing.

12/03/2000 to 01/28/2001   CURRENT WORKS IN CLAY
The recent works of ceramist Joanne Schnabel exploring geometric and organic forms .

CEDAR RAPIDS

Cedar Rapids Museum of Art
410 Third Ave., S.E., Cedar Rapids, IA 52401

☎: 319-366-7503 ◉ www.crma.org
Open: 10-4 Tu-W & Fr-Sa, 10am-7pm Th, Noon-4 Su **Closed:** Mo, LEG/HOL!
ADM: Adult: $4.00   **Children:** Free under 7   **Students:** $3.00   **Seniors:** $3.00
♿ ℗ Lot behind museum building; some metered parking on street **Museum Shop**
Group Tours: education office   **Drop-In Tours**: !
Historic Building Carnegie
Permanent Collection: REG: ptgs 20; PTGS, SCULP, GR, DEC/ART, PHOT 19-20

IOWA

Cedar Rapids Museum of Art - continued

Spanning a city block, the Cedar Rapids Museum of Art Houses 16 galleries in one wing and a museum shop, art library and multi-media center in another. A regionally focused museum, it was observed that by The Other Museums that, "No museum of art in this country is more deeply rooted in its own community." **NOT TO BE MISSED:** Museum includes restored 1905 Beaux Art building, formerly the Carnegie Library (free to the public); collections of Grand Wood & Marvin Cone paintings, Malvina Hoffman sculptures, & Mauricio Lasansky prints and drawings

ON EXHIBIT 2000

11/19/1999 to 01/30/2000   MAURICIO LASANSKY AND THE IOWA PRINT GROUP
Celebrating the Museum's ten year anniversary in the new building, Lasansky's work and works by artists trained with this Group are surveyed as is their collective contribution to American printmaking. *Catalog*

01/15/2000 to 03/26/2000   21ST CENTURY: 7 COMPOSERS/3 MINUTES PROJECT
Seven composers have been chosen art which will be their inspiration for a piece of music commissioned for Jan Boland and John Dowdall.

01/15/2000 to 03/26/2000   PETER SIS. CHILDREN'S BOOK ILLUSTRATOR EXHIBITION
Peter Sis is the next installment in this series on children's book illustrators.

04/15/2000 to 06/25/2000   KANSAS CITY: THE CITY SERIES
The third exhibition in this series is a seven gallery exploration f the best in contemporary art from a major mid-continent city.

29/03/2000 to 03/26/2000   TURN OF THE CENTURY AT THE TURN OF THE CENTURY
Work by contemporary artists continuing to be inspired by the work of Bonnard, Picasso, Matisse, Derain and Gris. Masterpieces from the turn of the century will be shown with their 21st c. descendants.

DAVENPORT

Davenport Museum of Art
1737 W. Twelfth St., Davenport, IA 52804
☎: 319-326-7804
Open: 10-4:30 Tu-Sa, 1-4:30 Su, till 8pm Th   **Closed:** Mo, LEG/HOL!
Sugg/Cont:
& ℗ Free   **Museum Shop   Group Tours   Sculpture Garden**
Permanent Collection: AM/REG; AM: 19-20; EU: 16-18; OM; MEXICAN COLONIAL; HAITIAN NAIVE

Works by Grant Wood and other American Regionalists are on permanent display at the Davenport Museum, the first public art museum established in the state of Iowa (1925). **NOT TO BE MISSED:** Grant Wood's "Self Portrait"

ON EXHIBIT 2000
12/26/1999 to 03/12/2000   EDOUARD DUVAL-CARRIE: THE MIGRATION OF THE SPIRIT
One of the premiere artists working in the US, this is the first major retrospective of his work to travel here.

DES MOINES

Des Moines Art Center
4700 Grand Ave., Des Moines, IA 50312-2099
☎: 515-277-4405 ◙ under construction
Open: 11-4 Daily, 12-4 Su, 11-9 Th & 1st Fr of the month   **Closed:** Mo, LEG/HOL!
ADM:
& ℗ Free   **Museum Shop**
�11: 11-2 lunch Tu-Sa; dinner 5;30-9 Th (by res.), 5-8 1ST F (light dining)
Group Tours: ex. 15
Permanent Collection: AM: ptgs, sculp, gr 19-20; EU: ptgs, sculp, gr 19-20; AF

Des Moines Art Center - continued

Its parklike setting is a perfect compliment to the magnificent structure of the Des Moines Art Center building, designed by Eliel Saarinen in 1948, with a south wing by the noted I. M. Pei & Partners added in 1968. Another spectacular wing, recognized as a masterpiece of contemporary architecture, was designed and built, in 1985, by Richard Meier & Partners. **NOT TO BE MISSED:** "Maiastra" by Constantin Brancusi; Frank Stella's "Interlagos"

ON EXHIBIT 2000

12/08/1999 to 02/13/2000   WORKS ON PAPER: THE 20TH CENTURY
Part two of the exhibition featuring works on paper from the Center's collection

02/26/2000 to 05/21/2000   LEE KRASNER: PALINGENESIS
Retrospective of paintings and collages from 1930-1970.

06/03/2000 to 08/06/2000   PAT STEIR: THE WATERFALL
20 paintings tracking the waterfall as a these in Steir's work.

08/19/2000 to 10/29/2000   IOWA ARTISTS 2000
Survey exhibition of Iowa Artists

11/11/2000 to 01/21/2001   TONY OURSLER: MID-CAREER SURVEY

Hoyt Sherman Place

1501 Woodland Ave., Des Moines, IA 50309
☎: 515-243-0913
Open: 8-4 Mo-Tu & Th-Fr; Closed on We from OCT.1-end of MAY   **Closed:** LEG/HOL!
&. Ⓟ Free   **Museum Shop**
Group Tours   Drop-In Tours: often available upon request
Historic Building Complex of 1877 House, 1907 Art Museum, 1923 Theater
Permanent Collection: PTGS; SCULP; DEC/ART 19; EU; sculp; B.C. ARTIFACTS

A jewel from the Victorian Era, the Hoyt Sherman Art Galleries offer an outstanding permanent collection of 19th century American and European art, complimented by antique decorative arts objects that fill its surroundings. Listed NRHP **NOT TO BE MISSED:** Major works by 19th century American masters including Church, Innes, Moran, Frieseke and others

---

DUBUQUE

Dubuque Museum of Art

7th at Washington Park, 701 Locust, Dubuque, IA 52001
☎: 319-557-1851
Open: 10-5 Tu-Fr; 1-4 Sa, Su   **Closed:** Mo, 1/1, EASTER, 7/4, THGV, 12/25
ADM: Adult: $3.00   **Children:** Free under 12   **Students:** $2.00   **Seniors:** $2.00
&. Ⓟ Metered street parking   **Museum Shop**
Group Tours   Drop-In Tours: daily upon request
Permanent Collection: REG

The inaugural exhibition in the new building was held August 1999. Exhibitions from the permanent collection are displayed on a rotating basis..

IOWA

Dubuque Museum of Art - continued
ON EXHIBIT 2000

12/15/1999 to 03/10/2000   EARTH, FIRE AND WATER: CONTEMPORARY FORGED METAL
Works by 16 artists across the country who use a variety of techniques from ancient blacksmithing methods to industrial welding. *Will Travel*

03/14/2000 to 07/02/2000   GRANT WOOD, AND MARVIN CONE: THE ORIGINS OF REALISM
Development of the artists style from post-impressionist to the flat treatment of paint and stylized forms of Regionalism in the 30's. *Will Travel*

FORT DODGE

Blanden Memorial Art Museum
920 Third Ave. South, Fort Dodge, IA 50501
☎: 515-573-2316
Open: 10-5 Tu-Fr, till 8:30 T, 1-5 Sa & Su
♿ Ⓟ Street parking and limited parking area behind the museum   **Museum Shop   Group Tours**
Permanent Collection: AM: ptgs, sculp, gr 19-20; EU: ptgs, sculp, drgs, gr 15-20; OR: 16-20; P/COL

Established in 1930 as the first permanent art facility in the state, the Blanden's neo-classic building was based on the already existing design of the Butler Institute of American Art in Youngstown, Ohio. Listed NRHP
NOT TO BE MISSED: "Central Park" by Maurice Prendergast, 1901; "Self-Portrait in Cap & Scarf" by Rembrandt (etching, 1663)

GRINNELL

Grinnell College Print & Drawing Study Room
Affiliate Institution: Grinnell College
Burling Library, Grinnell, IA 50112-0806
☎: 515-269-3371
Open: 1-5 Su-Fr during the academic year   **Closed:** 7/4, THGV, 12/25 THROUGH 1/1
♿ Ⓟ Available at 6th Ave. & High St.   **Museum Shop**
Permanent Collection: WORKS ON PAPER (available for study in the Print & Drawing Study Room)

1,400 works on paper, ranging from illuminated manuscripts to 16th century European prints and drawings to 20th century American lithographs, are all part of the study group of the Grinnell College Collection that started in 1908 with an original bequest of 28 etchings by J. M. W. Turner. A new gallery, designed by Cesar Pelli, is scheduled to open in the spring of 1998. **NOT TO BE MISSED:** Etching: "The Artist's Mother Seated at a Table" by Rembrandt

---

IOWA CITY

University of Iowa Museum of Art
150 North Riverside Dr., 112 Museum of Art, Iowa City, IA 52242-1789
☎: 319-335-1727   🖥 www.uiowa.edu/~artmus
Open: 10-5 Tu-Sa, Noon-5 Su   **Closed:** Mo, 1/1, THGV, 12/25
♿ Ⓟ Metered lots directly across Riverside Drive & north of the museum   **Museum Shop**
Group Tours   Sculpture Garden
Permanent Collection: AM: ptgs, sculp 19-20; EU: ptgs, sculp 19-20; AF; WORKS ON PAPER

University of Iowa Museum of Art - continued

Over nine thousand objects form the basis of the collection at this 30 year old university museum that features, among its many strengths, 19th & 20th century American and European art, and the largest group of African art in any university museum collection. **NOT TO BE MISSED:** "Karneval" by Max Beckman: "Mural, 1943" by Jackson Pollock

Central Iowa Art Association

Affiliate Institution: Fisher Community College
Marshalltown, IA 50158
📞: 515-753-9013
Open: 11-5 Mo-Fr; 1-5 Sa, Su (APR 15-OCT 15) **Closed:** LEG/HOL!
Vol/Cont: **Sugg/Cont:**
🚻 Ⓟ Free parking in front of building **Museum Shop Group Tours Sculpture Garden**
Permanent Collection: FR/IMPR: ptgs; PTGS; CER

You don't have to be a scholar to enjoy the ceramic study center of the Central Iowa Art Association, one of the highlights of this institution. 20th century paintings and sculpture at the associated Fisher Art Gallery round out the collection. **NOT TO BE MISSED:** The Ceramic Study Collection

Charles H. MacNider Museum

303 2nd St., S.E., Mason City, IA 50401-3988
📞: 515-421-3666
Open: 9-9 Tu-Sa, Su; 1-5 **Closed:** Mo, LEG/HOL!, PM 12/24, PM 12/31
🚻 Ⓟ **Museum Shop Group Tours Drop-In Tours**: available upon advance request during museum hours
Permanent Collection: AM: ptgs, gr, drgs, cer; REG: ptgs, gr, drgs, cer; the "Bil Baird World of Puppets"

A lovely English Tudor mansion built in 1921, complete with modern additions, is the repository of an ever growing collection that documents American art and life. Though only a short two block walk from the heart of Mason City, the MacNider sits dramatically atop a limestone ravine surrounded by trees and other beauties of nature. **NOT TO BE MISSED:** For young and old alike, a wonderful collection of Bil Baird Marionettes; "Gateways to the Sea", by Alfred T. Bricher; "Spring Tryout," by Thomas Hart Beuton; "The Clay Wagon," by Arthur Dove

ON EXHIBIT 2000

11/21/1999 to 01/09/2000 IOWA CRAFTS: 32

01/13/2000 to 02/27/2000 BIL: COLLECTOR
A collection of puppets from master puppeteer Bill Baird.

03/02/2000 to 04/09/2000 SEEING THE EXTRAORDINARY
Have ever visualized or imagined people, places, or objects in the clouds? When you look at a form and imagine it to be something else you are seeing the extraordinary.

04/13/2000 to 05/21/2000 PEOPLE WATCHERS: Isabel Bishop; Adolf Dehn ; Reginald Marsh; and Grant Wood
Artists turn everyday situations & moments into inspirational art.

05/25/2000 to 07/16/2000 RECENT ACQUISITIONS
This temporary exhibit focuses on the process of building the collection and presents in one gallery selections given to or presented to the Museum in preceding months.

07/21/2000 to 09/03/2000 20TH CERRO GORDO PHOTO SHOW
A very popular annual photo show featuring local residents.

IOWA

Muscatine Art Center

1314 Mulberry Ave., Muscatine, IA 52761
☎: 319-263-8282
Open: 10-5 Tu, We, Fr; 10-5 & 7-9 Th; 1-5 Sa, Su   **Closed:** Mo, LEG/HOL!
Vol/Cont:
&. ℗ Free   **Museum Shop**
Group Tours   Drop-In Tours: self guided   **Historic Building** 1908 Edwardian Musser Mansion
Permanent Collection: AM: ptgs, sculp, gr, drgs, dec/art 19-20; NAT/AM: ptgs

The original Musser Family Mansion built in Edwardian Style in 1908, has been joined since 1976 by the contemporary 3 level Stanley Gallery to form the Muscatine Art Center. In addition to its fine collection of regional and national American art, the center has received a bequest of 27 works by 19 important European artists including Boudin, Braque, Pissaro, Degas, Matisse and others. **NOT TO BE MISSED:** The "Great River Collection" of artworks illustrating facets of the Mississippi River from its source in Lake Itasca to its southernmost point in New Orleans.

Sioux City Art Center

225 Nebraska St., Sioux City, IA 51101-1712
☎: 712-279-6272   ◙ www.sc-artcenter.com
Open: 10-5 Tu-W & Fr-Sa, 12-9 Th, 1-5 Su   **Closed:** Mo, LEG/HOL!
&. ℗ Metered street parking & city lots within walking distance of the museum   **Museum Shop**
Group Tours: 712-279-6272 ext. 200   **Drop-In Tours**: By reservation
Permanent Collection: NAT/AM; 19-20; CONT/REG; PTGS, WORKS ON PAPER; PHOT

Begun as a WPA project in 1938, the Center features a 900 piece permanent collection that includes regional art. A stunning new $9 million Art Center building, designed by the renowned architectural firm of Skidmore, Owings and Merril, that features a three-story glass atrium, and a state-of-the-art Hands-On Gallery for children. **NOT TO BE MISSED:** In the new facility, a hands-on gallery for children featuring creative activity stations.

ON EXHIBIT 2000

04/22/1999 to 07/02/2000   MIDWESTERN GLASS

04/27/1999 to 07/06/2000   DAVID WEST RETROSPECTIVE

11/11/1999 to 02/20/2000   MARK L. MOSEMAN: AGRARIAN LEGACY
In his pastel paintings, Kansas City artist M. L. Moseman celebrates the relationship between people and nature.

12/02/1999 to 01/30/2000   SUITED TO A TEA
25 Midwestern Artists have been invited to the first Midwestern Ceramic Invitational.

12/02/1999 to 01/30/2000   MIDWESTERN CERAMICS

02/12/2000 to 04/09/2000   UPPER MIDWEST JURIED EXHIBITION

04/15/2000 to 07/16/2000   DAVID WEST/EDNA SMITH-WEST RETROSPECTIVE
An exhibition which will cover the career of this Sioux City artist from his abstract images to his recent representational landscape paintings.

06/01/2000 to 08/03/2000   LOUISE KAMES
A printmaker who is now creating installation works.

Sioux City Art Center - continued
07/07/2000 to 01/30/2001   PHOTOGRAPHIC IMAGES FROM THE PERMANENT COLLECTION

07/15/2000 to 10/15/2000   MIDWEST ABSTRACTION

08/12/2000 to 10/01/2000   JO STEALEY
Stealey has been working with papermaking and is now focused on three dimensional paper vessels paper vessels. The traditions and rituals of various cultures inspire her pieces.

09/15/2000 to 10/29/2000   SIOUX CITY CAMERA CLUB

09/19/2000 to 10/29/2000   DIOCESE 2000
The Sioux City Diocese will show their works and collection of ob jects and the history of how they were used by the church.

11/05/2000 to 12/21/2000   THE JOHN A. AND MARGERET HILL COLLECTION OF AMERICAN WESTERN ART
This collection of landscapes, portraits of cowboys, Native American subjects, etc. that stretch the scope of the American West. *Will Travel*

WATERLOO

Waterloo Museum of Art
225 Commercial St., Waterloo, IA 50701
☎: 319-291-4490   ◉   www.wplwloo.lib.ia.us/waterloo/arts.html
Open: 10-5 Mo-Sa; 1-4 -Su   **Closed:** LEG/HOL!
Vol/Cont:
&. Ⓟ Ample and free   **Museum Shop**
Group Tours
Permanent Collection: REG: ptgs, gr, sculp; HATIAN: ptgs, sculp; AM: dec/art

This museum notes as its strengths its collection of Midwest art including works by Grant Wood and Marvin Cone, an outstanding collection of Haitian paintings, metal sculpture and sequined banners, and an American decorative arts collection with particular emphasis on pottery and American art collection. **NOT TO BE MISSED:** Small collection of Grant Wood paintings, lithographs, and drawings. The largest public collection of Haitian art in US.

ON EXHIBIT 2000
ONGOING   SELECTED PERMANENT COLLECTION & PERMANENTLY INSTALLED SCULPTURE ON DISPLAY IN THE GRAND FOYER

12/10/1999 to 02/13/2000   PAINTINGS BY BURTON CHENET

KANSAS

Walker Art Collection of the Garnett Public Library

125 W. 4th Ave., Garnett, KS 66032

☎: 913-448-3388 ◙ www.kanza.net/garnett
Open: 10-8 Mo, Tu, Th; 10-5:30 We, Fr; 10-4 Sa **Closed:** 1/1, MEM/DAY, 7/4, THGV, 12/25
Vol/Cont:
&. ℗ Free and abundant street parking **Museum Shop** **Drop-In Tours**: Upon request if available
Permanent Collection: AM: ptgs: 20; REG

Considered one of the most outstanding collections in the state, the Walker was started with a 110 piece bequest in 1951 by its namesake, Maynard Walker, a prominent art dealer in New York during the 1930's & 40's. Brilliantly conserved works by such early 20th century American artists as John Stuart Curry, Robert Henri, and Luigi Lucioni are displayed alongside European and Midwest Regional paintings and sculpture. All works in the collection have undergone conservation in the past few years and are in pristine condition. **NOT TO BE MISSED:** "Lake in the Forest (Sunrise)" by Corot; "Girl in Red Tights" by Walt Kuhn; "Tobacco Plant" by John Stuart Curry

Spencer Museum of Art

Affiliate Institution: University of Kansas
1301 Mississippi St., Lawrence, KS 66045

☎: 785-864-4710
Open: 10-5 Tu-Sa, Noon-5 Su, till 9pm Th **Closed:** 1/1, 7/4, THGV & FOLLOWING DAY, 12/24, 12/25
&. ℗ Metered spaces in lot north of museum & parking anywhere when school not in session. **Museum Shop**
Group Tours: School year only
Permanent Collection: EU: ptgs, sculp, gr 17-18; AM: phot; JAP: gr; CH: ptgs; MED: sculp

The broad and diverse collection of the Spencer Museum of Art, located in the eastern part of the state not far from Kansas City, features particular strengths in the areas of European painting and sculpture of the 17th & 18th centuries, American photographs, Japanese and Chinese works of art, and Medieval sculpture. **NOT TO BE MISSED:** "La Pia de Tolommei" by Rosetti; "The Ballad of the Jealous Lover of Lone Green Valley" by Thomas Hart Benton

ON EXHIBIT 2000

01/29/2000 to 03/11/2000 The Art of 20-th Century Zen: Paintings and Calligraphy by Japanese Masters
This show examines modern examples of the traditional Zen artforms of painting and calligraphy. The works contain traditional visual motifs such as enso, a circle that symbolizes perfection, as well as new themes.

Birger Sandzen Memorial Gallery

401 N. 1st St., Lindsborg, KS 67456-0348

☎: 785-227-2220
Open: 1-5 We-Su **Closed:** Mo, Tu, LEG/HOL!
ADM: Adult: $2.00 **Children:** $.50 grades 1-12 **Seniors:** $2.00
&. ℗ Free in front of gallery and in lot behind church across from the gallery **Museum Shop**
Group Tours
Permanent Collection: REG: ptgs, gr, cer, sculp; JAP: sculp

Birger Sandzen Memorial Gallery - continued

Opened since 1957 on the campus of a small college in central Kansas, about 20 miles south of Salina, this facility is an important cultural resource for the state. Named after Birger Sandzen, an artist who taught at the College for 52 years, the gallery is the repository of many of his paintings. PLEASE NOTE: There is reduced rate of $5.00 for families of 5 or more people. **NOT TO BE MISSED:** "The Little Triton" fountain by sculptor Carl Milles of Sweden located in the courtyard.

ON EXHIBIT 2000
04/05/2000 to 05/28/2000   101ST ANNUAL MIDWEST ART EXHIBITION

LOGAN

Dane G. Hansen Memorial Museum

110 W. Main, Logan, KS 67646

☎: 785-689-4846

Open: 9-12 & 1-4 Mo-Fr, 9-12 & 1-5 Sa, 1-5 Su & Holidays   **Closed:** 1/1, THGV, 12/25

   ⓟ Free   **Museum Shop**   **Group Tours**: 785-689-4846   **Drop-In Tours**
Permanent Collection: OR; REG

Part of a cultural complex completed in 1973 in the heart of downtown Logan, the Hansen Memorial Museum, a member of the Smithsonian Associates, also presents regional artists. Also, Annual Labor Day Celebration, Labor Day Sunday. Car show, live entertainment, fireworks at dark, volleyball tournament and much, much more. All Free. **NOT TO BE MISSED:** Annual Hansen Arts & Craft Fair (3rd Sa of Sept) where judges select 12 artists to exhibit in the Hansen's artist corner, one for each month of the year.

ON EXHIBIT 2000
11/12/1999 to 01/09/2000   HOPI KATSINAS *Will Travel*

02/11/2000 to 06/04/2000   BUGS EYE VIEW

06/23/2000 to 08/20/2000   100 YEARS OF VAN BRIGGLE POTTERY *Brochure Will Travel*

10/06/2000 to 12/01/2000   DINEH "THE PEOPLE" LIFE AND CULTURE OF THE NAVAJO *Brochure Will Travel*

OVERLAND PARK

Johnson County Community College Gallery of Art

Affiliate Institution: Johnson County Community College

12345 College Blvd., Overland Park, KS 66210

☎: 913-469-8500

Open: 10-5 Mo, Th, Fr; 10-7 Tu, We; 1-5 Sa, Su   **Closed:** LEG/HOL!; Su, June - August

   ⓟ Free   **Museum Shop**   ↑↑
Group Tours: 913-469-8500 x3789   **Sculpture Garden**
Permanent Collection: AM/ CONT: ptgs, cer, phot, works on paper

The geometric spareness of the buildings set among the gently rolling hills of the campus is a perfect foil for the rapidly growing permanent collection of contemporary American art. Sculptures by Jonathan Borofsky, Barry Flanagan, Judith Shea, Louise Bourgeois, and Magdalena Abakanowicz are joined by other contemporary works in the Oppenheimer-Stein Sculpture Collection sited over the 234-acre campus. Seven exhibitions of contemporary art are presented annually. **NOT TO BE MISSED:** Oppenheimer-Stein Sculpture Collection

KANSAS

Salina Art Center
242 S. Santa Fe, Salina, KS 67401
☎: 785-827-1431 ◙ www.salinaartcenter.org
Open: 12-5 Tu-Sa; 1-5 Su; till 7 Th **Closed:** Mo, LEG/HOL!
& ℗ Free handicapped parking **Museum Shop**
Group Tours: school year only **Drop-In Tours**: 9-5 Tu-Fr; call to schedule

Recognized across the Midwest for bringing together art, artists, and audiences in innovative ways, the Salina Art Center specializes in exhibiting and interpreting contemporary American art. Rotating high quality original multicultural exhibitions, traveling exhibitions (often featuring works by international artists), and a permanent Discovery Area hands-on laboratory for children are its main features. **NOT TO BE MISSED:** A state of the art movie facility, Art Center Cinema, one block from the gallery, features the best current international and American film. Open Th-Su weekly. Cinema phone: 785-452-9868

ON EXHIBIT 2000

11/21/1999 to 01/23/2000 21st ANNUAL JURIED EXHIBITION
Five state Juried show.

02/06/2000 to 03/26/2000 NARRATIVES
Paintings and drawings from Tonya Hartman's "From the Nursery" and "Words and Pictures". Wall paintings by Ruth Moritz, paintings by Ed Rath

04/09/2000 to 06/25/2000 WILLIAM KENTRIDGE: WEIGHING AND WANTING
South African artist Kentridge 18 charcoal drawings and a laser disc video projection. Viewers respond to his beautiful drawings, emotional use of color and moving sound track.

07/09/2000 to 09/02/2000 GIRLFRIEND! THE BARBIE SESSIONS BY DAVID LEVINTHAL
Large format color saturated Polaroid photographs which blur the boundaries between fact and fiction. This series of 40 images, portraying Barbie dressed impeccably for a variety of occasions, continues Leventhal's on-going inquest into the realm where fantasies become plausible realities. *Will Travel*

09/16/2000 to 10/22/2000 ROBERT REGIER

11/18/2000 to 01/13/2000 22ND ANNUAL JURIED EXHIBITION

Gallery of Fine Arts-Topeka & Shawnee County
1515 W. 10th, Topeka, KS 66604-1374
☎: 913-233-2040
Open: 9-9 Mo-Fr, 9-6 Sa, 2-6 Su **Closed:** LEG/HOL!
& ℗ Free **Museum Shop** ⅰ: for 2002 new facility
Group Tours
Permanent Collection: REG: ptgs, gr 20; W/AF; AM: cer, glass paperweights

Although the fine art permanent collection is usually not on view, this active institution presents rotating exhibitions that are mainly regional in nature. PLEASE NOTE: Beginning 6/15/97, the museum will be closed until the year 2002 due to a major construction project that will more than double its exhibition space and allow for more of the permanent collection to be on display. **NOT TO BE MISSED:** Glass paperweights; Akan gold weights from Ghana and the Ivory Coast, West Africa

Mulvane Art Museum
Affiliate Institution: Washburn University
17th & Jewell, Topeka, KS 66621-1150

☎: 785-231-1124
Open: SEPT-MAY: 10-7 Tu-We, 10-4 T & Fr, 1-4 Sa, Su; SUMMER: 10-4 Tu-Fr
Closed: Mo, LEG/HOL! & during exhibit installations
Vol/Cont:
♿ Ⓟ Free **Museum Shop Group Tours**: 785-231-1010 x1322 **Drop-In Tours**: by appointment, 10-3 Tu-Fr
Historic Building Oldest Art Museum in State of Kansas (1924) on the campus of Washburn University. **Sculpture Garden**
Permanent Collection: EU: dec/art 19-20; AM: dec/art 19-20; JAP: dec/art 19-20; REG: cont ptgs; GR; SCULP; CER; PHOT

Opened in 1924, the Mulvane is the oldest art museum in the state of Kansas located on the campus of Washburn University. In addition to an ever growing collection of works by artists of Kansas and the Mountain-Plains region, the museum counts both an international and a Japanese print collection among its holdings.

ON EXHIBIT 2000
01/07/2000 to 02/27/2000 PHILLIP HERSHBERGER/GAIL GREGG

03/04/2000 to 04/23/2000 ABSTRACT ART FROM THE PERMANENT COLLECTION

05/27/2000 to 07/16/2000 PERSONAL CALLIGRAPHY: EMMI WHITEHORSE, JAUNE QUICK TO SEE SMITH AND LEE MANN

07/28/2000 to 09/17/2000 JANTZEN EXHIBIT - MENNONITE FURNITURE

09/29/2000 to 11/06/2000 FACULTY EXHIBIT

11/17/2000 to 01/07/2001 CORPORATE TOPEKA COLLECTS

WICHITA

Edwin A. Ulrich Museum of Art
Affiliate Institution: Wichita State University
1845 Fairmount St., Wichita, KS 67260-0046

☎: 316-978-3664 ▣ www.twsu.edu/~ulrich
Open: 12-5 Daily **Closed:** 1/1, 1/18, MEM/DAY, EASTER, 7/4, 7/5, LAB/DAY, THGV, 12/24-25
♿ Ⓟ Visitor lot available. **Museum Shop Group Tours**: 316-978-6413 **Drop-In Tours**: by appt
Historic Building Marble & glass mosaic mural by Spanish artist Joan Miro on museum facade **Sculpture Garden**
Permanent Collection: AM: 19-20; EU: 19-20; PRIM; AM: gr; EU: gr; PHOT

The Edwin A. Ulrich Museum of Art at Wichita State University is recognized among university museums for its outdoor sculpture collection and for the quality of its exhibition program. 19th and 20th century European and American sculpture, prints, drawings, and paintings form the core of the 7,300 object collection. A major aspect of the collection is the 64-piece outdoor sculpture collection, named in honor of the founding director of the museum, placed around the 330 acre campus of Wichita State University. The collection contains a cross-section of 19th and 20th century sculptures by artists such as Auguste Rodin, Henry Moore, Louise Nevelson, George Rickey, Lynn Chadwick, and Luis Jimenez, among others. The museum is easily recognized by the centerpiece of this outdoor collection is the mosaic, Personnages Oiseaux, by Joan Miró, commissioned by the University in 1979. Consisting of nearly one million pieces of Venetian glass and marble, the mural depicts whimsical bird characters that inhabited the imagination of the artist. The Ulrich has an outstanding exhibition program and acts as a visual laboratory for the students of the University as well as the community. Exhibitions range from established art work - often from the museum's collection - to more contemporary exhibitions highlighting prominent artists working today. **NOT TO BE MISSED:** Sculpture collection on grounds of university; Collection of marine paintings by Frederick J. Waugh

KANSAS

Edwin A. Ulrich Museum of Art - continued

ON EXHIBIT 2000

ONGOING   THE KOURI SCULPTURE TERRACE
Rotating presentations of works from the Museum's sculpture collection.

10/17/1999 to 01/02/2000   GARTH EVANS: THE YADDO DRAWINGS

01/24/2000 to 03/05/2000   THE GRAND MOVING PANORAMA: PILGRIMS PROGRESS (1851)

28/05/2000 to 05/28/2000   THE DIALECTICS OF SPACE: SHEILA MOSS AND SARA GOOD

Indian Center Museum

650 N. Seneca, Wichita, KS 67203
☎: 316-262-5221   ◉ WWW2.SOUTHWIND.NET/~ICM/MUSEUM/ICM
Open: 10-5 Mo-Sa, (closed Mo JAN-MAR)   **Closed:** Su, LEG/HOL!
ADM: **Adult:** $2.00   **Children:** Free 6 & under   **Students:** $1.00   **Seniors:** $1.00
Ⓟ Free   **Museum Shop   Group Tours**
Permanent Collection: NAT/AM

The artworks and artifacts in this museum preserve Native American heritage and provide non-Indian people with insight into the culture and traditions of Native Americans. In addition to the art, Native American food is served on Tuesday from 11-4. **NOT TO BE MISSED:** Blackbear Bosin's 44 foot "Keeper of the Plains" located on the grounds at the confluence of the Arkansas & Little Arkansas Rivers.

Wichita Art Museum

619 Stackman St., Wichita, KS 67203-3296
☎: 316-268-4921   ◉ www.feist.com/~wam
Open: 10-5 Tu-Sa, 12-5 Su   **Closed:** Mo, LEG/HOL
♿   Ⓟ Free   **Museum Shop**   ⅋: Truffles Cafe open 11:30-1:30 Tu-Sa & 12-2 Su
Group Tours: 316-268-4907   **Historic Building** 1977 designed by Edward Larabee Barnes
Permanent Collection: AM: ptgs, ge, drgs; EU: gr, drgs; P/COL; CHARLES RUSSELL: ptgs, drgs, sculp; OM: gr

Outstanding in its collection of paintings that span nearly 3 centuries of American art, the Wichita is also known for its Old Master prints and pre-Columbian art. **NOT TO BE MISSED:** The Roland P. Murdock Collection of American Art

ON EXHIBIT 2000

ONGOING   AN AMERICAN HOMECOMING
The Homecoming exhibition reviews the relationship of the nations art in 130 masterpieces from the permanent collection. It is presented in 9 thematic sections including "American Character";" Americans Abroad" ; and "Independent American Visions".

To 01/02/2000   MAURICE PRENDERGAST: THE STATE OF THE ESTATE
45 works by American Impressionist *Will Travel*

to 01/02/2000   MAURICE PRENDERGAST AND HIS ASSOCIATES
Watercolors from the Wichita Museum collection

to 01/13/2000   AMERICANA FROM HEARTH AND HOME
Quilts, coverlets and kitchen utensils from the collection

01/09/2000 to 04/02/2000   COMIC VIEWPOINTS
Cartoons and comic narrative from 20th C. American artists from the collection.

Wichita Art Museum - continued

01/23/2000 to 04/02/2000   DANCING AT THE LOUVRE: FAITH RINGOLD'S FRENCH COLLECTION AND OTHER STORY QUILTS
The first museum exhibition of selected quilt paintings including some from the 1980s. The exhibition will focus on two history-based series, both made of acrylic on canvas with pieced fabric. The "French Connection" combines a revisionist view of the early 20th C. School of Paris with a fictional biography of an African-American artist and model who lived in Paris during the 1920s. The "American Collection" continues the story through the life of the artist's daughter who becomes an artist in America. *Catalog Will Travel*

03/05/2000 to 11/12/2000   BRITISH WATERCOLORS AND DECORATIVE ARTS FROM THE COLLECTION
Presented in two segments during the dates shown.

03/18/2000 to 05/27/2000   CRAFT IS A VERB
A significant view of the development of contemporary craft since the 1950's.   104 examples showing the creative range .

04/09/2000 to 06/25/2000   PROFILE OF A PATRON PURCHASE COLLECTION
Watercolors purchased by Emprise Bank in its 20 year history of patronage of the Kansa Watercolor Society Competition.

04/23/2000 to 06/04/2000   KANSAS WATERCOLOR SOCIETY SEVEN-STATE EXHIBITION
A juried competition for works on paper in a water-based medium. Janet Fish is juring this year's exhibition and her painting will be presented.

06/25/2000 to 08/27/2000   COMMERCE BANCSHARES COLLECTION
40 20th C American paintings from this corporate collection with it's strength in contemporary realism

07/02/2000 to 11/12/2000   AN AIR OF REFINEMENT
The taste of the Aesthetic movement in British and American graphic works from the collection.

09/09/2000 to 11/14/2000   LATINO ART: TREASURES FROM THE SMITHSONIAN'S MUSEUM OF AMERICAN ART
The vitality of Latino art traditions and innovations from the 18th thru the 20th C is divided into 6 thematic sections.:" Puerto Rican Religious Tradition" ;"Honoring People"; "Establishing Place" ; "Activism/Dialogue"; "Imagination and Dreams". *Catalog Will Travel*

09/24/2000 to 11/19/2000   THE GILDED AGE: TREASURES FROM THE SMITHSONIAN'S NATIONAL MUSEUM OF AMERICAN ART
American paintings and sculpture from 1880-1915 highlighting the period when artists traveled abroad in large numbers. *Will Travel*

12/10/2000 to 02/25/2001   BEN SHAHN'S NEW YORK: THE PHOTOGRAPHY OF SOCIAL CONSCIENCE
Focusing on Shahn's 1930's photographs and his application of photography to drawings, paintings and mural projects which promoted social reform. *Catalog Will Travel*

Wichita Center for the Arts
9112 East Central, Wichita, KS 67206
☎: 316-634-2787
Open: 1-5 Tu-Su   **Closed:** Mo, LEG/HOL!
 ⚕ ℗ on-site free parking spaces   **Museum Shop**
Group Tours
Permanent Collection: DEC/ART: 20; OR; PTGS; SCULP; DRGS; CER; GR

Midwest arts, both historical and contemporary, are the focus of this vital multi-disciplinary facility. **NOT TO BE MISSED:** 1,000 piece Bruce Moore Collection

KENTUCKY

University of Kentucky Art Museum
Rose & Euclid Ave., Lexington, KY 40506-0241

📞: 606-257-5716
Open: 12-5 Tu-Su   **Closed:** Mo, ACAD!
Vol/Cont:
  ♿ ℗ Limited parking available in the circular drive in front of the Center.   **Museum Shop**
Group Tours: 606-257-8164   **Drop-In Tours**: By Appt
Permanent Collection: OM: ptgs, gr: AM: ptgs 19; EU: ptgs 19; CONT/GR; PTGS 20; AF; Asian; WPA WORKS

Considered to be one of Kentucky's key cultural resources, this museum houses over 3,500 art objects that span the past 2,000 years of artistic creation.

ON EXHIBIT 2000

09/1999 to 03/2000   TOWN AND COUNTRY: LANDSCAPES IN THE COLLECTION

09/1999 to 03/2000   ON THE BRINK: THE MILLENNIUM NEARS

11/14/1999 to 02/27/2000   HENRY CHODOWSKI: MAVOS LABYRINTHOS SERIES, 1986-1998

J. B Speed Art Museum
2035 S. Third St., Louisville, KY 40208

📞: 502-634-2700   ◙   www.speedmuseum.org
Open: 10:30-4 Tu-We, Fr 10:30-5 Sa, 12-5 Su, till 8pm Th   **Closed:** LEG/HOL!,
  ♿ ℗ Adjacent to the museum - $2.00 fee for non-members   **Museum Shop**
🍴: Bristol Cafe,11:30-2 Tu-Sa, 12-3 Su (Reservations suggested 637-7774)
Group Tours: 502-634-2725   **Drop-In Tours**: 2pm Sa, 1&3pm Su, 7pm Th   **Sculpture Garden**
Permanent Collection: AM: dec/art; PTGS; SCULP: GR; PRIM; OR; DU:17; FL:17; FR: ptgs 18; CONT

Founded in 1927, and located on the main campus of the University of Louisville, the newly renovated J. B. Speed Art Museum is the largest (over 3,000 works) and the most comprehensive (spanning 6,000 years of art history) public art collection in Kentucky. Free "Especially For Children" tours are offered at 11:00 each Saturday. PLEASE NOTE: A fee is charged for selected exhibitions. Two recently discovered masterpieces by Sir Edward Burne-Jones, Rash gift including Chagall, Matisse Picasso Klee and DuBuffet **NOT TO BE MISSED:** New acquisition: "Saint Jerome in the Wilderness" by Hendrick van Somer, 1651; "Head of a Ram", a 2nd century marble Roman sculpture (recent acquisition); "Colossal Head of Medusa", polychromed fiberglass sculpture by Audry Flack (recent acquisition)

ON EXHIBIT 2000

05/22/1999 to 04/2000   PRODIGAL SON TAPESTRY

01/25/2000 to 04/09/2000   REMBRANDT TO GAINSBOROUGH: MASTERPIECES FROM ENGLAND'S DULWICH PICTURE GALLERY
A selection of masterworks from England's oldest public art museum and the home of Europe's most celebrated Old Master collections. Features 90 works - many of which have never been shown in the U.S. - by such artists as Canaletto, Gainsborough, Poussin, Rembrandt, Rubens, and Tiepolo.

06/27/2000 to 08/27/2000   ART AND NATURE: THE HUDSON RIVER SCHOOL
Twenty-six nineteenth-century paintings by the Hudson River School artists, who are known for their dramatic depictions of nature and subjects ranging from sublime views of the wilderness to pastoral scenes and allerorical pictures with moral messages.

J. B. Speed Art Museum - continued
06/27/2000 to 06/27/2000   KARL BODMER'S EASTERN VIEWS: A JOURNEY IN NORTH AMERICA
Drawn entirely from the Joslyn Art Museum renowned Maximilian-Bodmer collection and consisting of nearly 100 watercolors, drawings, prints and documents, this exhibition illuminates an important aspect of Bodmer's work.

09/19/2000 to 11/12/2000   LINDA MCCARTNEY'S SIXTIES: PORTRAIT OF AN ERA
An exhibition of photographs by Linda McCartney, Beatle icon Paul McCartney's late wife and an important photographer in her own right. Pictures include The Rolling Stones, The Beatles, The Grateful Dead and other Rock icons.

Photographic Archives
Affiliate Institution: University of Louisville Libraries
Ekstrom Library, University of Louisville, Louisville, KY 40292
\: 502-852-6752   ◙   http://www.louisville.edu/library/ekstrom/special/pa-info.html
Open: 10-4 Mo-Fr, 10-8 Th   **Closed:** Sa, Su, LEG/HOL!
⑤   ⓟ Limited (for information call 502-852-6505)   **Museum Shop   Group Tours**
Permanent Collection: PHOT; GR

With 33 individual collections, and over one million items, the Photographic Archives is one of the finest photography and research facilities in the country. **NOT TO BE MISSED:** 2,000 vintage Farm Security Administration photos; more than 1500 fine prints "from Ansel Adams to Edward Weston"

OWENSBORO

Owensboro Museum of Fine Art
901 Frederica St., Owensboro, KY 42301
\: 502-685-3181
Open: 10-4 Tu-Fr; 1-4 Sa, Su   **Closed:** Mo, LEG/HOL!
Vol/Cont: ADM: Adult: $2.00   **Children:** $1.00
⑤   ⓟ Free   **Museum Shop   Group Tours:** 502-685-3181
Historic Building 1909 Carnegie Library Building (listed NRHP), restored pre-Civil War era John Hampden Smith House
Permanent Collection: AM: ptgs, drgs, gr, sculp 19-20; BRIT: ptgs, drgs, gr, sculp 19-20; FR: ptgs, sculp, drgs, gr 19-20; CONT/AM; DEC/ART 14-18

The collection of the Owensboro Museum, the only fine art institution in Western Kentucky, features works by important 18-20th century American, English, and French masters. Paintings by regional artists stress the strong tradition of Kentucky landscape painting. There is a restored Civil War era mansion, the John Hampdem Smith House, serves as a decorative arts wing for objects dating from the 15th to 19th century. **NOT TO BE MISSED:** 16 turn-of-the-century stained glass windows by Emil Frei (1867-1941) permanently installed in the new wing of the museum; revolving exhibitions of the museum's collection of Appalachian folk art.

PADUCAH

Yeiser Art Center
200 Broadway, Paducah, KY 42001-0732
\: 270-442-2453   ◙   www.yeiser.org
Open: 10-4 Tu-Sa, 1-4 Su   **Closed:** Mo, LEG/HOL! & JAN.
ADM: Adult: $1.00   **Children:** Free under 12   **Students:** $0.50   **Seniors:** $0.50
⑤   ⓟ Free   **Museum Shop   Group Tours   Drop-In Tours:** Usually available upon request
Historic Building Located in the historic Market House (1905)
Permanent Collection: AM, EU, AS & AF: 19-20

The restored 1905 Market House (listed NRHP), home to the Art Center and many other community related activities, features changing exhibitions that are regional, national, and international in content. **NOT TO BE MISSED:** Annual national fiber exhibition mid Mar thru Apr (call for exact dates)

LOUISIANA

Alexandria Museum of Art
933 Main St., Alexandria, LA 71301-1028
☎: 318-443-3458 ◉ www.themuseum.org
Open: 9-5 Tu-Fr 1-5 Sa-Su   **Closed:** Mo, LEG/HOL!
ADM: Adult: $4.00   **Children:** $2.00   **Students:** $3.00   **Seniors:** $3.00
♿ ⓟ Free General, Handicap and Bus parking in front of building.   **Museum Shop**
❚❙ Catered lunch can be pre-arranged in atrium café.
Group Tours: 318-443-3458 ext. 18   **Drop-In Tours:** often available upon request!
Historic Building 1900 Bank Building   **Sculpture Garden**
Permanent Collection: CONT: sculp, ptgs; REG; FOLK

The grand foyer of the new wing of the Alexandria Museum of Art, was constructed and opened to the public in March of 1998. The Museum was founded in 1977 and originally occupied the Historic Rapides Bank Building, circa 1898, listed on the National Historic Register. The expanded AMoA is the centerpiece of Alexandria's riverfront, situated on the entire 900 block of Main Street. **NOT TO BE MISSED:** Native expression exhibit of Louisiana art and children's gallery.

ON EXHIBIT 2000
11/22/1999 to 01/10/2000   ARTISTS OF THE AMERICAN WEST
The artists featured include -John J. Audubon, Albert Bierstadt , Karl Bodmer, George Catlin, Frederick Remington, and John Mix Stanley, among others–were key participants in the discovery of a "new world."

01/08/2000 to 03/11/2000   POETRY AND ART: COLLABORATIVE WORK BY LOUISIANA POETS AND ARTISTS
40 new works by artists who use Poets as a catalyst.

01/08/2000 to 03/11/2000   THE PHOTOGRAPHIC GUILD SURVEY

04/01/2000 to 05/27/2000   JOHN CLEMMER: A FIFTY YEAR RETROSPECTIVE
The development of Clemmer's career from his early figurative work in the late 40's to his uniquely personal abstractions of the60's and early 70's to his current experiments with urban scenes and landscapes.

06/03/2000 to 07/29/2000   BOTANICA: CONTEMPORARY ART AND THE WORLD OF PLANTS
Images, systems and/or the metaphorical potential of botany as the basis for art will be seen in the works on display by notable contemporary artists from the U.S. and abroad. *Catalog Will Travel*

08/18/2000 to 10/28/2000   18TH ANNUAL SEPTEMBER COMPETITION

11/11/2000 to 12/30/2000   HASMIG VARTANIAN/JEFF COOK
Seventh in a series of exhibitions related to work by contemporary Louisiana artists

Louisiana Arts and Science Center
100 S. River Rd., Baton Rouge, LA 70802
☎: 225-344-5272 ◉   www.lasc.lsu.edu
Open: 10-3 Tu-Fr, 10-4 Sa, 1-4 Su   **Closed:** Mo, .LEG/HOL!
Free Day: First Su of month   **ADM: Adult:** $3.00   **Children:** $2.00 (2-12)   **Students:** $2.00   **Seniors:** $2.00
♿ ⓟ Limited free parking in front of building and behind train; other parking areas available within walking distance
Museum Shop   Group Tours: 225-344-9478
Historic Building Housed in reconstructed Illinois Central Railroad Station   **Sculpture Garden**
Permanent Collection: SCULP; ETH; GR; DRGS; PHOT; EGT; AM: ptgs 18-20; EU: ptgs 18-20

Louisiana Arts and Science Center - continued

LASC, housed in a reconstructed Illinois Central Railroad Station, offers art exhibitions, and Egyptian tomb and mummies, and a five-car train (undergoing restoration). Hands-on areas for children include Discovery Depot-an "edutainment" area-and Science Station, an interactive physical science gallery. The Challenger Learning Center is a stimulated space station and mission control center (reservations required). **NOT TO BE MISSED:** Works by John Marin, Charles Burchfield, Asher B. Durand; Baroque, Neo-Classic, & Impressionist Works; Native American totem pole; 2nd largest collection in the U.S. of sculpture by Ivan Mestrovic.

JENNINGS

Zigler Museum

411 Clara St., Jennings, LA 70546
☎: 318-824-0114 ◉ www.JeffDavis.org
Open: 9-5 Tu-Sa, 1-5 Su **Closed:** Mo, LEG/HOL!
Sugg/Cont: **ADM: Adult:** $2.00 **Children:** $1.00
&. ℗ Free **Museum Shop Group Tours Drop-In Tours:** Usually available upon request
Permanent Collection: REG; AM; EU

The gracious colonial style structure that had served as the Zigler family home since 1908, was formerly opened as a museum in 1970. Two wings added to the original building feature many works by Louisiana landscape artists in addition to those by other American and European artists. PLEASE NOTE: The museum is open every day for the Christmas festival from the first weekend in Dec. to Dec. 22. **NOT TO BE MISSED:** Largest collection of works by African-American artist, William Tolliver

ON EXHIBIT 2000

01/16/2000 to 02/20/2000 BLACK HISTORY EXHIBIT: EUGENE J.. MARTIN, CHARLES SIMMS

01/22/2000 to 02/20/2000 MARDI GRAS EXHIBIT
Costumes from the area's crews

03/04/2000 to 03/31/2000 2000 AND BEYOND: ART FORMS EXHIBIT

04/08/2000 to 04/30/2000 ZIGLER MUSEUM'S 30TH YEAR CELEBRATION
Featuring Jeff Davis artists

05/06/2000 to 06/11/2000 ASSOCIATED LOUISIANA ARTISTS SHOWCASE

06/24/2000 to 07/30/2000 LOUISIANA ARTISTS

08/05/2000 to 09/17/2000 LOUISIANA ARTISTS

10/07/2000 to 11/12/2000 FRIENDS OF THE ZIGLER MUSEUM JURIED ART COMPETITION

12/02/2000 to 12/22/2000 FESTIVAL OF CHRISTMAS - CHRISTMAS AROUND THE WORLD

LAFAYETTE

University Art Museum

Joel L. Fletcher Hall, 2nd Floor, East Lewis & Girard Park Dr., Lafayette, LA 70504
☎: 318-482-5326
Open: 9-4 Mo-Fr, 10-4 Sa, closed on Sa during summer '98
Closed: Su, 1/1, MARDI GRAS, EASTER, THGV, 12/25, LEG/HOL!
&. ℗ Free with validation in paylot **Museum Shop**
Group Tours: 318-482-5326 **Drop-In Tours:** reservation only; Mo-Fr 9 -11:30 and 1:30 -3:30
Permanent Collection: AM/REG: ptgs, sculp, drgs, phot 19-20; JAP: gr; PLEASE NOTE: Selections from the permanent collection are on display approximately once a year (call for specifics)

LOUISIANA

University Art Museum - continued
The University Art Museum is situated on the beautiful campus of The University of Southwestern Louisiana, home of Cypress Lake. The UAM offers visitors art exhibitions of regional, national and international acclaim. The Permanent Collection is housed in an 18th century style plantation home on the corner of Girard Park Drive and St. Mary Boulevard. Permanent holdings include works by Henri Le Sidaner, Franz Marc, Sir Godfrey Kneller, G.P.A. Healy, Henry Pember Smith, and Adolph Rinck to name only a few. Overlooking Girard Park, touring exhibits can be seen in the more modern Fletcher Hall Gallery located in the Art & Architecture Building on the U.S.L. campus.

MONROE

Masur Museum of Art
1400 S. Grand, Monroe, LA 71202
☎: 318-329-2237
Open: 9-5 Tu-Th, 2-5 Fr-Su **Closed:** Mo, LEG/HOL!
& Ⓟ Free **Museum Shop Group Tours Drop-In Tours**: call for hours **Historic Building Sculpture Garden**
Permanent Collection: AM: gr 20; REG/CONT

Twentieth century prints by American artists, and works by contemporary regional artists, form the basis of the permanent collection of this museum which is housed in a stately modified English Tudor estate situated on the tree-lined banks of the Ouachita River.

ON EXHIBIT 2000
07/05/1999 to 08/16/2000 EARTH, FIRE AND WATER: CONTEMPORARY FORGED METAL
Works by 16 artists across the country who use a variety of techniques from ancient blacksmithing methods to industrial welding.

09/24/1999 to 01/07/2000 BEYOND THE HORIZON: SUDLOW AND JACOBSHAGEN
In the mid-1970's, Robert Sudlow emerged as a major figure in the regional painting. Since that time, his large canvases, depicting the subtle forms and spare beauty of the Kansas prairie, have achieved public acclaim and ever increasing critical recognition.

NEW ORLEANS

Historic New Orleans Collection
533 Royal St., New Orleans, LA 70130
☎: 504-523-4662 ◙ www.hnoc.org
Open: 10-4:30 Tu-Sa **Closed:** Su, Mo. LEG/HOL!
Free Day: MAIN EXHIBITION HALL Tu-Sa **ADM: Adult:** $4.00
& **Museum Shop**
Group Tours: 504-523-4662 **Drop-In Tours**: 10, 11, 2 & 3 DAILY **Historic Building** 1792 Jean Francois Merieult House Located in French Quarter
Permanent Collection: REG: ptgs, drgs, phot; MAPS; RARE BOOKS, MANUSCRIPTS

Located within a complex of historic French Quarter buildings, the Historic New Orleans Collection serves the public as a museum and research center for state and local history. Merieult House, one of the most historic buildings of this complex, was built in 1792 during Louisiana's Spanish Colonial period. It is one of the few structures in the French Quarter that escaped the fire of 1794. The Williams Research Center, 410 Chartres St., part of this institution, contains curatorial, manuscript and library material relating to the history and culture of Louisiana. **NOT TO BE MISSED:** Tours of the LA. History Galleries and Founders Residence

ON EXHIBIT 2000
11/02/1999 to 04/08/2000 FROM PANIC TO OCCUPATION: NEW ORLEANS IN THE AGE OF T.K. WHARTON

Louisiana State Museum
751 Chartres St., Jackson Square, New Orleans, LA 70116

📞: 800-568-6968
Open: 9-5 Tu-Su   **Closed:** Mo, LEG/HOL!
ADM: Adult: $4.00   **Children:** Free 12 & under   **Students:** $3.00   **Seniors:** $3.00
⚅   **Museum Shop**
Group Tours   Drop-In Tours: Gallery talks on weekends - call for specifics   **Historic Building**
Permanent Collection: DEC/ART; FOLK; PHOT; PTGS; TEXTILES

Several historic buildings, located in the famous New Orleans French Quarter are included in the Louisiana State Museum complex, provide the visitor with a wide array of viewing experiences that run the gamut from fine art to decorative art, textiles, Mardi Gras memorabilia, and even jazz music. The Cabildo, Presbytere, and 1850 House (all located on Jackson Square) and the Old U.S. Mint are currently open to the public. PLEASE NOTE THE FOLLOWING: (1) Although the entry fee of $4.00 is charged per building visited, a discounted rate is offered for a visit to two or more sites. (2) 1850 House features special interpretive materials for handicapped visitors. **NOT TO BE MISSED:** Considered the State Museum's crown jewel, the recently reopened Cabildo features a walk through Louisiana history from Colonial times through Reconstruction. Admission to the Arsenal, featuring changing exhibits, is included in the entry fee to the Cabildo.

New Orleans Museum of Art
1 Collins Diboll Circle, City Park, P.O. Box 19123, New Orleans, LA 70119-0123

📞: 504-488-2631   ◉ www.noma.org
Open: 10-5 Tu-Su   **Closed:** Mo, LEG/HOL!
Free Day: 10-noon Th for Louisiana residents only except for some special exh   **ADM: Adult:** $6.00   **Children:** $1.00
(3-17)   **Students:** $5.00   **Seniors:** $5.00
⚅   ℗ Free   **Museum Shop**   ⑆: Courtyard Cafe 10:30-4:30 Tu-Su (children's menu available)
Group Tours   Drop-In Tours: 11:00 & 2:00 Tu-Su and by appointment for groups of 10 or more   **Sculpture Garden**
Permanent Collection: AM; OM: ptgs; IT/REN: ptgs (Kress Collection); FR; P/COL: MEX; AF; JAP: gr; AF; OC; NAT/AM; LAT/AM; AS; DEC/ART: 1st. A.D.-20; REG; PHOT; GLASS

Located in the 1,500 acre City Park, the 75 year old New Orleans Museum recently completed a $23 million dollar expansion and renovation program that doubled its size. Serving the entire Gulf South as an invaluable artistic resource, the museum houses over one dozen major collections that cover a broad range of fine and decorative art. **NOT TO BE MISSED:** Treasures by Faberge; Chinese Jades; French Art; Portrait Miniatures; New 3rd floor showcase for Non-Western Art; The stARTing point, a new hands-on gallery area with interactive exhibits and 2 computer stations designed to help children and adults understand the source of artists' inspiration.

ON EXHIBIT 2000
Special admission for exhibitions is often charged
11/12/1999 to 01/07/2000   HENRY CASSELLI: MASTER OF THE AMERICAN WATERCOLOR

11/20/1999 to 01/02/2000   THE TRIUMPHANT SPIRIT: PORTRAIT AND STORIES OF HOLOCAUST SURVIVORS :PHOTOGRAPHS BY NICK DEL CALZO

12/04/1999 to 02/06/2000   LEWIS WICKES HINE: THE FINAL YEARS
These 169 photographs were given to the Museum by Hine in 1979 and have never been shown to the public. They show the oeuvre for the first time of the last years of one of America's most important photographers and a seminal figure in the history of the medium.

12/14/1999 to 02/06/2000   SWEDISH ART NOUVEAU PORCELAIN FROM THE ROBERT SCHREIBER COLLECTION

LOUISIANA

New Orleans Museum of Art - continued
01/2000 to 04/2000   KADOJIN: A MODERN NAGA MASTER

03/03/2000 to 04/18/2000   JOHN SINGER SARGENT: THE WERTHEIMER PORTRAITS *Will Travel*

03/03/2000 to 05/18/2000   SONG CERAMICS FROM THE ROBERT BARRON COLLECTION

05/2000 to 08/2000   AT WORK AND PLAY: EVERYDAY LIFE IN JAPANESE PAINTINGS

06/03/2000 to 08/27/2000   UNLOCKED DOORS: THE ART OF GORDON PARKS

09/2000 to 12/2000   MATSUMURA GOSHUN AND FOLLOWERS

09/11/2000 to 10/28/2000   HOWARD HODGKIN: RETROSPECTIVE PRINTS

11/12/2000 to 01/07/2001   MAGNIFICENT, MARVELOUS MARTELE: SILVER FROM THE COLLECTION OF ROBERT AND JULIE SHELTON

SHREVEPORT

Meadows Museum of Art of Centenary College
2911 Centenary Blvd., Shreveport, LA 71104-1188

📞: 318-869-5169   ◙   centenary.edu
Open: 12-4 Tu-Fr, 1-4 Sa, Su   **Closed:** Mo, LEG/HOL!
♿ Ⓟ Free behind the building   **Museum Shop**
Group Tours: 318-869-5169   **Drop-In Tours**: Upon request if available
Permanent Collection: PTGS, SCULP, GR, 18-20; INDO CHINESE: ptgs, gr

This museum, opened in 1976, serves mainly as a repository for the unique collection of works in a variety of media by French artist Jean Despujols and the Centenary College collection. The Museum's galleries also boast a series of temporary exhibitions throughout the year. **NOT TO BE MISSED:** The permanent collection itself which offers a rare glimpse into the people & culture of French Indochina in 1938. Also includes American and European paintings and works on paper from the college collection.

ON EXHIBIT 2000
11/14/1999 to 02/27/2000   ART AND SOUL I: , RUSSIAN ICONS, THEIR ART AND HISTORY FROM THE COLLECTION OF DANIEL R. BIBB/ WINDOWS TO HEAVEN WILL HAVE PIECES NEVER BEFORE SEEN IN PUBLIC.
This first exhibition in the Art and Soul project features icons spanning more than 300 years. The Windows in Heaven project shows many icons in their resident kliots, specially constructed boxes with glass fronts.

01/16/2000 to 02/13/2000   PORTRAIT 2000 : PHOTOGRAPHS OF PEOPLE OF SHREVEPORT AND BOSSIER CITY AT THE TURN OF THE MILLENNIUM
The goal of this exhibition is to present a true cross-section of the community depicting people from all walks of life.

02/20/2000 to 04/30/2000   CELEBRATING THE CREATIVITY OF LOUISIANA'S WOMEN:: LUCILLE REED: DISCOVERIES 1950-2000
Lucille Reed began making art and followed in the footsteps of the women in her family who practiced the craft of weaving.. She has created constructions of painted wood and fabric.

03/12/2000 to 06/11/2000   CELEBRATING THE CREATIVITY OF LOUISIANA'S WOMEN: MATERIALS GIRL LYNDA BENGLIS
Seen by many art critics as significant in relation what one critic called the contemporary "counter-tradition." This exhibition is a retrospective of her astonishing career but as a selective survey of her oeuvre.

Meadows Museum of Art of Centenary College - continued
05/07/2000 to 06/20/2000 THROUGH THE NEEDLES EYE: SELECTIONS FROM THE EMBROIDERY GUILD OF AMERICA

06/11/2000 to 07/30/2000 THE PAINTINGS OF JOHN CLEMMER

09/2000 to 11/2000 CLYDE CONNELL: DAUGHTER OF THE BAYOU

11/2000 to 01/2001 LOUISIANA TREASURE HOUSE

R. W. Norton Art Gallery
4747 Creswell Ave., Shreveport, LA 71106

☎: 318-865-4201 ◉ www.softdisk.com/comp/norton
Open: 10-5 Tu-Fr; 1-5 Sa, Su **Closed:** Mo, LEG/HOL!
♿ ℗ Free **Museum Shop**
Group Tours Drop-In Tours: reg hours
Permanent Collection: AM: ptgs, sculp (late 17-20); EU: ptgs, sculp 16-19; BRIT: cer

With its incomparable collections of American and European art, the Norton, situated in a 46 acre wooded park, has become one of the major cultural attractions in the region since its opening in 1966. Among its many attractions are the Bierstadt Gallery, the Bonheur Gallery, and the Corridor which features "The Prisons", a 16-part series of fantasy etchings by Piranesi. Those who visit the museum from early to mid April will experience the added treat of seeing 13,000 azalea plants that surround the building in full bloom. **NOT TO BE MISSED:** Outstanding collections of works by Frederic Remington & Charles M. Russell; The Wedgewood Gallery (one of the finest collections of its kind in the southern U.S.)

MAINE

Bowdoin College Museum of Art
9400 College Station, Brunswick, ME 04011-8494

☎: 207-725-3275 ◉ www.bowdoin.edu/cwis/resources/museums.html

Open: 10-5 Tu-Sa, 2-5 Su **Closed:** Mo, LEG/HOL! ALSO CLOSED WEEK BETWEEN 12/25 & NEW YEARS DAY
Vol/Cont:

 ♿ ⓟ All along Upper Park Row **Museum Shop** ⑪: on campus, in town

Group Tours: 207-725-3276 **Historic Building** 1894 Walker Art Building Designed by Charles Follen McKim

Permanent Collection: AN/GRK; AN/R; AN/EGT; AM: ptgs, sculp, drgs, gr, dec/art; EU: ptgs, sculp, gr, drgs, dec/art; AF: sculp; INTERIOR MURALS BY LAFARGE, THAYER, VEDDER, COX

From the original bequest of artworks given in 1811 by James Bowdoin III, who served as Thomas Jefferson's minister to France and Spain, the collection has grown to include important works from a broad range of nations and periods. **NOT TO BE MISSED:** Winslow Homer Collection of wood engravings, watercolors, drawings, and memorabilia (available for viewing during the summer months only).

ON EXHIBIT 2000

ONGOING BOYD GALLERY:
14th to 20th-century European art from the permanent collection.

ONGOING BOWDOIN GALLERY:
American art from the permanent collection.

ONGOING SOPHIA WALKER GALLERY: ART AND LIFE IN THE ANCIENT MEDITERRANEAN
4th century B.C. to 4th century A.D. Assyrian, Egyptian, Cypriot, Greek and Roman objects will be featured in an installation that highlights one of the museum's great strengths.

01/27/2000 to 03/19/2000 POLLY APFELBAUM - INSTALLATION

04/06/2000 to 06/04/2000 GOODBYE FOR NOW: PERMANENT COLLECTION FAVORITES

04/07/2000 to 07/04/2000 TERRY WINTERS: PRINTS

Bates College Museum of Art
Affiliate Institution: Bates College
Olin Arts Center, Bates College, Lewiston, ME 04240

☎: 207-786-6158 ◉ www.bates.edu/acad/museum

Open: 10-5 Tu-Sa, 1-5 Su **Closed:** Mo, LEG/HOL!

 ♿ ⓟ Free on-street campus parking **Museum Shop**

Group Tours: by appt

Permanent Collection: AM: ptgs, sculp; GR 19-20; EU: ptgs, sculp, gr; drgs:

The recently constructed building of the Museum of Art at Bates College houses a major collection of works by American artist Marsden Hartley. It also specializes in 20th-century American and European prints, drawings, and photographs, and has a small collection of 20th century American paintings. **NOT TO BE MISSED:** Collection of Marsden Hartley drawings and memorabilia

ON EXHIBIT 2000
ONGOING HIGHLIGHTS FROM THE PERMANENT COLLECTION

09/08/2000 to 11/03/2000 THE PEOPLE'S CHOICE

Ogunquit Museum of American Art

181 Shore Rd., Ogunquit, ME 03907

☎: 207-646-4909
Open: (open 7/1 through 9/30 ONLY) 10:30-5 Mo-Sa, 2-5 Su   **Closed:** LAB/DAY
ADM: **Adult:** $4.00   **Children:** Free under 12   **Students:** $3.00   **Seniors:** $3.00
♿ ℗ Free on museum grounds   **Museum Shop**
Group Tours   Drop-In Tours: Upon request if available   **Sculpture Garden**
Permanent Collection: AM: ptgs, sculp 20

Situated on a rocky promontory overlooking the sea, this museum has been described as the most beautiful small museum in the world! Built in 1952, the Museum houses many important 20th century American paintings and works of sculpture in addition to site-specific sculptures spread throughout its three acres of land. **NOT TO BE MISSED:** "Mt. Katadhin, Winter" by Marsden Hartley; "The Bowrey Drunks" by Reginald Marsh; "Pool With Four Markers" by Dozier Bell; "Sleeping Girl" by Walt Kuhn

ON EXHIBIT 2000

07/01/2000 to 08/2000   A CENTURY RE-DISCOVERED: WORKS FROM THE PERMANENT COLLECTION

08/2000 to 09/30/2000   AMERICAN IMPRESSIONISM & GEORGE LLOYD: A RETROSPECTIVE

University of Maine Museum of Art

5712 Carnegie Hall, Orono, ME 04469-5712

☎: 207-581-3255   ▣   www.ummm.umecah.maine.edu
Open: 9-4:30 Mo-Sa; (summer hours 9-4)   **Closed:** Su, STATE & LEG/HOL!
♿ ℗ Free with visitor permits available in director's office.   **Museum Shop**
Group Tours: by appt   **Historic Building** 1904 Library of Palladian Design
Permanent Collection: AM: gr, ptgs 18-20; EU: gr, ptgs 18-20; CONT; REG

Housed in a beautiful 1904 structure of classic Palladian design, this university art museum, located just to the north east of Bangor, Maine, features American and European art of the 18th-20th centuries, and works by Maine based artists of the past and present. The permanent collection is displayed throughout the whole university and in the main center-for-the-arts building.

Portland Museum of Art

Seven Congress Square, Portland, ME 04101

☎: 207-775-6148   ▣   www.portlandmuseum.org
Open: 10-5 Tu, We, Sa, Su; 10-9 Th, Fr; noon-5 Su; (open 10-5 Mo MEM/DAY to Columbus Day)
Closed: LEG/HOL!, 12/25, 1/1, THGV
Free Day: 5-9 Fr   **ADM**: **Adult:** $6.00   **Children:** $1.00 (6-12)   **Students:** $5.00   **Seniors:** $5.00
♿ ℗ Nearby garages   **Museum Shop**   ᵀ♔: Museum Café
Group Tours: 207-775-6148   **Drop-In Tours**: 2 & 6 Th, Fr
Permanent Collection: AM; ptgs, sculp 19-20; REG; DEC/ART; gr

The Portland Museum of Art is the oldest and largest art museum in the state of Maine. Established in 1882, the outstanding museum features Impressionist and American master works housed in an award-winning building designed by renowned architect I.M. Pei & Partners. PLEASE NOTE: Also, there is a toll free number (1-800-639-4067) for museum recorded information.

MAINE

Portland Museum of Art - continued
ON EXHIBIT 2000

ONGOING   FROM MONET TO MATISSE: THE ORIGINS OF MODERNISM

ONGOING   PHILLIPE HALSMAN: A GALLERY OF STARS

09/22/1999 to 01/23/2000   CUT FROM THE CLOTH OF LIFE: THE FABRIC COLLAGES OF ELIZABETH B. NOYCE
Noyce used her gifts with the needle to create "Cut from the Cloth of Life" of more than 40 appliqués. She also collected portraits of women sewing! *Will Travel*

11/4/1999 to 01/02/2000   THE GRAND MOVING PANORAMA OF BUNYAN'S PILGRIM'S PROGRESS

01/19/2000 to 03/19/2000   ANSEL ADAMS AND PHOTOGRAPHERS OF THE AMERICAN WEST

02/05/2000 to 05/07/2000   HAMILTON EASTER FIELD ART FOUNDATION COLLECTION

04/05/2000 to 06/04/2000   LASTING IMPRESSIONS: CONTEMPORARY PRINTS FROM THE BRUCE BROWN COLLECTION

ROCKLAND

Farnsworth Art Museum and Wyeth Center
352 Main St., Rockland, ME 04841-9975
☏: 207-596-6457   ◙   www.wyethcenter.com; www.midcoast.com/~farnsworth
Open: SUMMER: 9-5 daily; WINTER: 10-5 Tu-Sa, 1-5 Su   **Closed:** LEG/HOL!
ADM: Adult: $9.00   **Children:** Free under 17   **Students:** $5.00   **Seniors:** $7.00
& Ⓟ Free   **Museum Shop**
Group Tours: ex 104   **Drop-In Tours**
Historic Building 1850 Victorian Homestead and Olson House open MEM/DAY to Columbus Day.
Permanent Collection: AM: 18-20; REG; PHOT; GR

Nationally acclaimed for its collection of American Art, the Farnsworth, located in the mid coastal city of Rockland, counts among its important holdings the largest public collection of works by sculptor Louise Nevelson. The museum's 8 galleries offer a comprehensive survey of American art. Recently, the museum opened the Wyeth center, a new gallery building and study center, to house the works of Andrew, N.C. and Jamie Wyeth. **NOT TO BE MISSED:** Major works by N.C., Andrew & Jamie Wyeth, Fitz Hugh Lane, John Marin, Edward Hopper, Neil Welliver, Louise Nevelson; The Olson House, depicted by Andrew Wyeth in many of his most famous works

ON EXHIBIT 2000

ONGOING   MAINE IN AMERICA
The history of American art with a special emphasis on works related to Maine will be seen in the examples on view from the permanent collection.

ONGOING   HOMAGE TO LOUISE NEVELSON
In addition to the wood and terracotta sculptures for which she is best noted, this exhibition includes paintings, drawings, mixed media constructions and some personal items of jewelry and photography, all gifted to the museum by the late sculptor and her family.

02/10/2000 to 04/30/2000 CUT FROM THE CLOTH OF LIFE: FABRIC COLLAGES OF ELIZABETH B NOYCE
Noyce used her gifts with the needle to create "Cut from the Cloth of Life" of more than 40 appliqués. She also collected portraits of women sewing!

Colby College Museum of Art
Mayflower Hill, Waterville, ME 04901
📞: 207-872-3228   ◉ www.colby.edu/museum
Open: 10-4:30 Mo-Sa, 2-4:30 Su   **Closed:** LEG/HOL!
& ℗ Free   **Museum Shop**
Group Tours
Permanent Collection: AM: Impr/ptgs, folk, gr; Winslow Homer: watercolors; OR: cer

Located in a modernist building on a campus dominated by neo-Georgian architecture, the museum at Colby College houses a distinctive collection of several centuries of American Art. Included among its many fine holdings is a 36 piece collection of sculpture donated to the school by Maine native, Louise Nevelson. **NOT TO BE MISSED:** 25 watercolors by John Marin; "La Reina Mora" by Robert Henri (recent acquisition)

ON EXHIBIT 2000

07/05/2000 to 08/03/2000   QUILT NATIONAL
A juried exhibition of international art quilts.

07/21/2000 to 10/17/2000   NARRATIVES OF AFRICAN AMERICAN ART AND IDENTITY: THE DAVID DRISKELL COLLECTION
The transformation of African American identity is brought to life in art and archival material.

08/11/2000 to 10/17/2000   ECHOES: THE ART OF DAVID DRISKELL 1955-1997
Selections from the artist-collectors own work

MARYLAND

Mitchell Gallery
Affiliate Institution: St. John's College
60 College Ave., Annapolis, MD 21404-2800
☎: 410-626-2556 ◙ www.sjca.edu/gallery/gallery.html
Open: 12-5 Tu-Su; 7-8 Fr ; closed for the summer **Closed:** Mo, LEG/HOL!
& ℗ 2 hour metered street parking near museum; parking at the U.S. Naval & Marine Corps Stadium on Rowe Blvd. with free shuttle bus service; call ahead to arrange for handicap parking. **Museum Shop** ᛏᛚ: College Coffee Shop open 8:15-4
Group Tours   Historic Building

Established in 1989 primarily as a center of learning for the visual arts, this institution, though young in years, presents a rotating schedule of educational programs and high quality exhibitions containing original works by many of the greatest artists of yesterday and today.

ON EXHIBIT 2000
01/2000 to 02/2000   THE PHELAN COLLECTION OF WESTERN ART
This collection is as vivid and expressive a representation of man's gradual expansion into the American west. The 45 paintings, prints and drawings embody the beauty of the subjects and capture the beauty of an expanding nation. *Will Travel*

03/2000 to 04/2000   PICASSO CERAMIC EDITIONS FROM THE EDWARD WESTON COLLECTION
The 60 limited edition ceramics in this exhibition were created by Pablo Picasso during the years he worked at the Madoura pottery workshop of George and Susan Ramie from 1947 to 1971. *Will Travel*

09/2000 to 10/2000   FROM SHIP TO SHORE: MARINE PAINTINGS FROM THE BUTLER MUSEUM OF AMERICAN ART
Over 60 paintings, ranging from ship portraiture to ocean views, highlight the general fascination with marine culture since colonial times. Included are works by William Bradford, Alfred Thompson Bricher, James Butterworth and William Trost Richards. *Will Travel*

American Visionary Art Museum
800 Key Highway & Covington in the Baltimore Inner Harbor, Baltimore, MD 21202-3940
☎: 410-244-1900
Open: 10-6 Tu-Su **Closed:** THGV, 12/25
ADM: Adult: $6.00   **Children:** Free under 4   **Students:** $4.00   **Seniors:** $4.00
& ℗ $3.00 parking in large lot across the street from the Museum; many 24-hour metered spaces on Covington. **Museum Shop** ᛏᛚ: Joy America Cafe open 11:30am - 10pm Tu-S, Sunday Brunch 11-4:30 (call 410-244-6500 to reserve)
Historic Building 1913 elliptical brick building **Sculpture Garden**
Permanent Collection: Visionary art

Dedicated to intuition, The American Visionary Art Museum, designated by congress, is the nation's official repository for original self-taught (a.k.a. "outsider") visionary art. Among the many highlights of the 4,00 piece permanent collection are Gerlad Hawkes' one-of-a-kind matchstick sculptures, 400 original pen and ink works by postman/visionary Ted Gordon, and the entire life archive of the late Otto Billig, M.D., an expert in transcultural psychiatric art who was the last psychiatrist to Zelda Fitzgerald. **NOT TO BE MISSED:** Towering whirligig by Vollis Simpson, located in outdoor central plaza, which is like a giant playwheel during the day and a colorful firefly-like sculpture when illuminated at night; Joy America Cafe featuring ultra organic gourmet food created by four-star chef Peter Zimmer, formerly of The Inn of the Anazazi in Santa Fe, NM.; Wildflower sculpture garden complete with woven wood wedding chapel by visionary artist Ben Wilson.

ON EXHIBIT 2000
Fall/1999 to Fall/2000   WE ARE NOT ALONE: ANGELS AND ALIENS

Baltimore Museum of Art
Art Museum Drive, Baltimore, MD 21218-3898

☎: 410-396-7100   ◉ www.artbma.org
Open: 10-5 We-Fr, 11-6 Sa, Su; 5-9 1st Th of month   **Closed:** Mo Tu, 1/1, 7/4,THGV, 12/25
Free Day: Th   **ADM**: **Adult:** $6.00   **Children:** Free 18 & under   **Students:** $4.00   **Seniors:** $4.00
&   ℗ Metered & limited on site; or parking on weekends at The Johns Hopkins University adjacent to Museum
Museum Shop   ⑪: Gertrudes at the BMA 410-889-3399
Group Tours: 410-396-6320   **Historic Building** 1929 bldg designed by John Russell Pope   **Sculpture Garden**
Permanent Collection: Ptgs, Ren-20; OM/drgs 15-20; CONT; Sculp 15-20; dec/art; OR; p/col ;

One of the undisputed jewels of this important artistic collection is the Cone Collection of works by Matisse, the largest of its kind in the Western hemisphere new 17 gallery wing for contemporary art, the first and largest for this institution and for the state. Works by Andy Warhol from the second largest permanent collection of paintings by him are on regular display. **NOT TO BE MISSED:** The new installation (fall 2000) of the Cone Collection, American dec/arts; Antioch mosaics; Sculpture Garden; Am Paintings 19; OM paintings

ON EXHIBIT 2000
07/07/1999 to 02/2000   SELECTIONS FROM THE CONE COLLECTION

09/01/1999 to 02/27/2000   ROBES OF DELIVERANCE: RITUAL GARMENTS OF THE BUDDHIST PRIESTS OF JAPAN
17th, 18th-20th century garments worn by priests and primarily drawn from the BMA collection *Will Travel*

10/10/1999 to 01/30/2000   FACES OF IMPRESSIONISM: PORTRAITS FROM AMERICAN COLLECTIONS
Impressionist artists and their progressive approach to portraiture are the focus of this ground breaking exhibition . Included for the first time are works by Cassatt, Gauguin, Cézanne, Degas, Manet, Monet, Morisot and Renoir. This is the first attempt to provide insight into the genre as it was practiced by masters of this influential movement. *Catalog Will Travel*

01/23/2000 to 05/21/2000   JOYCE SCOTT: A THIRTY YEAR RETROSPECTIVE (working title)
Working in a broad range of mediums, including textiles, sculpture, site-specific installations and performance pieces. Her mother is the artist Elizabeth Scott. The exhibit will place her work in context particularly in relation to the craft tradition

03/12/2000 to 05/28/2000   NADAR/WARHOL: PARIS/NEW YORK
In pairing the work of the Parisian portrait photographer (1820-1910) and Andy Warhol (1928-1987) whose photography is just becoming the subject of museum exhibitions. Both befriended and photographed some of the most famous figures of their time. The exhibition includes 40 salt and albumen prints by Nadar and 43 gelatin silver and Polaroid prints by Warhol

03/12/2000 to 07/16/2000   FRENCH MASTER PAINTINGS FROM BALTIMORE (working title)
Drawn from the BMA and the Walters Art Gallery, the exhibition surveys French paintings from the 19th and early 20th C *Catalog*

04/05/2000 to 09/10/2000   CHANTILLY: THE BLACK LACE (working title)
Superb examples of shawls, parasols, face veils, and fans that illustrate the sophistication and exquisite design of the world's most beautiful laces.

06/11/2000 to 09/24/2000   WPA PRINTMAKERS AS CULTURAL WORKERS (working title)
One of the New Deal Projects was to provide work for thousands of destitute artists. 80 examples of the thousand prints underscore the social, historical and art historical content of the prints.

09/24/2000 to 01/07/2000   ART FOR THE PRESIDENTS (working title)
The aesthetic tastes which have defined the American presidency and the ideology showcases 200 years of presidential portraiture. Divided into two sections "Regal Courts and National Identity" it illustrates the importance of regal backdrop to the American Presidency *Catalog*

10/15/2000 to 01/07/2001   BOOK ARTS IN THE AGE OF Dürer
40 books and 40 loose sheets underscore the importance of Dürer in the development of book arts. It also provides a history of early book production

MARYLAND

The Contemporary
601 N. Howard St., Baltimore, MD 21201
☎: 410-333-8600   ◉ http://www.softaid.net/the contemporar
Open: For administrative office only: usually 12-5 Tu-Su
Sugg/Cont:
Museum Shop

Considering itself an "un-museum" The Contemporary is not a permanent facility but rather an institution dedicated to the presentation of exhibitions at various venues throughout the city of Baltimore. It is suggested that visitors call ahead to verify the location (or locations), hours of operation, and information on their schedule of exhibitions.

Evergreen House
Affiliate Institution: The Johns Hopkins University
4545 N. Charles St., Baltimore, MD 21210-2693
☎: 410-516-0341
Open: 10-4 Mo-Fr, 1-4 Sa, Su   **Closed:** LEG/HOL!
ADM: Adult: $6.00   **Children:** Free under 5   **Students:** $3.00   **Seniors:** $5.00
& ℗ Free   **Museum Shop** ❕: Call ahead for box lunches, high tea & continental breakfast for groups
Group Tours: 410-516-0344 (Groups more than 20 $5 pp)   **Drop-In Tours:** call for specifics
Historic Building 1850-1860 Evergreen House
Permanent Collection: FR: Impr, Post/Impr; EU: cer; OR: cer; JAP

Restored to its former beauty and reopened to the public in 1990, the 48 rooms of the magnificent Italianate Evergreen House (c 1878), with classical revival additions, contain outstanding collections of French and Post-Impressionist works of art collected by its founders, the Garrett family of Baltimore. PLEASE NOTE: All visitors to Evergreen House are obliged to go on a 1 hour tour of the house with a docent. It is recommended that large groups call ahead to reserve. It should be noted that the last tour of the day begins at 3:00.S **NOT TO BE MISSED:** Japanese netsuke and inro; the only gold bathroom in Baltimore; private theatre designed by Leon Bakst.

ON EXHIBIT 2000
04/29/2000 to 11/01/2000   SCULPTURE AT EVERGREEN
Newly created, site specific outdoor sculptures . Ten artists will be invited to participate.

10/27/2000 to 01/31/2001   THE SECOND ANNUAL COLLECTORS SERIES: THE CARRETT BOOK COLLECTION: THE GARRETT BOOK COLLECTION
A celebration of the Garrett Collection of 30,000 rare books and contemporary books as well.

Peale Museum
225 Holliday St., Baltimore, MD 21202
☎: 410-396-3525
Open: 10-5 Tu-Sa, Noon-5 Su   **Closed:** LEG/HOL!
ADM: Adult: $2.00   **Children:** $1.50 (4-18)   **Seniors:** $1.50
& ℗ Metered street parking and pay parking in the Harbor Park Garage on Lombard St., one block from the museum.
Museum Shop
Group Tours   Historic Building First building built as a museum in U.S. by Rembrandt Peale, 1814   **Sculpture Garden**
Permanent Collection: REG/PHOT; SCULP; PTGS; 40 PTGS BY PEALE FAMILY ARTISTS

The Peale, erected in 1814, has the distinction of being the very first museum in the U.S. One of the several City Life Museums in Baltimore. Over 40 portraits by members of the Peale Family are displayed in an ongoing exhibition entitled "The Peales, An American Family of Artists in Baltimore". PLEASE NOTE: The museum is temporarily closed till further notice.

Walters Art Gallery
600 N. Charles St., Baltimore, MD 21201
📞: 410-547-9000　◉ www.thewalters.org
Open: 10-4 Tu-Fr; 11-5 Sa, Su; till 8pm Th　**Closed:** 12/25
ADM: **Adult:** $6.00　**Children:** Free 18 & under　**Students:** $3.00　**Seniors:** $4.00
♿ Ⓟ Ample parking on the street and nearby lots
Museum Shop　❢❢: Cafe Troia (lunch) 11-4 Tu-S; (dinner) 5:30-11 W-S; Brunch Sa, Su
Group Tours: ex 232　**Drop-In Tours:** 1:00 We, (1:30 S during SEP & OCT)
Historic Building 1904 building modeled after Ital. Ren. & Baroque palace designs
Permanent Collection: AN/EGT; AN/GRK; AN/R; MED; DEC/ART 19; OM: ptgs; EU: ptgs & sculp; DEC/ART

The Walters, considered one of America's most distinguished art museums, features a broad-ranging collection that spans more than 5,000 years of artistic achievement from Ancient Egypt to Art Nouveau. Remarkable collections of ancient, medieval, Islamic & Byzantine art, 19th century paintings and sculpture, and Old Master paintings are housed within the walls of the magnificently restored original building and in a large modern wing as well. PLEASE NOTE: 1. For the time being there will be a reduction in the Museum's hours of operation. Please call for updates. 2. For restaurant reservations and information call 410-752-2887. 3. As of May, 1998, the Museum's wing, built in 1974, will be closed until the year 2000 for renovation and repair. **NOT TO BE MISSED:** Hackerman House, a restored mansion adjacent to the main museum building, filled with oriental decorative arts treasures.

ON EXHIBIT 2000
ONGOING AT HACKERMAN HOUSE　JAPANESE CLOISONNÉ ENAMELS

ONGOING AT HACKERMAN HOUSE　A MEDLEY OF GERMAN DRAWINGS

10/26/1999 to 01/16/2000　VIVE LA FRANCE! FRENCH TREASURES FROM THE MIDDLE AGES TO MONET
From the intricate Migration metalwork of the early Middle Ages through to the revolutionary jewelry design of René Lalique at the turn of this century, and including popular masterpieces by Edouard Manet and Claude Monet, over 1500 years and every major trend of French art within this period is represented in the collections of the Walters Art Gallery..

03/05/2000 to 05/28/2000　GOLD OF THE NOMADS: SCYTHIAN TREASURES FROM ANCIENT UKRAINE
A major exhibition of ancient gold treasures of the Scythians, the fierce nomadic horsemen who roamed the European steppe from the fifth to the third centuries B.C., will come to the United States for the first time in over two decades. These proud marauders, who grew rich on trade with the Greeks, were patrons of some of the finest Greek goldsmiths, and commissioned lavish gold objects for adornment, ceremony and battle. Many of the objects included in this show were only recently unearthed and will be seen for the first time outside Ukraine. 🎧

10/01/2000 to 12/10/2000　A MILLION AND ONE NIGHTS: ORIENTALISM IN AMERICAN CULTURE 1870-1930 (working title)
At the turn of the century, Americans were intrigued and fascinated by their own fanciful images of the "Orient." Exotic images of the region, which in the popular mind encompassed Anatolia, Palestine, and North Africa, found their way not only into silent film and products of popular culture but also filled the dreamlike canvases of such 19th-century painters as John Singer Sargent and Jean-Léon Gérôme. Although knowledge of the area was growing from increased travel, trade and political interaction, paintings, photographs, decorative arts objects and ephemera of the time retained the romantic imagery conjured from a blending of Biblical tradition and Arabian Nights lore. The exhibition will explore the range of influences orientalism had on American culture, from the era of Frederic Church to that of Rudolph Valentino.

EASTON

Academy of the Arts
106 South Sts., Easton, MD 21601
📞: 410-822-ARTS　◉ WWW.ART-ACADEMY.ORG
Open: 10-4 Mo-Sa, till 9 We　**Closed:** Su, LEG/HOL! month of Aug
♿ Ⓟ Free with 2 hour limit during business hours; handicapped parking available in the rear of the Academy.
Museum Shop　Group Tours: 410-822-5997　**Historic Building** Housed in Old Schoolhouse
Permanent Collection: PTGS; SCULP; GR: 19-20; PHOT

MARYLAND

Academy of the Arts - continued

Housed in two 18th century buildings, one of which was an old school house, the Academy's permanent collection contains an important group of original 19th & 20th century prints. This museum serves the artistic needs of the community with a broad range of activities including concerts, exhibitions and educational workshops. **NOT TO BE MISSED:** "Slow Dancer" sculpture by Robert Cook, located in the Academy Courtyard; Works by James McNeil Whistler, Grant Wood, Bernard Buffet, Leonard Baskin, James Rosenquist, and others.

HAGERSTOWN

Washington County Museum of Fine Arts

91 Key St., City Park, Box 423, Hagerstown, MD 21741

☎: 301-739-5727 ◉ www.washcomuseum.org
Open: 10-5 Tu-Sa, 1-5 Su **Closed:** LEG/HOL!
Vol/Cont:
♿ ℗ Free and ample. **Museum Shop   Group Tours   Drop-In Tours**: 2 weeks notice   **Sculpture Garden**
Permanent Collection: AM: 19-20; REG; OM; 16-18; EU: ptgs 18-19; CH

In addition to the permanent collection of 19th and 20th century American art, including works donated by the founders of the museum, Mr. & Mrs. William H. Singer, Jr., the Museum has a fine collection of Oriental Art, African Art, American pressed glass, and European paintings, sculpture and decorative arts. Hudson River landscapes, Peale family paintings, and works by "The Eight", all from the permanent collection, are displayed throughout the year on an alternating basis with special temporary exhibitions. The museum is located in the northwest corner of the state just below the Pennsylvania border. **NOT TO BE MISSED:** "Sunset Hudson River" by Frederic Church

ON EXHIBIT 2000

11/07/1999 to 01/02/2000   GEORGE SAKKAL

Mead Art Museum

Affiliate Institution: Amherst College

Amherst, MA 01002-5000

☎: 413-542-2335 ◙ www.amherst.edu/~mead (SEE FOR UPDATED INFO ABOUT MUSEUM)

Open: SEPT-MAY: 10-4:30 Weekdays, 1-5 Weekends; Summer: 1-4 Tu-Su

Closed: LEG/HOL!; ACAD!; MEM/DAY; LAB/DAY

& ℗ **Museum Shop**

Drop-In Tours

Permanent Collection: AM: all media; EU: all media; DU: ptgs 17; PHOT; DEC/ART; AN/GRK: cer; FR: gr 19

Surrounded by the Pelham Hills in a picture perfect New England setting, the Mead Art Museum, at Amherst College, houses a rich collection of 14,000 art objects dating from antiquity to the present. PLEASE NOTE: Summer hours are 1-4 Tu-S. **NOT TO BE MISSED:** American paintings and watercolors including Eakins "The Cowboy" & Homer's "The Fisher Girl"

University Gallery, University of Massachusetts

Affiliate Institution: Fine Arts Center

University of Massachusetts, Amherst, MA 01003

☎: 413-545-3670

Open: 11-4:30 Tu-Fr; 2-5 Sa, Su **Closed:** JAN.

& **Museum Shop Group Tours Sculpture Garden**

Permanent Collection: AM: ptgs, drgs, phot 20

With a focus on the works of contemporary artists, this museum is best known as a showcase for the visual arts. It is but one of a five college complex of museums, making a trip to this area of New England a worthwhile venture for all art lovers. PLEASE NOTE: Due to construction of The Fine Arts Center's Atrium project, there will be no exhibitions after 5/5/98. The Gallery hopes to reopen in November with an exhibition celebrating the history of the permanent collection.

Addison Gallery of American Art

Affiliate Institution: Phillips Academy

Andover, MA 01810-4166

☎: 978-749-4015 ◙ www.andover.edu/addison

Open: 10-5 Tu-Sa, 1-5 Su **Closed:** Mo, LEG/HOL!; 12/24

& ℗ Limited on street parking **Museum Shop**

Group Tours Drop-In Tours: Upon request **Sculpture Garden**

Permanent Collection: AM: ptgs, sculp, phot, works on paper 17-20

Since its inception in 1930, the Addison Gallery has been devoted exclusively to American art. The original benefactor, Thomas Cochran, donated both the core collection and the neo-classic building designed by noted architect Charles Platt. With a mature collection of more than 12,000 works, featuring major holdings from nearly every period of American art history, a visit to this museum should be high on every art lover's list. **NOT TO BE MISSED:** Marble fountain in Gallery rotunda by Paul Manship; " The West Wind" by Winslow Homer; R. Crosby Kemper Sculpture Courtyard

MASSACHUSETTS

Addison Gallery of American Art - continued

ON EXHIBIT 2000

11/1999 to 01/2000   NATHAN LYONS: RIDING FIRST CLASS ON THE TITANIC
A 200 photograph exhibition . *Catalog Will Travel*

01/2000 to 03/2000   WENDY EWALD: A RETROSPECTIVE

04/2000 to 07/2000   ELIE NADELMAN: CLASSICAL FOLK *Catalog Will Travel*

04/2000 to 07/2000   PHILLIPS ACADEMY: A LEGACY OF DESIGN: 1778 TO THE PRESENT
A major exhibition focused on the history and meaning of the Philips Academy campus.

BOSTON

Boston Athenaeum

10 1/2 Beacon St., Boston, MA 02108
☎: 617-227-0270
Open: JUNE-AUG: 9-5:30 Mo-Fr; SEPT-MAY: 9-5:30 Mo-Fr, 9-4 Sa   **Closed:** LEG/HOL!
  ⚹   **Museum Shop   Group Tours**: ex 221   **Historic Building** National Historic Landmark Building
Permanent Collection: AM: ptgs, sculp, gr 19

The Athenaeum, one of the oldest independent libraries in America, features an art gallery established in 1827. Most of the Athenaeum building is closed to the public EXCEPT for the 1st & 2nd floors of the building (including the Gallery). In order to gain access to many of the most interesting parts of the building, including those items in the "do not miss" column, free tours are available on Tu & T at 3pm. Reservations must be made at least 24 hours in advance by calling The Circulation Desk, 617-227-0270 ex 221. **NOT TO BE MISSED:** George Washington's private library; 2 Gilbert Stuart portraits; Houdon's busts of Benjamin Franklin, George Washington, and Lafayette from the Montecello home of Thomas Jefferson.

Boston Museum of Fine Arts

465 Huntington Ave., Boston, MA 02115
☎: 617-267-9300   ◙   www.mfa.org
Open: 10-4:45 Mo & Tu; 10-9:45 We-Fr; 10-5:45 Sa, Su   **Closed:** THGV, 12/24, 12/25
ADM: Adult: $10.00   **Children:** Free 17 & under   **Students:** $8.00   **Seniors:** $8.00
  ⚹   ℗ $3.50 first hour, $1.50 every half hour following in garage on Museum Rd. across from West Wing entrance.
Museum Shop   ⅋ Cafe, Restaurant & Cafeteria
Group Tours: ex 368   **Drop-In Tours**: on the half hour from 10:30-2:30 M-F
Permanent Collection: AN/GRK; AN/R; AN/EGT; EU: om/ptgs; FR: Impr, post/Impr; AM: ptgs 18-20; OR: cer

A world class collection of fine art with masterpieces from every continent is yours to enjoy at this great Boston museum. Divided between two buildings the collection is housed both in the original (1918) Evans Wing, with its John Singer Sargeant mural decorations above the Rotunda, and the dramatic West Wing (1981), designed by I.M. Pei. PLEASE NOTE: 1. There is a "pay as you wish" policy from 4pm-9:45 PM on Wed. and a $2.00 admission fee on T & F evenings. 2. The West Wing ONLY is open after 5pm on T & F. **NOT TO BE MISSED:** Egyptian Pectoral believed to have decorated a royal sarcophagus of the Second Intermediate Period (1784 - 1570 B.C.), part of the museum's renowned permanent collection of Egyptian art.

ON EXHIBIT 2000

ONGOING   NUBIA: ANCIENT KINGDOMS OF AFRICA
500 objects including stone sculptures, gold jewelry, household articles, clothing and tools that form this comprehensive permanent collection of Nubian art, considered the finest of its kind in the world, is on view indefinitely. CAT

Boston Museum of Fine Arts - continued

ONGOING   BEYOND THE SCREEN: CHINESE FURNITURE OF THE 16TH AND 17TH CENTURIES
Exquisite Ming period Chinese furniture will be displayed within gallery space that has been converted especially for it into the rooms and courtyards of a Chinese home.

ONGOING   AMERICAN TRADITIONS: ART OF THE PEOPLE

ONGOING   THE ELIZABETH PARKE AND HARVEY S. FIRESTONE COLLECTION OF FRENCH SILVER

ONGOING   A NEW WAY OF LOOKING: THE EUROPEAN PAINTINGS GALLERY

09/29/1999 to 01/17/2000   THE PAINTINGS OF MARTIN JOHNSON HEADE
The art of Martin Johnson Heade (1819–1904) is perhaps the most varied and inventive of any nineteenth-century American painter. This definitive exhibition of some seventy of Heade's finest paintings, drawn from public and private collections across the nation. This show examines Heade as a painter of remarkable originality, the only major artist to devote equal attention to landscape, marine, and still-life subjects. Included in the exhibition are the greatest of Heade's evocative Newburyport marsh scenes, his powerful thunderstorms-at-sea subjects, scintillating small studies of flowers in vases, and an outstanding group of orchid-and-hummingbird compositions, a dramatic combination invented by Heade. In addition, the important group of sixteen hummingbird studies called "The Gems of Brazil" has been lent from the distinguished private collection of Richard Manoogian. The show concludes with a series of five of Heade's most sensuous renderings of the magnolia blossom, a subject he came to specialize in after moving to Florida in 1883. *Will Travel*

10/4/1999 to 01/23/2000   SECRET GARDENS: "PAISLEY" MOTIFS FROM KASHMIR TO EUROPE

10/15/1999 - 04/12/2000   EBRU: CONTEMPORARY MARBLING BY FERIDUN OZGOREN

11/08/1999 to 05/15/2000   SASHES AND MOUSTACHES: MEN'S FASHION IN INDIAN PORTRAITURE

11/14/1999 to 02/06/2000   PHARAOHS OF THE SUN: AKHENATEN, NEFERTITI, TUTANKHAMEN
Pharaohs of the Sun: Akhenaten, Nefertiti, Tutankhamen, captures the revolutionary epoch known as the Amarna Age (1353 to 1336 B.C.) when the Pharaoh Akhenaten assumed the throne of Egypt at its peak of imperial glory. One of the most important international presentations of Egyptian art and culture in recent decades. *Will Travel*

11/24/1999 to 04/30/2000   VIEW FROM ABOVE: THE PHOTOGRAPHS OF BRADFORD WASHBURN

02/16/2000 to 05/14/2000   MICHAEL MAZUR: A PRINT RETROSPECTIVE

03/01/2000 to 06/25/2000   CROWNING GLORIES: TWO CENTURIES OF TIARAS

03/19/2000 to 05/29/2000   EDWARD WESTON AND MODERNISM
A chronological survey of the key themes of this American photographer's landmark career. Included are early constructivist-inspired portraits, views of the Armco Steel Plant in Middletown, Ohio, and examples of several of his best-known images-close-up depictions of peppers, nudes and ordinary objects. Also included are selections from his abstract studies of trees, dunes, and rocks. *Catalog Will Travel*

03/29/2000 to 07/23/2000   SAMPLERS

05/20/2000 to 10/29/2000   DUTCH WORKS ON PAPER: 17TH AND 18TH CENTURIES

07/02/2000 to 09/24/2000   VAN GOGH PORTRAITS
The Detroit Institute, The Boston Museum of Fine Arts, and the Philadelphia Museum have five major portraits. These will be joined by pivotal works from each part of his life. His intense portraits of friends in Paris as well as his success in capturing of his mostly poor and unnamed subjects earlier.. *Catalog Will Travel*

07/25/2000 to 11/05/2000   VAN GOGH TO MONDRIAN: DUTCH WORKS ON PAPER

11/05/2000 to 02/24/2001   FROM RENAISSANCE TO ROCK: A CELEBRATION OF GUITAR DESIGN

12/06/2000 to 03/24/2001   F. HOLLAND DAY

MASSACHUSETTS

Boston Public Library

Copley Square, Boston, MA 02117-3194

☎: 617-536-5400

Open: OCT 1-MAY 22!: 5-9 Mo-Th, 9-5 Fr-Sa, 1-5 Su **Closed:** LEG/HOL! & 5/28

& **Museum Shop**

Group Tours: ex 216 **Drop-In Tours:** 2:30 M; 6:00 Tu, Th; 11am Fr, Sa, 2:00 S Oct-May

Historic Building Renaissance "Palace" designed in 1895 by Charles Follen McKim

Permanent Collection: AM: ptgs, sculp; FR: gr 18-19; BRIT: gr 18-19; OM: gr, drgs; AM: phot 19, gr 19-20; GER: gr; ARCH/DRGS

Architecturally a blend of the old and the new, the building that houses the Boston Public Library, designed by Charles Follon McKim, has a facade that includes noted sculptor Augustas Saint-Gauden's head of Minerva which serves as the keystone of the central arch. A wing designed by Philip Johnson was added in 1973. PLEASE NOTE: While restoration of the McKim Building is in progress, some points of interest may temporarily be inaccessible. **NOT TO BE MISSED:** 1500 lb. bronze entrance doors by Daniel Chester French; staircase mural painting series by Puvis de Chavannes; Dioramas of "Alice in Wonderland", "Arabian Nights" & "Dickens' London" by Louise Stimson.

ON EXHIBIT 2000

There are a multitude of changing exhibitions throughout the year in the many galleries of both buildings. Call for current information.

Boston University Art Gallery

855 Commonwealth Ave., Boston, MA 02215

☎: 617-353-3329

Open: mid SEPT to mid DEC & mid JAN to mid MAY: 10-5 Tu-Fr; 1-5 Sa, Su **Closed:** 12/25

& Ⓟ On-street metered parking; pay parking lot nearby **Museum Shop**

Several shows in addition to student exhibitions are mounted annually in this 35 year old university gallery which seeks to promote under-recognized sectors of the art world by including the works of a variety of ethnic artists, women artists, and those unschooled in the traditional academic system. Additional emphasis is placed on the promotion of 20th century figurative art.

Institute of Contemporary Art

955 Boylston St., Boston, MA 02115-3194

☎: 617-266-5152

Open: 12-5 We, Fr-Su, 12-9 Th **Closed:** Mo, Tu

Free Day: Th after 5 **ADM: Adult:** $6.00 **Children:** Free under 12 **Students:** $4.00 **Seniors:** $4.00

& Ⓟ pay lots nearby **Museum Shop**

Group Tours: 617-927-6607 **Drop-In Tours:** Th, 3.:30; 4:30 5:30 6:30 & Fr 12:30 **Historic Building**

Originally affiliated with the Modern Museum in New York, the ICA, founded in 1936, has the distinction of being the oldest non-collecting contemporary art institution in the country. By presenting contemporary art in a stimulating context, the ICA has, since its inception, been a leader in introducing such "unknown" artists as Braque, Kokoshka, Munch and others who have changed the course of art history.

ON EXHIBIT 2000

11/10/1999 to 01/02/2000 SITES UNSEEN : SHIMON ATTIE

Isabella Stewart Gardner Museum
280 The Fenway, Boston, MA 02115
📞: 617-566-1401 ◙ www.boston.com/gardner
Open: 11-5 Tu-Su **Closed:** Mo, LEG/HOL!
ADM: Adult: $10.00, weekdays: $11.00 weekends **Children:** Free under 18 **Students:** $5.00 **Seniors:** $7.00
♿ ⓟ Street parking plus garage two blocks away on Museum Road
Museum Shop ⏹ Cafe 11:30-4 Tu-Fr 11-4 Sa, Su
Group Tours: 617-278-5147 **Drop-In Tours**: 2:30 Fr Gallery tour **Historic Building Sculpture Garden**
Permanent Collection: PTGS; SCULP; DEC/ART; GR; OM ◠

Located in the former home of Isabella Stewart Gardner, the collection reflects her zest for amassing this most exceptional and varied personal art treasure trove. PLEASE NOTE: 1. The admission fee of $5.00 for college students with current I.D. is $3.00 on Wed.; 2.Children under 18 admitted free of charge; 3. The galleries begin closing at 4:45pm. **NOT TO BE MISSED:** Rembrandt's "Self Portrait"; Italian Renaissance works of art

ON EXHIBIT 2000

10/22/1999 to 01/30/2000 THREADS OF DISSENT
Six works by contemporary artists will be related to tapestries from the collection, These will be installed to illuminate the social, aesthetic and political values of the living artists.

02/18/2000 to 04/30/2000 THE LIVING ROOM
Mingwei Lee was born in Taiwan and spent 8 summers in a Buddhist monastery. Still a practicing Zen Buddhist he uses minimal props to create situations where an exchange of objects, money, ideas takes place between artist and viewer.

06/16/2000 to 08/27/2000 A GARDENER'S DIARY
Joan Bankemper has installed a number of garden projects in New York and Texas. Here she includes gouache drawings and ceramic works inspired by plants in the Museum's courtyard and greenhouses.

09/22/2000 to 01/07/2001 REMBRANDT CREATES REMBRANDT: AMBITION AND VISION IN LEIDEN, 1629-1631
Ten paintings will illuminate Rembrandt's evolving etching and painting technique.

Museum of the National Center of Afro-American Artists
300 Walnut Ave., Boston, MA 02119
📞: 617-442-8614
Open: 1-5 Tu-Su
ADM: Adult: $4.00 **Children:** Free under 5 **Students:** $3.00 **Seniors:** $3.00
Museum Shop Group Tours Historic Building 19th C
Permanent Collection: AF/AM: ptgs; sculp; GR

Art by African-American artists is highlighted along with art from the African continent itself.

BROCKTON

Fuller Museum of Art
455 Oak St., Brockton, MA 02301-1399
📞: 508-588-6000 ◙ www.art-online.com/fuller.htm
Open: Noon-5 Tu-Su **Closed:** 1/1, 7/4, LAB/DAY, THGV, 12/25
ADM: Adult: $3.00 **Children:** Free under 18 **Seniors:** $2.00
♿ ⓟ Free **Museum Shop** ⏹ Cafe 11:30 -2 Tu-F **Group Tours**: ex 125 **Drop-In Tours Sculpture Garden**
Permanent Collection: AM: 19-20; CONT: reg

A park-like setting surrounded by the beauty of nature is the ideal site for this charming museum that features works by artists of New England with particular emphasis on contemporary arts and cultural diversity.

Fuller Museum of Art - continued

ON EXHIBIT 2000

01/28/2000 to 03/16/2000   PURE VISION: AMERICAN BEAD ARTISTS
From intimate necklace forms to large wall constructions, this exhibition of works by 28 artists demonstrates the broad range of individual creativity and artistic expression possible through beadwork, a medium that is enjoying a renaissance among contemporary American artists.

CAMBRIDGE

Arthur M. Sackler Museum
Affiliate Institution: Harvard University
485 Broadway, Cambridge, MA 02138
☎: 617-495-9400   ◉   www.artmuseums.harvard,edu
Open: 10-5 Mo-Sa, 1-5 Su   **Closed:** LEG/HOL!
Free Day: Wed and Sa 10-12   **ADM: Adult:** $5.00   **Children:** Free under 18   **Students:** $3.00   **Seniors:** $4.00
♿   ℗ $5.00 3-hour valet parking for the museums at Harvard Inn, 1201 Mass. Ave.
Museum Shop
Group Tours: 617-496-8576   **Drop-In Tours:** 2:00 Mo-Fr
Permanent Collection: AN/ISLAMIC; AN/OR; NAT/AM

Opened in 1985, the building and its superb collection of Ancient, Asian, and Islamic art were all the generous gift of the late Dr. Arthur M. Sackler, noted research physician, medical publisher, and art collector. **NOT TO BE MISSED:** World's finest collections of ancient Chinese jades; Korean ceramics; Japanese woodblock prints; Persian miniatures

ON EXHIBIT 2000

10/09/1999 to 01/02/2000   A GRAND LEGACY: ARTS OF THE OTTOMAN EMPIRE

10/09/1999 to 01/02/2000   LETTERS IN GOLD: OTTOMAN CALLIGRAPHY FROM THE SAKIP SABANJI COLLECTION, ISTANBUL

02/05/2000 to 04/30/2000   BEN SHAHN'S NEW YORK: THE PHOTOGRAPHY OF SOCIAL CONSCIENCE
Focusing on Shahn's 1930's photographs and his application of photography to drawings, paintings and mural projects which promoted social reform. *Catalog Will Travel*

Busch-Reisinger Museum
Affiliate Institution: Harvard University
32 Quincy St., Cambridge, MA 02138
☎: 617-495-9400
Open: 10-5 Mo-Sa, 1-5 Su   **Closed:** LEG/HOL!
ADM: Adult: $5.00   **Children:** Free under 18   **Students:** $3.00   **Seniors:** $4.00
♿   ℗ $5.00 3-hour valet parking for the museums at Harvard Inn, 1201 Mass. Ave.   **Museum Shop**
Group Tours   Drop-In Tours: 1:00 Mo-Fr
Permanent Collection: GER: ptgs, sculp 20; GR; PTGS; DEC/ART; CER 18; MED/SCULP; REN/SCULP

Founded in 1901 with a collection of plaster casts of Germanic sculpture and architectural monuments, the Busch-Reisinger later acquired a group of modern "degenerate" artworks purged by the Nazi's from major German museums. All of this has been enriched over the years with gifts from artists and designers associated with the famous Bauhaus School, including the archives of artist Lyonel Feininger, and architect Walter Gropius. **NOT TO BE MISSED:** Outstanding collection of German Expressionist Art

Fogg Art Museum
Affiliate Institution: Harvard University
32 Quincy St., Cambridge, MA 02138
℡: 617-495-9400
Open: 10-5 Mo-Sa, 1-5 Su **Closed:** LEG/HOL!
ADM: Adult: $5.00 **Children:** Free under 18 **Students:** $3.00 **Seniors:** $4.00.
 ♿ ℗ $5.00 3 hour valet parking for the museums at Harvard Inn, 1201 Mass. Ave. **Museum Shop**
Group Tours: 617-496-8576 **Drop-In Tours:** 11:00 Mo-Fr
Permanent Collection: EU: ptgs, sculp, dec/art; AM: ptgs, sculp, dec/art; GR; PHOT, DRGS

The Fogg, the largest university museum in America, with one of the world's greatest collections, contains both European and American masterpieces from the Middle Ages to the present. Access to the galleries is off of a two story recreation of a 16th century Italian Renaissance courtyard. **NOT TO BE MISSED:** The Maurice Wertheim Collection containing many of the finest Impressionist and Post-Impressionist paintings, sculptures and drawings in the world.

ON EXHIBIT 2000
ONGOING   INVESTIGATING THE RENAISSANCE
A reinstallation of 3 galleries of one of the most important collections of early Italian Renaissance paintings in North America.

ONGOING   FRANCE AND THE PORTRAIT, 1799-1870
Changing conventions in and practices of portraiture in France between the rise of Napoleon and the fall of the Second Empire will be examined in the individual images on view from the permanent collection.

ONGOING   CIRCA 1874: THE EMERGENCE OF IMPRESSIONISM
Works by Bazille, Boudin, Johgkind, Monet, Degas and Renoir selected from the Museum's collection reveal the variety of styles existing under the single "new painting" label of Impressionism.

ONGOING   THE PERSISTENCE OF MEMORY: CONTINUITY AND CHANGE IN AMERICAN CULTURES
From pre-contact Native American to African to Euro-American, the 60 works of art on exhibit reflect the personal immigrant histories and cultures of each of the artists who created them.

ONGOING   SUBLIMATIONS: ART AND SENSUALITY IN THE NINETEENTH CENTURY
19th century artworks chosen to convey the sensual will be seen in an exhibition that demonstrates how these often erotic images impacted on the social, personal and religious lives of the times.

ONGOING   THE ART OF IDENTITY: AFRICAN SCULPTURE FROM THE TEAL COLLECTION
A diverse group of sub-Saharan African sculptures, collected over a 35 year period, is featured in this exhibition.

MIT-List Visual Arts Center
20 Ames St., Wiesner Bldg., Cambridge, MA 02142
℡: 617-253-4680 ■ web.mit.edu/lvac/www
Open: 12-6 Tu-Th, Sa, Su; till 8 Fr **Closed:** Mo, LEG/HOL
Sugg/Cont: **ADM: Adult:** $5.00
♿ ℗ Corner of Main & Ames Sts.
Museum Shop 🍴: Nearby restaurants
Group Tours: 617-253-4400 **Historic Building** 1985 I.M. Pei building **Sculpture Garden**
Permanent Collection: SCULP; PTGS; PHOT; DRGS; WORKS ON PAPER

Approximately 10 temporary exhibitions of contemporary art are mounted annually in MIT's List Visual Arts Center .with an interior mural by Kenneth Noland and seating by Scott Burton. Artists featured have included Jessica Brawson, Alfredo Jaar, Lewis de Soto and Kiki Smith. **NOT TO BE MISSED:** Alexander Calder, "The Big Sail" (1965), MIT's first commissioned public outdoor sculpture.

MASSACHUSETTS

McMullen Museum of Art Boston College
Affiliate Institution: Boston College
Devlin Hall, 140 Commonwealth Ave., Chestnut Hill, MA 02167-3809
☎: 617-552-8587 or 8100   ◙ www.bc.edu:80/bc_org/avp/cas/artmuseum/
Open: FEB-MAY -Fr; 12-5 Sa, Su JUNE-AUG: 11-3 Mo-Fr   **Closed:** LEG/HOL!
ᕲ ℗ 1 hour parking on Commonwealth Ave.; in lower campus garage on weekends & as available on weekdays (call 617-552-8587 for availability)   **Museum Shop**   ☖: On campus   **Group Tours   Historic Building**
Permanent Collection: IT: ptgs 16 & 17; AM: ptgs; JAP: gr; MED & BAROQUE TAPESTRIES 15-17

Devlin Hall, the Neo-Gothic building that houses the museum, consists of two galleries featuring a display of permanent collection works on one floor, and special exhibitions on the other. **NOT TO BE MISSED:** "Madonna with Christ Child & John the Baptist" By Ghirlandaio, 1503-1577)

ON EXHIBIT 2000
02/2000 to 05/2000 FRAGMENTED DEVOTIONS: MEDIEVAL OBJECTS FROM THE SCHNUTGEN MUSEUM IN COLOGNE
The primary goal of the exhibition will be in three sections, modes of collecting, displaying and interpreting fragments of medieval art, and to invite viewers to reflect on the use and abuse of Christian imagery from the medieval period to the present The works are from the collection of Alexander Schnutgen (1843-1918) a Catholic priest and collector. Most of these objects have never been shown before nor published since the 19thC catalog. A series of rooms will be reconfigured to recreate the setting in which they were viewed . *Only Venue Catalog*

Concord Art Association
37 Lexington Rd., Concord, MA 01742
☎: 978-369-2578
Open: 10-4:30 Tu-Sa   **Closed:** LEG/HOL!
ᕲ ℗ Free street parking   **Museum Shop   Group Tours**
Historic Building Housed in building dated 1720   **Sculpture Garden**
Permanent Collection: AM: ptgs, sculp, gr, dec/art

Historic fine art is appropriately featured within the walls of this historic (1720) building. The beautiful gardens are perfect for a bag lunch picnic during the warm weather months. **NOT TO BE MISSED:** Ask to see the secret room within the building which was formerly part of the underground railway.

ON EXHIBIT 2000
Rotating exhibits of fine art and crafts are mounted on a monthly basis.

Cahoon Museum of American Art
4676 Falmouth Rd., Cotuit, MA 02635
☎: 508-428-7581   ◙ www.cahoonmuseum.org
Open: 10-4 Tu-Sa   **Closed:** Su, Mo, LEG/HOL!; Also closed FEB.
Vol/Cont:
ᕲ ℗ Free   **Museum Shop   Group Tours   Drop-In Tours**: Gallery talks 11:00 Fr
Historic Building 1775 Former Cape Cod Colonial Tavern
Permanent Collection: AM: ptgs 19-20; CONT/PRIM

Cahoon Museum of American Art - continued
Named in honor of the contemporary primitive painters, R & M Cahoon, their work is shown with works by prominent American Luminists and Impressionists. The Museum is approximately 9 miles west of Hyannis. **NOT TO BE MISSED:** Gallery of marine paintings

ON EXHIBIT 2000
The Cahoon Museum's permanent collection of American paintings is on display between special exhibitions.

03/03/2000 to 04/29/2000   **WOMEN CREATING: INVITATIONAL AND JURIED EXHIBITION**

05/05/2000 to 05/27/2000   **PASTEL PAINTERS SOCIETY OF CAPE COD**

06/02/2000 to 07/08/2000   **SAILOR'S VALENTINES: SANDI BLANDA**

07/14/2000 to 08/19/2000   **MARJORIE KEARY: PAINTINGS**

08/25/2000 to 09/23/2000   **TWENTY AT TRURO**

11/17/2000 to 12/30/2000   **THE WORLD OF JAYNE SHELLEY- PIERCE**

DENNIS

Cape Museum of Fine Arts
Rte. 6A, Dennis, MA 02638-5034
☎: 508-385-4477
Open: 10-5 Tu-Sa, 1-5 Su, till 7:30 Th, open Mo May-Sep   **Closed:** LEG/HOL!
ADM: Adult: $5.00   **Children:** Free 16 and under
♿ ⓟ Free and ample parking   **Museum Shop**   **Group Tours:** 508-385-4477 x16   **Drop-In Tours:** !
Permanent Collection: REG

Art by outstanding Cape Cod artists, from 1900 to the present, is the focus of this rapidly growing permanent collection which is housed in the restored former summer home of the family of Davenport West, one of the original benefactors of this institution. New galleries provide wonderful new space for permanent collections and special exhibitions. On the grounds of the Cape Playhouse and Cape Cinema.

DUXBURY

Art Complex Museum
189 Alden St. Box 2814, Duxbury, MA 02331
☎: 781-934-6634
Open: 1-4 We-Su   **Closed:** Mo, Tu, LEG/HOL!
♿ ⓟ Free   **Museum Shop**   **Group Tours**
Sculpture Garden
Permanent Collection: OR: ptgs; EU: ptgs; AM: ptgs; gr

In a magnificent sylvan setting that compliments the naturalistic wooden structure of the building, the Art Complex houses a remarkable core collection of works on paper that includes Rembrandt's "The Descent from the Cross by Torchlight". An authentic Japanese Tea House, complete with tea presentations in the summer months, is another unique feature of this fine institution. The museum is located on the eastern coast of Massachusetts just above Cape Cod. **NOT TO BE MISSED:** Shaker furniture; Tiffany stained glass window

MASSACHUSETTS

Art Complex Museum - continued

ON EXHIBIT 2000

05/14/2000 to 09/10/2000   THE OLD BALLGAME
Historically and significantly works relating to Baseball

05/14/2000 to 09/10/2000   MILLENNIUM MASTERPIECES
A historical overview from the collection of works from 1000 - 2000 from the collection. Highlighted will be major artistic accomplishments and universal themes

09/24/2000 to 01/14/2001   SHAKER CHAIRS
An opportunity for visitors to view the collection of Shaker chairs and Contemporary Studio Furniture. Unique seats installed on Museum grounds will show outdoor furniture.

FITCHBURG

Fitchburg Art Museum
185 Elm St., Fitchburg, MA 01420
☎: 978-345-4207
Open: 11-4:00 Tu-Sa, 1-4 Su   **Closed:** LEG/HOL!
ADM: Adult: $3.00   **Children:** Free under 18   **Seniors:** $2.00
 ⅋ ℗ Free on-site parking   **Museum Shop**
Group Tours   Sculpture Garden
Permanent Collection: AM: ptgs 18-20 EU: ptgs 18-20; PRTS & DRGS: 15-20; PHOT 20; AN/GRK; AN/R; AS; ANT; ILLUSTRATED BOOKS & MANUSCRIPTS 14-20

Eleanor Norcross, a Fitchburg artist who lived and painted in Paris for 40 years, became impressed with the number and quality of small museums that she visited in the rural areas of northern France. This led to the bequest of her collection and personal papers, in 1925, to her native city of Fitchburg, and marked the beginning of what is now a 40,000 square foot block long museum complex. The museum is located in north central Massachusetts near the New Hampshire border. **NOT TO BE MISSED:** "Sarah Clayton" by Joseph Wright of Derby, 1770

FRAMINGHAM

Danforth Museum of Art
123 Union Ave., Framingham, MA 01702
☎: 508-620-0050   ◙   www.e-guide.com/sites/Danforth
Open: Noon-5 We-Su   **Closed:** LEG/HOL! AUG!
ADM: Adult: $3.00   **Children:** Free 12 & under   **Students:** $2.00   **Seniors:** $2.00
 ⅋ ℗ Free   **Museum Shop   Group Tours   Drop-In Tours:** 1:00 We (Sep-May)
Permanent Collection: PTGS; SCULP; DRGS; PHOT; GR

The Danforth, a museum that prides itself on being known as a community museum with a national reputation, offers 19th & 20th century American and European art as the main feature of its permanent collection. **NOT TO BE MISSED:** 19th & 20th c American works with a special focus on the works of New England artists

ON EXHIBIT 2000

ONGOING   HARVEY WANG: PHOTOGRAPHS OF OLDER AMERICANS AT WORK
Taken by documentary photographer Wang on his many trips crisscrossing the U.S. since 1979, the photographs on view feature images of the hands and faces of older persons whose skills and occupations recall the nation's past and dramatize the dignity of the work ethic.

GLOUCESTER

Cape Ann Historical Association

27 Pleasant St., Gloucester, MA 01930
☏: 978 283-0455
Open: 10-5 Tu-Sa **Closed:** Su, Mo, LEG/HOL!; FEB
Free Day: Month of January **ADM: Adult:** $4.00 **Children:** Free under 6 **Students:** $2.50 **Seniors:** $3.50
♿ ⓟ In the lot adjacent to the museum and in the metered public lot across Pleasant St. from the museum.
Museum Shop   Group Tours
Historic Building 1804 Federal period home of Captain Elias Davis is part of museum
Permanent Collection: FITZ HUGH LANE: ptgs; AM: ptgs, sculp, DEC/ART 19-20; MARITIME COLL

Within the walls of this most charming New England treasure of a museum is the largest collection of paintings (39), drawings (100), and lithographs by the great American artist, Fitz Hugh Lane. A walking tour of the town takes the visitor past many charming small art studios & galleries that have a wonderful view of the harbor as does the 1849 Fitz Hugh Lane House itself. Be sure to see the famous Fisherman's Monument overlooking Gloucester Harbor. **NOT TO BE MISSED:** The watercolor by Fitz Hugh Lane which is his earliest known work

ON EXHIBIT 2000

PLEASE NOTE: There are several exhibitions a year usually built around a theme that pertains in some way to the locale and its history!

LINCOLN

DeCordova Museum and Sculpture Park

Sandy Pond Rd., Lincoln, MA 01773-2600
☏: 781-259-8355 ◉ www.decordova.org
Open: 11-5 Tu-Su **Closed:** LEG/HOL!
ADM: Adult: $6.00 **Children:** Free 5 & under **Students:** $4.00 **Seniors:** $4.00
♿ ⓟ Free
Museum Shop 🍴: Terrace Cafe open 11-4 W-Sa
Group Tours   Drop-In Tours: 1:00 We & 2:00 S
Sculpture Garden
Permanent Collection: AM: ptgs, sculp, gr, phot 20; REG

In addition to its significant collection of modern and contemporary art, the DeCordova features the only permanent sculpture park of its kind in New England. While there is an admission charge for the museum, the sculpture park is always free and open to the public from 8am to 10pm daily. The 35 acre park features nearly 40 site-specific sculptures. PLEASE NOTE: The museum IS OPEN on SELECTED Monday holidays! **NOT TO BE MISSED:** Annual open air arts festival first Sunday in June; summer jazz concert series from 7/4 - Labor Day

ON EXHIBIT 2000

06/19/1999 to 6/14/2000   ROBERT ARNESON: BRONZE SELF PORTRAITS AND DRAWINGS
"Provocative, confrontational, and witty," are just a few of the words used to describe the artist Arneson. The exhibition presents a selection of bronzes and works on paper that capture Arneson's satirical and often ironic approach to art.

09/18/1999 to 01/02/2000   SCOTT PRIOR RETROSPECTIVE

01/2000 to 03/2000   NEW WORK/NEW ENGLAND

MASSACHUSETTS

LOWELL

Whistler House Museum of Art and Parker Gallery
243 Worthen St., Lowell, MA 01852-1822
☎: 978-452-7641 ◉ www.valley.uml.edu/lowell/historic/museums/whistler.html
Open: May-Oct 11-4 We-Sa, 1-4 Su; Nov, Dec, Mar, Apr 11-4 We-Sa **Closed:** Mo, Tu, LEG/HOL! JAN. & FEB.
ADM: Adult: $3.00 **Children:** Free under 5 **Students:** $2.00 **Seniors:** $2.00
& ℗ On street; commercial lots nearby
Museum Shop
Group Tours: 978-452-7641 **Drop-In Tours:** Upon request
Historic Building   Sculpture Garden
Permanent Collection: AM: ptgs

Works by prominent New England artists are the highlight of this collection housed in the 1823 former home of the artist. **NOT TO BE MISSED:** Collection of prints by James A.M. Whistler

ON EXHIBIT 2000
Rotating exhibitions of contemporary regional art presented on a bi-monthly basis.

03/01/2000 to 04/15/2000   WOMEN ARTISTS: A COLLABORATIVE PROGRAM WITH THE LOWELL NATIONAL HISTORIC PARK

MEDFORD

Tufts University Art Gallery
Affiliate Institution: Tufts University
Aidekman Arts Center, Medford, MA 02115
☎: 617-627-3518
Open: SEPT to mid DEC & mid JAN to MAY: 12-8 We-Sa, 12-5 Su **Closed:** LEG/HOL!; ACAD!; SUMMER
& **Museum Shop**
Group Tours   Sculpture Garden
Permanent Collection: PTGS, GR, DRGS, 19-20; PHOT 20; AN/R; AN/GRK; P/COL

Located just outside of Boston, most of the Tufts University Art Museum exhibitions feature works by undergraduate students and MFA candidates.

NORTH ADAMS

Massachusetts Museum of Contemporary Art
87 Marshall St., North Adams, MA 01247
☎: 413-664-4481 ◉ www.massmoca.org
Open: 6/1-10/31 10-5 daily; till 8 Sa 11/1-5/31 10-4 Tu-Su) **Closed:** 1/1, THGV, 12/25
ADM: Adult: $8.00 **Children:** Free under 6, $5.00
& ℗ **Museum Shop** ⫪: Mass Moca Café
Group Tours: 413-664-4481
Historic Building Museum is located in a late 19th-century industrial site.
Permanent Collection: The Museum has two permanent works of sound art in its collection; the majority of work shown here will be long-term loans of oversized or sited works from major museum collections.

Massachusetts Museum of Contemporary Art - continued

Opened in late spring 1999, the much anticipated Massachusetts Museum of Contemporary Art (MASS MoCA), created from a 27-building historic mill complex on 13 acres in the Berkshires of Western Massachusetts, promises to be an exciting multi-disciplinary center for visual and performing arts. International in scope, MASS MoCA will offer exhibitions of work on loan from the Solomon R. Guggenheim Museum in New York City and other major museum collections, as well as special exhibitions of contemporary art.

ONGOING   BILLBOARD

The first retrospective installation of artist-designed billboards of the last thirty years, coupled with five newly commissioned pieces by such artists as Sue Coe, Gary Simmons, and Leon Golub, appear on commercial billboard sites throughout Berkshire County.

ONGOING   TRISHA BROWN & TERRY WINTERS

Acclaimed choreographer and dancer Trisha Brown is also a visual artist; MASS MoCA presents an exhibition of her works, created in collaboration with artist-designer Terry Winters.

ONGOIN   GHOSTCATCHING

This motion-capture video installation by dancer Bill T. Jones and Riverbed Studios multiplies images of Jones's body into an ensemble of three-dimensional drawings.

NORTHAMPTON

Smith College Museum of Art

Elm St. at Bedford Terrace, Northampton, MA 01063

☎: 413-585-2760   ◙   www.smith.edu/artmuseum

Open: SEPT-JUNE: 9:30-4 Tu, Fr, Sa; 12-8 Th, Noon-4 We, Su; JUL & AUG: Noon-4 Tu-Su

Closed: Mo, 1/1, 7/4, THGV, 12/25

♿ Ⓟ Nearby street parking with campus parking available on evenings and weekends only; Handicapped parking behind Hillyer art building.   **Museum Shop**

Permanent Collection: AM: ptgs, sculp, gr, drgs, dec/art 17-20; EU: ptgs, gr, sculp, drgs, dec/art 17-20; PHOT; DU:17; ANCIENT ART

With in-depth emphasis on American and French 19th & 20th century art, and literally thousands of superb artworks in its permanent collection, Smith College remains one of the most highly regarded college or university repositories for fine art in the nation. PLEASE NOTE: Print Room hours are 1-4 Tu-F & 1-5 T from Sep. to May - other hours by appointment only. **NOT TO BE MISSED:** "Mrs. Edith Mahon" by Thomas Eakins; "Walking Man" by Rodin

---

Words & Pictures Museum

140 Main St., Northampton, MA 01060

☎: 413-586-8545   ◙   wordsandpictures.org

Permanent Collection: Original contemporary sequential/comic book art & fantasy illustration, 1970's - present

The Words & Pictures Museum on Northampton's Main Street closed it's doors to the public on July 16, 1999. "After long consideration, discussion and calculation, the key members of staff and myself have decided to close the building and invest our funds into a Virtual Museum," Kevin B. Eastman, Museum Trustee, said recently. "By creating an entirely Virtual Museum, an enormous expansion of our current web site, we can reach millions and millions of interested fans globally. Fans that could never make the trip to Northampton," he continued. The Virtual Museum will continue to fulfill the mission of the Museum and offer exhibits, archives and programming for a global audience.

MASSACHUSETTS

Berkshire Museum

39 South St., Pittsfield, MA 01201

☎: 413-443-7171   ▣ www.berkshiremuseum.org
Open: 10-5 Tu-Sa, 1-5 Su; Open 10-5 Mo JUL & AUG   **Closed:** Mo LEG/HOL!
Free Day: 3-5 We and on one's birthday   **ADM: Adult:** $6.00   **Children:** $4.00 (4-18), Free under 3   **Seniors:** $5.00
Ⅾ Ⓟ Metered street parking; inexpensive rates at the nearby Crowne Plaza Hotel and municipal parking garage.
Museum Shop   ⅱ: Snacks at the Vendo-Mat Café
Group Tours: 413-443-7171 x11   **Drop-In Tours:** 11 am Sa in Jun, Jul, Aug
Historic Building 1903 Italian Renaissance Revival
Permanent Collection: AM: 19-20; EU: 15-19; AN/GRK; AN/R; DEC/ART; PHOT; Natural Science; Aquarium

Three Museums in one - art, natural science and history - set the stage for a varied and exciting visit to this complex in the heart of the beautiful Berkshires. In addition to its rich holdings of American art of the 19th and 20th-centuries, the Museum has an interactive aquarium and exciting changing exhibitions. **NOT TO BE MISSED:** "Hudson River School Collection" Special family exhibitions February thru May

Provincetown Art Association and Museum

460 Commercial St., Provincetown, MA 02657

☎: 508-487-1750   ▣ www.CapeCodAccess.com/Gallery/PAAM.html
Open: SUMMER: 12-5 & 8-10 daily; SPRING/FALL: 12-5 Fr, Sa, Su; WINTER: 12-4 Sa, Su
Closed: Open most holidays!; open weekends only Nov-Apr
Sugg/Cont: **ADM: Adult:** $3.00   **Students:** $1.00   **Seniors:** $1.00
Ⅾ   **Museum Shop**
Group Tours: by appt   **Sculpture Garden**
Permanent Collection: PTGS; SCULP; GR; DEC/ART; REG

Works by regional artists is an important focus of the collection of this museum. **NOT TO BE MISSED:** Inexpensive works of art by young artists that are for sale in the galleries

Mount Holyoke College Art Museum

South Hadley, MA 01075-1499

☎: 413-538-2245   ▣ www.mtholyoke.edu/offices/artmuseum
Open: 11-5 Tu-Fr, 1-5 Sa-Su   **Closed:** LEG/HOL!, ACAD!
Ⅾ Ⓟ Free   **Museum Shop**
Group Tours: 413-538-2085   **Drop-In Tours:** by appointment at least 3 weeks prior
Sculpture Garden
Permanent Collection: AS; P/COL; AN/EGT; IT: med/sculp; EU: ptgs; AN/GRK; AM: ptgs, dec/art, gr, phot; EU: ptgs, dec/art, gr, phot

A stop at this leading college art museum is a must for any art lover traveling in this area. Founded in 1876, it is one of the oldest college museums in the country. **NOT TO BE MISSED:** Albert Bierstadt's "Hetch Hetchy Canyon"; A Pinnacle from Duccio's "Maesta" Altarpiece; Head of Faustina the Elder, 2nd century AD, Roman

George Walter Vincent Smith Art Museum

At the Quadrangle, Corner State & Chestnut Sts., Springfield, MA 01103

☎: 413-263-6800   ◙   www.quadrangle.org
Open: 12-4 We-Su   **Closed:** Mo, Tu, LEG/HOL
ADM: Adult: $4.00   **Children:** $1.00 (6-18)   **Students:** $4.00   **Seniors:** $4.00 Sen day We $2.00
& Ⓟ Free parking in Springfield Library & Museum lots on State St. & Edwards St.
Museum Shop ¶ year-round café
Group Tours: 413-263-6800 x472   **Drop-In Tours:** by reservation   **Historic Building** Built in 1896
Permanent Collection: ENTIRE COLLECTION OF 19th C AMERICAN ART OF GEORGE WALTER VINCENT SMITH; OR; DEC/ART 17-19; CH: jade; JAP: bronzes, ivories, armour, tsuba 17-19; DEC/ART: cer; AM: ptgs 19

With the largest collection of Chinese cloisonné in the western world, the G. W. V. Smith Art Museum, built in 1895 in the style of an Italian villa, is part of a four museum complex that also includes The Museum of the Fine Arts. The museum reflects its founder's special passion for collecting the arts of 17th to 19th century Japan and American art by his contemporaries. **NOT TO BE MISSED:** Early 19th century carved 9' high wooden Shinto wheel shrine

ON EXHIBIT 2000

10/06/1999 to 01/02/2000   TEMPLE AND VILLAGE: PATTERNS AND PRINTS OF INDIA
The rich regional diversity in hand printed, dyed and embroidered fabric. Evidence indicates that embroidery existed in India perhaps as early as 3000 b.c.

11/14/1999 to 01/09/2000   ON THE ROAD WITH THOMAS HART BENTON: IMAGES OF A CHANGING AMERICA
How drawing, one of Benton's greatest talents and travel, a passion combined to produce some of his most significant works. *Catalog Will Travel*

02/02/2000 to 04/30/2000   KATHMANDU
Created to complement the exhibition "The Mystical Arts of Tibet" this recreation of a Nepal-Tibetan temple will serve as a backdrop for performances, demonstrations and other activities.

Museum of Fine Arts

At the Quadrangle, Corner of State & Chestnut Sts., Springfield, MA 01103

☎: 413-263-6800   ◙   www.quadrangle.org
Open: We-Su 12-4 (Tu-Su July & Aug)   **Closed:** Mo, Tu, LEG/HOL
ADM: Adult: $4.00 single adm provides entry to all four museums   **Children:** $1.00 (6-18)   **Students:** $4.00   **Seniors:** $4.00
& Ⓟ Free in Springfield Library & Museum lots on State St. and Edwards St.
Museum Shop ¶
Group Tours: ex 472   **Drop-In Tours:** by reservation
Permanent Collection: AM: 19-20; FR: 19-20; IT Baroque; Dutch + Flemish

Part of a four museum complex located on The Quadrangle in Springfield, the Museum of Fine Arts, built in the 1930's Art Deco Style, offers an overview of European and American art. Single admission fee provides entry to all four museums on the Quadrangle. **NOT TO BE MISSED:** "The Historical Monument of the American Republic, 1867 & 1888 by Erastus S. Field, a monumental painting in the court of the museum

ON EXHIBIT 2000

11/14/1999 to 01/09/2000   ON THE ROAD WITH THOMAS HART BENTON: IMAGES OF A CHANGING AMERICA
How drawing, one of Benton's greatest talents and travel, a passion combined to produce some of his most significant works. *Catalog Will Travel*

02/02/2000 to 04/30/2000   MANDALA SAND PAINTINGS
A display created over a series of days by Buddhist monks. It will then be ritually destroyed on the last day of the exhibition.

Museum of Fine Arts - continued
02/03/2000 to 04/30/2000   THE MYSTICAL ARTS OF TIBET
Sacred objects from the personal collection of the Dalai Lama as well as ancient objects from the monastery, contemporary objects made by Tibetan refugees, and 21 photos from the Tibet Image Bank, London.

06/07/2000 to 08/13/2000   DREAMINGS: ABORIGINAL ART OF THE WESTERN DESERT FROM THE DONALD KAHN COLLECTION
An exhibition which introduces viewers to an art that is based on ritual and a concept of time in which past, present and future simultaneously exist.

06/28/2000 to 08/20/2000   BILL ROHAN: MINDSCAPES
Rohan uses the egg as a metaphor in his paintings, sculpture and collages, he explores the human experience.

09/20/2000 to 12/31/2000   RETROSPECTIVE 2000: DOUG AND DAVE BREGA
Work of twin brothers includes Doug Brega's realistic renderings of people and places in New England, and Dave Brega's trompe L'oiel paintings

---

STOCKBRIDGE

Chesterwood
Off Rte. 183, Glendale Section, Stockbridge, MA 01262-0827
📞: 413-298-3579
Open: 10-5 Daily (MAY 1-OCT 31)   **Closed:** None during open season
ADM: **Adult:** $7.50   **Children:** $4.00 (13-18), $2.00 (6-12)   **Students:** $2.50 (10 or more)
& Ⓟ Ample   **Museum Shop**
Group Tours: ex 11   **Drop-In Tours**: hourly throughout the day
Historic Building Two Buildings (1898 studio & 1901 house) of Daniel Chester French   **Sculpture Garden**
Permanent Collection: SCULP; PTGS; WORKS OF DANIEL CHESTER FRENCH; PHOT

Located on 120 wooded acres is the original studio Colonial Revival house and garden of Daniel Chester French, leading sculptor of the American Renaissance. Working models for the Lincoln Memorial and the Minute Man, his most famous works, are on view along with many other of his sculptures and preliminary models. PLEASE NOTE: There are reduced admission rates to see the grounds only, and a special family admission rate of $16.50 for the museum buildings, grounds and tour. **NOT TO BE MISSED:** Original casts and models of the seated Abraham Lincoln for the Memorial.

Norman Rockwell Museum at Stockbridge
Stockbridge, MA 01262
📞: 413-298 4100 ◉ www.nrm.org
Open: MAY-OCT 10-5 daily ; Nov-Apr 10-4 Mo-Fr 10-5 Sa, Su & Hols   **Closed:** THGV, 12/25
ADM: **Adult:** $9.00 (fam 2 ad, 2 ch under 18 $20.00)   **Children:** $2.00 (Free under 5)   **Students:** $7.00   **Seniors:** $4.50 (We, Nov-Apr)
& Ⓟ Free   **Museum Shop**
Group Tours: ex 220   **Drop-In Tours**: tours daily on the hour
Historic Building Built by Edward Larabee Barnes-Museum is housed in 1859 Georgian House
Permanent Collection: Am; gr, ptgs, sculp19-20;Eu gr, ptgs, sculp 19-20 P/Col, Af,Or Nat/Am

Aside from an impressive collection of 20th C American and European Art, the Museum is home to the most comprehensive collection of works by William Glackens and others of his contemporaries known as "The Eight" or the Ashcan School. It also is home to the largest collection of CoBrA art in this country.

Norman Rockwell Museum at Stockbridge - continued
ON EXHIBIT 2000

09/18/1999 to 01/23/2000   EYE ON AMERICA: EDITORIAL ILLUSTRATIONS IN THE 1990'S
An exhibition documenting the editorial art which has appeared in major publications of our times. The broad range of styles includes Dellesert , Parker, Sorel, Arisman Jetter, etc.

11/13/1999 to 04/02/2000   BEFORE TV: AMERICAN CULTURE, ILLUSTRATION AND THE SATURDAY EVENING POST
A showcase of the importance of the Saturday Evening Post in our culture. Reaching one in ten households, it was the most popular and influential media outlet in this first half of this century. The power of illustrated images to communicate ideas, tell stories and sell products will be shown versus what TV brings into our homes today.

03/18/2000 to 08/27/2000   IN ROCKWELL WE TRUST
For a brief period illustrators were as popular as movie stars before being eclipsed by television and its stars.

04/15/2000 to 06/18/2000   24 FRAMES A SECOND – THE STORY OF ANIMATION
This lively and entertaining exhibition features cell, background drawings, character sketches, rough and finished animation drawings, movie posters, and the storyboards that demonstrate the way in which animated cartoons have been created in the past decades.

07/01/2000 to 10/29/2000   DISTANT SHORES: THE ODYSSEY OF ROCKWELL KENT
Kent was one of the 20th C artists whose remote areas inspired an art of spiritual beauty. His wilderness paintings of his sojourns in Maine, Alaska, Newfoundland, Terra Del Fuego and Greenland will come to life in the exhibit.

09/02/2000 to 01/28/2001   NORMAN ROCKWELL'S 322 SATURDAY EVENING POST COVERS
An archival exhibit showing his first at age 22 to his last in 1963. His covers were so popular that hundreds of thousands of magazines were added to the print run when his illustration appeared on the cover to handle increased demand. .

WALTHAM

Rose Art Museum
Affiliate Institution: Brandeis University
415 South St., Waltham, MA 02254-9110
☎: 781-736-3434   ◉ www.brandeis.edu/rose
Open: 12-5 Tu-Su 12-9 Th   **Closed:** Mo, LEG/HOL!
♿ Ⓟ Visitor parking on campus   **Museum Shop   Group Tours   Drop-In Tours**: by advance reservation
Permanent Collection: AM: ptgs, sculp 19-20; EU: ptgs, sculp 19-20; CONT; ptgs, drgs, sculp, phot. PLEASE NOTE: The permanent collection is not always on veiw!

The Rose Art Museum, founded in 1961, and located on the campus of Brandeis University, just outside of Boston, features one of the largest collections of contemporary art in New England. Selections from the permanent collection, and an exhibition of the works of Boston area artists are presented annually. PLEASE NOTE: Tours are given by advance reservation only.

ON EXHIBIT 2000

01/20/2000 to 03/19/2000   TWENTY FIVE YEARS OF GREATER BOSTON ART: THE LOIS FOSTER EXHIBITION OF BOSTON AREA ARTISTS

01/20/2000 to 03/19/2000   STEPHEN ANTONAKOS: TIME BOXES 2000, WITH RICHARD ARTSCHWAGER, DANIEL BURAN, SOL LEWITT, AND ROBERT RYMAN
Commissioned for the Museum's rotunda is this installation of a "room" by Antonakos, an artist known for his large-scale interior and exterior "neons" and "rooms".

03/30/2000 to 05/28/2000   JONATHAN LASKER: SELECTIVE IDENTITY: PAINTINGS FROM THE 1990'S

03/30/2000 to 05/28/2000   LASKER CURATES SELECTIONS FROM THE BRANDEIS UNIVERSITY ART COLLECTIONS

MASSACHUSETTS

Davis Museum and Cultural Center

Affiliate Institution: Wellesley College

106 Central St., Wellesley, MA 02181-8257

☎: 781-283-2051   ◙ www.wellesley.edu/DavisMuseum/davismenu.html

Open: 11-5 Tu & Fr-Sa, 11-8 We, Th, 1-5 Su;   **Closed:** 1/1, 12/25

& Ⓟ Free   **Museum Shop**   ᵢ: Cafe Collins open M-F (call 781-283-3379 for hours and info.)

Group Tours: 617-283-2081

Permanent Collection: AM: ptgs, sculp, drgs, phot; EU: ptgs, sculp, drgs, phot; AN; AF; MED; REN

Established over 100 years ago, the Davis Museum and Cultural Center, formerly the Wellesley College Museum, is located in a stunning 61,000 square foot state-of-the-art museum building. One of the first encyclopedic college art collections ever assembled in the United States, the museum is home to more than 5,000 works of art. PLEASE NOTE: The museum closes at 5pm on W & T during the month of Jan. and from 6/15 to 8/15). **NOT TO BE MISSED:** "A Jesuit Missionary in Chinese Costume", a chalk on paper work by Peter Paul Rubens (recent acquisition)

Sterling and Francine Clark Art Institute

225 South St., Williamstown, MA 01267

☎: 413-458-9545

Open: 10-5 Tu-Su; also Mo during JUL & AUG; open MEM/DAY, LAB/DAY, COLUMBUS DAY

Closed: 1/1, THGV, 12/25

& Ⓟ **Museum Shop** ᵢ

Group Tours: 413-458-2303 ex 324   **Drop-In Tours:** 3:00 Tu-Fr during Jul & Aug

Permanent Collection: IT: ptgs 14-18; FL: ptgs 14-18; DU: ptgs 14-18; OM: ptgs, gr, drgs; FR: Impr/ptgs; AM: ptgs 19

More than 30 paintings by Renoir and other French Impressionist masters as well as a collection of old master paintings and a significant group of American works account for the high reputation of this recently expanded, outstanding 40 year old institution. PLEASE NOTE: Recorded tours of the permanent collection are available for a small fee. **NOT TO BE MISSED:** Impr/ptgs; works by Homer, Sargent, Remington, Cassatt; Silver coll.; Ugolino Da Siena Altarpiece; Porcelain gallery

ON EXHIBIT 2000

06/10/2000 to 09/04/2000   A MILLION AND ONE NIGHTS: ORIENTALISM IN AMERICAN CULTURE 1870-1930

This exhibit is the first exploration of American orientalism in all of it's guises. It examines the fascination with exotic locales such as North Africa, the Middle East and India. Artists include Sargent, Chase, Weeks, LaFarge, Bridgeman, Gifford and Tiffany.

Williams College Museum of Art

Main St., Rte. #2, Williamstown, MA 01267

☎: 413-458-2429   ◙ www.williams.edu/wcma

Open: 10-5 Tu-Sa, 1-5 Su (open Mo on MEM/DAY, LAB/DAY, COLUMBUS DAY)   **Closed:** Mo, 1/1, THGV, 12/25

& Ⓟ Limited in front of and behind the museum, and behind the Chapel. A public lot is available at the foot of Spring St.

Museum Shop

Group Tours   **Drop-In Tours:** 2:00 We & Su Jul & Aug ONLY

Historic Building 1846 Brick Octagon by Thomas Tefft; 1983-86 additions by Chas. Moore

Permanent Collection: AM: cont & 18-19; ASIAN & OTHER NON-WESTERN CIVILIZATIONS; BRIT: ptgs 17-19; SP: ptgs 15-18; IT/REN: ptgs ; PHOT; GR/ARTS; AN/GRK; AN/R

Williams College Museum of Art - continued

Considered one of the finest college art museums in the U.S., the Museum's collection of 11,000 works that span the history of art, features particular strengths in the areas of contemporary & modern art, American art from the late 18th century to the present, and non-Western art. The original museum building of 1846, a two-story brick octagon with a neoclassic rotunda, was joined, in 1986, by a dramatic addition designed by noted architect Charles Moore. **NOT TO BE MISSED:** Works of Maurice and Charles Prendergast

ON EXHIBIT 2000

ONGOING   AN AMERICAN IDENTITY: 19TH-CENTURY AMERICAN ART FROM THE PERMANENT COLLECTION
Works by Eakins, Harnett, Homer, Innes, Kensett, LaFarge, Whistler and others examine the ways in which creative artists helped define a national image for the new republic.

ONGOING   ART OF THE ANCIENT WORLDS
From the permanent collection, a selection of ancient sculpture, vases, artifacts, and jewelry from Greece, Rome, Egypt, the Near East, Southeast Asia and the Americas.

ONGOING   OUTDOOR SCULPTURE FROM THE "KNOTS" AND "TAICHI" SERIES BY THE CHINESE ARTIST, JU MING

ONGOING   INTERNATIONAL BIRD MUSEUM
Mounted on the outside of the Museum, this unusual, elaborate structure constructed of 10,000 quarter-inch glazed bricks, is intentionally placed high enough off the ground so that only boards can visit the exhibitions.

ONGOINH   INVENTING THE TWENTIETH CENTURY: SELECTIONS FROM THE PERMANENT COLLECTION (1900-1950)
Aspects of "The New" as contemporary art evolved will be explored in thematic groupings of paintings, sculpture, drawings and photographs.

ONGOING   VITAL TRADITIONS: OLD MASTER WORKS FROM THE PERMANENT COLLECTION
300 years of artistic change, from the Renaissance to the Baroque, will be highlighted in the 17 paintings by Guardi, Ribera, van Ostade and others on view from the permanent collection.

07/24/1999 to 01/2000   THE PANAMA CANAL AND THE ART OF CONSTRUCTION
A selection of paintings, prints and photographs of canal construction.

10/16/1999 to 01/23/2000   AMY PODMORE: RECENT WORK

01/15/2000 to 06/25/2000   SELECTIONS FROM THE TEXTILE COLLECTION (working title))

03/04/2000 to 08/2000   CARRIE MAE WEEMS: THE HAMPTON PROJECT (working title) *Will Travel*

WORCESTER

Iris & B. Gerald Cantor Art Gallery

Affiliate Institution: College of Holy Cross
1 College St., Worcester, MA 01610
✆: 508-793-3356   ◉ www.holycross.edu/visitor/cantor/cantor/html
Open: 9-Noon & 1-4 Mo & Tu, Th & Fr, and by appointment   **Closed:** ACAD!, Su, LEG/ HOL!
& ℗ Free   **Museum Shop**
Group Tours: 205-932-8327   **Drop-In Tours:** daily during Museum hours   **Historic Building**
Permanent Collection: Am: ptgs 20; folk

Housed in a 1930's former schoolhouse, this collection consists of more than 3500 works of 20th century American art. **NOT TO BE MISSED:** One of the largest collections of folk art in the Southeast.

MASSACHUSETTS

Worcester Art Museum

55 Salisbury St., Worcester, MA 01609-3196

📞: 508-799-4406 ◉ www.woresterart.org

Open: 11-5 We-Fr, 10-5 Sa, 11-5 Su; Closed Su JUL & AUG   **Closed:** 7/4, THGV, 12/25

ADM: Adult: $6.00   **Children:** Free under 12   **Students:** $4.00   **Seniors:** $4.00

  Ⓕ Free parking in front of museum and along side streets; handicapped parking at the Hiatt Wing entrance off Tuckerman Street.   **Museum Shop** ‖ Cafe 11:30-2 W-Sa (ex. 3068)

Group Tours: ex 3061   **Drop-In Tours:** 2:00 most Su Sep-May; 2:00 Sa   **Sculpture Garden**

Permanent Collection: AM: 17-19; JAP: gr; BRIT: 18-19; FL: 16-17; GER: 16-17; DU: 17; P/COL; AN/EGT; OR: sculp; MED: sculp; AM: dec/art

Opened to the public in 1898, the Worcester Art Museum is the second largest art museum in New England. Its exceptional 35,000-piece collection of paintings, sculpture, decorative arts, photography, prints and drawings is displayed in 36 galleries and spans 5,000 years of art and culture, ranging from Egyptian antiquities and Roman mosaics to Impressionist paintings and contemporary art. Throughout its first century, the Museum has proven itself a pioneer. Among its many "firsts," the Museum was the first American museum to purchase work by Claude Monet (1910) and Paul Gauguin (1921); the first museum to bring a medieval building to America; a sponsor of the first major excavation at Antioch, one of the four great cities of ancient Rome (1932); the first museum to organize a Members' Council (1949); and the first museum to create an Art All-State program for high school artists.   **NOT TO BE MISSED:** Antiochan Mosaics ; American Portrait miniatures; New Roman Art Gallery; New Contemporary Art Gallery

MICHIGAN

University of Michigan Museum of Art
525 S. State St. at S. Univ., Ann Arbor, MI 48109
📞: 734-764-0395 ◉ www.umich.edu/~umma/
Open: 10-5 Tu-Sa, till 9 Th, 12-5 Su **Closed:** Mo, 1/1, 7/4, THGV, 12/25
Sugg/Cont: $3.00 ♿ Ⓟ Limited on-street parking with commercial lots nearby **Museum Shop**
Group Tours Drop-In Tours: 12:10-12:30 Th; 2pm Su
Permanent Collection: CONT; gr, phot; OM; drgs 6-20; OR; AF; OC; IS

This museum, which houses the second largest art collection in the state of Michigan, also features a changing series of special exhibitions, family programs, and chamber music concerts. With over 12,000 works of art ranging from Italian Renaissance panel paintings to Han dynasty Tomb figures, this 50 year old university museum ranks among the finest in the country. **NOT TO BE MISSED:** Works on paper by J. M. W. Whistler

ON EXHIBIT 2000
ONGOING   PERSONAL FAVORITES
Artworks from the collection chosen for viewing by Museum staff, faculty, and students and by members of the community at large.

ONGOING   A CLOSER LOOK
Major recent acquisitions, newly conserved objects and recent research discoveries are highlighted in a series of featured works that change approximately every 8 weeks.

09/25/1999 to 01/02/2000   WHEN TIME BEGAN TO RANT AND RAGE: FIGURATIVE PAINTING FROM 20TH CENTURY IRELAND
Taking the title from William Butler Yeats this exhibition will explore the full range of figurative painting during the past 100 years. Two vital issues are discussed: the development of a distinctively Irish identity in the visual arts, and the involvement of Irish artists in international art movements. *Will Travel*

01/23/2000 to 03/26/2000   THE ORCHID PAVILION GATHERING: CHINESE PAINTING FROM THE UNIVERSITY OF MICHIGAN MUSEUM OF ART
Works from the Southern Sung Dynasty (1126-1280) are shown. *Catalog Will Travel*

04/15/2000 to 06/11/2000   STILL TIME: PHOTOGRAPHS BY SALLY MANN
A survey of Mann's work from 1971-1991 selected by the photographer herself. *Will Travel*

07/01/2000 to 09/10/2000   WHITE HOUSE COLLECTION OF AMERICAN CRAFTS
The furniture, ceramics glass, woodworking sculpture, etc. represent the highest level of technical mastery

07/08/2000 to 09/17/2000   AMISH QUILTS FROM THE COLLECTION OF FAITH AND STEPHEN BROWN
The extraordinary beauty of Amish quilts from Indiana and Ohio from the 19th and 20th C. will be shown here.

12/02/2000 to 01/28/2001   ED WEST –PHOTOGRAPHS
The role of black people in South African society is shown here.

Art Center of Battle Creek
265 E. Emmett St., Battle Creek, MI 49017-4601
📞: 616-962-9511
Open: 10-5 Tu-Sa; 12-4 Su, till 7pm Th **Closed:** Mo, LEG/HOL
Sugg/Cont: ♿ Ⓟ 70 spaces with handicapped access at building **Museum Shop**
Group Tours: 616-962-9511 **Historic Building** core of bldg is an old church
Permanent Collection: REG

The mission of the Art Center is to present quality exhibitions and programming in the visual arts for the education, enrichment and enjoyment of the southwestern Michigan region. **NOT TO BE MISSED:** KIDSPACE, a hands-on activity gallery for children.

MICHIGAN

BLOOMFIELD HILLS

Cranbrook Art Museum

1221 North Woodward Ave., Bloomfield Hills, MI 48303-0801

: 248-645-3323 ◙ www.cranbrook.edu/museum

Open: 11-5 Tu-Su, till 9pm Th **Closed:** Mo, LEG/HOL!

ADM: **Adult:** $5.00 **Children:** Free 7 and under **Students:** $3.00 **Seniors:** $3.00

♿ Ⓟ **Museum Shop** **Group Tours**: 248-645-3323 **Drop-In Tours**: varies

Historic Building Designed by noted Finnish-Amer. architect, Eliel Saarinen **Sculpture Garden**

Permanent Collection: ARCH/DRGS; CER; PTGS; SCULP; GR 19-20 ; DEC/ART 20

The newly restored Saarinen House, a building designed by noted Finnish-American architect Eliel Saarinen, is part of Cranbrook Academy, the only institution in the country solely devoted to graduate education in the arts. In addition to outdoor sculpture on the grounds surrounding the museum, the permanent collection includes important works of art that are influential on the contemporary trends of today. PLEASE NOTE: Please call ahead (248-645-3323) for specific information on tours and admission fees for Cranbrook House, Cranbrook Gardens (for the architecture & sculpture tour), Cranbrook Art Museum, and Saarinen House. **NOT TO BE MISSED:** Works by Eliel Saarinen; carpets by Loja Saarinen

DETROIT

Detroit Institute of Arts

5200 Woodward Ave., Detroit, MI 48202

: 313-833-7900 ◙ www.dia.org

Open: 11-4 We-Fr; 11-5 Sa, Su **Closed:** Some Holidays

Sugg/Cont: **ADM**: **Adult:** $4.00 **Children:** $1.00 **Students:** $1.00

♿ Ⓟ Underground parking adjacent to museum; metered street parking **Museum Shop**

🍴: Kresge Court Cafe (833-1932), Gallery Grille (833-1857)

Group Tours: 313-833-7981 **Drop-In Tours**: 1:00 We-Sa; 1 & 2:30 Su

Permanent Collection: FR: Impr; GER: Exp; FL; ptgs; AS; EGT; EU: 20; AF; CONT; P/COL; NAT/AM; EU: ptgs, sculp, dec/art; AM: ptgs, sculp, dec/art 🎧

With holdings that survey the art of world cultures from ancient to modern times, The Detroit Institute of Arts, founded in 1885, ranks fifth largest among the nation's fine art museums. **NOT TO BE MISSED:** "Detroit Industry" by Diego Rivera, a 27 panel fresco located in the Rivera court.

ON EXHIBIT 2000

03/02/1999 to 03/05/2000 GLASS, GLASS, GLASS

This exhibition consists of seventy pieces of twentieth-century studio glass from the permanent collection of the Detroit Institute of Arts. Many of these artworks have not been on display for years while many others are recent gifts.

EAST LANSING

Kresge Art Museum

Affiliate Institution: Michigan State University

East Lansing, MI 48824-1119

: 517-355-7631 ◙ www.msu.edu/unit/kamuseum

Open: 9:30-4:30 Mo-We, Fr; 12-8 Th; 1-4 Sa, Su; SUMMER: 11-4 Mo-Fr; 1-4 Sa, Su **Closed:** LEG/HOL! ACAD!; August

Vol/Cont: ♿ Ⓟ Small fee at designated museum visitor spaces in front of the art center. **Museum Shop**

Group Tours: 517-353-9834 **Sculpture Garden**

Permanent Collection: GR 19-20; AM: cont/ab (1960'S), PHOT

Founded in 1959, the Kresge, an active teaching museum with over 6,000 works ranging from prehistoric to contemporary, is the only fine arts museum in central Michigan. **NOT TO BE MISSED:** "St. Anthony" by Francisco Zurbaran; "Remorse" by Salvador Dali; Contemporary collection

Flint Institute of Arts

1120 E. Kearsley St., Flint, MI 48503-1991
☏: 810-234-1695 ◉ www.flintarts org
Open: 10-5 Tu-Sa, 1-5 Su **Closed:** Mo, LEG/HOL!
Vol/Cont:
♿ &#9física; Free
Museum Shop
Group Tours: 810-234-1695 **Drop-In Tours**: 10-5 Tu-Sa
Permanent Collection: AM: ptgs, sculp, gr 19-20; EU: ptgs, sculp, gr 19-20; FR/REN: IT/REN: dec/art; CH; cer, sculp

The Flint Institute of Arts, founded in 1928, has grown to become the largest private museum collection of fine art in the state. In addition to the permanent collection with artworks from ancient China to modern America, visitors to this museum can enjoy the renovated building itself, a stunning combination of classic interior gallery space housed within the walls of a modern exterior. **NOT TO BE MISSED:** Bray Gallery of French & Italian Renaissance decorative art.

ON EXHIBIT 2000

09/25/1999 to 01/16/2000 CHILDE HASSAM AS PRINTMAKER: GRAPHICS FROM THE FIA COLLECTION
As a leading exponent of impressionism in the US Hassam at age 56 turned to printmaking to express his artistic needs. This is a rare opportunity to observe artistic experimentation of this American master.

11/26/1999 to 01/02/2000 THE ART OF COLLECTING
Artworks from more than 25 galleries in New York, Birmingham and Chicago are to show the visitor the wide range of purchasing opportunities in the art market and to develop connoisseurship and collecting. Works represent many time periods, styles, media, and techniques.

01/29/2000 to 03/05/2000 CAN I GET A WITNESS: PHOTOGRAPHS BY JAMES PERRY WALKER
40 photographs will be on view documenting the role of religion in contemporary African American life.

01/29/2000 to 03/19/2000 LOVE EVERLASTING : THE ART OF ROMANCE THROUGH THE MILLENNIA
More than 30 works will embody some of the world's greatest artistic achievements in commemoration of romantic love.

01/29/2000 to 08/06/2000 TO HAVE AND TO HOLD: ANCIENT AND MODERN VESSELS FROM AROUND THE WORLD
The differences and similarities of containers from around the world in a variety of cultures.

03/11/2000 to 05/07/2000 MICHIGAN DIRECTIONS: THE DAS PRINT CO.
The DAS Pint Co. was until recently the association of 4 printmakers to explore print media and produce limited, hand-pulled editions.

04/15/2000 to 06/11/2000 CARL MILLES: SCULPTURE
Milles, best known in Sweden then worked with Rodin who directly influenced his work.
As resident sculptor at Cranbrook Academy he became known as a premier designer of major public fountains

05/13/2000 to 07/02/2000 KAREL APPEL: PRINTS FROM THE FIA COLLECTION
As a founding member of the CoBrA movement, Appel bold prints and mask like faces continue to have a influence on the mainstream of modern art.

MICHIGAN

Calvin College Center Art Gallery
Affiliate Institution: Calvin College
Grand Rapids, MI 49546
☎: 616-957-6271
Open: 9-9 Mo-Th, 9-5 Fr, Noon-4 Sa   **Closed:** Su, ACAD!
&. ℗   **Museum Shop   Group Tours**: 616-957-6271   **Drop-In Tours**: Available upon request
Permanent Collection: DU: ptgs, drgs 17-19; GR, PTGS, SCULP, DRGS 20

17th & 19th century Dutch paintings are one of the highlights of the permanent collection.

Grand Rapids Art Museum
155 N. Division, Grand Rapids, MI 49503
☎: 616-831-1000   ◙   www.gram.mus.mi.us
Open: 11-6; Fr-11-9   **Closed:** Mo, LEG/HOL!
Free Day: Fr 5-9   **ADM:** Adult: $3.00   **Children:** Free under 5 w/ adult, $1.00 6-17   **Students:** $2.00   **Seniors:** $2.00
&. ℗ Less than 1 block from the museum   **Museum Shop**
Group Tours   Historic Building Beaux Arts Federal Building
Permanent Collection: REN: ptgs; FR: ptgs 19; AM: ptgs 19-20; GR; EXP/PTGS; PHOT; DEC/ART

Located in a former Federal Building, the Grand Rapids Art Museum, founded in 1911, exhibits paintings and prints by established and emerging artists, as well as photographs, sculpture, and a collection of furniture & decorative arts from the Grand Rapids area and beyond. **NOT TO BE MISSED:** "Harvest" by Karl Schmidt-Rottluff; "Ingleside" by Richard Diebenkorn, and other works by Alexander Calder, Childe Hassam, Max Pechstein, Grach Hartigan, and Christo. Fri eve, Rhythm and Blues. Cash Bar There are admission fees for some special exhibitions

ON EXHIBIT 2000

02/11/2000 to 04/23/2000   CONTEMPORARY ART FROM CUBA: IRONY AND SURVIVAL ON THE UTOPIAN ISLAND
Opening in the centenary anniversary year of Cuban independence from Spain, this exhibition of works reflective of contemporary Cuban life, examines the satire and irony incorporated within these works as a means of survival.

Kalamazoo Institute of Arts
314 South Park St., Kalamazoo, MI 49007
☎: 616-349-7775   ◙   www.kiarts.org
Open: 10-5 Tu, We, Fr, Sa, 10-8 Th, 12-5 Su   **Closed:** Mo, LEG/HOL
Vol/Cont:
&. ℗   **Museum Shop**
Group Tours: 616-349-7775, ext 3132   **Historic Building** architecturally significant   **Sculpture Garden**
Permanent Collection: sculp, ptgs, drgs, cer, gr, photo

The Kalamazoo Institute, established in 1924, is known for its collection of 20th century American art and European graphics, as well as for its outstanding art school. More than 3,000 objects are housed in a building that in 1979 was voted one of the most significant structures in the state and in 1998 underwent a significant expansion. **NOT TO BE MISSED:** The state of the art interactive gallery and permanent collection installations, including "La Clownesse Aussi (Mlle. Cha-U-Ka-O)" by Henri de Toulouse Lautrec; "Sleeping Woman" by Richard Diebenkorn; "Simone in a White Bonnet" by Mary Cassatt

Kalamazoo Institute of Arts - continued

ON EXHIBIT 2000

12/18/1999 to 02/20/2000   ITALY IN THE SHADOW OF TIME: PHOTOGRAPHS BY LINDA BUTLER
These beautifully printed photographs capture the timeless spirit of Italy in haunting images of architecture, landscapes and antique objects. Linda Butler strayed far from the standard tourist paths to discover subjects that evoke the creativity and sense of tradition that is so much a part of the Italian heritage.

01/08/2000 to 03/12/2000   ART AND NATURE: THE HUDSON RIVER SCHOOL
Twenty-six paintings, dating from 1825 through the late 1870s, by Hudson River artists known for their dramatic depictions of nature. Subjects range from sublime views of the wilderness, to beautiful pastoral scenes, to allegorical pictures with moral messages, all meant to celebrate the presence of God in nature. Artists include Thomas Cole, Asher B. Durand, Frederic Church, Jasper F. Cropsey and George Inness, among many others.

03/25/2000 to 05/14/2000   THE A.M. TODD COLLECTION
A.M. Todd, one of Kalamazoo's principal philanthropists, assembled an extraordinary collection of art during his long lifetime. After his death, the collection was dispersed to a variety of educational institutions, as well as to family members. This exhibition brings the paintings Todd collected together for the first time since his death. Curated by J.Gray Sweeney, the show is documented in a fully illustrated and thoroughly researched catalogue.

04/15/2000 to 05/28/2000   DANCING AT THE LOUVRE: STORY QUILTS BY FAITH RINGGOLD
Fiber artist Ringgold, credited with bringing quiltmaking and craft-oriented processes into the artistic mainstream, has created a series of quilt paintings that reflect her experiences as an African American in the 20th-century art world. The stories told by these quilts not only involve Ringgold's personal experiences, but her own revisionist view of the School of Paris painting.

05/27/2000 to 08/26/2000   2000 WEST MICHIGAN AREA SHOW
The annual Area Show, selected by a nationally known juror (yet to be selected), will feature the finest works in all media produced by artists in 14 counties in Southwest Michigan.

06/10/2000 to 08/12/2000   DRAWINGS AND PAINTINGS BY ETHEL GROOS
For over 30 years, Ethel Groos maintained a lively involvement in the KIA - as an artist, member and major benefactor. While her landscapes were always outstanding, it was portraiture that offered the greater challenges and rewards. The large body of portraits Groos created over the years reveal the high quality and technical accomplishment of her painting. More importantly, they provide a revealing and sympathetic visual record of her many friends and fellow artists. This exhibition is a history of Groos' painting career and a tribute to her great talent.

MUSKEGON

Muskegon Museum of Art
296 W. Webster, Muskegon, MI 49440
\: 231-720-2570   ◙ www.muskegon/mma/Default.html
Open: 10-5 Tu-Fr; 12-5 Sa, Su   **Closed:** Mo, LEG/HOL!
Vol/Cont:
♿ ℗ Limited street and adjacent mall lots; handicapped parking at rear of museum   **Museum Shop**
Permanent Collection: AM: ptgs, gr 19-early 20; EU: ptgs; PHOT; SCULP; OM: gr; CONT: gr

The award winning Muskegon Museum, which opened in 1912, and has recently undergone major renovation, is home to a permanent collection that includes many fine examples of American and French Impressionistic paintings, Old Master through contemporary prints, photography, sculpture and glass. The museum features a diverse schedule of changing exhibitions. Call for possible date changes! **NOT TO BE MISSED:** American Art Collection

ON EXHIBIT 2000

12/02/1999 to 01/23/2000   TWO HUNDRED YEARS OF FOLLY: GOYA'S CAPRICHIOS
Goya's prints with contemporary artists responses.

Muskegon Museum of Art - continued
12/16/1999 to 02/13/2000   MOMENTS OF GRACE: NEW REGIONAL PAINTING
New works by regional artists showing the vigorous rebirth of realism and spiritualism in art today.

02/05/2000 to 04/16/2000   SHADOWY EVIDENCE: EDWARD S CURTIS AND HIS CONTEMPORARIES
Curtis created masterpiece images of Native American people incorporated with works of 33 other photographers between 1900 and 1928.

02/19/2000 to 03/26/2000   KYOUNG AE CHO
Fiber and natural material constructions by this well known artist.

02/27/2000 to 04/05/2000   BEYOND THE MOUNTAINS: THE CONTEMPORARY AMERICAN LANDSCAPE
Paintings from the 1980's and 1990's by Amenoff, Katz, Leslie, Moskowitz, Porter and Theibaud. *Will Travel*

04/01/2000 to 05/14/2000   CHILDREN'S LITERATURE AND ILLUSTRATIONS BY BRIAN AND ANDREA PINKNEY
Many award winning books including "Sukey and the Mermaid", "The Boy and the Ghost", etc. were written and illustrated by these artists.

05/13/2000 to 07/04/2000   REALITY AND SPIRITUALITY: DUTCH AND GERMAN PRINTS FROM THE PERMANENT COLLECTION
500 years of images drawn from the Bible, and daily life.

08/27/2000 to 10/22/2000   ROBERT ARNESON: SCULPTURE
The exhibition explores the nature of portraiture in the contemporary and historical scene. *Will Travel*

11/05/2000 to 12/31/2000   FROM SHIP TO SHORE: MARINE PAINTINGS FROM THE BUTLER INSTITUTE FOR AMERICAN ART
Images of ships, boating and seascapes from the mid 1800's to the 1950's *Will Travel*

10/21/2001 to 12/16/2001   AFRICAN AMERICAN WORKS ON PAPER
Prints, drawings and watercolors by America's greatest African American artists. *Will Travel*

02/03/2002 to 03/24/2002   GRANT WOOD AND MARVIN COHN: THE ORIGINS OF REGIONALISM
Paintings that highlight the work of Grant Wood and a lesser known fellow artist. It reveals the origins of Regionalism in the 1930's *Will Travel*

10/14/2002 to 11/25/2002   OXYMORONS: ABSURDLY LOGICAL QUILTS
Quilts that feature word play . *Will Travel*

PETOSKEY

Crooked Tree Arts Council
461 E. Mitchell St., Petoskey, MI 49770
📞: 616-347-4337   ◉   www.crookedtreecrg
Open: 10-5 Mo-Fr 11-4 Sa   **Closed:** Su, LEG/HOL!
♿ Ⓟ 60 parking spaces on city lot next door to museum   **Museum Shop**
Group Tours
Historic Building 1890 Methodist Church
Permanent Collection: REGIONAL & FINE ART

This fine arts collection makes its home on the coast of Lake Michigan in a former Methodist church built in 1890.

ROCHESTER

Meadow Brook Art Gallery
Affiliate Institution: Oakland University
Rochester, MI 48309-4401
☎: 248-370-3005
Open: 1-5 Tu-Fr; 2-6:30 Sa, Su (7-9:30 Tu-Fr theater performance days)
♿ ⓟ Free **Museum Shop Group Tours Sculpture Garden**
Permanent Collection: AF; OC; P/COL; CONT/AM: ptgs, sculp, gr; CONT/EU: ptgs, gr, sculp

Located 30 miles north of Detroit on the campus of Oakland University, the Meadow Brook Art Gallery offers four major exhibitions annually.

SAGINAW

Saginaw Art Museum
1126 N. Michigan Ave., Saginaw, MI 48602
☎: 517-754-2491 ◙ www.cris.com/~jKerman/SAM.shtml
Open: 10-5 We, Fr, Sa; 10-6:30 Tu, Th; 1-5 Su **Closed:** Mo, LEG/HOL!
♿ ⓟ Free **Museum Shop Group Tours**: 517-754-2491 (ask for Dona) **Drop-In Tours**: by appointment
Historic Building former 1904 Clark Lombard Ring Family Home
Permanent Collection: EU: ptgs, sculp 14-20; AM: ptgs sculp; OR: ptgs, gr, dec/art; JAP: GR; JOHN ROGERS SCULP; CHARLES ADAM PLATT: gr

The interesting and varied permanent collections of this museum, including an important group of John Rogers sculptures, are housed in a gracious 1904 Georgian-revival building designed by Charles Adam Platt. The former Clark Lombard Ring Family home is listed on the state & federal registers for historic homes. **NOT TO BE MISSED:** T'ang Dynasty Marble Buddha

ON EXHIBIT 2000
06/08/1999 to 07/09/2000 ALMA COLLEGE PRINT SHOW

01/2000 to 01/2000 ALL AREA SHOW
A juried show of works in all media by artists from a 27 county area.

01/29/2000 to 03/26/2000 BIRDS IN ART
An annual autumn exhibition which brings together international artists whose work celebrates the beauty and bounty of the avian kingdom.

04/2000 to 04/2000 ALL AREA PHOTO SHOW

05/2000 to 05/2000 LATINO ART EXHIBITION

ST. JOSEPH

Krasl Art Center
707 Lake Blvd., St. Joseph, MI 49085
☎: 616-983-0271 ◙ http//ww.asama.org
Open: 10-4 Mo-Th & Sa, 10-1 Fr, 1-4 Su **Closed:** Sa, Su, LEG/HOL!
♿ ⓟ Free **Museum Shop**
Group Tours: 334-636-3303 **Drop-In Tours**: by appt
Permanent Collection: ptgs, sculp, gr.all on the single theme of American sports heros

MICHIGAN

Krasl Art Center - continued
One of the largest collections of sports art in America may be found at this museum which also features works highlighting an annual sport artist of the year. Of special interest is the two-story high mural on an outside wall of the Academy entitled "A Tribute to the Human Spirit". Created by world-renowned Spanish artist Cristobal Gabarron, the work pays tribute to Jackie Robinson on the 50th anniversary of his breaking the color barrier in major league baseball. **NOT TO BE MISSED:** "The Pathfinder", a large sculpture of a hammerthrower by John Robinson where the weight of the ball of the hammer is equal to the rest of the entire weight of the body of the figure.

TRAVERSE CITY

Dennos Museum Center
Affiliate Institution: Northwestern Michigan College
1701 East Front St., Traverse City, MI 49686
☎: 616-922-1055 ◙ dmc.nmc.edu
Open: 10-5 Mo-Sa, 1-5 Su **Closed:** LEG/HOL!
ADM: Adult: $2.00 **Children:** $1.00 **Students:** $1.00 **Seniors:** $2.00
& ℗ Reserved area for museum visitors adjacent to the museum. **Museum Shop**
Group Tours Drop-In Tours: by appointment **Sculpture Garden**
Permanent Collection: Inuit art; CONT: Canadian Indian graphics; AM; EU; NAT/AM

With a collection of more than 1600 works, the Dennos Museum Center houses one of the largest and most historically complete collections of Inuit art from the peoples of the Canadian Arctic. The museum also features a "hands-on" Discovery Gallery. **NOT TO BE MISSED:** The Power Family Inuit Gallery with over 880 Inuit sculptures and prints; The Thomas A. Rutkowski interactive "Discovery Gallery"

DULUTH

Tweed Museum of Art
Affiliate Institution: Univ. of Minn.
10 University Dr., Duluth, MN 55812

📞: 218-726-8222 ◙ www.d.umn.edu/tma
Open: 9-8 Tu, 9-4:30 We-Fr, 1-5 Sa-Su **Closed:** Mo, ACAD!
Sugg/Cont:
⅏ ℗ **Museum Shop**
Group Tours: 218-726-8527
Historic Building on campus of University of Minnesota Duluth **Sculpture Garden**
Permanent Collection: OM: ptgs; EU: ptgs 17-19; F: Barbizon ptgs 19; AM: all media 19-20; CONT; AF; JAP: cer; CONT/REG

Endowed with gifts of American and European paintings by industrialist George Tweed, for whom this museum is named, this fine institution also has an important growing permanent collection of contemporary art. One-person exhibitions by living American artists are often presented to promote national recognition of their work. **NOT TO BE MISSED:** "The Scourging of St. Blaise", a 16th century Italian painting by a follower of Caravaggio

ON EXHIBIT 2000
10/19/1999 to 01/09/2000 WORKS ON PAPER SERIES:PRINTS FROM THE PRESSES PART I
SELECTED PRINTS FROM PRESSES FROM DIFFERENT PARTS OF THE COUNTRY

11/02/1999 to 04/02/2000 COMMUNITY CURATORS PROJECT
Individuals and curators are invited to view the collections and to curate a series of installations of their own.

01/11/2000 to 12/24/2000 FOCUS ON TWEED COLLECTIONS / 50TH ANNIVERSARY

01/18/2000 to 05/19/2000 WORKS ON PAPER SERIES: PRINTS FROM PRESSES PART II

03/21/2000 to 07/09/2000 CONTEMPORARY FIGURATIVE SCULPTURE
Traditional and innovative approaches to making figurative sculpture

05/27/2000 to 07/09/2000 CONTEMPORARY REGIONAL ARTISTS SERIES

07/18/2000 to 10/01/2000 THE RICHARD AND DOROTHY NELSON COLLECTION OF CONTEMPORARY AMERICAN INDIAN ART

MINNEAPOLIS

Frederick R. Weisman Art Museum at the University of Minnesota
Affiliate Institution: University of Minnesota
333 East River Road, Minneapolis, MN 55455

📞: 612-625-9494 ◙ hudson.acad.umn.edu
Open: 10-5 Tu, We, Fr; 10-8 Th; 11-5 Sa, Su **Closed:** Mo, ACAD!, LEG/HOL!
⅏ ℗ Paid parking in the Museum Garage is $1.60 per hour with a weekend flat rate of $3.50 per day.
Museum Shop
Group Tours: 612-625-9656 **Drop-In Tours**: 1 PM Sa, Su
Historic Building Terra-cotta brick & stainless steel bldg. (1993) by Frank O. Gehry
Permanent Collection: AM: ptgs, sculp, gr 20; KOREAN: furniture 18-19; Worlds largest coll of works by Marsden Hartley & Alfred Maurer (plus major works by their contemporaries such as Feninger & O'Keeffe

MINNESOTA

Frederick R. Weisman Art Museum at the University of Minnesota - continued
Housed since 1993 in a striking, sculptural stainless steel and brick building designed by architect Frank Gehry, the Weisman Art Museum offers a convenient and friendly museum experience. The museum's collection features early 20th-century American artists, such as Georgia O'Keeffe and Marsden Hartley, as well as a selection of contemporary art. A teaching museum for the University and the community, the Weisman provides a multidisciplinary approach to the arts through an array of programs and a changing schedule of exhibitions. **NOT TO BE MISSED:** "Oriental Poppies", by Georgia O'Keeffe

ON EXHIBIT 2000
ONGOING   SELECTIONS FROM THE WEISMAN ART FOUNDATION

ONGOING   REINSTALLATION OF THE WEISMAN PERMANENT COLLECTION

09/11/1999 to 01/02/2000   WORLD VIEWS: MAPS AND ART
A contemplation of the cultural and aesthetic significance of maps on our global society and how they have influenced contemporary artists.

05/20/2000 to 08/13/2000   HOSPICE: A PHOTOGRAPHIC INQUIRY
A unique exhibition featuring the work of 5 outstanding American photographers, Jim Goldberg, Nan Golden, Sally Mann, Jack Radcliff and Kathy Vargas. Each project documents the emotional and collaborative experience of living and working in a hospice environment. *Will Travel*

Minneapolis Institute of Arts
2400 Third Ave. So., Minneapolis, MN 55404
📞: 612-870-3000 ▣ www.mtn.org/MIA
Open: 10-5 Tu-Sa, 10-9 Th, Noon-5 Su   **Closed:** 7/4, THGV, 12/25
🚹 ℗ Free and ample
Museum Shop 🍴: Restaurant 11:30-2:30 Tu-S
Group Tours: 612-870-3140   **Drop-In Tours:** 2:00 Tu-S, 1:00 Sa & S, 7pm Th
Historic Building 1915 NEO-CLASSIC BUILDING BY McKIM MEAD & WHITE
Permanent Collection: AM: ptgs, sculp; EU: ptgs, sculp; DEC/ART; OR; P/COL; AF; OC; ISLAMIC; PHOT; GR; DRGS; JAP: gr

Distinguished by a broad-ranging 80,000 object collection housed within its walls, this landmark building consists of a 1915 neo-classic structure combined with 1974 Japanese inspired additions. With the recent completion of a 50 million dollar renovation project, the museum has reinstalled its redesigned 20th-century galleries on the 1st & 2nd floors of the East Wing. PLEASE NOTE: There is a charge for some special exhibitions. **NOT TO BE MISSED:** Rembrandt's "Lucretia"

ON EXHIBIT 2000
10/01/1999 to 02/27/2000   COPPER INTO GOLD: ETCHINGS AND DRYPOINTS BY JAMES MACNEIL WHISTLER

10/24/1999 to 01/16/2000   CHOKWE! ART AND INITIATION AMONG CHOKWE AND RELATED PEOPLES
In the first exhibition of its kind in the U.S., the 200 artifacts on view, gathered from important public and private collections here and in Europe, highlight the artistry of the Chokwe and related peoples of Angola, Zaire and Zambia. Interactive elements and innovative video techniques will be integrated into this gallery installation to provide a rich contextural setting for the items.

10/30/1999 to 02/06/2000   PORTRAITS OF JEREMIAH GURNEY

11/1999 to 01/2000   HOW PRINTS ARE MADE

12/05/1999 to 02/13/2000   LOUISE BOURGEOIS:1989-1998
Her powerful and evocative prints are the focus of this exhibition

Minneapolis Institute of Arts - continued
02/27/2000 to 06/04/2000   STAR WARS: THE MAGIC OF MYTH
Original artwork, props, models, costumes, characters and other artifacts used to create the original STAR WARS TRILOGY.

07/22/2000 to 09/17/2000   SYMBOLS OF FAITH AND BELIEF: ART OF THE NATIVE AMERICAN CHURCH

08/20/2000 to 10/29/2000   AMERICAN IMPRESSIONISM
Led by the example of James McNeil Whistler, a generation of American artist studied abroad to absorb the new palette and compositions that were modernizing painting. Landscapes, figure, and still life paintings by Hassam, Twatchman, Dewing, Merrit Chase and Robinson marked a distinct departure from academic styles.

10/21/2000 to 01/14/2001   THE ART OF TWENTIETH CENTURY ZEN
The first exhibition in America to present a survey of painting and calligraphy by Japan's greatest Zen masters of the 20th C.
Catalog Will Travel

Walker Art Center
Vineland Place, Minneapolis, MN 55403
☎: 612-375-7622   ◉ www.walkerart.org
Open: Gallery: 10-5 Tu-Sa, 11-5 Su, till 8pm Th   **Closed:** LEG/HOL!
ADM: Adult: $4.00   **Children:** Free under 12   **Students:** $3.00   **Seniors:** $3.00
♿ ℗ Hourly metered on-street parking & pay parking at nearby Parade Stadium lot   **Museum Shop** ¶ Sculpture Garden 11:30-3 Tu-S; Gallery 8 Restaurant 11:30-3, till 8 W
Group Tours: 612-375-7609   **Drop-In Tours:** 2pm Sa, Su; 2 & 6pm Th (Free with adm.)   **Sculpture Garden**
Permanent Collection: AM & EU CONT: ptgs, sculp; GR; DRGS ☊

Housed in a beautifully designed building by noted architect Edward Larabee Barnes, the Walker Art Center, with its superb 7,000 piece permanent collection, is particularly well known for its major exhibitions of 20th century art. PLEASE NOTE: 1. The sculpture garden is open free to all from 6am to midnight daily. There is a self-guided audio tour of the Garden available for rent at the Walker lobby desk. 2. For information on a wide variety of special needs tours or accommodations call 612-375-7609. **NOT TO BE MISSED:** Minneapolis Sculpture Garden at Walker Art Center (open 6-Midnight daily; ADM F); "Standing Glass Fish" by F. Gehry at Cowles Conservatory (open 10 -8 Tu-Sa, 10-5 S; ADM F)

ON EXHIBIT 2000
10/10/1999 to 01/02/2000   2000 BC: THE BRUCE CONNER STORY PART II
This exhibition will consist of some 150 works in a wide variety of media by the celebrated artist Bruce Conner. While including works from the entire span of Conner's career (1954 to the present) the exhibition will not attempt to be an inclusive retrospective, but will focus instead on common concerns that run through his work in different media, including film, painting, drawing, sculpture, collage, printmaking, and photography. In particular it will highlight his lifelong engagement with the physical, metaphorical, and metaphysical properties of light and dark.

12/19/1999 to 03/05/2000   GLOBAL CONCEPTUALISM: POINTS OF ORIGIN, 1950S-1980S
The first major exhibition to explore in depth the history of conceptual art as it developed around the world, Global Conceptualism: Points of Origin, 1950s-1980s challenges the perception that conceptual art was one movement that spread internationally. By presenting conceptual art in relation to the conditions and times in which it was made, this exhibition acknowledges the local circumstances that influenced artists to make idea-based art in regions around the world. Highlighted, in particular, will be work made from the mid-1950s through the 1980s in North America, Western Europe, Eastern Europe (and the former Soviet Union), Africa, Latin America, Asia, and Australia.

02/12/2000 to 04/30/2000   LET'S ENTERTAIN
Today's consumer society produces a massive overflow of visual stimuli--a sea of images and information generated by television, movies, video, newspapers, magazines, cartoons, billboards, posters, and commercial packaging that transforms our everyday life into an endless loop of multi-sensory spectacles in which we all participate. The international, multidisciplinary exhibition Let's Entertain features work by more than 50 artists who focus on entertainment not only to amuse or engage viewers, but also to interrogate contemporary social phenomena.

MINNESOTA

Minnesota Museum of American Art
Landmark Center - 75 West Fifth St., St. Paul, MN 55102-1486

☏: 612-292-4355
Open: 11-4 Tu-Sa, 11-7:30 Th, 1-5 Su   **Closed:** LEG/HOL!
Sugg/Cont: **ADM: Adult:** $2.00
♿ ℗ Street parking and nearby parking facilities   **Museum Shop**   ‖: 11:30-1:30 Tu-F; 11-1 S
Group Tours: 612-292-4367   **Drop-In Tours**: Group tours scheduled daily, regular Museum hours
Historic Building   Sculpture Garden
Permanent Collection: AM

Begun in 1927 as the St. Paul School of Art, the Minnesota Museum is one of the oldest visual arts institutions in the area. Housed in two historic buildings, the museum's exhibitions focus of the multicultural diversity of the Upper Midwest as expressed through the artists of the region.

George E. Ohr Arts and Cultural Center
136 George E. Ohr St., Biloxi, MS 39530
☎: 601-374-5547 ◙ www.georgeohr.org
Open: 9-5 Mo-Sa **Closed:** 1/1, 7/4, THGV, 12/25
ADM: Adult: $2.00 **Seniors:** $1.00
& ℗ Free parking in the lot across the street from the museum. **Museum Shop**
Group Tours: 601-374-5547 **Drop-In Tours**
Permanent Collection: George Ohr pottery

In addition to a 300 piece collection of pottery by George Ohr, a man often referred to as the mad potter of Biloxi, this museum features a gallery dedicated to the promotion of local talent and another for rotating and traveling exhibitions. **NOT TO BE MISSED:** Art Activity, a program for children from 10-12 on the 2nd Saturday of the month, led each time by a different artist using a different medium.

Mississippi Museum of Art
201 E. Pascagoula St., Jackson, MS 39201
☎: 601-960-1515 ◙ www.msmuseumart.org
Open: 10-5 Mo-Sa, Noon-5 Su **Closed:** LEG/HOL
ADM: Adult: $3.00 **Children:** $2.00 (Free under 3) **Students:** $2.00 **Seniors:** $2.00
& ℗ Pay lot behind museum **Museum Shop** ‖: Palette Restaurant (open for lunch 11:30-1:30 M-F)
Group Tours: 960-1515 x2242 **Drop-In Tours:** Upon request if available **Sculpture Garden**
Permanent Collection: AM: 19-20; REG: 19-20; BRIT: ptgs, dec/art mid 18-early 19; P/COL: cer; JAP: gr

Begun as an art association in 1911, the Mississippi Museum now has more than 3,100 works of art in a collection that spans more than 30 centuries.

ON EXHIBIT 2000
11/13/1999 to 02/06/2000 CROSSING THE THRESHOLD
As we approach a new millennium this exhibition reflects on the artistic milestones of women artists during the past 100 years. While striving for equality, the women included here will be remembered for challenging and overcoming the traditional social mores of our American culture. Artists include Louise Bourgeois, Elizabeth Catlett, Helen Frankenthaler, Nell Blaine, Agnes Martin, Nancy Spiro, Lois Mailou Jones and others.

02/19/2000 to 08/06/2000 THE ANNE LAURIE SWAIM HEARIN MEMORIAL EXHIBITION

Lauren Rogers Museum of Art
5th Ave. at 7th St., Laurel, MS 39441-1108
☎: 601-649-6374
Open: 10-4:45 Tu-Sa, 1-4 Su **Closed:** LEG/HOL!
& ℗ New lot at rear of museum and along side of the museum on 7th Street
Museum Shop
Group Tours Drop-In Tours: 10-12 & 1-3 Tu-Fr
Permanent Collection: AM:19-20; EU: 19-20; NAT/AM; JAP: gr 18-19; NAT/AM: baskets; ENG: silver

MISSISSIPPI

Lauren Rogers Museum of Art - continued

Located among the trees in Laurel's Historic District, the Lauren Rogers, the first museum to be established in the state, has grown rapidly since its inception in 1922. While the original Georgian Revival building still stands, the new adjoining galleries are perfect for the display of the fine art collection of American and European masterworks. **NOT TO BE MISSED:** One of the largest collections of Native American Indian baskets in the U.S.; Gibbons English Georgian Silver Collection

ON EXHIBIT 2000

12/14/1999 to 01/16/2000   LAUREN ROGERS MUSEUM OF ART COLLECTION: WORKS ON PAPER

MERIDIAN

Meridian Museum of Art

25th Ave. & 7th St., Meridian, MS 39301
☎: 601-693-1501
Open: 1-5 Tu-Su   **Closed:** LEG/HOL!
ⓟ Free but very limited   **Museum Shop   Group Tours   Drop-In Tours**: Upon request if available
Permanent Collection: AM: phot, sculp, dec/art; REG; WORKS ON PAPER 20; EU: portraits 19-20

Housed in the landmark Old Carnegie Library Building, built in 1912-13, the Meridian Museum, begun in 1933 as an art association, serves the cultural needs of the people of East Mississippi and Western Alabama. **NOT TO BE MISSED:** 18th century collection of European portraits

---

OCEAN SPRINGS

Walter Anderson Museum of Art

510 Washington Ave. P.O. Box 328, Ocean Springs, MS 39564
☎: 228-872-3164   ◙ www.motif.org
Open: 10-5 Mo-Sa, 1-5 Su   **Closed:** 1/1, EASTER, THGV, 12/25
ADM: Adult: $4.00   **Children:** $1.50(6-12), Free under 6   **Students:** $3.00   **Seniors:** $3.00
♿ ⓟ Limited free parking at the adjacent Community Center and on the street.   **Museum Shop**
Permanent Collection: Works by Walter Inglis Anderson (1903-1965), in a variety of media and from all periods of his work.

This museum celebrates the works of Walter Inglis Anderson, whose vibrant and energetic images of plants and animals of Florida's Gulf Coast have placed him among the forefront of American painters of the 20th century. **NOT TO BE MISSED:** "The Little Room", a room with private murals seen only by Anderson until after his death when it was moved in its entirety to the museum.

TUPELO

Tupelo Artist Guild Gallery

211 W. Main St., Tupelo, MS 38801
☎: 601-844-ARTS
Open: 10-4 Tu-Th 1-4 Fr   **Closed:** Mon,1/1, 7/4, THGV, 12/25
♿ ⓟ   **Museum Shop   Group Tours   Drop-In Tours**: Upon request if available

Housed in the former original People's Bank Building (1904-05) this small but effective non-collecting institution is dedicated to bringing traveling exhibitions from all areas of the country to the people of the community and its visitors.

COLUMBIA

Museum of Art and Archaeology
Affiliate Institution: MU campus, University Of Missouri
1 Pickard Hall, Columbia, MO 65211
☎: 573-882-3591 ◉ www.researchmissouriedu/museum/
Open: 9-5 Tu, We, Fr; 12-5 Sa, Su; 9-5 & 6-9 Th **Closed:** Mo. LEG/HOL!; 1/1, 12/25
Vol/Cont:
♿ ℗ Parking is available at the university visitors' garage on University Avenue; metered parking spaces on Ninth St.
Museum Shop Group Tours: 2 wks notice
Historic Building
Permanent Collection: AN/EGT; AN/GRK; AN/R; AN/PER; BYZ; DRGS 15-20; GR 15-20; AF; OC; P/COL; CH; JAP; OR

Ancient art and archaeology from Egypt, Palestine, Iran, Cyprus, Greece, Etruria and Rome as well as early Christian and Byzantine art, the Kress study collection, and 15th-20th century European and American artworks are among the treasures from 6 continents and five millennia that are housed in this museum. **NOT TO BE MISSED:** "Portrait of a Musician", 1949

KANSAS CITY

Kemper Museum of Contemporary Art
4420 Warwick Blvd., Kansas City, MO 64111-1821
☎: 816-753 5784 ◉ www.kemperart.org
Open: 10-4 Tu-Th, 10-9 Fr, 10-5 Sa, 11-5 Su **Closed:** Mo, 1/1, 7/4, THGV, 12/25
♿ ℗ Free
Museum Shop ⊪: Café Sebastienne 11-2:30 Tu-Su, 6-9pm Fr
Group Tours Drop-In Tours Sculpture Garden
Permanent Collection: WORKS BY MODERN, CONTEMPORARY, EMERGING AND ESTABLISHED ARTISTS

Designed by architect Gunnar Birkerts, the stunning Kemper Museum of Contemporary Art (a work of art in itself) houses a rapidly growing permanent collection of modern and contemporary works, and hosts temporary exhibitions and creative programs designed to both entertain and challenge. A Museum Shop and the lively Café Sebastienne round out the Museum's amenities. **NOT TO BE MISSED:** Louise Bourgeois's bronze "Spider" sculptures; a Waterford crystal chandelier by Dale Chihuly; Ursula Von Rydingsvaard's "Bowl with Sacks"; "Ahulani" bronze sculpture by Deborah Butterfield; Frank Stella's "The Prophet"; "The History of Art" in Café Sebastienne, a 110-painting cycle by Frederick James Brown.

ON EXHIBIT 2000
11/05/1999 to 01/28/2000   HERB RITTS: WORK
More than 200 photographs will be on view in the first full-scale exhibition devoted to the work of American photographer Ritts.

11/19/1999 to 02/11/2000   LEZLEY SAAR
These mixed media works are an accumulation of layers of found objects creating a visual history. Her work often comments on issues of gender, race and identity.

12/15/2000 to 03/04/2001   DEFINING MOMENTS IN CONTEMPORARY CERAMICS: STUDIO CERAMICS FROM THE LOS ANGELES COUNTY MUSEUM OF ART, THE SMITS COLLECTION AND RELATED WORKS
Defining Moments In Contemporary Ceramics surveys the major stylistic movements in ceramic history during the last half of the 20th century, and aims to illumine the great experiences of contemporary studio ceramics through exhibiting and publishing 200 works selected from the vast holdings of the Los Angeles County Museum of Art.

MISSOURI

The Nelson-Atkins Museum of Art
4525 Oak St., Kansas City, MO 64111-1873
☎: 816-751-IART ◉ www.nelson-atkins.org and www.kansascity.com
Open: 10-4 Tu-Th, 10-9 Fr, 10-5 Sa, 1-5 Su **Closed:** 1/1, 7/4, THGV, 12/25
ADM: Adult: $5.00 **Children:** $1 (6-18) **Students:** $2.00 (with ID)
& ℗ Free lot on 45th St; parking lot for visitors with disabilities at Oak St. Business Entrance on west side of the Museum
Museum Shop ‖: Rozzelle Court Restaurant 10-3 Tu-T, 10-8F (closed 3-5), 10-3 Sa, 1-3
Group Tours: 816-751-1238
Drop-In Tours: 10:30, 11, 1,& 2 Tu-Sa; 1:30, 2, 2:30, 3 S
Sculpture Garden
Permanent Collection: AM: all media; EU: all media; PER/RMS; NAT/AM; OC; P/COL; OR ◠

Among the many fine art treasures in this outstanding 65 year old museum is their world famous collection of Oriental art and artifacts that includes the Chinese Temple Room with its furnishings, a gallery displaying delicate scroll paintings, and a sculpture gallery with glazed T'ang dynasty tomb figures. **NOT TO BE MISSED:** Largest collection of works by Thomas Hart Benton; Kansas City Sculpture Park; "Shuttlecocks", a four-part sculptural installation by Claes Oldenburg and Coosje van Bruggen located in the grounds of the museum

---

POPLAR BLUFF

Margaret Harwell Art Museum
421 N. Main St., Poplar Bluff, MO 63901
☎: 573-686-8002 ◉ www.mham
Open: 1-4 We-Su **Closed:** Mo, Tu, LEG/HOL!
Vol/Cont:
& **Museum Shop Group Tours Historic Building** Located in 1883 mansion
Permanent Collection: DEC/ART; REG; CONT

The 1880's mansion in which this museum is housed is a perfect foil for the museum's permanent collection of contemporary art. Located in the south-eastern part of the state, just above the Arkansas border, the museum features monthly exhibitions showcasing the works of both regional and nationally known artists.

ON EXHIBIT 2000
01/08/2000 to 01/30/2000 THE ART OF PENNY LYONS
Slumped-fused and leaded glass presented in masques and floor standing as well as small panels, also original ink and watercolor paintings.

02/05/2000 to 02/27/2000 CELEBRATION: AFRICAN-AMERICAN MONTH AT THE MHAM
The art of Katerina (Kuumba) Powell and Tom Sleet, working in acrylic/oils and three dimensional.

03/04/2000 to 04/23/2000 THE ART OF SHARON PATTEN
During her short 16 year career her large body of towering scale works and personal statements were in bold, vibrant and rich patterns.

06/04/2000 to 06/25/2000 THE WATERCOLORS OF JANICE RUSHING O'QUINN
Pure watercolor techniques with a wet-in-wet method producing a misty soft effect for landscapes and controlled detail for buildings.

Albrecht-Kemper Museum of Art
2818 Frederick Avenue, Saint Joseph, MO 64506
📞: 816-233-7003 💻 www.albrecht-kemper.org
Open: 10-4 Tu-Sa, till 8pm Th, 1-4 Su
Closed: 1/1, EASTER, 7/4, THGV, 12/25, MEM/DAY, LAB/DAY
Free Day: Su **ADM:** Adult: $3.00 (18 & over) **Children:** Free under 12 **Students:** $1.00 **Seniors:** $2.00
♿ ℗ Free on-site parking
Museum Shop 🍴: Special Events Only
Group Tours: 816-233-7003
Sculpture Garden
Permanent Collection: AM: ldscp ptgs, Impr ptgs, gr, drgs 18-20

Considered to have the region's finest collection of 18th through 20th century American art, the Albrecht-Kemper Museum of Art is housed in the expanded and transformed 1935 Georgian-style mansion of William Albrecht. **NOT TO BE MISSED:** North American Indian Portfolio by Catlin: illustrated books by Audubon; Thomas Hart Benton collection

ON EXHIBIT 2000
12/05/1999 to 01/16/2000 HANDWOVEN TAPESTRIES BY JEROME REGNIER
A series of tapestries by this self-taught artist.

12/05/1999 to 02/27/2000 JIM LEEDY: RETROSPECTIVE
Leedy is a well known regional artist

01/20/2000 to 02/27/2000 25TH ANNUAL MEMBERSHIP EXHIBITION

03/05/2000 to 06/04/2000 HALLMARK MASTER ARTISTS

04/09/2000 to 06/04/2000 CRAIG BARBER: PHOTOGRAPHY

Springfield Art Museum
1111 E. Brookside Dr., Springfield, MO 65807-1899
📞: 417-837-5700
Open: 9-5 Tu, We, Fr, Sa; 1-5 Su; till 8pm Th **Closed:** LOCAL & LEG/HOL!
Vol/Cont:
♿ ℗ West parking lot with 55 handicapped spaces; limited on-street parking north of the museum
Museum Shop Group Tours
Permanent Collection: AM: ptgs, sculp, drgs, gr, phot 18-20; EU: ptgs, sculp, gr, drgs, phot 18-20; DEC/ART; NAT/AM; OC; P/COL

Watercolor U.S.A., an annual national competition is but one of the features of the Springfield Museum, the oldest cultural institution in the city. **NOT TO BE MISSED:** New Jeannette L. Musgrave Wing for the permanent collection; John Henry's "Sun Target", 1974, a painted steel sculpture situated on the grounds directly east of the museum; paintings and prints by Thomas Hart Benton

MISSOURI

ST. LOUIS

Forum For Contemporary Art
3540 Washington Avenue, St. Louis, MO 63103
☎: 314-535-4660   ▣ www. forumart.org
Open: 10-5 Tu-Sa   **Closed:** Su, Mo, LEG/HOL! & INSTALLATIONS
Vol/Cont: $2.00
♿ ℗ Street or public parking (nominal fee) at the Third Baptist Church parking lot on Washington.   **Museum Shop**
Group Tours   Drop-In Tours: By Appointment during museum hours
Permanent Collection: No permanent collection. Please call for current exhibition information not listed below.

Experimental cutting-edge art of the new is the focus of The Forum which presents exhibitions of important recent national and international art enhanced by educational programming and public discussions.

ON EXHIBIT 2000
11/19/1999 to 01/08/2000   MICHAEL RESS: WYSIWYG
Wysiwig is an acronym for what you see is what you get. This project combines 20th century technologies with centuries old concepts of creation.

11/19/1999 to 01/08/2000   DOUG ISCHER: RECENT WORK
A video artist who will install among others a work called "Seam". A video camera is installed in a man's dress shirt lying on the floor.

01/21/2000 to 03/18/2000   BRAD CLOEPFILL AND ALLIED WORKS
Cloepfil was selected as the architect for a new Museum building in the Grand Center Area.

01/21/2000 to 03/18/2000   WILLIAM KENTRIDGE: WEIGHING... AND WANTING
South African artist Kentridge 18 charcoal drawings and a laser disc video projection. Viewers respond to his beautiful drawings, emotional use of color and moving sound track. *Will Travel*

03/31/2000 to 05/13/2000   ALLEN WEXLER: CUSTOM BUILT
Culture, ritual, design and symbol are examined through works that blur the lines between sculpture, architecture, design and furniture.

03/31/2000 to 05/18/2000   WENDY JACOB
Urban landscapes and homelessness are examined in the installation.

06/02/2000 to 07/29/2000   ANDREW CONNELLY: PERFORMANCE INSTALLATION
A site specific work dealing with the emotional; territory of relationships.

06/02/2000 to 07/29/2000   VAN MCELWEE: RECENT WORKS
McElwee has been producing and exhibiting experimental videotapes since 1976. He mutates images of ancient and industrial structures into beautiful kaleidoscopic imagery.

08/25/2000 to 10/21/2000   MOIRA DRYER: PAINTINGS
Large scale abstractions by the late painter who was a gifted colorist

11/10/2000 to 01/13/2001   STEPHAN BALKENHOF
Large scale carved wooden figures by this German sculptor.

Laumeier Sculpture Park Museum
12580 Rott Rd., St. Louis, MO 63127
☎: 314-821-1209
Open: Park: 7am-1/2 hour after sunset; Museum: 10-5 Tu-Sa & 12-5 Su   **Closed:** Park & Museum: 1/1, THGV, 12/25
♿ ℗ Free   **Museum Shop** ⅋ Picnic Area
Group Tours: 314-821-1298 ($10 groups less than 25)   **Drop-In Tours**: 1st & 3rd Su of month at 2pm (May - Oct)
Sculpture Garden
Permanent Collection: CONT/AM; sculp: NATIVE SCULP & ART; SITE SPECIFIC SCULP

Laumeier Sculpture Park Museum - continued

More than 75 internationally acclaimed site-specific sculptures that complement their natural surroundings are the focus of this institution whose goal is to promote greater public involvement and understanding of contemporary sculpture. In addition to audio cassettes that are available for self-guided tours, there are, for the visually impaired, 12 scale models of featured works, accompanied by descriptive braille labels, that are placed near their full sized outdoor counterparts. **NOT TO BE MISSED:** Works by Alexander Liberman, Beverly Pepper, Dan Graham, Jackie Ferrara

Saint Louis Art Museum

1 Fine Arts Park, Forest Park, St. Louis, MO 63110-1380

☎: 314-721-0072 ◉ www.slam.org
Open: 1:30-8:30 Tu, 10-5 We-Su **Closed:** Mo, 1/1, THGV, 12/25
Free Day: special exh is free Tu
♿ ℗ Free parking in small lot on south side of building; also street parking available.
Museum Shop ⅋: Cafe 11-3:30 & 5-8 Tu; 11-3:30 We-Sa; 10-2 Su (brunch); Snack Bar also
Group Tours: ex 484 **Drop-In Tours:** 1:30 We-Fr (30 min.); 1:30 Sa, Su (60 min.)
Historic Building Located in a 1904 World's Fair Exhibition Building designed by Cass Gilbert
Sculpture Garden
Permanent Collection: AN/EGT; AN/CH; JAP; IND; OC; AF; P/COL; NAT/AM; REN; PTGS:18-CONT; SCULP: 18-CONT

Just 10 minutes from the heart of downtown St. Louis, this museum is home to one of the most important permanent collections of art in the country. A global museum featuring pre-Columbian and German Expressionist works that are ranked among the best in the best in the world, this institution is also known for its Renaissance, Impressionist, American, African, Oceanic, Asian and Ancient through Contemporary art. **NOT TO BE MISSED:** The Sculpture Terrace with works by Anthony Caro, Pierre Auguste Renoir, Henry Moore, Alexander Calder, and Aristide Maillol; Egyptian mummy and Cartonnage on display with a full-size x-ray of the mummy.

ON EXHIBIT 2000

02/01/2000 to 04/16/2000 ABELARDO MORELL AND THE CAMERA EYE
The first major exhibit to explore the most fundamental of photographic principles which while fully understood have not been fully expressed as images, and the full extent of his work.

02/19/2000 to 05/14/2000 THE WORK OF CHARLES AND RAY EAMES: A LEGACY OF INVENTION
Admission Fee

07/01/2000 to 09/24/2000 WONDERLAND
The work of 10-15 contemporary artists showing the most inventive, exciting and compelling art being produced at the dawn of the 21st century. Wonderland will incorporate viewers into inventive installations and full scale aesthetic environments.
Catalog Admission Fee

11/04/2000 to 01/07/2001 PAINTING ON LIGHT: DRAWINGS AND STAINED GLASS IN THE AGE OF Dürer AND HOLBEIN
Preparatory drawings with painted glass panels in the exhibition will examine the relationship between the designers and the glass painters. The beliefs, concerns and lives of people from all walks of life in German Renaissance society. Religion, history sporting all come to life in the luminous meticulously crafted painted glass panels evoking the spirit of the Renaissance.
Catalog Admission Fee Will Travel

MISSOURI

Washington University Gallery of Art, Steinberg Hall

One Brookings Drive, St. Louis, MO 63130-4899

☎: 314-935-5490 ▣ www.proserve.wustle.edu/~wugallery

Open: Sept-May: 10-4:30 Mo-Fr & 1-5 Sa, Su; CLOSED mid May-early Sept. **Closed:** LEG/HOL! Occasionally closed for major installations; Call (314-935-4523)

♿ Ⓟ Free North side of the building   **Museum Shop**

Group Tours   Drop-In Tours: call

Permanent Collection: EU: ptgs, sculp 16-20; OM: 16-20; CONT/GR; AM: ptgs, sculp 19-20; DEC/ART; FR: academic; AB/EXP; CUBISTS

With a well-deserved reputation for being one of the premier university art museums in the nation, the more than 100 year old Gallery of Art at Washington University features outstanding examples of works by Picasso (25 in all) and a myriad of history's artistic greats. Including Depre, Daumier, Church, and Gifford, Picasso, Ernst, deKooning and Pollock among a host of other artists. **NOT TO BE MISSED:** Hudson River School Collection

ON EXHIBIT 2000

01/21/2000 to 03/19/2000   JAPANESE PAINTINGS AND CERAMICS FROM A PRIVATE COLLECTION

01/21/2000 to 03/19/2000   FIRST ART: ORIGINS OF THE WASHINGTON UNIVERSITY COLLECTION: OLD MASTER AND 19TH C PAINTINGS

BILLINGS

Yellowstone Art Museum
410 N. 27th St., Billings, MT 59101

☎: 406-256-6804   ◉ yellowstone.artmuseum.org
Open: 11-5 Tu-Sa, Noon-5 Su, till 8pm Th; Open one hour earlier in summer   **Closed:** Mo, LEG/HOL!
ADM: Adult: $3.00   **Children:** $1.00 6-18; Free under 6   **Students:** $2.00   **Seniors:** $2.00
♿ ⓟ Pay lot next to building is free to museum patrons.   **Museum Shop**
Group Tours: 406-256-6804   **Drop-In Tours:** 10-2 Tu-Fr   **Historic Building** Original building built in 1884. Completed expansion and remodel in Feb 28, 1998. 30,000 sq. ft. added to orig. structure.
Permanent Collection: CONT/HISTORICAL: ptgs, sculp, cer, phot, drgs, gr

Situated in the heart of downtown Billings, the focus of the museum is on displaying the works of contemporary regional artists and on showcasing artists who have achieved significant regional or national acclaim. With nearly 2,000 objects in its permanent collection, the museum is well-known for its "Montana Collection" dedicated to the preservation of art of the West. The museum collection includes work by notable artists such as Rudy Autio, John Buck, Deborah Butterfield, Clarice Dreyer, Peter Voulkos and Theodore Waddell. Additionally, the museum houses a collection of 90 abstract expressionist paintings from the George Poindexter family of New York and the largest private collection of work by cowboy author and illustrator Will James. The museum re-opened its doors February 28, 1998 after closing for two years to complete a 6.2 million dollar expansion and renovation project. The expansion added 30,000 square feet to the original structure. In addition to tripling the exhibition space, other visitor amenities were added including: an education classroom/studio, public meeting room, courtyard and enhanced museum store. The museum is fully accessible with ramped entrances and elevators to assist handicapped patrons. Wheel chairs are also available.

ON EXHIBIT 2000

11/1999 to 01/2000   HOLIDAY EXHIBITION(S)

01/2000 to 02/2000   32ND ART AUCTION EXHIBITION

04/29/2000 to 07/25/2000   TRASHFORMATIONS: RECYCLED MATERIALS IN CONTEMPORARY AMERICAN ART AND DESIGN
Works in various media featuring the varied and inventive use of recycled materials in American art and design. *Will Travel*

07/2000 to 08/2000   CHRISTO AND JEAN-CLAUDE: THE ARKANSAS RIVER PROJECT

GREAT FALLS

C. M. Russell Museum
400 13th St. North, Great Falls, MT 59401-1498

☎: 406-727-8787   ◉ www.cmrussell.org
Open: MAY 1-SEPT 30: 9-6 Mo-Sa & 12-5 Su; WINTER: 10-5 Tu-Sa & 1-5 Su   **Closed:** 1/1, EASTER, THGV, 12/25
Free Day: Dec - Feb Su-2-5   **ADM:** Adult: $4.00   **Children:** Free under 6   **Students:** $2.00   **Seniors:** $3.00
♿ ⓟ Free   **Museum Shop**
Group Tours   Drop-In Tours: 9:15 & 1:15 Mo-Fr June-Aug   **Historic Building**
Permanent Collection: REG; CONT; CER

Constructed mainly of telephone poles, the log cabin studio of the great cowboy artist C. M. Russell still contains the original cowboy gear and Indian artifacts that were used as the artist's models. Adjoining the cabin, and in contrast to it, is the fine art museum with its modern facade. It houses more than 7,000 works of art that capture the flavor of the old west and its bygone way of life. **NOT TO BE MISSED:** Collection of Western Art by many of the American greats

MONTANA

Paris Gibson Square Museum of Art

1400 1st Ave., North, Great Falls, MT 59401-3299
☎: 406-727-8255
Open: 10-5 Tu-Fr; Noon-5 Sa, Su; 7-9 Th; Also open Mo MEM/DAY to LAB/DAY   **Closed:** LEG/HOL!
♿ ℗ Free and ample   **Museum Shop** ⑂ Lunch Tu-Fr
Group Tours
Historic Building 19th C Romanesque structure built in 1895 as a high school
Sculpture Garden
Permanent Collection: REG: ptgs, sculp, drgs, gr

Contemporary arts are featured within the walls of this 19th century Romanesque building which was originally used as a high school.

ON EXHIBIT 2000

12/22/1999 to 02/07/2000   RICHARD NOTKIN RETROSPECTIVE

02/17/2000 to 04/20/2000   NATIVE AMERICAN CONTEMPORARY ART

04/28/2000 to 05/30/2000   GREAT FALLS PUBLIC SCHOOLS ALL-CITY ART EXHIBIT

06/08/2000 to 08/07/2000   A PASSION FOR PRINTMAKING

KALISPELL

Hockaday Center for the Arts

Second Ave E. & Third St, Kalispell, MT 59901
☎: 406-755-5268
Open: 10-6 Tu-Sa, 10-8 We   **Closed:** Mo, LEG/HOL!
Free Day: We   **ADM: Adult:** $2.00   **Children:** Free   **Students:** $1.00   **Seniors:** $1.00
♿ ℗   **Museum Shop**
Group Tours: 406-755-5268   **Drop-In Tours**: Upon request if available
Historic Building
Sculpture Garden
Permanent Collection: CONT/NORTHWEST: ptgs, sculp, gr, port, cer

The Hockaday Center for the Arts which places strong emphasis on contemporary art is housed in the renovated Carnegie Library built in 1903. A program of rotating regional, national, or international exhibitions is presented approximately every 6 weeks. **NOT TO BE MISSED:** The Hockaday permanent collection of works by NW Montana artists and our museum shop featuring fine arts and crafts.

ON EXHIBIT 2000
ONGOING   PERMANENT COLLECTION INSTALLATION: HUGH HOCKADAY

ONGOING   PERMANENT COLLECTION INSTALLATION: RUSSEL CHATHAM

Fall/2000   TWO PARKS, TWO VIEWS: PHOTOS BY LEE SILLIMAN AND MARSHALL NOICE

Spring/2000   ROBOTIC PORTRAITURE: DEENA DES RIOUX

Custer County Art Center

Water Plant Rd., Miles City, MT 59301
☎: 406-232-0635
Open: 1-5 Tu-Su   **Closed:** 1/1, EASTER, THGV, 12/25
Vol/Cont:
♿ ℗ **Museum Shop**
Group Tours   Historic Building Located in the old holding tanks of the water plant (member NRHP)
Permanent Collection: CONT/REG; 126 EDWARD S. CURTIS PHOTOGRAVURES; 81 WILLIAM HENRY JACKSON PHOTOCHROMES, 200 REGIONAL ARTIST'S WORKS ON DISPLAY

The old holding tanks of the water plant (c. 1914) provide an unusual location for the Custer Art Center. Situated in the southeastern part of the state in a park-land setting overlooking the Yellowstone River, this facility features 20th century Western and contemporary art. The gift shop is worthy of mention due to the emphasis placed on available works for sale by regional artists. **NOT TO BE MISSED:** Annual Western Art Roundup & Quick Draw Art Auction 3rd weekend in May

Art Museum of Missoula

335 North Pattee, Missoula, MT 59802
☎: 406-728-0447
Open: Noon-6 Tu-Su, till 8pm Tu   **Closed:** LEG/HOL!
ADM: Adult: $2.00   Children: Free under 18   **Students:** $2.00   **Seniors:** $2.00
♿ ℗ Limited metered on-street parking   **Museum Shop**
Group Tours   **Historic Building**
Permanent Collection: REG: 19-20

International exhibitions and regional art of Montana and other Western states is featured in this lively community-based museum which is housed in the early 20th century Old Carnegie Library building in downtown Missoula.

Museum of Fine Arts

Affiliate Institution: School of Fine Arts, University of Montana
Missoula, MT 59812
☎: 406-243-4970
Open: 9-12 & 1-4 Mo-Fr   **Closed:** STATE/HOL & LEG/HOL!
♿ ℗ Free on-street parking and in Springfield Library & Museum lots on State St. and Edwards St.   **Museum Shop**
Permanent Collection: REG

Great American artists are well represented in this University museum with special emphasis on Western painters and prints by such contemporary artists as Motherwell and Krasner. The permanent collection rotates with exhibitions of a temporary nature.

ON EXHIBIT 2000

06/19/2000 to 08/11/2000   DREAMINGS: ABORIGINAL ART OF THE WESTERN DESERT FROM THE DONALD KAHN COLLECTION
Paintings by aboriginal artists who live and work in central Australia's Western desert region. Works in this region are governed by the Aboriginal law of "Tjukurrpa", defined as the explanation of existence by two physical manifestations: the land and the people.

NEBRASKA

Museum of Nebraska Art
Affiliate Institution: University of Nebraska at Kearney
24th & Central, Kearney, NE 68848
☎: 308-865-8559
Open: 11-5 Tu-Sa,1-5 Su   **Closed:** LEG/HOL!
   ⑆   ℗   **Museum Shop**   **Group Tours**   **Historic Building**   **Sculpture Garden**
Permanent Collection: REG: Nebraskan 19-present

The museum building, listed in the National Register of Historic Places, has been remodeled and expanded with new gallery spaces and a sculpture garden. Featured is the Nebraska Art Collection-artwork by Nebraskans from the Artist-Explorers to the contemporary scene. **NOT TO BE MISSED:** 'The Bride', by Robert Henri

Great Plains Art Collection
Affiliate Institution: University of Nebraska
215 Love Library, Lincoln, NE 68588-0475
☎: 402-472-6220   ◙   www.unl.edu/plains/artcoll
Open: 9:30-5 Mo-Fr, 10-5 Sa, 1:30-5 Su   **Closed:** closed holiday weekends, between exhibits and ACAD
Vol/Cont:
   ⑆   ℗ Limited metered parking   **Group Tours**
Permanent Collection: WESTERN: ptgs, sculp 19,20; NAT/AM

This collection of western art which emphasizes the Great Plains features sculptures by such outstanding artists as Charles Russell & Frederic Remington, and paintings by Albert Bierstadt, John Clymer, Olaf Wieghorst, Mel Gerhold and others. **NOT TO BE MISSED:** William de la Montagne Cary, (1840-1922), 'Buffalo Throwing the Hunter', bronze

ON EXHIBIT 2000
01/12/2000 to 02/18/2000   EDWARD BOREIN: THE ARTIST'S LIFE AND WORK *Will Travel*

03/2000 to 04/2000   SPECIAL EXHIBITION IN CONJUNCTION WITH THE CENTER FOR GREAT PLAIN'S STUDIES

Sheldon Memorial Art Gallery and Sculpture Garden
Affiliate Institution: University of Nebraska
12th and R Sts., Lincoln, NE 68588-0300
☎: 402-472-2461   ◙   www. Sheldon.unl.edu
Open: 10-5 Tu-Sa, 7-9 Th-Sa, 2-9 Su   **Closed:** Mo, LEG/HOL!
Vol/Cont:
   ⑆   ℗   **Museum Shop**
Group Tours   **Drop-In Tours**: during public hours   **Historic Building**   **Sculpture Garden**
Permanent Collection: AM: ptgs 19,20,sculp, phot, w/col, drgs, gr

This highly regarded collection is housed in a beautiful Italian marble building designed by internationally acclaimed architect Philip Johnson. It is located on the University of Nebraska-Lincoln campus and surrounded by a campus-wide sculpture garden consisting of over 34 key examples by artists of renown including di Suvero, Lachaise, David Smith, Heizer, Shea, Serra and Oldenburg. **NOT TO BE MISSED:** "Torn Notebook", a new 22 foot monumental sculpture by Claes Oldenburg and Coosje van Bruggen, 3 pieces.

Sheldon Memorial Art Gallery and Sculpture Garden - continued
ON EXHIBIT 2000
01/24/1999 to 01/02/2000   ROBERT COLESCOTT: RECENT PAINTINGS, 47TH VENICE BIENNIAL
The 19 provocative paintings on view, created over the past decade by Arizona-based artist Colescott, contain his highly personal narrative figurative imagery blended with ironic viewpoints that address major contemporary social issues. One of the most important U.S. artists working today, Colescott was the first painter since Jasper Johns, in 1988, to be included in the 47th Venice Biennale. He was also the first American ever to be given a solo exhibition at that prestigious event.

09/01/1999 to 01/02/2000   BLACK IMAGE AND IDENTITY: AFRICAN AMERICAN ART

11/16/1999 to 01/09/2000   HEROS AND HEROINES: COMIC ART ORIGINALS

11/23/1999 to 01/23/2000   JUDY BURTON VISUAL NUANCES

OMAHA

Joslyn Art Museum
2200 Dodge St., Omaha, NE 68102-1292
☎: 402-342-3300   ◙   www.joslyn.org
Open: 10-4 Tu-Sa, 12-4 Su   **Closed:** Mo, LEG/HOL!
Free Day: 10-12 Sa   **ADM: Adult:** $5.00   **Children:** 5-17 $2.50, under 5 Free   **Students:** $3.00   **Seniors:** $3.00
&   ℗ Free
Museum Shop ⊮: Tu-Sa 11-3:30, Su 12-3:30
Group Tours: ext 206   **Drop-In Tours:** We, 1pm; Sa 11am
Historic Building
Permanent Collection: AM: ptgs 19,20; WESTERN ART; EU: 19,20

Housing works from antiquity to the present the Joslyn, Nebraska's only art museum with an encyclopedic collection, has recently completed a major $16 million dollar expansion and renovation program. **NOT TO BE MISSED:** World-renowned collection of watercolors and prints by Swiss artist Karl Bodmer that document his journey to the American West 1832-34; Noted collection of American Western art including works by Catlin, Remington, and Leigh.

ON EXHIBIT 2000
11/06/1999 to 01/09/2000   DECK THE HALLS: HOLIDAY PHOTOGRAPHY BY ROGER MERTIN AND CHRISTINA PATOSKI

11/23/1999 to 01/02/2000   THE GREAT AMERICAN POP ART STORE: MULTIPLES OF THE SIXTIES
From a ray gun and cast baked potato by Claes Oldenburg and shopping bags by Roy Lichtenstein to Robert Indiana's LOVE ring and Andy Warhol's Brillo boxes, the 100 items featured in this exhibition document the popularity of the Pop movement in the art and culture of the 1960's. *Will Travel*

11/23/1999 to 01/23/2000   AFRICAN ART FROM THE HAN CORAY COLLECTION, 1916-1928

02/12/2000 to 06/04/2000   DALE CHIHULY: INSTALLATIONS
A showcase of three decades of work by America's foremost glass artist. Individual glass blown sculptures and large scale environments, for which he is best known, comprise this stunning exhibition of luminous glass work. *Will Travel*

02/19/2000 to 04/30/2000   PACIFIC ARCADIA: IMAGES OF CALIFORNIA, 1600-1914
Images in all media tracking the artistic views of California from an unspoiled paradise in the 17th and 18th C. "Land of plenty and opportunity" in the 19th C.

05/13/2000 to 06/25/2000   SOON COME: THE ART OF CONTEMPORARY JAMAICA
40 paintings and mixed media sculptures by 20 Jamaican artists are included in this display of vibrant art.

NEBRASKA

Joslyn Art Museum - continued
05/13/2000 to 07/02/2000   MIDLANDS INVITATIONAL 2000: WORKS ON PAPER
Regional art from Nebraska and 6 contiguous states.

07/08/2000 to 09/24/2000   MARSDEN HARTLEY: AMERICAN MASTERS
Superb examples of Harley's work from each period of his output: early post-impressionist Maine mountain scenes, Pre WWI abstractions made in Paris and Berlin, Provincetown landscapes and abstracts, New Mexican landscapes, still-lifes from the 1920's and 1930's, Bavarian mountain pastels, 1930's portraits and late Maine landscapes. *Will Travel*

07/15/2000 to 09/10/2000   TWENTIETH CENTURY AMERICAN DRAWINGS FROM THE ARKANSAS ART CENTER COLLECTION *Will Travel*

10/14/2000 to 01/07/2001   AN AMERICAN CENTURY OF PHOTOGRAPHY FROM DRY-PLATE TO DIGITAL: THE HALLMARK PHOTOGRAPHIC COLLECTION *Will Travel*

Nevada Museum of Art/E. L. Weigand Gallery
160 W. Liberty Street, Reno, NV 89501
☎: 775-329-3333 ◉ nevadaart.org
Open: 10-4 Tu, We, Fr: 10-7-Th 12-4 Sa, Su **Closed:** Mo, LEG/HOL!
Free Day: Su **ADM: Adult:** $5.00 **Children:** $1.00 (6-12) **Students:** $3.00 **Seniors:** $3.00
& ℗ **Museum Shop**
Group Tours Drop-In Tours: 2pm Sa
Permanent Collection: AM: ptgs 19,20, NAT/AM; REG

As 'the only collecting fine art museum in the state of Nevada', this 60 year old institution has made art and artists of the Great Basin & the American West its primary focus. PLEASE NOTE: The permanent collection is on display only during specific exhibitions. Call for specifics. **NOT TO BE MISSED:** A 'welcome' collage of neon tubes & fragmented glass placed over the entryway to the museum

ON EXHIBIT 2000

12/11/1999 to 02/06/2000 DREAMINGS: ABORIGINAL EXPLORATIONS BY SUZANNE KANATSIZ
A combination of sculptural and two dimensional pieces as a result of her travels in Australia. The use of diverse materials the viewer will be conceptually exposed to Aboriginal art forms.

12/11/1999 to 02/06/2000 EDWARD BOREIN: ON THE RANGE
Romantic images of the cowboy in the west.

02/12/2000 to 04/30/2000 BEYOND BORDERS: ENRIQUE CHAGOYA
The works look at the cultural collisions between Western art and the Pre-Columbia art world.

02/12/2000 to 06/18/2000 AMERICAN VISIONS: PAINTINGS FROM THE HUDSON RIVER SCHOOL
Over 65 paintings by Bierstadt, Durand, Cole and others will be shown in looking at the roots of American landscape painting.

07/01/2000 to 09/04/2000 TWENTIETH CENTURY IMAGES: THE SBC COMMUNICATIONS COLLECTION
This outstanding collection of corporate art focuses on 20th C. American art . Included are works by Pollack, O'Keeffe, and de Kooning.

09/16/2000 to 11/12/2000 CHIHULY OVER VENICE
Chihuly and his team of glass blowers traveled to Finland, Ireland and Mexico collaborating with masters from each country on huge colored-glass chandeliers which he then hung in a dramatic installation over the canals of Venice. Included also are Chihuly pieces from local collections.

09/16/2000 to 11/12/2000 CHIHULY OVER VENICE
Chihuly and his team of glass blowers traveled to Finland, Ireland and Mexico collaborating with masters from each country on huge colored-glass chandeliers which he then hung in a dramatic installation over the canals of Venice. Included also are Chihuly pieces from local collections.

NEW HAMPSHIRE

CORNISH

Saint-Gaudens
St. Gaudens Rd, Cornish, NH 03745-9704
✆: 603-675-2175 ▣ www.sgnhs.org./or/abc/www.nps.gov/saga
Open: 9:30-4:30 Daily, last weekend May-Oct
Free Day: Aug 25th **ADM:** **Adult:** $4.00 **Children:** Free
ⓟ **Museum Shop**
Group Tours Drop-In Tours: adv res req **Historic Building Sculpture Garden**
Permanent Collection: AUGUSTUS SAINT GAUDENS: sculp

The house, the studios, and 150 acres of the gardens of Augustus Saint-Gaudens (1848-1907), one of America's greatest sculptors.

ON EXHIBIT 2000
Exhibits of contemporary art throughout the season. Concert Series Sundays at 2 PM, July and August.

DURHAM

Art Gallery, University of New Hampshire
Paul Creative Arts Center, 30 College Road, Durham, NH 03824-3538
✆: 603-862-3712
Open: 10-4 Mo-We, 10-8 Th, 1-5 Sa-Su (Sep-May) **Closed:** Fr. ACAD!
♿ ⓟ Metered or at Visitors Center
Group Tours: 603-862-3713
Permanent Collection: JAP: gr 19; EU & AM: drgs 17-20; PHOT; EU: works on paper 19,20

Each academic year The Art Gallery of the University of New Hampshire presents exhibitions of historical to contemporary art in a variety of media. Exhibitions also include work by the University art faculty, alumni, senior art students and selections from the permanent collection.

ON EXHIBIT 2000
01/25/2000 to 03/09/2000 PAST INTO PRESENT : PAINTINGS BY M. ZABARSKY
A retrospective of the 28 years of paintings professor M. Zabarsky

01/25/2000 to 04/25/2000 RELIGION: CONTEMPORARY INTERPRETATIONS BY WOMEN
Gallery closed March 10-19 and April 23rd. Women artists whose work addresses religion from a personal or cultural point of view.

03/25/2000 to 04/25/2000 THOUGHTFUL MECHANISMS: THE LYRICAL ENGINEERING OF ARTHUR GANSON
Describing himself as a cross between a mechanical engineer and a choreographer, Ganson creates sculptures that dance, flutter, tumble and breathe.

HANOVER

Hood Museum Of Art
Affiliate Institution: Dartmouth College
Wheelock Street, Hanover, NH 03755
✆: 603-646-2808
Open: 10-5 Tu, Th-Sa, 10-9 We, 12-5 Su **Closed:** LEG/HOL!
♿ ⓟ **Museum Shop** ⫙
Permanent Collection: AM: ptgs 19,20; GR; PICASSO; EU: ptgs

226

Hood Museum Of Art - continued

The Museum houses one of the oldest and finest college collections in the country in an award-winning post-modern building designed by Charles Moore and Chad Floyd. **NOT TO BE MISSED:** Panathenaic Amphora by the Berlin Painter 5th C. BC.

KEENE

Thorne-Sagendorph Art Gallery

Affiliate Institution: Keene State College
Wyman Way, Keene, NH 03435-3501
✆: 603-358-2720 ◙ www.keene.edu/FACILITIES/TSAG
Open: 12-4 Mo-We, 12-7, Tu-Fr, 12-4 Sa, Su **Closed:** ACAD!
Vol/Cont:
も Ⓟ Free
Group Tours **Drop-In Tours**: by appt
Permanent Collection: REG: 19; AM & EU: cont, gr

Changing exhibitions as well as selections from the permanent collection are featured in the contemporary space of this art gallery.

MANCHESTER

Currier Gallery of Art

201 Myrtle Way, Manchester, NH 03104
✆: 603-669-6144 ◙ www.currier.org
Open: 11-5 Mo, We, Th, Su, 11-8 Fr, 10-5 Sa **Closed:** Tu, LEG/HOL!
Free Day: 10-1 Sa **ADM: Adult:** $5.00 **Children:** Free under 18 **Students:** $4.00 **Seniors:** $4.00
も Ⓟ Adjacent on-street parking **Museum Shop** ⑪
Group Tours: 603-626-4154 **Historic Building** Registered in National Landmark of historic places (Circa 1929)
Permanent Collection: AM & EU: sculp 13-20; AM: furniture, dec/art

Set on beautifully landscaped grounds, The Gallery is housed in a elegant, newly renovated 1929 Beaux Arts building reminiscent of an Italian Renaissance villa. **NOT TO BE MISSED:** Zimmerman House (separate admission: Adults $7, Seniors and Students $5) designed in 1950 by Frank Lloyd Wright. It is one of five Wright houses in the Northeast and the only Wright designed residence in New England that is open to the public.

ON EXHIBIT 2000

11/26/1999 to 01/23/2000 MAXFIELD PARRISH, 1870-1966
A major retrospective of the work of one of the Academy's most distinguished alumni exploring the artistic influences, his work as one of the century's most popular illustrators and as a painter. Also to be explored is the qualities of his work which have led to his "rediscovery" by many contemporary artists. *Catalog Will Travel*

02/11/2000 to 04/17/2000 PHILIPPE HALSMAN: A RETROSPECTIVE
From the 1940s through the 1970s, Philippe Halsman's portraits of world-famous figures appeared on the covers, and in the pages, of the major picture magazines, such as Look and the Saturday Evening Post. The 73 vintage prints on exhibit-from the Halsman Family Collection-span the photographer's career, beginning in the 1930s in Paris with portraits of French writers Andre Gide and Andre Malraux. During the next 40 years, virtually every major personality in the arts and a long list of important world figures sat for his camera including Pablo Picasso, Judy Garland, Marlon Brando, Winston Churchill, John Steinbeck, John F. Kennedy, Marian Anderson, John Kenneth Galbraith, Ingrid Bergman, Aldous Huxley, Alfred Hitchcock, Martha Graham, Sammy Davis Jr., Barbra Streisand and Joan Baez.

NEW JERSEY

Stedman Art Gallery
Affiliate Institution: The State Univ of NJ
Rutgers Fine Arts Center, Camden, NJ 08102
☎: 609-225-6245
Open: 10-4 Mo-Sa   **Closed:** MEM/DAY, 7/4, LAB/DAY, THGV, 12/24-1/2
♿ ℗
Permanent Collection: AM & EU: Cont works on paper

Located in southern New Jersey, the gallery brings visual arts into focus as an integral part of the human story.

JERSEY CITY

Jersey City Museum
472 Jersey Ave, Jersey City, NJ 07302
☎: 201-547-4514
Open: 10:30-5 Tu, Th-Sa, 10:30-8 We, closed Sa in summer   **Closed:** LEG/HOL!, 12/24, 12/31
♿ ℗ Street
Group Tours: 201-547-4380   **Historic Building**
Permanent Collection: AUGUST WILL COLLECTION: views of Jersey City, 19; AM: ptgs, drgs, gr, phot; HIST: dec/art; JERSEY CITY INDUSTRIAL DESIGN

Established in 1901, the museum is located in the historic Van Vorst Park neighborhood of Jersey City in the 100-year old public library building. In addition to showcasing the works of established and emerging contemporary regional artists, the museum presents exhibitions from the permanent collection documenting regional history.

MILLVILLE

Museum of American Glass at Wheaton Village
Affiliate Institution: 998-4552
1501 Glasstown Road, Millville, NJ 08332-1566
☎: 609-825-6800 or 800-
Open: 10-5 daily(Apr-Dec), 10-5 We-Su (Jan-Mar)   **Closed:** 1/1, Easter, THGV, 12/25
ADM: Adult: $6.50   **Children:** Free under 5   **Students:** $3.50   **Seniors:** $5.50
♿ ℗ Free   **Museum Shop**   ‖: 7am-9pm, PaperWaiter Restaurant and Pub, adjacent to Village
Group Tours: 800-998-4552, ext. 2730   **Drop-In Tours**: by appt   **Historic Building**   **Sculpture Garden**
Permanent Collection: AM/GLASS

Wheaton Village focuses on American glass, craft and art. The collection features more than 6500 0bjects ranging from paperweights to fiber optics, mason jars to Tiffany masterpieces. Also featured are Crafts and Trades Row, Folklife Center, a Stained Glass Studio, unique museum stores, a train ride and picnic area. **NOT TO BE MISSED:** Featured in addition to the Museum are a fully operational glass factory with daily narrated demonstrations as well as demonstrations in pottery, woodworking, glass lampworking and stained glass.

ON EXHIBIT 2000

01/2000   A CENTURY OF INNOVATION

MONTCLAIR

Montclair Art Museum
3 South Mountain Ave, Montclair, NJ 07042
☎: 973-746-5555 ◉ www.montclair-art.com
Open: 11-5 Tu, We, Fr, Sa, 1-5 Th, Su, Summer hours 12-5 We-Su, 7/4-LAB/DAY **Closed:** Mo, LEG/HOL!
Free Day: Sa, 11-2 **ADM: Adult:** $5.00 **Children:** Free under 12 **Students:** $4.00 **Seniors:** $4.00
♿ ℗ Free on site parking **Museum Shop** ‖ nearby restaurants
Group Tours: 973-746-5555 x221 **Drop-In Tours**: most Su, 2pm !
Permanent Collection: NAT/AM: art 18-20; AM: ldscp, portraits 19; AM; Hudson River School: Am Impressionists

Located just 12 miles west of midtown Manhattan and housed in a Greek Revival style building, this museum, founded in 1914, features an impressive American art collection of a quality not usually expected in a small suburb.

ON EXHIBIT 2000

09/28/1999 to 1/02/2000 AMERICAN TONALISM: SELECTIONS FROM THE METROPOLITAN MUSEUM OF ART AND THE MONTCLAIR ART MUSEUM
An outstanding selection of turn-of-the-century masterpieces with muted hues and misty effects by Inness, Whistler, Ryder, Steichen, Twachtman, Davies and many others.

09/28/1999 to 1/16/2000 PARIS 1900: THE "AMERICAN SCHOOL" AT THE UNIVERSAL EXPOSITION
A millennial recreation of the American display at the Paris Exposition featuring the major artists of the 19th century. It was the first time that the existence of a uniquely "American School" was established in parity with the European Schools. Admission: $10 *Admission Fee*

02/13/2000 to 04/22/2000 PEOPLE'S CHOICE
The public will select favorite works.

04/2000 to 06/2000 NORTHWEST COAST ART
Native American works from the Northwest are included.

05/14/2000 to 08/20/2000 WILL BARNET RETROSPECTIVE / WILL BARNET IN CONTEXT
A survey of the work of this American modernist

09/2000 to 01/2001 GEORGIA O'KEEFFE: THE ARTISTS LANDSCAPE'
Photographs by Todd Webb of the landscape that inspires this artist. *Will Travel*

09/10/2000 to 01/07/2001 NATIVE SOIL: ART AND THE AMERICAN LAND
The theme of native soil as a pervasive concept that came to embody Americanism and nationalism.

NEW BRUNSWICK

Jane Voorhees Zimmerli Art Museum
Affiliate Institution: Rutgers, The State University of New Jersey
Corner George & Hamilton Streets, New Brunswick, NJ 08903
☎: 732-932-7237
Open: 10-4:30 Tu-Fr, Noon-5 Sa, Su **Closed:** LEG/HOL! 12/25 thru 1/1; Month of August, Mo, Tu in July
Free Day: 1st Su each month **ADM: Adult:** $3.00 **Children:** Free **Students:** $3.00 **Seniors:** $3.00
♿ ℗ Nearby or metered **Museum Shop** **Group Tours** **Drop-In Tours**: res req **Historic Building**
Permanent Collection: FR: gr 19; AM: 20; EU: 15-20; P/COL: cer; CONT/AM: gr; THE NORTON AND NANCY DODGE COLLECTION OF NONCONFORMIST ART FROM THE SOVIET UNION

Housing the Rutgers University Collection of more than 50,000 works, this museum also incorporates the International Center for Japonisme which features related art in the Kusakabe-Griffis Japonisme Gallery. **NOT TO BE MISSED:** The George Riabov Collection of Russian Art; The Norton and Nancy Dodge Collection of Nonconformist Russian Art from the Soviet Union.

NEW JERSEY

Newark Museum

49 Washington Street,, Newark, NJ 07101-0540
☎: 973-596-6550
Open: 12-5 We-Su   **Closed:** 1/1, 7/4, THGV, 12/25
  ⚹ Ⓟ $4.25 in the museum's adjacent parking lot
Museum Shop   ⅠⅠ Cafe in Engelhard Court noon-3:30 W-S (wheelchair accessible)
Group Tours: 973-596-6615   **Drop-In Tours:** 12:30-3:30 We-Su   **Historic Building** Ballantine House, schoolhouse
Permanent Collection: AM: ptgs 17-20; AM: folk; AF/AM; DEC/ARTS; GLASS; JAP; CONT; AM: Hudson River School
ptgs; AF; AN/GRK; AN/R; EGT

Established in 1909 as a museum of art and science, The Newark Museum features one of the finest collection
of Tibetan art in the world. The museum encompasses 80 galleries and includes the historic 1885 Ballantine
House, a landmark Victorian mansion; New Jersey's first planetarium; a Mini Zoo; and an 18th-century one-
room schoolhouse. **NOT TO BE MISSED:** Joseph Stella's 5-panel mural "The Voice of the City of New York
Interpreted," 1920-22; the Tibetan Altar, consecrated in 1990 by His Holiness the 14th Dalai Lama.

ON EXHIBIT 2000
ONGOING   HOUSE AND HOME: BALLANTINE HOUSE EXHIBITION
The Victorian origins of today's concept of "home" through the restored rooms and new thematic galleries that showcase the
Museum's extensive decorative arts collection. This 1885 national landmark building is the only urban Victorian mansion open
to the public in the Tri-state area. Included is an interactive computer game allowing the players to chose items for their own
fantasy house.

**09/1999 to 1/2000   MOUNTAINS AND VALLEYS, CASTLES AND TENTS: TIBETAN ART FROM THE
NEWARK MUSEUM COLLECTION**

Newark Public Library

5 Washington Street, Newark, NJ 07101
☎: 973-733-7745
Open: 9-5:30 Mo, Fr, Sa, 9-8:30 Tu, We, Th   **Closed:** LEG/HOL!
  ⚹ **Historic Building**
Permanent Collection: AM & EU: gr

Since 1903 the library can be counted on for exhibitions which are of rare quality and well documented.

Noyes Museum of Art

Lily Lake Rd, Oceanville, NJ 08231
☎: 609-652-8848   ◙ users.jerseyscape.com/thenoyes
Open: 11-4 We-Su   **Closed:** Mo, Tu, LEG/HOL!
Free Day: Fr   **ADM: Adult:** $3.00   **Children:** Free under 18   **Students:** $2.00   **Seniors:** $2.00
  ⚹ Ⓟ Free   **Museum Shop**
Group Tours: 800-669-2203   **Drop-In Tours:** Schedule in advance
Permanent Collection: AM: 19th, 20th C., craft, folk; NJ: reg; VINTAGE BIRD DECOYS

Nestled in a peaceful lakeside setting, the Museum displays rotating exhibitions of American art and craft.
Southern New Jersey's only fine art museum, it is a hidden treasure worth discovering and is located only 15
minutes from Atlantic City. **NOT TO BE MISSED:** Purple Martin Palace, view of Lily Lake

NEW JERSEY

Noyes Museum of Art - continued
ON EXHIBIT 2000

10/17/1999 to 1/16/2000   AMBIENCE AND ENERGY: EXPRESSIONIST PAINTERS GIVE LIFE TO SPACES
Three emerging expressionists: David Brewster, Jeff Epstein, and William Smith.

10/17/1999 to 1/19/2000   BRIAN MEUNIER
Whimsical sculptures based on nature.

ORADELL

Hiram Blauvelt Art Museum
705 Kinderkamack Road, Oradell, NJ 07649
☎: 201-261-0012
Open: 10-4 We-Fr, 2-5 Sa, Su   **Closed:** Mo, Tu, LEG/HOL
Vol/Cont:
&. Ⓟ Free   **Museum Shop**
Group Tours: 201-261-0012   **Drop-In Tours**: by appt   **Historic Building   Sculpture Garden**
Permanent Collection: WILDLIFE ART; AUDUBON FOLIO; IVORY GALLERY; BIG GAME ANIMALS, EXTINCT BIRDS, REPTILES

Founded in 1957 the museum is dedicated to bringing awareness to issues facing the natural world and to showcasing the artists who are inspired by it. It is located in an 1893 shingle and turret style carriage house. The 1679 Demarest House in River Edge, NJ is also owned by the Blauvelt-Demarest Foundation. **NOT TO BE MISSED:** Carl Rungius oil

ON EXHIBIT 2000

02/04/2000 to 06/11/2000   THE POWER OF BLACK AND WHITE

09/06/2000 to 12/17/2000   THE PAINTINGS OF ARTHUR SINGER

PRINCETON

Art Museum, Princeton University
Affiliate Institution: Princeton University
Nassau Street, Princeton, NJ 08544-1018
☎: 609-258-3788   ◙   www.princeton, edu
Open: 10-5 Tu-Sa, 1-5 Su   **Closed:** Mo, LEG/HOL!
&.   Ⓟ On-street or nearby garages; special parking arrangements for the handicapped are available (call ahead for information)   **Museum Shop**
Group Tours: 609-258-3043   **Drop-In Tours**: 2:00 Sa   **Historic Building** original 1890 Romanesque revival building designed by A. Page Brown
Permanent Collection: AN/GRK; AN/R+Mosaics; EU: sculp, ptgs 15-20; CH: sculp, ptgs; GR; P/COL; OM: ptgs, drgs; AF

An outstanding collection of Greek and Roman antiquities including Roman mosaics from Princeton University's excavations in Antioch is but one of the features of this highly regarded eclectic collection housed in a modern building on the lovely Princeton University campus. **NOT TO BE MISSED:** Picasso sculpture, ' Head of a Woman'

ON EXHIBIT 2000

11/23/1999 to 01/02/2000   CONTEMPORARY PHOTOGRAPHS

10/09/2000 to 01/02/2000   THE TRAPPINGS OF GENTILITY: NINETEENTH CENTURY BRITISH ART AT PRINCETON

NEW JERSEY

New Jersey Center For Visual Arts

68 Elm Street, Summit, NJ 07901
☎: 908-273-9121 ◙ www.njmuseums.com/njcva/index.htm
Open: 12-4 Mo-Fr, 7:30-10 Th, 2-4 Sa, Su **Closed:** LEG/HOL! & last 2 weeks in August
ADM: Adult: $1.00 **Children:** Free under 12 **Students:** $1.00
ও ℗ Free **Museum Shop**
Group Tours Drop-In Tours: ! **Sculpture Garden**
Permanent Collection: non-collecting institution

The Center presents exhibitions of contemporary art by artists of national and international reputation as well as classes for people of all ages and levels of ability.

African Art Museum of the S. M. A. Fathers

23 Bliss Ave, Tenafly, NJ 07670
☎: 201-894-8611 ◙ www.smafathers.org
Open: 10-5 Daily **Closed:** LEG/HOL! MO
ও ℗ Free
Group Tours Drop-In Tours: by appt
Permanent Collection: AF; sculp, dec/art

Located in a cloistered monastery with beautiful gardens in the gracious old town of Tenafly, this museum features changing collection and loan exhibitions.

ON EXHIBIT 2000

02/03/2000 to 05/31/2000 FOR BODY AND SOUL: TEXTILES OF SUB-SAHARAN AFRICA

06/22/2000 to 03/31/2000 TOTEMS, MYTHS, AND ENCHANTED LIZARDS: DOOR LOCKS OF THE BAMBARA PEOPLE OF MALI FROM THE COLLECTION OF Dr. Pascal JAMES AND ELEANOR IMPERATO

06/22/2000 to 01/07/2001 TRANSFORMATIONS: CERAMICS FROM THE PERMANENT COLLECTIONS

New Jersey State Museum

205 West State Street, CN530, Trenton, NJ 08625-0530
☎: 609-292-6464 ◙ www.state.nj.us/state/museum/usidx.html
Open: 9-4:45 Tu-Sa, 12-5 Su **Closed:** LEG/HOL!
ADM: Adult: Planetarium $1.00 **Children:** Planetarium $1.00 **Students:** $1.00 **Seniors:** $1.00
ও ℗ Free parking available in garage near museum **Museum Shop**
Group Tours
Permanent Collection: AM: cont, gr; AF/AM

The museum is located in the Capitol Complex in downtown Trenton. The fine art collections cover broad areas of interest with a special focus on New Jersey and culturally diverse artists. **NOT TO BE MISSED:** Ben Shahn Graphics Collection

---
ABIQUIU

Georgia O'Keeffe Home and Studio

Affiliate Institution: The Georgia O'Keeffe Foundation

Abiquiu, NM 87510

☎: 505-685-4539

Open: open by reservation only! 1 hr Tours seasonally on Tu, Th, Fr **Closed:** LEG/HOL

ADM: Adult: $20 interior $15 ext **Students:** $15.00 **Seniors:** $15.00

  Ġ Ⓟ no buses

Group Tours Historic Building

Permanent Collection: Home and studio of artist Georgia O'Keeffe

---
ALBUQUERQUE

University of New Mexico Museum

Affiliate Institution: The University of New Mexico

Fine Arts Center, Albuquerque, NM 87131-1416

☎:Fine Arts Center: 505-277-4001 Jonson Gallery: 1909 Las Lomas, 505-277-4967

Open: 9-4 Tu-Fr, 5-8 Tu, 1-4 Su, Jonson Gallery closed on weekends **Closed:** Mo, Sa, LEG/HOL!

  Ġ Ⓟ Limited free parking **Museum Shop**

Group Tours Sculpture Garden

Permanent Collection: CONT; 19, 20; GR; PHOT; SP/COL; OM

In addition to changing exhibitions of work drawn from the permanent collection the Museum features significant New Mexico and regional artists working in all media.

ON EXHIBIT 2000

10/19/1999 to 05/12/2000 RAYMOND JONSON: SELECTIONS FROM THE PERMANENT COLLECTION
A retrospective view of the pioneer modernist American painter who founded the Jonson Gallery in 1950.

06/05/2000 to 09/01/2000 50TH YEAR ANNIVERSARY FOR THE FOUNDING OF THE JONSON GALLERY
The connections between Johnson, Emil Bisstram, Nicholas Roerich and others through the Arsuna school of Fine Arts that opened in 1938 and operated for only a few years.

LOS ALAMOS

Art Center at Fuller Lodge

2132 Central Avenue, Los Alamos, NM 87544

☎: 505-662-9331 ▣ www.losalamos.org/flac.htm

Open: 10-4 Mo-Sa **Closed:** Su, LEG/HOLS

Sugg/Cont: $2.00 pp

  Ġ Ⓟ **Museum Shop**

Group Tours Drop-In Tours Historic Building

Located in historic Fuller Lodge, this art center presents changing exhibitions of local and regional fine arts and crafts. **NOT TO BE MISSED:** Shop sells artist work

233

NEW MEXICO

Roswell Museum and Art Center
100 West 11th, Roswell, NM 88201
📞: 505-624-6744 ☉ www.roswellmuseum.org
Open: 9-5 Mo-Sa, 1-5 Su & HOL   **Closed:** 1/1, THGV, 12/24, 12/25
Vol/Cont: **Sugg/Cont:** $2.00 pp
& ℗   **Museum Shop**
Group Tours: x 22, 1 week advance notice   **Drop-In Tours**
Historic Building original WPA arts center 1937   **Sculpture Garden**
Permanent Collection: SW/ART; HISTORY; SCIENCE; NM/ART; NAT/AM

16 galleries featuring works by Santa Fe and Taos masters and a wide range of historic and contemporary art in its impressive permanent collection make this museum one of the premier cultural attractions of the Southwest. Temporary exhibitions of Native American, Hispanic, and Anglo art are often featured. **NOT TO BE MISSED:** Rogers Aston Collection of Native American and Western Art

ON EXHIBIT 2000
09/10/1999 to 01/30/2000   **INVITATIONAL EXHIBITION : JIM WAID**

10/29/1999 to 01/02/2000   **MARY JOSEPHSON**

01/07/2000 to 12/31/2000   **EQUSS AND THE SOUTHWEST**

01/14/2000 to 03/12/2000   **PANOS**

02/25/2000 to 07/16/2000   **RANCHWOMEN OF NEW MEXICO**

02/25/2000 to 08/09/2000   **VISIONS OF THE BOMB**

03/24/2000 to 03/2001   **PHOTOGRAPHY: SELECTIONS FROM THE PERMANENT COLLECTION**

07/28/2000 to 09/10/2000   **ERIC SNELL ARTIST IN RESIDENCE EXHIBITION**

07/28/2000 to 09/10/2000   **KATIE KAHN-ARTIST IN RESIDENCE EXHIBITION**

08/18/2000 to 12/31/2000   **INGER JIRBY**

09/29/2000 to 02/18/2001   **2000 NATIVE AMERICAN INVITATIONAL**

Institute of American Indian Arts Museum
108 Cathedral Place, Santa Fe, NM 87501
📞: 505-988-6281 ☉ www.iaiancad.org
Open: 9-5 daily June-September;10-5 daily Oct-May   **Closed:** 1/1, 04/4, 12/25: Easter: THGV
ADM: Adult: $4.00; F NAT/AM   **Children:** Free under 16   **Students:** $2.00   **Seniors:** $2.00
& ℗ Local garages available   **Museum Shop**
Group Tours   Sculpture Garden

The Museum cares for and presents the National Collection of Contemporary Indian Art which chronicles the development 1960-present. Contemporary Native American arts and crafts and Alaskan native arts are featured. **NOT TO BE MISSED:** Admission to Allan Houser Art Park with Museum adm

Institute of American Indian Arts Museum - continued
ON EXHIBIT 2000
05/06/2000 to 06/06/2000   INDIAN TIMES: ART IN THE NEW MILLENNIUM
An exploration of the creative, individual visions of what the future may hold for the first peoples in this land. The art work represents some of the finest by contemporary Native-American artists from across Canada and the US.

08/20/2000 to 03/31/2000   SWIAI MONUMENTAL SCULPTURE
An annual presentation and competition of monumental works by the Southwestern Association for Indian Arts, Inc presented in Allan Houser Art Park

Museums of New Mexico
113 Lincoln Ave., Santa Fe, NM 87501
✆: 505-827-6451 ◉ www.nmculture.org
Open: All Museums 10-5 Tu-Su!, Monuments, 8:30-5 daily   **Closed:** Mo, LEG/HOL
ADM: Adult: $10, 4 day pass all   **Children:** Free under 17   **Seniors:** Free We
& Ⓟ   **Museum Shop**
Group Tours: 505-827-6452   **Drop-In Tours**: ! each Museum   **Historic Building**
Permanent Collection: (5 Museums with varied collections): TAOS & SANTA FE MASTERS; PHOT; SW/REG ;NAT/AM; FOLK; 5 State Monuments

In 1917 when it opened, the Museum of Fine Arts set the Santa Fe standard in pueblo-revival architecture. The Palace of the Governors, built by Spanish Colonial and Mexican governors, has the distinction of being the oldest public building in the US. Its period rooms and exhibitions of life in New Mexico during the Colonial Period are unique. Also included in the Museum is the Museum of Indian Arts and culture and the Museum of International Folk Art. The new Georgia O'Keeffe Museum is America's first museum dedicated to the work of a woman artist of international stature. Although it is a private, non-profit museum, it is in close partnership with the Museum of New Mexico. It is included in the 4 day pass. **NOT TO BE MISSED:** The entire complex

ON EXHIBIT 2000
PALACE OF THE GOVERNORS ON THE PLAZA
  ART OF ANCIENT AMERICA
  ANOTHER MEXICO: SPANISH LIFE ON THE UPPER RIO GRANDE
  SEGESSER HIDE PAINTINGS
  PERIOD ROOMS

MUSEUM OF FINE ARTS ON THE PLAZA

MUSEUM OF INDIAN ARTS AND CULTURE
  HERE NOW AND ALWAYS
  THE BUCHSBAUM GALLERY OF SOUTHWESTERN POTTERY

MUSEUM OF INTERNATIONAL FOLK ART
  MULTIPLE VISIONS: A COMMON BOND
  FAMILIA Y FE: FAMILY AND FAITH

THE GEORGIA O'KEEFFE MUSEUM

NEW MEXICO STATE MONUMENTS: call for admission cost
  FORT SELDEN STATE MONUMENT
  FORT SUMNER STATE MONUMENT
  JEMEZ STTE MONUMENT
  LINCOLN STATE MONUMENT
  CORONADO STATE MONUMENT

to 03/04/2000   Museum of International Folk Art   EXTRAORDINARY IN THE ORDINARY

NEW MEXICO

Museums of New Mexico - continued

06/06/1999 to 09/05/2000   Museum of International Folk Art   ANTECEDENTES: HISPANA AND HISPANO ARTISTS OF THE EARLY TWENTIETH CENTURY

01/24/1999 to 07/02/2000   Museum of International Folk Art   NEW MEXICAN MADONNAS, 1775-1998

060/6/1999 to 099/5/2000   Museum of International Folk Art   ZIA NOMBRE: HISPANO AND HISPANA ARTISTS OF THE NEW DEAL ERA

06/27/1999 to 05/2000   Museum of American Indian Arts and Crafts   OF STONES AND STORIES: VOICES FROM THE DINETAH

02/04/2000 to 08/13/2000   Museum of Fine Arts   NEW ACQUISITIONS IN PHOTOGRAPHY

03/10/2000 to 05/21/2000   Museum of Fine Arts   ADOLPH GOTTLIEB AND THE WEST

03/11/2000 to 05/20/2000   Museum of American Indian Arts and Crafts   CURATORS CHOICE

03/12/2000 to 09/12/2000   Palace of The Governors   FOLLOWING SOLOMAN NUNES CARVALHO

03/24/2000 to 06/25/2000   Museum of Fine Arts   BATHYSPHERE: ANDREW DAVIS

05/04/2000 to 10/01/2001   Museum of International Folk Art   THROUGH THE LOOKING GLASS

05/06/2000 to 10/29/2000   Museum of Fine Arts   TERM LIMITS

OPENS 6/18/2000   Palace of The Governors   JEWISH PIONEERS OF NEW MEXICO

OPENS 6/18/2000   Palace of The Governors   ART OF ANCIENT AMERICA

OPENS 6/18/2000   Palace of The Governors   SPANISH LIFE ON THE UPPER RIO GRANDE

06/11/2000 to 09/17/2000   Museum of American Indian Arts and Crafts   STRONG HEARTS

06/23/2000 to 09/17/2000   Museum of Fine Arts   CROSSING BOUNDARIES: CONTEMPORARY ART FROM MAYA ORTIZ

07/07/2000 to 10/15/2000   Museum of Fine Arts   TOM ASHCROFT

07/17/1999 to 12/31/2000   Museum of International Folk Art   LA CASA COLONIAL

09/15/2000 to 02/25/2001   Museum of Fine Arts   JAROMIR FUNKE: EARLY MODERN CZECH PHOTOGRAPHER

09/23/2000 to 12/31/2000   Museum of International Folk Art   TO HONOR AND COMFORT

10/08/2000 to 04/23/2000   Museum of Fine Arts   NEW MEXICO 2000

10/13/2000 to 04/22/2001   Museum of Fine Arts   DRAWINGS, PORTRAITS AND CARICATURES

Wheelwright Museum of the American Indian

704 Camino Lejo, Santa Fe, NM 87502
☎: 505-982-4636   ◉ www.wheelwright.org
Open: 10-5 Mo-Sa, 1-5 Su   **Closed:** 1/1, 12/25, THGV
& Ⓟ in front of building   **Museum Shop**
Group Tours   Drop-In Tours: 2pm Mo, Tu, Fr,: 11 Sa   **Historic Building   Sculpture Garden**
Permanent Collection: NAT/AM, Navajo; SW Ind (not always on view)

Wheelwright Museum of the American Indian - continued

Inside this eight sided building, shaped like a Navajo 'hooghan' or home, on a hillside with vast views, you will find breathtaking American Indian art. **NOT TO BE MISSED:** Case Trading Post museum shop.

ON EXHIBIT 2000

ONGOING SKYLIGHT GALLERY: CHANGING EXHIBITS OF EMERGING NATIVE AMERICAN ARTISTS

11/09/1999 to 04/2000 PAINTINGS BY JUDITH LOWRY (Mountain Maidu/Hammawi-Pit River) (working title) Judith Lowery's heritage is of California Native Peoples. Figuration and accessibility are most important to her. She uses ideas from stories she has heard from family and other images from her family history.

TAOS

Harwood Museum of the University of New Mexico

Affiliate Institution: University of New Mexico
238 Ledoux St, Taos, NM 87571
☎: 505-758-9826 ◉ www.nonculture.org
Open: 10-5 Tu-Sa, 12-5 Su **Closed:** Mo, LEG/HOL!
Free Day: Su **ADM: Adult:** $5.00
&. ℗ **Museum Shop**
Group Tours **Historic Building**
Permanent Collection: Hispanic and 19th C. Retablos; Bulhos, American Mod.

Many of the finest artists who have worked in Taos are represented in this collection. The building is one of the first twentieth-century that set the Pueblo Revival architectural style which became popular in northern New Mexico. Expansion completed 1997. **NOT TO BE MISSED:** 'Winter Funeral' by Victor Higgins, Agnes Martin Gallery ; Hispanic traditions gallery

ON EXHIBIT 2000

ONGOING THROUGHOUT THE YEAR SELECTIONS FROM THE PERMANENT COLLECTION ARE SHOWN IN THE FIVE OTHER GALLERIES.

12/05/1999 to 02/2000 BURTON PHILLIPS: ARTIST AND COLLECTOR

06/2000 to 08/2000 PICTURES OF TAOS

Millicent Rogers Museum

Museum Road, 4 miles N of Taos, Taos, NM 87571
☎: 505-758-2462
Open: 10-5 Daily Apr-Oct, closed Mo Nov-Mar **Closed:** 1/1, EASTER, SAN GERONIMO DAY 9/30, THGV, 12/25
Free Day: Su **ADM: Adult:** $6.00 **Children:** 6-16 $1.00 **Students:** $5.00 **Seniors:** $5.00
&. ℗ **Museum Shop**
Group Tours Drop-In Tours: ! **Historic Building Sculpture Garden**
Permanent Collection: NAT/AM & HISP: textiles, basketry, pottery, jewelry; REG

Dedicated to the display and interpretation of the art and material of the Southwest, the Millicent Rogers Museum places particular focus on New Mexican cultures. **NOT TO BE MISSED:** Extensive collection of pottery by Maria Martinez

NEW YORK

Albany Institute of History and Art
125 Washington Ave, Albany, NY 12210
☎: 518-463-4478 ◙ www.albanyinstitute.org
Open: 12-5 We-Su **Closed:** Mo, Tu, LEG/HOL!
Free Day: We **ADM: Adult:** $3.00 **Children:** Free under 12
♿ ℗ Nearby pay garage **Museum Shop Group Tours Historic Building**
Permanent Collection: PTGS: Hudson River School & Limner; AM: portraits 19; CAST IRON STOVES; DEC/ARTS: 19

Founded in 1791, this museums, one of the oldest in the nation presents permanent displays and changing exhibitions throughout the year. There are over 20,000 objects in the permanent collection.
The Museum will be under construction and renovation beginning in April 1999 and reopening in 2001. Please call ahead for exhibition information. **NOT TO BE MISSED:** Hudson River School paintings by Cole, Durand, Church, Kensett, Casilear and the Hart Brothers

University Art Museum
Affiliate Institution: University At Albany, State University of NY
1400 Washington Ave,, Albany, NY 12222
☎: 518-442-4035 ◙ www.albany.edu/museum
Open: 10-5 Tu-Fr, 12-4 Sa, Su **Closed:** Mo, LEG/HOL!
♿ ℗ Free ‖: In Campus Center
Permanent Collection: AM: gr, ptng, dr 20

This museum, the largest of its kind among the State University campuses and one of the major galleries of the Capitol District, features work from student and mid-career to established artists of national reputation. **NOT TO BE MISSED:** Richard Diebenkorn,' Seated Woman', 1966, (drawing)

Center for Curatorial Studies Museum
Bard College, Annandale on Hudson, NY 12504
☎: 914-758-7598 ◙ www.bard.edu/ccs
Open: 1-5 We-Su **Closed:** Mo. Tu,12/31, 1/1, MEM/DAY, 7/4, THGV, 12/25
♿ ℗
Group Tours: 914-758-7598
Permanent Collection: CONT: all media; VIDEO: installation 1960-present

Housed in a facility which opened in 1992, the CCS Museum features changing exhibitions of contemporary art curated by director Amada Cruz, internationally renowned guest curators and graduate thesis candidates.

American Museum of the Moving Image
35th Ave at 36th St, Astoria, NY 11106
☎: 718-784-0077 ◙ www.ammi.org
Open: 12-5 Tu-Fr, 11-6 Sa-Su **Closed:** 12/25
ADM: Adult: $8.00 **Children:** $4.00 (5-18) under 4 Free **Students:** $5.00 **Seniors:** $5.00
♿ ℗ street parking available **Museum Shop** ‖: cafe
Group Tours: 718-784-4520 **Historic Building**

American Museum of the Moving Image - continued
Permanent Collection: BEHIND THE SCREEN, combination of artifacts, interactive experiences, live demonstrations and video screenings to tell the story of the making, marketing and exhibiting of film, television and digital media. Especially popular are Automated Dialogue Replacement where visitors can dub their own voices into a scene from a movie and Video Flipbook where visitors can create a flipbook of themselves that they can pick up at the gift shop as a memento.

The only Museum in the US devoted exclusively to film, television, video and interactive media and their impact on 20th century American life. **NOT TO BE MISSED:** 'Tut's Fever Movie Palace', Red Grooms and Lysiane Luongs interpretation of a 1920's neo-Egyptian movie palace showing screenings of classic movie serials daily.

AUBURN

Schweinfurth Memorial Art Center
205 Genesee St, Auburn, NY 13021
☎: 315-255-1553
Open: 10-5 Tu-Sa, 1-5 Su (extended hours during Quilt Show)   **Closed:** Mo, THGV, 12/25
ADM: Adult: $3.00   **Children:** Free under 12   **Seniors:** $3.00
♿ ℗   **Museum Shop   Group Tours**

Regional fine art, folk art and crafts are featured in changing exhibitions at this cultural center located in central New York State. **NOT TO BE MISSED:** Made in New York gift shop featuring regional fine arts and crafts.

BAYSIDE

QCC Art Gallery
Affiliate Institution: Queensborough Community College
222-05 56th Ave., Bayside, NY 11364-1497
☎: 718-631-6396
Open: 9-5 Mo-Fr and by appt.   **Closed:** Sa, Su, ACAD!
♿   **Museum Shop**   ⏸: 9am-2pm   **Group Tours   Historic Building**
Permanent Collection: AM: after 1950; WOMEN ARTISTS

The Gallery which reflects the ethnic diversity of Queensborough Community College and its regional residents also highlights the role art plays in the cultural history of people.

BINGHAMTON

Roberson Museum Science Center
30 Front St., Binghamton, NY 13905-4779
☎: 607-772-0660   ◙   www.roberson.org
Open: 10-5 Mo-Sa, 12-5 Su   **Closed:** LEG/HOL!
ADM: Adult: $5.00   **Children:** Free under 4   **Students:** $3.00   **Seniors:** $3.00
♿ ℗   **Museum Shop   Group Tours   Historic Building**
Permanent Collection: Reg TEXTILES; PHOT; PTGS; DEC/ART: late 19,20, agricultural tools and archeological materials

A regional museum featuring 19th and 20th c art, history, folklife, natural history and technology. It includes a 1907 mansion, a museum, a Planetarium, and the off-site Kopernik Observatory. **NOT TO BE MISSED:** 'Blue Box' trainer circa 1942 by Edwin Link; mammoth tusk and mammoth tooth c.9000 B.C.

NEW YORK

Roberson Museum Science Center - continued
ON EXHIBIT 2000
to 02/06/2000   REFUGE: THE NEWEST NEW YORKERS
Photographs by Mel Rosenthal of recently arrived refugees which reveal the hopes and aspirations of thousands who have found safe havens and new lives in New York.

to Summer/2000   SUSQUEHANNA STREET: IMMIGRANTS AND NEIGHBORS

02/07/2000 to 07/2000   ART AND SPIRIT: THE ICON PAINTINGS OF VLADISLAV ANDREJEV

03/25/2000 to 08/2000   TIME DETECTIVES

BLUE MOUNTAIN LAKE

Adirondack Museum
Blue Mountain Lake, NY 12812
☎: 518-352-7653   ◙ www.adkmuseum.org
Open: Normal season Mem/Day-Col/Day 2000 changed for opening of Visitor's Center.
Free Day: call for dates and times   **ADM**: **Adult:** $10.00   **Children:** 7-16 $6.00   **Seniors:** $9.00
& ℗   **Museum Shop**   ⵐ **Historic Building**
Permanent Collection: AM: Pntgs, GR, Drwgs, 1850-present

The Museum tells the stories of how people lived, moved, worked and played in the Adirondacks. There are 23 indoor and outdoor exhibit areas featuring special events and programs. Just an hour from Lake Placid and Lake George, the museum has a cafeteria overlooking Blue Mountain Lake.

ON EXHIBIT 2000
ONGOING   THE VIEW FROM ASGAARD: ROCKWELL KENT'S ADIRONDACK LEGACY
An exploration of Kent's life and creativity through paintings, commercial art and artifacts inspired by the Adirondack wilderness.

ONGOING   A PEOPLED WILDERNESS
The first part of a two- phase exhibition of the changing relationship between people and the Adirondack environment. It explores the impact of the environment on the settlement and use of the land.

BRONX

Bronx Museum of the Arts
1040 Grand Concourse, Bronx, NY 10456
☎: 718-681-6000
Open: 3-9 We; 10-5 Th-Fr; 12-6 Sa, Su   **Closed:** Mo, Tu, THGV, 12/25
Free Day: We   **Sugg/Cont:**   **ADM**: **Adult:** $3.00   **Children:** Free under 12   **Students:** $2.00   **Seniors:** $2.00
& ℗ nearby garage   **Museum Shop**   **Group Tours**: 718-681-6000, Ex132
Permanent Collection: AF: LAT/AM: SE/ASIAN: works on paper 20; CONT/AM: eth

Noted for its reflection of the ethnically diverse NYC metro area it is the only fine arts museum in the Bronx. The collection and exhibitions are a fresh perspective on the urban experience. And its commitment to stimulating audience participation in the visual arts.

ON EXHIBIT 2000
11/18/1999 to 02/27/2000   AMNESIA
16 contemporary artists from South America who examine the themes of memory, loss, and desire and issues related to mortality and the temporal nature of mortality.

11/18/1999 to 02/27/2000   RECENT ACQUISITIONS FROM THE PERMANENT COLLECTION

240

Hall of Fame for Great Americans
Affiliate Institution: Bronx Community College
University Ave and W. 181 St, Bronx, NY 10453
☏: 718-289-5161   ◙ www.bcc.cuny.edu
Open: 10-5 Daily
Ġ Ⓟ ¶¶
Group Tours   Drop-In Tours: by appt   **Historic Building   Sculpture Garden**
Permanent Collection: COLONNADE OF 98 BRONZE BUSTS OF AMERICANS ELECTED TO THE HALL OF FAME
SINCE 1900 (includes works by Daniel Chester French, James Earle Fraser, Frederick MacMonnies, August Saint-Gaudens

Overlooking the Bronx & Harlem Rivers, this beautiful Beaux arts style architectural complex, once a
Revolutionary War fort, contains a Stanford White designed library modeled after the Pantheon in Rome. 98
recently restored bronze portrait busts of famous Americans elected to the Hall of Fame since 1900 and placed
within the niches of the 'Men of Renown' classical colonnade allow the visitor to come face-to-face with
history through art.

BROOKLYN

The Brooklyn Museum of Art
200 Eastern Parkway, Brooklyn, NY 11238
☏: 718-638-5000   ◙ www.brooklynart.org
Open: 10-5 We-Fr, 11-6 Sa, open 11-11 first Sa of month 11-6 Su   **Closed:** Mo, Tu, THGV, 12/25, 1/1
Sugg/Cont: ADM: Adult: $4.00   **Children:** Free under 12   **Students:** $2.00   **Seniors:** $1.50
Ġ Ⓟ Pay parking on site   **Museum Shop**   ¶¶ open until 4 weekdays, till 5 Weekends & holidays, coffee/wine bar Sa eve
Group Tours: 718-638-5000, ext 221   **Drop-In Tours:** Th, Fr 1pm, Sa, Su, 1 & 3pm   **Historic Building   Sculpture
Garden**
Permanent Collection: EGT; AM-EU ptgs, scupl, dec/art 18-20; AS; AF; OC; NW/AM; W/COL

The Brooklyn Museum of Art is one of the nation's premier art institutions. Housed in a Beaux-Arts structure
designed in 1893 by McKim, Mead & White, its collections represent virtually the entire history of art from
Egyptian artifacts to modern American paintings. **NOT TO BE MISSED:** Newly renovated and brilliantly
installed Charles A. Wilbour Egyptian Collection

ON EXHIBIT 2000
10/02/1999 to 01/09/2000   SENSATION: YOUNG BRITISH ARTISTS FROM THE SAATCHI COLLECTION
Sections of animals in formaldehyde, sexual identity transformation and commercialism, fleshy female forms, etc. *Catalog*

10/29/1999 to 02/06/2000   EASTMAN JOHNSON: PAINTING AMERICA
Johnson is one of the most important American artists of the 19th Century. Famous for images of American life including rural
genre subjects, Civil War scenes, interior scenes, and portraiture. The exhibition is a comprehensive exploration of the entire
range of his work. *Catalog Will Travel*

**11/19/1999 to 04/16/2000   WITHIN THE PALE: JEWISH TOMBSTONES IN THE UKRAINE AND MOLDOVA:
PHOTOGRRAPHS BY DAVID GUBERMAN**
The vanishing art of stone carvers dating back to the 17th C ,it also provides a story of Jewish life in Russia over more than
three centuries.

02/05/2000 to 04/16/2000   THE BOOK ARTS: WORKING IN BROOKLYN
Artists books are a work of art on its own. It is conceived specifically for the book form and often published by the artist.

02/11/2000 to 05/07/2000   GUENNOL: A COLLECTION OF THE IMAGINATION
Alistair B. Martin and his late wife had a diverse and unique collection of decorative objects from almost every culture
throughout the world from Olmec Jade to a William de Kooning painting. The collection is a work of art in itself. The criteria
which shaped their choices made visible the unity from vastly different cultures *Catalog*

The Brooklyn Museum of Art - continued

05/06/2000 to 09/03/2000   GLASS
Celebrating the glass art conferences being held in Brooklyn in May 2000, it is part of a series of events happening in the boro. It will bring together the Urban Glass Center and the ancient Egyptians and Louis Comfort Tiffany and compare historical techniques.

05/26/2000 to 08/06/2000   MAXFIELD PARRISH, 1870-1966
100 works including easel paintings, murals, drawings, prints, ephemera and material artifacts illustrating how prolific Parrish was. Organized chronologically the exhibition starts with book and magazine illustration in the 1890's and early 1900's. It reveals his nationalist spirit and obsession with American identity in the current post-modern period. *Catalog Will Travel*

05/26/2000 to 08/13/2000   WILLIAM MERRITT CHASE: PAIINTING IN BROOKLYN AND MANHATTAN, 1886-1891 (working title)
Chase was known for elaborate interior scenes, still-lifes, and portraits. This exhibition of carefully chosen oils and pastels will show a group of landscapes which are his first concentrated explorations of the American landscape. It will show some of his choicest works landscapes and examine this crucial period in his career. *Catalog*

06/23/2000 to 09/04/2000   DECADE: THE BROOKLYN MUSEUM OF ART'S TWENTY-SIXTH PRINT NATIONAL
The Print National originated at the Brooklyn Museum of Art in 1947. The last one was held in 1989. The Annual will examine the developments of collaborative printmaking and technological advances focusing on different regions of the United States *Catalog*

09/29/2000 to 01/07/2001   MASTERPIECES OF FASHION
The Museum's fashion collection is one of the oldest and largest in the country. Here it will be divided into four main groupings: fashion and historicism; fashion and exotic inspirations; art and fashion; and American fashion. *Catalog*

10/06/2000 to 01/07/2001   LEE KRASNER

10/27/2000 to 01/21/2001   SCYTHIAN GOLD IN THE UKRAINE
Although known as warring barbarians, the Scythians left behind them a wealth of Greek gold pieces which were fashioned by craftsmen in the black sea region. *Catalog Will Travel*

Rotunda Gallery

33 Clinton Street, Brooklyn, NY 11201
☎: 718-875-4047
Open: 12-5 Tu-Fr, 11-4 Sa   **Closed:** Su, Mo, LEG/HOL!
♿ ℗ Metered street parking; nearby pay garage
Group Tours   Drop-In Tours: 10-11:30 Mo-Fr
Permanent Collection: non-collecting institution

The Gallery's facility is an architecturally distinguished space designed for exhibition of all forms of contemporary art. It is located in Brooklyn Heights which is well known for its shops, restaurants and historic brownstones.

Rubelle & Norman Schafler Gallery

Affiliate Institution: Pratt Institute
200 Willoughby Ave, Brooklyn, NY 11205
☎: 718-636-3517
Open: 9-5 Mo-Fr   **Closed:** Sa, Su, L EG/HOL!
♿ ℗ on street parking only
Permanent Collection: Currently building a collection of Art and Design Works by Pratt Alumni, Faculty and Students

Varied programs of thematic, solo, and group exhibitions of contemporary art, design and architecture are presented in this gallery.

Albright Knox Art Gallery
1285 Elmwood Ave, Buffalo, NY 14222
☎: 716-882-8700 ◙ www.albrightknox.org
Open: 11-5 Tu-Sa, 12-5 Su **Closed:** Mo, THGV, 12/25, 1/1
Free Day: 11-1 Sa **ADM: Adult:** $4.00 **Children:** Free under 12 **Students:** $3.00 **Seniors:** $3.00
&. ℗ **Museum Shop** ⑂ **Group Tours** **Drop-In Tours:** 12:15 W-Th, 1:30 Sa-Su
Historic Building Sculpture Garden
Permanent Collection: AB/EXP; CONT: 70's & 80's; POST/IMPR; POP; OP; CUBIST; AM & EU: 18-19

With one of the world's top international surveys of twentieth-century painting and sculpture, the Albright-Knox is especially rich in American and European art of the past fifty years. The permanent collection which also offers a panorama of art through the centuries dating from 3000 BC., is housed in a 1905 Greek Revival style building designed by Edward B. Green with a 1962 addition by Gordon Bunshaft of Skidmore, Owings and Merrill.

ON EXHIBIT 2000

01/07/2000 to 04/02/2000 SEAN SCULLY: WORKS ON PAPER 1975-1996
One of a new generation of abstract painters, Scully expands the potential of his work with paint, canvas and steel.

01/22/2000 to 03/05/2000 NEW ROOM OF CONTEMPORARY ART: EUGENE LEROY
Composed of layer on layer of gnarled paint on canvas They slowly reveal the classic subjects, still-lives, landscapes, interiors, portraits and the French icon -the female nude. *Brochure*

01/22/2000 to 03/05/2000 IN WESTERN NEW YORK 2000
A biennial invitational exhibition of work in all media done by artists living in the eight counties of Western New York. *Brochure*

03/25/2000 to 07/02/2000 JAMES TISSOT: VICTORIAN LIFE/MODERN LOVE
The works shown here particularly emphasize works done in London which reflect his penetrating insight into Victorian life. The exhibition is arranged into thematic sections: Historical Subjects: modern life in France: Modern Life In Britain: Prints: La Femme a Paris: and Biblical illustrations. *Catalog Will Travel*

07/22/2000 to 09/10/2000 CLIFFORD STILL
The Albright Knox owns the largest public collection of Still's work.

07/22/2000 to 09/10/2000 NEW ROOM OF CONTEMPORARY ART: CATHY DE MONCHAUX
British artist de Monchaux will install a series of sculptures looking at the tensions between opposites. Her constructions confuse gender, the beautiful and repulsive, the hard and soft.

Burchfield Penney Art Center
Affiliate Institution: Buffalo State College
1300 Elmwood Ave, Buffalo, NY 14222-6003
☎: 716-878-6011 ◙ www.burchfield-penney.org
Open: 10-5 Tu, Th-Sa, 10-7:30 We, 1-5 Su **Closed:** Mo, LEG/HOL!
Vol/Cont:
&. ℗ Some on campus and metered parking. **Museum Shop** ⑂: on college grounds
Group Tours Drop-In Tours: by appt **Historic Building**
Permanent Collection: AM; WEST/NY: 19,20: CHARLES A BURCHFIELD; CHARLES CARY RAMSEY, Roycroft, Photo,

The Burchfield-Penney Art Center is dedicated to the art and artists of Western New York. Particular emphasis is given to the works of renowned American watercolorist Charles E. Burchfield. The museum holds the largest archives and collection in the world of his works. **NOT TO BE MISSED:** Burchfield's' Appalachian Evening'; 'Oncoming Spring', 'Fireflies and Lightening' hand crafted objects by Roycroft Arts and Crafts community artists, sculpture by Charles Cary Rumsey. Hands-on gallery-USEUM.

NEW YORK

Burchfield Penney Art Center - continued
ON EXHIBIT 2000

12/18/1999 to 02/13/2000   BEGINNING A NEW CENTURY, EMERGING ARTISTS IN WESTERN NEW YORK
To usher in a new century, this exhibition will highlight approximately fifty of the strongest and most promising artists in the region. With a team of curatorial advisors, the curatorial staff will select artists from the eight counties of Western New York. All media will be represented. A catalog illustrating a work by each artist will accompany the show. The exhibition is the fifth in a series promoting the work of emerging and under-represented artists. In previous years funding had been provided by Wilson Greatbatch Ltd., a firm developed by the inventor of the heart pacemaker.

REOPENS 2000   THE ROYCROFT LEGACY MOVES TO GALLERY 4
Examples of hand-crafted copper objects, furniture, and publications, and Buffalo China dinnerware made for the Roycroft Inn. Roycroft is the trade name for an arts community established in 1895 in East Aurora, New York. Founder Elbert Hubbard was both a visionary and consummate businessman able to promote a humble American aesthetic that also reflected his own socially and politically challenging ideas.

02/26/2000 to 05/21/2000   THE FILMIC ART OF PAUL SHARITS
The Center will present the first retrospective exhibition of Paul Sharits' works to include both his films and his two-dimensional works. Sharits, who died in 1993 at the age of 50, has been recognized internationally as a pioneering experimental filmmaker; however, he was trained as a painter. In the early 1970s he utilized structuralist theory and painting strategies to create non-narrative, non-objective works he called "flicker films" that were about the elements of film itself.

02 or 03/2000   DECOMPOSITIONS
An exhibition of fourteen Ektacolor photographs with fourteen poems that were inspired by them. Pfahl's photographs are large, colorful semi-abstractions of his backyard compost pile taken at various times of the year, and include watermelon rinds, bean pods, ginko leaves and other organic materials in various stages of decay. Weiss' poems deal with mortality, love, time and other large and small issues-each in a different format. Some are formal and dense, others are like haiku, and still others like concrete poetry. John Pfahl is an internationally renowned photographer living in Buffalo. David Weiss is a writer and poet living in Ithaca and teaching at Hobart and William Smith College.

06/30/2000 to 08/27/2000   THE ART OF THE CHAIR
The exhibition will survey furniture making in the region, including historic and classic designs as well as works by artists who challenge conventions by putting design before function. Artists will include Bob Booth, Wendell Castle, Mark Griffis, Bill Herod, Sanford Hubbard, Kittinger Furniture artisans, Joseph Moran, Edith Lunt Small, Roycroft artisans, Thomas W. Stender, Gustav Stickley, Barry Yavener.)and others.

CANAJOHARIE

Canajoharie Library and Art Gallery
2 Erie Blvd, Canajoharie, NY 13317
📞: 518-673-2314   🖳 www.claj.org
Open: 10-4:45 Mo-We, Fr, 10-8:30 Th, 10-1:30 Sa   **Closed:** Su, LEG/HOL!
♿ ⓟ   **Museum Shop   Group Tours   Sculpture Garden**
Permanent Collection: WINSLOW HOMER; AMERICAN IMPRESSIONISTS; 'THE EIGHT'

Located in downtown Canajoharie, the gallery's collection includes 21 Winslow Homers.

CLINTON

Emerson Gallery
Affiliate Institution: Hamilton College
198 College Hill Road, Clinton, NY 13323
📞: 315-859-4396
Open: 12-5 Mo-Fr, 1-5 Sa, Su, closed weekends June, July & Aug   **Closed:** LEG/HOL! & ACAD/HOL
♿ ⓟ
Permanent Collection: NAT/AM; AM & EU: ptgs, gr 19,20; WEST INDIES ART

Emerson Gallery - continued

While its ultimate purpose is to increase the educational scope and opportunity for appreciation of the fine arts by Hamilton students, the gallery also seeks to enrich campus cultural life in general, as well as to contribute to the cultural enrichment of the surrounding community. **NOT TO BE MISSED:** Outstanding collection of works by Graham Sutherland

ON EXHIBIT 2000

08/25/2000 to 10/15/2000   **ROMARE BEARDEN IN BLACK AND WHITE: PHOTOMONTAGE PROJECTION ,1969**

CORNING

Corning Museum of Glass

One Corning Glass Center, Corning, NY 14830-2253

☎: 800-732-6845, 607-937-5371   ◙   www.cmog.org
Open: 9-5 daily, 9-8 July & Aug   **Closed:** 1/1, THGV, 12/24, 12/25!
ADM: **Adult:** $7.00, family $16   **Children:** $5 (6-17)   **Students:** $6.00   **Seniors:** $6.00
&   ℗
Museum Shop   ⑪
Group Tours: 607-974-2000   **Drop-In Tours:** by reservation
Historic Building
Permanent Collection: GLASS: worldwide 1500 BC - present

The Museum houses the world's premier glass collection – more than 30,000 objects representing 3500 years of achievements in glass design and craftsmanship. New hot-glass studio presents workshops, classes and demonstrations. In June 1999, the New Glass Innovation Center and the Sculpture Gallery open. **NOT TO BE MISSED:** The Hot Glass show where visitors can watch artisans make glass objects. The new Glass Innovation Center

Rockwell Museum

111 Cedar St., Corning, NY 14830

☎: 607-937-5386   ◙   www.stny.lrun.com/RockwellMuseum
Open: 9-5 Mo-Sa, 12-5 Su   **Closed:** 1/1, THGV, 12/24, 12/25
Free Day: 12-5 Su (Dec Apr),
ADM: Adult: $5.00, family $12.50   **Children:** $2.50, 6-17, Free under 6   **Students:** $4,50   **Seniors:** $4.50
&   ℗ Municipal lot across Cedar St.
Museum Shop
Group Tours   Drop-In Tours: 10am & 2pm wkdays (Jun - Sep), other times by appointment and extra fee
Historic Building 1893 City Hall, Corning, NY
Permanent Collection: PTGS & SCULP: by Western Artists including Bierstadt, Remington and Russell 1830-1920; FREDERICK CARDER STEUBEN GLASS; ANT: toys

Located in the 1893 City Hall of Corning, NY, and nestled in the lovely Finger Lakes Region of NY State is the finest collection of American Western Art in the Eastern U.S. The museum building is in a Romanesque revival style and served as a City Hall, firehouse and jail until the 1970s. It is also home to the worlds most comprehensive collection of Frederick Carder Steuben glass. **NOT TO BE MISSED:** Model of Cyrus E. Dallin's famous image, 'Appeal to the Great Spirit'.

NEW YORK

Dowd Fine Arts Gallery
Affiliate Institution: State University of New York College at Cortland
SUNY Cortland, Cortland, NY 13045
☎: 607-753-4216
Open: 11-4 Tu-Sa **Closed:** Mo, ACAD!
Vol/Cont:
  ᚼ ℗ Adjacent to building **Group Tours Drop-In Tours**: scheduled by request **Sculpture Garden**
Permanent Collection: Am & EU: gr,drgs 20; CONT: art books

Temporary exhibitions of contemporary and historic art which are treated thematically are presented in this university gallery.

ON EXHIBIT 2000
02/04/2000 to 03/10/2000 THE MILLENNIUM: VIEWS OF ROME AND JERUSALEM AND ALBRECHT Dürer'S "THE APOCALYPSE" THE DREADED APPROACH OF 1500

03/31/2000 to 04/28/2000 THE JEFFREY RYAN COLLECTION OF CONTEMPORARY AMERICAN PRINTS

Guild Hall Museum
158 Main Street, East Hampton, NY 11937
☎: 516-324-0806 ◙ guild-hall.org
Open: 11-5 daily (Summer), 11-5 We-Sa, 12-5 Su (Winter) **Closed:** THGV, 12/25, 1/1, LEG/HOL!
Sugg/Cont: $3.00
  ᚼ ℗ **Museum Shop Group Tours**: 516-324-0806 **Historic Building Sculpture Garden**
Permanent Collection: AM: 19,20 :reg

Located in one of America's foremost art colonies this cultural center combines a fine art museum and a 400 seat professional theater.

ON EXHIBIT 2000
06/17/2000 to 07/30/2000 AMERICAN IMPRESSIONISM
Led by the example of James McNeil Whistler, a generation of American artist studied abroad to absorb the new palette and compositions that were modernizing painting. Landscapes, figure, and still life paintings by Hassam, Twatchman, Dewing, Merrit Chase and Robinson marked a distinct departure from academic styles.

Islip Art Museum
50 Irish Lane, East Islip, NY 11730
☎: 516-224-5402
Open: 10-4 We-Sa, 2-4:30 Su **Closed:** Mo, Tu, LEG/HOL!
Vol/Cont:
  ᚼ ℗ **Museum Shop**
Group Tours: 516-224-5402 **Drop-In Tours**: by request **Historic Building**
Permanent Collection: AM/REG: ptgs, sculp, cont

The Islip Museum is the leading exhibition space for contemporary and Avant Garde Art on LI. The Carnegie House Project Space, open in the summer and fall, features cutting-edge installations and site-specific work. A satellite gallery called the Anthony Giordamo Gallery is at Dowling College in Oakdale, LI.

Islip Art Museum - continued

ON EXHIBIT 2000

11/04/1999 to 01/28/2000   PURE VISION: AMERICAN BEAD ARTISTS
From intimate necklace forms to large wall constructions, this exhibition of works by 28 artists demonstrates the broad range of individual creativity and artistic expression possible through beadwork, a medium that is enjoying a renaissance among contemporary American artists.

ELMIRA

Arnot Art Museum

235 Lake St, Elmira, NY 14901-3191
📞: 607-734-3697
Open: 10-5 Tu-Sa, 1-5 Su   **Closed:** THGV, 12/25, 1/1
ADM: Adult: $2.00   **Children:** $.50 (6-12)   **Students:** $1.00   **Seniors:** $1.00
& Ⓟ Free   **Museum Shop   Group Tours   Drop-In Tours   Historic Building**
Permanent Collection: AM: salon ptgs 19,20; AM: sculp 19

The original building is a neo-classical mansion built in 1833 in downtown Elmira. The museum modern addition was designed by Graham Gund. **NOT TO BE MISSED:** Matthias Arnot Collection; one of last extant private collections housed intact in its original showcase

---

FLUSHING

Godwin-Ternbach Museum

Affiliate Institution: Queens College
65-30 Kissena Blvd, Flushing, NY 11367
📞: 718-997-4734
Open: 11-7 Mo-Th Call!   **Closed:** ACAD!
& Ⓟ On campus
Permanent Collection: GR: 20; ANT: glass; AN/EGT; AN/GRK; PTGS; SCULP

This is the only museum in Queens with a broad and comprehensive permanent collection which includes a large collection of WPA/FAP prints.

GLENS FALLS

Hyde Collection

161 Warren St,, Glens Falls, NY 12801
📞: 518-792-1761   ▣ www.hydeartmuseum.org
Open: 10-5 Tu-Fr 10-7 Th, 12-5 Su   **Closed:** Mo, LEG/HOL!
Vol/Cont:
& Ⓟ   **Museum Shop   Group Tours:** ext 15   **Drop-In Tours:** 1 & 4 PM   **Historic Building   Sculpture Garden**
Permanent Collection: O/M: ptgs; AM: ptgs; ANT; IT/REN; FR: 18

The central focus of this museum complex is an Italianate Renaissance style villa built in 1912 which houses an exceptional collection of noted European Old Master and significant modern European and American works of art from 4th C. to 20th C. They are displayed among an important collection of Renaissance and French 18th century furniture. The collection spans western art from the 4th c B.C.-20th c. Since 1985 temporary exhibitions and year round programming are offered in the Edward Larabee Barnes Education Wing. **NOT TO BE MISSED:** 'Portrait of a Young Man' by Raphael; 'Portrait of Christ' by Rembrandt; 'Coco' by Renoir; 'Boy Holding a Blue Vase' by Picasso; 'Geraniums' by Childe Hassam

NEW YORK

Picker Art Gallery
Affiliate Institution: Colgate University
Charles A Dana Center For the Creative Arts, Hamilton, NY 13346-1398
☎: 315-228-7634 ◙ www.picker.colgate.edu
Open: 10-5 Daily **Closed:** ACAD!; (also open by request!)
& Ⓟ 2 large lots nearby
Group Tours Sculpture Garden
Permanent Collection: ANT; PTGS & SCULP 20; AS; AF

Located on Colgate University campus, the setting of the Charles A. Dana Art Center is one of expansive lawns and tranquility. Exhibition information: 315-228-774

Hofstra Museum
Affiliate Institution: Hofstra University
112 Hofstra University, Hempstead, NY 11549
☎: 516-463-5672
Open: 10-9 Tu, 10-5 We-Fr, 1-5 Sa, Su! varying hours in galleries **Closed:** Mo, EASTER WEEKEND, THGV WEEKEND, LEG/HOL
Vol/Cont:
& Ⓟ **Museum Shop** ⊪ **Historic Building Sculpture Garden**
Permanent Collection: SCULP: Henry Moore, HJ. Seward Johnson,Jr, Tony Rosenthal

Hofstra University is a living museum. Five exhibition areas are located throughout the 238-acre campus, which is also a national arboretum. **NOT TO BE MISSED:** Sondra Rudin Mack Garden designed by Oehme, Van Sweden and Assoc. Henry Moore's 'Upright Motive No. 9', and 'Hitchhiker', and Tony Rosenthal's 'T's.

ON EXHIBIT 2000
09/18/2000 to 12/15/2000 FOUR OBJECTS; FOUR ARTISTS; TEN YEARS
In 1986 four American still-life painters–Janet Fish, Sondra Freckelton, Nancy Hagin, and Harriet Shorr–agreed that each would select an object that they would all include in a painting. Ten years later they decided to repeat the project. The results of their efforts reveal the wide spectrum of choices which artists make during the creative process.

Olana State Historic Site
State Route 9G, Hudson, NY 12534
☎: 518-828-0135
Open: 10-4 We-Su 4/1-11/1, MEM/DAY, 7/4, LAB/DAY, COLUMBUS DAY , Mo Holidays **Closed:** Nov-Mar
ADM: Adult: $3.00 **Children:** $1.00(5-12) **Seniors:** $2.00
& Ⓟ Limited **Museum Shop**
Group Tours: 518-828-0135 **Historic Building**
Permanent Collection: FREDERIC CHURCH: ptgs, drgs; PHOT COLL; CORRESPONDENCE

Olana, the magnificent home of Hudson River School artist Frederic Edwin Church, was designed by him in the Persian style, and furnished in the Aesthetic style. He also designed the picturesque landscaped grounds. Many of Church's paintings are on view throughout the house. The house is only open by guided tour. Visitor's Center and grounds are open 7 days a week.

HUNTINGTON

Heckscher Museum of Art
2 Prime Ave, Huntington, NY 11743
☎: 516-351-3250
Open: 10-5 Tu-Fr, 1-5 Sa, Su, 1st Fr till 8:30
ADM: Adult: $3.00   **Children:** $1.00   **Students:** $1.00   **Seniors:** $1.00
ᵭ ℗   **Museum Shop**
Group Tours: 516-357-3250   **Drop-In Tours:** 2:30 & 3:30 Sa, Su; 1 & 3 We   **Historic Building**
Permanent Collection: AM: ldscp ptg 19; AM: Modernist ptgs, drgs, works on paper

Located in a 18.5 acre park, the museum, whose collection numbers more than 900 works, was presented as a gift to the people of Huntington by philanthropist August Heckscher. **NOT TO BE MISSED:** 'Eclipse of the Sun', by George Grosz' (not always on view!)

ON EXHIBIT 2000
The Museum closes for several days for installation of an exhibition. Call!

Fall/1999 to Winter/2000   MILLENNIUM MESSAGES
Based on the concept of the time capsule, approximately 40 major artists, architects and designers will create individual time capsules filled with either existing or newly made objects to identify significant aspects of the 20th C and to speak to people of future generations.

ITHACA

Herbert F. Johnson Museum of Art
Affiliate Institution: Cornell University
Cornell University, Ithaca, NY 14853-4001
☎: 607-255-6464   ◉ www.museum.cornell.edu
Open: 10-5 Tu-Su   **Closed:** Mo, MEM/DAY, 7/4, THGV + F
ᵭ ℗ Metered   **Group Tours:** 607-255-6464   **Drop-In Tours:** 12 noon every other Th;1 Sa, Su!
Historic Building IM Pei built in 1973   **Sculpture Garden**
Permanent Collection: AS; AM: gr 19,20

The Gallery, in an IM Pei building, with a view of Cayuga Lake, is located on the Cornell Campus in Ithaca, NY. **NOT TO BE MISSED:** 'Fields in the Month of June', by Daubigny

ON EXHIBIT 2000
10/30 1999 to 01/16/2000   IDENTITY AND EMPIRE: ANCIENT COINS FROM THE OSTRANDER COLLECTION
In recent years Robert Ostrander, Cornell Class of 1952, has been giving a series of Roman Imperial and Near Eastern coins to the Museum. This exhibition gives a sense of this wide ranging collection, which brings to life the politics and economics of the ancient world.

11/6/1999 to 10/15/2000   WHERE WE ARE NOW: RECENT ACQUISITIONS IN CONTEMPORARY PRINTS
With several important purchases as well as a stellar gift from the Berley Collection, this exhibition explores contemporary prints, their makers and techniques.

01/29/2000 to 03/26/2000   FRESH WOODS AND PASTURES NEW: 17TH CENTURY DUTCH LANDSCAPE DRAWINGS FROM THE PECK COLLECTION
A rare public look at an outstanding private collection includes works by Rembrandt, Jacob van Ruisdael, Jan van Goyen, and many other masters of the period.

01/29/2000 to 03/26/2000   LIGHT CONSTRUCTION: PHOTO-SCULPTURES BY DOUG PRINCE
Combining two-dimensional photographic images with the three-dimensional sculptural medium, Prince's work creates carefully constructed worlds of fact and fiction.

NEW YORK

Herbert F. Johnson Museum of Art - continued
01/29/2000 to 03/26/2000   WOMEN'S WORKS
Images made by women from many cultures, drawn from the Museum's permanent collection.

04/08/2000 to 05/28/2000   INDIAN TEXTILES 1400-1900
Drawn from a major private collection, this exhibition features splendid temple hangings, saris, shawls, and other fabrics showing a wide range of Indian textile traditions.

03/11/2000 to 06/04 2000   ANDY GOLDSWORTHY II
Goldsworthy returns to Cornell for an exhibition of photographs, drawings and sculpture in the galleries.

04/18/2000 to 06/18/2000   THE COLLECTOR'S EYE: AUDREY AND BERNARD BERMAN
A recent gift of German Expressionist prints and Pop Art multiples from a major private collection.

06/03/2000 to 08/06/2000   CUBA! THE JAY AND ANITA HYMAN COLLECTION
New interest in Cuban art makes this exhibition of works by important 20th century Cuban artists very timely.

06/10/2000 08/13/2000   PHOTOGRAPHS FROM THE SIEGEL COLLECTION
Alan Siegel, of the Cornell Class of 1960, has avidly collected classic, unusual, and beautiful photographs of the 20th century.

KATONAH

Caramoor Center for Music and the Arts
149 Girdle Ridge Road, Katonah, NY 10536
☎: 914-232-5035   ◙ www.caramoor.com
Open: 11-4 Tu-Sa, 1-4 Su Jun-Sep, 11-4 We-Su Oct-May, by appt Mo-Fr Nov-May   **Closed:** Mo, LEG/HOL!
ADM: Adult: $6.00   **Children:** Free under 12   **Students:** $6.00   **Seniors:** $6.00
& Ⓟ Free   **Museum Shop** ᵼᵼ: Picnic facilities and snack bar
Group Tours   Drop-In Tours: art tour at 2 W-S May-Oct, & by request   **Historic Building   Sculpture Garden**
Permanent Collection: FURNITURE; PTGS; SCULP; DEC/ART; REN; OR: all media

Built in the 1930s by Walter Rosen as a country home, this 54 room Italianate mansion is a treasure trove of splendid collections spanning 2000 years. There are six unusual gardens including the Marjorie Carr Sense Circle (for sight-impaired individuals). Tours of the gardens are by appt spring and fall and every weekend during the festival at 2:30 PM. Caramoor also presents a festival of outstanding concerts each summer and many other programs throughout the year. At 11 Wed Apr-Nov a short recital in the music room is followed by a tour of the house. **NOT TO BE MISSED:** Extraordinary house-museum with entire rooms from European villas and palaces

Katonah Museum of Art
Route 22 at Jay Street, Katonah, NY 10536
☎: 914-232-9555   ◙ www.katonah-museum.org
Open: 1-5 Tu-Fr, Su, 10-5 Sa: summer 12-5 Tu-Fr,   **Closed:** Mo, 1/1, MEM/DAY; PRESIDENTS/DAY, 7/4, THGV, 12/25
ADM: Adult: $3.00
& Ⓟ Free   **Museum Shop   Group Tours   Drop-In Tours**: 2:30pm   **Sculpture Garden**
Permanent Collection: No Permanent Collection

Moved to a building designed by Edward Larabee Barnes in 1990, the museum has a commitment to outstanding special exhibitions which bring to the community art of all periods, cultures and mediums.

ON EXHIBIT 2000
07/18/1999 to 01/02/2000   KEITH HARING: THE STORY OF RED AND BLUE
21 silk screens created for the children of his German dealer create a charming exhibition telling a playful story of the colors in relation to objects and images.

Katonah Museum of Art - continued
10/17/1999 to 01/02/2000 REFLECTIONS OF TIME AND PLACE: LATIN AMERICAN STILL LIFE IN THE 20TH CENTURY

01/16/2000 to 04/02/2000 DÉJA VU
The concept of appropriation, using ideas, motifs and manners of working from the past in view of the large number of contemporary artists looking to the past for inspiration.

04/30/2000 to 07/04/2000 HOPE PHOTOGRAPHS
Hope is a future oriented desire-childhood, science, the arts, sports and death are featured in testimony to the power of art in overcoming malaise.

07/16/2000 to 09/24/2000 MAINE AND THE MODERN SPIRIT
The myth that Maine is a uniquely modern American Eden Because of its isolation, seasonal communities rugged life and social conservatism, it has fueled 20th C. artist's imagination and influenced many early modernists.

10/08/2000 to 12/31/2000 THE ART OF THE PUZZLE: ASTOUNDING AND CONFOUNDING
Puzzle solving entails thought, imagination, knowledge and observation. 200 mechanical and Jigsaw puzzles are examined and related to decorative art, mathematics, psychology and education. Puzzles will be provided to give first hand information.

LONG ISLAND CITY

Isamu Noguchi Garden Museum
32-37 Vernon Blvd, Long Island City, NY 11106
✆: 718-721-1932   ◙ www.noguchi.org
Open: 10-5, We-Fr,11-6 Sa, Su (Apr-Oct only)
ADM: **Adult:** $4.00   **Children:** $2.00   **Students:** $2.00   **Seniors:** $2.00
♿ Ⓟ Street parking   **Museum Shop**   🍴 Café
Group Tours: 718-721-1932 x203   **Drop-In Tours:** 2 PM daily, not for groups   **Historic Building   Sculpture Garden**
Permanent Collection: WORKS OF ISAMU NOGUCHI

Designed by Isamu Noguchi,(1904-1988), this museum offers visitors the opportunity to explore the work of the artist on the site of his Long Island City studio. The centerpiece of the collection is a tranquil outdoor sculpture garden. The Museum is in 13 galleries of a converted warehouse and surrounding gardens. PLEASE NOTE: A shuttle bus runs to the museum on Sat. & Sun. every hour on the half hour starting at 11:30am from the corner of Park Ave. & 70th St, NYC, and returns on the hour every hour till 5pm. The round trip fare is $5.00 and DOES NOT include the price of museum admission. **NOT TO BE MISSED:** Permanent exhibition of over 250 sculptures as well as models, drawings, and photo-documentation of works of Noguchi; stage sets designed for Martha Graham; paper light sculptures called Akari

P. S. 1 Contemporary Arts Center
2225 Jackson Avenue, Long Island City, NY 11101
✆: 718-784-2084
Open: 12-6 We-Su   **Closed:** MEM/DAY, 7/4, LAB/DAY, THGV, 12/25
ADM: **Adult:** $4.00   **Children:** $2.00   **Students:** $2.00   **Seniors:** $2.00
♿ Ⓟ on street and near-by garages   🍴 coffee shop   **Sculpture Garden**
Permanent Collection: CONT, AM

P.S.1 recognizes and introduces the work of emerging and lesser known artists. **NOT TO BE MISSED:** 'Meeting' by James Turrell, 1986

ON EXHIBIT 2000
11/07/1999 to 01/2000 CHILDREN OF BERLIN: CULTURAL DEVELOPMENTS 1989-1999
Berlin Artists, spaces, associations, etc are featured .

NEW YORK

Storm King Art Center

Old Pleasant Hill Rd, Mountainville, NY 10953

☎: 914-534-3115
Open: 11-5:30 Daily (Apr-Nov.14), Special eve hours Sa, June, July, Aug   **Closed:** closed 11/15-3/31
ADM: Adult: $7.00   **Children:** Free under 5   **Students:** $3.00   **Seniors:** $5.00
♿ ℗   **Museum Shop**
Group Tours: 914-534-3115 x110   **Drop-In Tours:** 2pm daily   **Historic Building   Sculpture Garden**
Permanent Collection: SCULP: Alice Aycock, Alexander Calder, Mark di Suvero, Andy Goldsworthy, Louise Nevelson, Isamu Noguchi, Richard Serra, David Smith, Kenneth Snelson

America's leading open-air sculpture museum features over 120 masterworks on view amid 500 acres of lawns, fields and woodlands. Works are also on view in a 1935 Normandy style building that has been converted to museum galleries. **NOT TO BE MISSED:** ''Momo Taro', a 40 ton, nine-part sculpture by Isamu Noguchi designed for seating and based on Japanese Folk tale

ON EXHIBIT 2000
05/15/2000 to 11/15/2000   ANDY GOLDSWORTHY

Genesee Country Village & Museum

410 Flint Hill Road, P.O. box 310, Mumford, NY 14511

☎: 716-538-6822   ◙   www.gcv.org
Open: 10-5 Tu-Su Jul, Aug; 10-4 Tu-Fr, 10-5 Sa, Su Spring and Fall, season May-Oct   **Closed:** Mo
ADM: Adult: $11   **Children:** 4-16 $6.50, under 3 Free   **Students:** $9.50   **Seniors:** $9.50
♿ ℗ Free   **Museum Shop**   🍽
Group Tours: ext 248   **Sculpture Garden**
Permanent Collection: AM,Ptgs, sculpt;AM\SW;late 19;NAT/AM;sculpt;WILDLIFE art;EU&AM sport art 17-20

The outstanding J. F. Wehle collection of sporting art is housed in the only museum in New York specializing in sport, hunting and wildlife subjects. The collection and carriage museum are part of an assembled village of 19th century shops, homes and farm buildings.

Samuel Dorsky Museum of Art

Affiliate Institution: State University of New York at New Paltz
New Paltz, NY 12561

☎: 914-257-3844   ◙   www.newpaltz.edu/artgallery
Open: 11-4 Tu-Fr, 1-4, Sa, Su ; 7-9 Tu eve   **Closed:** Mo, LEG/HOL, ACAD HOL!
♿ ℗   **Museum Shop**
Group Tours
Permanent Collection: AM; gr,ptgs 19,20; JAP: gr; CH: gr; P/COL; CONT: phot

The Samuel Dorsky Museum of Art is the second largest museum in the State University system. Not only does the museum enhance the educational mission of the college, it promotes cross disciplinary research and collaboration . It serves as a cultural resource for the Hudson Valley. **NOT TO BE MISSED:** The opening of the gallery and installation of the permanent collection which Spans over 4000 years

NEW YORK CITY

See Astoria, Bayside, Bronx, Brooklyn, Flushing, Long Island City, New York, Queens and Staten Island

NEW YORK

Alternative Museum
594 Broadway, New York, NY 10012
☎: 212-966-4444 ◙ www.alternativemuseum.org
Open: 11-6 Tu-Sa **Closed:** Mo 12/25
Sugg/Cont: **ADM: Adult:** $3.00
& ℗ Nearby pay garage only
Permanent Collection: CONT

This contemporary arts institution is devoted to the exploration and dissemination of new avenues of thought on contemporary art and culture.

Americas Society
680 Park Avenue, New York, NY 10021
☎: 212-249-8950 ◙ www.americas-society.org
Open: 12-6 Tu-Su **Closed:** Mo 7/4,THGV,12/24,12/25
& ℗ Nearby pay Garage **Museum Shop** **Group Tours** **Historic Building**
Permanent Collection: No permanent collection

Located in a historic neo federal townhouse built in 1909, the goal of the Americas Society is to increase public awareness of the rich cultural heritage of our geographic neighbors.

Asia Society
725 Park Ave., New York, NY 10021
☎: 212-517-ASIA ◙ www.asiasociety.org
Open: 11-6 Tu-Sa, 11-8 Th, 12-5 Su **Closed:** Mo, LEG/HOL!
Free Day: Th, 6-8pm **ADM: Adult:** $4.00 **Children:** $2.00, Free under 12 **Students:** $2.00 **Seniors:** $2.00
& ℗ Nearby pay garages **Museum Shop** **Group Tours**: 212-288-6400 **Drop-In Tours**: 12:30 Tu-Sa, 6:30 Th, 2:30 Su
Permanent Collection: The Mr. and Mrs. John D. Rockefeller 3rd Collection of Asian Art

The Asia Society is America's leading institution dedicated to fostering understanding of Asia and communication between Americans and the peoples of Asia and the Pacific.

ON EXHIBIT 2000

Spring/2000 SHEER REALITIES: BODY, POWER, AND CLOTHING IN THE 19TH CENTURY PHILIPPINES
75 to 100 items will look at the action between the external indigenous cultural influences of the Philippines over the past century. They will be shown with other materials including hardwoods, ivories, silver, etc. The exhibition will be held at the Grey Art Gallery at New York University.

Fall/2000 IN TRANSIT: PUBLIC ART PROJECT-ASIAN/ASIAN/AMERICAN AS AMERICAN ARTISTS IN NEW YORK SPACES
Ground breaking exhibitions will commission artists to realize works on the streets of New York The six to eight artists will be chosen for their ability to question fixed stereotypes of nation, culture and identity and replace these with new visions and visual language. Sites will include Rockefeller Center, Central Park, Battery Park, the foyers of major corporate institutions, etc.

NEW YORK

Chaim Gross Studio Museum
526 LaGuardia Place, New York, NY 10012
☎: 212-529-4906
Open: 12-5 Tu-Sa. **Closed:** Su, Mo, LEG/HOL
 ♿ Ⓟ Nearby pay parking **Museum Shop**
Group Tours **Drop-In Tours:** by appt **Historic Building**
Permanent Collection: Sculp, wood, stone, bronze; sketches, w/c, prints

A seventy year sculpture collection of several hundred Chaim Gross (1904-1991) works housed on three floors of the Greenwich Village building which was the artist's home and studio for thirty-five years. The studio is left intact and is also open to the public. **NOT TO BE MISSED:** "Roosevelt and Hoover in a Fistfight" 1932, Mahogany 72x20x1 1/2. The 1932 cubist inspired wood sculptures were done in the only year when Gross submitted to modernist influences.

China Institute Gallery, China Institute in America
125 East 65th Street, New York, NY 10021=7088
☎: 212-744-8181 ▣ www.chinainstitute.org
Open: 10-5 Mo & We-Sa, 1-5 Su, 10-8 Tu & Th **Closed:** LEG/HOL!, CHINESE NEW YEAR
ADM: Adult: $5.00 **Children:** Free **Students:** $3.00 **Seniors:** $3.00
♿ Ⓟ Pay garage nearby, limited street parking **Museum Shop**
Group Tours **Drop-In Tours:** Varies **Historic Building**
Permanent Collection: Non-collecting institution

The only museum in New York and one of five in the entire country specializing in exhibitions of Chinese art and civilization. The Gallery reaches out to people interested in learning about and staying connected to China.

ON EXHIBIT 2000

03/21/2000 to 06/20/2000 **EARLY CHINESE CERAMICS FROM THE MEIYINTANG COLLECTION**

09/14/2000 to 12/17/2000 **THE PAINTER AS POET**
Paintings from the Song Dynasty thru the 20th C. Woodblock printed books and Western paintings will be included to draw comparisons. *Catalog*

The Cloisters
Affiliate Institution: The Metropolitan Museum of Art
Fort Tryon Park, New York, NY 10040
☎: 212-923-3700 ▣ www.metmuseum.org
Open: 9:30-5:15 Tu-Su (3/1-10/30), 9:30-4:45 Tu-Su (11/1-2/28) **Closed:** Mo, 1/1, THGV, 12/25
ADM: Adult: $10 inc Met Museum on the same day **Children:** Free under 12 **Students:** $5.00 **Seniors:** $5.00
♿ Ⓟ Free limited street parking in Fort Tryon Park **Museum Shop**
Group Tours: 212-650-2280 **Drop-In Tours:** 3pm Tu-Fr, 12 & 2pm Sa: 12 Su
Historic Building 1938 bldg resembling medieval monastery, incorporates actual medieval architectural elements
Permanent Collection: ARCH: Med/Eu; TAPESTRIES; ILLUMINATED MANUSCRIPTS; STAINED GLASS; SCULP; LITURGICAL OBJECTS

This unique 1938 building set on a high bluff in a tranquil park overlooking the Hudson River recreates a medieval monastery in both architecture and atmosphere. Actual 12th - 15th century medieval architectural elements are incorporated within various elements of the structure which is filled with impressive art and artifacts of the era. **NOT TO BE MISSED:** 'The Unicorn Tapestries'; 'The Campin Room'; Gardens; Treasury; the 'Belles Heures' illuminated manuscript of Jean, Duke of Berry

254

Cooper-Hewitt, National Design Museum, Smithsonian Institution

2 East 91st Street, New York, NY 10128

☎: 212-849-8300 ◙ www.si.edu/ndm
Open: 10-9 Tu, 10-5 We, Sa, 12-5 Su **Closed:** Mo, LEG/HOL!
Free Day: Th 5-9 **ADM: Adult:** $5.00 **Children:** Free under 12 **Students:** $3.00 **Seniors:** $3.00
& ℗ Nearby pay garages **Museum Shop**
Group Tours: 212-849-8380 **Drop-In Tours:** times vary; call 212-849-8389 **Historic Building Sculpture Garden**
Permanent Collection: DRGS; TEXTILES; DEC/ART; CER

Cooper Hewitt, housed in the landmark Andrew Carnegie Mansion, has more than 250,000 objects which represent 3000 years of design history from cultures around the world. It is the only museum on Museum Mile with an outdoor planted garden and lawn open during regular museum hours-weather permitting.

ON EXHIBIT 2000

10/12/1999 to 1/09/2000 THE WORK OF CHARLES AND RAY EAMES: A LEGACY OF INVENTION
The first posthumous retrospective of the work of the American husband and wife team considered among the greatest designers of the 20th C will present more than 500 objects created between the 1940s and 1970s. *Will Travel*

03/07/2000 to 08/06/2000 NATIONAL DESIGN TRIENNIAL
The museum is inaugurating a new program which will look, every three years, at the impulses driving design practice, focusing on the work of 100 designers including emerging talent as well as a selection of mature leaders.

10/03/2000 to 03/04/2001 GREAT DESIGN: 100 MASTERPIECES FROM THE VITRA MUSEUM
A major exhibition highlighting the concepts styles and materials central to furniture design in the modern era. Works by Thonet , Hoffman, Reitveld, Aalto Breuer and the Eames'.

Dahesh Museum

601 Fifth Avenue, New York, NY 10017

☎: 212-759-0606 ◙ www.daheshmuseum.org
Open: 11-6 Tu-Sa **Closed:** S, Mo, LEG/HOL!
Vol/Cont:
& ℗ pay parking nearby **Museum Shop Group Tours Drop-In Tours:** lunchtime daily
Permanent Collection: Acad pntg;19,20

More than 2000 works collected by writer, philosopher Salimoussa Achi who was known as Dr. Dahesh form the collection of this relatively new museum housed on the second floor of a commercial building built in 1911. Included are works by Auguste Bonheur, Jean-Leon Genose, Alexandre Cabance, Lord Leighton and Edwin Long.

ON EXHIBIT 2000

01/18/2000 to 05/13/2000 OVERCOMING ALL OBSTACLES: THE WOMEN OF THE ACADEMIE JULIAN
The Julian was particularly important because it was the principal atelier which accepted women until the end of the 19th C. Among the Americans who studied there were Anna Klumpke, Elizabeth Gardner Bouguereau and Celia Beaux. Early in the 20th C Louise Bourgeouis studied there.

05/30/2000 to 08/19/2000 IN THE FOOTSTEPS OF GOETHE: PAINTINGS AND DRAWINGS FROM GERMAN COLLECTIONS

Dia Center for the Arts

548 West 22nd Street, New York, NY 10011

☎: 212-989-5566 ◙ www.diacenter.org
Open: 12-6 Th-Su Sep-Jun **Closed:** LEG/HOL!
ADM: Adult: $4.00 **Children:** Free under 10 **Students:** $2.00 **Seniors:** $2.00
& **Museum Shop** ⃫: Rooftop café and video lounge
Permanent Collection: not permanently on view

NEW YORK

Dia Center for the Arts - continued
With several facilities and collaborations Dia has committed itself to working with artists to determine optimum environments for their most ambitious and uncompromising works which are usually on view for extended exhibition periods. **NOT TO BE MISSED:** Two Walter De Maria extended exhibitions, THE NEW YORK EARTH ROOM at the gallery at 141 Wooster Street and THE BROKEN KILOMETER at 393 Broadway. Both are open 12-6 W-Sa, closed July and August, adm F

ON EXHIBIT 2000

ONGOING   JOSEPH BEUYS: 7000 OAKS
In 1988 Dia installed five basalt stone columns, each paired with a tree, along the street in front of its exhibition facility, continuing 7000 Eichen (7000 Oaks), a project by German artist Joseph Beuys that was initiated at Documenta 7 in Kassel, Germany. During 1996, eighteen additional pairs of trees and stones were installed along both sides of West 22nd Street, furthering Beuys' intention to continue the project beyond the city of Kassel.

09/09/1999 to 03/2000   STAN DOUGLAS AND DOUGLAS GORDON: DOUBLE VISION
This exhibition of the work of Canadian artist Stan Douglas and Scottish artist Douglas Gordon includes a new media installation by each artist. Stan Douglas presents a work entitled "Win, Place or Show," which takes as its point of departure a fundamental transformation in the organization of North American civic space in the 1960s. Douglas Gordon's new work, "left is right and right is wrong and left is worng and right is right," appropriates a little-known film made in 1949 by Hollywood director Otto Preminger titled Whirlpool. Juxtaposed, the two works, which both utilize dual projection, reveal surprising correspondences with one another, while simultaneously permitting each artists's singular concerns to emerge sharply.

09/16/1999 to 02/2000   THOMAS SCHÜTTE: IN MEDIAS RES
In this unusually extended tripartite installation, lasting some eighteen months, Dia explores in detail the vast range of work created over the past twenty years by this renowned mid-career German artist. This exhibition, devised in three segments with distinct points of reference, reveals the extraordinary inventiveness and diversity of Schütte's production. "In Medias Res," the third and final phase, will focus on recent figure sculpture and ceramics, which will be shown together with a new series of works on paper.

10/14/1999 to 06/2000   RODNEY GRAHAM AND VERA LUTTER: TIME TRACED
Like the camera obscura, the pinhole camera was an influential precursor to that most sophisticated of mechanical tools, the modern multilens camera. At a time when it, in turn, is being challenged by newer reproductive technologies, such rudimentary modes of image making are, paradoxically, proving unexpectedly vital. In their recent works, both Canadian artist Rodney Graham and German Vera Lutter draw on these pioneering techniques and historical models to construct vividly arresting representations.

11/17/1999 to 06/18/2000   DONALD JUDD: UNTITLED, 1976
Acquired by Dia earlier this year from the Chinati Foundation in Marfa, Texas, this work, comprised of fifteen plywood boxes, is a centerpiece of Dia's historical collection, and exemplifies Judd's ability to produce exquisitely complex works by combining essential geometry and common industrial materials.

Drawing Center
35 Wooster Street, New York, NY 10013
☎: 212-219-2166
Open: 10-6 Tu-Fr; 11-6 Sa   **Closed:** Su, Mo, 12/25, 1/1, all of AUG, THGV
Vol/Cont:
♿ Ⓟ On street and nearby pay garages   **Museum Shop**
Group Tours   Historic Building
Permanent Collection: non collecting institution

Featured at The Drawing Center are contemporary and historical drawings and works on paper both by internationally known and emerging artists.

El Museo del Barrio
1230 Fifth Ave, New York, NY 10029-4496
☎: 212-831-7272 ◙ www.elmuseo.org
Open: 11-5 We-Su, 11-6 Th SUMMER 6/6-9/26 **Closed:** LEG/HOL!
ADM: **Adult:** $4.00 **Children:** Free under 12 **Students:** $2.00 **Seniors:** $2.00
♿ Ⓟ Discount at Merit Parking Corp 12-14 E 107 St.
Permanent Collection: LAT/AM: P/COL; CONT: drgs, phot, sculp

One of the foremost Latin American cultural institutions in the United States, this museum is also the only one in the country that specializes in the arts and culture of Puerto Rico. **NOT TO BE MISSED:** Santos: Sculptures Between Heaven and Earth

Equitable Gallery
787 Seventh Avenue, New York, NY 10019
☎: 212-554-4818
Open: 11-6 Mo-Fr 12-5 Sa **Closed:** Su LEG/HOL, 12/24
♿ Ⓟ pay **Museum Shop** 🍴 3 fine restaurants located in the space overlooking the Galleria
Permanent Collection: 'PUBLIC ART IN LOBBY OF EQUITABLE TOWER: Roy Lichtenstein's Mural with Blue Brushstroke

The gallery presents works from all fields of the visual arts that would not otherwise have a presence in New York City.

Frick Collection
1 East 70th Street, New York, NY 10021
☎: 212-288-0700 ◙ www.frick.org
Open: 10-6 Tu-Sa, 1-6 Su, also open 2/12, Election Day, 11/11 **Closed:** Mo, 1/1, 7/4, THGV, 12/24, 12/25
ADM: **Adult:** $7.00 **Children:** under 10 not adm **Students:** $5.00 **Seniors:** $5.00
♿ Ⓟ Pay garages nearby **Museum Shop**
Historic Building Sculpture Garden
Permanent Collection: PTGS; SCULP; FURNITURE; DEC/ART; Eur, Or, PORCELAINS 🎧

The beautiful Henry Clay Frick mansion built in 1913-14, houses this exceptional collection while preserving the ambiance of the original house. In addition to the many treasures to be found here, the interior of the house offers the visitor a tranquil respite from the busy pace of city life outside of its doors. PLEASE NOTE: Children under 10 are not permitted in the museum and those from 11-16 must be accompanied by an adult. **NOT TO BE MISSED:** Boucher Room; Fragonard Room; Paintings by Rembrandt, El Greco, Holbein and Van Dyck

ON EXHIBIT 2000
10/20/1999 to 01/09/2000 WATTEAU AND HIS WORLD: FRENCH DRAWINGS FROM 1700-1750
The drawings of Watteau are an unrivaled achievement of observation and imagination, a window onto the lost world, and a glimpse into the creative mind that came to define his age. This comprehensive survey of drawings by Watteau and some of his leading contemporaries will include over sixty-five drawings. A core of some thirty-five drawings by Watteau himself will demonstrate the evolution and range of his graphic art. Other sections of the exhibition will be devoted to his artistic forebears, to his contemporary followers, and to a group of later artists indebted to the example of his work. Among those represented will be Boucher, Gillot, Lancret, Lemoyne, Liotard, Natoire, Oudry, Pater, and Portail. *Catalog Will Travel*

11/16/1999 to 01/16/2000 VELÁZQUEZ IN NEW YORK MUSEUMS
To mark the four-hundredth anniversary of the birth of Diego Rodríguez de Silva y Velázquez (1599–1660), The Frick Collection will bring together for the first time six of the Spanish master's portraits belonging to public collections in New York. The exhibition will demonstrate the variety and power of the Spanish master's work over a lifetime.

NEW YORK

Frick Collection - continued

04/11/2000 to 06/04/2000   FROM MICHELANGELO TO PICASSO: MASTER DRAWINGS FROM THE ALBERTINA, VIENNA

This major spring exhibition features masterpieces on paper selected to demonstrate not only the superb holdings of this illustrious Austrian institution, but to chronicle the major assets acquired during the tenure of each of its directors. Works by Rembrandt and Dürer will be featured as well as twentieth-century masters acquired by the present regime.

09/12/2000 to 11/12/2000   A BRUSH WITH NATURE: THE GERE COLLECTION OF LANDSCAPE OIL SKETCHES

Collecting of small-scale landscape oil sketches on paper, created by eighteenth- and nineteenth-century artists working out of doors, was pioneered by the distinguished art historians John and Charlotte Gere, as recently as the 1950s when they began to gather these intimate and compelling documents of artists at work. Today, what is perhaps the most comprehensive collection includes seventy works and continues to expand.

12/12/2000 to 02/25/2001   THE DRAFTSMAN'S ART: MASTER DRAWINGS FROM THE NATIONAL GALLERY OF SCOTLAND

A survey of five centuries of draftsmanship by British, Dutch, Flemish, French, German, and Italian artists, this exhibition brings together roughly eighty masterworks on paper — comprising watercolor, chalk, oil, and silverpoint — that highlight various schools and traditions throughout Europe and allow for comparisons among different generations from the same nationality. Spanning the fifteenth to the nineteenth centuries, The Draftsman's Art includes examples by masters such as Leonardo da Vinci, Raphael, Peter Paul Rubens, François Boucher, William Blake, Jean-Auguste-Dominique Ingres, and Georges Seurat, as well as by less prominent artists such as Giovanni Battista Lusieri and Ernest Hébert.

George Gustav Heye Center of the National Museum of the American Indian

Affiliate Institution: Smithsonian Institution
One Bowling Green, New York, NY 10004

☎: 212-668-6624   ◉   www.si.edu/nmai
Open: 10-5 daily, 10-8 Th   **Closed:** 12/25
&   ⓟ Nearby pay   **Museum Shop**   **Group Tours**: 212-825-8096   **Drop-In Tours**: daily!   **Historic Building**
Permanent Collection: NAT/AM; Iroq silver, jewelry, NW Coast masks

The Heye Foundation collection contains more than 1,000,000 works which span the entire Western Hemisphere and present a new look at Native American peoples and cultures. Newly opened in the historic Alexander Hamilton Customs House it presents masterworks from the collection and contemporary Indian art.

ON EXHIBIT 2000

ONGOING   ORIENTATION INSTALLATION

This orientation installation, which begins outside the Heye Center, provides a brief history of the Lenni Lenape (Delaware), one of the first groups to inhabit Manhattan Island. The exhibition also provides information on the mission of the museum, the architecture of the Custom House, and other points of interest in lower Manhattan.

ONGOING   CREATION'S JOURNEY: MASTERWORKS OF NATIVE AMERICAN IDENTITY AND BELIEF

Objects of beauty and historical significance, representing numerous cultures throughout the Americas, ranging from 3200 B.C. to the present will be on display. CAT

ONGOING   ALL ROADS ARE GOOD: NATIVE VOICES ON LIFE AND CULTURE

Artifacts chosen by 23 Indian selectors. CAT

ONGOING   THIS PATH WE TRAVEL: CELEBRATIONS OF CONTEMPORARY NATIVE AMERICAN CREATIVITY

Collaborative exhibition featuring works by 15 contemporary Indian artists. CAT

ONGOING   SPIRIT CAPTURE: NATIVE AMERICANS AND THE PHOTOGRAPHIC IMAGE.

Photographs which will reveal new and deeper images in the development of cultural Stereotypes.

10/17/1999 to 03/2000   RESERVATION X

Installation pieces by native artists

Grey Art Gallery
Affiliate Institution: New York University Art Collection
100 Washington Square East, New York, NY 10003-6619
☎: 212-998-6780 ◉ www.nyu.edu/greyart
Open: 11-6 Tu, Th, Fr, 11-8 We, 11-5 Sa **Closed:** Su, Mo, LEG/HOL!
ADM: Adult: $2.50 **Children:** $2.50 **Students:** $2.50 **Seniors:** $2.50
♿ Ⓟ Nearby pay garages
Permanent Collection: AM: ptgs 1940-present; CONT; AS; MID/EAST

Located at Washington Square Park and adjacent to Soho, the Grey Art Gallery occupies the site of the first academic fine arts department in America established by Samuel F. B. Morse in 1835.

ON EXHIBIT 2000
11/16/1999 to 01/29/2000   INVERTED ODYSSEYS: CLAUDE CAHUN, MAYA DEREN, SINDY SHERMAN
Collages, books, photographs, films and props by 3 20th C women artists who special ize in self-portraiture.. Expanding concepts of individuality in modernist space and time and one's expanded self. *Catalog Will Travel*

02/16/2000 to 04/22/2000   SHEER REALITIES: POWER AND CLOTHING IN THE NINETEENTH CENTURY PHILIPPINES
75 to 100 items will look at the action between the external indigenous cultural influences of the Philippines over the past century. They will be shown with other materials including hardwoods, ivories, silver, etc. The exhibition will be held at the Grey Art Gallery at New York University.

05/09/2000 to 07/15/2000   RUDY BURKHARDT AND FRIENDS: NEW YORK ART OF THE 1950'S AND 60'S
Burkhardts photographs of artists will be shown with works from those artists. It will show how one artist chose to portray another. It will also show his outstanding cityscapes and films.

Guggenheim Museum Soho
575 Broadway at Prince St, New York, NY 10012
☎: 212-423-3500 ◉ www.guggenheim.org
Open: 11-6 Th-Mo **Closed:** Tu, We, 1/1, 12/25
♿ Ⓟ Nearby pay garages **Museum Shop** ⏸ **Group Tours   Historic Building**
Permanent Collection: INTERNATIONAL CONT ART

As a branch of the main museum uptown, this facility, located in a historic building in Soho, was designed as a museum by Arata Isozaki.

ON EXHIBIT 2000
Ongoing   THE LAST SUPPER by ANDY WARHOL

Hispanic Society of America
155th Street and Broadway, New York, NY 10032
☎: 212-926-2234 ◉ www.hispanicsociety.org
Open: 10-4:30 Tu-Sa, 1-4,Su **Closed:** Mo, LEG/HOL!
Vol/Cont:
♿ Ⓟ Nearby pay garage **Museum Shop**
Group Tours: ext. 254 **Historic Building   Sculpture Garden**
Permanent Collection: SP: ptgs, sculp; arch; HISPANIC

Representing the culture of Hispanic peoples from prehistory to the present, this facility is one of several diverse museums located within the same complex on Audubon Terrace in NYC. **NOT TO BE MISSED:** Paintings by El Greco, Goya, Velazquez

ON EXHIBIT 2000
11/16/1999 to 01/16/2000   VELAZQUEZ IN NEW YORK MUSEUMS
The Hispanic Society will collaborate with The Frick Collection to present a selection of works in New York public collections. It presents an opportunity for audiences never before possible. *Catalog*

NEW YORK

International Center of Photography
1130 Fifth Avenue & Midtown, 1133 Avenue of the Americas, 10036, New York, NY 10128
☎: 212-860-1777 ◙ www.icp.org
Open: 10-5 Tu-Th, 10-8 Fr, 10-6 Sa, Su **Closed:** Mo., I/I, 7/4. THGV. 12/25
Free Day: 5-8 Fr, Vol. Contribution **ADM: Adult:** $6.00 **Students:** $4.00 **Seniors:** $4.00
& ℗ Nearby pay garages **Museum Shop** ᵼᵼ: Nearby
Group Tours: 212-860-1777 x154 Drop-In Tours **Historic Building**
Permanent Collection: PRIMARILY DOCUMENTARY PHOT: 20

ICP was established in 1974 to present exhibitions of photography, to promote photographic education at all levels, and to study 20th century images, primarily documentary. The uptown museum is housed in a 1915 Neo-Georgian building designed by Delano and Aldrich.

Japan Society Gallery
333 E. 47th Street, New York, NY 10017
☎: 212-832-1155 ◙ www.jpn.org
Open: 11-6 Tu-Fr, 11-5 Sa, Su **Closed:** Mo LEG/HOL!
Sugg/Cont: **ADM: Adult:** $5.00 **Students:** $5.00 **Seniors:** $5.00
& ℗ Nearby pay garages
Group Tours: 212-715-1253 **Historic Building** **Sculpture Garden**
Permanent Collection: JAPANESE ART

Exhibitions of the fine arts of Japan are presented along with performing and film arts at the Japan Society Gallery which attempts to promote better understanding and cultural enlightenment between the peoples of the U.S. and Japan.

ON EXHIBIT 2000

09/22/1999 to 01/02/2000   DAIDO MORIYAMA: FIRST AMERICAN RETROSPECTIVE -TWO PART EXHIBITION AT THE JAPAN SOCIETY AND THE METROPOLITAN MUSEUM OF ART
One of Japan' moist innovative and important photographers. "Stray Dog" presents several of his most important series. It will present 130 vintage photographs at the Japan Society and "Hunter will be concurrently shown at the Metropolitan Museum of Art.

Jewish Museum
1109 5th Ave., New York, NY 10128
☎: 212-423-3200 ◙ www.thejewishmuseum.org
Open: 11-5:45 Su, Mo, We & Th, 11-8 Tu **Closed:** Fr, Sa, JEWISH/HOL, Martin Luther King Day, THGV
Free Day: Tu after 5 **ADM: Adult:** $8.00 **Children:** Free under 12 **Students:** $5.50 **Seniors:** $5.50
& ℗ Nearby pay garages **Museum Shop** ᵼᵼ: Cafe Weissman, kosher cuisine
Group Tours: 212-423-3225 **Drop-In Tours**: 12:15, 2:15, 4:15 Mo-Th, 6:15 Tu **Historic Building**
Permanent Collection: JUDAICA: ptgs by Jewish and Israeli artists; ARCH; ARTIFACTS

27,000 works of art and artifacts covering 4000 years of Jewish history created by Jewish artists or illuminating the Jewish experience are displayed in the original building (the 1907 Felix Warburg Mansion), and in the new addition added in 1993. The collection is the largest of its kind outside of Israel. **NOT TO BE MISSED:** "The Holocaust" by George Segal

ON EXHIBIT 2000

ONGOING   CULTURE AND CONTINUITY: THE JEWISH JOURNEY
The centerpiece of the Museum is a core exhibition on the Jewish experience that conveys the essence of Jewish identity–the basic ideas, values and culture developed over 4000 years.

Jewish Museum - continued
11/07/1999 to 02/06/2000   JOHN SINGER SARGENT: PORTAITS OF THE WERTHEIMER FAMILY
The paintings will be shown for the first time together since they were in the London residence of the Wertheimer family 70 years ago. *Catalog Will Travel*

11/14/1999 to 04/25/2000   BERLIN METROPOLIS: JEWS AND THE NEW CULTURE, 1890-1918
This unique exhibition will feature 250 objects-paintings, sculpture, drawings, prints letters, posters and theater memorabilia from the period revealing the vitality and diversity of art forms created at the turn of the century. It will also look at the role Jews played in the in the cultural language and its effect on the 20th C. *Catalog*

Metropolitan Museum of Art
5th Ave at 82nd Street, New York, NY 10028
☎: 212-879-5500   ◉ www.metmuseum.org
Open: 9:30-5:30 Tu-Th, Su; 9:30-9pm Fr, Sa   **Closed:** Mo, THGV,12/25, 1/1
Sugg/Cont: ADM: Adult: $10.00   **Children:** Free under 12   **Students:** $5.00   **Seniors:** $5.00
♿ ⓟ Pay garage   **Museum Shop** 🍴
Group Tours: 212-570-3711   **Historic Building   Sculpture Garden**
Permanent Collection: EU: all media; GR & DRGS: Ren-20; MED; GR; PHOT; AM: all media; DEC/ART: all media; AS: all media; AF; ISLAMIC; CONT; AN/EGT; AN/R; AN/AGR; AN/ASSYRIAN

The Metropolitan is the largest world class museum of art in the Western Hemisphere. Its comprehensive collections includes more than 2 million works from the earliest historical artworks thru those of modern times and from all areas of the world. Just recently, the museum opened the Florence & Herbert Irving Galleries for the Arts of South & Southeast Asia, one of the best and largest collections of its kind in the world. **NOT TO BE MISSED:** Temple of Dendur; The 19th century European Paintings & Sculpture galleries (21 in all), designed to present the permanent collection in chronological order and to accommodate the promised Walter Annenberg collection now on view approximately 6 months annually.

ON EXHIBIT 2000
NEW AND RECENTLY OPENED INSTALLATIONS:
   SCULPTURE AND DECORATIVE ARTS OF THE QUATTROCENTO
   NEW CHINESE GALLERIES
   THE NEW AMARNA GALLERIES: EGYPTIAN ART 1353-1295 B.C.
   **PHASE 1 OF THE NEW GREEK AND ROMAN ART GALLERIES: THE ROBERT AND RENEE
      BELFER COURT**
   STUDIOLO FROM THE PALACE OF DUKE FEDERICO DE MONTEFELTRO AT GUBBIO
   THE AFRICAN GALLERY
   ANTONIO RATTI TEXTILE CENTER

09/02/1999 to 01/09/2000   THE ARTIST AS COLLECTOR: MASTERPIECES OF CHINESE PAINTING FROM THE C.C.WANG FAMILY COLLECTION
12 promised gifts from this renowned collection including "Riverbank" one of the earliest and most important landscape hanging scrolls from the collection is included. Spanning ten centuries of painting history it illuminates the tradition of scholar painting. *Catalog*

09/14/1999 to 01/02/2000   KLEE PAINTINGS
These paintings from 1920 to 1937 from the Bergruen Klee Collection are being shown for the first time.

09/14/1999 to 01/23/2000   FAROUK HOSNY/ADAM HENEIN: CONTEMPORARY EGYPTIAN ARTISTS AND HEIRS TO AN ANCIENT TRADITION
Known for it's ancient art, contemporary artists work in all media drawing on Egypt's rich past. *Catalog*

09/16/1999 to 01/02/2000   THE NATURE OF ISLAMIC ORNAMENT, PART 1V: FIGURAL REPRESENTATION
The last in a series examining the basic forms and sources of Islamic ornament.

09/16/1999 to 01/09/2000   EGYPTIAN ART IN THE AGE OF THE PYRAMIDS
These works were created during the third millennium BCE, the period of the Old Kingdom.

NEW YORK

Metropolitan Museum of Art - continued

09/22/1999 to 01/02/2000   DAIDO MORIYAMA: HUNTER
Photographer Daido Moriyama found his country in great change from Western mores and mass media. These images are dedicated to Jack Kerouac and are virtually unknown in this country.

10/05/1999 to 01/02/2000   PORTRAITS BY INGRES: IMAGE OF AN EPOCH
Rare books and richly decorated objects from the Museum's collection including swords, daggers, shields , and gauntlets all of which tell the story of teaching the use of civilian swords and related arms. *Catalog Will Travel*

10/05/1999 to 01/09/2000   CARLETON WATKIINS: THE ART OF PERCEPTION
Watkins was the finest American landscape photographer of the 19th C. *Catalog*

10/07/1999 to 01/02/2000   RODIN'S MONUMENT TO VICTOR HUGO
20 figures from a small terra cotta sketch to a life size marble and bronze castings

11/10/1999 to 11/12/2000   CELEBRATING THE AMERICAN WING: NOTABLE ACQUISITIONS 1980-1999
All these additions are explained with labels describing their significance in the light of the Museum collection.

11/16/1999 to 02/27/2000 ONLY THE BEST:" MASTERPIECES OF THE CALOUSTE GULBENKIAN MUSEUM, LISBON
This extraordinary collection includes paintings from Renaissance to Impressionism, illuminated manuscripts and spectacular jeweled pieces by Lalique, as well as French furniture and silver, and paintings by Rubens, Fragonard, Turner, Manet and Monet.

11/27/1999 to 01/09/2000   ANNUAL CHRISTMAS TREE AND NEAPOLITAN BAROQUE CRECHE
Lighting ceremony Friday and Saturday evenings at 7.00 PM.

12/09/1999 to 03/19/2000   ROCK STYLE
Classic Rock and Roll performers and their pervasive influence on fashion.

12/14/1999 to 03/26/2000   A CENTURY OF DESIGN, PART 1: 1900-1925
The first in a four part series surveying design in the 20th C.

01/11/2000 to 03/12/2000   SEAN SCULLY
Recent watercolors, pastels, and photographs by American artist Scully.

01/25/2000 to 03/26/2000   MASTERPIECES OF KOREAN CERAMICS FROM THE MUSEUM OF ORIENTAL CERAMICS, OSAKA

01/25/2000 to 01/2001   EUROPEAN HELMETS, 1450-1650
Helmets are the earliest known body armor. Some 75 helmets will reveal the depth of the collection and a glimpse of objects rarely on display.

02/01/2000 to 05/14/2000   WALKER EVANS
175 VINTAGE PRINTS OF American photographer Evans will be shown . They span his long and productive career. Included will be the artist's short stories, important letters and critical essays.

02/01/2000 to 08/20/2000   THE WORLD OF SCHOLARS ROCKS: GARDENS, STUDIOS AND PAINTINGS
Rocks have been admired in China as an essential ingredient in gardens. These will be accompanied by 100 paintings from the 11th to 20th C. from the collection.

02/01/2000 to 09/03/2000   PERFECT DOCUMENTS:: WALTER EVANS AND AFRICAN ART 1935
In 1935 The Museum of Modern Art showed African Negro Art as sculpture, rather than ethnographic objects. Evans created a portfolio for the show. The exhibition will display 50 of these documents.

02/10/2000 to 05/14/2000   TILMAN RIEMENSCHNEIDER: MASTER SCULPTOR OF THE LATE MIDDLE AGES
The first major survey of master sculptor Tilman Riemenschneider in almost seventy years presents more than fifty of his finest works in a variety of media, including fragments of altarpieces, independent figures, objects for private devotion, and models he created for assistants. Reimenschneider struck a balance between elegance and expressive strength. He was solidly anchored in the late Gothic tradition while expressing humanist concerns. *Will Travel*

02/15/2000 to 05/07/2000   MUMMY FACES: MUMMY PORTRAITS FROM ROMAN FACES
These portraits with their direct full gaze and strong presence were at once Greco-Roman in style and Egyptian in purpose.

262

Metropolitan Museum of Art - continued
03/08/2000 to 12/31/2000   BONNARD TO BALTHUS: PAINTERS OF THE SCHOOL OF PARIS

03/30/2000 to 06/25/2000   JAPANESE ART FROM THE MARY BURKE COLLECTION
This collection, the most renowned in the West, features masterpieces in various media.

04/2000 to 08/13/2000   DRAWN TO PAINTING: LEON KOSSOFF'S DRAWINGS AND PRINTS AFTER NICOLAS POUSSIN
Kossoff's response to the 1995 Poussin retrospective in London. *Catalog*

04/11/2000 to 08/20/2000   SUBJECTS AND SYMBOLS IN AMERICAN SCULPTURE

04/26/2000 to 07/30/2000   ART AND ORACLE: AFRICAN ART AND RITUALS OF DIVINATION
Sculpture in a full range of media

05/2000 to 10/2000   A CENTURY OF DESIGN, PART II: 1925-1980
A four part series surveying design in the 20th C.

05/2000 to 10/2000   AMERICAN MODERN: DESIGN FOR A NEW AGE 1925-1940
Objects of all kinds will be on display including clocks, furniture, appliances, etc from the first generation of American industrial designers.

05/2000 to 11/2000   THE ANNENBERG COLLECTION OF IMPRESSIONIST AND POSTIMPRESSIONIST MASTERPIECES
Acknowledged as one of the most distinguished private collections of its kind.

05/02/2000 to Late Fall 2000   IRIS AND GERALD B. CANTOR ROOF GARDEN
Wonderful views, beverage and sandwich service as weather permits.

06/2000 to 08/2000   FIREWORKS
More than 100 prints and drawings illustrating fireworks marking special occasions from the 15th to 20th C.

06/06/2000 to 09/10/2000   JOHN SINGER SARGENT: BEYOND THE PORTRAIT STUDIO, PAINTINGS AND DRAWINGS FROM THE COLLECTION

06/27/2000 to 09/17/2000   CHARDIN
Chardin's distinguished career as a still-life and genre painter will be surveyed.

Summer 2000   PHOTOGRAPHY: PROCESSES, PRESERVATION, TREATMENT
Celebrating the opening of the Photograph Conservation Lab the exhibit will explain these processes.

09/28/2000 to 01/09/2000   NORTHERN DRAWINGS OF THE SEVENTEENTH AND EIGHTEENTH CENTURIES IN THE ROBERT LEHMAN COLLECTION
Dutch, Flemish, French and British drawings. *Catalog*

Miriam and Ira D. Wallach Art Gallery
Affiliate Institution: Columbia University
Schermerhorn Hall, 8th Fl.116th St. and Broadway, New York, NY 10027
☎: 212-854-7288
Open: 1-5 We-Sa The gallery is open only when there is an exhibition!
Closed: Mo, Tu, Su, 1/1, week of THGV, 12/25, 6/3-10/10, MEM Day wkend
♿ ⓟ Nearby pay garages **Group Tours   Drop-In Tours   Historic Building**
Permanent Collection: non-collecting institution

Operated under the auspices of Columbia University and situated on its wonderful campus, the gallery functions to complement the educational goals of the University.

ON EXHIBIT 2000

02/2000 to 03/2000   PENNSYLVANIA STATION: CONSTRUCTION, DEMOLITION, REDEVELOPMENT

10/2000 to 12/2000   ARCHITECT OF DREAMS: THE THEATRICAL VISION OF JOSEPH URBAN

NEW YORK

Morgan Library
29 East 36th Street, New York, NY 10016-3490

☎: 212-685-0610

Open: 10:30-5 Tu-Fr, 10:30-6 Sa, noon-6 Su   **Closed:** Mo, LEG/HOL!

Sugg/Cont: **ADM**: **Adult:** $6.00   **Children:** Free under 12   **Students:** $4.00   **Seniors:** $4.00

& Ⓟ Nearby pay garage   **Museum Shop**   ⑪: Cafe open daily for luncheon and afternoon tea 212-685-0008, ext 401

Group Tours: 212-695-0008, ext. 390   **Drop-In Tours**: daily ! ext 390   **Historic Building**

Permanent Collection: MED: drgs, books, ptgs, manuscripts, obj d'art

Both a museum and a center for scholarly research, the Morgan Library is a perfect Renaissance style gem both inside and out. Set in the heart of prosaic NY, this monument comes to the city as a carefully thought out contribution to the domain for the intellect and of the spirit. **NOT TO BE MISSED:** Stavelot Triptych, a jeweled 12th century reliquary regarded as one of the finest medieval objects in America; Pierpont Morgan's private study and Library

ON EXHIBIT 2000

09/16/1999 to 01/2/2000   THE GREAT EXPERIMENT: GEORGE WASHINGTON AND THE AMERICAN REPUBLIC
Using Washington's career and the 200th anniversary of his death as a vehicle, the exhibition will present the creation of the American republic as a genuinely revolutionary process, which produced the first successful republican nation in the modern world. *Catalog Will Travel*

01/2000 to 04/2000   CAXTON: COLOGNE, BRUGES, AND WESTMINSTER:
The Morgan Library houses the largest collection of Caxton's (1422-1491) work outside of England. He is renowned as England's first printer. Showcased will be nearly 70 books and contemporary bookbindings from the collection. Examples of works of his immediate successors in England and colleagues on the Continent will also be shown.

02/04/2000   NETHERLANDISH AND FLEMISH DRAWING IN THE MORGAN LIBRARY
Surveying the finest Northern drawings in the Library's collections, this exhibition will feature over eighty-five works spanning the Gothic through the Flemish Baroque periods. A small selection of drawings by artists working in the tradition of Van Eyck and Van der Goes also will be included.

Museum for African Art
593 Broadway, New York, NY 10012

☎: 212-966-1313   ◙   www.africanart.org

Open: 10:30-5:30 Tu-Fr; 12-6 Sa, Su   **Closed:** Mo, LEG/HOL!

ADM: **Adult:** $5.00   **Children:** $2.50   **Students:** $2.50   **Seniors:** $2.50

& Ⓟ Nearby pay garages   **Museum Shop**   **Group Tours**   **Drop-In Tours**: !   **Historic Building**

Permanent Collection: AF: all media

This new facility in a historic building with a cast iron facade was designed by Maya Lin, architect of the Vietnam Memorial in Washington, D.C. Her conception of the space is 'less institutional, more personal and idiosyncratic'. She is using 'color in ways that other museums do not, there will be no white walls here'.

ON EXHIBIT 2000

09/15/1999 to 01/03/2000 LIBERATED VOICES: CONTEMPORARY SOUTH AFRICAN ART SINCE MANDELA
Works dating from 1994, the end of apartheid. A landmark exhibition it is the first to show the works of young African artists rather than South Africans of European decent.

02/2000 to 08/2000 HEADLINES: THE LANGUAGE OF HAIR IN AFRICAN ART AND CULTURE (working title)
Throughout Africa, self-adornment serves as a communications system, revealing much about social and religious position in society. Artworks, photographs and objects examine the role of hair.

264

Museum of American Folk Art

Two Lincoln Square, New York, NY 10023-6214

☎: 212-595-9533   ◙   www.folkartmus.org
Open: 11:30-7:30 Tu-Su   **Closed:** LEG/HOL!
&   ℗ pay garage nearby   **Museum Shop**
Group Tours
Permanent Collection: FOLK: ptgs, sculp, quilts, textiles, dec/art

The museum is known both nationally and internationally for its leading role in bringing quilts and other folk art to a broad public audience. **NOT TO BE MISSED:** 'Girl in Red with Cat and Dog', by Ammi Phillips; major works in all areas of folk art

ON EXHIBIT 2000

ONGOING   AMERICA'S HERITAGE
Major works from the permanent collection shown on a rotating basis.

Museum of Modern Art

11 West 53rd Street, New York, NY 10019-5498

☎: 212-708-9400   ◙   www.moma.org   www.ticketweb.com for advance adm. tickets (service fee on ticketweb)
Open: 10:30-6 Sa-Tu, Th; 10:30-8:30 Fr   **Closed:** We, THGV12/25
Free Day: Fr 4:30-8:15 vol cont
ADM: Adult: $9.50   **Children:** Free under 16 with adult   **Students:** $6.50   **Seniors:** $6.50
&   ℗ Pay nearby   **Museum Shop**   ᝀ: Garden Cafe and Sette Moma (open for dinner exc We & Su)
Group Tours: 212-708-0400   **Drop-In Tours:** !Weekdays, Sa, Su 1 & 3   **Historic Building** 1939 Bldg by Goodwin & Stone considered one of first examples of Int. Style   **Sculpture Garden**
Permanent Collection: WORKS BY PICASSO, MATISSE, Van Gogh, Warhol and Monet, DESIGN 20 ∩

The MOMA offers the world's most comprehensive survey of 20th century art in all media as well as an exceptional film library. **NOT TO BE MISSED:** Outstanding collection of 20th century photography, film and design.

MOMA Bookstore hours: 10-6:30 Sa-Tu, Th, 10-9 Fr
MOMA Design Store: 10-6:00 Sa-Tu, Th, 10-8 Fr
Garden Cafe   11-5 Sa-Tu, Th, 11-7:45 Fr
Sette MOMA   12-3, 5-10:30 daily exc. We

ON EXHIBIT 2000

10/1999 to 08/2000   END OF CENTURY
Three cycles of exhibitions celebrate the multiplicity of modernism's that comprise the visual arts since the 1880's and provide an unparalleled overview of some of the century's most powerful art.

10/9/1999 to 02/01/2000   MODERN STARTS: PEOPLE
As part of the first cycle of MoMA2000, this exhibition examines the period of early modern figurative art, ranging from the figure compositions of Matisse and Picasso to the prints of Munch and Redon. ∩

10/28/1999 to 03/14/2000   MODERN STARTS: PLACES
Part of the first cycle of MoMA2000, this exhibition considers the geographical sites represented in works created between 1880 and 1920. It includes images by French landscape artists from Cézanne to Atget, images of the modern city by de Chirico and Léger, and the interiors of Guimard. ∩

11/21/1999 to 03/14/2000   MODERN STARTS: THINGS
Also part of the first cycle of MoMA2000, this exhibition addresses the importance of object-like works of art to the early modern period, from Duchamp's readymades to the sculpture of Brancusi, from still life paintings to advertising posters. ∩

NEW YORK

Museum of the City of New York

Fifth Ave. at 103rd Street, New York, NY 10029

☎: 212-534-1672 ◙ www.mcny.org
Open: 10-5 We-Sa, 1-5 Su:;10-2 Tu for pre-registered groups only   **Closed:** Mo, LEG/HOL!
ADM: Adult: $5.00: family $10.00   **Children:** $4.00   **Students:** $4.00   **Seniors:** $4.00
& ℗ Nearby pay garages   **Museum Shop   Group Tours**: 212-534-1672 ext 206   **Drop-In Tours:** !   **Historic Building**
Permanent Collection: NEW YORK: silver 1678-1910; INTERIORS: 17-20; THE ALEXANDER HAMILTON
COLLECTION; PORT OF THE NEW WORLD MARINE GALLERY

Founded in 1933 this was the first American museum dedicated to the history of a major city. The Museum's
collections encompass the City's heritage, from its exploration and settlement to the NY of today **NOT TO
BE MISSED:** Period Rooms

ON EXHIBIT 2000

ONGOING   BROADWAY
A survey of the magical Broadway comedies, dramas and musicals from 1866 to the present.

ONGOING   BROADWAY CAVALCADE
The history of the street known as Broadway from its origins as a footpath in Colonial New York to its development into the
City's most dynamic, diverse and renowned boulevard.

ONGOING   FAMILY TREASURES: TOYS AND THEIR TALES
Toys from the Museum's renowned collection present a history of New York City through their individual stories.

ONGOING   ISADORA DUNCAN
A display focusing on the provocative life of the dancer who transformed the concept of dance into an art form.

02/18/1999 to 08/20/2000   NEW YORK NOW 2000
A new series of exhibitions showcasing the work of contemporary artists who choose New Yorkers and New York as their
subjects. Media will be alternated with Prints, photographs and slides in 2000 and paintings and sculpture in 2001.

09/25/1999 to 01/02/2000   AMERICANS: LATINO LIFE IN THE UNITED STATES
A portrait of a growing community that is a part of our cultural heritage. Photographs explore the breadth and variety of the
Latino experience in the US.

10/09/1999 to 02/25/2000   FORGOTTEN GATEWAY: THE ABANDONED BUILDINGS OF ELLIS ISLAND
A photographic journey through Ellis Island past and present. *Will Travel*

11/20/1999 to 04/02/2000   KIDS MAKE HISTORY
Photographs and essays by New York City high school students exploring the changing neighborhoods of some of the most
dynamic immigrant communities.

11/20/1999 to 07/08/2000   THE NEW YORK CENTURY–WORLD CAPITOL, HOMETOWN
Drawn primarily from the collections it evokes the experience of New York City during the 20th C. It is a visually exciting
informative and memorable journey to scholarly and popular programs that represent the City's experience during the last 100
years

03/18/2000 to 09/24/2000   ELEGANT PLATE: THREE CENTURIES OF PRECIOUS METALS IN New York City
The Museum' s silver and precious metal collection will document the material culture. *Catalog*

**04/12/2000 to 06/25/2000   PAINTING THE TOWN: CITYSCAPES FROM THE MUSEUM OF THE CITY OF NEW
YORK**
The cityscape paintings document the development of New York from a small colonial settlement to the world's foremost
metropolis. 45 paintings will be on view at Paine Webber Gallery. *Catalog*

09/13/2000 to 01/14/2000   A COMMUNITY OF MANY WORLDS: ARAB AMERICANS IN NEW YORK CITY
The Museum will undertake a much needed history of Arab Americans. The faiths to which they belong, material culture and
imagery and the four generation history in the US.

11/04/2000 to 02/25/2001   EUGENE ATGET AT WORK (working title)
Over a period of thirty years Atget photographed Paris, its buildings, monuments, ancient streets, civic spaces, public parks
and gardens, picturesque villages and royal gardens. He took an estimated 8500 negatives. His approach and method and
the interplay between technical procedures and interpretive strategies over the period.

National Academy Museum and School of Fine Arts

1083 Fifth Avenue, New York, NY 10128

☎: 212-369-4880
Open: 12-5 We-Su, 12-8 Fr   **Closed:** LEG/HOL!
Free Day: Fr, 5-8 pay-as-you-wish   **ADM:** **Adult:** $5.00   **Students:** $3.50   **Seniors:** $3.50
& ℗ Nearby pay garage   **Museum Shop   Group Tours**
Permanent Collection: AM: all media 19-20

With outstanding special exhibitions as well as rotating exhibits of the permanent collection, this facility is a school as well as a resource for American Art. **NOT TO BE MISSED:** The oldest juried annual art exhibition in the nation is held in spring or summer with National Academy members only exhibiting in the odd-numbered years and works by all U.S. artists considered for inclusion in even-numbered years.

National Arts Club

15 Gramercy Park South, New York, NY 10024

☎: 212-475-3424
Open: 1-6 daily   **Closed:** LEG/HOL!
& ℗ Nearby pay garage, some metered street parking   **Museum Shop**   ⓘ For members   **Historic Building**
Permanent Collection: AM: ptgs, sculp, works on paper, dec/art 19,20; Ch: dec/art

The building which houses this private club and collection was the 1840's mansion of former Governor Samuel Tilden. The personal library of Robert Henri which is housed here is available for study on request.

New Museum of Contemporary Art

583 Broadway, New York, NY 10012

☎: 212-219-1222   ◙ www.newmuseum.org
Open: 12-6 We & Su, 12-9 Th-Sa   **Closed:** Mo, Tu, 1/1, 12/25
Free Day: 6-8 Th   **ADM:** **Adult:** $5.00, ARTISTS $3.00   **Children:** Free under 18   **Students:** $3.00   **Seniors:** $3.00
& ℗ Nearby pay garages   **Museum Shop   Group Tours:** ext 216   **Historic Building** Astor Building
Permanent Collection: Semi-permanent collection

The museum is a premiere site dedicated to contemporary art in New York City as well as internationally. Solo exhibitions as well as group shows reflect the global nature of art today. It presents an exciting array of work in all media from around the world.

ON EXHIBIT 2000

11/19/1999 to 03/05/2000   CILDO MEIRELES
Room scale installations, walk through environments and sculptures spanning a 25 year period in the retrospective of this Brazilian artist. He creates pieces which require the viewer to abandon the traditionally passive role for a visitor for a direct interaction with the installations.

03/30/2000 to 07/02/2000   PICTURING THE MODERN AMAZON
The hypermuscular and physically strong women , examining their image and reality. Their relationship between body and social power and images of women by more than 45 contemporary artists. *Catalog*

New-York Historical Society

170 Central Park West, New York, NY 10024

☎: 212-873-3400   ◙ www.nyhistory.org
Open: 11-5 Tu-Su, Library 11-5 Tu-Sa   **Closed:** Mo, LEG/HOL!
ADM: **Adult:** $5.00   **Students:** $3.00   **Seniors:** $3.00
& ℗ Pay garages nearby   **Museum Shop**
Group Tours: 212-501-9233   **Drop-In Tours:** 1 & 3pm
Historic Building
Permanent Collection: AM: Ptgs 17-20; HUDSON RIVER SCHOOL; AM: gr, phot 18-20; TIFFANY GLASS; CIRCUS & THEATER: post early 20; COLONIAL: portraits (includes Governor of NY dressed as a woman)

NEW YORK

New-York Historical Society - continued

Housed in an elegant turn of the century neoclassical building is a collection of all but 2 of the 435 'Birds of America' watercolors by John James Audubon. In addition there are 150 works from Tiffany Studios. **NOT TO BE MISSED:** 435 original W/Col by John James Audubon

ON EXHIBIT 2000

08/31/1999 to 01/02/2000 PUTTING IT ON PAPER: TWO HUNDRED YEARS OF AMERICAN DRAWINGS AND WATERCOLORS FROM THE COLLECTION OF THE NEW-YORK HISTORICAL SOCIETY
Selected entirely from the Historical Society's collection, this exhibition features artists who worked primarily in New York. New York views and portraits of individuals who are significant in New York and/or national history will be shown. Many rarely seen works from artists including Asher B. Durand, Beatrice Wood, William Sidney Mount, Thomas Cole, John J. Audubon, and Fredric Remington will be on view.

09/21/1999 to 03/09/2000 $24: MANHATTAN'S MYTH OF ORIGIN
The myth of the infamous Manhattan purchase-told with historical prints, maps, books, wampum string and other colonial era items from the Historical Society collections-is debunked and the true story revealed.

OPENING 09/28/1999   MASTERWORKS OF NINETEENTH CENTURY AMERICAN PAINTINGS FROM THE COLLECTION OF THE NEW-YORK HISTORICAL SOCIETY
Closed to the public since 1992, Dexter Hall reopens as a permanent public gallery featuring thirty American masterpieces from the Historical Society's magnificent collection of 18th- and 19th-century oil paintings. Many of the paintings from artists such as Asher B. Durand, George Healey, Thomas Hill and Francis William Edmonds, have not been exhibited for nearly 25 years.

10/11/1999 to 02/20/20000   THE ITALIANS OF NEW YORK
The complex five century story of the Italians in New York City from Giovanni Verrazano in 1524 to Rudolph Giuliani today.

07/11/2000   INVENTING THE SKYLINE: THE ARCHITECTURE OF CASS GILBERT
From the Historical Society's archives, ten renowned structures by American architect Cass Gilbert (1859-1934) are followed from drawings through completion. Gilbert's most renowned works include the Woolworth Building, the Custom House at Bowling Green and the New York Life Insurance Building.

Pratt Manhattan Gallery

295 Lafayette Street, 2nd floor, New York, NY 10012
☎: 718-636-3517
Open: 10-5 Mo-Sa   **Closed:** LEG/HOL!
 ♿ ⓟ Nearby pay garage
Historic Building Puck Building
Permanent Collection: Not continuously on view.

Pratt Manhattan and Schaffler Galleries in Brooklyn present a program of exhibitions of contemporary art, design, and architecture in thematic exhibitions as well as solo and group shows of work by faculty, students and alumni.

Salmagundi Museum of American Art

47 Fifth Avenue, New York, NY 10003
☎: 212-255-7740
Open: 1-5 daily   **Closed:** LEG/HOL!
♿ ⓟ Nearby pay garage   ⑪: Members Only
Group Tours: 212-255-7740   **Drop-In Tours**: can be arranged
Historic Building
Permanent Collection: AM: Realist ptgs 19,20

An organization of artists and art lovers in a splendid landmark building on lower 5th Avenue.

Sidney Mishkin Gallery of Baruch College
135 East 22nd Street, New York, NY 10010

✆: 212-802-2690
Open: 12-5 Mo-We, Fr, 12-7 Th **Closed:** Sa, Su, ACAD!
  ♿ ℗ Nearby pay garages
Historic Building
Permanent Collection: GR; PHOT 20

The building housing this gallery was a 1939 Federal Courthouse erected under the auspices of the WPA. **NOT TO BE MISSED:** Marsden Hartley's 'Mount Katadin, Snowstorm', 1942

Society of Illustrators Museum of American Illustration
128 East 63rd St, New York, NY 10021

✆: 212-838-2560 ◙ www.societyillustraors.org
Open: 10-5 We-Fr, 10-8 Tu, 12-4 Sa **Closed:** Su, Mo, LEG/HOL!
  ♿ ℗ Nearby pay garages **Museum Shop** ‖: by membership @ $150/Yr **Group Tours** **Historic Building**
Permanent Collection: NORMAN ROCKWELL

A very specialized collection of illustrations familiar to everyone.

Solomon R. Guggenheim Museum
1071 Fifth Ave, New York, NY 10128

✆: 212-423-3500 ◙ www.guggenheim.org
Open: 10-6 Su–We, 10-8 Fr, Sa **Closed:** Th, 12/25,1/1
ADM: Adult: $12.00 **Children:** Free under 12 w/adult **Students:** $7.00 **Seniors:** $7.00
  ♿ ℗ Nearby pay garages **Museum Shop** ‖
Group Tours: 212-423-3652 Drop-In Tours
Historic Building Sculpture Garden
Permanent Collection: AM & EU: ptgs, sculp; PEGGY GUGGENHEIM COLL: cubist, surrealist, & ab/exp artworks; PANZA diBIUMO COLL: minimalist art 1960's -70's ◠

Designed by Frank Lloyd Wright in 1950, and designated a landmark building by New York City, the museum was recently restored and expanded. Originally called the Museum of Non-Objective Painting, the Guggenheim houses one of the world's largest collections of paintings by Kandinsky as well as prime examples of works by such modern masters as Picasso, Giacometti, Mondrian and others. **NOT TO BE MISSED:** Kandinsky's 'Blue Mountain'

ON EXHIBIT 2000

10/08/1999 to 01/09/2000 CLEMEMTE

Studio Museum in Harlem
144 West 125th Street, New York, NY 10027

✆: 212-864-4500 ◙ www.studiomuseuminharlem.org
Open: 10-5 We-Fr, 1-6 Sa, Su **Closed:** Mo, Tu, LEG/HOL!
ADM: Adult: $5.00 **Children:** $1.00 (under 12) **Students:** $3.00 **Seniors:** $3.00
  ♿ ℗ pay garages nearby **Museum Shop Sculpture Garden**
Permanent Collection: AF/AM; CARIBBEAN; LATINO

This is the premier center for the collection, interpretation and exhibition of the art of Black America and the African Diaspora. The five-story building is located on 125th Street, Harlem's busiest thoroughfare and hub of it's commercial rebirth and redevelopment.

NEW YORK

Studio Museum in Harlem - continued

ON EXHIBIT 2000

11/17/1999 to 01/17/2000   PASSAGES: CONTEMPORARY ART IN TRANSITION
New installations by Chakaia Booker, Leonardo Dre, Nari Ward and Sana Musasama. These works test the sanctioned boundaries of contemporary art and reflect the persistence of important movements in minimalism, conceptualism, modernism and post-modernism

02/02/2000 to 06/18/2000   AFRICAN-AMERICAN ARTISTS AND AMERICAN MODERNISM
In the 20th C many African-American artists experimented with modernism to express the black experience or reflect the constant changing characteristics of mainstream American art.

Summer 2000   BEADS, BODY AND SOUL: ART AND LIGHT IN THE YORUBA UNIVERSE
The exhibition examines the extraordinary variety and complexity of Yoruba beaded arts. This is the first major exhibition to explore the historical and philosophical dimensions of the Yoruba universe through beads, and considers the web of ideas, images, and forms that connect and define the Yoruba aesthetic over hundreds of years and thousands of miles.

Summer/Fall 2000   FROM THE STUDIO: ARTISTS IN RESIDENCE, 1999-2000
This annual exhibition features the works of the 1998-1999 Artists-in-Residence: Nicole Awai, Sanford L. Biggers and Terry Bodie. Chosen from among hundreds of applicants, the 1999-2000 program participants represent a variety of ethnic and educational backgrounds and stylistic approaches.

Whitney Museum of American Art

945 Madison Ave, New York, NY 10021
📞: 212-570-3676   ◙ www.echony.com/nwhitney
Open: 11-6 Tu, We, Fr, Sa, Su, 1-8 Th   **Closed:** Mo. 1/1, THGV, 12/25
ADM: Adult: $12.50   **Children:** Free under 12   **Students:** $10.50   **Seniors:** $10.50
♿ ⓟ Nearby pay parking lots   **Museum Shop** ¶
Group Tours: 212-570-7720
Drop-In Tours: We-Su, & Th eve 212-570-3676
Historic Building
Sculpture Garden
Permanent Collection: AM: all media, 20

Founded by leading American art patron Gertrude Vanderbilt Whitney in 1930, the Whitney is housed in an award winning building designed by Marcel Breuer. The museum's mandate, to devote itself solely to the art of the US, is reflected in its significant holdings of the works of Edward Hopper (2,500 in all), Georgia O'Keeffe, and more than 850 works by Reginald Marsh. New directions and developments in American art are featured every 2 years in the often cutting edge and controversial 'Whitney Biennial'. **NOT TO BE MISSED:** Alexander Calder's 'Circus'

Satellite Galleries:
Whitney Museum of American Art at Philip Morris,120 Park Ave, NYC

Whitney Museum of American Art at Champion, Stamford, CT

ON EXHIBIT 2000

09/26/1999 to 02/13/2000   THE AMERICAN CENTURY ART AND CULTURE 1900-2000
The exhibition examines the evolution of American identity as seen through the eyes of American artists over the last century and examines the impact of immigration, mass media and technology. There will be a major internet based program for the exhibition. *Bilingual*

03/2000 to 06/2000   2000 BIENNIAL EXHIBITION
An invitational show of work produced in America in the preceding two years *Catalog*

07/2000 to 10/2000   BARBARA KRUGER
First comprehensive overview of Kruger's work covering all varieties of her output. *Catalog Will Travel*

Yeshiva University Museum
2520 Amsterdam Avenue, New York, NY 10033
☎: 212-960-5390 ◙ www.yu.edu/museum/index.html
Open: 10:30-5 Tu-Th, 12-6 Su **Closed:** LEG/HOL!, JEWISH/HOL!
ADM: **Adult:** $3.00 **Children:** $2.00, 4-16 **Students:** $2.00 **Seniors:** $2.00
 ♿ Ⓟ neighboring streets and pay lots
Museum Shop 🍴: Cafeteria on campus
Group Tours
Permanent Collection: JEWISH: ptgs, gr, textiles, ritual objects, cer

Major historical and contemporary exhibitions of Jewish life and ceremony are featured in this museum. **NOT TO BE MISSED:** Architectural models of historic synagogues

---

NIAGARA FALLS

Castellani Art Museum-Niagara University
Niagara Falls, NY 14109
☎: 716-286-8200 ◙ www.niagara.edu/~cam
Open: 11-5 We-Sa, 1-5 Su **Closed:** ACAD!
♿ Ⓟ
Group Tours
Permanent Collection: AM: ldscp 19; CONT: all media; WORKS ON PAPER: 19-20; PHOT: 20

Minutes away from Niagara Falls, Artpark, and the New York State Power Vista, the Castellani Art Museum features an exciting collection of contemporary art and a permanent folk arts program in a beautiful grey marble facility. **NOT TO BE MISSED:** 'Begonia', 1982, by Joan Mitchell

ON EXHIBIT 2000
10/07/1999 to 01/09/2000 A COMMUNITY BETWEEN TWO WORLDS
The Arab-American Community in Greater Detroit

02/2000 to 03/2000 JAZZ PHOTOGRAPHS

NORTH SALEM

Hammond Museum
Deveau Rd. Off Route 124, North Salem, NY 10560
☎: 914-669-5033 ◙ www.hammondmuseum.org.com
Open: 12-4 We-Sa **Closed:** 12/25, 1/1
ADM: **Adult:** $4.00 **Children:** Free under 12 **Students:** $3.00 **Seniors:** $3.00
♿ Ⓟ **Museum Shop** 🍴: Apr through Oct
Group Tours Drop-In Tours: Res
Permanent Collection: Changing exhibitions

The Hammond Museum and Japanese Stroll Garden provide a place of natural beauty and tranquility to delight the senses and refresh the spirit.

NEW YORK

Frederic Remington Art Museum

303/311 Washington Street, Ogdensburg, NY 13669

☎: 315-393-2425　◙　www.remington.museum.org

Open: 9-5 Mo, Sa,1-5 Su (5/1-10/31), 11-5 Tu-Sa (11/1-4/30) 1-5 Su　**Closed:** LEG/HOL!

ADM: **Adult:** $4.00　**Children:** Free under 5　**Students:** $3.00　**Seniors:** $3.00

&　℗

Museum Shop
Group Tours
Historic Building
Permanent Collection: REMINGTON: ptgs, w/col, sculp, works on paper

The library, memorabilia, and finest single collection of Frederic Remington originals are housed in a 1809-10 mansion with a modern gallery addition. **NOT TO BE MISSED:** 'Charge of the Rough Riders at San Juan Hill'

Yager Museum

Oneonta, NY 13820

☎: 607-431-4480

Open: 11-5 Tu-Sa, 1-4 Su　**Closed:** Mo, LEG/HOL!

&　℗

Museum Shop　Group Tours

Permanent Collection: NAT/AM: artifacts; P/COL: pottery; VAN ESS COLLECTION OF REN, BAROQUE & AM (ptgs 19); masks; shells; botanical specimens

An excellent college museum with community involvement and traveling exhibitions which reflects its unique collections ranging from fine art of the Renaissance, 19th and 20th C. American paintings, upper Susquehanna area, archeology, ethnologic, mesoamerican and north American.

Plattsburgh State Art Museum

Affiliate Institution: State University Of New York

State University of New York, Plattsburgh, NY 12901

☎: 518-564-2474　◙　www.plattsburgh.edu/museum

Open: 12-4 daily　**Closed:** LEG/HOL!

&　℗ Free

Museum Shop　‖: on campus across from museum

Group Tours: 518-564-2813　**Drop-In Tours:** by appt

Sculpture Garden

Permanent Collection: ROCKWELL KENT: ptgs, gr, cer; LARGEST COLLECTION OF NINA WINKEL SCULPTURE

This University Museum features a 'museum without walls' with late 19th and 20th century sculptures, paintings, and graphics displayed throughout its campus and in four secure galleries. **NOT TO BE MISSED:** Largest collection of Rockwell Kent works

Roland Gibson Gallery

Affiliate Institution: State University College
State University College at Potsdam, Potsdam, NY 13676-2294

☎: 315-267-2250
Open: 12-5 Mo-Fr, 12-4 Sa, Su, 7-9:30 Mo-Th eve   **Closed:** LEG/HOL!
♿ Ⓟ
Group Tours
Sculpture Garden
Permanent Collection: CONT: sculp; WORKS ON PAPER; JAP: ptgs

Based on the New York State University campus in Potsdam, this is the only museum in northern New York that presents a regular schedule of exhibitions. **NOT TO BE MISSED:** 'Untitled', by Miro

Frances Lehman Loeb Art Center at Vassar College

Affiliate Institution: Vassar College
124 Raymond Ave., Poughkeepsie, NY 12601

☎: 914-437-5235 ◉ vassun.vassar.edu/~orfuac/
Open: 10-5 Tu-Sa, 1-5 Su **Closed:** Mo, EASTER, THGV, 12/25-1/1
♿ Ⓟ
Museum Shop
Group Tours: 914-437-5237   **Drop-In Tours**
Sculpture Garden
Permanent Collection: AM, EU: ptgs, sculp; AN/GR & AN/R: sculp; GR: old Master to modern

Housed in a newly built facility, this is the only museum between Westchester County and Albany exhibiting art of all periods. **NOT TO BE MISSED:** Magoon Collection of Hudson River Paintings

ON EXHIBIT 2000

01/27/2000 to 03/19/2000 MODELING FEMININITY: ART AND THE MORAL EDUCATION OF NINETEENTH CENTURY WOMEN
The link between women's education and the moral mission of art. is investigated . The images from the Magoon collection showed students in the early years of the college, heroines like Joan of Arc, Lady Jane Grey and contemporary domestic managers to show what they wanted them to become. *Brochure*

04/06/2000 to 06/11/2000 MAKING LIGHT: PHOTOGRAPHY AND HUMOR
This survey of photography's 160 year history shows that the camera has long provided humorists with a potent and adaptable tool. The works shown here include early stereographic images to present computer-aided ones and from staged arrangements to candid street scenes *Catalog*

06/30/2000 to 09/17/2000 KUNIE SUGIURA
30 works from series produced in the past decade . Her chosen medium is photograms , without a camera, and placing objects on photographic paper and exposing them to light. Her work incorporates the intimate nature studies which define a long Japanese visual tradition. *Catalog Will Travel*

NEW YORK

Donald M. Kendall Sculpture Gardens at Pepsico

700 Anderson Hill Road, Purchase, NY 10577
📞: 914-253-2082
Open: 9-5 daily   **Closed:** LEG/HOL!
🚹 Ⓟ Free
Sculpture Garden
Permanent Collection: 44 SITE-SPECIFIC SCULPTURES BY 20TH CENTURY ARTISTS

44 site-specific sculptures are located throughout the 168 magnificently planted acres that house the headquarters of PepsiCo, corporate sculpture gardens designed in 1970 by noted architect Edward Durell Stone. A large man-made lake and wandering ribbons of pathway invite the visitor to enjoy the sculptures within the ever-changing seasonal nature of the landscape. The garden, located at a corporate headquarters in Westchester County about 30 miles outside of NYC, is an art lover's delight.

Neuberger Museum of Art

Affiliate Institution: Purchase College, SUNY
735 Anderson Hill Rd, Purchase, NY 10577-1400
📞: 914-251-6100   ◙ www.neuberger.org
Open: 10-4 Tu-Fr 11-5 Sa, Su   **Closed:** Mo LEG/HOL
ADM: Adult: $4.00   **Children:** Free under 12   **Students:** $2.00   **Seniors:** $2.00
🚹 Ⓟ Free   **Museum Shop**   ‖: Museum Cafe 11:30-2:30 Tu-F, 12-4 Sa, Su
Group Tours: 914-251-6110   **Drop-In Tours:** 1pm Tu-Fr; 2 and 3pm Su
Permanent Collection: PTGS, SCULP, DRGS 20; ROY R. NEUBERGER COLLECTION; EDITH AND GEORGE RICKEY COLLECTION OF CONSTRUCTIVIST ART; AIMEE HIRSHBERG COLLECTION OF AFRICAN ART; HANS RICHTER BEQUEST OF DADA AND SURREALIST OBJECTS; ANC GRK, ETR VASES GIFT OF NELSON A. ROCKEFELLER

On the campus of Purchase College, SUNY, the Neuberger Museum of Art houses a prestigious collection of 20th century art. **NOT TO BE MISSED:** Selections from the Roy R. Neuberger Collection of 20th century American art

ON EXHIBIT 2000

ONGOING   ROY R. NEUBERGER COLLECTION
More than sixty works from the permanent collection displayed on a rotating basis form the heart and soul of the Museum's collection and include major works by Romare Bearden, Jackson Pollack, Edward Hopper, Georgia O'Keeffe and others.

ONGOING   OBJECT AND INTELLECT: AFRICAN ART FROM THE PERMANENT COLLECTION
Over forty objects created in the 19th and 20th century reflect African tradition, rites and religious beliefs. The exhibition presents the African view of the universe as being composed of two inseparable realms: a visible, tangible world of the living and an invisible world of the sacred.

ONGOING   INTERACTIVE LEARNING CENTER
Interactive video program enables visitors to delve into the style, history and artistic vocabulary of 200 works of art from the Roy R. Neuberger Collection of 20th century paintings and sculpture.

09/13/1999 to 01/10/2000   KILENGI: THE BAREISS COLLECTION OF AFRICAN ART
Selections from a world renowned collection depict the creation of new art forms that meet the changing needs of the people who use them.

01/16/2000 to 04/02/2000   THE SELF- CONSCIOUS EYE: 1890-1900 AND 1990-2000
The ends of this century and the last through art. European achievements at the end of the last century and American efforts at the end of the 20th. The work may shed light on cultural tendencies as civilization moves to millennium markers.

274

Neuberger Museum of Art - continued
01/29/2000 to 04/14/2000   INNER EYE: CONTEMPORARY ARTS FROM THE MARC AND LIVIA STRAUSS COLLECTION
Paintings, sculpture and photography from both emerging artists selected from the almost 100 works in this collection.

01/30/2000 to 04/16/2000   25 YEARS/25ARTISTS
Artists who have been associated with the Museum in solo or group exhibitions.

04/23/2000 to 08/27/2000   WHITFIELD LOVELL: PORTRAYALS
This African American artist portrays his penchant for portrait drawing and interest in found objects.

05/07/2000 to 08/27/2000   WELDED: SCULPTURES OF THE TWENTIETH CENTURY
A survey of welded sculpture in the twentieth century. Welding will be shown in all its techniques that is formalistic, figurative and humorous or playful.

09/17/2000 to 01/07/2001   MARY FRANK: ENCOUNTERS
A comprehensive overview of works completed during the past 15 years. Franks sensual dream penetrates her current oeuvre and memory and poetic sensibilities. *Catalog*

QUEENS

Queens Museum of Art
New York City Building, Flushing Meadows, Corona Park, Queens, NY 11368-3393
☎: 718-592-9700   ◉ www.queensmuse.org
Open: 10-5 We-Fr, 12-5 Sa, Su, Tu groups by appt   **Closed:** Mo, Tu, 1/1, THGV, 12/25
ADM: Adult: $4.00   **Children:** Free under 5   **Students:** $2.00   **Seniors:** $2.00
& Ⓟ Free   **Museum Shop**
Group Tours   Drop-In Tours: Tours of Panorama 3pm Sa
Historic Building
Permanent Collection: CHANGING EXHIBITIONS OF 20TH CENTURY ART AND CONTEMPORARY ART

The Panorama is where all of NYC fits inside one city block. You will feel like Gulliver when you experience it for the first time. The building was built for the 1939 World's Fair and was later used for United Nations meetings. Satellite Gallery at Bulova Corporate Center, Jackson Heights, Queens. **NOT TO BE MISSED:** 'The Panorama of NYC', largest architectural scale model of an Urban Area. "Tiffany in Queens: Selections from the Neustadt Museum Collection". Lamps, desk objects and a window on long term loan.

ROCHESTER

George Eastman House, International Museum of Photography and Film
900 East Ave, Rochester, NY 14607
☎: 716-271-3361   ◉ www.eastman.org
Open: 10-4:30 Tu-Sa, 1-4:30 Su   **Closed:** Mo, LEG/HOL!
ADM: Adult: $6.50   **Children:** $2.50 (5-12)   **Students:** $5.00   **Seniors:** $5.00
& Ⓟ   **Museum Shop** ⑪
Group Tours: 716-271-3361, ext 238   **Drop-In Tours**: 10:30 & 2 Tu-Sa, 2 Su
Historic Building
Permanent Collection: PHOT: prints; MOTION PICTURES; MOTION PICTURE STILLS; CAMERAS; BOOKS

The historic home of George Eastman, founder of Eastman Kodak Co. includes a museum that contains an enormous and comprehensive collection of over 400,000 photographic prints, 21,000 motion pictures, 25,000 cameras, 41,000 books and 5,000,000 motion picture stills. **NOT TO BE MISSED:** Discovery room for children

NEW YORK

George Eastman House, International Museum of Photography and Film - continued
ON EXHIBIT 2000
ONGOING   THROUGH THE LENS: SELECTIONS FROM THE PERMANENT COLLECTION

ONGOING   AN HISTORICAL TIMELINE OF PHOTO IMAGING

ONGOING   A PICTURE-PERFECT RESTORATION: GEORGE EASTMAN'S HOUSE AND GARDEN

ONGOING   ENHANCING THE ILLUSION: THE ORIGINS AND PROGRESS OF PHOTOGRAPHY

ONGOING   GEORGE EASTMAN IN FOCUS

Memorial Art Gallery
Affiliate Institution: University of Rochester
500 University Ave, Rochester, NY 14607
\: 716-473-7720   ◉ www.rochester.edu/MAG
Open: 12-9 Tu, 10-4 We-Fr, 10-5 Sa, 12-5 Su   **Closed:** Mo, LEG/HOL!
ADM: Adult: $5.00, $2 Tu 5-9   **Children:** 6-8 $3.00, Free 5 and under   **Students:** $4.00   **Seniors:** $4.00
♿ ℗   **Museum Shop** ⑪
Group Tours   Drop-In Tours: 2pm, Fr, Sa; 7:30 PM Tu
Historic Building   Sculpture Garden
Permanent Collection: MED; DU: 17; FR: 19; AM: ptgs, sculp 19,20; FOLK

The Gallery's permanent collection of 10,000 works spans 50 centuries of world art and includes masterworks by artists such as Monet, Cézanne, Matisse, Homer and Cassatt. An interactive learning center focuses on Learning to Look. Also included is an interactive CD-ROM "tour" of the Gallery. **NOT TO BE MISSED:** 'Waterloo Bridge, Veiled Sun' 1903, by Monet

ON EXHIBIT 2000
08/31/1999 to 01/09/2000   LYNNE FELDMAN: GOOD YONTIF
30 small paintings for a children's book depicting family celebrations for nine Jewish holidays. Good Yontif is the expression used when people greet each other on the holidays.

09/21/1999 to 01/16/2000   BEYOND MOSAIC
Mosaic is an ancient method of putting small pieces of colored glass, stone pr other material. together Recently artists have experimented with new materials and techniques. Many examples will be shown and the highlight is a 6 foot digital mosaic of Van Gogh's "Starry Night" composed of small images relating to the exploration of space.

12/12/1999 to 01/30/2000   THOMAS HOVINGS 20 FOR 2000
A dazzling array of objects in all media created at the turn of the last century, greets the millennium. He suggests never buy art for investment-only buy contemporary art. 32 up and coming artists as well as Frankenthaler and Wyeth.

02/21/2000 to 04/30/2000   MAXFIELD PARRISH, 1870-1966
A major retrospective of the work of one of the Academy's most distinguished alumni exploring the artistic influences, his work as one of the century's most popular illustrators and as a painter. Also to be explored is the qualities of his work which have led to his "rediscovery" by many contemporary artists. *Catalog Will Travel*

05/21/2000 to 07/16/2000   THE STONEWARE OF CHARLES FERGUS BINNS: FATHER OF AMERICAN STUDIO CERAMICS
Between 1900 and 1934, Binns created beautiful, functional ceramics . Sixty of his wheel-thrown vases, bottles, jars and bowls illustrate his mastery of science versus art.

06/11/2000 to 08/20/2000   TWENTIETH- CENTURY STILL LIFE PAINTINGS FROM THE PHILLIPS COLLECTION
The Phillips believed that "art was personal, art is passionate. These 60 examples run the gamut from purely representational to abstract including works by Graves, Picasso, Rousseau and Weston.

Memorial Art Gallery - continued
08/06/2000 to 10/15/2000   ABOUT TIME: WENDELL CASTLE
Wendell Castle has been known for organic, incorporating elements of painting, in his recent works. Celebrating the millennium, he features 17 clocks and time measuring installations including 3 which do not have clock faces, but address the issues of time.

09/24/2000 to 01/07/2001   THE ART OF WILL EDMUNDSON
In 1937, Edmundson was the first African American to have a one man exhibition at the Museum of Modern Art. He is a self0-tought artist and his work is inspired by his religious beliefs, African American folklore and popular culture. 40 limestone sculptures, and 25 period photographs of him and his work.

ROSLYN HARBOR

Nassau County Museum of Fine Art
Northern Blvd & Museum Dr, Roslyn Harbor, NY 11576
📞: 516-484-9338   ◙ www.nassaumuseum.org
Open: 11-5 Tu-Su   **Closed:** LEG/HOL!
ADM: Adult: $4.00   **Children:** $2.00   **Students:** $2.00   **Seniors:** $3.00
&. ℗ Free   **Museum Shop** ⃒⃒
Group Tours   Drop-In Tours: 2pm Tu-Sa   **Historic Building   Sculpture Garden**
Permanent Collection: AM: gr, sculp

Situated on 145 acres of formal gardens, rolling lawns and meadows, the museum presents four major exhibitions annually and is home to one of the east coasts' largest publicly accessible outdoor sculpture gardens.

SARATOGA SPRINGS

Schick Art Gallery
Affiliate Institution: Skidmore College
Skidmore Campus North Broadway, Saratoga Springs, NY 12866-1632
📞: 518-584-5000   ◙ dom.skidmore.edu/academics/art/mosaic/schick
Open: 9-5 Mo-Fr ; 9-4 Mo-Fr, (summer) 1-3:30 Sa   **Closed:** LEG/HOL!, ACAD!
&. ℗ On campus ⃒⃒ **Group Tours:** 518-580-5049

Theme oriented or one person exhibitions that are often historically significant are featured in this gallery located on the beautiful Skidmore Campus.

SOUTHAMPTON

Parrish Art Museum
25 Job's Lane, Southampton, NY 11968
📞: 516-283-2118
Open: 11-5 Mo, Tu, Fr, Sa, 1-5 Su; Open Daily Jun 1 - Sep 15   **Closed:** 1/1, EASTER, 7/4, THGV, 12/25
Sugg/Cont: ADM: Adult: $2.00   **Students:** Free (with valid ID)   **Seniors:** $1.00
&. ℗   **Museum Shop   Group Tours   Historic Building   Sculpture Garden**
Permanent Collection: AM: ptgs, gr 19; WILLIAM MERRITT CHASE; FAIRFIELD PORTER

Situated in a fashionable summer community, this Museum is a 'don't miss' when one is near the Eastern tip of Long Island. It is located in an 1898 building designed by Grosvenor Atterbury.

NEW YORK

Jacques Marchais Museum of Tibetan Art

338 Lighthouse Ave., Staten Island, NY 10306

☏: 718-987-3500 ◉ www.tibetanmusem.com

Open: 1-5 We-Su (Apr-mid Nov or by appt. Dec-Mar)1-5 We-Fr

Closed: Mo, Tu, EASTER, 7/4, LAB/DAY, THGV & day after, 12/25, 1/1

ADM: Adult: $3.00   **Children:** $1.00 (under 12)   **Students:** $3.00   **Seniors:** $2.50

 ♭ **Museum Shop**

Group Tours

Sculpture Garden

Permanent Collection: TIBET; OR: arch; GARDEN, BUDDHIST, HIMALAYAN: ASIAN

This unique museum of Himalayan art within a Tibetan setting consists of two stone buildings resembling a Buddhist temple. A quiet garden and a goldfish pond help to create an atmosphere of serenity and beauty. It is the only museum in this country devoted primarily to Tibetan art.

John A. Noble Collection at Snug Harbor

Affiliate Institution: Snug Harbor Cultural Center

270 Richmond Terrace, Staten Island, NY 10301

☏: 718-447-6490 ◉ www.mcns10.med.nyu.edu.noble

Open: 10-9 Th-Sa, 1-5 Su   **Closed:** Mo, Tu, We, LEG/HOL

ADM: Adult: $6.00   **Children:** under 12 $4.00   **Seniors:** $4.00

♭ ℗

Museum Shop

Group Tours

Historic Building

Permanent Collection: PTGS; LITHOGRAPHS; DOCUMENTS AND ARTIFACTS; SALOON HOUSEBOAT OF JOHN A. NOBLE

John Noble wrote 'My life's work is to make a rounded picture of American Maritime endeavor of modern times'. He is widely regarded as America's premier marine lithographer. The collection is in a new site at historic Snug Harbor Cultural Center.

Snug Harbor Cultural Center

Affiliate Institution: Newhouse Center for Contemporary Art

1000 Richmond Terrace, Staten Island, NY 10301

☏: 718-448-2500

Open: 12-5 We-Su   **Closed:** Mo, LEG/HOL!

ADM: Adult: $2.00

♭ ℗ Free **Museum Shop** ¶¶

Group Tours

Historic Building   **Sculpture Garden**

Once a 19th century home for retired sailors Snug Harbor is a landmark 83 acre, 28 building complex being preserved and adapted for the visual and performing arts. The Newhouse Center for Contemporary art provides a forum for regional and international design and art. **NOT TO BE MISSED:** The award winning newly restored 1884 fresco ceiling in the Main Hall.

Staten Island Institute of Arts and Sciences
75 Stuyvesant Place, Staten Island, NY 10301

☎: 718-727-1135
Open: 9-5 Mo-Sa, 1-5 Su   **Closed:** LEG/HOL!
ADM: **Adult:** $2.50   **Students:** $1.50   **Seniors:** $1.50
 ♿ Ⓢ Pay lot across the street   **Museum Shop**   **Group Tours**
Permanent Collection: PTGS; DEC/ART; SCULP; STATEN ISLAND: arch

One of Staten Island's oldest and most diverse cultural institutions, this facility explores and interprets the art, natural resources and cultural history of Staten Island. **NOT TO BE MISSED:** Ferry Collection on permanent exhibition. This exhibition on the history of the world-famous ferry service is located in the Staten Island Ferry terminal.

ON EXHIBIT 2000

ONGOING   THE STATEN ISLAND FERRY COLLECTION OF SIIAS
The history of the world's most famous Ferry Line is explored in an exhibition in the Staten Island Ferry waiting room, St. George. open daily 9-2 Suggested donation: adults $1.00; children under 12 $.25

STONY BROOK

Museums at Stony Brook
1208 Rte. 25A, Stony Brook, NY 11790-1992

☎: 516-751-0066   ▪ www.museumsatstonybrook.org
Open: 10-5 We-Sa, 12-5 Su, July, Aug 10-5 Mo-Sa, 12-5 Su   **Closed:** Mo, Tu, 1/1, THGV, 12/24, 12/25
Free Day: We, for Students   **ADM: Adult:** $4.00   **Children:** $2.00, 6-17, under 6 Free   **Students:** $2.00   **Seniors:** $3.00
 ♿ Ⓢ   **Museum Shop**   **Group Tours**: EXT.248   **Drop-In Tours**: !
Permanent Collection: AM: ptgs; Horse Drawn Carriages; Miniature Rooms; ANT: decoys; Costumes; Toys

A museum complex on a nine acre site with art, history, and carriage museums, blacksmith shop, 19th century one room schoolhouse, carriage shed and 1794 barn. **NOT TO BE MISSED:** Paintings by William Sidney Mount (1807-1868), 100 horse drawn carriages.

ON EXHIBIT 2000

10/08/1999 to 01/23/2000   THE TILE CLUB AND THE AESTHETIC MOVEMENT (1877-1887)

SYRACUSE

Everson Museum of Art
401 Harrison Street, Syracuse, NY 13202

☎: 315-474-6064   ▪ www.everson.org
Open: 12-5 Tu-Fr; 10-5 Sa; 12-5 Su   **Closed:** Mo, LEG/HOL
Sugg/Cont: **ADM**: **Adult:** $2.00
 ♿ Ⓢ Nearby pay garages, limited metered on street   **Museum Shop**   ││
Group Tours   **Drop-In Tours**: !   **Historic Building**   **Sculpture Garden**
Permanent Collection: AM: cer; AM: ptgs 19,20; AM: Arts/Crafts Movement Objects

When it was built, the first museum building designed by I.M. Pei was called 'a work of Art for Works of Art'. The Everson's Syracuse China Center for the Study of Ceramics is one of the nation's most comprehensive, ever increasing collection of America's ceramics housed in an open-storage gallery. The installation is arranged chronologically by culture and includes samples from the ancient classical world, the Americas, Asia and Europe. **NOT TO BE MISSED:** One of the largest, most comprehensive permanent exhibitions of American and world ceramics

Everson Museum of Art - continued

ON EXHIBIT 2000

ONGOING   ONE HUNDRED FIFTY YEARS OF AMERICAN ART
An overview of American art featuring turn of the century portraits and genre paintings, late 19th century landscapes and American modernism through the 1950s, including American Scene painting by some of America's best known artists.

ONGOING   INTERNATIONAL CONTEMPORARY CERAMICS

ONGOING   SYRACUSE CHINA CENTER FOR THE STUDY OF AMERICAN CERAMICS

ONGOING   10/02/1999 to 02/13/2000   FRANK GILLETTE: DIGITAL IMAGES, 1994-1999
Since 1991, Manhattan-based artist Frank Gillette has worked in a "virtual" studio, becoming proficient on a high-end computer with allied scanners, archival storage systems, monitors, and printers. During the subsequent years, he has created over 300 pictures by these means. For his solo show at the Everson, the artist will exhibit digitally-composed work created during the past five years, including 24 large-scale Iris prints and 12 smaller ink-jet prints.

ONGOING   10/02/1999 to 12/31/2002   200 YEARS OF AMERICAN ART, 1740-1940
About 40 artworks from the time period spanning 1746 to 1946 to both illustrate leading themes of American art history and portray to advantage the Everson's collection. The installation is broken down into four broad categories: portraiture, landscape, the culture of entertainment, and still life.

TARRYTOWN

Kykuit

Affiliate Institution: Historic Hudson Valley,
150 White Plains Road, Tarrytown, NY 10591
☎: 914-631-9491   ▣   www.hudsonvalley.org
Open   Closed: Open mid-April through October
ADM: Adult: $18.00   **Children:** not rec under 12   **Seniors:** $16.00
&   ℗ Free at Visitor's Center   **Sculpture Garden**

The six story stone house which was the Rockefeller home for four generations is filled with English and American furnishings, portraits and extraordinary collections of Asian ceramics. In the art galleries are paintings and sculpture by Andy Warhol, George Segal, Alexander Calder, Robert Motherwell and many others. Visitors also view the enclosed gardens and terraces with their collections of classical and 20th century sculpture and stunning river views. The Coach Barn contains horse-drawn carriages and classic automobiles. The Beaux-Arts gardens were designed by William Welles Bosworth and are filled with an extraordinary collection of modern sculpture.

UTICA

Munson-Williams Proctor Institute Museum of Art

310 Genesee Street, Utica, NY 13502
☎: 315-797-0000   ▣   www.mwpi.edu
Open: 10-5 Tu-Sa, 1-5 Su   **Closed:** Mo, LEG/HOL!
Sugg/Cont:
&   ℗   **Museum Shop**   ‖: Mo-Fr 11:30-3
Group Tours: 315-797-0000, ext 2170   **Drop-In Tours:** by appt
Historic Building   Sculpture Garden
Permanent Collection: AM: ptgs, dec/art; EU: manuscripts, gr, drgs

The Museum is a combination of the first art museum designed by renowned architect Philip Johnson (1960) and Fountain Elms, an 1850 historic house museum which was the home of the museum's founders.

Munson-Williams Proctor Institute Museum of Art - continued
ON EXHIBIT 2000
11/18/2000 to 02/04/2001   AMERICAN IMPRESSIONISM
Led by the example of James McNeil Whistler, a generation of American artist studied abroad to absorb the new palette and compositions that were modernizing painting. Landscapes, figure, and still life paintings by Hassam, Twatchman, Dewing, Merrit Chase and Robinson marked a distinct departure from academic styles.

YONKERS

Hudson River Museum
511 Warburton Ave, Yonkers, NY 10701-1899
📞: 914-963-4550   ◉   www.hrm.org
Open: 12-5 We-Su, (Oct-Apr), 12-5 We, Th, Sa, Su, 12-9 Fr (May-Sept)   **Closed:** Mo, Tu, LEG/HOL!
ADM: Adult: $3.00   **Children:** $1.50 under 12   **Seniors:** $1.50
♿ ℗ Free   **Museum Shop** 🍴: The Hudson River Cafe overlooking the Hudson River
Group Tours: 914-963-4550 ext 40   **Drop-In Tours**: by appt   **Historic Building   Sculpture Garden**
Permanent Collection: AM: ldscp/ptgs 19,20; DEC/ART; GR: 19,20; COSTUMES; PHOT: 19,20.

The Hudson River Museum overlooking the Palisades, provides a dramatic setting for changing exhibitions of art, architecture, design, history and science - many designed for families. Discover the Hudson River's special place in American life as you enjoy the art. The Museum Shop was designed by Pop artist Red Grooms. There are Planetarium Star Shows in the Andrus Planetarium at 1:30, 2:30, 3:30 Sa, Su. **NOT TO BE MISSED:** Hiram Powers ''Eve Disconsolate', marble statue, 1871,(gift of Berol family in memory of Mrs. Gella Berolzheimer, 1951). Also, woodwork and stencils in the decorated period rooms of the 1876 Glenview Mansion.

ON EXHIBIT 2000

ONGOING   GLENVIEW MANSION
Completed in 1877 and overlooking the Hudson and the Palisades, four period rooms of the Mansion have been restored to reflect the lifestyle of its turn-of-the-century inhabitants, the John Trevor Bond family. This building is considered one of the finest examples of an Eastlake interior open to the public.

ONGOING   THE ANDRUS PLANETARIUM
Star shows Sa, Su 1:30, 2:30 and 3:30 PM; Fr 7

07/02/1999 to 01/09/2000   HUNTERS OF THE SKY
For hundreds of years birds of prey have maintained a fierce grip on the human imagination. The ways in which they have adapted to their ecological niches is examined through their use as symbols in art, literature, and religions of the world from ancient times to the present day.

NORTH CAROLINA

Asheville Art Museum
2 S. Pack Square, Asheville, NC 28801
☎: 704-253-3227
Open: 10-5 Tu-Fr, Summer hours June-Oct also 1-5 Sa, Su, and until 8 Fr
Closed: Mo, 1/1,MEM/DAY,7/4,LAB/DAY,THGV,12/25
Free Day: 1st W 3-5pm   **Sugg/Cont:** for special exh $2.00
ADM: Adult: $3.00   **Children:** 4-14 $2.50   **Students:** $2.50   **Seniors:** $2.50
&. ℗ on street
Group Tours: 800-935-0204   **Drop-In Tours   Historic Building**
Permanent Collection: AM/REG:ptgs,sculp,crafts 20

The Museum is housed in the splendidly restored Old Pack Memorial Library, a 1920 Beaux Arts Building.
NOT TO BE MISSED: ART IS...The Museum's collection of 20th century art asks this question and there
are historical and contemporary responses by noted artists.

Ackland Art Museum
Columbia & Franklin Sts-Univ. Of North Carolina, Chapel Hill, NC 27599
☎: 919-966-5736   ▣ www.ackland.org
Open: 10-5 We-Sa, 1-5 Su   **Closed:** Mo, Tu, 12/25, 12/31, 1/1, 7/4
Sugg/Cont: $3.00
&. ℗ in nearby municipal lots
Group Tours: 919-962-3342
Permanent Collection: EU & AM: ptgs, gr 15-20; PHOT; REG .Asian Cont, African

The Ackland, with a collection of more than 14,000 works of art ranging from ancient times to the present,
includes a wide variety of categories conveying the breadth of mankind's achievements. **NOT TO BE
MISSED:** Large Asian collection, only one of its kind in North Carolina

ON EXHIBIT 2000
10/03/1999 to 01/02/2000   DUTCH LANDSCAPE DRAWINGS FROM THE PECK COLLECTION

12/19/1999 to 03/26/2000   TRANSATLANTIC DIALOGUES : AFRICAN/AFRICAN-AMERICAN ART

**01/23/2000 to 03/26/2000   FROM THE MOLECULAR TO THE GALACTIC: SCIENTIFIC IMAGERY IN THE
ART OF MAX ERNST AND ALPHONSE OSSORIO**

04/16/2000 to 05/21/2000   NEW CURRENTS IN CONTEMPORARY ART

06/11/2000 to 09/02/2000   CONTEMPORARY ART

09/2000 to 11/2000   WETHEIMER PORTRAITS OF JOHN SINGER SARGENT *Will Travel*

09/2000 to 09/2002   TANTRIC BUDDHISM : THE HIMALAYAN ART OF TIBET AND NEPAL
A rare opportunity to see sculpture and religious objects from Nepal and Tibet.

**09/20/2000 to 10/29/2000   REFLECTIONS IN A LOOKING GLASS: A CENTENARY LEWIS CARROLL
EXHIBITION**

10/03/2000 to 01/03/2001   DÜRER AND THE APOCALYPSE IN ART

11/2000 to 01/07/2001   BIENNIAL FACULTY EXHIBITION

CHARLOTTE

Mint Museum of Art
2730 Randolph Road, Charlotte, NC 28207-2031
☎: 704-337-2000   ◙ www.mintmuseum.org
Open: 10-10 Tu, 10-5 We-Sa, 12-5 Su   **Closed:** Mo, LEG/HOL
Free Day: Tu 5-10, 2nd Su of month   **ADM: Adult:** $6.00   **Children:** Free under 12   **Students:** $4.00   **Seniors:** $4.00
♿ ℗ Free   **Museum Shop**
Group Tours: 704-337-2032   **Drop-In Tours:** 2 PM daily   **Historic Building**
Permanent Collection: EU & Am ptgs, REN, CONT,: CH; DEC/ART; AM pottery, glass: Brit cer,

The building, erected in 1836 as the first branch of the US Mint, produced 5 million dollars in gold coins before the Civil war. In 1936 it opened as the first art museum in North Carolina. When the museum was moved to its present parkland setting the facade of the original building was integrated into the design of the new building The Mint Museum of Craft and Design is located at 220 North Tryon Street in Center City. Hours and admissions are the same as the Museum. Second Su of Month is Free..   **NOT TO BE MISSED:** Extensive Delhom collection of English pottery, beautifully displayed

ON EXHIBIT 2000

07/24/1999 to 01/16/2000   DALE CHIHULY: INSTALLATIONS
A showcase of three decades of work by America's foremost glass artist. Individual glass blown sculptures and large scale environments, for which he is best known, comprise this stunning exhibition of luminous glass work.

11/27/1999 to 02/27/2000   NEW FRONTIERS: DARIO ROBLETO
Pop and conceptual art are combined by this San Francisco artist to create objects that engage contemporary mass culture.

01/15/2000 to 04/02/2000   THE DEFINING MOMENT VICTORIAN NARRATIVE PAINTINGS FROM THE FORBES COLLECTION:
A specific moment rendered in paint, accompanied by an aptly selected title, can weave a sometimes complex narrative that does not have literary familiarity. *Catalog*

02/03/2000 to 04/22/2000   A MILLION AND ONE NIGHTS: ORIENTALISM AND AMERICAN CULTURE 1870-1930
This exhibit is the first exploration of American orientalism in all of it's guises. It examines the fascination with exotic locales such as North Africa, The Middle East and India. Artists include Sargent, Chase, Weeks, LaFarge, Bridgeman, Gifford and Tiffany.

02/05/2000 to 04/30/2000   SPIRIT OF THE CLOTH: CONTEMPORARY AFRICAN AMERICAN QUILTS

02/26/2000-09/17/2000   AN INAUGURAL GIFT: THE FOUNDERS CIRCLE COLLECTION

05/06/2000 to 08/12/2000   TO HAVE AND TO HOLD: 115 YEARS OF WEDDING FASHIONS
In western society, the bridal gown has reflected the elegance of the occasion as well as current fashion trends.

05/20/2000 to 10/08/2000   TURNING WOOD INTO ART: MASTERWORKS FROM THE ARTHUR AND JANE MASON COLLECTION
Wood bowls, vessels and sculptural forms represent the subject of this major exhibition.

09/09/2000 to 12/31/2000   UNSEEN TREASURES: IMPERIAL RUSSIA AND THE NEW WORLD
The story of Imperial Russia and its connection to the New World in the 18th and 19th C is told in 300 art objects and artifacts. Included are the Baroque Coronation sleigh of Catherine the Great and the Tula Steel armchair of Alexander I, etc. *Catalog*

11/04/2000 to 05/27/2001   THE ALLAN CHASANOFF CERAMIC COLLECTION
Functional, sculptural and decorative forms which demonstrate diverse approaches to ceramics and subject matter.

NORTH CAROLINA

Gaston County Museum of Art and History
131 W. Main Street, Dallas, NC 28034

☎: 704-922-7681
Open: 10-5 Tu-Fr, 1-5 Sa, 2-5 4th Su of month   **Closed:** Mo, Su, other than 4th of month, LEG/HOL!
& Ⓟ   **Museum Shop**
Group Tours: 704-923-8103   **Drop-In Tours**: Th, Sa at 3 PM
Historic Building
Permanent Collection: CONT; ARTIFACTS RELATING TO THE U.S, N.C., & THE SOUTHEAST

The museum, housed in the 1852 Hoffman Hotel located in historic Court Square, features contains period rooms and contemporary galleries and furnishings . Regional history from the 1840s to the present. **NOT TO BE MISSED:** Carriage exhibit, the largest public collection of horse drawn vehicles in the Southeast

William H. Van Every Gallery and Edward M. Smith Gallery
Davidson College, Visual Arts Center, 315 N. Main Street, Davidson, NC 28036

☎: 704-892-2519
Open: 10-6 Mo-Fr, 12-42 Sa, Su (Sep-June)   **Closed:** LEG/HOL! ACAD
Vol/Cont:
& Ⓟ
Group Tours
Historic Building designed by Graham Gund 1993
Permanent Collection: WORKS ON PAPER, PTGS Hist,Cont

In the fall of 1993 the Gallery moved to a new building designed by Graham Gund where selections from the 2,500 piece permanent collection are displayed at least once during the year. The Gallery also presents a varied roster of contemporary and historical exhibitions. **NOT TO BE MISSED:** Auguste Rodin's 'Jean d'Aire', bronze

Duke University Museum of Art
Affiliate Institution: Duke University
Buchanan Blvd at Trinity, Durham, NC 27701

☎: 919-684-5135 ◙ www.duke.edu/web/duma
Open: 10-5 Tu-Fr, 11-2 Sa, 2-5 Su (open We, 10-9 Sept-May)   **Closed:** Mo LEG/HOL!
& Ⓟ   **Museum Shop**
Group Tours
Permanent Collection: MED: sculp; DEC/ART; AF: sculp; AM & EU: all media

Duke University Art Museum, with its impressive collection ranging from ancient to modern works includes the Breumner collection of Medieval art, widely regarded as a one of a kind in the US, and a large pre-Columbian collection from Central and South America as well as a collection of contemporary Russian art.

ON EXHIBIT 2000
01/20/2000 to 04/02/2000   EMERGING ARTISTS FROM THE PROJECT AT HARLEM

02/04/2000 to 05/21/2000   DON EDDY: FROM LOGIC TO MYSTERY

Duke University Museum of Art - continued

02/10/2000 to 04/09/2000   IN THE DARK OF THE DAY: WORKS BY CORRINE COLORRUSO

04/06/2000 to 05/14/2000 SAVy SELECTS REPRESENTATIONS OF THE "OTHER" FROM THE COLLECTION OF THE DUKE UNIVERSITY MUSEUM OF ART

05/19/2000 to 06/11/2000   PARTICULAR VISIONS: DURHAM SCHOOL OF THE ARTS

06/09/2000 to 09/10/2000   NEW ART IN THE TRIANGLE

10/15/2000 to 12/01/2000   TO CONSERVE A LEGACY AMERICAN ART FROM HISTORICALLY BLACK COLLEGES AND UNIVERSITIES
The collections of 6 historically Black colleges will be showcased in a exhibition of over 150 artworks. *Will Travel*

FAYETTEVILLE

Fayetteville Museum of Art
839 Stamper Road, Fayetteville, NC 28303
📞: 910-485-5121 ◙ www,fayetteville.comefmaster
Open: 10-5 Mo-Fr, 1-5 Sa, Su   **Closed:** Mo, 1/1, EASTER, 7/4, THGV, 12/23-12/31
& Ⓟ   **Museum Shop**
Group Tours: 910-485-0548   **Drop-In Tours**
Sculpture Garden
Permanent Collection: CONT: North Carolina art; PTGS, SCULP, CER, AF artifacts

The museum, whose building was the first in the state designed and built as an art museum, also features an impressive collection of outdoor sculpture on its landscaped grounds. **NOT TO BE MISSED:** 'Celestial Star Chart', by Tom Guibb

ON EXHIBIT 2000
11/13/1999 to 01/09/2000   RUTH OGLE AND RUTH BLACKWELL RODGERS
Mixed media and two dimensional work.

01/15/2000 to 03/12/2000   THE ARTISTS OF GREENVILLE
WORKS SHOWCASING ARTISTS AND THEIR WORK FROM MAJOR METRO AREAS 0F THE State

03/19/2000 to 05/14/2000   TWENTY EIGHTH ANNUAL COMPETITION FOR NORTH CAROLINA ARTISTS
Works of artist living or native to North Carolina. One of the Southeast's moat distinguished and competitive professional exhibitions.

05/20/2000 to 07/30/2000   BOB TIMBERLAKE
From furniture to painting and print making, the show will feature his early works.

08/05/2000 to 09/03/2000   SELECTIONS FROM THE PERMANENT COLLECTION
Works by North Carolina artists

09/08/2000 to 11/12/2000   DALE CHIHULY: SEAFORMS
Exceptional examples of American master Chihuly's glass sculptures resembling brilliant undulating marine life will be on exhibit with a number of his working drawings.

NORTH CAROLINA

Weatherspoon Art Gallery

Affiliate Institution: The University of North Carolina
Spring Garden & Tate Street, Greensboro, NC 27402-6170
📞: 336-334-5770 ◉ www.uncg.edu/wag
Open: 10-5 Tu,Th, Fr, 1-5 Sa-Su, 10-8 We **Closed:** Mo, ACAD! and vacations
&. Ⓟ **Museum Shop** ᵞ: Many restaurants nearby
Group Tours Drop-In Tours: 1st Su 2pm !
Historic Building Sculpture Garden
Permanent Collection: AM: 20; MATISSE PRINTS AND BRONZE SCULPTURES; OR

Designed by renowned architect, Romaldo Giurgola, the Weatherspoon Art Gallery features six galleries showcasing special exhibitions and a predominantly 20th century collection of American art with works by Willem de Kooning, Alex Katz, Louise Nevelson, David Smith, and Robert Rauschenberg. **NOT TO BE MISSED:** The Cone Collection of Matisse prints and bronzes

ON EXHIBIT 2000
ONGOING HENRI MATISSE: PRINTS AND BRONZES FROM THE CONE COLLECTION

11/13/1999 to 01/23/2000 HIGHLIGHTS FROM THE DILLIARD COLLECTION
75 works demonstrating the remarkable breadth of the collection include Brice Marden, Louise Bourgois. Christo, Joan Brown, Stuart Davis, Eva Hesse, Romare Bearden, Max Weber, Jim Dine, Frank Stella and Katherine Porter among others. *Catalog*

02/13/2000 to 04/23/2000 IN COMPANY: ROBERT CREELEY'S COLLABORATIONS
Poet Robert Creeley and many leading contemporary artists including Warhol, Clemente, Johns and Rosenquist did highly productive collaborations. *Will Travel*

05/14/2000 to 08/06/2000 NORTH CAROLINA ARTIST FELLOWSHIP WINNERS *Catalog*

Fall/2000 CHILDHOOD DEPLOYED: PICTORIALISM AND SOCIAL DOCUMENTARY IN THE US (1890-1925)
Images by photographers including Riis, Stieglitz, Hine, Steichlin Day, Broughton, Kassabier and others. The working class and middle class child will be presented.

Greenville Museum of Art Inc.

802 Evans Street, Greenville, NC 27834
📞: 252-758-1946 ◉ gma.greenvillene.com
Open: 10-4:30 Th, Fr, 1-4 Su **Closed:** Mo-We LEG/HOL!
&. Ⓟ
Group Tours
Permanent Collection: AM: all media 20

Founded in 1939 as a WPA Gallery, the Greenville Museum of Art focuses primarily on the achievements of 20th century American art. Many North Carolina artists are represented in its collection which also includes works by George Bellows, Thomas Hart Benton, Robert Henri, Louise Nevelson, and George Segal, to name but a few. **NOT TO BE MISSED:** Major collection of Jugtown pottery

Wellington B. Gray Gallery
Affiliate Institution: East Carolina University
Jenkins Fine Arts Center, Greenville, NC 27858
☎: 919-757-6336   ◙ www.ecu.edu/art/home.html
Open: 10-5 Mo-We, Fr & Sa, 10-8 Th   **Closed:** LEG/HOL!, ACAD/HOL
& ℗ Limited metered   **Sculpture Garden**
Permanent Collection: CONT;AF

One of the largest contemporary art galleries in North Carolina. Reopens Jan 2000 – call for information unavailable at press time **NOT TO BE MISSED:** Print portfolio, Larry Rivers 'The Boston Massacre'; African Art Collection

HICKORY

Hickory Museum of Art
243 Third Ave. NE, Hickory, NC 28601
☎: 704-327-8576   ◙ www.hickorymuseumofart.org
Open: 10-5 Tu-Fr, 10-4 Sa, 1-4 Su   **Closed:** LEG/HOL!
& ℗   **Museum Shop   Group Tours   Historic Building**
Permanent Collection: AM: all media 19,20 ; ART POTTERY; AM: Impr

The second oldest art museum in North Carolina and the first in the southeast US to collect American art, the museum is located in one of Hickory's finest examples of neo-classic revival architecture. **NOT TO BE MISSED:** William Merritt Chase painting (untitled)

ON EXHIBIT 2000
08/21/1999 to 05/12/2000   NORTH CAROLINA ARTISTS FROM THE PERMANENT COLLECTION
North Carolina artists included in the Museum's Permanent collection will be featured in a new installation. The exhibition will include paintings, works on paper, sculpture, outsider art, pottery and glass.

01/22/2000 to 03/05/2000   THE UNIFOUR COLLECTS
This exhibition features works of art drawn from private collection across the Unifour.

03/24/2000 to 05/29/2000   DOROTHY GILLESPIE: A RETROSPECTIVE
The career of one of America's foremost painters and sculptors will be examined in a retrospective of her works from 1944 through 1997. Whether on canvas, paper, or metal, whether two- or three- dimensional, Gillespie's work explodes and scintillates with iridescence and visual excitement. Its playfulness belies the careful precision of its construction. Catalog

10/7/2000 to 12/31/2000   CONRAD FELIXMULLER AND THE ART SCENE IN DRESDEN – GRAPHIC WORKS FROM 1913 – 1933
This exhibition features works on paper from the Lindenau Museum in Altenburg, Germany. Altenburg is the Unifour's sister city. This exhibition begins an exchange between the two institutions and provides a survey of the role of Dresden in the development of German art in the 20th century.

NORTH WILKESBORO

Wilkes Art Gallery
800 Elizabeth Street, North Wilkesboro, NC 28659
☎: 910-667-2841
Open: 10-5 Tu-Fr, 12-4 Sa   **Closed:** 1/1, EASTER, EASTER MONDAY, 7/4, 12/25
& ℗   **Museum Shop**
Permanent Collection: REG & CONT: all media

This 80 year old neighborhood facility which was formerly the Black Cat Restaurant presents monthly changing exhibitions often featuring minority artists.

NORTH CAROLINA

North Carolina Museum of Art
2110 Blue Ridge Road, Raleigh, NC 27607-6494

☎: 919-715-5923 ◙ www.ncartmuseum.org

Open: 9-5 Tu-Th, Sa, 9-9 Fr, 11-6 Su   **Closed:** Mo, LEG/HOL!

♿ ℗

Museum Shop ¶: Cafe serves lunch daily & dinner Fri 5:30-8:45

Group Tours: 919-839-6262, ext. 2145

Drop-In Tours: 1:30 daily

Permanent Collection: EU/OM: ptgs; AM: ptgs 19; ANCIENT ART; AF; REG; JEWISH CEREMONIAL ART

The Kress Foundation, in 1960, added to the museum's existing permanent collection of 139 prime examples of American and European artworks, a donation of 71 masterworks. This gift was second in scope and importance only to the Kress bequest to the National Gallery in Washington, D.C. **NOT TO BE MISSED:** Kress Collection

ON EXHIBIT 2000

02/27/2000   REOPENING OF AFRICAN AND NEW WORLD GALLERIES

04/16/2000 to 08/13/2000   RODIN SCULPTURES FROM THE IRIS AND GERALD B. CANTOR COLLECTION
In addition to the works from the collection, more than 50 have been borrowed from public and private collections in the US and France. These explore works in his oeuvre - movement in sculpture, dance and human poses and gestures.

09/17/2000 to 12/03/2000   INTERIORS
Shelter is a basic human requirement as is the need to create a place of one's own. The exhibition explores how changing defines the ways it defines a sequence of enclosure and space-mental, physical and spiritual. One's space can be a refuge or a prison.

10/08/2000 to 01/07/2000   IN PRAISE OF NATURE: ANSEL ADAMS AND PHOTOGRAPHERS OF THE AMERICAN WEST
An eclectic and varied photographic record of the American West during the first century of photography (1850-1950). In addition to Adams, the 150 works will include images by Jackson, Watkins, Muybridge and Fiske as well as Lange, Evans, Rothstein and Cunningham. ADM: Adults, $6.00; SR, STU $4.00; under 12 F *Will Travel*

10/21/2000 to 01/07/2001   DESIGNING IN RAFFIA: KUBA EMBROIDERIES FROM THE CONGO
Exhibiting this collection as a group will enable the design and technique to be appreciated.

North Carolina State University Gallery of Art & Design
Cates Ave., University Student Center, Raleigh, NC 27695-7306

☎: 919-515-3503 ◙ www.fis.ncsu.edu/

Open: 12-8 We-Fr, 2-8 Sa, Su   **Closed:** ACAD!

♿ ℗ ¶

Group Tours: 919-515-3503

Permanent Collection: AM: cont, dec/art, phot, outsider art, textiles, ceramics, paintings

The Center hosts exhibitions of contemporary arts and design of regional and national significance and houses research collections of photography, historical and contemporary ceramics, textiles, glass and furniture.

Blount Bridgers House/Hobson Pittman Memorial Gallery
130 Bridgers Street, Tarboro, NC 27886
📞: 252-823-4159 ◙ www2.coastalnet.com/ng3f3w5rm
Open: 10-4 Mo-Fr, 2-4 Sa, Su **Closed:** LEG/HOL!, good Fri, Easter
ADM: Adult: $2.00
♿ Ⓟ Street
Group Tours Drop-In Tours: Mo-Fr 10-4, Sa, Su, 2-4
Historic Building
Permanent Collection: AM: 20; DEC/ART

In a beautiful North Carolina town, the 1808 Plantation House and former home of Thomas Blount houses decorative arts of the 19th Century and the Hobson Pittman (American, 1899-1972) Collections of paintings and memorabilia. **NOT TO BE MISSED:** "The Roses," oil, by Hobson Pittman

St. John's Museum of Art
114 Orange Street, Wilmington, NC 28401
📞: 910-763-0281 ◙ www.wilmington.org/stjohnsart
Open: 10-5 Tu-Sa, 12-4 Su **Closed:** LEG/HOL!
Free Day: 1st Su of month **Vol/Cont:** **ADM: Adult:** $2.00 **Children:** $1.00 under 18
♿ Ⓟ
Museum Shop
Group Tours Drop-In Tours
Historic Building
Permanent Collection: AM: ptgs, sculp

Housed in three architecturally distinctive buildings dating back to 1804, St. John's Museum of Art is the primary visual arts center in Southeastern North Carolina. The Museum highlights two centuries of North Carolina and American masters. **NOT TO BE MISSED:** Mary Cassatt color prints

Reynolda House, Museum of American Art
Reynolda Road, PO Box 11765, Winston-Salem, NC 27116
📞: 336-725-5325, 888-663-1149 ◙ www.reynoldahouse.org
Open: 9:30-4:30 Tu-Sa, 1:30-4:30 Su **Closed:** Mo, 1/1, THGV, 12/25
ADM: Adult: $6.00 **Children:** $3.00 **Students:** $3.00 **Seniors:** $5.00
♿ Ⓟ
Group Tours Drop-In Tours
Historic Building
Permanent Collection: AM: ptgs 18-present; HUDSON RIVER SCHOOL; DOUGHTY BIRDS

Reynolda House, an historic home designed by Charles Barton Keen, was built between 1912 and 1917 by Richard Joshua Reynolds, founder of R.J. Reynolds Tobacco Company, and his wife, Katharine Smith Reynolds **NOT TO BE MISSED:** Costume Collection

NORTH CAROLINA

Southeastern Center for Contemporary Art

750 Marguerite Drive, Winston-Salem, NC 27106

☎: 910-725-1904 ◙ www.electricpaving.com/secca/index.html

Open: 10-5 Tu-Sa, 2-5 Su **Closed:** Mo, LEG/HOL!

ADM: Adult: $3.00 **Children:** Free under 12 **Students:** $2.00 **Seniors:** $2.00

& ℗ Free **Museum Shop Group Tours**: 910-725-1904, Ext 14 **Historic Building Sculpture Garden**

Outstanding contemporary art being produced throughout the nation is showcased at the Southeastern Center for Contemporary Art, a cultural resource for the community and its visitors.

ON EXHIBIT 2000

10/1999 to 02/2000 MILLENNIUM

Significant moments of the last 20th C. as interpreted by a select group of contemporary artists, roughly 25 years, the lifespan of "contemporary" art. Artists considered for inclusion include Baird, Bedia, Durham, Fury, Noland, Rath, Spero, Wall and Warhol.

FARGO

Plains Art Museum
704 First Avenue North, Fargo, ND 58102-2338
☎: 702-232-3821 ◙ www.plainsart.org
Open: 10-5 Mo, 10-8 Tu, Th, 10-6 We-Fr, Sa, 12-6 Su   **Closed:** LEG/HOL!
Free Day: 2nd & 4th Tu of month   **ADM: Adult:** $3.00   **Children:** $2.00   **Students:** $2.50   **Seniors:** $2.50
 ♿ ℗ **Museum Shop** ⅋
Group Tours: ext 101   **Historic Building** Renovated turn of century warehouse
Permanent Collection: AM/REG;NAT/AM;AF;PHOT 20

The historically significant warehouse which has been turned into a state of the art facility. It blends the old with the new with a result that is both stunning and functional. Large permanent collection. 9000 feet of exhibit space.

ON EXHIBIT 2000

ONGOING ARTIST AND PRINTER: THE COLLABORATIVE PROCESS
This touring exhibition is being developed by the museum. Its goal is to show the process of making a fine art print and of translating an artwork from one discipline to another.

06/09/2000 to 08/11/2000 THE POTTERS OF MATA ORTIZ: TRANSFORMING A TRADITION
Innovative ceramic vessels by contemporary Mexican potters inspired by traditional Casas Grandes ceramics. Also shown will be rugs, kachina dolls and Illinois Native American materials.

GRAND FORKS

North Dakota Museum of Art
Affiliate Institution: University of North Dakota
Centennial Drive, Grand Forks, ND 58202
☎: 701-777-4195 ◙ www.ndmoa.com
Open: 9-5 Mo-Fr, 1-5 Sa, Su   **Closed:** 7/4, THGV, 12/25
 ♿ ℗ Metered on street   **Museum Shop** ⅋: Coffee bar
Group Tours Historic Building Sculpture Garden
Permanent Collection: CONT: Nat/Am; CONT: reg ptgs, sculp; REG HIST (not always on display)

In ARTPAPER 1991 Patrice Clark Koelsch said of this museum "In the sparsely populated state that was the very last of all the US to build an art museum,...(The North Dakota Museum of Art) is a jewel of a museum that presents serious contemporary art, produces shows that travel internationally, and succeeds in engaging the people of North Dakota."

OHIO

Akron Art Museum
70 East Market Street, Akron, OH 44308-2084
\: 330-376-9185 ◙ www.akronartmuseum.org
Open: 11-5 daily   **Closed:** LEG/HOL!
& ℗ $2.00 for 2 1/2 hrs; $5 for over 2 1/2 hrs
Group Tours: 330-376-9185, ext 229   **Drop-In Tours**: Museum hours, free guided tour 2:30 S
Historic Building 1899 Italian Renaissance Revival structure, listed NRHP   **Sculpture Garden**
Permanent Collection: EDWIN C. SHAW COLLECTION; AM: ptgs, sculp, phot

Conveniently located in the heart of downtown Akron, the Museum offers three floors of galleries exhibiting art from collections across the country and abroad. The museum's own collection presents a distinctive look at some of the finest regional, national and international art from 1850 to the present, with special focus on contemporary art and photography. **NOT TO BE MISSED:** Claus Oldenberg's ' Soft Inverted Q', 1976; The Myers Sculpture Courtyard

ON EXHIBIT 2000
10/31/1999 to 01/23/2000   RAPHAEL GLEITSMANN: RECENT ACQUISITIONS
A new and intimate glimpse into the mind of Raphael Gleitsmann, one of Akron's best-known, mid-century artists, is provided by recent gifts. On view for the first time, newly received paintings, works on paper and sketches reveal the character of his work and how radically it was changed by his experiences serving in World War II.

12/11/1999 to 02/20/2000   STRUCTURE AND SURFACE: CONTEMPORARY JAPANESE TEXTILES
Textile artists and designers currently working in Japan are combining traditional techniques with modern industrial methods to yield new expressions which are having an extraordinary worldwide impact on textiles, interior design and fashion. A selection of 110 works by 29 of Japan's most influential textile artists, designers and manufacturers are presented in this exhibition. These works of astonishing beauty reassert the artistic potential of textiles and highlight the revolution in the creation of textiles during the past decade.

01/30/2000 to 04/16/2000   THE TIRE SCULPTURES OF CHAKAIA BOOKER
From tires that have outlived their usefulness for transportation, New York artist Chakaia Booker creates dense, black writhing masses. Her coiled strips stretch the rubber to its limit. The works are metaphorical and are meant to evoke personal and social issues, many of which relate to the artist's life as a black woman in America. Tires suggest mobility, yet their round form also implies going in circles-being bound to old ideas, attitudes and behaviors. Booker likens the rubber's blackness to the skin color of Africans and the tire tread to African patterns for fabric and body decoration. By interweaving the strips into a unified whole, Booker sets the stresses of an individual's life against the hope for positive social change achieved through collective effort.

03/11/2000 to 05/28/2000   LIZA LOU: BEAD THE WORLD
Liza Lou takes mundane objects and scenes of suburban domestic bliss and transforms them into dazzling reflections on the American ideal. The Kitchen-a 168 square foot room size installation in which every surface is covered with glittering glass beads-took five years to complete; The Backyard, with over 250,000 hand-beaded blades of grass took two. In between, Liza beaded the American Presidents, an installation containing 42 beaded portraits of our country's leaders.

06/10/2000 to 08/27/2000   LEE KRASNER
Lee Krasner is widely acknowledged as one of the premier abstract expressionist painters of this century. She is also the only woman accorded that rank. This exhibition-the first retrospective of Krasner's work since her death in 1984-surveys the breadth of Krasner's career and includes over 60 works. From the figure studies she produced in the 1930s as a student, to her late masterful collages produced in the early 1980s, Krasner is revealed as a fascinating artist who produced radically different yet compelling bodies of work throughout the years. In constant dialogue with the greatest artists of her time- Picasso, Mondrian, de Kooning, and her husband Jackson Pollock- Krasner carved out her own unique and influential identity.

06/10/2000 to 08/27/2000   EXPLORE & DISCOVER XIX
This exhibition returns for its 19th year with all new hands-on activities plus the old favorites.

09/09/2000 to 11/26/2000   THE LURE OF THE WEST FROM THE NATIONAL MUSEUM OF AMERICAN ART
Sixty-eight paintings and sculptures by artists who explored the untamed West from 1820 to 1940 are included in this exhibition which views the expanding United States through art. Albert Bierstadt, George Caitlin, Charles Bird King and Frederic Remington are among the many artists featured in this story of the frontier.

Akron Art Museum - continued
12/09/2000 to 02/25/2001   MATERIAL WORLD: OBJECTS IN SPACE
This traveling exhibition focuses on new work by five to six emerging or underexposed artists currently working in a three-dimensional idiom. It will investigate how a new generation of artists is re-thinking sculpture through dynamic new approaches to materials, processes, and space. These artists may range from those who make subtle or radical adjustments to the architectural space of the gallery using common construction materials to others who accumulate or reconfigure the detritus of their daily lives into compelling scenarios.

ATHENS

Kennedy Museum of Art
Affiliate Institution: Ohio University
Lin Hall, Athens, OH 45701-2979
☎: 740-593-1304   ◙ www.cats.ohiou.edu.kenmus
Open: 12-5 Tu, We, Fr; 12-8 Th; Sa, Su, 1-5   **Closed:** Mo, LEG/HOL!
&   ℗
Group Tours   Historic Building
Permanent Collection: NAT/AM; AM art

Housed in the recently renovated 19th century Lin Hall, the Museum collections include the Edwin L and Ruth Kennedy Southwest Native American, American textiles and jewelry, and the Martha and Foster Harmon Collection which is on long term loan.

CANTON

Canton Museum of Art
Affiliate Institution: .
1001 Market Ave. N., Canton, OH 44702
☎: 330-453-7666   ◙ www.canton-museum of art
Open: 10-5 & 7-9 Tu-Th, 10-5 Fr, Sa, 1-5 Su   **Closed:** Mo,1/1, THGV, 12/25
Vol/Cont: ADM: **Adult:** $2.50   **Children:** $1.25   **Seniors:** $1.25
&   ℗   **Museum Shop   Group Tours   Sculpture Garden**
Permanent Collection: WORKS ON PAPER; AM & EU: ptgs 19-20; CER: after 1950

Located in the Cultural Center for the Arts, the Canton Museum of Art is the only visual arts museum in Stark County. A mix of permanent with traveling exhibitions creates a showcase for a spectrum of visual art. **NOT TO BE MISSED:** Painting by Frank Duveneck 'Canal Scene with Washer Women, Venice'

CINCINNATI

Cincinnati Art Museum
935 Eden Park Drive, Cincinnati, OH 45202-1596
☎: 513-639-2995   ◙ www.cincinarttmuseum.org
Open: 10-5 Tu-Sa, 12-6 Su   **Closed:** Mo, 1/1, THGV, 12/25
Free Day: Sa   ADM: **Adult:** $5.00   **Children:** Free under 17   **Students:** $4.00   **Seniors:** $4.00
&   ℗ Free   **Museum Shop** ¶
Group Tours: 513-639-2975   **Drop-In Tours:** 1pm weekdays, 1 & 2 PM weekends   **Sculpture Garden**
Permanent Collection: AS; AF; NAT/AM: costumes, textiles; AM & EU: ptgs, dec/art, gr, drgs, phot

One of the oldest museums west of the Alleghenies, the Cincinnati Art Museum's collection includes the visual arts of the past 6000 years from almost every major civilization in the world. **NOT TO BE MISSED:** 'Undergrowth with Two Figures,' Vincent van Gogh, 1890

OHIO

Cincinnati Art Museum - continued

ON EXHIBIT 2000

10/24/1999 to 01/02/2000   JIM DINE: WALKING MEMORY, 1959-1969
Presented by the Lois and Richard Rosenthal Foundation this first major survey of the Pop artist traces his multi faceted exploration for personal identity through more than 50 works.

02/20/2000 to 05/28/2000   MASTERPIECES OF 19TH CENTURY AMERICAN FURNITURE FROM THE MUNSON-WILLIAMS-PROCTOR INSTITUTE
A first analysis of the beauty, breadth and quality of American workmanship.

03/19/2000 to 05/14/2000   NARRATIVES OF AFRICAN AMERICAN ART AND IDENTITY: THE DAVID C. DRISKELL COLLECTION
The transformation of African American identity is brought to life in art and archival material. *Will Travel*

04/16/2000 to 06/11/2000   ANSEL ADAMS, A LEGACY: MASTERWORKS FROM THE FRIENDS OF PHOTOGRAPHY COLLECTION
A most popular and influential photographer, he is the focus of more than 100 works in a broad cross section of his images. *Will Travel*

06/25/2000 to 08/06/2000   SLEEPING BEAUTY: TAPESTRIES BY MAUD RYDIN MARCH
Tapestries full of bold and graphics with abstract figures, landscapes and seascapes.

07/16/2000 to 09/24/2000   THE ROYAL ACADEMY IN THE AGE OF QUEEN VICTORIA (1837-1901): 19TH CENTURY PAINTINGS FROM THE PERMANENT COLLECTION
This exhibition which includes a selection by William Blake, Sir John Millais, Sir Lawrence Alma Tadema and many contemporaries. A growing appreciation of these works is beginning to take hold in the art wor-ld.

Contemporary Arts Center

115 E. 5th St., Cincinnati, OH 45202-3998
☎: 513-345-8400   ◙ www.spiral.org
Open: 10-6 Mo-Sa, 12-5 Su   **Closed:** LEG/HOL!
Free Day: Mo   **ADM**: **Adult:** $3.50   **Children:** Free under 12   **Students:** $2.00   **Seniors:** $2.00
& ℗ Pay garage 1 block away under Fountain Square   **Museum Shop   Group Tours**: 513-345-8400
Permanent Collection: Non-collecting Institution

This is one of the first contemporary art museums in the United States, founded in 1939. Art of today in all media including video is presented.

ON EXHIBIT 2000

ONGOING   TOWARD A NEW CAC: THE ARCHITECTURE OF ZAHA HADID
Hadid is an architect, but her works are art and this exhibit lets one see the evolution of the new CAC and the process of the building.

11/13/1999 to 01/16/2000   CUSTOM BUILT: A 20 YEAR SURVEY OF THE WORK OF ALLAN WEXLER
Wexler describes himself as an architect trapped inside the body of an artist His work includes functional and non functional structures. Works will include built and unbuilt projects. *Catalog*

01/29/2000 to 03/26/2000   FROM HERE TO EAR: CELESTE BOURSIER-MOUGENOT
This young French composer explores the musicality of day-to-day objects and living creatures.. Pools of water, peeping birds, chiming dishes are included.

01/29/2000 to 04/02/2000   VIEWS OF THE GARDEN: JACCI DEN HARTOG
These are wall mounted and free standing sculptural landscapes inspired by Chinese landscape traditions.

01/29/2000 to 04/02/2000   DAVID BYRNE
Using photographs and the Acoustiguide (a listening device shaped like telephone which gives tour information) he has produced a wry critique of mass media and today's culture.

Contemporary Arts Center - continued
04/08/2000 to 06/111000   CONTINUOUS REPLAY: THE PHOTOGRAPHY OF ARNIE ZANE
Zane is a combination of photographer and choreographer. It shows his wide range of styles and focus on depicting a wide range of styles.

04/08/2000 to 06/11/2000   LILY VAN DER STOKKER
The wall paintings of van der Stokker are all we think high art is not. They are decorative. She will design a site-specific wall painting project for the museum.

04/08/2000 to 06/11/2000   CHARLES KRAFT: THE PORCELAIN WAR MUSEUM PROJECT
In 1995 Kraft traveled to Slovenia and moved by war torn Croatia, he produced the on-going recreation of weapons used in the Balkan conflicts. It has become a beautiful memorial to senseless destruction of human life.

06/17/2000 to 08/27/2000   STEPHAN BALKENHOL
Balkenhol celebrates "Everyman" and "Everywomen" through human and animal forms roughly carved from blocks of wood.
Catalog

06/27/2000 to 08/20/2000   LESLEY DILL AND NARI WARD
Ward looks for found objects, Dill recalls traditional women's crafts of stitching, needlepoint and dressmaking. Together they will do a large scale installation.

Taft Museum
316 Pike Street, Cincinnati, OH 45202-4293
\: 513-241-0343
Open: 10-5 Mo-Sa, 1-5 S & HOL!   **Closed:** 1/1, THGV, 12/25
Free Day: We   **ADM: Adult:** $4.00   **Children:** Free under 8   **Students:** $2.00   **Seniors:** $2.00
& ℗ Limited free parking   **Museum Shop**
Group Tours   Drop-In Tours: by appt   **Historic Building**
Permanent Collection: PTGS; CH: Kangzi-period cer; FR/REN: Limoges enamels; EU & AM: furniture 19

Collections include masterpieces by Rembrandt, Hals, Gainsborough, Turner and Corot, arranged within the intimate atmosphere of the 1820 Baum-Taft house, a restored Federal-period residence. **NOT TO BE MISSED:** 'At The Piano' 1858-59 by James A. McNeill Whistler; French Gothic ivory Virgin and Child from the Abbey Church of St. Denis, ca. 1260.

CLEVELAND

Cleveland Museum of Art
11150 East Blvd, Cleveland, OH 44106
\: 216-421-7340   ◉ www.clemusart.com
Open: 10-5 Tu, Th, Sa, Su, 10-9 We, Fr   **Closed:** Mo, 1/1, 7/4, THGV, 12/25
& ℗ Pay and street   **Museum Shop**   ⵏ
Group Tours: 216-421-7340, ex6t 380   **Drop-In Tours:** by appt   **Historic Building   Sculpture Garden**
Permanent Collection: ANCIENT: Med, Egt, Gr, R; EU; AM; AF; P/COL; OR; phot, gr, text, drgs

One of the world's major art museums, The Cleveland Museum of Art is known for the exceptional quality of its collections with exquisite examples of art spanning 5000 years. Especially noteworthy are the collections of Asian and Medieval European art and the renovated 18th-20th c galleries. A portion of the museum includes a wing designed in 1970 by Marcel Breuer. Some special exhibitions have admission fees. **NOT TO BE MISSED:** Guelph Treasure, especially the Portable Altar of Countess Gertrude (Germany, Lower Saxony, Brunswick, c 1040; gold, red porphyry, cloisonné, enamel, niello, gems, glass, pearls; 'La Vie' by Picasso; 'Burning of the Houses of Parliament' by J. M. W. Turner; works by Faberge.

OHIO

Cleveland Museum of Art - continued

ON EXHIBIT 2000

10/31/1999 to 1/9/2000 STILL-LIFE PAINTINGS FROM THE NETHERLANDS, 1550-1720
In a cooperative project with the Rjksmuseum, Amsterdam this survey will look at the accomplishments of Dutch and Flemish still-life painters of the 17th century emphasizing the connections between still-lifes and contemporary life. Principal artists include Aertsen, Peeters, Heda, Rembrandt, Snyders, and de Heem.

11/14/1999 to 1/23/2000 A PAINTING IN FOCUS: NICHOLAS POUSSIN'S 'HOLY FAMILY ON THE STEPS'
This exhibition will bring together the painting of this subject purchased by the Cleveland Museum in 1981 and the one in the collection of the National Gallery of Art, Washington, D.C. There has been much discussion as to which is the Poussin and which a later copy. X-radiograms, preparatory drawings and prints and other paintings relating to this work will also be shown.

12/19/1999 to 02/27/2000   THE JEANNE MILES BLACKBURN COLLECTION OF ILLUMINATED MANUSCRIPTS.
The 70 single leaves in this collection range in date from the 13th through the 16th centuries. Included are works by de Brailles, the Master of the Queen Mary Psalter,
the Gold Scrolls Group, Guilebeert de Mets, the Limbourg Circle, and a humanistic leaf by Benedetto Bordone.

2/21/1999 to 05/2/1999 DIEGO RIVERA: ART AND REVOLUTION (working title)
A major retrospective featuring 120 works exploring the artist's contribution to symbolism, cubism, the neoclassical revival of the 1910s-1920s, social realism, surrealism, and muralism. Included are 2 murals in true fresco and other masterworks never before exhibited in the US.

05/28/2000 to 07/30/2000 FACES OF IMPRESSIONISM: PORTRAITS FROM AMERICAN COLLECTIONS
Impressionist artists and their progressive approach to portraiture are the focus of this ground breaking exhibition . Included for the first time are works by Cassatt, Gauguin, Cézanne, Degas, Manet, Monet, Morisot and Renoir. This is the first attempt to provide insight into the genre as it was practiced by masters of this influential movement.

COLUMBUS

Columbus Art Museum

480 East Broad Street, Columbus, OH 43215
📞: 614-221-6801 ◙ www.dispatch.com/museum-of-art
Open: 10-5:30 Tu, We, Fr-Su, 10-8:30 Th   **Closed:** LEG/HOL!
Free Day: Th 5:30-8:30   **Sugg/Cont:**
ADM: Adult: $3.00   **Children:** Free under 5   **Students:** $2.00   **Seniors:** $2.00
 ♿ ℗ $2.00 **Museum Shop** ⫯⫯: Palette Cafe
Group Tours: 614-629-0359   **Drop-In Tours**: Fr noon, Sa 2   **Historic Building   Sculpture Garden**
Permanent Collection: EU & AM: ptgs 20

Located in downtown Columbus in a Renaissance-revival building, the Museum is an educational and cultural center for the people of central Ohio and its visitors.

ON EXHIBIT 2000

ONGOING   FLASH: THE ART OF PHOTOGRAPHY Portrait, documentary, landscape and art photography

ONGOING   AN OHIO PORTFOLIO
Central Ohio landscapes

ONGOING   RECENT WORK BY FOURTEEN OHIO PHOTOGRAPHERS

ONGOING   CLARENCE WHITE OF NEWARK, OHIO: THE BIRTH OF PICTORIAL PHOTOGRAPHY
15 early 20th century photographs by one of the most important photographers at the beginning of the 20th century.

10/23/1999 to 01/02/2000   THIS LAND IS YOUR LAND: PHOTOGRAPHS BY MARILYN BRIDGES
An aerial photographer now focuses her attention on America's backyards. It provides a fresh perspective on our land.

Columbus Art Museum - continued
11/19/1999 to 01/30/2000   SPECTACULAR ST. PETERSBURG: 100 YEARS OF RUSSIAN THEATRE DESIGN

01/15/2000 to 07/23/2000   CRAFTING A JEWISH STYLE : THE ART OF BEZALEL
The school was founded in Jerusalem in 1906 to instruct the first generation of Jewish artists in Israel

02/18/2000 to 04/30/2000   ILLUSIONS OF EDEN: VISIONS OF THE AMERICAN HEARTLAND
The character and values of the American Midwest have a profound influence on the way the nation views itself. Four installations look at the cultural identity of the region.

04/01/2000 to 05/28/2000   FACING DEATH: PORTRAITS FROM CAMBODIA'S KILLING FIELDS
Nearly 14,000 people were killed between 1975-79. These prints were found in the archives in 1993. *Will Travel*

05/18/2000 to 08/13/2000   PARIS 1900: THE "AMERICAN SCHOOL" AT THE UNIVERSAL EXPOSITION
The Pennsylvania Academy was a major lender to the Paris Exposition of 1900 which played a critical role in defining "American" artistic influences at the time. It featured all the major artists of the late 19th century. Approximately 50 of the paintings and sculpture will be featured here. *Catalog Will Travel*

10/07/2000 to 12/31/2000   NO ORDINARY LAND: ENCOUNTERS IN A CHANGING ENVIRONMENT
Large format photographs showing how people interact with the landscape in places as diverse as Sri Lanka, Iceland, Costa Rica and New York.

11/03/2000 to 12/31/2000   A BOUNTIFUL PLENTY: FOLK ART FROM THE SHELBURNE MUSEUM

Schumacher Gallery
Affiliate Institution: Capital University
2199 East Main Street, Columbus, OH 43209-2394
📞: 614-236-6319
Open: 1-5 Mo-Fr, 2-5 Sa Closed May through August   **Closed:** Su, LEG/HOL!; ACAD!
 ♿ ⓟ   **Group Tours**
Permanent Collection: ETH; AS; REG; CONT; PTGS, SCULP, GR 16-19

In addition to its diverse 1600 object collection, the gallery, located on the 4th floor of the University's library building, hosts exhibitions which bring to the area artworks of historical and contemporary significance.

ON EXHIBIT 2000
01/14/2000 to 02/24/2000   BEXLEY ART ASSOCIATION LEAGUE

03/10/2000 to 04/08/2000   MICHAEL MCEWAN

Wexner Center for the Arts
Affiliate Institution: The Ohio State University
1871 N. High Street, Columbus, OH 43210-1393
📞: 614-292-3535 ◙ www.wexarts.org
Open: 10-6 Tu, We, Fr-Sa, 10-9 Th,12-6 Su   **Closed:** Mo, LEG/HOL!
Free Day: 5-9 Th   **ADM:** Adult: $3.00   **Children:** Free under 12   **Students:** $2.00   **Seniors:** $2.00
 ♿ ⓟ pay garage nearby   **Museum Shop** ‖: Café 7-4, Mo-Fr
Group Tours: 614-292-6982   **Drop-In Tours:** 1:00 Sa, Su   **Historic Building**
Permanent Collection: ART OF THE 70's

Located on the campus of The Ohio State University, the Wexner Center is a multi-disciplinary contemporary arts center dedicated to the visual, performing, and media arts with a strong commitment to new work. Its home, designed by Peter Eisenmann and the late Richard Trott. It has been acclaimed as a landmark of postmodern architecture.

OHIO

Wexner Center for the Arts - continued

ON EXHIBIT 2000

09/18/1999 to 01/02/2000   JULIE TAYMOR: PLAYING WITH FIRE
Taymor's work has always been a mix of dance, music and puppetry. The designer of "The Lion King", this is the first museum retrospective devoted to her.

01/28/2000 to 04/16/2000   ERNESTO NETO
Neto is an Argentine artist in a country where hedonism is taken seriously and makes art fun. He tents nylon hosiery stretched and stuffed with materials from lead to sand and spices. His works are often room sized.

01/28/2000 to 04/16/2000   RAY JOHNSON: CORRESPONDENCES
Collagist and 'mail artist' Johnson was much respected and influential in the art world from 1950's-1990's. This is a first opportunity to examine his use of found images and materials and use of subjects drawn from popular culture. He chopped apart his abstract canvases and from the pieces constructed a series of collages by adding images of iconic pop figures such as Shirley Temple, Marilyn Monroe and Elvis Presley. He also created highly personal performances and virtually invented "mail Art" -a network of hundreds of friends with whom he communicated by distributing ideas and art works by mail.

01/28/2000 to 04/16/2000   IN MEMORY OF MY FEELINGS: FRANK O'HARA AND AMERICAN ART
O'Hara was one of the most perceptive writers on what later was known as the New York School. Included were Larry Rivers, Grace Hartigan, Franz Kline as well as works created in homage to him by Johns, deKooning, Johnston, Mitchell and Motherwell. *Will Travel*

05/13/2000 to 08/13/2000   SHIRIN NESHAT: ARTIST RESIDENCY
During her residency, Iranian born Neshat will develop a commissioned project specifically for the Wexner Center.

05/13/2000 to 08/13/2000   UDOMSACK KRISANAMIS
This Thai born artist is a rising star in the art world. He creates rich shimmering pieces that from afar evoke star studded night skies. A close-up view reveals a more chaotic world.

05/13/2000 to 08/13/2000   JAMES WELLING: PHOTOGRAPHS 1974-1999
A first mid-career survey of Welling's work. He is equally interested in the 19th C. spirit of industrial optimism and in the digital power of the 20th C. *Catalog*

DAYTON

Dayton Art Institute
456 Belmonte Park North, Dayton, OH 45405

☎: 937-223-5277   ◙ www.daytonartinstitute.org
Open: 10-5 daily, 10-9 Th
  ❧ ℗ **Museum Shop** ¶: Café Monet 11-4 daily, 5-8:30 Th
Group Tours: 937-223-5277, ext 337   **Drop-In Tours:** Tu-Su 12 & 2, Th 7   **Historic Building   Sculpture Garden**
Permanent Collection: AM; EU; AS; OCEANIC; AF; CONT; PRE/COL

The Dayton Art Institute is located at the corner of Riverview Avenue and Belmonte Park North in a Edward B. Green designed Italian Renaissance style building built in 1930. **NOT TO BE MISSED:** 'Water Lilies', by Monet; 'Two Study Heads of an Old Man'' by Rubens; 'St. Catherine of Alexandria in Prison', by Preti; 'High Noon', by Hopper

ON EXHIBIT 2000

08/15/2000   COLOR CONNECTIONS
Color , light and the relationship between art, science and daily life.

10/30/1999 to 10/02/2000   IN PRAISE OF NATURE: ANSEL ADAMS AND PHOTOGRAPHERS OF THE AMERICAN WEST
An eclectic and varied photographic record of the American West during the first century of photography (1850-1950). In addition to Adams, the 150 works will include images by Jackson, Watkins, Muybridge and Fiske as well as Lange, Evans, Rothstein and Cunningham. ADM: Adults, $6.00; SR, STU $4.00; under 12 F *Admission Fee Will Travel*

Dayton Art Institute - continued
01/22/2000 to 03/26/2000   RODIN: SCULPTURE FROM THE IRIS AND B. GERALD CANTOR COLLECTION
60 sculptures by Rodin from this world famous collection. Adm: Adults $6.00, Students, Seniors $4.00 *Admission Fee Will Travel*

04/22/2000 to 06/04/2000   REFLECTIONS IN THE LOOKING GLASS: A CENTENARY LEWIS CARROLL EXHIBITION *Will Travel*

06/24/2000 to 08/27/2000   SHAPED WITH A PASSION: THE CARL A. WYERHAEUSER COLLECTION OF JAPANESE CERAMIC FROM THE 1970

12/16/2000 to 03/04/2001   OUT OF AFRICA: MASTERWORKS FROM THE DAYTON COLLECTION

Wright State University Galleries
Affiliate Institution: Wright State University
A 128 CAC Colonel Glenn Highway, Dayton, OH 45435
✆: 937-775-2978
Open: 10-4 Tu-Fr, 12-5 Sa, Su   **Closed:** ACAD!
 ᗕ Ⓟ
Permanent Collection: PTGS, WORKS ON PAPER, SCULP 20

The Museum is located on the Wright State University campus. **NOT TO BE MISSED:** Aimee Rankin Morgana's "The Dream," 1988

GRANVILLE

Denison University Gallery
Burke Hall of Music & Art, Granville, OH 43023
✆: 740-587-6610
Open: 1:00-4 daily   **Closed:** ACAD!
 ᗕ Ⓟ
Group Tours: on request
Permanent Collection: BURMESE & SE/ASIAN; EU & AM: 19; NAT/AM

Located on the Denison University Campus

KENT

Kent State University Art Galleries
Affiliate Institution: Kent State University
Kent State University, School of Art, Kent, OH 44242
✆: 330-672-7853
Open: 10-4 Mo-Fr; 2-5 Su   **Closed:** ACAD!
 ᗕ **Museum Shop**
Group Tours
Permanent Collection: GR & PTGS: Michener coll; IGE COLL: Olson photographs; GROPPER PRINTS: (political prints)

Operated by the School of Art Gallery at Kent State University since its establishment in 1972, the gallery consists of two exhibition spaces both exhibiting Western and non-Western 20th century art and craft.

OHIO

Cleveland Artists Foundation at the Beck Center for the Arts

17801 Detroit Ave, Lakewood, OH 44107

☎: 216-521-2540 ◉ www.clevelandartistsorg
Open: 1-6 Tu, Th, Fr, Sa **Closed:** Su, Mo, We LEG/HOL!
♿ ℗ Free
Permanent Collection: Reg. Ptgs, sculpt, gr

The Beck Center is a multi-arts facility featuring an art gallery, Main Stage Theater, Studio Theater, etc. The Center offers exciting juried, non-juried and travelling art exhibitions. The Gallery is home to a cooperative of local, highly acclaimed artists whose works are on display throughout the year.

ON EXHIBIT 2000

11/19/1999 to 01/23/2000 CITY LIFE
Art featuring people at work and play using and living in the city.

02/06/2000 to 03/26/2000 FROM THE POTTERS HAND: OBJECTS OF UTILITY AND COMFORT BY NORTHEAST OHIO CERAMIC ARTISTS
Focusing on functional pieces.

04/07/2000 to 05/26/2000 CARL GAERTNER AND THE AMERICAN SCENE

06/09/2000 to 07/30/2000 AN IMPASSIONED JOURNEY: THE ART AND LIFE OF DAVID BATZ
Sculpture, handmade paper, prints and ceramics from private collections.

08/11/2000 to 10/20/2000 RORIMER-BROOKS: DESIGNING FOR CLEVELAND

Allen Memorial Art Museum

Affiliate Institution: Oberlin College
87 North Main Street, Oberlin, OH 44074

☎: 440-775-8665 ◉ www.oberlin.edu/allenart
Open: 10-5 Tu-Sa,1-5 Su **Closed:** Mo, LEG/HOL!
Vol/Cont:
♿ ℗ Free **Museum Shop**
Group Tours: 440-775-8048 **Historic Building Sculpture Garden**
Permanent Collection: DU & FL: ptgs; CONT/AM: gr; JAP: gr; ISLAMIC: carpets

Long ranked as one of the finest college or university art collections in the nation, the Allen continues to grow in size and distinction. The museum's landmark building designed by Cass Gilbert was opened in 1917. PLEASE NOTE: The Weitzheimer/Johnson House, one of Frank Lloyd Wright's Usonian designs, was recently opened. It is open on the first Sunday and third Saturday of the month from 1-5pm with tours on the hour. Admission is $5.00 pp with tickets available at the Museum. **NOT TO BE MISSED:** Hendrick Terbrugghen's 'St. Sebastian Attended by Irene', 1625; Modigliani 'Nude With Coral Necklace'.

ON EXHIBIT 2000

The Museum Shop and Gallery "Uncommon Objects" is a combined effort with the Firelands Association of Visual Arts New Union Center for the Visual Arts-39 S Main St. Oberlin, OH.

08/27/1999 to 08/2000 AN ECLECTIC ENSEMBLE: THE HISTORY OF THE ASIAN ART COLLECTION AT OBERLIN

Allen Memorial Art Museum - continued
08/27/1999 to 01/30/2000   GERMAN RENAISSANCE PRINTS 1470-1550

10/19/1999 to 01/23/2000   ART AND ARTIFACT: THREE-DIMENSIONAL MASTERPIECES FROM THE PERMANENT COLLECTION

10/29/1999 to 05/2000   ART FROM 13TH-CENTURY THROUGH THE 20TH-CENTURY: A NEW FOCUS ON THE PERMANENT COLLECTION

01/2000 to 05/29/2000   ART OF THE 1980S AND 1990S: FOCUS ON RECENT ACQUISITIONS

OXFORD

Miami University Art Museum
Affiliate Institution: Miami University
Patterson Ave, Oxford, OH 45056
☎: 513-529-2232
Open: 11-5 Tu-Su   Closed: LEG/HOL! ACAD!
&ㅁ ℗   Group Tours
Permanent Collection: AM: ptgs, sculp; FR: 16-20; NAT/AM; Ghandharan, sculp

Designed by Walter A. Netsch, the museum building is located in an outstanding natural setting featuring outdoor sculpture.

PORTSMOUTH

Southern Ohio Museum and Cultural Center
825 Gallia Street, Portsmouth, OH 45662
☎: 614-354-5629
Open: 10-5 Tu-Fr, 1-5 Sa, Su   Closed: Mo, LEG/HOL!
Free Day: Fr   ADM: Adult: $1.00   Children: $0.75   Students: $0.75   Seniors: $1.00
&ㅁ ℗ Free on street and municipal lot   Museum Shop
Group Tours: 740-354-5629   Drop-In Tours: by arrangement   Historic Building
Permanent Collection: PORTSMOUTH NATIVE ARTIST CLARENCE CARTER; ANT: doll heads

Constructed in 1918, this beaux art design building is located in the heart of Portsmouth.

ON EXHIBIT 2000
ONGOING   CLARENCE HOLBROOK CARTER: THE PERMANENT COLLECTION

SPRINGFIELD

Springfield Museum of Art
107 Cliff Park Road, Springfield, OH 45501
☎: 937-325-4673 ▣ www.spfld-museum-of-art.com
Open: 9-5 Tu, Th, Fr, 9-9 We, 9-3 Sa, 2-4 Su   Closed: Mo, MEM/DAY, 7/4, LAB/DAY, THGV WEEKEND, 12/24-1/1
&ㅁ ℗   Museum Shop
Group Tours: 937-324-3729   Drop-In Tours: by appt
Permanent Collection: AM & EU: 19,20; ROOKWOOD POTTERY; REG: ptgs, works on paper

OHIO

Springfield Museum of Art - continued

Located in Cliff Park along Buck Creek in downtown Springfield, this 51 year old institution is a major and growing arts resource for the people or Southwest Ohio. Its 1,400 piece permanent collection attempts to provide a comprehensive survey of American art enhanced by works that represent all of the key movements in the development of Western art during the past two centuries. **NOT TO BE MISSED:** Gilbert Stuart's "Portrait of William Miller," 1795

ON EXHIBIT 2000

12/4/1999 to 01/09/2000   THE WESTERN OHIO WATERCOLOR SOCIETY JURIED EXHIBITION

03/13/2000 to 04/15/2001   NANCY FLETCHER CASSELL: RECENT WORK
Cincinnati installation artist Nancy Fletcher Cassell transforms the Chakeres Gallery with an array of her organic, environmental and sensual drawings.

04/21/2000 to 05/27/2001   GEORGE HAGEMAN: Recent Work
Formally derived from Oriental prototypes and decorated with traditional American salt glaze techniques, Dayton (Ohio's) George Hageman's ceramic vessels are evocative, sophisticated and beautiful.

04/21/2000 to 05/27/2001   TOMOKO PARRY: Recent Works
This Japanese-American Artist, now living in Dayton Ohio presents 30 of her expressive, lush and lavish floral watercolors and drawing in her first, solo exhibition.

04/22/2000 to 05/28/2000   PATRICIA BRUTCHIN: RECENT WORK
Wilmington sculptress Pat Brutchin presents her figural works in cast bronze and terra cotta.

04/22/2000 to 05/28/2000   JON BARLOW HUDSON: Recent work
Yellow Springs sculptor Jon Barlow Hudson explore symbology and spirituality as expressed in massive and contrasting materials.

TOLEDO

The Toledo Museum of Art

2445 Monroe Street, Toledo, OH 43697
℡: 419-255-8000 ⬛ www.toledomuseum.org
Open: 10-4 Tu-Th, Sa, 10-10 Fr, 11-5 Su   **Closed:** Mo, 1/1, 7/4, THGV, 12/25
&. ℗ $1.00 in lot on Grove St.   **Museum Shop** ⑪
Group Tours: x 352   **Drop-In Tours**: by appt   **Historic Building**
Permanent Collection: EU: glass, ptgs, sculp, dec/art; AM: ptgs; AF;IND;OR ◯

Founded in 1901 by Edward Drummond Libbey of Libbey Glass, the Museum is internationally known for the quality and depth of its collections. Housed in a perfectly proportioned neo-classical marble building designed by Edward Green, the Museum features American, European, African, Chinese, and Indian art, along with strength in glass and decorative arts. Award winning architect Frank Gehry designed the adjacent Center for the Visual Arts which opened in 1993. **NOT TO BE MISSED:** 'The Crowning of St. Catherine" Peter Paul Rubens, 1633; "The Architect's Dream" Thomas Cole, 1840

ON EXHIBIT 2000

10/01/1999 to 01/20/2000   AN AMERICAN TREASURY: MASTER QUILTS FROM THE MUSEUM OF AMERICAN FOLK ART
50 quilts from the mid 1800's to modern times examine the art and stories and hidden meanings of families and history are revealed.

11/07/1999 to 01/16/2000 PICASSO: GRAPHIC MAGICIAN–PRINTS FROM THE NORTON SIMON MUSEUM
The 120 drawings shown here look at Picasso's career over three-quarters of a century providing insight into the artist, his career, his family, friends and loves. *Will Travel*

The Toledo Museum of Art - continued
11/14/1999 to 01/09/2000   PHILIPPE HALSMAN: A RETROSPECTIVE
"Life" and celebrity photographer captures famous faces that shaped the 20th C. *Will Travel*

03/01/2000 to 04/16/2000   82ND ANNUAL TOLEDO AREA ARTISTS EXHIBITION
One of the oldest juried competitions in the country.

06/05/2000 to 08/13/2000   GREAT AMERICAN POP ART STOR: MULTIPLES OF THE SIXTIES
Pop art defined one culture and ended the innocence of another. These mass produced works were supervised by the artists.
Will Travel

10/2000 to 12/2000   AMERICAN WESTERN ART: FROM MYTH TO REALITY
The truths and tall tales of the cowboys and indians in the works of Remington, Bierstadt and others.

YOUNGSTOWN

Butler Institute of American Art
524 Wick Ave, Youngstown, OH 44502

☎: 330-743-1711   ◙ www.butlerart.com
Open: 11-4 Tu-Th-Sa, 11-8 We, 12-4 Su   **Closed:** Mo, 1/1, EASTER, 7/4, THGV, 12/25
& ℗ Adjacent   **Museum Shop** ¶: adjacent
Group Tours: 330-743-1711, ext 114   **Drop-In Tours:** by appt   **Historic Building   Sculpture Garden**
Permanent Collection: AM: ptgs 19,20; EARLY/AM: marine coll; AM/IMPR; WESTERN ART; AM: sports art

Dedicated exclusively to American Art, this exceptional museum, containing numerous national artistic treasures is often referred to as "America's Museum." It is housed in a McKim, Mead and White building that was the first structure erected in the United States to house a collection of American art. **NOT TO BE MISSED:** Winslow Homer's "Snap the Whip",1872, oil on canvas.

ON EXHIBIT 2000
BUTLER INSTITUTE OF AMERICAN ART/SALEM
343 East State St. Salem, Oh 44460
330-332-8213

BUTLER INSTITUTE OF AMERICAN ART/TRUMBULL
9350 East Market Street Howland, OH 44484
330-609-9900

Both satellite museums have hours 11-4 Th, Fr; 10-3 Sa; 12-4 S; Closed Leg/Hol

07/99/1999 to 01/09/2000   NOM JUNE PAIK

11/14/1999 to 01/02/2000   LANCE RICHBOURG
at Trumbull branch

01/09/2000 to 03/05/2000   GREGORY GILLESPIE
Renaissance technique, expressionistic vigor, and symbolism from around the world are merged in these paintings with obsessive forays into philosophy and sexuality.

01/16/2000 to 02/27/2000   DENNIS ASHBAUGH

03/05/2000 to 06/04/2000   LYN CHADWICK
at Trumbull Branch

Fall/2000   JUDY CHICAGO

OHIO

Zanesville Art Center

620 Military Road, Zanesville, OH 43701
: 740-452-0741
Open: 10-5 Tu, We, Fr, 10-8:30 Th, 1-5 Sa, Su   **Closed:** Mo, LEG/HOL
  ⊛   **Museum Shop**
Group Tours   Drop-In Tours
Permanent Collection: ZANESVILLE: cer; HAND BLOWN EARLY GLASS; CONT; EU

In addition to the largest public display of Zanesville art pottery (Weller, Roseville & J. B. Owens), the Art Center also has a generally eclectic collection including Old and Modern Masters, African, Oriental and European, Indian, Pre-Columbian, Mexican and regional art. **NOT TO BE MISSED:** Rare areas (unique) hand blown glass & art pottery; 300 year old panel room from Charron Garden, London

ON EXHIBIT 2000

01/29/2000 to 03/26/2000   ART OF THE JAZZ AGE IN PARIS:1914-1940
Photographs, audio and video and a variety of artifacts this Smithsonian Institution exhibition describes the expatriate scene between the first and second World Wars. *Will Travel*

04/27/2000 to 06/01/2000   HOT AND COOL CONTEMPORARY GLASS WORKS
The last 35 years have ushered in great changes in production and perception. This exhibit emphasizes the new techniques.

Charles B. Goddard Center for Visual and Performing Arts

First Ave & D Street SW, Ardmore, OK 73401
☎: 405-226-0909
Open: 9-4 Mo-Fr, 1-4 Sa, Su   **Closed:** LEG/HOL!
♿ ⓟ
Group Tours
Permanent Collection: PTGS, SCULP, GR, CONT 20; AM: West/art; NAT/AM

Works of art by Oklahoma artists as well as those from across the United States & Europe are featured in this multicultural center.

Woolaroc Museum

Affiliate Institution: The Frank Phillips Foundation, Inc
State Highway, 123, Bartlesville, OK 74003
☎: 918-336-0307   ◉ www.woolaroc.org
Open: 10-5 Tu-Su, Mem day-Lab day 10-5 daily   **Closed:** Mo, THGV, 12/25
ADM: **Adult:** $5.00   **Children:** Free under 12   **Students:** $4.00   **Seniors:** $4.00
♿ ⓟ   **Museum Shop**   ⑪: Snack bar w/sandwiches, etc.
Group Tours: written arrangement
Historic Building   Sculpture Garden
Permanent Collection: WEST: ptgs; sculp

Brilliant mosaics surround the doors of this museum situated in a wildlife preserve. The large Western art collection includes Remington, Russell, Leigh and others. The original country home of oilman Frank Phillips called his Lodge (built in 1926-27) is completely restored. On the upper level is the Woolaroc monoplane, winner of the 1927 race across the Pacific to Hawaii. **NOT TO BE MISSED:** The Lodge is a separate building.

Five Civilized Tribes Museum

Agency Hill, Honor Heights Drive, Muskogee, OK 74401
☎: 918-683-1701
Open: 10-5 Mo-Sa, 1-5 Su   **Closed:** 1/1, THGV, 12/25
ADM: **Adult:** $2.00   **Children:** Free under 6   **Students:** $1.00   **Seniors:** $1.75
♿ ⓟ   **Museum Shop**
Group Tours   Drop-In Tours   Historic Building
Permanent Collection: NAT/AM

Built in 1875 by the US Government as the Union Indian Agency, this museum was the first structure ever erected to house the Superintendency of the Cherokee, Chickasaw, Choctaw, Creek and Seminole Tribes.

OKLAHOMA

Fred Jones Jr. Museum of Art
Affiliate Institution: University of Oklahoma
410 West Boyd Street, Norman, OK 73019-0525
☎: 405-325-3272 ◙ www.ou.edu/fjjma
Open: 10-4:30 Tu, We, Fr, 10-9 Th, 1-4:30 Sa, Su, Summer 12-4:30 Tu-Su
Closed: Mo, LEG/HOL!; ACAD!; HOME FOOTBALL GAMES 10-kickoff
& ℗ Free passes available at admission desk **Museum Shop**
Group Tours Drop-In Tours: 10 days advance notice req.
Permanent Collection: AM: ptgs 20; NAT/AM; PHOTO; cont cer; GR 16-present

Considered one of the finest university museums in the country with a diverse permanent collection of nearly 6000 objects, it also hosts the states most challenging exhibitions of contemporary art. **NOT TO BE MISSED:** State Department Collection

National Cowboy Hall of Fame and Western Heritage Center
1700 N.E. 63rd Street, Oklahoma City, OK 73111
☎: 405-478-2250 ◙ www.cowboyhalloffame.com
Open: 9-5 daily (Lab/Day-Mem/Day), 8:30-6 daily (Mem/Day-Lab/Day) **Closed:** LEG/HOL, 12/25
ADM: Adult: $6.50 **Children:** 6-12 $3.25 **Seniors:** $5.50
& ℗ **Museum Shop** ⊺⏐: overlooking gardens Group Tours: Ext. 277 **Drop-In Tours**: no guide **Sculpture Garden**
Permanent Collection: WEST/ART

Housing the largest collection of contemporary Western art available for public view, this unusual and unique museum features work by Frederic Remington, Charles M. Russell, Charles Schreyvogel, Nicolai Fechin, and examples from the Taos School. Cowboy and Native historical exhibits from the Museum's impressive holdings are on display. New galleries are opening as expansion continues. Westerntown (14,000 sf), American Cowboy Gallery, American Rodeo gallery opens summer 1999. **NOT TO BE MISSED:** Gerald Balclair's 18' Colorado yule marble "Canyon Princess"; Wilson Hurley's 5 majestic landscape paintings, 7 ft bronze of former President Ronald Reagan

Oklahoma City Art Museum
3113 Pershing Blvd, Oklahoma City, OK 73107
☎: 405-946-4477 ◙ www.oakhartmuseum.com
Open: 10-5 Tu-Sa, 10-9 T, 1-5 Su, Fairgrounds 10-8 Th **Closed:** Mo, LEG/HOL!
ADM: Adult: $3.50 **Children:** Free under 12 **Students:** $2.50 **Seniors:** $2.50
& ℗ **Museum Shop** ⊺⏐: Lobby Bistro
Group Tours Drop-In Tours Sculpture Garden
Permanent Collection: AM: ptgs, gr 19,20; ASHCAN SCHOOL COLLECTION

The Museum complex includes the Oklahoma City Art Museum at the Fairgrounds built in 1958 (where the design of the building is a perfect circle with the sculpture court in the middle), **NOT TO BE MISSED:** Works by Washington color school painters and area figurative artists are included in the collection of modern art from the former Washington Gallery.

ON EXHIBIT 2000
03/25/1999 to 04/30/2000 ELIZABETH LAYTON: FACE TO FACE
This exhibition chronicles the 15 years of Elizabeth Layton's remarkable, inspiring career. It opens with her first drawing, done at the age of 68 in her first and only art class, and closes with the drawing she was working on shortly before her death in 1993. *Will Travel*

OMNIPLEX
2100 NE 52nd, Oklahoma City, OK 73111
📞: 405-609-6664　◉　www.omniplex.org
Open: 9-6 MoSa, 11-6 Su (Mem/Day-Lab/Day), 9:00-5 Mo-Fr, 9-6 Sa,11-6 Su (Winter months)　**Closed:** THGV, 12/25
ADM: **Adult:** $6.50 + tax　**Children:** 3-12,$5.25 + tax　**Students:** $6.50　**Seniors:** $5.25
&　Ⓟ Free
Museum Shop　🍴: Limited
Group Tours: 405-608-3760: 800-532-7652
Permanent Collection: VARIED; REG; AF; AS

Omniplex includes the Kirkpatrick Science and Air Space Museum; the International Photography Hall of Fame and Museum; Red Earth Indian Center as well as the Kirkpatrick Planetarium; Conservatory and Botanical Garden and numerous galleries. **NOT TO BE MISSED:** Sections of the Berlin Wall : traveling exhibits

ON EXHIBIT 2000
PLANETARIUM AND GARDEN EXHIBITS ARE PLANNED EACH MONTH - CALL

01/2000　EVEREST
This film details the true dramatic story of Everst expeditions, etc.

02/11/2000 to 08/27/2000　REMEMBER THE CHILDREN: DANIEL'S STORY
The experiences of a Jewish family during the Holocaust.

03/03/2000 to 04/02/2000　OKLAHOMA ART GUILD
A juried mixed media exhibition.

04/07/2000 to 05/08/2000　FIBERWORKS/ CONTEMPORARY QUILTERS
Outstanding fiber artists and stitching highlights the show.

05/15/2000 to 06/18/2000　ORIENTAL BRUSHWORKS
Watercolors painted on natural fibers, rice paper and silk. The beauty and technique is shown in the works.

05/20/2000 to 06/19/2000　OKLAHOMA WATERCOLOR ASSOCIATION
A juried show judged by nationally known watercolorists.

09/2000 to 10/2000　NATIONAL WATERCOLOR-OKLAHOMA

SHAWNEE

Mabee-Gerer Museum of Art
1900 West MacArthur Drive, Shawnee, OK 74801
📞: 405-878-5300
Open: 10-4 Tu-Sa, 1-5 Su　**Closed:** 1/1, GOOD FRI, HOLY SAT, EASTER, THGV, 12/25
Sugg/Cont:　**ADM:** **Adult:** $3.00　**Children:** $1.00　**Students:** $3.00　**Seniors:** $3.00
&　Ⓟ Free　**Museum Shop**
Group Tours　Sculpture Garden
Permanent Collection: EU: ptgs (Med-20); AN/EGT; NAT/AM; GRECO/ROMAN; AM: ptgs

The oldest museum collection in Oklahoma. **NOT TO BE MISSED:** Egyptian mummy 32nd Dynasty and associated funerary and utilitarian objects.

OKLAHOMA

Gilcrease Museum

1400 Gilcrease Museum Road, Tulsa, OK 74127-2100

☎: 918-596-2700 ◙ www.gilcrease.org
Open: 9-5 Tu-Sa, 1-5 Su and Holidays, Mem Day-Lab Day open Mo **Closed:** 12/25
Sugg/Cont: **ADM:** **Adult:** $3.00 (Fam $5) **Children:** Free under 18
& ℗ Free **Museum Shop** ¶: Rendezvous Restaurant open 11-2 Tu-SuRes.918-596-2720
Group Tours: 918-596-2712 **Drop-In Tours:** 2pm daily **Sculpture Garden**
Permanent Collection: THOMAS MORAN, FREDERIC REMINGTON, C.M. RUSSELL, ALBERT BIERSTADT,ALFRED JACOB MILLER, GEORGE CATLIN, THOMAS EAKINS

Virtually every item in the Gilcrease Collection relates to the discovery, expansion and settlement of North America, with special emphasis on the Old West and the American Indian. The Museum's 460 acre grounds include historic theme gardens. **NOT TO BE MISSED:** "Shoshone Falls on the Snake River, Idaho'', by Thomas Moran

ON EXHIBIT 2000

ONGOING LAS ARTES DE MEXICO
The story of Mexico from pre-Columbian times to the present in a permanent, hands-on installation.

ONGOING DECLARING A NATION
Historical documents and art focused on the formative years of our nation. On display is the only surviving certified copy of the Declaration of Independence signed by John Hancock, Benjamin Franklin, Charles Thomson and Silas Deane.

12/03/1999 to 02/27/2000 GIFTS OF PRIDE AND LOVE: THE CULTURAL SIGNIFICANCE OF KIOWA AND COMANCHE LATTICE CRADLES
The historical and aesthetic significance of cradleboards in Native American culture.

04/28/2000 to 06/25/2000 GILCREASE RENDEZVOUS 2000
The featured artists will be Joe Bohler and Mehl Lawrence. Retrospective pieces will be shown.

05/05/2000 to 07/16/2000 POWERFUL IMAGES: PORTRAYALS OF NATIVE AMERICA
The history of fine art, popular culture and media representation of Native American cultures and their members

05/06/2000 to 07/16/2000 POWERFUL IMAGES: PORTRAYALS OF NATIVE AMERICA
The history of fine art, popular culture and media representation of Native American cultures and their members

06/24/2000 to 08/20/2000 CREATIVITY AND RESISTANCE: MAROON CULTURES OF THE AMERICAS
Contemporary Maroon peoples of Jamaica, Surinam and the Seminole community in the US with their cultural expressions, historical documentation and personal experiences.

10/08/2000 to 12/03/2000 ON THE ROAD WITH THOMAS HART BENTON: IMAGES OF A CHANGING AMERICA
How drawing, one of Benton's greatest talents and travel, a passion combined to produce some of his most significant works.

Philbrook Museum of Art Inc

2727 South Rockford Road, Tulsa, OK 74114

☎: 918-749-7941 or 800-324-7941 ◙ www.philbrook.org
Open: 10-5 Tu-Sa, 10-8 Th 11-5 Su **Closed:** Mo, LEG/HOL
Free Day: Twice each year in May & Oct! **ADM:** **Adult:** $5.00 plus tax **Children:** Free 12 & under **Students:** $3.00 plus tax **Seniors:** $3.00 plus tax
& ℗ Free **Museum Shop** ¶: 11-2 Tu-Su, Su Brunch, Cocktails 5-7 Th
Group Tours: 918-749-5309 **Drop-In Tours:** Upon request
Historic Building Sculpture Garden
Permanent Collection: NAT/AM; IT/REN: ptgs, sculp; EU & AM: ptgs 19-20;

Philbrook Museum of Art Inc - continued

An Italian Renaissance style villa built in 1927 on 23 acres of formal and informal gardens and grounds. The collections, more than 6000 works, are from around the world, more than half of which are by Native-Americans. Visitors enter a 75,000 square foot addition via a striking rotunda which was completed in 1990 and is used for special exhibitions, a shop, a restaurant.

ON EXHIBIT 2000

09/19/1999 to 01/02/2000   THE ARTIST' BOOK: THE BOOK AS A WORK OF ART
Artists in the last half century have strived to make the book "a thing of beauty" with fine bindings and illustrations

03/26/2000 to 06/18/2000   LAND OF THE WINGED HORSEMEN: ART IN POLAND, 1571-1764
In the first major display in America of works in all media from Poland during the 16th-18th c. Paintings, ceramics, glass, furniture, weaponry, metalworks, and textiles including a captured Turkish tent) will be shown. *Will Travel*

08/13/2000 to 11/05/2000   WOVEN WORLDS: BASKETRY FROM THE CLARK FIELD COLLECTION OF NATIVE AMERICAN ART

11/19/2000 to 12/03/2000   FESTIVAL OF TREES

OREGON

COOS BAY

Coos Art Museum
235 Anderson, Coos Bay, OR 97420
\: 541-267-3901 ◙ www.coos.or.us/~cam/
Open: 11-5 Tu-Fr, 1-4 Sa   **Closed:** LEG/HOL!
& Ⓟ Free
Museum Shop
Historic Building
Permanent Collection: CONT: ptgs, sculp, gr; AM; REG

This cultural center of Southwestern Oregon is the only art museum on the Oregon coast. It's collection includes work by Robert Rauschenberg, Red Grooms, Larry Rivers, Frank Boyden, Henk Pander and Manuel Izquierdo. Newly added is the Prefontaine Room, a special memorial to the late Olympic track star who was a native of Coos Bay. **NOT TO BE MISSED:** 'Mango, Mango', by Red Grooms

EUGENE

University of Oregon Museum of Art
Affiliate Institution: University of Oregon
1430 Johnson Lane, Eugene, OR 97403
\: 541-346-3027 ◙ www.uoma.uoregon.edu
Open: 12-5 Th-Su, 12-8 We   **Closed:** Mo, Tu, 1/ 1, 7/4, THGV. 12/25 ACAD
Free Day: We 5-8   **ADM: Adult:** $3.00
& **Museum Shop**
Group Tours: 541-346-0968   **Drop-In Tours:** 2 PM Su
Historic Building
Permanent Collection: CONT: ptgs, phot, gr, cer; NAT/AM

Enjoy one of the premier Visual art experiences in the Pacific Northwest. The second largest museum of in the state, the museum collection features more than 12,500 objects from throughout the world as well as contemporary Northwest art and photography. **NOT TO BE MISSED:** Museum Fountain Courtyard

KLAMATH FALLS

Favell Museum of Western Art and Indian Artifacts
125 West Main Street, Klamath Falls, OR 97601
\: 541-882-9996
Open: 9:30-5:30 Mo, Sa   **Closed:** Su, LEG/HOL!
ADM: Adult: $4.00   **Children:** $2.00 (6-16)   **Students:** $3.00   **Seniors:** $3.00
& Ⓟ
Museum Shop
Drop-In Tours
Permanent Collection: CONT/WEST: art; NAT/AM; ARTIFACTS; MINI FIREARMS

The museum is built on an historic campsite of the Klamath Indians. There are numerous artifacts–some of which have been incorporated into the stone walls of the museum building itself.

Douglas F. Cooley Memorial Art Gallery
Affiliate Institution: Reed College
3203 S.E. Woodstock Blvd., Portland, OR 97202-8199
☎: 503-777-7790   ◉   http://web.reed.edu/resources/gallery/
Open: 12-5 Tu-Su   **Closed:** Mo, LEG/HOL
  ⓅAdjacent
Permanent Collection: AM: 20; EU: 19

The gallery is committed to a program that fosters a spirit of inquiry and questions the status quo.

ON EXHIBIT 2000
02/2000 to 03/2000   LIAO AND HAN DYNASTY TOMBS (LOANS FROM HUBEI, PR CHINA WITH HSING YUAN TSAO

04/2000 to 06/2000   DAVID SMITH: TWO INTO THREE DIMENSIONS

08/2000 to 10/2000   CLASSICISM AND THE EDUCATION OF ARTISTS (working title) FROM THE DAHESH MUSEUM

Portland Art Museum
1219 S.W. Park Ave., Portland, OR 97205
☎: 503-226-2811   ◉   www.pam.org
Open: 10-5 Tu-Su, 10-9 We (begin Oct thru winter) & 1st Th   **Closed:** Mo, LEG/HOL!
ADM: Adult: $6.00   **Children:** Free under 5   **Students:** $2.50   **Seniors:** $4.50
  Museum Shop
Group Tours: 503-226-2811 ext 889
Historic Building
Permanent Collection: NAT/AM; P/COL; AS; GR; EU & AM: ptgs; CONT: ptgs   ♫

Designed by Pietro Belluschi, the Portland Art Museum has a permanent collection that spans 35 centuries of international art. It is the region's oldest and largest visual arts and media center. The museum also hosts a Jazz series, Museum After Hours. Note: Some exhibitions may have extended hours and/or admission fees.

ON EXHIBIT 2000
11/19/1999 to 01/23/2000   MONET TO MOORE: THE MILLENNIUM GIFT OF THE SARA LEE CORPORATION
The exhibition offers a comprehensive survey of French avant-garde painting and sculpture of the late 19th and early 20th centuries. Because the collection is being donated to 19 American museums, including the Portland Art Museum, the exhibition is a rare chance to see the works before they are dispersed. Particular strengths include Impressionist painting and early 20th century sculpture by artists such as Camille Pissarro, Claude Monet, Henri Matisse, Pablo Picasso and Edouard Vuillard.

02/19/2000 to 05/31/2000   STROGANOFF: THE PALACE AND COLLECTIONS OF A RUSSIAN NOBLE FAMILY
Stroganoff is one of the most familiar names in Russian history, that of an extraordinary family whose impact over five centuries included aggressive entrepreneurship as well as social vision and patronage of the arts. The exhibition includes icons and antiquities, palace furnishings and paintings of the greatest European masters from Botticelli to Poussin. These will be arrayed as they were in the Stroganoff Palace, one of the grandest 18th century buildings in St. Petersburg.   ♫

08/2000   PROJECT FOR THE MILLENNIUM: BUILDING A LEGACY WHERE ART LIVES

OREGON

Museum at Warm Springs Oregon
Affiliate Institution: Confederated Tribes of the Warm Springs Reservation
Warm Springs, OR 97761

☎: 541-553-3331
Open: 10-5 daily   **Closed:** 12/25, 1/1, THGV
ADM: Adult: $6.00   **Children:** $3.00 5-12 ; Free under 5   **Seniors:** $5.00
 ♧ &#9business;   **Museum Shop**
Group Tours
Permanent Collection: NAT/AM: art, phot, artifacts

The Museum at Warm Springs draws from a rich collection of native artwork, photographs and stories that tell the long history of the three tribes (Wasco, Warm Springs and Paiute) that comprise the Confederated Tribes of Warm Springs. It is architecturally designed to evoke a creekside encampment among a stand of cottonwoods. **NOT TO BE MISSED:** A trio of traditional buildings built by tribal members; the tule mat wickiup, or house of the Paiutes, the Warm Springs summer teepee, and the Wasco wooden plank house.

ALLENTOWN

Allentown Art Museum

Fifth & Court Street, Allentown, PA 18105

☎: 610-432-4333 ◙ www.allentownartmuseum.org

Open: 11-5 Tu-Sa, 12-5 Su **Closed:** Mo, LEG/HOL!

ADM: Adult: $4.00 **Children:** Free under 12 **Students:** $2.00 **Seniors:** $3.00

♿ Ⓟ On street meters and several pay garages

Museum Shop 🍴 small cafe

Group Tours: 610-432-4333,ext. 32 **Drop-In Tours:** by appt

Permanent Collection: EU: Kress Coll; AM; FRANK LLOYD WRIGHT: library; OM: gr; gem collection ◠

Discover the intricate and visual riches of one of the finest small art museums in the country. **NOT TO BE MISSED:** 'Piazetti in Venice', by Canaletto

ON EXHIBIT 2000

ONGOING   INSTALLATIONS OF PERMANENT COLLECTION

European Paintings and Sculpture

American Art

Decorative Arts 1875-1925

The James C. Fuller Gem Collection

American Studio Ceramics

10/1999 to 01/2000   VINCENT DESIDERIO

Desiderio emerged as a leader of the new "History Painting" in the mid-1980's making monumental paintings with subjects generated by personal tragedy and hope.

01/16/2000 to 04/09/2000   GREAT DESIGN: 100 MASTERPIECES FROM THE VITRA DESIGN MUSEUM COLLECTION

A major exhibition highlighting the concepts styles and materials central to furniture design in the modern era. Works by Thonet , Hoffman, Reitveld, Aalto Breuer and the Eames'. *Catalog Will Travel*

04/23/2000 to 07/02/2000   MODERNIST PAINTINGS FROM THE NATIONAL MUSEUM OF AMERICAN ART

Catalog Will Travel

AUDUBON

Mill Grove The Audubon Wildlife Sanctuary

Paulings and Audubon Roads, Audubon, PA 19407-7125

☎: 610-666-5593

Open: 10-4 Tu-Sa, 1-4 Su grounds open dawn to dusk Tu-Su **Closed:** Mo, 1/1, EASTER, 7/4, THGV, 12/24, 12/25, 12/31

Vol/Cont:

♿ Ⓟ **Museum Shop**

Group Tours: by appt **Historic Building**

Permanent Collection: JOHN JAMES AUDUBON: all major published artwork, (complete 19th C editions) and related items

Housed in the 1762 National Historic Landmark building which was the first American home of John James Audubon, artist/naturalist. This site is also a wildlife sanctuary complete with nature trails and feeding stations. Grounds self-guide map Free. **NOT TO BE MISSED:** Exceptionally large oil painting by Audubon called "Eagle and the Lamb"

PENNSYLVANIA

Lehigh University Art Galleries

Affiliate Institution: Zoellner Arts Center
420 East Packer Ave, Bethlehem, PA 18015-3007
☎: 610-758-3615
Open: 11-5 We-Sa; 1-5, Su; Some galleries are open late, others closed weekends !   **Closed:** Mo, Tu, LEG/HOL!
 ♿ ℗ Limited   **Museum Shop**   ⊮: In Iacocca Bldg. open until 2 PM
Group Tours   Sculpture Garden
Permanent Collection: EU & AM: ptgs; JAP: gr; PHOT

The Galleries do not permanently exhibit all the important works in its collections. Call to inquire. **NOT TO BE MISSED:** Outdoor sculpture throughout 3 Campuses, including work by Henry Moore, David Cerulli and Menash Kadishman

ON EXHIBIT 2000

More than 20 temporary exhibitions a year in five campus galleries introduce students and the community to current topics in art, architecture, history, science and technology.

Glencairn Museum: Academy of the New Church

1001 Cathedral Road, Bryn Athyn, PA 19009
☎: 215-938-2600
Open: 9-5 Mo-Fr by appt, 2-5 second Su each month (except Jul & Aug)   **Closed:** Sa, LEG/HOL!
ADM: Adult: $4.00   **Children:** $2.00   **Students:** $2.00   **Seniors:** $3.00
♿ ℗
Group Tours: 215-914-2981
Permanent Collection: MED, GOTHIC & ROMANESQUE: sculp; STAINED GLASS; EGT, GRK & ROMAN: cer, sculp; NAT/AM

Glencairn is a unique structure built in the Romanesque style using building processes unknown since the middle ages. It is the former home of Raymond and Mildred Pitcairn. **NOT TO BE MISSED:** French Medieval stained glass and sculpture

Trout Gallery, Weiss Center for the Arts

Affiliate Institution: Dickinson College
High Street PO box 1773, Carlisle, PA 17013
☎: 717-245-1344   ◙ www.dickinson.edu/departments/trout
Open: 10-4 Tu-Su   **Closed:** Mo, LEG/HOL!; ACAD!
♿ ℗
Group Tours: 717-245-1492
Permanent Collection: GR; 19,20; AF

The exhibitions and collections here emphasize all periods of art history. **NOT TO BE MISSED:** Gerofsky Collection of African Art and the Carnegie Collection of prints. Rodin's 'St. John the Baptist' and other gifts from Meyer P. and Vivian Potamkin.

Trout Gallery, Weiss Center for the Arts - continued
ON EXHIBIT 2000
11/05/1999 to 01/15/2000   RESISTANCE AND AFFIRMATION: PRINTS AND POSTERS OF RUPERT GARCIA
Rupert Garcia is known as a man of artistic flair and as a man of action. He first became known for his political posters in the late 1960s and early 1970s, a time of turmoil in the United States and a time when Garcia was most engaged in Mexican-American and Latino cultural programs and policies. He quickly became well known for his unique blend of topical messages and his bold style that incorporated elements of Pop art and commercial art with his own unique color sensibilities.

03/03/2000 to 04/08/2000   EAST MEETS WEST: RENE BOLL/SOZUN MATSUBA

09/08/2000 to 11/25/2000   WRITING ON HANDS: KNOWLEDGE AND MEMORY IN EARLY MODERN EUROPEAN CULTURE

CHADDS FORD

Brandywine River Museum
U.S. Route 1, Chadds Ford, PA 19317
☎: 610-388-2700   ◉ www.brandywinemuseum.org
Open: 9:30-4:30 Daily   **Closed:** 12/25
ADM: **Adult:** $5.00   **Children:** Free under 6   **Students:** $2.50   **Seniors:** $2.50
  ᕈ ℗   **Museum Shop**   ⑪: 11-3 (Closed M and Tu Jan through Mar)
Group Tours: 610-388-8366   **Historic Building**
Permanent Collection: AM: ptgs by three generations of the Wyeth Family

Situated in a pastoral setting in a charming converted 19th century grist mill, this museum is devoted to displaying the works of three generations of the Wyeth family and other Brandywine River School artists. Particular focus is also placed on 19th c American still-life & landscape paintings and on works of American illustration. Su 10-3:15. Timed tickets must be purchased at the Museum. There is a shuttle bus.

ON EXHIBIT 2000
ONGOING   BRANDYWINE HERITAGE GALLERIES
Works by Pyle, his students and other artists of the period.

ONGOING   ANDREW WYETH GALLERY
Works from various stages of his career

CHESTER

Widener University Art Collection and Gallery
Affiliate Institution: Widener University
14th and Chestnut Street, Chester, PA 19013
☎: 610-499-1189
Open: 10-4:30 We-Sa, 10-7 Tu (call for summer hours)   **Closed:** Su, Mo, LEG/HOL
  ᕈ ℗ nearby pay garages
Permanent Collection: AM & EU: ptgs 19,20

The Museum is located in the new University Center on 14th St on the main campus. It includes in its holdings the Widener University Collection of American Impressionist paintings, the Alfred O. Deshong Collection of 19th and 20th c European and American painting, 19th c Asian art and pre-Columbian pottery.
PLEASE NOTE: Children under 16 must be accompanied by an adult.

PENNSYLVANIA

COLLEGEVILLE

Philip and Muriel Berman Museum of Art at Ursinus College
Main Street, Collegeville, PA 19426-1000

☎: 610-409-3500 ◙ www.ursinus.edu
Open: 10-4 Tu-Fr, Noon-4:30 Sa, Su **Closed:** Mo, LEG/HOL!
Vol/Cont:
♿ Ⓟ On campus adjacent to Museum
Group Tours: 609-409-3500 **Drop-In Tours**: by appt **Historic Building Sculpture Garden**
Permanent Collection: AM: ptgs 19,20; EU: ptgs 18; JAP: ptgs; PENNSYLVANIA GERMAN ART: cont outdoor sculp

With 145 works from 1956-1986, the Berman Museum of Art holds the largest private collection of sculpture by Lynn Chadwick in a U.S. museum, housed in the original Georgian Style stone facade college library built in 1921. **NOT TO BE MISSED:** 'Seated Couple on a Bench' (1986 bronze), by Lynn Chadwick (English b. 1914)

ON EXHIBIT 2000
10/1999 to 01/2000 STEVEN QUILLER WATERCOLORS

11/12/1999 to 01/23/2000 FOUR OBJECTS; FOUR ARTISTS; TEN YEARS
In 1986 four American still-life painters–Janet Fish, Sondra Freckelton, Nancy Hagin, and Harriet Shorr–agreed that each would select an object that they would all include in a painting. Ten years later they decided to repeat the project. The results of their efforts reveal the wide spectrum of choices which artists make during the creative process. *Catalog Will Travel*

02/2000 to 04/2000 JOHN GWINN - RETROSPECTIVE

05/2000 to 07/2000 HANS MOLLER RETROSPECTIVE

08/2000 to 10/2000 JAPANESE SCROLLS FROM THE BERMAN COLLECTION

DOYLESTOWN

James A. Michener Art Museum
138 South Pine Street, Doylestown, PA 18901

☎: 215-340-9800 ◙ www.michenerartmuseum.org
Open: 10-4:30 Tu-Fr, till 9pm We, 10-5 Sa, Su **Closed:** Mo, LEG/HOL!
ADM: Adult: $5.00 **Children:** Free under 12 **Students:** $1.50 **Seniors:** $4.50
♿ Ⓟ Free **Museum Shop** 🍴 Espresso Café
Group Tours: ext 126 **Drop-In Tours**: 2pm, Sa, Su, & by appt **Historic Building Sculpture Garden**
Permanent Collection: AM: Impr/ptgs 19-20; BUCKS CO: 18-20; AM: Exp 20; SCULP 20; NAKASHIMA READING ROOM; CREATIVE BUCKS COUNTY

Situated in the handsomely reconstructed buildings of the antiquated Bucks County prison, the Museum provides an invigorating environment for viewing a wonderful collection of 19th and 20th century American art. **NOT TO BE MISSED:** Redfield, Garber & New Hope School

ON EXHIBIT 2000
ONGOING CREATIVE BUCKS COUNTY: A CELEBRATION OF ART AND ARTISTS
A multi-media exhibition in the new Mari Sabusawa Michener Wing which tells the story of Bucks County's rich artistic tradition. Included are individual displays on 12 of the country's best known artists, a video theater, and a comprehensive database containing information on hundreds of Bucks County artists, both living and deceased. The featured artists are Pearl S. Buck, Daniel Garber, Oscar Hammerstein II, Moss Hart, Edward Hicks, George S. Kaufman, Henry Chapman Mercer, Dorothy Parker, S. J. Perelman, Charles Sheeler, Edward Redfield, and Jean Toomer.

James A. Michener Art Museum - continued
ONGOING   JAMES A MICHENER: A LIVING LEGACY
Michener's Bucks County office is installed at the Museum and included are a video, the Presidential Medal of Freedom and the original manuscript of 'The Novel'.

ONGOING   NAKASHIMA READING ROOM
Classic furniture from the studio of internationally known woodworker George Nakashima.

ONGOING   VISUAL HERITAGE OF BUCKS COUNTY
A comprehensive exhibition based on the permanent collection which traces art in the region from Colonial times through to the present.

ONGOING   INSIDE OUR VAULT: SELECTIONS FROM THE COLLECTION
A small-scale exhibition of delights and surprises in the Museum's rapidly expanding collection.

ONGOING   OUTDOOR SCULPTURE:
Regional and National sculptors explore the human figure and its possibilities.

09/25/1999 to 01/02/2000   AN EDWARD HICKS SAMPLER
Hicks lived in Bucks County for all of his life In honor of the major exhibition opening at the Philadelphia Museum the Michener is celebrating his life and work.

12/04/1999 to 02/27/2000   LET CHILDREN BE CHILDREN: LEWIS WICKES HINE'S CRUSADE AGAINST CHILD LABOR
Hine documented the abuses against children and his photographs were instrumental in the passing of the Child Labor Act.

01/22/2000 to 04/02/2000   THE JAZZ AGE IN PARIS 1914-1940
Photographs, audio and video and a variety of artifacts this Smithsonian Institution exhibition describes the expatriate scene between the first and second World Wars.

03/11/2000 to 06/04/2000   NO ORDINARY LAND: ENCOUNTERS IN A CHANGING ENVIRONMENT
Photographers Virginia Beahan and Laura McPhee have explored the way that people interact with the environments in which they live as diverse as Sri Lanka, Iceland, Costa Rica and New York..

04/15/2000 to 07/02/2000   BUCKS COUNTY INVITATIONAL IV
Artists in all media are invited to participate in this regional show.

06/17/2000 to 09/03/2000   SUBLIME SERVERS: A CELEBRATION OF THEATRICAL POSSIBILITIES AS THE TABLE
30 artists provide a cornucopia of ceramic sculpture and vessels of infinite possibilities.

10/99/2001 to 01/09/2000   INTIMATE VISTAS: THE POETIC LANDSCAPES OF WILLIAM LANGSON LATHROP
Lathrop was one of the most respected landscape painter in the beginning of the 20th C. He and his wife were instrumental in the formation of the New Hope Art Colony. Many of the works shown here have never been exhibited before.

EASTON

Lafayette College Art Gallery, Williams Center for the Arts
Hamilton and High Streets, Easton, PA 18042-1768
☎: 610-330-5361 ◙ www.lafayette.edu
Open: 10-5 Tu, Th, Fr; 10-8 We; 12-5 Mo, Su Sep-May   **Closed:** ACAD!
♿ Ⓟ On-street
Group Tours
Permanent Collection: AM: ptgs, portraits, gr

Located in Easton, Pennsylvania, on the Delaware River, the collection is spread throughout the campus.
NOT TO BE MISSED: 19th c American history paintings and portraits

PENNSYLVANIA

ERIE

Erie Art Museum
411 State Street, Erie, PA 16501
📞: 814-459-5477 ▣ www.erie.net/~erieartm/
Open: 11-5 Tu-Sa, 1-5 Su **Closed:** Mo, LEG/HOL!
Free Day: We **ADM: Adult:** $2.00 **Children:** $.50 (under 12) **Students:** $1.00 **Seniors:** $1.00
♿ ℗ Street parking
Museum Shop
Group Tours Drop-In Tours: 11-5
Historic Building
Permanent Collection: IND: sculp; OR; AM & EU: ptgs, drgs, sculp gr; PHOT

The museum is located in the 1839 Greek Revival Old Customs House built as the U. S. Bank of PA. Building plans are underway to provide more gallery space in order to exhibit works from the 4,000 piece permanent collection. **NOT TO BE MISSED:** Soft Sculpture installation ' The Avalon Restaurant'

ON EXHIBIT 2000

10/21/1999 to 03/05/2000 PLASTIC SKETCHES
Pictorial bas relief tiles by Arthur Osborne (1855-1942) created for the J. G. Low Art Tile Works of Chelsea, Massachusetts in the 1880's

12/31/1999 to 04/16/2000 MARC BROWN
Works by beloved the children's book illustrator and creator of Arthur the Aardvark

03/15/2000 THEREMIN EXHIBIT

04/29/2000 to 06/18/2000 THE 77TH ANNUAL SPRING SHOW: JURIED

GREENSBURG

Westmoreland Museum of American Art
221 North Main Street, Greensburg, PA 15601-1898
📞: 412-837-1500 ▣ www.wmuseumaa.org
Open: 11-5 We-Su, 11-9 Th **Closed:** Mo, Tu, LEG/HOL!
Sugg/Cont: ADM: Adult: $3.00 **Children:** Free under 12
♿ ℗ Free **Museum Shop**
Group Tours Drop-In Tours: by appt
Permanent Collection: AM: ptgs (18-20), sculp, drgs, gr, fruniture, dec/art

This important collection of American art is located in a beautiful Georgian style building situated on a hill overlooking the city. The collection has been re-installed in a more cohesive and dramatic fashion.. **NOT TO BE MISSED:** Portraits by William Merritt Chase and Cecilia Beaux; Largest known collection of paintings by 19th century southwestern Pennsylvania artists.

ON EXHIBIT 2000

11/26/1999 to 01/16/2000 HOLIDAY TOY AND TRAIN EXHIBITION: CHRISTMAS: PAST, PRESENT AND FUTURE
The Museum collection will be supplemented by loans from private collections, representing toys highlighted and manufactured during each decade of the 20th century.

318

State Museum of Pennsylvania

3rd and North Streets, Harrisburg, PA 17108-1026
☎: 717-787-7789
Open: 9-5 Tu-Sa, 12-5 Su   **Closed:** LEG/HOL
♿ **Museum Shop**
Group Tours: 717-772-6997   **Drop-In Tours**: !
Permanent Collection: VIOLET OAKLEY COLL; PETER ROTHERMEL MILITARY SERIES; PA: cont

A newly renovated Art Gallery collecting, preserving, and interpreting contemporary art & historical works relating to Pennsylvania's history, culture and natural heritage is the main focus of this museum whose collection includes 4000 works of art from 1650 to the present produced by residents/natives of Pennsylvania. **NOT TO BE MISSED:** The 16' X 32' 'Battle of Gettysburg: Pickett's Charge', by P. F. Rothermel (the largest battle scene on canvas in North America)

ON EXHIBIT 2000

10/1999 to 04/2000   THE MILLENNIUM MAZE

University Museum

Affiliate Institution: Indiana University
John Sutton Hall, Indiana University of Penn, Indiana, PA 15705-1087
☎: 412-357-7930   ◉ www.iup.edu/fa/museum
Open: 11-4 Tu-Fr, 7-9 Th, 1-4 Sa, Su   **Closed:** Mo, ACAD!
ADM: **Adult:** $3.00   **Children:** Free under 12   **Students:** $3.00   **Seniors:** $3.00
♿ ⓟ Metered lot just East of the Student Center (next to the football stadium)   **Group Tours**
Permanent Collection: AM: 19,20; NAT/AM; MILTON BANCROFT: ptgs & drgs; INUIT: sculp

The University Museum at Indiana University of Pennsylvania, one of just three university museums in Pennsylvania, offers a diverse program of changing exhibits, related cultural events, and educational activities to the university community and residents of the four-county area. Each year, the museum stages more than six exhibitions, designed to appeal to a variety of interests. Local, regional and international artists display contemporary works in a wide range of media. Special interdisciplinary exhibits explore the cultural heritage of the region and other themes from an aesthetic viewpoint. Rotating displays drawn from the museum's permanent collection round out the exhibit schedule. The museum's permanent collection, started in 1946 and refined during the early 1990s, consists of more than 1200 works. An active program of new acquisitions focuses on American fine and folk art and native arts of North and Central America

Bucknell Art Gallery

Affiliate Institution: Bucknell University
Seventh Street and Moore Ave, Lewisburg, PA 17837
☎: 570-577-3792   ◉ http://www.departments.bucknell.edu/center_gallery/index.html
Open: 11-5 Mo-Fr, 1-4 Sa, Su   **Closed:** LEG/HOL!
♿ ⓟ Free   **Museum Shop**   ⑪ Not in museum but in bldg.
Drop-In Tours
Permanent Collection: IT/REN: ptgs; AM: ptgs 19,20; JAP

Bucknell Art Gallery - continued

The permanent collection, which numbers approximately 8,000 objects has been established primarily through large bequests and gifts. Most impressive are the 24 items from the Samuel H. Kress Foundation,including the earliest documented painting by Pontormo, Cupid and Apollo, a very early Rosso Fiorentino, Madonna and Child, and works by Tintoretto, Veronese, Francesco Cossa, Agostino Tassi and Andrea Sansovino; the Andrew J. Sordoni Collection of Japanese art which includes 500 objects, mostly 19th century netsuke, okimono, and inro boxes of extremely high quality; and the Cook Collection of 156 musical instruments from all over the world and dating back as far as the 18th century. **NOT TO BE MISSED:** 'Cupid Apollo', by Pontormo

---

LORETTO

Southern Alleghenies Museum of Art

Affiliate Institution: Saint Francis College
Saint Francis College Mall, P. O. Box 9, Loretto, PA 15940
☎: 814-472-3920 ◙ www.sama-sfc.org
Open: 10-4 Mo-Fr, 1:30-4:30 Sa, Su   **Closed:** LEG/HOL
 ᚷ ℗ ᵀᴵ: Nearby and on college campus
Group Tours: by appt   **Drop-In Tours**: by appt   **Sculpture Garden**
Permanent Collection: AM: ptgs 19, 20; sculp; drwg; gr

The museum was founded to bring museum services to this geographically isolated rural region and to provide the audience with an opportunity to view important trends in American Art. Also: Southern Alleghenies Museum of Art, Brett Bldg, 1210 11th Ave, Altoona, PA 16602 814-946-4464   Southern Alleghenies Museum of Art at Pasquerilla Performing Arts Center, University of Pittsburgh at Johnstown, PA 15904 814-946-4464. Southern Alleghenies Museum of Art at Ligonier Valley, One Boucher Lane, Route 711S, Ligonier, PA 15658 724-238-6015 **NOT TO BE MISSED:** John Sloan's 'Bright Rocks'

MERION STATION

Barnes Foundation

300 North Latch's Lane, Merion Station, PA 19066
☎: 610-667-0290
Open: 9:30-5 Fr, Sa, 9:30-5-Su (subject to change !) by advance reservation only   **Closed:** Mo-Th, 12/25
ADM: Adult: $5.00, additional $7.00 for audio
 ᚷ ℗   **Museum Shop**
Group Tours: 610-664-5191
Permanent Collection: FR: Impr, post/Impr; EARLY FR MODERN; AF; AM: ptgs,sculp 20

The core of the collection includes a great many works by Renoir, Cézanne, and Matisse, but also contains works by Picasso, van Gogh, Seurat, Braque, Modigliani, Soutine, Monet and Manet. Various traditions are displayed in works by El Greco, Titian, Corbet, Corot, Delacroix and others. Works are displayed among American antique furniture, ironwork, ceramics and crafts. The building has just undergone a 3 year, $12 million renovation. **NOT TO BE MISSED:** This outstanding collection should not be missed.

MILL RUN

Fallingwater
Rt. 381, Mill Run, PA 15464

☎: 724-329-8501   ◙ www.paconserve.org
Open: 11/21-12/20, 2/27-3/14, weekends only, Xmas week 10-4 Tu-Su, Closed Jan/Feb   **Closed:** Mo, some LEG/HOL!
Free Day: Fayette Country Day   **ADM: Adult:** $8.00 Tu-F;$12 wknds
& ℗ Free   **Museum Shop**   ‖: Open 5/1 - 11/1
Group Tours   Historic Building National Historic Landmark   **Sculpture Garden**
Permanent Collection: ARCH; PTGS; JAP: gr; SCULP; NAT/AM

Magnificent is the word for this structure, one of Frank Lloyd Wrights most widely acclaimed works. The key to the setting of the house is the waterfall over which it is built. Fallingwater is undergoing some renovation. Special hours are listed. 3/15-11/15 hours will be 10-4 Tu-Su 11/1-4/1 weekends only. 2 hour in depth tours are available by advance reservation only. $30 per person weekdays, $35 weekends. **NOT TO BE MISSED:** View of the House from the Overlook

PHILADELPHIA

African-American Museum in Philadelphia
701 Arch Street, Philadelphia, PA 19106

☎: 215-574-0380   ◙ www.aampmuseum.org
Open: 10-5 Tu-Sa, 12-5 Su   **Closed:** Mo, LEG/HOL
Free Day: Martin Luther King Jr. day   **ADM: Adult:** $6.00   **Children:** $4.00   **Students:** $4.00   **Seniors:** $4.00
& ℗ Pay parking nearby   **Museum Shop**
Group Tours: x228
Permanent Collection: JACK FRANK COLL: phot; PEARL JONES COLL: phot drgs, dec/art: JOSEPH C. COLEMAN personal papers, photos and awards

A diverse and unique showplace, this is the first museum built by a major city to house and interpret collections of African-American art, history, and culture primarily in, but not limited to the Commonwealth of Pennsylvania. The museum contains over 300,000 objects.

ON EXHIBIT 2000
ONGOING   INTRODUCTION TO THE MUSEUM AND ITS COLLECTION

12/12/1999 to 02/28/2000   TUSKEGEE AIRMEN

03/10/2000 to 05/27/2000   SHOUT OUT
A exhibition of women who celebrate womenhood through their particular artforms and whose present and future roles in their art reflect their views.

03/23/2000 to 06/04/2000   THE MONUMENT DRAWINGS: BARBARA CHASE RIBOUD
This Philadelphia born artist and sculptor shows 24 works which represent the major body of her graphic work since 1973.

06/01/2000 to 09/03/2000   STATE OF THE BLUES: THE LIVING LEGACY OF THE DELTA
A showcase and tribute to the richness of the southern blues tradition and to some of the great performers of that time including B.B. King, Koko Taylor, Charlie Russell, Clarence "Gatemouth" Brown , and others. Photos by Jeff Dunas.

06/16/2000 to 09/17/2000   PAUL ROBESON: SPIRIT OF A CULTURE
Photographs and documents taking one through the life of Robeson.

09/14/2000 to 04/01/2001   BIENNIAL EXHIBITION
Highlighting the regions finest artists working in several disciplines.

09/28/2000 to 12/03/2000   UNTOLD STORIES FROM THE JACK T. FRANKLIN PHOTOGRAPHIC COLLECTION
Selections from the Museum's permanent collection.

PENNSYLVANIA

Institute of Contemporary Art
Affiliate Institution: University of Pennsylvania
118 South 36th Street at Sansom, Philadelphia, PA 19104-3289
☎: 215-898-7108   ◙ www.upenn.edu/ica
Open: 10-5 We, Fr-Su, 10-7 Th   **Closed:** Mo, Tue, 1/1, 12/25
Free Day: Su, 10-12   **ADM: Adult:** $3.00   **Children:** $2.00, Free under 12   **Students:** $2.00   **Seniors:** $2.00.
& ℗ lots nearby
Group Tours: 215-898-7108   **Drop-In Tours:** Th, 5:15
Historic Building Contemporary Building designed by Adele Naude Santos
Permanent Collection: non-collecting institution

The Museum was founded in 1963 and is one of the premier institutions solely dedicated to the art of our time.

ON EXHIBIT 2000

11/20/1999 to 01/16/2000   DAVID GRAHAM

11/20/1999 to 01/16/2000   NANCY DAVIDSON

02/05/1999 to 04/16/2000   AGAINST DESIGN

02/05/1999 to 04/16/2000   FOR MODERN LIVING ART

05/13/2000 to 07/30/2000   WALL POWER: BARRY MCGEE AND STEPHEN POWERS

05/13/2000 to 07/30/2000   JOSEPH BARTSCHERER

La Salle University Art Museum
Affiliate Institution: LaSalle University
20th and Olney Ave, Philadelphia, PA 19141
☎: 215-951-1221
Open: 11-4 Tu-Fr, 2-4 Su, Sep-Jul   **Closed:** ACAD!
& ℗ Campus lot
Permanent Collection: EU: ptgs, sculp, gr 15-20; AM: ptgs

Many of the major themes and styles of Western art since the Middle ages are documented in the comprehensive collection of paintings, prints, drawings and sculpture at this museum.

Museum of American Art of the Pennsylvania Academy of the Fine Arts
Broad Street and Cherry Street, Philadelphia, PA 19102
☎: 215-972-7600   ◙ www.pafa.org/-pafa
Open: 10-5 Mo-Sa, 11-5 Su   **Closed:** LEG/HOL!
Free Day: 3-5 Su   **ADM: Adult:** $5.95   **Children:** $3.95 Free under 5   **Students:** $4.95   **Seniors:** $4.95
& ℗ Public parking lots nearby ($2.00 discount at Parkway Corp. lots at Broad & Cherry and 15th & Cherry); some street parking   **Museum Shop** ⑪
Group Tours: 215-972-1667   **Drop-In Tours:** Sa, Su 12:30 & 2   **Historic Building**
Permanent Collection: AM: ptgs, sculp 18-20 ◠

The Museum of American Art is housed in a Victorian Gothic masterpiece designed by Frank Ferness and George Hewitt located in the heart of downtown Philadelphia. Its roster of past students includes some of the most renowned artists of the 19th & 20th centuries.

322

Museum of American Art of the Pennsylvania Academy of the Fine Arts - continued
ON EXHIBIT 2000

10/16/1999 to 01/02/2000   IMPRESSIONISM : IN AN AMERICAN LIGHT
Selected works from the permanent collection featured in a neighboring gallery.

10/9/1999 to 1/2/2000   JOHN HENRY TWACHTMAN: AN AMERICAN IMPRESSIONIST
The first retrospective in more than 30 years featuring over 50 oils and pastels covering four periods of the artist's production-Early Works, European Period, Connecticut Years, and Gloucester, late Period. *Catalog Will Travel*

02/2000 to 04/2000   VIEWS FROM ABROAD: NINETEENTH CENTURY DRAWINGS FROM THE COLLECTION
Selected drawings from the permanent collection by expatriate artists.

02/12/2000 to 04/16/2000   PARIS 1900: THE "AMERICAN SCHOOL" AT THE UNIVERSAL EXPOSITION
The Pennsylvania Academy was a major lender to the Paris Exposition of 1900 which played a critical role in defining "American" artistic influences at the time. It featured all the major artists of the late 19th century. Approximately 50 of the paintings and sculpture will be featured here. *Catalog Will Travel*

06/2000 to 07/2000   A CELEBRATION OF THE REPUBLIC
Works of political significance from the collection.

06/18/2000 to 08/13/2000   ROBERT GWATHMEY:1903-88
Approximately 60 paintings and graphics surveying the life and career of this noted social realist. There is special emphasis on images of African-American life and the Southern Scene. *Will Travel*

Summer/2000   UNCENSORED: THE NEA AT PAFA

09/2000   VIDEO INSTALLATION

Fall/2000   AMERICAN WATERCOLORS AT THE PENNSYLVANIA ACADEMY: A CENTENNIAL CELEBRATION
18TH-20TH C. watercolors from the collection and local private collections.

Fall/2000   VIRGIL MARTI
site specific works for the Tyler School

12/10/2000 to 02/05/2000   BARRY GOLDBERG
Work from this recent Pennsylvania Academy Graduate.

The Philadelphia Museum of Art
26th Street & Benjamin Franklin Parkway, Philadelphia, PA 19130
☎: 215-763-8100 ▣ www.philamuseum.org
Open: 10-5 Tu-Su, 10-8:45 We   **Closed:** Mo, LEG/HOL!
Free Day: Su, 10-1   **ADM: Adult:** $8.00   **Children:** $5.00   **Students:** $5.00   **Seniors:** $5.00
& Ⓟ Free   **Museum Shop** ⅋: Tu-Sa 11:30-2:30, We 5-7:30, Su 11-3:30
Group Tours   Drop-In Tours: on the hour 10-3   **Historic Building   Sculpture Garden**
Permanent Collection: EU: ptgs 19-20; CONT; DEC/ART; GR; AM: ptgs, sculp 17-20 ◠

With more than 400,000 works in the permanent collection the Philadelphia Art Museum is the 3rd largest art museum in the country. Housed within its more than 200 galleries are a myriad of artistic treasures from many continents and cultures. **NOT TO BE MISSED:** Van Gogh's 'Sunflowers"; A Ceremonial Japanese Teahouse; Medieval & Early Renaissance Galleries (25 in all) which include a Romanesque cloister, a Gothic chapel, and a world-class collection of early Italian & Northern paintings.

ON EXHIBIT 2000
10/10/1999 to 01/02/2000   WORLDLY GOODS: THE ARTS OF PENNSYLVANIA, 1690-1758
A comprehensive look at the important developments between the decorative and fine arts which developed in Philadelphia and the surrounding colony.

PENNSYLVANIA

The Philadelphia Museum of Art - continued
10/10/1999 to 01/02/2000   THE KINGDOMS OF EDWARD HICKS
The first retrospective devoted to the life and work of Bucks County, Pennsylvania artist Edward Hicks. Included are paintings, decorated objects and important manuscripts which illustrate his deep spirituality and talent as an artist and his involvement in the doctrinal controversies that divided the Quakers in the early 19th C. *Catalog Will Travel*

Early/2000   ALICE NEAL, 1900-1984
The first major museum retrospective of Neal's career will open in the her native city and celebrates her centennial year. On view will be five decades of work, many never before seen by the public. They will reveal the depth and breadth of her work far beyond the portraits for which she is best known. *Catalog Will Travel*

03/2000 to 05/2000   ART IN ROME IN THE EIGHTEENTH CENTURY
290 works of art in all media representing the work of 160 artists will reveal the rich vitality of Rome's artistic life as it approached the end of its independent existence as a secular-state.

08/2000 to 10/2000   HON'AMI KOETSU: JAPANESE RENAISSANCE MASTER
An in-depth exhibition of 60 works from Japanese, American, and European collections celebrating this central figure in the early 17th C. artistic world in Japan. He is universally acknowledged as a master whose wide-ranging talents influenced numerous areas of Japanese art. *Catalog*

10/22/2000 to 01/14/2001   VAN GOGH PORTRAITS
The Detroit Institute, The Boston Museum of Fine Arts, and the Philadelphia Museum have five major portraits. These will be joined by pivotal works from each part of his life. His intense portraits of friends in Paris as well as his success in capturing of his mostly poor and unnamed subjects earlier.. *Catalog Will Travel*

Rodin Museum
Benjamin Franklin Parkway at 22nd Street, Philadelphia, PA 19130
☎: 215-763-8100   ◙   www.rodinmuseum.org
Open: 10-5 Tu-Su   **Closed:** Mo, LEG/HOL!
Sugg/Cont: ADM: **Adult:** $3.00   **Students:** $3.00   **Seniors:** $3.00
& ℗ Free on-street   **Museum Shop**
Group Tours   Drop-In Tours   Historic Building   Sculpture Garden
Permanent Collection: RODIN: sculp, drgs

The largest collection of Rodin's sculptures and drawings outside of Paris is located in a charming and intimate building designed by architects Paul Cret and Jacques Greber. **NOT TO BE MISSED:** 'The Thinker', by Rodin . PLEASE NOTE: The Museum will be closed from 11/1/99 to 7/1/2000

Rosenbach Museum & Library
2010 DeLancey Place, Philadelphia, PA 19103
☎: 215-732-1600   ◙   www.rosenbach.org
Open: 11-4 Tu-Su   **Closed:** Mo, LEG/HOL! August thru 2nd Tu after Labor Day
Free Day: Bloomsday, June 16th   **ADM: Adult:** $5.00 incl guide   **Children:** $3.00   **Students:** $3.00   **Seniors:** $3.00
& **Museum Shop**
Group Tours   Drop-In Tours   Historic Building
Permanent Collection: BRIT & AM: ptgs; MINI SCALE DEC/ARTS; BOOK ILLUSTRATIONS; Rare books and Manuscripts

In the warm and intimate setting of a 19th-century townhouse, the Rosenbach Museum & Library retains an atmosphere of an age when great collectors lived among their treasures. It is the only collection of its kind open to the public in Philadelphia. **NOT TO BE MISSED:** Maurice Sendak drawings

Rosenwald-Wolf Gallery, The University of the Arts
Broad and Pine Streets, Philadelphia, PA 19102
☎: 215-717-6480 ◙ www.uarts.edu
Open: 10-5 Mo, Tu & Th, Fr, 10-8 We, 12-5 Sa, Su, (10-5 weekdays Jun & Jul) **Closed:** ACAD!
♿ Ⓟ Pay garages and metered parking nearby **Group Tours**
Permanent Collection: non-collecting institution

This is the only university in the nation devoted exclusively to education and professional training in the visual and performing arts. The gallery presents temporary exhibitions of contemporary art.

ON EXHIBIT 2000
01/14/2000 to 03/03/2000 LEBBEUS WOODS

03/20/2000 to 05/15/2000 REE MORTON: THE MATING HABITS OF LINES: SKETCHBOOKS AND NOTEBOOKS OF REE MORTON

University of Pennsylvania Museum of Archaeology and Anthropology
Affiliate Institution: University of Pennsylvania
33rd and Spruce Streets, Philadelphia, PA 19104
☎: 215-898-4000 ◙ www.upenn.edu/mus
Open: 10-4:30 Tu-Sa, 1-5 Su, closed Su Mem day-Lab day **Closed:** Mo, LEG/HOL
ADM: Adult: $5.00 **Children:** Free under 6 **Students:** $2.50 **Seniors:** $2.50
♿ Ⓟ **Museum Shop** ⑪
Group Tours: 215-898-4015 **Drop-In Tours:** 1:30 Sa, Su (mid Sep-mid May)! **Sculpture Garden**
Permanent Collection: GRECO/ROMAN; AF; AN/EGT; ASIA; MESOPOTAMIA; MESOAMERICAN; POLYNESIAN; AMERICAS

Dedicated to the understanding of the history and cultural heritage of humankind, the museum's galleries include objects from China, Ancient Egypt, Mesoamerica, South America, North America (Plains Indians), Polynesia, Africa, and the Greco Roman world. **NOT TO BE MISSED:** Bull headed lyre, gold, lapis lazuli, shell on wooden construction; Ur, Iraq ca. 2650-2550 B.C.

ON EXHIBIT 2000
ONGOING TIME AND RULERS AT TIKAL: ARCHITECTURAL SCULPTURE OF THE MAYA

ONGOING ANCIENT MESOPOTAMIA: THE ROYAL TOMBS OF UR

ONGOING THE EGYPTIAN MUMMY: SECRETS AND SCIENCE

ONGOING RAVEN'S JOURNEY: THE WORLD OF ALASKA'S NATIVE PEOPLE

ONGOING BUDDHISM: HISTORY AND DIVERSITY OF A GREAT TRADITION

10/10/1999 to 10/01/2000 POMO INDIAN BASKET WEAVERS: THEIR BASKETS AND THE ART MARKET
125 superb examples of turn-of-the-century California Pomo basketry looks at the complex relationship of between art, artist and society, tradition and change and the outside market forces which influenced the Native American traditions in the 19th and 20th centuries.

04/2000 CELEBRITY EYES IN A MUSEUM STOREROOM (tentative title)
In celebration of the millennium and the groundbreaking for the new Culture storage and Study Wing, international celebrities from diverse fields were invited to visit. Included are Kevin Bacon, actor[Robert Runcie, 102nd Archbishop of Canterbury and Maha Chakri Sirindhorn, Princess of Thailand.

09/18/2000 to 01/02/2000 ODUNDE: AFRICAN AMERICAN FESTIVAL
One of the oldest African American street festivals in the country is the subject of 30 photographs by Thomas Morton. The festival began in 1975. Odunde means Happy New Year in Yoruba language of Nigeria. The Dancers, drummers and performers all visit Oshin, a Yuroba river goddess in a procession to the Schuylkill River to make fruit and flower offerings.

PENNSYLVANIA

Woodmere Art Museum
9201 Germantown Ave, Philadelphia, PA 19118
📞: 215-247-0476
Open: 10-5 Tu-Sa, 1-5 Su   **Closed:** Mo, 1/1, EASTER, 7/4, THGV, 12/25
ADM: **Adult:** $5.00   **Children:** Free under 12   **Students:** $3.00   **Seniors:** $3.00
♿ ℗ Free   **Museum Shop   Group Tours**
Permanent Collection: AM: ptgs 19,20, prints, gr, drgs; EU (not always on view()

The Woodmere Art Museum, located in a mid 1850's Victorian eclectic house, includes a large rotunda gallery. The collection of local, Philadelphia area and Pennsylvania Impressionist art is outstanding. **NOT TO BE MISSED:** Benjamin West's 'The Death of Sir Phillip Sydney'

ON EXHIBIT 2000
11/21/1999 to 01/06/2000   PHILADELPHIA WATER COLOR CLUB ANNUAL
The year 2000 is the 100th anniversary of the Club.

02/20/2000 to 03/26/2000   WOODMERE ART MUSEUM 60TH ANNUAL JURIED EXHIBITION
One of the longest running exhibitions of its kind in the Philadelphia region shows a spectrum of artistic styles and technique.

02/20/2000 to 03/26/2000   60th ANNUAL JURIED EXHIBITION
Hundreds of artists submit their work in hopes of being selected from the world of art or museums.

04/09/2000 to 06/25/2000   DISTINGUISHED COLLECTORS SERIES: THE PERRY OTTENBERG COLLECTION OF ARTHUR B. CARLES ART AND EPHEMERA
A new series focusing on local private collectors who share the Museum's keen interest in preserving, promoting and praising the artistic heritage of Philadelphia.

04/09/2000 to 06/25/2000   ARTHUR B. CARLES & STUDENTS
Carles was a talent both as an artist and a teacher. The exhibit was assembled by the Hollis Taggart Galleries

07/09/2000 to 08/29/2000   ANNUAL MEMBER'S EXHIBITION
A museum tradition since 1940, each member is invited to submit a work of art made during the last year. Hundreds participate!

09/10/2000 to 01/28/2001   WOMEN IN THE HISTORY OF PHILIDELPHIA FINE ARTS: AN HISTORICAL SURVEY
An ambitious survey using works from the collection as well as loans, of the work of women artists throughout the history of Philadelphia.

Spring/2001   ROBERT VENTURI: MOTHER'S HOUSE
Venturi is one of the world's most esteemed architects. Featured will be preliminary models and drawings for his mother's Chestnut Hill home.

PITTSBURGH

Andy Warhol Museum
417 Sandusky Street, Pittsburgh, PA 15212-5890
📞: 412-237-8300 ◉ www.warhol.org/warhol
Open: 11-6 We, Su, 11-8 Th-Sa
ADM: **Adult:** $6.00   **Children:** $4.00   **Students:** $4.00   **Seniors:** $5.00
♿ ℗ 2 pay lots adjacent to the museum (nominal fee charged); other pay lots nearby   **Museum Shop**   🍴 Cafe
Group Tours   Historic Building Former Vokwein building renovated by Richard Gluckman Architects
Permanent Collection: ANDY WARHOL ARTWORKS

The most comprehensive single-artist museum in the world, this 7 story museum with over 40,000 square feet of exhibition space permanently highlights artworks spanning every aspect of Warhol's career. A unique feature of this museum is a photo booth where visitors can take cheap multiple pictures of themselves in keeping with the Warhol tradition. **NOT TO BE MISSED:** Rain Machine, a 'daisy waterfall' measuring 132'by 240'; 'Last Supper' paintings; 10' tall 'Big Sculls' series

PENNSYLVANIA

Carnegie Museum of Art
4400 Forbes Ave, Pittsburgh, PA 15213
☎: 412-622-3131 ◙ www.clpgh.org
Open: 10-5 Tu-Sa, 1-5 Su, 10-5 Mo, 10-9 Fr July/Aug only **Closed:** LEG/HOL!
ADM: **Adult:** $6.00 **Children:** $4.00 **Students:** $4.00 **Seniors:** $5.00
⟡ Ⓟ Pay garage **Museum Shop** ⑂ cafe open weekdays; coffee bar daily
Group Tours: 412-622-3289 **Drop-In Tours:** 1:30 Tu-Sa, 3 Su **Historic Building** **Sculpture Garden**
Permanent Collection: FR/IMPR: ptgs; POST/IMPR: ptgs; AM: ptgs 19,20; AB/IMPR; VIDEO ART

The original 1895 Carnegie Institute, created in the spirit of opulence by architects Longfellow, Alden and Harlowe, was designed to house a library with art galleries, the museum itself, and a concert hall. A stunning light filled modern addition offers a spare purity that enhances the enjoyment of the art on the walls. **NOT TO BE MISSED:** Claude Monet's 'Nympheas' (Water Lilies)

Frick Art Museum
7227 Reynolds Street, Pittsburgh, PA 1520821
☎: 412-371-0600
Open: 10-5:30 Tu-Sa, 12-6 Su **Closed:** LEG/HOL!
⟡ Ⓟ Free **Museum Shop** **Group Tours:** 412-371-0600, ext. 158 **Drop-In Tours:** We, Sa, Su 2pm
Permanent Collection: EARLY IT/REN: ptgs; FR & FLEM: 17; BRIT: ptgs; DEC/ART

The Frick Art Museum features a permanent collection of European paintings, sculptures and decorative objects and temporary exhibitions from around the world.

Clayton House: Admission, Adults $6.00, Seniors $5.00, Students $4.00
Car and Carriage Museum: Adults $4.00, Seniors $3.00, Students $2.00Combination admission Adults $7.00, Seniors $6.00, Students $5.00

Hunt Institute for Botanical Documentation
Affiliate Institution: Carnegie Mellon University
Pittsburgh, PA 15213-3890
☎: 412-268-2440 ◙ www.huntbot.andrew.cmu.edu/HIBD
Open: 9-12 & 1-5 Mo-Fr **Closed:** Sa, Su, LEG/HOL!,12/24-1/1
⟡ Ⓟ Pay parking nearby **Museum Shop**
Permanent Collection: BOTANICAL W/COL 15-20; DRGS; GR

30,000 botanical watercolors, drawings and prints from the Renaissance onward represented in this collection.

ON EXHIBIT 2000
09/16/1999 to 02/29/2000 INDIAN TREES: PAINTINGS BY ARUNDHATI VARTAK
Working in Mumbai and Pune, Vartak has devoted herself to painting portraits of common Indian trees in a most distinctive style. About 40 sketches will be shown as part of "The Year of South Asia". *Catalog*

Spring/2000 JOHN MATYAS "IN THE REALM OF EDEN"
Watercolors of the Costa Rican rainforest.

Fall/2000 to Winter/2000 WINTER SHOW–CHARLES PITCHER'S TREES, RICHARD CARROLL'S FOREST LITTER AND OTHER PAINTINGS OF COLORED LEAVES, ETC
The beauty of the season will be displayed.

04/2000 to 07/2000 CHELSEA PHYSIC GARDEN FLORILEGIUM SOCIETY
Botanical paintings by members of the society.

PENNSYLVANIA

Mattress Factory Ltd
500 Sampsonia Way, satellite bldg at 1414 Monterey, Pittsburgh, PA 15212
☎: 412-231-3169 ▣ www.mattress.org
Open: 10-5 Tu-Sa, 1-5 Su (Sep-Jul by appt) **Closed:** Mo, /1, EASTER, LEG/HOL
Free Day: Th **Sugg/Cont:** **ADM:** Adult: $4.00 **Students:** $3.00 **Seniors:** $3.00
♿ Ⓟ **Museum Shop**
Group Tours
Historic Building **Sculpture Garden**
Permanent Collection: Site-specific art installations completed in residency

A museum of contemporary art that commissions, collects and exhibits site-specific art installations. Founded in 1977 in a six story warehouse in the historic Mexican War Streets of Pittsburgh's North Side. **NOT TO BE MISSED:** Yayoi Kusama, "Repetitive Vision" 1997 and James Torrrell: permanent installations

ON EXHIBIT 2000
10/31/1999 to 07/31/2000 MATTRESS FACTORY 2000: NEW INSTALLATIONS BY ASIAN ARTISTS

10/2000 NEW WORKS PRODUCED IN RESIDENCE BY ARTISTS WORKING WITH SOUND

READING

Freedman Gallery
Affiliate Institution: Albright College
Center for the Arts, 13th and Bern Streets, Reading, PA 19604
☎: 610-921-2381
Open: 12-8 Tu; 12-6 We-Fr, 12-4 Sa, Su; Summer 12-4 We-Su **Closed:** Mo, LEG/HOL!, ACAD! Summer Mo, Tu
♿ Ⓟ
Group Tours: 610-921-7541
Permanent Collection: CONT: gr, ptgs

The only gallery in Southeastern Pennsylvania outside of Philadelphia that presents an on-going program of provocative work by today's leading artists. **NOT TO BE MISSED:** Mary Miss Sculpture creates an outdoor plaza which is part of the building

SCRANTON

Everhart Museum
1901 Mulberry Street, Nay Aug Park, Scranton, PA 18510
☎: 717-346-7186 ▣ http://everhart-museum.org/
Open: 12-5 daily, 12-8 Th 4/1-10/12, 12-5 We-Su 12-8 Th 10/13-3/30 **Closed:** THGV, 12/25
Sugg/Cont: **ADM:** Adult: $3.00 **Children:** $1.00, Free under 6 **Seniors:** $2.00
♿ Ⓟ **Museum Shop**
Group Tours **Drop-In Tours:** by appt
Permanent Collection: AM: early 19,20; WORKS ON PAPER; AM: folk, gr; AF; Glass; Nat/Hist

This art, science, and natural history museum is the only wide-ranging museum of its type in Northeastern Pennsylvania.

UNIVERSITY PARK

Palmer Museum of Art
Affiliate Institution: The Pennsylvania State University
Curtin Road, University Park, PA 16802-2507
☎: 814-865-8608 ◙ weww.psu.edu/dept/palmermuseum
Open: 10-4:30 Tu-Sa, 12-4 Su **Closed:** Mo, LEG/HOL!, 12/25-1/1
Vol/Cont:
& ℗ Limited meter, nearby pay **Museum Shop** ‖: Java Market next door
Group Tours: 814-865-7672 **Drop-In Tours Sculpture Garden**
Permanent Collection: AM; EU; AS; S/AM: ptgs, sculp, works on paper, ceramics

A dramatic and exciting new facility for this collection of 35 centuries of artworks. **NOT TO BE MISSED:** The building by Charles Moore, a fine example of post-modern architecture

ON EXHIBIT 2000
01/04/2000 to 03/05/2000 **PSU COLLECTS WPA**

03/14/2000 to 06/11/2000 **ANDY WARHOL: COWBOYS AND INDIANS**

06/27/2000 to 09/11/2000 **ABE AJAY: CONSTRUCTIONS AND COLLAGES**

09/19/2000 to 01/03/2001 **AN INTERLUDE AT GIVERNY: THE FRENCH CHEVALIER BY FREDERICK MACMONNIES**

10/10/2000 to 12/10/2000 **OLD MASTER DRAWINGS FROM THE COLLECTION OF ALFRED MOIR**

20/06/2000 to 06/04/2000 **SEYMOUR LIPTON: AN AMERICAN SCULPTOR**

VALLEY FORGE

Wharton Esherick Museum
Horseshoe Trail, Valley Forge, PA 19301
☎: 610-644-5822
Open: 10-4 Mo-Fr, 10-5 Sa, 1-5 Su, (Mar-Dec) **Closed:** LEG/HOL!
ADM: Adult: $6.00 **Children:** $3.00 under 12 **Seniors:** $6.00
& ℗ **Museum Shop Group Tours Drop-In Tours:** Hourly, (reservations required) **Historic Building**
Permanent Collection: WOOD SCULP; FURNITURE; WOODCUTS; PTGS

Over 200 works in all media, produced between 1920-1970 which display the progression of Esherick's work are housed in his historic studio and residence. **NOT TO BE MISSED:** Oak spiral stairs

WILKES-BARRE

Sordoni Art Gallery
Affiliate Institution: Wilkes University
150 S. River Street, Wilkes-Barre, PA 18766-0001
☎: 717-408-4325
Open: 12-5 daily **Closed:** LEG/HOL!
& ℗
Permanent Collection: AM: ptgs 19,20; WORKS ON PAPER

Located on the grounds of Wilkes University, in the historic district of downtown Wilkes-Barre, this facility is best known for mounting both historical and contemporary exhibitions.

RHODE ISLAND

Fine Arts Center Galleries, University of Rhode Island
105 Upper College Road, Suite 1, Kingston, RI 02881-0820
☎: 401-874-2775 or 2131
Open: Main Gallery 12-4 & 7:30-9:30 Tu-Fr, 1-4 Sa, Su, Phot Gallery 12-4 Tu-Fr, 1-4 Sa, Su   **Closed:** LEG/HOL!; ACAD!
 ♿ Ⓟ   **Group Tours   Drop-In Tours**: !
Permanent Collection: non-collecting institution

A university affiliated 'kunsthalle' distinguished for the activity of their programming (20-25 exhibitions annually) and in generating that programming internally. Contemporary exhibitions in all media are shown as well as film and video showings. The Corridor Gallery is open from 9-9 daily.

Newport Art Museum
76 Bellevue Avenue, Newport, RI 02840
☎: 401-848-8200
Open: 10-4 Mo-Sa, 12-4 Su (Col Day-Mem Day Mo-Sa, 12-5 Su)   **Closed:** THGV, 12/25, 1/1
Free Day: Sa 10-12   **ADM: Adult:** $4.00   **Children:** Free under 5   **Students:** $2.00   **Seniors:** $3.00
 ♿ Ⓟ   **Museum Shop**
Group Tours: by appt   **Drop-In Tours**: Sa, Su aft !   **Historic Building**
Permanent Collection: AM: w/col 19,20

Historic J. N. A. Griswold House in which the museum is located was designed by Richard Morris Hunt in 1862-1864.

Redwood Library and Athenaeum
50 Bellevue Avenue, Newport, RI 02840
☎: 401-847-0292   ▣   www.redwood1747.org
Open: 9:30-5:30 Mo, Fr Sa, Tu, Th 9:30-8, 1-5 Su   **Closed:** LEG/HOL!
 ♿ Ⓟ
Group Tours   Drop-In Tours: 1:30 &3:30 We; 1:30 Su   **Historic Building**
Permanent Collection: AM: gr, drgs, phot, portraits, furniture, dec/art 18,19

Established in 1747, this facility serves as the oldest circulating library in the country. Designed by Peter Harrison, considered America's first architect, it is the most significant surviving public building from the Colonial period. **NOT TO BE MISSED:** Paintings by Gilbert Stuart and Charles Bird King

David Winton Bell Gallery
Affiliate Institution: Brown University
List Art Center, 64 College Street, Providence, RI 02912
☎: 401-863-2932   ▣   www.brown.cav/facilities/david-winton-bell-gallery
Open: 11-4 Mo-Fr., 1-4 Sa-Su   **Closed:** 1/1, THGV, 12/25
 ♿ Ⓟ On-street
Permanent Collection: GR & PHOT 20; WORKS ON PAPER 16-20; CONT: ptgs

Located in the List Art Center, an imposing modern structure designed by Philip Johnson, the Gallery presents exhibitions which focus on the arts and issues of our time.

Rhode Island School of Design Museum
Affiliate Institution: Rhode Island School of Design
224 Benefit Street, Providence, RI 02903

☎: 401-454-6100
Open: 10:30-5 Tu, We, Fr, Sa; 12-8 T; 2-5 Su, Hol; 12-5 We-Sa (6/30-Lab day)   **Closed:** LEG/HOL!
Free Day: Sa   **ADM: Adult:** $2.00   **Children:** $.50 (5-18)   **Students:** $0.50   **Seniors:** $1.00
♿   **Museum Shop**
Group Tours: CATR!   **Sculpture Garden**

The museum's outstanding collections are housed on three levels: in a Georgian style building completed in 1926, in Pendleton House, completed in 1906, and in The Daphne Farago Wing, a center dedicated to the display and interpretation of contemporary art in all media. **NOT TO BE MISSED:** "Mantled Figure" 1993

ON EXHIBIT 2000
ONGOING   THE CENTER CANNOT HOLD: ART FROM 1900 TO 1920
This inaugural exhibition of a new suite of galleries includes paintings, sculptures, drawings, decorative arts, and textiles devoted to art of the 20th-century. Among the treasure trove are paintings by Picasso, Braque and Matisse.

ONGOING   FOCUS ON FORM: AMERICAN FURNITURE FROM THE MUSEUM'S COLLECTION
While Pendleton House is closed for renovation, over 100 selections of furniture and paintings will be on view in the Main Gallery. The works will be arranged in groups of similar forms (desks, chests of drawers, tables, etc.) on two-tiered platforms and combined with a frieze of paintings and chairs hung on the walls overhead.

Rhode Island Black Heritage Society
202 Washington Street, Providence, RI 02903

☎: 401-751-3490
Open: 10-5 Mo-Fr, 10-2 Sa & by appt   **Closed:** LEG/HOL!
♿ Ⓟ on street and nearby pay garages   **Museum Shop**
Permanent Collection: PHOT; AF: historical collection

The Society collects documents and preserves the history of African-Americans in the state of Rhode Island with an archival collection which includes photos, rare books, and records dating back to the 18th century. **NOT TO BE MISSED:** Polychrome relief wood carvings by Elizabeth N. Prophet

SOUTH CAROLINA

CHARLESTON

City Hall Council Chamber Gallery
Broad & Meeting Streets, Charleston, SC 29401

☎: 803-724-3799
Open: 9-5 Mo-Fr, closed 12-1   **Closed:** LEG/HOL!
Vol/Cont:
&
Group Tours   Drop-In Tours: 9-5 (closed 12-1)
Historic Building
Permanent Collection: AM: ptgs 18,19

What is today Charleston's City Hall was erected in 1801 in Adamsesque style to be the Charleston branch of the First Bank of the United States. **NOT TO BE MISSED:** 'George Washington', by John Trumbull is unlike any other and is considered one of the best portraits ever done of him.

Gibbes Museum of Art
135 Meeting Street, Charleston, SC 29401

☎: 843-722-2706   ▣ www.gibbes.com
Open: 10-5 Tu-Sa, 1-5 Su   **Closed:** Mo LEG/HOL!
ADM: Adult: $6.00   **Children:** $4.00   **Students:** $5.00   **Seniors:** $5.00
&   ℗ Municipal   **Museum Shop**
Group Tours   Drop-In Tours: 1st We of month at 2:30pm
Historic Building   Sculpture Garden
Permanent Collection: AM: reg portraits, miniature portraits; JAP: gr

Charleston's only fine arts museum offers a nationally significant collection of American art, American Renaissance period (1920's-40's) room interiors done in miniature scale, and a miniature portrait collection, the oldest and finest in the country. **NOT TO BE MISSED:** 'John Moultie and Family' ca 1782 by John, Francis Rigaud

ON EXHIBIT 2000
11/23/1999 to 01/30/2000   THE CHARLESTON RENAISSANCE
Inspired by the city's rich cultural heritage a group of artists and writers undertook a cultural renewal. It fostered civic pride and the Charleston dramatic cultural renewal.

03/31/2000 to 06/11/2000   AUDUBON
Audubon is known today for his "Birds in America: Their exquisite color, elaborate detail and fine sense of design lend distinctive personal quality to his art.

07/02/2000 to 09/10/2000   THE ASHEPON, COMBAHEE AND EDISTO RIVERS
The rice planters who cultivated land along the landscape of the low country rivers provide inspiration for this exhibit.

09/29/2000 to 12/31/2000   HENRY BENBRIDGE AND COLONIAL CHARLESTON (signature series)
Paintings and miniatures created by this portrait painter look at artists and their connection to Charleston and the Southeast.

09/29/2000 to 12/31/2000   COMMUNION OF SPIRITS: AFRICAN-AMERICAN QUILTERS, PRESERVERS, AND THEIR STORIES.
More than 20 years of Freeman's documentation of African American quilt makers . The scope of the exhibition is both national and inclusive. Tracing it from its Southern roots.

332

COLUMBIA

Columbia Museum of Arts
Main at Hampton, Columbia, SC 29202
☎: 803-799-2810 ◙ www.colmusart.org
Open: 10-5 Tu-Fr, 10-9 We, 10-5 Sa, 1-5 Su **Closed:** Mo, 1/1, Mem/Day, 7/4, LAB/DAY, THGV, 12/24, 12/25
Free Day: 1st Sa each month **ADM: Adult:** $4.00 **Children:** Free under 6 **Students:** $2.00 **Seniors:** $2.00
& Ⓟ **Museum Shop**
Group Tours Drop-In Tours: Su, 2-3, We eve, Th, 12-15-1!
Permanent Collection: KRESS COLL OF MED, BAROQUE & REN; AS; REG

The museum emphasizes a broad spectrum of European and American fine arts dating from the 145th C to the present. It also has one of the Southeast's most important collections of Italian Renaissance and Baroque paintings, sculpture and decorative art by the Old Masters.

ON EXHIBIT 2000
01/22/2000 to 03/19/2000   THE CECIL FAMILY COLLECTS: FOUR CENTURIES OF DECORATIVE ARTS FROM BURGHLEY HOUSE
Burghley House is one of the oldest and grandest Elizabethan houses in England. The 120 crafted works from its collection will document the evolution of taste and collecting in Britain in the course of four centuries. *Catalog Will Travel*

FLORENCE

Florence Museum of Art, Science & History
558 Spruce Street, Florence, SC 29501
☎: 843–662-3351
Open: 10-5 Tu-Sa, 2-5 Su **Closed:** Mo, LEG HOL
& Ⓟ **Museum Shop**
Group Tours Drop-In Tours   Historic Building
Permanent Collection: AM/REG: ptgs; SW NAT/AM; pottery; CER

Founded to promote the arts and sciences, this museum, located in a 1939 art deco style building originally constructed as a private home, is surrounded by the grounds of Timrod Park. **NOT TO BE MISSED:** 'Francis Marion Crossing to Pee Dee', by Edward Arnold

ON EXHIBIT 2000
Spring/2000   SPECIAL EXHIBIT OF COMPUTER ART

GREENVILLE

Bob Jones University Collection of Sacred Art
Jones University, Greenville, SC 29614
☎: 864-242-5100 ◙ www.bju.edu/artgallery/
Open: 2-5 Tu-Su **Closed:** Mo, 1/1, 7/4, 12/20 thru 12/25, Commencement Day (early May)
ADM: Adult: $5.00 **Children:** Free 6-12, under 6 not admitted **Students:** Free
& Ⓟ Nearby **Museum Shop**
Group Tours: ext 1050
Permanent Collection: EU: ptgs including Rembrandt, Tintoretto, Titian Veronese, Sebastiano del Piombo

One of the finest collections of religious art in America.

SOUTH CAROLINA

Greenville County Museum of Art
420 College Street, Greenville, SC 29601

☎: 864-271-7570 ◙ www.greenvillemuseum.org
Open: 10-5 Tu-Sa, 1-5 Su **Closed:** Mo, LEG/HOL!
Vol/Cont:
   ⑤ ⑫ **Museum Shop Group Tours**
Permanent Collection: AM: ptgs, sculp, gr; REG

The Southern Collection is nationally recognized as one of the countries best regional collections. It provides a survey of American art history from 1726 to the present through works of art that relate to the South. The Museum resettle acquired 24 watercolors by Andrew Wyeth which the artist described as one of the best collections of his watercolors in any public museum in this country.

ON EXHIBIT 2000
ONGOING PHOTOGRAPHS FROM THE MUSEUM COLLECTION

ONGOING NEW WORLDS: TWO HUNDRED YEARS OF REALISM FROM THE MUSEUM COLLECTION

ONGOING STEPHEN SCOTT YOUNG: A PORTRAIT OF GREENVILLE

ONGOING ANDREW WYETH: THE GREENVILLE COLLECTION

02/16/2000 to 04/30/2000 JACK SPENCER
A self taught photographer whose sepia toned photos capture people and landscapes of the deep south which seem to have been undisturbed by progress.

03/01/2000 to 05/21/2000 YOUNG AMERICA: TREASURES FROM THE SMITHSONIAN'S MUSEUM OF AMERICAN ART
54 works by the era's most famous artists, trace the transformation of the colonies into nationhood from the 1760s to the Civil War. Includes portraits by Gilbert Stuart, Charles Willson Peale; paintings by Benjamin West, Washington Allston; landscapes by Thomas Cole, Alvan Fisher; genre paintings by John Quidor, Lily Martin Spencer. Hudson River School landscapes by Asher B. Durand, Frederic E. Church. Sculptures by Horatio Greenough, Hiram Powers. Civil War era paintings by Samuel Colman, Homer Dodge Martin. *Catalog Will Travel*

04/07/2000 to 06/04/2000 LEWIS WICKES HINE: THE FINAL YEARS
These 169 photographs were given to the Museum by Hine in 1979 and have never been shown to the public. They show the oeuvre for the first time of the last years of one of America's most important photographers and a seminal figure in the history of the medium. *Will Travel*

MURRELLS INLET

Brookgreen Gardens
1931 Brookgreen Gardens Drive, Murrells Inlet, SC 29576

☎: 803-237-4218
Open: 9:30-4:45 daily, ! for summer hours **Closed:** 12/25
ADM: Adult: $7.50 **Children:** $3.00 6-12 **Students:** $7.50 **Seniors:** $7.50
   ⑤ ⑫ **Museum Shop** ¶: Terrace Cafe open year round
Group Tours: 800-849-1931 **Drop-In Tours:** ! seasonal **Historic Building Sculpture Garden**
Permanent Collection: AM: sculp 19,20

The first public sculpture garden created in America is located on the grounds of a 200-year old rice plantation. It is the largest permanent outdoor collection of American Figurative Sculpture in the world with 542 works by 240 American sculptors on permanent display. **NOT TO BE MISSED:** 'Fountain of the Muses', by Carl Milles

Spartanburg County Museum of Art
385 South Spring Street, Spartanburg, SC 29306

☏: 864-582-7616

Open: 9-5 Mo-Fr, 10-2 Sa, 2-5 Su   **Closed:** LEG/HOL!, EASTER, 12/24

♿ ℗ Adjacent to the building   **Museum Shop**

Group Tours

Permanent Collection: AM/REG: ptgs, gr, dec/art

A multi-cultural Arts Center that presents 20 exhibits of regional art each year. **NOT TO BE MISSED:** 'Girl With The Red Hair', by Robert Henri

ON EXHIBIT 2000

11/29/1999 to 01/02/2000   GROUP LANDSCAPE SHOW

Stephen Chesley, William Jamison, Marshall McCAll. Margaret McCann (oils with Roman theme), holiday invitational of local artists.

SOUTH DAKOTA

South Dakota Art Museum

Medary Ave at Harvey Dunn Street, Brookings, SD 57007-0899

☎: 605-688-5423

Open: 8-5 Mo-Fr, 10-5 Sa, 1-5 Su, Holidays   **Closed:** 1/1, THGV, 12/25

♿ Ⓟ   **Museum Shop**

Group Tours   Sculpture Garden

Permanent Collection: HARVEY DUNN: ptgs; OSCAR HOWE: ptgs; NAT/AM; REG 19, 20

Many of the state's art treasures including the paintings by Harvey Dunn of pioneer life on the prairie, a complete set of Marghab embroidery from Madeira, outstanding paintings by regional artist Oscar Howe, and masterpieces from all the Sioux tribes are displayed in the 6 galleries of this museum established in 1970.

Friends of the Middle Border Museum of American Indian and Pioneer Life

1311 S. Duff St., PO Box 1071, Mitchell, SD 57301

☎: 605-996-2122

Open: 8-6 Mo-Sa & 10-6 S (Jun-Aug), 9-5 Mo-Fr & 1-5 Sa,S (May-Sep), by appt(Oct-Apr)   **Closed:** 1/1, THGV, 12/25

ADM: Adult: $3.00   **Children:** Free under 12   **Seniors:** $2.00

♿ Ⓟ   **Museum Shop**

Group Tours

Historic Building   Sculpture Garden

Permanent Collection: AM: ptgs 19,20; NAT/AM

This Museum of American Indian and Pioneer life also has an eclectic art collection in the Case Art Gallery, the oldest regional art gallery including works by Harvey Dunn, James Earle Fraser, Gutzon Borglum, Oscar Howe, Childe Hassam, Charles Hargens, Anna Hyatt Huntington and many others. **NOT TO BE MISSED:** Fraser's 'End of the Trail' and Lewis and Clark Statues

Oscar Howe Art Center

119 W. Third, Mitchell, SD 57301

☎: 605-996-4111

Open: 9-5 Mo-Sa   **Closed:** Su, LEG/HOL!

Vol/Cont: **ADM: Adult:** $2.50   **Children:** $1.00   **Seniors:** $2.00

♿ Ⓟ   **Museum Shop**

Group Tours: 605-996-4111   **Drop-In Tours:** Upon request   **Historic Building**

Permanent Collection: OSCAR HOWE: ptgs, gr

Housed in a beautifully restored 1902 Carnegie Library, the Oscar Howe Art Center displays both a collection of work by Yanktonai Sioux artist Oscar How and rotating exhibits of work by regional artists. **NOT TO BE MISSED:** 'Sun and Rain Clouds Over Hills', dome mural painted by Oscar Howe in 1940 as a WPA project (Works Progress Administration)

PINE RIDGE

Heritage Center Inc
Affiliate Institution: Red Cloud Indian School
Pine Ridge, SD 57770
☎: 605-867-5491 ◉ www.basic.net/rcheritaqe
Open: 9-5 Mo-Fr **Closed:** Sa, S, EASTER, THGV, 12/25
& ℗ **Museum Shop Group Tours Historic Building**
Permanent Collection: CONT NAT/AM; GR; NW COAST; ESKIMO: 19,20

The Center is located on the Red Cloud Indian school campus in an historic 1888 building built by the Sioux and operated by them with the Franciscan sisters. The Holy Rosary Mission church built in 1998 has stained glass windows designed by the students.

RAPID CITY

Dahl Fine Arts Center
713 Seventh Street, Rapid City, SD 57701
☎: 605-394-4101 ◉ http://blackhills-info.com/dahl/
Open: 9-5 Mo-Sa, 1-5 S (winter), 9-7 Mo-Th, 9-5 Fr, Sa, 1-5 Su (summer) **Closed:** LEG/HOL!
& ℗ Metered **Museum Shop**
Group Tours
Permanent Collection: CONT; REG: ptgs; gr 20

The Dahl presents a forum for all types of fine arts: visual, theatre, and music, that serve the Black Hills region, eastern Wyoming, Montana, and Western Nebraska. **NOT TO BE MISSED:** 200 foot cyclorama depicting the history of the US.

ON EXHIBIT 2000
01/09/2000 to 03/05/2000 UNIQUE AMERICAN VISIONS: THE PAINTINGS OF GREGORY GILLESPIE

02/17/2000 to 04/14/2000 A CERAMIC CONTINUUM: FIFTY YEARS OF THE ARCHIE BRAY INFLUENCE
The contribution of the Archie Bray Foundation for Ceramic Art to its residency program and ceramic art showing 85 works.

03/19/2000 to 04/30/2000 GEORGE DEGROAT

09/24/2000 to 11/05/2000 DANIEL STOLPE

Sioux Indian Museum
222 New York Street, Rapid City, SD 57701
☎: 605-394-2381 ◉ www.sdsmt.edu/journey
Open: 8-7daily summer; 10-4 Mo-Sa, 11-4 Su winter **Closed:** 1/1, THGV, 12/25
Vol/Cont see web site!
& ℗ **Museum Shop**
Group Tours: 605-394-6923
Permanent Collection: SIOUX ARTS

The rich diversity of historic and contemporary Sioux art may be enjoyed in the Journey Museum, location of the Sioux Indian Museum. This museum with rotating exhibitions, and interactive displays dramatically reveal the geography, people and historical events that shaped the history and heritage of the Black Hills area. **NOT TO BE MISSED:** THE JOURNEY, Black Hills History thru sight, sound and touch

SOUTH DAKOTA

Washington Pavilion of Arts and Sciences
Affiliate Institution: Visual Arts Center
235 West Tenth Street, Sioux Falls, SD 57102
☎: 605-367-7397 ◙ www.washingtoonpavillion.orgsiouxfalls.org/members/cfa
Open: 9-5 Mo-Sa, 1-5 Su & HOL **Closed:** THGV, 12/25
& ℗ **Museum Shop** ⁌ **Group Tours**: ext 2319 Drop-In Tours **Historic Building Sculpture Garden**
Permanent Collection: REG/ART: all media

Opening in June 1999 is the 250,000 square foot Washington Pavilion of the Arts and Science featuring the Visual Arts Center, Kirby Science Discovery Center, Wells Fargo CineDome and the Husby Performing Arts Center

ON EXHIBIT 2000
02/11/2000 to 04/06/2000 HOT AND COOL CONTEMPORARY GLASS WORKS
The last 35 years have ushered in great changes in production and perception. This exhibit emphasizes the new techniques.

Tekakwitha Fine Arts Center
401 South 8th Street W., Sisseton, SD 57262
☎: 605-698-7058 ◙ http://swcc.cc.sd.us/tek.htm
Open: 10-4 daily (Mem day-Lab day),10-4 Tu-Fr & 12:30-4 Sa-Su (mid Sep-mid May) **Closed:** LEG/HOL!
& ℗ **Museum Shop**
Group Tours
Permanent Collection: TWO DIMENSIONAL ART OF LAKE TRAVERSE DAKOTA SIOUX RESERVATION

It is the vision that the Tekakwitha Fine Arts Center at Sisseton, South Dakota, be a gathering place and a bridge to all cultures. The effort at Tekakwitha is to provide a respectful presence in which both the visitor and the paintings, drawings and sketches can be comfortable and to make their statement in peace. This unique collection of visual art was created by Native American artists, who at the time the works were created, were residents of the triangle shaped Lake Traverse Dakotah Sioux Reservation. Of the 37 artists whose works are included in the permanent collection, only one was not of the Dakotah

University Art Galleries
Affiliate Institution: University of South Dakota
Warren M. Lee Center, 414 E. Clark Street, Vermillion, SD 57069-2390
☎: 605-677-5481 ◙ http://www.usd.edu/cfa/Art/gallery.html
Open: 10-4 Mo-Fr, 1-5 Sa, Su **Closed:** ACAD!
& ℗ **Group Tours**: 605-677-5481
Permanent Collection: Sioux artist OSCAR HOWE; HIST REG/ART

The University Art Galleries, established in 1976, exists in recognition of a commitment to the visual arts which may be traced to the founding of the University in 1862. The University Art Galleries' major purpose is to support the formal educational process of the University, but its impact extends beyond the academic community to serve artists and audiences in South Dakota and the region. The University Art Galleries is responsible for the operation of the Main Gallery, Gallery 110, several on-campus exhibition spaces, the University Permanent Collection, the Campus Beautification Project, and a touring exhibition program.

338

CHATTANOOGA

Hunter Museum of American Art
10 Bluff View, Chattanooga, TN 37403-1197
☎: 423-267-0968 ◉ www.huntermuseum.org
Open: 10-4:30 Tu-Sa, 1-4:30 Su **Closed:** Mo, LEG/HOL!
Free Day: 1st F of month **ADM:** **Adult:** $5.00 **Children:** $2.50, 3-12 **Students:** $3.00 **Seniors:** $4.00
 ᕦ ℗ **Museum Shop** **Group Tours** **Drop-In Tours** **Historic Building** **Sculpture Garden**
Permanent Collection: AM: ptgs, gr, sculp, 18-20

Blending the old and the new, the Hunter Museum consists of a recently restored 1904 mansion with a 1975 contemporary addition.

ON EXHIBIT 2000
03/04/1999 to 04/16/2000   HARVEY LITTLETON: REFLECTIONS 1946-1994 *Will Travel*

12/04/1999 to 01/30/2000   HELEN FRANKENTHALER, TALES OF THE GENJI

12/11/1999 to 02/06/2000   LARGE DRAWINGS
40 of the best examples in the collection are divided in two sections: "Structural Foundations of Clarity" and "Expressive Voices of the Meaningful". In addition to the traditional drawing media works on paper represent acrylic and oil and incorporate collage, photography and printmaking. Artists include Barnet, Stackhouse, Sultan and Wesselmann.

01/08/2000 to 02/20/2000   IRV GINSBURG

02/12/2000 to 04/02/2000   NORTHWEST PASSAGE: PHOTOGRAPHS BY ROBERT GLENN KETCHUM

03/04/2000 to 04/16/2000   HARVEY LITTLETON: REFLECTIONS 1946-1994 *Will Travel*

04/2000   ARTSCENE

04/15/2000 to 06/04/2000   CESSNA AND ELIZABETH DECOSIMO: SCULPTURE

04/29/2000 to 06/11/2000   BARRY MOSER: ILLUSTRATIONS FOR THE BIBLE (working title)

05/2000   ARTSTRVAGANZA

06/2000   SUMMER EXHIBITIONS

06/27/2000 to 08/27/2000   THE GILDED AGE FROM THE NATIONAL MUSEUM OF AMERICAN ART *Will Travel*

09/09/2000 to 10/15/2000   GEORGE CRESS

12/02/2000 to 02/11/2001   MIRIAM SHAPIRO
The first retrospective exhibition of the artist's works on paper. *Will Travel*

KNOXVILLE

Knoxville Museum of Art
1050 World's Fair Park Drive, Knoxville, TN 37916-1653
☎: 615-525-6101 ◉ www.knoxart.org
Open: 10-5 Tu-Th, Sa, 10-9 Fr, 12-5 Su **Closed:** Mo, LEG/HOL!
ADM: **Adult:** $4.00 **Children:** $1 under12,$2,13-17 **Students:** $3.00 **Seniors:** $3.00
 ᕦ ℗ Free parking across the street **Museum Shop** ⑪
Group Tours **Drop-In Tours**: 3pm Su for focus exh.
Permanent Collection: CONT; GR ; AM: 19

Knoxville Museum of Art - continued

Begun in 1961 as the Dulin Gallery of art, located in a ante bellum mansion, the Museum because of its rapidly expanding collection of contemporary American art then moved to the historic Candy Factory. It now occupies a building designed in 1990 by Edward Larabee Barnes. PLEASE NOTE: Some exhibitions have admission charge. **NOT TO BE MISSED:** Historic Candy Factory next door; the nearby Sunsphere, trademark building of the Knoxville Worlds Fair

---

MEMPHIS

Dixon Gallery & Gardens

4339 Park Ave, Memphis, TN 38117

℡: 901-761-5250 ◙ www.dixon.org

Open: 10-5 Tu-Sa, 1-5 Su, Gardens only Mo 1/2 price **Closed:** Mo, LEG/HOL!

Free Day: Th, Seniors only **ADM**: **Adult:** $5.00 **Children:** $1.00 under 12 **Students:** $3.00 **Seniors:** $4.00

♿ Ⓟ Free **Museum Shop**

Group Tours **Drop-In Tours**: !

Historic Building **Sculpture Garden**

Permanent Collection: FR: Impr, 19; GER: cer

Located on 17 acres of woodlands and formal gardens, the Dixon was formerly the home of Hugo and Margaret Dixon, collectors and philanthropists.

Memphis Brooks Museum of Art

Overton Park, 1934 Poplar Ave., Memphis, TN 38104-2765

℡: 901-722-3500 ◙ www.brooksmuseum.org

Open: 9-4 Tu-Fr, 9-8 We during Art in the Evenings, 9-5 Sa, 11:30-5 Su **Closed:** Mo, 1/1, 7/4, THGV (open 10-1), 12/25

Free Day: We (except during "Ancient Gold: Wealth of the Thracians" **ADM**: **Adult:** $5.00 **Children:** $2.00, (7-17) **Students:** $2.00 **Seniors:** $4.00

♿ Ⓟ Free **Museum Shop**

🍴: Brushmark Restaurant; Lunch 11:30-2:30; Cocktails and dinner 5-8, W

Group Tours: 901-722-3515 **Drop-In Tours**: 10:30, 1:30 Sa; 1:30 Su

Historic Building

Permanent Collection: IT/REN, NORTHERN/REN, & BAROQUE: ptgs; BRIT & AM: portraits 18,19; FR/IMPR; AM: modernist

Founded in 1916, the Memphis Brooks Museum of Art is the oldest and largest fine arts museum in the state of Tennessee, housing one of the most outstanding collections of fine art dating from antiquity to the present. Strengths of the collection include Italian Renaissance and Baroque paintings and sculpture, principally gifts of the Kress Foundation, English portraits, European and American paintings, sculpture and decorative arts, and a significant collection of works on paper, including drawings, watercolors, prints and photographs. The Museum also hosts world-class traveling exhibitions and several long-term, continuing loans. **NOT TO BE MISSED:** Global Survey Galleries

ON EXHIBIT 2000

12/12/1999 to 02/13/2000 THE PRINTED WORLD OF PIETER BREUGEL THE ELDER

Although he himself etched only one print (The Rabbit Hunt, 1566) Pieter Breugel the Elder was an artist whose work was transferred into print often in the 16th century.. This exhibition presents a remarkable selection of prints that illustrate the rich and varied imagery of his world. *Catalog Will Travel*

MURFREESBORO

Baldwin Photographic Gallery
Affiliate Institution: Middle Tennessee State University
Learning Resources Center, Murfreesboro, TN 37132
\: 615-898-5628
Open: 8-4:30 Mo-Fr, 8-noon Sa, 6-10pm Su   **Closed:** EASTER, THGV, 12/25
& Ⓟ Free parking 50 yards from gallery
Permanent Collection: CONT: phot

A college museum with major rotating photographic exhibitions.

NASHVILLE

Cheekwood - Tennessee Botanical Garden and Museum of Art
1200 Forrest Park Drive, Nashville, TN 37205-4242
\: 615-356-8000 ◙ www.cheekwood.org
Open: 9-5 Mo-Sa, 11-5 Su (Grounds open 11-5 Su)   **Closed:** 1/1, THGV, 12/25,
ADM: Adult: $8.00   **Children:** $5.00 (6-17)   **Students:** $7.00   **Seniors:** $7.00
& Ⓟ **Museum Shop** ⑪ 11-2   **Group Tours**: 615-353-2155   **Historic Building   Sculpture Garden**
Permanent Collection: AM: ptgs, sculp, dec/art 19-20

One of the leading cultural centers in the South, the Museum of Art is a former mansion built in the 1930s. Located in a luxuriant botanical garden, it retains a charming homelike quality. **NOT TO BE MISSED:** New Contemporary Galleries and Sculpture Garden trail

The Parthenon
Centennial Park, Nashville, TN 37201
\: 615-862-8431 ◙ www.parthenon.org
Open: 9-4:30 Tu-Sa, 12:30-430 Su; (April - Sept Su 12:30-8)   **Closed:** Mo, LEG/HOL!
ADM: Adult: $2.50   **Children:** $1.25, 4-17   **Students:** $1.25   **Seniors:** $1.25
& Ⓟ Free   **Museum Shop**
Group Tours   Drop-In Tours: !   **Historic Building**
Permanent Collection: AM: 19,20; The Cowan Collection

First constructed as the Art Pavilion for the Tennessee Centennial Exposition, in 1897, The Parthenon is the world's only full size reproduction of the 5th century B.C. Greek original complete with the 42 foot statue of Athena Parthenos. **NOT TO BE MISSED:** 'Mt. Tamalpais', by Albert Bierstadt; 'Autumn in the Catskills' by Sanford Gifford

ON EXHIBIT 2000
06/03/2000 to 09/24/2000   WINSLOW HOMER: THE MOVE TOWARD ABSTRACTION

Tennessee State Museum-Polk Culture Center
5th and Deadeick, Nashville, TN 37243-1120
\: 615-741-2692
Open: 10-5 Tu-Sa; 1-5 Su   **Closed:** Mo, 1/1, Easter, THGV, 12/25
& Ⓟ **Museum Shop**

TENNESSEE

Tennessee State Museum-Polk Culture Center - continued

This museum offers a fascinating look at the history of Tennessee, from prehistoric times through the 20th century. Displays include collections of prehistoric Indian artifacts, firearms, silver, quilts, paintings and pottery. There is an extensive collection of Civil War uniforms, battle flags and weapons. You can learn about the long hunters such as Daniel Boone, who hunted in the area beginning in the 1760s, as well as interesting political figures such as Andrew Jackson and Sam Houston.

ON EXHIBIT 2000

PLEASE NOTE: admission charges for some special exhibitions

09/23/1999 to 01/30/2000   PRESERVING OUR STORIES: 150 YEARS OF THE TENNESSEE HISTORICAL SOCIETY
Selected items from the collection. *Will Travel*

11/02/1999 to 02/01/2000   GEORGE WASHINGTON: THE MAN BEHIND THE MYTHS
The Presidents life at Mount Vernon with a large collection of decorative items and letters in his hand.

03/01/2000 to 05/31/2000   COLD WAR-ERA SOVIET ART (not official title)
Beautiful 20th C. landscapes of Russia and Soviet workers.

04/01/2000 to 05/31/2000   CHESTNUT MOUNTAIN: PHOTOGRAPHS BY HOWARD BAKER

06/20/2000 to 08/20/2000   SCENES OF AMERICAN LIFE
65 realist works from the National Museum of American Art including Hopper, Benton, Sloan, Wyeth and others.

09/2000 to 12/2000   BUFFALO BILL'S WILD WEST
Artifacts that chronicle the life of Buffalo Bill and the phenomenon of the Wild West show in America

University Galleries

Affiliate Institution: Fisk University
1000 17th Avenue North, Nashville, TN 37208-3051
☎: 615-329-8720
Open: 9-5 Tu-Fr, 1-5 Sa-Su, summer closed Su   **Closed:** Mo, ACAD!
Vol/Cont:
♿ ⓟ   **Museum Shop   Group Tours   Historic Building**
Permanent Collection: EU; AM; AF/AM: ptgs; AF: sculp

The Museum is housed in an historic (1888) building and in the University library. **NOT TO BE MISSED:** The Alfred Stieglitz Collection of Modern Art

Vanderbilt University Fine Arts Gallery

23rd at West End Ave, Nashville, TN 37203
☎: 615-322-0605   ◙   www.vanderbilt.edu/AnS/finearts/gallery.html
Open: 12-4 Mo-Fr, 1-5 Sa, Su, Summer 12-4 Tu-Fr; 1-5 Sa   **Closed:** Note summer hours ACAD!
ⓟ
Group Tours   Historic Building
Permanent Collection: OR: Harold P. Stern Coll; OM & MODERN: gr (Anna C. Hoyt Coll); CONTINI-VOLTERRA PHOT ARCHIVE; EU: om/ptgs (Kress Study Coll)

The history of world art may be seen in the more than 5,000 works from over 40 countries and cultures housed in this university gallery. Rich in contemporary prints and Oriental art, this historical collection is the only one of its kind in the immediate region. **NOT TO BE MISSED:** 'St. Sebastian', 15th century central Italian tempera on wood

Oak Ridge Arts Center

201 Badger Avenue, Oak Ridge, TN 37830

☎: 423-482-1441

Open: 9-5 Tu-Fr, 1-4 Sa-Mo   **Closed:** LEG/HOL!

Vol/Cont:

♿ Ⓟ

Group Tours   Drop-In Tours

Permanent Collection: AB/EXP: Post WW II

Two galleries with monthly changing exhibitions, educational programming and art lectures. Call for schedule.

TEXAS

Grace Museum, Inc
102 Cypress, Abilene, TX 79601
☎: 915-673-4587
Open: 10-5 Tu, We, Fr, Sa, 10:30 Th, 1-5 Su (closed Su, May 30-Sept 5)   **Closed:** Mo, LEG/HOL!
Free Day: Th -5-8:30   **ADM: Adult:** $3.00   **Children:** $1.00 (4-12)   **Students:** $2.00   **Seniors:** $2.00
 ♿ Ⓟ   **Museum Shop**
Group Tours
Historic Building
Permanent Collection: TEXAS/REG; AM: gr, CONT: gr; ABELINE, TX, & PACIFIC RAILWAY: 18-20

The museums are housed in the 1909 'Mission Revival Style' Railroad Hotel. **NOT TO BE MISSED:** Children's Museum

Old Jail Art Center
Hwy 6 South, Albany, TX 76430
☎: 915-762-2269 ▣ www.albanytexas.com
Open: 10-5 Tu-Sa, 2-5 Su   **Closed:** Mo, LEG/HOL!
 ♿ Ⓟ   **Museum Shop**
Group Tours
Historic Building   **Sculpture Garden**
Permanent Collection: AS, EU, BRIT cont, Mod, P/COL

The Old Jail Art Center is housed partly in a restored 1878 historic jail building with a small annex which opened in 1980 and new wings added in 1984 and 1998 featuring a courtyard, sculpture garden and educational center. **NOT TO BE MISSED:** 'Young Girl With Braids', by Modigliani; 37 Chinese terra cotta tomb figures

ON EXHIBIT 2000
11/27/1999 to 01/16/2000   JEAN CARRUTHERS WETTA: A SURVEY, 1883-98

Amarillo Museum of Art
2200 S. Van Buren, Amarillo, TX 79109
☎: 806-371-5050
Open: 10-5 Tu-Fr, 1-5 Sa, Su   **Closed:** LEG/HOL!
 ♿ Ⓟ
Drop-In Tours: by appt   **Sculpture Garden**
Permanent Collection: CONT AM; ptgs, gr, phot, sculp; JAP gr; SE ASIA sculp,textiles

Opened in 1972, the Amarillo Museum of Art is a visual arts museum featuring exhibitions, art classes, tours and educational programs. The building was designed by Edward Durell Stone.

Arlington Museum of Art
201 West Main St., Arlington, TX 76010

☎: 817-275-4600
Open: 10-5 We-Sa   **Closed:** S, Mo, Tu, LEG/HOL, 12/25-1/2!
Vol/Cont:
 Ġ **Museum Shop** **Group Tours** **Drop-In Tours**: Occasional
Permanent Collection: Non-collecting institution

Texas contemporary art by both emerging and mature talents is featured in this North Texas museum located between the art-rich cities of Fort Worth and Dallas. It has gained a solid reputation for showcasing contemporary art in the six exhibitions it presents annually.

Center for Research in Contemporary Arts
Fine Arts Bldg, Cooper Street, Arlington, TX 76019

☎: 817-273-2790
Open: 10-3 Mo-Th, 1-4 Sa-Su   **Closed:** ACAD!
Ⓟ

Permanent Collection: Non-collecting institution

A University gallery with varied special exhibitions.

Austin Museum of Art-Downtown
823 Congress Avenue, Austin, TX 78701

☎: 512-495-9224   ◙   www.amoa.org
Open: 10-6 Tu-Sa, 10-8 Th, 12-5 Su   **Closed:** Mo, LEG/HOL
ADM: **Adult:** $3.00, $1 day Th   **Children:** Free under 12   **Students:** $2.00   **Seniors:** $2.00
 Ġ **Museum Shop**
Group Tours **Drop-In Tours**: 2 PM Sa during exhibitions
Permanent Collection: AM: ptgs 19, 20; WORKS ON PAPER, photo

An additional facility for the Museum

ON EXHIBIT 2000
11/20/1999 to 01/30/2000   NEW WORKS III: EVE ANDREE LARAMEE
Installations, objects and drawings critiquing the realm of science of this artist.

11/20/1999 to 01/30/2000   ARCHITECTONIC THOUGHT FORMS: A SURVEY OF THE ART OF PAUL LAFFOLLY, 1968–1999
A survey of the work of this visionary painter.

02/12/2000 to 04/30/2000   NEW WORKS IV: BERNARD MAISNER: CONTEMPORARY ILLUMINATED MANUSCRIPTS AND PAINTINGS

02/12/2000 to 04/30/2000   THE LABYRINTH OF MEMORY: GERARDO SUTER
One of Latin America's most important young photographers are shown here.

05/11/2000 to 08/20/2000   LIBERATED VOICES: CONTEMPORARY SOUTH AFRICAN ART SINCE MANDELA
A first major exhibition of the younger generation of South African artists that has emerged.

TEXAS

Austin Museum of Art-Laguna Gloria

3809 W. 35th Street, Austin, TX 78703
📞: 512-458-8191 ◉ www.amo2.org
Open: 10-5 Tu-Sa, 10-8 Th, 1-5 Su **Closed:** Mo, LEG/HOL!
ADM: Adult: $2.00, $1.00 Th **Children:** Free under 16 **Students:** $1.00 **Seniors:** $1.00
& ℗ Free **Museum Shop**
Group Tours: 512-495-9224, ext 224 **Historic Building Sculpture Garden**
Permanent Collection: AM: ptgs 19,20; WORKS ON PAPER, photo

The Museum is Located on the 1916 Driscoll Estate which is listed in the National Register of Historic Places located in Mediterranean style villa on the banks of Lake Austin. PLEASE NOTE: THE GALLERIES AT THE MUSEUM AT LAGUNA GLORIA WILL UNDERGO RESTORATION BEGINNING IN JUNE 2000 **NOT TO BE MISSED:** The beautiful setting.

ON EXHIBIT 2000

AUSTIN MUSEUM OF ART DOWNTOWN
823 Congress Ave. Austin, TX 78701
512-495-9224
Fax: 512-495-9029

01/15/2000 to 03/12/2000 MASTERS OF MATA ORTIZ: POTTERY FROM NORTHWEST MEXICO *Will Travel*

Jack S. Blanton Museum of Art

Affiliate Institution: University of Texas at Austin
Art Bldg 23rd & 21st, Austin, TX 78712
📞: 512-471-7324 ◉ www.utexas.edu/cofa/hag
Open: 9-5 Mo, Tu, We, Fr, 9-9 Th, 1-5 Sa, Su **Closed:** MEM/DAY, LAB/DAY, THGV, XMAS WEEK
& ℗ **Museum Shop**
Group Tours: 512-471-5025 **Drop-In Tours:** !
Permanent Collection: LAT/AM; CONT; GR; DRGS,

The encyclopedic collection of this university gallery, one of the finest and most balanced in the southern US, features an artistic, cultural and historical record of Western European and American Art dating from antiquity to the present. Including 13,000 works spanning the history of western civilization. Please Note: selections from the permanent collection are shown at the Harry Ransom Center (21st and Guadalupe) while temporary exhibitions and the Clark room are in the art building. A current ongoing search for a architectural firm to create a new state of the art building to open in 2002 has reached its final stages. **NOT TO BE MISSED:** The Mari and James A. Michener Collection of 20th c. American Art; C. R. Smith Collection of Western American Art; Contemporary Latin American Collection

ON EXHIBIT 2000

02/19/2000 to 04/09/2000 BLURRING THE BOUNDARIES: INSTALLATION ART 1969-1996
This major traveling exhibition surveys developments in installation art as exemplified by works in the permanent collection of the Museum of Contemporary Art, San Diego.

08/31/2000 to 10/15/2000 LITHOGRAPHS OF JAMES McNEILL WHISTLER from the Collection of Steven Block
The 19th-century British artist James McNeil Whistler created hundreds of poignant portraits and landscapes, much praises for their romantic realism and delicacy of technique.

11/03/2000 to 12/10/2000   THE TEACHING COLLECTION OF MARVIN VEXLER '48: RECENT ACQUISITIONS
This exhibit presents 30 prints from the Renaissance to the 19th Century.

BEAUMONT

Art Museum of Southeast Texas
500 Main Street, Beaumont, TX 77701
☎: 409-832-3432 ◉ www.amset.org
Open: 9-5 Mo-Sa, 12-5 Su **Closed:** LEG/HOL!
&. ℗ Free **Museum Shop** ¶¶
Group Tours Drop-In Tours: We, noon **Sculpture Garden**
Permanent Collection: AM: ptgs, sculp, dec/art, FOLK: 19,20

This new spacious art museum with 4 major galleries and 2 sculpture courtyards is located in downtown Beaumont. **NOT TO BE MISSED:**

COLLEGE STATION

MSC Forsyth Center Galleries
Affiliate Institution: Texas A & M University
Memorial Student Center, Joe Routt Blvd, College Station, TX 77844-9081
☎: 409-845-9251 ◉ www.charlotte.tamu.edu/services/forsyth
Open: 9-8 Mo-Fr, 12-6 Sa-Su, 10-4:30 Mo-Fr, 12-4:30 Sa, Su May-Aug **Closed:** 7/4, THGV, 12/25-1/2
&. ℗ Underground
Group Tours Drop-In Tours: by appt
Permanent Collection: EU, BRIT,& AM; glass; AM: western ptgs

The Gallery is particularly rich in its collection of American Art glass, and has one of the finest collections of English Cameo Glass in the world. **NOT TO BE MISSED:** Works by Grandma Moses

Texas A&M University/J. Wayne Stark University Center Galleries
Mem Student Ctr. Joe Routt Blvd, College Station, TX 77844-9083
☎: 409-845-6081 ◉ www.starktamued
Open: 9-8 Tu-Fr, 12-6 Sa-Su **Closed:** Mo, ACAD
&. ℗
Group Tours
Permanent Collection: REG; GER 19

A University gallery featuring works by 20th century Texas artists

---
CORPUS CHRISTI

Art Museum of South Texas
1902 N. Shoreline, Corpus Christi, TX 78401
☎: 512-884-3844
Open: 10-5 Tu-Sa, 1-5 Su **Closed:** 1/1, 7/4, THGV, 12/25
Free Day: Th **ADM: Adult:** $3.00 **Children:** $1.00 (2-12) **Students:** $2.00 **Seniors:** $2.00
&. ℗ Free **Museum Shop** ¶¶
Sculpture Garden
Permanent Collection: AM; REG

The award winning building designed by Philip Johnson, has vast expanses of glass which provide natural light for objects of art and breathtaking views of Corpus Christi Bay.

TEXAS

Asian Cultures Museum and Educational Center
1809 North Chaparral, Corpus Christi, TX 78412

☎: 512-882-2641
Open: 12-5 Tu-Sa **Closed:** LEG/HOL!, EASTER
Vol/Cont: **ADM: Adult:** $4.00 **Children:** $2.50, 6-15 **Students:** $3.50 **Seniors:** $3.50
&. ℗ Street
Museum Shop
Group Tours **Drop-In Tours:** by request
Permanent Collection: JAP,CH,IND,AS CUL

An oasis of peace and tranquility as well as a resource of Asian history and information for the Corpus Christi Community. **NOT TO BE MISSED:** Cast bronze Buddha weighing over 1500 lb.

DALLAS

African American Museum
3536 Grand Avenue, Dallas, TX 75210

☎: 214-565-9026
Open: 12-5 Th-Fr, 10-5 Sa, 1-5 Su **Closed:** Mo, LEG/HOL!
&. ℗ **Museum Shop** ¶
Group Tours: 214-565-9026, ext 328 **Drop-In Tours:** by appt
Historic Building **Sculpture Garden**
Permanent Collection: AF/AM: folk

The African American Museum collects, preserves, exhibits and researches artistic expressions and historic documents which represent the African-American heritage. Its mission is to educate and give a truer understanding of African-American culture to all.

ON EXHIBIT 2000
03/18/2000 to 05/14/2000 **THE ART OF NELLIE MAE ROWE: NINETY NINE AND A HALF WON'T DO**
A self-taught artist from Georgia, filled her home with drawings, sculpture, photocollages, and dolls that she made from such everyday items as cardboard, paper, cloth, felt-tip pens, and even chewing gum.

Biblical Arts Center
7500 Park Lane, Dallas, TX 75225

☎: 214-691-4661 ◙ www.biblicalarts.org
Open: 10-5 Tu-Sa, 10-9 Th, 1-5 Su **Closed:** Mo, 1/1, THGV, 12/24, 12/25
ADM: Adult: $4.00 **Children:** $2.50 (6-12) **Students:** $3.00 (13-18) **Seniors:** $3.50
&. ℗ Yes
Museum Shop
Group Tours
Permanent Collection: BIBLICAL ART

The sole purpose of this museum is to utilize the arts as a means of helping people of all faiths to more clearly envision the places, events, and people of the Bible. The building, in f Romanesque style, features early Christian era architectural details. **NOT TO BE MISSED:** 'Miracle at Pentecost', painting with light and sound presentation

Dallas Museum of Art
1717 N. Harwood, Dallas, TX 75201

☎: 214-922-1200   ◙ www.dm-art.org
Open: 11-4 Tu, We, Fr, 11-9 T, 11-5 Sa, Su   **Closed:** Mo, 1/1, THGV, 12/25
Free Day: Th after 5, spec exh
♿ ℗ Large underground parking facility   **Museum Shop** ᵀ᷏: 2 rest
Group Tours: 214-922-1331   **Drop-In Tours**: Tu, Fr 1pm, Sa, Su 2pm, Th 7PM   **Sculpture Garden**
Permanent Collection: P/COL; AF; AM: furniture; EUR: ptgs, sculp, Post War AM; AF; AS; CONT

Designed by Edward Larabee Barnes, the 370,000 square foot limestone building houses a broad and eclectic permanent collection. The art of the Americas from the pre-contact period (which includes a spectacular pre-Columbian gold Treasury of more than 1,000 works) through the mid-20th century is outstanding. **NOT TO BE MISSED:** 'The Icebergs' by Frederick Church; Claes Oldenburg's pop art 'Stake Hitch in the Barrel Vault'; Colonial and post-Colonial decorative arts: early and late paintings by Piet Mondrian

ON EXHIBIT 2000
The J. E. R. Chilton Galleries (Special Exhibition Galleries) have an admission charge: Adults $8.00; Students/Seniors $6.00; Children under 12 $2.00. Audio tour is included. Thursday after 5 adm is free-audio tour $4.00.

ONGOING   ETERNAL EGYPT
A three part installation on long term loan containing funerary art, sculptures of kings and gods, and other objects from tombs and temples in ancient Egypt. Views of everyday life and the afterlife are seen through vessels, jewelry and religious objects. Art of Nubia includes fine examples of blue faience vessels, weapons, lamps, etc., as well as a large group of 'shabti' tomb figures.

ONGOING   SOUTH ASIAN SCULPTURE
Exceptionally fine sculptures representing the artistic traditions of India, Nepal, Tibet, Thailand and Indonesia.

11/07/1999 to 01/30/2000   GEORGIA O'KEEFFE: THE POETRY OF THINGS
In 1915, Georgia O'Keeffe: divided a series of her early charcoal drawings into two categories: "landscapes" and "things". This exhibition focus on the "things" –including flowers, crosses, and animal skulls–in 63 still-life paintings and drawings, dating between 1908 and 1963.

01/30/2000 to 04/30/2000   DEGAS TO PICASSO: THE PAINTER, THE SCULPTOR AND THE CAMERA
The exhibition will explore the role of photography in the finished work and conceptual process of artists including Bonnard, Brancusi, Degas, Gauguin, Khnopff, Moreau, Mucha, Munch, Picasso, Rodin, Rosso, von Stuck, Valloton and Vuillard.

09/16/1999 to 02/13/2000   ART IN POST-REVOLUTIONARY MEXICO
More than 50 paintings, drawings, prints, and photographs by some of Mexico's most famous artists such as José Clemente Orozco, Diego Rivera, David Alfaro Siqueiros, and Rufino Tamayo. The exhibition presents the variety of ways that domestic and foreign artists worked in Mexico as a newly vitalized community, and contributed to the country's emergence for the first time as an artistic force in global culture.

07/22/2000 to -1/2000   CHINA & GLASS IN AMERICA, 1880–1980: FROM TABLETOP TO TV TRAY
Explore the fascinating topic of ceramic and glass tableware design in America. Features hundreds of beautiful objects designed for dining in the 20th century. Through innovative displays recreating department store showrooms and table settings from the past, this exhibit chronicles the progress of style in American dining, from finger bowls to Fiesta Ware.

10/2000 01/20001   THE JACQUES AND NATASHA GELMAN COLLECTION OF MODERN MEXICAN PAINTING
Jacques and Natasha Gelman assembled on of the most important collections of Mexican modernist painting in private hands. Containing masterpieces by giants of Mexican modernism such as Diego Rivera, Frida Kahlo, Rufino Tamayo, José Clemente Orozco, David Alfaro Siqueiros, and Carlos Mérida, the collection reflects the personal tastes of the collectors and includes a number of portraits, both of the Gelmans and self-portraits of the artists. Most notable are a striking group of self-portraits by Frida Kahlo, whose poignantly beautiful paintings blend her emotions with traditional Mexican themes and surrealism. The collection also includes Rivera's 1915 Última Hora, an early experiment with cubism, and his Calla Lily Vendor, derived from one of his 1920s mural projects.

TEXAS

Meadows Museum

Affiliate Institution: SMU School of the Arts
Bishop Blvd. at Binkley Ave., Dallas, TX 75275-0356
☏: 214-768-2516 ◉ www.smu.edu/meadows/museum
Open: 10-5 Mo, Tu, Fr, Sa, 10-8 Th, 1-5 Su **Closed:** W, 1/1, EASTER, 7/4, THGV, 12/25
Vol/Cont:
♿ ⓟ **Museum Shop**
Group Tours: 214-823-7644 **Drop-In Tours:** 2pm, Su, Sept-May **Sculpture Garden**
Permanent Collection: SP; ptgs, sculp, gr, drgs; AM: sculp 20,

The collection of Spanish Art is the most comprehensive in the US with works from the last years of the 10th century through the 20th century. **NOT TO BE MISSED:** 'Sibyl With Tabula Rasa' by Diego Rodriquez de Silva y Velazquez, Spanish, 1599-1660

ON EXHIBIT 2000

09/11/1999 to 01/02/2000 EL GRECO AND THE IMAGE OF SAINT FRANCIS

09/24/1999 to 01/02/2000 THE ART OF WAR: GOYA'S DISASTERS

01/21/2000 to 03/05/2000 CYNTHIA LIN: PAINTINGS AND DRAWINGS

03/24/2000 to 05/28/2000 CHRISTINA GARCIA RODERO: PHOTOGRAPHIC EYE OF SPAIN

EL PASO

El Paso Museum of Art

1211 Montana Ave, El Paso, TX 79902-5588
☏: 915-541-4040
Open: 9-5 Tu, We, Fr, Sa, 9-9 Th, 1-5 Su **Closed:** LEG/HOL!
♿ ⓟ Free **Museum Shop**
Group Tours
Permanent Collection: EU: Kress Coll 13-18; AM; MEX: 18,19; MEX SANTOS: 20; REG

The museum houses the renowned permanent Kress collection of works by European masters; one of the most important concentrations of Mexican Colonial art; American painting (1800 to the present); and over 2000 works on paper by Dürer, Degas, Miro, Benton, Rivera and Orozco. Two changing galleries display work by recognized contemporary regional artists.

FORT WORTH

Amon Carter Museum

3501 Camp Bowie Blvd, Fort Worth, TX 76107-2695
☏: 817-738-1933 ◉ www.cartermuseum.org
Open: 10-5 Tu-Sa, 12-5 Su! Call for Info **Closed:** Mo, 1/1, 7/4, THGV,12/25
♿ ⓟ Free **Museum Shop**
Group Tours
Permanent Collection: AM: ptgs, sculp, gr, phot 19,20

One of the foremost museums of American Art, the Amon Carter is located in Fort Worth's cultural district. It represents the Western experience and embraces the history of 19th and 20th century American Art.0 **NOT TO BE MISSED:** 'Swimming', by Thomas Eakins

350

Amon Carter Museum - continued
The Amon Carter Museum will close to the public on Sunday, August 1, 1999, to start a building expansion program that will more than triple the size of the galleries to display the Museum's collection of American art.

The Carter Downtown allows patrons to view samples of the exceptional exhibitions of American art they have come to expect from the Carter. With 2,700 square feet of space, the Carter Downtown displays approximately 30 works of art at a time. The downtown location also has a well-stocked Museum Store and houses expansion information, including models, architectural renderings, computer-aided design stills, and site elevations, to keep patrons up-to-date with the expansion. The Carter Downtown is open Tuesday through Sunday, with extended evening hours on Thursday, Friday, and Saturday. It is closed on Monday and major holidays. Admission is free. Located at 500 Commerce Street, the Carter Downtown is across the street from Bass Hall, next to The Grape Escape.

Kimbell Art Museum
3333 Camp Bowie Blvd, Fort Worth, TX 76107-2792
☎: 817-332-8451   ◉ www.kimbellart.org
Open: 10-5 Tu-Th, Sa, 12-8 Fr, 12-5 Su   **Closed:** Mo, 1/1, 7/4, THGV, 12/25
Free Day: Perm Coll. Free daily, Adm is for Special exhibitions   **ADM: Adult:** $10.00   **Children:** 6-12 $6.00   **Students:** $8.00   **Seniors:** $8.00
&. ℗   **Museum Shop** ¶
Group Tours: 817-332-8451, ext. 229   **Drop-In Tours**: 2pm Tu-Fr, Su, exh tours 2pm Su, 3:00 Su   **Sculpture Garden**
Permanent Collection: EU: ptgs, sculp 14-20; AS; AF; Med/Ant

Designed by Louis I. Kahn, this classic museum building is perhaps his finest creation and a work of art in its own right. It was the last building completed under his personal supervision. It is often called 'America's best small museum'. The permanent collection of the Museum is free. Admission is for Special exhibitions **NOT TO BE MISSED:** "The Cardsharps" by Caravaggio

ON EXHIBIT 2000

to early 2000   PERMANENT COLLECTION
The Kimbell Art Museum's internationally renowned permanent collection will be on display in a new installation through 1999 and early 2000. The regular schedule of traveling exhibitions will resume in the year 2000.

07/02/2000 to 10/01/2000   STROGANOFF: THE PALACE AND COLLECTIONS OF A RUSSIAN NOBLE FAMILY
Stroganoff is one of the most familiar names in Russian history, that of an extraordinary family whose impact over five centuries included aggressive entrepreneurship as well as social vision and patronage of the arts. The exhibition includes icons and antiquities, palace furnishings and paintings of the greatest European masters from Botticelli to Poussin. These will be arrayed as they were in the Stroganoff Palace, one of the grandest 18th century buildings in St. Petersburg.

11/12/2000 to 02/25/2001   FROM RENOIR TO PICASSO: MASTERPIECES FROM THE MUSÉE DE L'ORANGERIE

Modern Art Museum of Fort Worth
1309 Montgomery Street, Fort Worth, TX 76107
☎: 817-738-9215   ◉ www.mamfw.org
Open: 10-5 Tu-Fr, 11-5 Sa, 12-5 Su   **Closed:** Mo, LEG/HOL!
&. ℗   **Museum Shop**
Group Tours   Drop-In Tours: Sa PM   **Sculpture Garden**
Permanent Collection: AM; EU; CONT; ptgs, sculp, works on paper, photo, 14 new works by Modern and Contemporary photographers and artists.

TEXAS

Modern Art Museum of Fort Worth - continued

Chartered in 1892 (making it one of the oldest museums in the western U.S.), this museum has evolved into a celebrated and vital showcase for works of modern and contemporary art. Great emphasis at the Modern is placed on the presentation of exceptional traveling exhibitions making a trip to this facility and others in this 'museum rich' city a rewarding experience for art lovers. **NOT TO BE MISSED:** Important collections of works by Robert Motherwell, Jackson Pollock, Morris Louis and Milton Avery as well as contemporary photography.

ON EXHIBIT 2000

11/07/1999 to 01/23/2000   PERMANENT COLLECTION
This exhibition, featuring a broad range of artists, including Baselitz, Borofsky, Calle, Celmins, Gilbert & George, Guston, Jess, Kiefer, Pollock, Rothenberg, Rothko, Still, Viola, Warhol, offers an all too rare opportunity for viewing the Modern Art Museum of Fort Worth's impressive holdings. The scope and depth of Permanent Collection provides viewers content and context for art made in the last fifty years. The exhibition follows the progression of art over five decades. Paintings, photographs and video chart the development of ideas and technology as the work in this exhibition reflects a relatively recent past and provides a window to the future.

11/07/1999 to 01/23/2000   ANN HAMILTON
Hamilton who is known for large-scale material laden installations using huge quantities of common materials such as 14,000 tons of work clothes or 15,000 human teeth, has begun to incorporate technology into her environments including video, sound and mechanical apparatuses. She is creating a new, site-specific installation for the Museum.

02/06/2000 to 04/23/2000   2000 BC: THE BRUCE CONNOR STORY PART II
Famous for landmark nylon shrouded assemblages from the 50's and 60's and as a post war independent film maker, Connor has explored most media during his 40 year career.

09/2000 to 01/2001   WAYNE THIEBAUD

Modern at Sundance Square

Affiliate Institution: The Modern Art Museum
410 Houston Street, Fort Worth, TX 76102
☎: 817-335-9215   ◙ www.mamfw.org
Open: 11-6 Mo-Th, 11-10 Fr & Sa, 1-5 Su   **Closed:** LEG/HOL
& **Museum Shop**
Historic Building
Permanent Collection: AM, EU CONT ptg, sculp, works on paper, CONT photo

Opened in 1995 in the historic Sanger Building in downtown Fort Worth as an annex for both the permanent collections and temporary exhibitions of the Modern Art Museum.

Sid Richardson Collection of Western Art

309 Main Street, Fort Worth, TX 76102
☎: 817-332-6554(888-332-6554   ◙ www.sidrmuseum.org
Open: 10-5 Tu, We, 10-8 Th, Fr, 11-8 Sa, 1-5 Su   **Closed:** Mo, LEG/HOL!
& Ⓟ 3 hours free at Chisholm Trail Lot-4th and Main with ticket validation.   **Museum Shop**
Group Tours   Historic Building
Permanent Collection: AM/WEST: ptgs

Dedicated to Western Art the museum is located in historic Sundance Square in a reconstructed 1890's building. The area, in downtown Fort Worth, features restored turn-of-the-century buildings housing shops, restaurant, theater and museum. **NOT TO BE MISSED:** 56 Remington and Russell paintings on permanent display

Contemporary Arts Museum

5216 Montrose Boulevard, Houston, TX 77006-6598

☎: 713-284-8250　◙ www.camh.org
Open: 10-5 Tu-Sa, 10-9 Th 12-5 Su　**Closed:** Mo, 1/1, THGV, 12/25
& ℗ On-street parking　**Museum Shop**　ⵌ: Starbucks cafe
Group Tours　**Sculpture Garden**
Permanent Collection: Non-Collecting Institution

Located in a metal building in the shape of a parallelogram this museum is dedicated to presenting the art of our time to the public.

Menil Collection

1515 Sul Ross Street, Houston, TX 77006

☎: 713-525-9400　◙ www.menil.org
Open: 11-7 We-Su　**Closed:** Mo Tu, LEG/HOL!
& ℗　**Museum Shop**
Group Tours　**Historic Building**　**Sculpture Garden**
Permanent Collection: PTGS, DRGS, & SCULP 20; ANT; TRIBAL CULTURES; MED; BYZ

The Menil Collection was founded to house the art collection of John and Dominique de Menil. Considered one of the most important privately assembled collections of the 20th c. it spans human creative efforts from antiquity to the modern era. The Renzo-Piano designed Museum building is renowned for its innovative architecture and naturally-illuminated galleries. **NOT TO BE MISSED:** In collaboration with the Dia Center for the Arts, NY, the Cy Twombly Gallery designed by Renzo Piano is a satellite space featuring works in all media created by Cy Twombly.

ON EXHIBIT 2000
ONGOING　SURREALISM + "WITNESSES" (A SURREALIST WUNDERKAMMER)

09/10/1999 to 01/02/2000　SAM FRANCIS: PAINTINGS 1947-1990
A major retrospective of the acclaimed abstract painter tracing the course of his long and productive career It provides a rare opportunity to see his early work.

11/01/1999 to 02/21/2000　BYZANTINE ART IN TEXAS
Treasures on loan from private collections as well as those of the Menil. Among the objects is a silver plate known as " paten" from the 6th C. and a 7th C. incense burner.

01/02/2000 to 03/04/2000　WILLEM DE KOONING: IN PROCESS/JOHN CHAMBERLAIN
Works done from 1968-1988 many never before exhibited. A chief feature will be tracings, photographs, drawings and other evidence of de Kooning's work "in process".

03/01/2000 to 06/04/2000　LUNAR LANDSCAPES (FOTOFEST)
Pictures from the moon as NASA received them, not as magazines touched up and reproduced them. These were beamed back to earth from lunar spacecraft in the 1960's and have not been seen before in an art context.

04/28/2000 to 08/06/2000　SECRETS OF THE WATER: ART FROM ALASKA AND BRITISH COLUMBIA
The great bounty of late 18th C expeditions as taken by James Cook, Malaspina and Peter the Great, and others including masks, helmets, clubs, and other weapons and shamanistic figures.

TEXAS

Museum of Fine Arts, Houston
1001 Bissonnet, Houston, TX 77005

☎: 713-639-7300 ◉ www.mfahorg
Open: 10-5 Tu-Sa, 5-9pm Th, 12:15-6 Su **Closed:** Mo, 1/1, 7/4, LAB/DAY, THGV, 12/25
Free Day: Th **ADM**: **Adult:** $5.00 **Children:** Free under 5, 6-18 $2.50 **Students:** $2.50 **Seniors:** $2.50
&. ℗ Free **Museum Shop** ¶
Group Tours: 713-639-7324 **Drop-In Tours**: 12 and by appt **Sculpture Garden**
Permanent Collection: STRAUS COLL OF REN & 18TH C WORKS; BECK COLL: Impr; GLASSELL COLL: Af gold

Over 31,000 works are housed in the largest and most outstanding museum in the southwest. **NOT TO BE MISSED:** Audrey Jone Beck building opening March 2000, designed by Raphael Moneo housing European art from antiquity to 1920, American art to 1945. Bayou Bend Collection and Gardens,a 28 room house with 2800 works of fine and decorative American arts from colonial to MID 19TH c. Separate admission and hours. 733-639-7750. Rienzi, a newly opened house museum showcasing an important collection of 18th and 19th C European art and antiques and English porcelain. Separate admission and hours. 713-639-7800

ON EXHIBIT 2000
ONGOING   AFRICAN GOLD: SELECTIONS FROM THE GLASSELL COLLECTION
Objects created by the Akan peoples of the Ivory Coast and Ghana as well as works from the Fulani of Mali and the Swahili of Kenya dating from the late 19th and 20th centuries are featured in this exhibition.

ONGOING   IMPRESSIONIST AND MODERN PAINTING: THE JOHN AND AUDREY JONES BECK COLLECTION

ONGOING   BAYOU BEND COLLECTION AND GARDENS
One of the nation's premier collections of decorative arts.

10/24/1999 to 01/09/2000   FROM REMBRANDT TO GAINSBOROUGH: MASTERPIECES FROM THE DULWICH MUSEUM
A rare look at Old Master paintings, many on view for the first time in the United States.

02/24/2000 to 05/07/2000 THE GOLDEN AGE OF CHINESE ARCHEOLOGY FROM THE PEOPLES REPUBLIC OF CHINA
The achievements of Chinese culture from 6000 B.C. to A.D.960.

03/25/2000 to 05/07/2000   FACES OF IMPRESSIONISM: PORTRAITS FROM AMERICAN COLLECTIONS
Impressionist artists and their progressive approach to portraiture are the focus of this ground breaking exhibition . Included for the first time are works by Cassatt, Gauguin, Cézanne, Degas, Manet, Monet, Morisot and Renoir. This is the first attempt to provide insight into the genre as it was practiced by masters of this influential movement.

06/18/2000 to 09/2000   THE ART OF ROME IN THE 18TH CENTURY *Will Travel*

06/25/2000 to 10/01/2000   MASKS: FACES OF CULTURE
Examples include a mummy mask of 800 B. C. to a bulletproof mask from the US made in 1989.

08/27/2000 to 11/16/2000   LAND OF MYTH AND FIRE: ART OF ANCIENT AND MEDIEVAL GEORGIA
The extraordinary span of Georgian culture and diversity over 25 centuries.

12/16/2000 to 02/28/2001   ROBERT THERRIEN
At the age of 50, Robert Therrien is one of the most highly respected artists working in Southern California. Known predominantly as a sculptor, over the last 25 years he has produced a unique body of work in which forms and images that recur in his sculpture have been recycled and reinterpreted with the aid of painting, drawing, and photography. This exhibition will present eight major sculptures, most done within the last five years. It will also include a group of smaller reliefs and two-dimensional works in a variety of media that will help to explicate Therrien's very personal and unusual creative process

Rice University Art Gallery
6100 Main Street, MS-21, Houston, TX 77005

📞: 713-527-6069 ◙ www.rice.edu-ruag
Open: 11-5 Tu-Sa, 11-8 Th 12-5 Su **Closed:** Mo, ACAD, Summer
♿ ℗ ⅂: Cafeteria on campus
Group Tours
Permanent Collection: Rotating Exhibitions

The Gallery features changing exhibitions of contemporary art with an emphasis on site-specific installations

KERRVILLE

Cowboy Artists of America Museum
1550 Bandera Hwy, Kerrville, TX 78028

📞: 210-896-2553 ◙ www.caamuseum.com
Open: 9-5 Mo-Sa, 1-5 Su **Closed:** 1/1, EASTER, THGV, 12/25
ADM: Adult: $3.00 **Children:** $1.00 (6-18) **Seniors:** $2.50
♿ ℗ Free **Museum Shop**
Group Tours Drop-In Tours: daily ! **Historic Building Sculpture Garden**
Permanent Collection: AM/WESTERN: ptgs, sculp

Located on a hilltop site just west of the Guadalupe River, the museum is dedicated to perpetuating America's western heritage. Exhibitions change quarterly.

LONGVIEW

Longview Museum of Fine Arts
215 E. Tyler St, Longview, TX 75601

📞: 903-753-8103 ◙ www.lmfa.org
Open: 10-4 Tu-Fr, 12-4 Sa **Closed:** Mo, Su 12/25, 1/1
Free Day: no charge for permanent exhibitions **Sugg/Cont:** Adult $3.00 Student $1.00
♿ ℗ Adjacent to the building **Museum Shop**
Group Tours: 903-753-8103 **Historic Building**
Permanent Collection: CONT TEXAS ART (1958-1999)

Located in downtown Longview, this renovated building was used by many businesses in the city's history. **NOT TO BE MISSED:** Millenium celebration highlighting LMFA's fine art permanent collection since 1959

ON EXHIBIT 2000

01/08/2000 to 02/19/2000 LMFA CELEBRATES THE MILLENNIUM : PERMANENT COLLECTION SINCE 1959

02/26/2000 to 04/01/2000 FROM LONGVIEW TO NEW HEIGHTS: FRANKLIN WILLIS AND CHASE YARBROUGH

05/12/2000 to 06/30/2000 PHOTOVIEW 2000 INVITATIONAL (45TH)

07/08/2000 to 09/02/2000 ART AND MACHINES: THE HARLEY DAVIDSON SHOW
Machines and a history of their development

09/09/2000 to 10/28/2000 PHOTOVIEW INVITATIONAL WINNERS

TEXAS

Museum of East Texas
503 N. Second Street, Lufkin, TX 75901
☎: 409-639-4434
Open: 10-5 Tu-Fr, 1-5 Sa-Su **Closed:** LEG/HOL!
 ♿ Ⓝ **Museum Shop**
Group Tours   **Historic Building**
Permanent Collection: AM, EU, & REG: ptgs

The Museum is housed in St. Cyprians Church, whose original Chapel was built in 1906. An award winning wing was completed in 1990. **NOT TO BE MISSED:** Historic photographic collection covering a period of over 90 years of Lufkin's history

Michelson Museum of Art
216 N. Bolivar, Marshall, TX 75670
☎: 903-935-9480
Open: 12-5 Tu-Fr, 1-4 Sa-Su **Closed:** Mo, EASTER, MEM/DAY, 7/4, THGV, 12/25
Vol/Cont:
♿ Ⓝ
Group Tours   Drop-In Tours: 12-5 daily   **Historic Building**
Permanent Collection: WORKS OF RUSSIAN AMERICAN ARTIST LEO MICHELSON, 1887-1978

The historic Southwestern Bell Telephone Corporation building in downtown Marshall is home to this extensive collection.

McAllen International Museum
1900 Nolana, McAllen, TX 78504
☎: 956-682-1564 ◉ www.hiline.net/mim
Open: 9-5 Mo-We, Sa ;Th 12-8; Su 1-5 **Closed:** THGV, 12/25
Free Day: 9-1 Sa **ADM: Adult:** $2:00 **Children:** $1.00 under 13 **Students:** $1.00 **Seniors:** $1.00
♿ Ⓝ **Museum Shop** 🍽 small café
Group Tours: 956-682-1564, ext. 116 **Drop-In Tours:** 8:30-11, 12-2:30
Permanent Collection: LAT/AM: folk; AM; EU: gr 20

The museum caters to art & science on an equal level. See the hands-on mobile exhibits.

ON EXHIBIT 2000

ONGOING METEOROLOGY
Includes a working weather station and related exhibits

ONGOING   THE TOUCH BASE
Investigation tables and curiosity drawers all dealing with Earth Science and Ethnography.

Museum of the Southwest
1705 W. Missouri Ave, Midland, TX 79701-6516

📞: 915-683-2882
Open: 10-5 Tu-Sa, 2-5 Su   **Closed:** Mo, LEG/HOL!
♿ ℗
Group Tours   Drop-In Tours: on request   **Sculpture Garden**
Permanent Collection: REG; GR; SW

The Museum of the Southwest is an educational resource in art including a Planetarium and Children's Museum. It focuses on the Southwest. Housed in a 1934 mansion and stables, the collection also features the Hogan Collection of works by founder members of the Taos Society of Artists. **NOT TO BE MISSED:** 'The Sacred Pipe', by Alan Houser, bronze

ON EXHIBIT 2000
ONGOING   THE SEARCH FOR ANCIENT PLAINSMEN: AN ARCHEOLOGICAL EXPERIENCE

ONGOING   THE COLLECTION
Selections including paintings, sculptures, graphics and photographs.

ONGOING   UNDER STARRY SKIES: DEFINING THE SOUTHWEST
An interpretive installation using loan and collection works by culturally diverse artists.

11/04/1999 to 01/02/2000   CURRIER AND IVES: PRINTMAKERS TO THE AMERICAN PEOPLE
The firm of Currier and Ives lasted from 1857 to 1907. During that period they produced over 7000 titles in unlimited quantities. Seventy prints from the collection of the Museum of the City of New York will be shown here.

12/02/1999 to 01/09/2000   SELECTIONS FROM THE COLLECTIONS OF THE MUSEUM

01/18/2000 to 03/26/2000   REFLECTIONS OF A JOURNEY: ENGRAVINGS AFTER KARL BODMER
In the early 1830s Prince Maximilian, a German naturalist and explorer and Swiss painter Bodmer made a journey up the Missouri River to record information about the American environment and people. These hand-colored aquatint engravings were the result of that journey. They were originally compiled in "Travels in the American Interior" published in the 1840s.

03/02/2000 to 04/09/2000   13TH ANNUAL MIDLAND ARTS ASSOCIATION SPRING JURIED ART EXHIBITION

04/02/2000 to 05/21/2000   AMERICAN LANDSCAPES: 47 WORKS BY HOMER, INNESS, WHISTLER, MORAN, BLAKELOCK, AND BIRCHER FROM THE PAINE ART CENTER, WISCONSIN

Stark Museum of Art
712 Green Ave, Orange, TX 77630

📞: 409-883-6661
Open: 10-5 We-Sa, 1-5 Su   **Closed:** Mo, Tu, 1/1, EASTER, 7/4, THGV, 12/25
♿ ℗   **Museum Shop**
Group Tours   Drop-In Tours: by appt   **Sculpture Garden**
Permanent Collection: AM: 1830-1950; STEUBEN GLASS; NAT/AM; BIRDS BY DOROTHY DOUGHTY & E.M. BOEHM

In addition to Great Plains and SW Indian crafts the Stark houses one of the finest collections of Western American art in the country. The museum also features the only complete Steuben Glass collection of 'The US in Crystal'. **NOT TO BE MISSED:** Bronze Sculptures by Frederic Remington

TEXAS

San Angelo Museum of Fine Arts

704 Burgess, San Angelo, TX 76903
📞: 915-658-4084 ◙ http://web2.airmail/net
Open: 10-4 Tu-Sa, 1-4 Su **Closed:** LEG/HOL!
ADM: Adult: $2.00 **Children:** Free under 6 **Seniors:** $1.00
& ℗ On-site **Museum Shop**
Group Tours Historic Building Sculpture Garden
Permanent Collection: AM: cont cer; REG; MEX: 1945-present

The completely renovated museum building was originally the 1868 quartermaster's storehouse on the grounds of Fort Concho, a National Historic Landmark. It is currently undergoing a major Capitol Building Campaign to construct a new museum to be started in the spring of 1997. **NOT TO BE MISSED:** 'Figuora Accoccolata', by Emilio Greco

McNay Art Museum

6000 N. New Braunfels Ave, San Antonio, TX 78209-4618
📞: 210-805-1757 ◙ www.mcnayart.org
Open: 10-5 Tu-Sa, 12-5 Su **Closed:** 1/1, 7/4, THGV, 12/25
& ℗ **Museum Shop**
Group Tours Drop-In Tours Historic Building Sculpture Garden
Permanent Collection: FR & AM: sculp 19,20; SW: folk ; GR & DRGS: 19,20; THEATER ARTS

Devoted to the French Post-Impressionist and early School of Paris artists, the McNay Art Museum also has an outstanding theatre arts collection containing over 20,000 books and drawings as well as models of stage sets. It is located on beautifully landscaped grounds in a classic mediterranean style mansion.

San Antonio Museum of Art

200 West Jones Street, San Antonio, TX 78215
📞: 210-978-8100 ◙ www.samuseum.org
Open: 10-5,We, Fr, Sa, 10-9 Tu, 12-5 Su **Closed:** Mo, THGV, 12/25
Free Day: Tu 3-9 **ADM: Adult:** $5.00 **Children:** $1.75 (4-11) **Students:** $4.00 **Seniors:** $4.00
& ℗ Free **Museum Shop** ‖
Group Tours: 210-978-8138 **Drop-In Tours:** most Su at 2pm ! **Historic Building Sculpture Garden**
Permanent Collection: AN/GRK; AN/R; EGT; CONT: ptgs, sculp

The San Antonio Museum of Art is located in the restored turn-of-the-century former Lone Star Brewery. In addition to its other varied and rich holdings it features the most comprehensive collection of ancient art in the south. **NOT TO BE MISSED:** The spectacular Ewing Halsell Wing for Ancient Art. The Nelson A. Rockefeller Center for Latin American Art is a 30,000 square foot addition to the Museum providing exhibition and storage space for the extensive collections of pre-Columbian art, Latin American folk art, Spanish Colonial and contemporary Latin American art.

ON EXHIBIT 2000

11/07/1999 to 01/30/2000 GOLD OF THE NOMADS

11/19/1999 to 03/19/2000 DELLSCHAU PRINTS

TYLER

Tyler Museum of Art

1300 S. Mahon Ave, Tyler, TX 75701

℡: 903-595-1001

Open: 10-5 Tu-Sa, 1-5 Su **Closed:** LEG/HOL!

♿ Ⓟ **Museum Shop** 🍴: Cafe open Tu-F 11-2

Group Tours **Historic Building**

Permanent Collection: PHOT; REG 20

The Museum is located in an architecturally award winning building.

ON EXHIBIT 2000

11/21/1999 to 01/21/2000 HOT AND COOL CONTEMPORARY GLASS WORKS

The last 35 years have ushered in great changes in production and perception. This exhibit emphasizes the new techniques.

WACO

Art Center of Waco

1300 College Drive, Waco, TX 76708

℡: 254-752-4371

Open: 10-5 Tu-Sa; 1-5 Su **Closed:** Mo, LEG/HOL!

Sugg/Cont: **ADM**: **Adult:** $2.00 **Children:** $1.00 **Students:** $1.00 **Seniors:** $1.50

♿ Ⓟ **Museum Shop**

Group Tours **Historic Building** **Sculpture Garden**

Permanent Collection: CONT; REG

Housed in the Cameron Home, The Art Center is located on the McLennan Community College campus. It features an exhibit of sculpture on the grounds. **NOT TO BE MISSED:** 'Square in Black', by Gio Pomodoro; 'The Waco Door' 6½ ton steel sculpture by Robert Wilson

WICHITA FALLS

Wichita Falls Museum and Art Center

Two Eureka Circle, Wichita Falls, TX 76308

℡: 817-692-0923

Open: 10-5 Tu-Sa, 1-5 Su **Closed:** LEG/HOL!

ADM: **Adult:** $3.00 **Children:** Free under 3, $2.00 **Students:** $2.00 **Seniors:** $2.00

♿ Ⓟ **Museum Shop**

Group Tours

Permanent Collection: AM: gr; CONT

The art collection has the singular focus of representing the history of American art through the medium of print making. **NOT TO BE MISSED:** The 'Magic Touch Gallery' featuring hands-on science and the 'Discovery Gallery' emphasizing family programming. Also high energy, high tech laser programs and planet shows in the planetarium.

UTAH

Nora Eccles Harrison Museum of Art
Affiliate Institution: Utah State University
650 N. 1100 E., Logan, UT 84322-4020
☎: 801-797-0163
Open: 10:30-4:30 Tu, Th, Fr, 10:30-8 We, 2-5 Sa-Su **Closed:** Mo, LEG/HOL!
♿ Ⓟ Within one block ⑪
Group Tours: 801-797-0165 **Drop-In Tours**
Sculpture Garden
Permanent Collection: NAT/AM; AM: cont art, cer 20

The Nora Eccles Harrison Museum of Art is the major center for the exhibition of the visual arts in Northern Utah. Emphasizing the breadth of artistic expression and the history of art in the western United States, the Museum's permanent collections include 20th century American sculpture, ceramics, paintings, graphic arts, photographs, and American Indian arts. Selections from the collection are always on view and are rotated periodically to reflect the continuing growth and refinement of the collection. In addition to installations of its permanent holdings, the Museum organizes temporary and traveling exhibitions and serves as a venue for exhibitions of national and international stature. Artist talks, films, docent tours, and educational activities are additional dimensions of the Museum's programs which are designed to interpret, present, and foster the development of the visual arts. **NOT TO BE MISSED:** 'Untitled' (Standing Woman), 1959, by Manuel Neri

Salt Lake Art Center
20 S.W. Temple, Salt Lake City, UT 84101
☎: 801-328-4201
Open: 10-5 Tu-Th, 10-9 Fr, 10-5 Sa, 1-5 Su **Closed:** LEG/HOL!
Sugg/Cont: **ADM: Adult:** $2.00pp
♿ Ⓟ Paid on street parking
Museum Shop ⑪
Group Tours Drop-In Tours
Permanent Collection: REG: all media

The 60 year old art center is located in the Bicentennial complex in the heart of downtown Salt Lake City.

Utah Museum of Fine Arts
101 AAC, University of Utah, Salt Lake City, UT 84112
☎: 801-581-7332
Open: 10-5 Mo-Fr, 2-5 Sa, Su **Closed:** LEG/HOL!
♿ Ⓟ Free on campus parking Sa & Su; metered parking on weekdays
Museum Shop Group Tours
Sculpture Garden
Permanent Collection: EU & AM: ptgs 17-19; AF; AS; EGT

With a permanent collection of over 10,000 works spanning a broad spectrum of the world's art history, this major Utah cultural institution is a virtual artistic treasure house containing the only comprehensive collection of art in the state or the surrounding region. **NOT TO BE MISSED:** "Dance Around The Maypole" by Pieter Breughel, The Younger

Springville Museum of Art
126 E. 400 S., Springville, UT 84663

☎: 801-489-2727

Open: 10-5 Tu-Sa, 2-5 Su, 10-9 We   **Closed:** 1/1, 12/25

& ℗   **Museum Shop   Group Tours**

Permanent Collection: UTAH: ptgs, sculp

The museum, housed in a Spanish colonial revival style building, features a collection noted for the art of Utah dating from pioneer days to the present.

VERMONT

Bennington Museum
W. Main Street, Bennington, VT 05201
☎: 802-447-1571
Open: 9-5 daily, Weekends 9-7, MEM/DAY-LAB/DAY   **Closed:** THGV
ADM: Adult: $5.00, family $ **Children:** Free under 12   **Students:** $3.50   **Seniors:** $4.50
♿ ℗   **Museum Shop   Group Tours   Historic Building**
Permanent Collection: AM: dec/art; MILITARY HIST; AM: ptgs

Visitors can imagine days gone by while gazing at a favorite Grandma Moses painting at The Bennington, one of the finest regional art and history museums in New England. The original museum building is the 1855 St. Francis de Sales church.

Robert Hull Fleming Museum
Affiliate Institution: University of Vermont
61 Colchester Ave., Burlington, VT 05405
☎: 802-656-0750 ▣ www.uvm.edu/~fleming
Open: 9-4 Tu-Fr, 1-5 Sa, Su, (summer May 1st-Labor/Day 12-4 Th, Fr, 12-5 Sa, Su   **Closed:** Mo, LEG/HOL!, ACAD!
ADM: Adult: $3.00, Fam $5.00   **Children:** $2.00   **Students:** $2.00   **Seniors:** $2.00
♿ ℗   **Museum Shop   Group Tours   Historic Building**
Permanent Collection: AN/EGT; CONT; Eu & Am; MID/EAST; AS; AF

Vermont's primary art and anthropology museum is located in a 1931 McKim, Mead and White building. **NOT TO BE MISSED:** Assyrian Relief

ON EXHIBIT 2000
02/2000 to 05/2000   AN AUTHOR'S VISION: PRINTS AND DRAWINGS BY GUNTER GRASS

05/2000 to 09/2000   PARIS POSTERS: ORIGINAL LITHOGRAPHS BY PICASSO, MATISSE, CHAGALL AND OTHERS

10/2000 to 12/2000   HERITAGE OF THE BRUSH: THE ROY AND MARILYN PAPP COLLECTION OF CHINESE PAINTINGS

Southern Vermont Art Center
West Road, Manchester, VT 05254
☎: 802-362-1405 ▣ www.svac.org
Open: Winter 10-5 Mo-Sa: Summer10-8:30 Tu-,10-5 We-Sa; 12-5 Su   **Closed:** Su in winter, MO in summer 1/1, COLUMBUS DAY, 12/25
Free Day: Sa, 10-1   **ADM: Adult:** $3.00   **Children:** Free under 13   **Students:** $0.50   **Seniors:** $3.00
♿ ℗   **Group Tours   Historic Building   Sculpture Garden**
Permanent Collection: PTGS, SCULP, PHOT, GR; CONT: 20

Built in 1917, by Mr. & Mrs. W. M. Ritter of Washington D.C., the Art Center is housed in a Georgian Colonial Mansion located on 450 acres on the eastern slope of Mt. Equinox. Included in the facility is a theater with dance, music and film programs. **NOT TO BE MISSED:** Works by Winslow Homer and Ogden Pleissner

362

Middlebury College Museum of Art
Middlebury College, Middlebury, VT 05753
☎: 802-443-5007 ◙ www.middlebury.edu/~museum
Open: 10-5 Tu-Fr, 12-5 Sa, Su   **Closed:** Mo, ACAD!, 12/18-1/1
♿ ℗ Free   **Museum Shop** ⎟⎟
Group Tours: 802-443-5007
Permanent Collection: Anc/R/Grk; ceramic, sculp, cer.sculp;: EU, AM sculp, drg ptgs, photos, and Cont all media

Designed by the New York firm of Hardy Holzman Pfeiffer Associates, the new (1992) Center for the Arts also includes a theater, concert hall, music library and dance studios. It is located midway between Rutland and Burlington. **NOT TO BE MISSED:** 'Bimbo Malato (Sick Child)', 1893 by Medardo Rosso (wax over plaster)

ON EXHIBIT 2000
ONGOING   19TH CENTURY ART FROM THE COLLECTION

ONGOING   20TH-CENTURY ART FROM THE COLLECTION

ONGOING   FACULTY CHOICES: ANCIENT, ASIAN, AND EUROPEAN ART FROM THE COLLECTIONS

01/18/2000 to 04/16/2000   FIFTY YEARS OF FACULTY ART AT MIDDLEBURY

05/19/2000 to 12/10/2000   MIDDLEBURY ALUMNI ARTISTS

09/14/2000 to 12/10/2000   MIDDLEBURY COLLEGE: 200 YEARS

Sheldon Art Museum, Archeological and Historical Society
1 Park Street, Middlebury, VT 05753
☎: 802-388-2117 ◙ www.middlebury.edu/~shel-mus
Open: 10-5 Mo-Sa, June-Oct, 12-4 some Su, 10-5 Mo-Fr late Oct-late May   **Closed:** LEG/HOL!, 1/1, MEM/DAY, 7/4, LAB/DAY, THGV
ADM: **Adult:** $4.00, $8.00 fam   **Children:** $1.00 6-18   **Students:** $3.50   **Seniors:** $3.50
♿ ℗ Public parking nearby   **Museum Shop**
Group Tours   Drop-In Tours   Historic Building
Permanent Collection: DEC/ART; PER/RMS; ARTIFACTS

Regional Vermont's exciting and interesting history is interpreted in this century old museum located in the 1829 Judd Harris house and Fletcher History Center. **NOT TO BE MISSED:** Portraits by itinerant artist Benjamin Franklin Mason.

ON EXHIBIT 2000
09/24/1999 to 01/02/2000   ROBERT COLESCOTT RECENT PAINTINGS: 47TH VENICE BIENNIAL
The 19 provocative paintings on view, created over the past decade by Arizona-based artist Colescott, contain his highly personal narrative figurative imagery blended with ironic viewpoints that address major contemporary social issues. One of the most important U.S. artists working today, Colescott was the first painter since Jasper Johns, in 1988, to be included in the 47th Venice Biennale. He was also the first American ever to be given a solo exhibition at that prestigious event.

11/15/1999 to 01/09/2000   HEROS AND HEROINES: COMIC ART ORIGINALS

11/23/1999 to 01/23/2000   JUDY BURTON: VISUAL NUANCES

VERMONT

T. W. Wood Gallery and Arts Center

Affiliate Institution: Vermont College
College Hall, Montpelier, VT 05602

☎: 802-828-8743
Open: 12-4 Tu-Su **Closed:** Mo, LEG/HOL!
Free Day: Su **ADM: Adult:** $2.00 **Children:** Free under 12 **Seniors:** $2.00
& ℗ on street **Museum Shop**
Group Tours **Historic Building**
Permanent Collection: THOMAS WATERMAN WOOD: ptgs; PORTRAITS; WPA WORKS

Included in the more than 200 oils and watercolors in this collection are the works of Thomas W. Wood and his American contemporaries of the 1920s and 30s including A. H. Wyant and Asher B. Durand. **NOT TO BE MISSED:** Exhibits of Vermont's artists and crafts people

Shelburne Museum

U.S. Route 7, Shelburne, VT 05482

☎: 802-985-3346 ◙ www.shelburnemuseum.org
Open: 10-5 Mo-Su Late-May through Late-Oct **Closed:** 1/1,Easter THGV, 12/25
ADM: Adult: $17.50 **Children:** $7.00 (6-14) **Students:** $10.50
& ℗ Free **Museum Shop** ⑪
Group Tours: 802-985-3348, ext 3392 **Drop-In Tours:** 1 PM late-Oct-late May **Historic Building**
Permanent Collection: FOLK; DEC/ART; HAVERMEYER COLL

37 historic and exhibition buildings on 45 scenic acres combine to form this nationally celebrated collection of American folk art, artifacts, and architecture. **NOT TO BE MISSED:** Steamboat Ticonderoga, "Louise Havemeyer and her Daughter Electra" by Mary Cassatt, 1895

St. Johnsbury Athenaeum

30 Main Street, St. Johnsbury, VT 05819

☎: 802-748-8291 ◙ www.kingcon,com/athena/
Open: 10:00-8:00 Mo, We, 10:00-5:30 Tu, Fr, 9:30-4 Sa **Closed:** Su, LEG/HOL!
ADM: Adult: $2.00pp
& ℗ Limited **Museum Shop**
Group Tours Drop-In Tours Historic Building
Permanent Collection: AM: ptgs 19; Hudson River School

The Athenaeum was built as a public library and presented to the townspeople of St. Johnsbury by Horace Fairbanks in 1871. In 1873 an art gallery, which today is an authentic Victorian period piece, was added to the main building. The collection of American landscapes and genre paintings is shown as it was in 1890 in the oldest unaltered art gallery in the US. **NOT TO BE MISSED:** 'Domes of The Yosemite', by Albert Bierstadt

CHARLOTTESVILLE

Bayly Art Museum of the University of Virginia
Rugby Road, Thomas H. Bayly Memorial Bldg, Charlottesville, VA 22903-2427

☎: 804-924-3592   ◙ www.virginia.edu/-bayly/bayly.html
Open: 1-5 Tu-Su   **Closed:** Mo, 12/24-1/2
Sugg/Cont: ADM: Adult: $3.00   **Seniors:** $3.00
& Ⓟ Limited parking behind the museum
Museum Shop
Group Tours: 804-924-7458   **Drop-In Tours**
Permanent Collection: NAT/AM; MESO/AM; AF; DEC/ART 18; OM: gr; AM: ptgs, sculp, works on paper, phot 20; P/COL,

This handsome Palladian-inspired building is located on the grounds of Jefferson's University of Virginia. With its wide ranging collection it serves as a museum for all ages and interests, for art lovers and scholars alike.

ON EXHIBIT 2000

01/08/2000 to 03/19/2000   KARA WALKER: WORKS ON PAPER

01/15/2000 to 04/02/2000   AMERICAN INDIAN ART FROM A LOCAL COLLECTION (working title)

01/21/2000 to 03/12/2000   CONTEMPORARY CERAMIC SCULPTURE

03/24/2000 to 06/13/2000   ADJA YUNKERS: TO INVENT THE GARDEN

04/08/2000 to 06/18/2000   PATI HILL: TONAL PRINTS

06/17/2000 to 08/20/2000   JAPANESE PRINTS

06/30/2000 to 08/20/2000   MILLENNIUM EXHIBITION: BILL VIOLA AND ANN HAMILTON

09/16/2000 to 11/05/2000   CHARLOTTESVILLE COLLECTS

11/11/2000 to 12/24/2000   WALTER NEIDICH

11/18/2000 to 01/14/2001   THE MYSTICAL ARTS OF TIBET
Sacred objects from the personal collection of the Dalai Lama as well as ancient objects from the monastery, contemporary objects made by Tibetan refugees, and 21 photos from the Tibet Image Bank, London.

Second Street Gallery
201 2nd Street, NW, Charlottesville, VA 22902

☎: 804-977-7284
Open: 10-5 T-Sa, 1-5 Su   **Closed:** Mo, LEG/HOL!
& Ⓟ On-street parking
Historic Building
Permanent Collection: Non-collecting Contemporary art space

Nationally known for its innovative programming, Second Street Gallery presents work of talented, regional, and national artists working in a variety of media from painting and photography, to sculpture and site-specific installations. The McGuffey Art Center which houses the Gallery is a historic former primary school building and is now an artist cooperative with open studios.

VIRGINIA

Allegheny Highlands Arts and Craft Center
439 East Ridgeway Street, Clifton Forge, VA 24422
☎: 703-862-4447
Open: 10:30-4:30 Mo-Sa May-Dec, 10:30-4:30 Tu-Sa Jan-Apr   **Closed:** THGV, 12/24-01/12
& ℗   **Museum Shop**
Group Tours: on request
Permanent Collection: Non-collecting institution

Housed in an early 1900's building, the galleries' changing exhibits feature works produced by Highlands and other artists.

Danville Museum of Fine Arts & History
975 Main Street, Danville, VA 24541
☎: 804-793-5644
Open: 10-5 Tu-Fr, 2-5 Sa, Su   **Closed:** Mo, LEG/HOL!
Sugg/Cont: **ADM**: **Adult:** $2.00   **Children:** $1.00   **Students:** $1.00   **Seniors:** $1.00
& ℗   **Museum Shop**
Group Tours   Drop-In Tours: by appt
Historic Building
Permanent Collection: REG: portraits, works on paper, dec/art, furniture, textiles

The Museum, located in Sutherlin Mansion built about 1857, was the residence of Confederate President Jefferson Davis for one week in April 1865. **NOT TO BE MISSED:** Restored Victorian Parlor

ON EXHIBIT 2000
03/19/2000 to 05/14/2000   THE SUBJECT OF THE MASK
Masks representing cultures of five continents, more than twenty five countries, and six Native American tribes, accompanied by photographs and prints to document their authentic usage.

Belmont, The Gari Melchers Estate and Memorial Gallery
224 Washington St., Fredericksburg, VA 22405
☎: 540-654-1015
Open: 10-5 Mo-Sa, 1-5 Su   **Closed:** 1/1, THGV, 12/24, 12/25, 12/31
ADM: **Adult:** $4.00   **Children:** Free under 6   **Students:** $1.00   **Seniors:** $3.00
& ℗   **Museum Shop**
Group Tours: 540-654-1841   **Drop-In Tours**: on the hour and half hour
Historic Building
Permanent Collection: EU & AM: ptgs (mostly by Gari Melchers)

This 18th century estate features many paintings by Gari Melchers (its former resident). Also on view are works by his American and European contemporaries as well as some old masters.

HAMPTON

Hampton University Museum
Hampton University, Hampton, VA 23668

📞: 757-727-5308 ◉ www.hamptonu.edu
Open: 8-5 Mo-Fr,12-4 Sa, Su **Closed:** LEG/HOL!, ACAD!
 ⅃ ℗ **Museum Shop**
Group Tours: 757-727-5508, child 757-727-5024
Permanent Collection: AF; NAT/AM: AM: ptgs 20

The Museum is housed in the spectacular, newly renovated Huntington Building, formerly the University Library. It is the oldest African American museum in the US and one of the oldest museums in Virginia. The collections include over 9000 objects including traditional African, Native American, Asian and Pacific Island art as well as a fine art collection. **NOT TO BE MISSED:** 'The Banjo Lesson', by Henry O. Tanner

---
LYNCHBURG

Maier Museum of Art
Affiliate Institution: Randolph-Macon Woman's College
2500 Rivermont Avenue, Lynchburg, VA 24503

📞: 804-947-8136 ◉ www.rmwc.edu/maier
Open: 1-5 Tu-Su Sep-May, 1-4 We-Su, June-Aug **Closed:** Mo, Acad/Hol !
 ⅃ ℗ Limited **Museum Shop**
Group Tours: ext 3 **Drop-In Tours**
Permanent Collection: AM: ptgs 19,20

19th and 20th century American paintings including works by Gilbert Stuart, Winslow Homer, Thomas Eakins, Thomas Cole, George Bellows, Mary Cassatt, Georgia O'Keeffe, and Andrew Wyeth, are among the many highlights of the Maier Museum of Art. **NOT TO BE MISSED:** George Bellows' 'Men of the Docks'

ON EXHIBIT 2000

01/15/2000 to 03/05/2000   30 VIEWS: SMALL PAINTINGS BY GREGORY AMENOFF

03/12/2000 to 04/23/2000   89TH ANNUAL EXHIBITION: GARNER TULLIS AND WORKS FROM THE GARNER TULLIS WORKSHOP

05/27/2000 to 08/13/2000   FRANK WHITEHOUSE PRINTS

08/19/2000 to 12/20/2000   JULIA NORELL PHOTO SHOW AND DIANA MITCHNER

NEWPORT NEWS

Peninsula Fine Arts Center
101 Museum Drive, Newport News, VA 23606

📞: 757-596-8175 ◉ www.pfac-vol.org
Open: 10-5 Mo-Sa, 1-5 Su; 10-9 Th **Closed:** 1/1, THGV, 12/24/pm, 12/25
Vol/Cont:
 ⅃ ℗ **Museum Shop**
Group Tours   Drop-In Tours: by appt **Sculpture Garden**
Permanent Collection: Non-collecting institution

VIRGINIA

Peninsula Fine Arts Center - continued

Changing exhibitions of primarily contemporary art by emerging artists that often contrast with exhibitions of historical significance are featured at this fine arts center which also has a Hands On For Kids gallery. The Center is located within the Mariner's Museum Park with the Noland Trail.

ON EXHIBIT 2000

11/13/1999 to 01/09/2000   A HUMAN PRESENCE: ZEUXIS
Zeuxis promotes contemporary artists to a intuitive approach to paintings and still-lifes.

11/13/1999 to 01/09/2000   EXPLORATIONS: WORKS BY MEMBERS OF THE PHOTOGRAPHIC ARTS NETWORK
Innovative approaches to photography using processes and techniques dating back to the 1900s.

11/13/1999 to 01/09/2000   ILLUSIONS OF GRANDEUR: WALTER GARDE
The visual aspect of his work and the sensual use of color creates an incredible illusion. He makes reality and illusion float back and forth as one sees his work.

01/29/2000 to 03/19/2000   SIX DEGREES OF INSPIRATION
A collaborative project with the Peninsula Fine Arts Center shows the diverse identity of the Hampton Roads region at the beginning of the 21st C. It focuses on large groups which have immigrated to the US within the past 50 years.

NORFOLK

Chrysler Museum of Art
245 West Olney Road, Norfolk, VA 23510-1587

☎: 757-664-6200 ▣ www.chrysler.org
Open: 10-5 Tu-Sa, 1-5 Su   **Closed:** Mo, 1/1, 7/4, THGV, 12/25
Free Day: We   **ADM: Adult:** $5.00   **Children:** $2.00, under 12 Free   **Students:** $3.00   **Seniors:** $3.00
♿ ℗ Free   **Museum Shop** ⅋: Phantoms
Group Tours: 757-664-6269 or 6283   **Drop-In Tours**
Historic Building
Permanent Collection: GLASS; IT/BAROQUE: ptgs; FR: 19; AN/EGT; AM: sculp, ptgs ⌒

Home to one of America's premier art collections spanning 5000 years of art history in an Italianate-Style building built on the picturesque Hague of the Elizabeth River. There are three historic houses. **NOT TO BE MISSED:** Gianlorenzo Bernini's 'Bust of the Savior'; Degas 'Dancer With Bouquet'

ON EXHIBIT 2000

09/14/1999 to 01/02/2000   MAN RAY'S "ELECTRICITE"

09/16/1999 to 01/02/2000   20/20 FASHION IN PHOTOGRAPHY

10/22/1999 to 01/09/2000   INNER EYE: CONTEMPORARY ART FROM THE MARK AND LIVIA STRAUS COLLECTION
Paintings, sculpture and photography from both emerging artists selected from the almost 100 works in this collection.

11/16/1999 to 08/2000   RAFAEL FERRER BEDROOM

11/23/1999 to 08/2000   FIRST IN THE HEARTS OF HIS COUNTRYMEN: AMERICA REMEMBERS GEORGE WASHINGTON, 1732-1799

01/28/2000 to 05/28/2000   PICTURES TELL THE STORY: ERNEST C. WITHERS

02/24/2000 to 05/21/2000   ANCIENT GOLD

Chrysler Museum of Art - continued
06/20/2000 to 10/01/2000   JAMES ABBE

09/21/2000 to 12/31/2000   RODIN: SCULPTURE FROM THE IRIS AND B. GERALD CANTOR COLLECTION
On loan from the most important and extensive private collections of its kind will be 52 sculptures by celebrated 19th century French sculptor, Rodin.

Hermitage Foundation Museum
7637 North Shore Road, Norfolk, VA 23505
☎: 757-423-2052
Open: 10-5 M-Sa, 1-5 Su   **Closed:** 1/1, THGV, 12/25
ADM: Adult: $4.00   **Children:** $1.00   **Seniors:** $4.00
&. ℗
Historic Building
Permanent Collection: OR; EU; AS; 16,17

Nestled in a lush setting along the Lafayette River is the 12 acre estate of the Hermitage Foundation Museum whose turn-of-the-century English Tudor home appears to have been frozen in time. It is, however, alive with treasures from the past. **NOT TO BE MISSED:** 1400 year old Buddha

---
RADFORD

Radford University Galleries
200 Powell Hall, Radford, VA 24142
☎: 540-831-5754   ◙   www.runet,edu/~rumuseum
Open: Sept-April 10-5 Mo-Fr 1-4 Su (5/1-7/30 Mo-Fr 10-4   **Closed:** Mo, August, ACAD
&. ℗
Group Tours   Drop-In Tours: by appt   **Sculpture Garden**
Permanent Collection: Cont works in all media

Located in the New River Valley, the gallery is noted for the diversity of its special exhibitions. NOT TO BE MISSED: Radford University Living Collection placed throughout the campus

---
RICHMOND

Anderson Gallery, School of the Arts
Affiliate Institution: Virginia Commonwealth University
907 1/2 W. Franklin Street, Richmond, VA 23284-2514
☎: 804-828-1522   ◙   www.vcu.edu/artweb/gallery/index.html
Open: 10-5 Tu-Fr, 1-5 Sa, Su   **Closed:** LEG/HOL! ACAD!
Vol/Cont: ADM: Adult: $3.00   **Children:** $1.00   **Students:** $1.00   **Seniors:** $1.00
&. ℗ Metered on-street parking   **Museum Shop**
Group Tours
Permanent Collection: CONT: gr, phot, ptgs, sculp

The gallery is well known in the US and Europe for exhibiting work of nationally and internationally renowned artists.

VIRGINIA

Marsh Art Gallery, University of Richmond
George M. Modlin Center for the Arts, Richmond, VA 23173
📞: 804-289-8276
Open: 1-5 Tu-Sa   **Closed:** ACAD !
  ⓟ Free 🍴 College Cafeteria
Permanent Collection: AM: AS: EU: cer,drgs,gr,photo,ptg,sculp

The new galleries feature outstanding exhibitions of contemporary and historical art. **NOT TO BE MISSED:** The new Cram-inspired building designed by the architectural firm of Marcellus, Wright, Cox and Smith.

Virginia Museum of Fine Arts
2800 Grove Ave, Richmond, VA 23221-2466
📞: 804-367-0844 ◙ www.vmfa.state.va.us
Open: 11-5 Tu-Su, 11-8 Th   **Closed:** Mo, 1/1, 7/4, THGV, 12/25
Sugg/Cont: $4.00 pp
  ⓟ Free **Museum Shop** 🍴
Group Tours: 804-367-0859   **Drop-In Tours**: 2:30 Tu-Su, 6pm Th except summer   **Sculpture Garden**
Permanent Collection: AM: ptgs, sculp; LILLIAN THOMAS PRATT COLL OF JEWELS BY PETER CARL FABERGE; EU: all media (Ren to cont) ⌒

Diverse collections and outstanding special exhibits abound in the internationally prominent Virginia Museum which houses one of the largest collections in the world of Indian, Nepalese, and Tibetan art. It also holds the Mellon Collection of British sporting art and the Sydney and Francis Lewis Collection of late 19th and early 20th century decorative arts, contemporary American paintings and sculpture. **NOT TO BE MISSED:** 'Caligula', Roman, AD 38-40 marble 80 ' high. Also the largest public collection of Faberge Imperial Easter eggs in the West.

ON EXHIBIT 2000
to 01/2000   HIGHLIGHTS OF LATE TWENTIETH-CENTURY ART FROM THE SYDNEY AND FRANCES LEWIS COLLECTION
The complete installation of this extraordinary modern art gift will open in March 2000. These form the core of the Museum's holdings in 20th C. art.

07/06/1999 to 02/13/2000   GOD, REFUGE, AND PROTECTION: IMAGES OF VISHNU
Paintings, textiles and sculptures revealing the forms and colorful myths associated with Vishnu.

02/2000 to 05/2000   PAINTINGS AND DRAWINGS BY GEORGE STUBBS
Paul Mellon was an admirer and collector of George Stubbs. Most of his holdings went to the Yale Center for British Art, the Virginia Museum and the National Gallery. Upon his death he left those in his home to the three institutions. This exhibition will be a never to be repeated opportunity to see his best works. *Catalog Will Travel*

03/2000 to 06/2000   VANITAS: MEDITATIONS ON LIFE AND DEATH IN CONTEMPORARY ART
Combining tradition with contemporary art the exhibition features an international selection of contemporary artists whose works explore an age old theme. This has long been an inspiration for Western cultures most ignorant works of art, notably 17th C. Dutch still life's with flowers, ripe fruit, snuffed candles, skulls and timepieces. It combines an appreciation of life's pleasures with the knowledge of their inevitable loss.

05/2000 to 06/2000   UKIYO-E PRINTS: THE C. COLEMAN MCGEHEE COLLECTION
" Pictures of the Floating World" are highly stylized, often brilliantly colored wood block prints that depict Japanese Kabuki theatre subjects and actors as well as river, teahouse and other scenes of Japanese life during the Edo period (1600-1868). They are printed on "Washi," a special form of hand molded paper. Many famous ukiyo-e masters are represented here. *Will Travel*

09/21/2000 to 12/10/2000   MONET, RENOIR AND THE IMPRESSIONIST LANDSCAPE
Two of impressionism greatest, along with Corot, Boudin, Pissaro, Sisley Degas, Cézanne , Gauguin , Van Gogh and others tell the story of how we see the world.

ROANOKE

Art Museum of Western Virginia
One Market Square, Roanoke, VA 24011
☎: 540-342-5760 ◉ www.artmuseumroanoke.org
Open: 10-5 Tu-Sa, 1-5 Su (10-2 12/24,12/31) **Closed:** Mo, 1/1, 12/25
&. ℗ Pay **Museum Shop**
Group Tours Sculpture Garden
Permanent Collection: AM & EU: ptgs 20; AM: folk, gr, phot

The collection reflects all cultures formerly and presently found there. By collecting, exhibiting, preserving and interpreting works of art, the Museum plays a significant role in the cultural history of the region. Exhibitions are of both national and regional significance **NOT TO BE MISSED:** Sidewalk Art Show, June 3-4. 2000

ON EXHIBIT 2000
to 01/02/2000 AMERICA AMERICA: STYLES OF INDEPENDENCE
New acquisitions of American paintings by Hassam, Homer, Potthast and Dewing. Extraordinary examples of decorative art from Baltimore, Philadelphia and Virginia.

to 06/25/2000 CELEBRATION AND CEREMONY: WEST AFRICAN COMMUNITY TRADITIONS
From two private area collections, this includes ceremonial headdresses, funerary sculptures, tools and textiles from west African cultures including the Yoruba, Kongo and Bamana.

10/22/1999 to 02/20/2000 OF DARKNESS AND LIGHT: RECENT AMERICAN LANDSCAPE PAINTING
Contemporary responses to the American landscape by artists including Rackstraw Downes, Alan Bray, April Gornik, Joan Nelson and others.

01/15/2000 to 04/30/2000 CELEBRATING THE CREATIVE SPIRIT: CONTEMPORARY SOUTHEASTERN FURNITURE
The works shown here emphasize the whimsical side of personal artistic expression. It is as much about aesthetics as it is about function.

SWEET BRIAR

Sweet Briar College Art Gallery
Sweet Briar College, Sweet Briar, VA 24595
☎: 804-381-6248 ◉ www.artgallery.sbc.edu
Open: Pannell: 12-9:30 Mo-Th-, 12-5 Fr-Su, Babcock: 9-9 daily **Closed:** ACAD!
&. ℗ **Museum Shop** ∦: On campus
Group Tours Historic Building Sculpture Garden
Permanent Collection: JAP: woodblock prints; EU: gr, drgs 19; AM: ptgs 20

Th exterior design of the 1901 building is a rare collegiate example of Ralph Adams Cram Georgian Revival Style architecture. **NOT TO BE MISSED:** 'Daisies and Anemones', by William Glackens

ON EXHIBIT 2000
01/16/2000 to 03/12/2000 CAPE SPLIT CYCLE: MONOTYPES BY KATHERINE KADISH; POEMS BY SUE STANDING
These two artists have worked on a process they call "commenting" on each other's world.

01/20/2000 to 04/02/2000 AMERICAN ART FROM THE SWEET BRIAR COLLECTION

03/16/2000 to 05/14/2000 WASHINGTON AND LEE UNIVERSITY ART FACULTY EXHIBITION
Katherine Stone, Paintings; Larry Stene, Sculpture; Frank Hobbs, Paintings will be shown in this faculty exchange exhibition.

VIRGINIA

Sweet Briar College Art Gallery - continued

08/19/2000 to 11/07/2000   WILLIAM HARRIS AND HUNTER PHARIS "BUCK" JOHNSON
William Harris is primarily an etcher of whimsical, poignant and amusing images, 9 year old "Buck" Johnson is inspired by the natural world and by comic book artists.

08/26/2000 to 10/17/2000   LAURA PHARIS: TONE WOOD
The title refers to the type of wood used to make stringed instruments

10/21/2000 to 01/09/2000   RETRO GIRLS: NADARA GOODWIN, CYANOTYPES AND WILLIE ANNE WRITE, PINHOLE PHOTOGRAPHS
Each of these artists has developed a large body of work using 19th C photographic techniques.

VIRGINIA BEACH

Contemporary Art Center of Virginia
2200 Parks Avenue, Virginia Beach, VA 23451
\: 757-425-0000   ◉   www.cacv.org
Open: 10-4 Tu-Sa, 12-4 Su   **Closed:** Mo, .LEG/HOL!
&   ℗   **Museum Shop**
Group Tours   Drop-In Tours   Sculpture Garden
Permanent Collection: Non-collecting institution

This non-profit center exists to foster awareness and understanding of the significant art of our time.

ON EXHIBIT 2000
11/04/1999 to 02/06/2000   CONTEMPORARY LIGHT
The Contemporary Art Center will be transformed for the holidays into an extravaganza of light. Featured will be contemporary artists who utilize light as their medium of choice.

11/26/1999 to 01/09/2000   DANCING AT THE LOUVRE: FAITH RINGGOLD'S STORY COLLECTION AND OTHER STORY QUILTS
Over 20 acrylic on canvas quilt paintings, each expressing ideas through images and narrative, are displayed. *Will Travel*

01/28/2000 to 03/19/2000   SIX DEGREES OF INSPIRATION
A collaborative project with the Peninsula Fine Arts Center shows the diverse identity of the Hampton Roads region at the beginning of the 21st C. It focuses on large groups which have immigrated to the US within the past 50 years.

WILLIAMSBURG

Abby Aldrich Rockefeller Folk Art Center
307 S. England Street, Williamsburg, VA 23185
\: 757-220-7698   ◉   www.colonialwilliamsburg.org
Open: 11-5 daily 1/5-3/20; 10-5 3/21-12/3
ADM: Adult: $10.00, combine
&   ℗ Free   **Museum Shop**   ᵀ⅃: Cafe in Dewitt Wallace Gallery (separate building)
Group Tours   **Historic Building**
Permanent Collection: AM: folk

Historic Williamsburg is the site of the country's premier showcase for American folk art. The museum, originally built in 1957 and reopened in its new building in 1992, demonstrates folk art's remarkable range and inventiveness in textiles, paintings, and decorative arts. The DeWitt Wallace Gallery houses the collection of English and American Decorative arts and is included in the Museums ticket cost.

Abby Aldrich Rockefeller Folk Art Center - continued
ON EXHIBIT 2000

ONGOING   THE DEWITT WALLACE DECORATIVE ARTS GALLERY (entered through the Public Hospital Building)
The gallery offers exhibitions of decorative arts, firearms, textiles and costumes.

TO 12/2000   AN INTRODUCTION TO AMERICAN FOLK ART

TO 12/2000   FOLK ART IN AMERICAN LIFE
The Center's permanent collection of paintings, sculpture, textiles, furniture and a variety of three-dimensional objects such as whirligigs, weather vanes and shop signs.

TO 08/2000   MEET THE MAKERS
Biographies of six distinctive artists and examples of their works.

TO 12/2000   "SELECTIONS FROM MRS. ROCKEFELLER'S COLLECTION
Major examples of folk art collected by Abby Aldrich Rockefeller in the 1930s.

WILLIAMSBURG

Muscarelle Museum of Art
College of William and Mary, PO Box 8795, Williamsburg, VA 23187-8795

☎: 757–221-2700 ◙ www.wm.edu/muscarelle
Open: 10-4:45 Mo-Fr, 12-4 Sa-Su   **Closed:** LEG/HOL!
Vol/Cont:
   P   **Museum Shop**
Group Tours: 757-221-2703   **Drop-In Tours**: by appt   **Historic Building**
Permanent Collection: BRIT & AM: portraits 17-19; O/M: drgs; CONT: gr; AB; EU & AM: ptgs

The 'worlds' first solar painting' by Gene Davis, transforms the south facade of the Museum into a dramatic and innovative visual statement when monumental tubes, filled with colored water are lit from behind. **NOT TO BE MISSED:** "Portrait of William Short" by Rembrandt Peale; "Teacup and Bread on Ledge" by John Frederick Peto; "Moonlit Landscape" by Henry Ossawa Tanner

ON EXHIBIT 2000

10/02/1999 to 01/16/2000   FOR POSTERITY: SELECTIONS FROM THE NATIONAL ACADEMY OF DESIGN
This is the largest group of important American paintings to be exhibited in Williamsburg. Artists include Durand, Inness, Church, Kensett, Gifford, Homer, Chase, Eakins, Hassam, Henri and Johnson.

01/22/2000 to 03/19/2000   LIFTING THE ROSE-COLORED GLASSES: THREE SOCIAL REALISTS

WASHINGTON

Bellevue Art Museum

301 Bellevue Square, Bellevue, WA 98004
📞: 425-454-3322 ◉ www.bellevueart.org
Open: 10-6 Mo, We-Sa, 10-8 Tu, 11-5 Su THE MUSEUM IS CLOSED BETWEEN EXHIBITIONS
Closed: 1/1,EASTER,7/4,MEM/DAY,LAB/DAY,THGVG,12/25
Free Day: Tu **ADM: Adult:** $3.00 **Children:** Free under 12 **Seniors:** $2.00
♿ Ⓟ Free **Museum Shop**
Group Tours: 425-454-3322, ext. 100 **Drop-In Tours**: 2:00 daily
Permanent Collection: Non-collecting institution

Located across Lake Washington about 10 minutes drive from Seattle, the museum is a place to see, explore and make art.

ON EXHIBIT 2000

11/20/1999 to 01/30/2000 GAME SHOW
Games and game theory shed light on aspects of the artistic process. The exhibition will include interactive stations and artists in residence. Game Show will serve as a prototype for the ongoing presence of artists and thinkers in the new museum.

02/12/2000 to 04/22/2000 FIRST DESCENT
The exhibition will investigate the relationship between art and the sport of snowboarding. A companion exhibit will focus on mountain terrain - the physical world of the sport and the culture.

05/06/2000 to 06/25/2000 KURDISTAN: IN THE SHADOW OF HISTORY
The story of the Kurdish people, their struggle for independence and survival over the past century through photographs, documents, and artifacts. The exhibit will tell the story of a people who struggle to define themselves visually, politically, and culturally. MacArthur Award winning photographer Susan Meiselas has collected images from family albums, cultural institutions, news outlets, military/intelligence sources, her own photography, and elsewhere to resurrect the lost history of the Kurdish people.

07/09/2000 to 09/03/2000 2000 PACIFIC NORTHWEST ANNUAL
Artists from the region will be invited to undertake projects that address different aspects of regional identity.

Whatcom Museum of History & Art

121 Prospect Street, Bellingham, WA 98225
📞: 360-676-6981 ◉ www.cob.org.museum
Open: 12-5 Tu-Su **Closed:** Mo. LEG/HOL!
♿ **Museum Shop**
Group Tours Historic Building
Permanent Collection: KINSEY: phot coll; HANSON: Naval arch drgs; NW/COAST: ethnography; VICTORIANA

An architectural and historic landmark, this museum building is situated in a 1892 former City Hall on a bluff with a commanding view of Bellingham Bay.

ON EXHIBIT 2000

10/26/1999 to 02/20/2000 THE WHATCOM MUSEUM CELEBRATES WESTERN WASHINGTON UNIVERSITY'S CENTENNIAL
This celebration includes Western Views: historic photographs of Western's campus from the Museum archives; a variety of student shows presented by WWU Associated Student Gallery (known as the VU Gallery); and, an exhibition of current faculty works.

Whatcom Museum of History & Art - continued

10/26/1999 to 12/31/2000 THE KINSEY COLLECTION: LOGGING INDUSTRY
This selection from the Whatcom Museum's internationally known Kinsey Collection documents the drama of giant cedars being felled and the resulting clear-cut hillsides in northwest Washington from 1890 to 1940, as photographed by Darius Kinsey.

11/13/1999 to 03/19/2000 LANNY BERGNER: UN/NATURAL WORLD
This installation is a retrospective of the past fifteen years of Bergner's fascinating work. Inspired by the natural world, he uses hands-on methods of twisting, fraying, wrapping and knotting industrial materials to create visually striking and technically inventive forms.

CLARKSTON

Valley Art Center, Inc

842-6th Street, Clarkston, WA 99403
✆: 509-758-8331
Open: 9-4 Mo-Fr, by appt other times   **Closed:** 7/4, THGV, 12/25-1/1
& ℗   **Museum Shop   Group Tours   Historic Building**
Permanent Collection: REG; NAT/AM

Valley Art Center is located in Southeast Washington at the Snake and Clearwater Rivers in the heart of the city's historic district made famous by Lewis and Clarke. **NOT TO BE MISSED:** Beadwork, Piute Cradle Board Tatouche

GOLDENDALE

Maryhill Museum of Art

35 Maryhill Museum Drive, Goldendale, WA 98620
✆: 509-773-3733   ◉ www.maryhillmuseum.org
Open: 9-5 daily, Mar 15-Nov 15.   **Closed:** Open HOL
ADM: Adult: $6.50   **Children:** Free under 6   **Students:** $1.50   **Seniors:** $6.00
& ℗ Free   **Museum Shop**   ⅋: cafe, picnic grounds
Group Tours: 509-773-3733   **Historic Building   Sculpture Garden**
Permanent Collection: AUGUST RODIN SCULP; ORTHODOX ICONS: 18; BRIT: ptgs; NAT/AM: baskets, dec/art; FURNISHINGS OF QUEEN MARIE of ROMANIA; INTERNATIONAL CHESS SETS

Serving the Pacific Northwest, the Maryhill Museum is a major cultural resource in the Columbia River Gorge region. **NOT TO BE MISSED:** Theatre de la Mode: 1946 French Fashion collection

LONGVIEW

Art Gallery, Lower Columbia College Fine Arts Gallery

1600 Maple Street, Longview, WA 98632
✆: 360-577-2300
Open: 10-4 Mo, Tu, Fr, 10-8 We, Th Sept-June   **Closed:** Sa, S, LEG/HOL, ACAD/HOL
& ℗   ⅋: cafeteria in student center   **Group Tours**: 360-577-2314
Permanent Collection: Non-collecting institution

A College Gallery that features temporary exhibitions by local, regional, and national artists.

WASHINGTON

Washington State Capitol Museum
211 West 21st Avenue, Olympia, WA 98501
📞: 360-753-2580   ◙   www.wshs.org
Open: 10-4 Tu-Fr, 12-4 Sa-Su   **Closed:** Mo, LEG/HOL!
ADM: Adult: $2.00,$5.00 Families   **Students:** $1.00   **Seniors:** $1.75
♿ Ⓟ   **Museum Shop**
Group Tours   Drop-In Tours: by appt   **Historic Building**
Permanent Collection: REG: NAT/AM: 18,19

The Museum is housed in the Lord Mansion, a 1924 Italian Renaissance Revival Style building. It also features a permanent exhibit on the history of Washington State government and cultural history. **NOT TO BE MISSED:** Southern Puget Sound American Indian exhibit welcome healing totem pole figure.

Museum of Art
Washington State University, Pullman, WA 99164
📞: 509-335-1910   ◙   www.wsu.ed/artmuse
Open: 10-4 Mo-Fr, 10-10 Tu, 1-5 Sa-Su   **Closed:** ACAD!
♿ Ⓟ Parking permits may be purchased at Parking Services, adjacent to the Fine Arts Center
Group Tours
Permanent Collection: NW: art; CONT/AM & CONT/EU: gr 19

The WSU Museum of Art, in the university community of Pullman, presents a diverse program of changing exhibitions, including paintings, prints, photography, and crafts.

Frye Art Museum
704 Terry Avenue, Seattle., WA 98104
📞: 206-622-9250   ◙   www.fryeart.org
Open: 10-5 Tu-Sa, 10-9 Th, 12-5 Su   **Closed:** Mo, 1/1, THGV, 12/25
♿ Ⓟ Free across from Museum   **Museum Shop**   ¶: 11-4 Tu-Sa, 11-7:30 Th, 12-4 Su
Group Tours: 2 weeks adv res   **Sculpture Garden**
Permanent Collection: AM Realist 19-20; EU Realist ptgs, Munich School

A mid-sized museum representing representational art from Colonial times to the present Hailed by the press as a "little gem of a museum" it presents European and American art . Charles and Emma Frye bequeathed their collection to create a free public art museum.

ON EXHIBIT 2000
09/18/1999 to 01/02/2000   VICTORIAN PAINTINGS FROM THE ROYAL ACADEMY

11/06/1999 to 01/02/2000   RIE MUNOZ: PORTRAIT OF ALASKA

12/03/1999 to 01/30/2000   JON SWIHART: PAINTINGS

01/07/2000 to 02/27/2000   PATRICK HUSE: LANDSCAPES

Frye Art Museum - continued
01/15/2000 to 04/16/2000   **HERSEN COLLECTION**

02/04/2000 to 04/02/2000   **DONALD BARTON: PHOTOGRAPHS**

03/03/2000 to 04/30/2000   **LISA ZWERLING**

04/07/2000 to 05/28/2000   **ROBERT SCHWARTZ: ENIGMAS AND SEDUCTIONS**

04/29/2000 to 06/25/2000   **ON THE ROAD WITH THOMAS HART BENTON**
How drawing, one of Benton's greatest talents and travel, a passion combined to produce some of his most significant works. *Will Travel*

05/05/2000 to 07/09/2000   **GRAHAM NICKSON**

06/02/2000 to 07/30/2000   **DAVID ROSENTHAL: VISIONS OF ANTARCTICA**

07/08/2000 to 09/17/2000   **NORTHWEST WATERCOLOR SOCIETY: SIXTIETH ANNIVERSARY**

07/14/2000 to 09/10/2000   **ANOTHER LOOK: WINOLD REISS**

08/04/2000 to 10/01/2000   **HELEN LUGGER: ETCHINGS AND DRAWINGS**

09/15/2000 to 11/05/2000   **SHELLEY JORDAN**

09/30/2000 to 11/26/2000   **TONY FOSTER:WORLDVIEWS**

10/06/2000 to 12/10/2000   **STEPHEN FISHER**

11/10/2000 to 01/07/2001   **ROBERT VAN VRANKEN**

12/09/2000 to 02/11/2001   **REPRESENTING LA : CONTEMPORARY REPRESENTATIONAL ARTISTS FROM LOS ANGELES**

Henry Art Gallery
Affiliate Institution: University of Washington
15th Ave. NE & NE 41st Street, Seattle, WA 98195-3070
☎: 206-543-2280   ◙   www.henryart.org
Open: 11-5 Tu, We, Fr-Su, 11-8 Th   **Closed:** Mo 1/1, 7/4, THGV, 12/25
Free Day: Th, 5-8pm pay what you wish   **ADM: Adult:** $5.00   **Children:** Free under 12   **Seniors:** $3.50
&. ℗ Pay   **Museum Shop**   ¶¶
Group Tours: 206-616-8782   **Drop-In Tours**: 2nd Sa, 3rd Th each month, 2pm   **Historic Building   Sculpture Garden**
Permanent Collection: PTGS: 19,20; PHOT; CER; ETH: textiles & W./Coast

The major renovation designed by Charles Gwathmey of Carl F. Gould's 1927 building reopened in April 1997. The expansion adds 10,000 square feet of galleries and additional visitor amenities and educational facilities.

ON EXHIBIT 2000
11/18/1999 to 03/05/2000   **INSIDE OUT: NEW CHINESE ART**
Concepts of "modernity" and "identity" are undergoing rapid transformation in the Chinese world as Asian societies evolve in the post-1980s climate of radical social, economic and political change. This major exhibition is the first to bring together more than 100 works from various parts of the Chinese world including Taiwan, Hong Kong and outside of Asia. The political and economic change will be traced in the work of artists who worked in Asia before Tiananmen and outside after. Some of the works will be at the P.S. 1 Contemporary Art Center in New York

01/14/2000 to 04/23/2000   **FUTURE FORWARD: PROJECTS IN NEW MEDIA**

02/10/2000 to 08/21/2000   **SHIFTING GROUND: TRANSFORMED VIEWS OF AMERICAN LANDSCAPE**

WASHINGTON

Nordic Heritage Museum
3014 N.W. 67th Street, Seattle, WA 98117

☎: 206-789-5707 **◉** WWW.NORDICMUSEUM.COM
Open: 10-4 Tu-Sa, 12-4 Su **Closed:** Mo, 12/24, 12/25, 1/1
Free Day: 1st Tu each month **ADM: Adult:** $4.00 **Children:** $2.00 (6-16) **Students:** $3.00 **Seniors:** $3.00
& **℗** Free **Museum Shop** **Group Tours**
Permanent Collection: SCANDINAVIAN/AM: folk; PHOT

Follow the immigrants journey across America in this museum located in Ballard north of the Ballard Locks.
NOT TO BE MISSED: "Dancing Angels" original bronze sculpture by Carl Milles

ON EXHIBIT 2000
12/03/1999 to 02/27/2000 IHOMEPLACES-HEIMAHAGAR ICELANDIC/AMERICAN PHOTOGRAPHY: OF ICELAND, THE LAND THEY LEFT AND THE LAND OF IMMIGRATION

02/2000 to 03/2000 INGER HODGSON: SWEDISH PAINTER

03/10/2000 to 05/28/2000 FAMILY PORTRAITS-NORWAY TO AMERICA YLVISAKER AND BLAENDEL
An American artist in Norway and a Norwegian artist in America–two views

04/2000 to 05/2000 JOAN GROUT: NORWEGIAN-AMERICAN PAINTER

06/02/2000 to 07/02/2000 PHOTOS - BILDSTUGAN
Photos from Norbotten, a province in Northern Sweden

07/08/2000 to 09/17/2000 ERIK HOGLAND: A RETROSPECTIVE
Studio glass by one of Sweden's foremost glass artists

09/29/2000 to 11/12/2000 THE NORDIC SOUND
musical instruments from pre-Christian to contemporary times loaned by museums in the five Nordic countries

12/01/2000 to 01/31/2001 STEVE JENSEN-NORWEGIAN AMERICAN SCULPTOR

Seattle Art Museum
100 University Street, Seattle, WA 98101-2902

☎: 206-625-8900 **◉** www.seattleartmuseum.org
Open: 10-5 Tu-Su, 10-9 Th, open Mo on Holidays **Closed:** Mo, except Hols, THGV, 12/25, 1/1
Free Day: 1st Tu, Sr.1st Fr **ADM: Adult:** $6.00 **Children:** Free under 12 **Students:** $4.00 **Seniors:** $4.00
& **℗** Limited pay parking **Museum Shop** **†|**
Group Tours: 206-654-3123 **Drop-In Tours**: 2 Tu-Su 7 Th, Sp exh 1 Tu-Su, 6 Th
Sculpture Garden
Permanent Collection: AS; AF; NW NAT/AM; CONT; PHOT; EU: dec/art; NW/CONT

Designed by Robert Venturi, architect of the new wing of the National Gallery in London, this stunning new five story building is but one of the reasons for visiting the outstanding Seattle Art Museum. The new downtown location is conveniently located within walking distance of many of Seattle's most interesting landmarks including Pike Place Market, and Historic Pioneer Square. The Museum features 2 complete educational resource centers with interactive computer systems. **NOT TO BE MISSED:** NW Coast Native American Houseposts; 48' kinetic painted steel sculpture 'Hammering Man' by Jonathan Borofsky

ON EXHIBIT 2000
ONGOING CONTEMPORARY NORTHWEST COAST BASKETRY
From the collection, a new case installation of masterworks by today's outstanding native weavers.

Seattle Art Museum - continued

02/24/2000 to 05/14/2000   WEEGEE'S WORLD: LIFE, DEATH AND THE HUMAN DRAMA
The late great photojournalist and maverick photographer, Weegee .

06/08/2000 to 09/10/2000   EASTMAN JOHNSON: PAINTING AMERICA
This retrospective exhibition of the genre painter includes 100 paintings and drawings.

Seattle Asian Art Museum

Volunteer Park, 1400 East Prospect Street, Seattle, WA
☎: 206-625-8900   ◉ www.seattleartmuseum.org
Open: 10-5 Tu-Su, 10-9 Th   **Closed:** Mo LEG/HOL
Free Day: 1st Th, Sr 1st Fr, First Sa   **ADM: Adult:** $3.00   **Children:** Free under 12
&   ℗ Free   **Museum Shop**
Group Tours: 206-654-3123   **Drop-In Tours**: !
Historic Building
Permanent Collection: WONDERS OF CLAY AND FIRE: CHINESE CERAMICS THROUGH THE AGES (WITH PARTIAL ROTATION)   A comprehensive survey of Chinese ceramic history from the fifth millennium BC through the 15th century AD

The historical preservation of the Carl Gould designed 1932 building (the first Art-Deco style art museum in the world) involved uniting all areas of the structure including additions of 1947, 1954, and 1955. Now a 'jewel box' with plush but tasteful interiors perfectly complementing the art of each nation. 900 0f the 7000 objects in the collection are on view.

ON EXHIBIT 2000

ONGOING   THE INDIVIDUALISTIC BRUSH: CHINESE PAINTINGS OF THE 17TH AND 18TH CENTURIES

to 04/02/2000   WOVEN SYMBOLS: CHINESE GARMENTS AND TEXTILES
The potent symbolism in traditional Chinese clothing is shown here.

to 04/02/2000   WORLDS OF FANTASY: CHINESE SHADOW PUPPETS
Mythical beasts, wild animals and human characters are in this rich array of characters..

to 07/25/2000   FLIGHTS OF FANCY: NATURAL AND SUPERNATURAL IMAGERY IN JAPANESE ART
Uninhibited images ranging from lyrical daydreams to surreal nightmares will be seen in the works on view.

to 08/22/2000   KOREAN SCREEN PAINTINGS AND BUDDHIST PRIEST PORTRAITS

04/29/1999 to 02/13/2000   MODERN MASTERS OF KYOTO: TRANSFORMATION OF JAPANESE PAINTING TRADITIONS 'NIHONGA' FROM THE GRIFFITH AND PATRICIA WAY COLLECTION
A third in a chronological series on Japanese painting. Featured are works from the late 19th into the 20th century. A full changeover will take place in October 1999.

10/23/1999 to 10/2000   EXPLORE KOREA: A VISIT TO GRANDFATHER'S HOUSE
A replica of a 1930's Korean home will be installed.

04/20/2000   HIMALAYAN ART

07/01/2000 to 01/01/2001   SHEER REALITIES: POWER, BODY AND CLOTHING IN THE 19TH CENTURY PHILIPPINES
75 to 100 items will look at the action between the external indigenous cultural influences of the Philippines over the past century. They will be shown with other materials including hardwoods, ivories, silver, etc.

WASHINGTON

Cheney Cowles Museum
2316 W. First Avenue, Spokane, WA 99204
📞: 509-456-3931
Open: 10-5 Tu-Sa, 10-9 We, 1-5 Su   **Closed:** LEG/HOL!
Free Day: We, 1/2 price   **ADM: Adult:** $4.00, Fam $10   **Children:** $2.50, 6-16   **Students:** $2.50   **Seniors:** $2.50
  Ⓟ   **Museum Shop**
Group Tours   Historic Building
Permanent Collection: NW NAT/AM; REG; DEC/ART

The mission of the Cheney Cowles Museum is to actively engage the people of the Inland Northwest in life-long learning about regional history, visual arts, and American Indian and other cultures especially those specific to the region. PLEASE NOTE: The museum will close on July 1, 1999 for major expansion and will remain closed until 2001. There will be programming and special events off-site. www.cheneycowles.org will be our updated website.

Tacoma Art Museum
12th & Pacific (downtown Tacoma), Tacoma, WA 98402
📞: 206-272-4258   ▣   www.tacomaartmuseum.org
Open: 10-5 Tu-Sa, 10-7 Th, 12-5 Su   **Closed:** 1/1, THGV, 12/25
Free Day: Tu   **ADM: Adult:** $3.00   **Children:** Free under 12   **Students:** $2.00   **Seniors:** $2.00
  Ⓟ Street parking   **Museum Shop**
Group Tours
Permanent Collection: CONT/NW; AM: ptgs

The only comprehensive collection of the stained glass of Dale Chihuly in a public institution. **NOT TO BE MISSED:** Chihuly Retrospective Glass Collection

ON EXHIBIT 2000
11/20/1999 to 05/03/2000   INSIDE OUT: NEW CHINESE ART
Inside Out is the first major international exhibition to present the dynamic new art being produced by artists in China, Taiwan, Hong Kong and select artist who emigrated to the West in the late 1980s. The exhibition focuses on artworks that explore the complex relationship between culturally specific issues and larger developments, such as the rapid pace of economic, social and political change in the region, of a modern/postmodern age.

Tacoma Public Library/Thomas Handforth Gallery
1102 Tacoma Avenue South, Tacoma, WA 98402
📞: 206-591-5666   ▣   www.tpl.lib.wa.us
Open: 9-9 Mo-Th, 9-6 Fr-Sa   **Closed:** S, LEG/HOL!
  Ⓟ
Historic Building
Permanent Collection: HISTORICAL; PHOT; ARTIFACTS

Built in 1903 as an original Andrew Carnegie Library, the Gallery has been serving the public since then with rotating exhibits by Pacific Northwest artists and touring educational exhibits **NOT TO BE MISSED:** Rare book room containing 750 prints including 'North American Indian', by Edward S. Curtice

Sheehan Gallery

Affiliate Institution: Whitman College
900 Isaacs- Olin Hall, Walla Walla, WA 99362

☏: 509-527-5249
Open: 10-5 Tu-Fr, 1-4 Sa-Su   **Closed:** Mo, ACAD!
♿ Ⓥ On campus
Group Tours
Permanent Collection: SCROLLS; SCREENS; BUNRAKY PUPPETS; CER

The Sheehan Gallery administrates the Davis Collection of Oriental Art which is not on permanent display.

WEST VIRGINIA

Sunrise Museum
746 Myrtle Road, Charleston, WV 25314
☎: 304-344-8035 ◙ (under construction) sunrisemuseum.org
Open: 11-5 We-Sa, 12-5 Su **Closed:** LEG/HOL!
ADM: Adult: $3.50 **Students:** $2.50 **Seniors:** $2.50
& ℗ **Museum Shop**
Group Tours **Historic Building Sculpture Garden**
Permanent Collection: AM: ptgs, sculp, gr; SCI COLL

This multi media center occupies two historic mansions overlooking downtown Charleston. Featured are a Science Hall, Planetarium, and an art museum.

Huntington Museum of Art, Inc
2033 McCoy Road, Huntington, WV 25701-4999
☎: 304-529-2701 ◙ www.hmoa.org
Open: 10-5 Tu-Sa, 12-5 Sa **Closed:** Mo, /1, 7/4, THGV, 12/25
& ℗ **Museum Shop**
Group Tours Drop-In Tours: 10:30, 11:30 Sa, 2, 3 Su **Historic Building Sculpture Garden**
Permanent Collection: AM: ptgs, dec/art 18-20; GLASS; SILVER

The serene beauty of the museum complex on a lovely hilltop surrounded by nature trails, herb gardens, an outdoor amphitheater and a sculpture courtyard is enhanced by an extensive addition designed by the great architect Walter Gropius. The Museum is home to the state's only plant conservatory.

ON EXHIBIT 2000

08/22/1999 to 01/09/2000 WINSLOW ANDERSON: AARTIST/DESIGNER
Andeerson was head designer at Blenko Glass and at Lenox China, and received the Museum of Modern Art award for design. This is a retrospective of his work in studio glass and porcelain ware.

11/07/1999 to 03/26/2000 COOL DESIGNS @ HMA
No one style defines the 20th C. but the look is unmistakable. Form and function have blended together to shape the landscape of our daily lives.

01/30/2000 THE AMERICANS
What is "American" in our culture. A selection of work in all media looks at the concepts of landscape and portraits . Furniture and porcelain are incorporated. To give a perspective on creative activity in the 19th and 20th C.

02/27/2000 to 04/23/2000 LINDA MCCARTNEY'S SIXTIES-PORTRAIT OF AN ERA
The 50 photographs in the exhibition were intimate shots taken in natural light. Her portraits of the rock stars of the era were unique.

03/26/2000 to 04/24/2000 SPRING FLOWER SHOW

04/09/2000 to 07/09/2000 FIVE ARTIST INVITATIONAL
Contemporary artists who have exhibited before to see what they are doing as the century changes

04/30/2000 to 05/28/2000 PORTFOLIO
Students and community members are exhibited here.

BELOIT

Wright Museum of Art
Affiliate Institution: Beloit College
Prospect at Bushnell, Beloit, WI 53511
☎: 608-363-2677 ◉ www.beloit.edu/~museum
Open: 9-5 Mo-Fr, 11-4 Sa, Su **Closed:** ACAD!
  ♿ ℗ **Museum Shop**
Group Tours
Permanent Collection: AS; KOREAN: dec/art, ptgs, gr; HIST & CONT: phot

The Wright Museum of Art had its beginnings in 1892. Over the years, the museum has obtained a large collection of Asian decorative arts, a large collection of Chinese snuff bottles, Japanese woodblock prints, Japanese sword fittings, Japanese sagemono and netsuke, Korean ceramics and Bhuddist sculpture and a wide variety of important works by major artists.

MADISON

Elvehjem Museum of Art
Affiliate Institution: University of Wisconsin-Madison
800 University Ave, Madison, WI 53706
☎: 608-263-2246
Open: 9-5 Tu-Fr 11-5 Sa, Su **Closed:** Mo. 1/1, THGV, 12/24, 12/25
  ♿ ℗ University lots 46 and 83 on Lake Street and City Lake St and Madison ramps. **Museum Shop**
Group Tours   Drop-In Tours: !
Permanent Collection: AN/GRK: vases & coins; MIN.IND PTGS: Earnest C. & Jane Werner Watson Coll; JAP: gr (Van Vleck Coll); OR: dec/arts); RUSS & SOVIET: ptgs (Joseph E. Davies Coll)

More than 15,000 objects that date from 2300 B.C. to the present are contained in this unique university museum collection.

ON EXHIBIT 2000
09/16/2000 to 12/03/2000   PARIS 1900: THE "AMERICAN SCHOOL" AT THE UNIVERSAL EXPOSITION
The Pennsylvania Academy was a major lender to the Paris Exposition of 1900 which played a critical role in defining "American" artistic influences at the time. It featured all the major artists of the late 19th century. Approximately 50 of the paintings and sculpture will be featured here. *Catalog Will Travel*

Madison Art Center
211 State Street, Madison, WI 53703
☎: 608-257-0158
Open: 11-5 Tu-Th, 11-9 Fr, 10-9 Sa, 1-5 Su **Closed:** LEG/HOL!
  ♿ ℗ Pay **Museum Shop**
Group Tours   Historic Building
Permanent Collection: AM: works on paper,ptgs,sculp; JAP; MEX; CONT

Located in the Old Capitol theatre, the Madison Art Center offers modern and contemporary art exhibitions and highlights from its permanent collections. **NOT TO BE MISSED:** 'Serenade' by Romare Bearden

WISCONSIN

MANITOWOC

Rahr-West Art Museum
610 North Eighth Street, Manitowoc, WI 54220

☎: 920-683-4501   ◙   link from www.manitowoc.org
Open: 10-4 Mo, Tu, Th, Fr, 10-8 We, 11-4 Sa-Su   **Closed:** LEG/HOL!
&   Ⓟ Free
Group Tours   **Historic Building**
Permanent Collection: AM: ptgs, dec/art 19; OR: ivory, glass; CONT: ptgs

Built between 1891 & 1893, this Victorian mansion combines with the West Wing added in 1975 and 1986. These showcase the Museum's 19th and 20th C. art, antiques while the West Gallery rotates a schedule of regional and nationally touring exhibitions. **NOT TO BE MISSED:** 'Birch and Pine Tree No 2', by Georgia O'Keeffe ; La Petite Boudeuse, 1888 o/c by William Adolphe Bougereau

ON EXHIBIT 2000
12/19/1999 to 01/09/2000   RAHR- WEST PERMANENT COLLECTION AND RECENT ACQUISITIONS

02/06/2000 to 02/20/2000   THE ART OF TABLESETTINGS
An annual exhibition of tableware and wall hangings.

04/16/2000 to 05/14/2000   WILL BARNET: AN AMERICAN MASTER PRINT RETROSPECTIVE

07/09/2000 to 08/20/2000   SUNLIGHT AND SHADOW: AMERICAN IMPRESSIONISM 1885-1945

09/03/2000 to 10/15/2000   THE JOHN AND MARGARET HILL COLLECTION OF AMERICAN WESTERN ART
This collection of landscapes, portraits of cowboys, Native American subjects, etc. that stretch the scope of the American West.

MILWAUKEE

Charles Allis Art Museum
1801 North Prospect Avenue, Milwaukee, WI 53202

☎: 414-278-8295
Open: 1-5 We-Su, 7-9 We   **Closed:** LEG/HOL!
ADM: Adult: $2.00
&   **Group Tours**   **Historic Building**
Permanent Collection: CH: porcelains; OR; AN/GRK; AN/R; FR: ptgs 19

With its diverse collection this museum is housed in a 1909 Tudor style house.

Milwaukee Art Museum
750 North Lincoln Memorial Drive, Milwaukee, WI 53202

☎: 414-224-3200   ◙   www.mam.org
Open: 10-5 Tu, We, Fr, Sa, 12-9 T, 12-5 Su   **Closed:** Mo, 1/1, THGV, 12/25
ADM: Adult: $5.00   **Children:** Free under 12   **Students:** $3.00   **Seniors:** $3.00
&   Ⓟ   **Museum Shop**   ⅋
Group Tours: 414-224-3825   **Historic Building**   **Sculpture Garden**
Permanent Collection: CONT: ptgs, sculp; GER; AM: folk art

The Milwaukee Museum features an exceptional collection housed in a 1957 landmark building by Eero Saarinen, which is cantilevered over the Lake Michigan shoreline. A dramatic addition designed by Santiago Calatrava is scheduled to open in 2000. **NOT TO BE MISSED:** Zurburan's 'St. Francis'

Milwaukee Art Museum - continued

ON EXHIBIT 2000

ONGOING   THE MICHAEL AND JULIE HALL COLLECTION OF AMERICAN FOLK ART
After a cross country tour the renowned collection acquired by the Museum in 1989 will be presented in an ongoing exhibition.

09/10/1999 to 01/02/2000   THE LAST SHOW OF THE CENTURY: A HISTORY OF THE 20TH CENTURY THROUGH ITS ART
Using a 20th-century time line, this exhibition will convey how artists witnessed, responded to, chronicled or interpreted virtually every major historical milestone in the past 100 years. Rather than tell the history of art in this century, this exhibit will show the complex history of this century through art.

09/24/1999 to 01/02/2000   ROY LICHTENSTEIN PRINTS
A survey of the extensive range of Pop graphics from one of America's preeminent artists.   Lichtenstein, who produced hundreds of prints that highlight the explosion of imagery in American popular culture, reworked our visual culture into sleek, new commodities, underscoring the reproducibility and marketability of just about everything in our midst.

01/21/2000 to 04/23/2000   INTERVENTIONS: NEW ART IN UNCONVENTIONAL SPACES
Recent works by about 12 leading international artists will be dispersed throughout the museum. To view the exhibition, visitors will navigate the entire facility, a configuration that has remained essentially unchanged since 1975. In 2000, the museum is scheduled to open a 125,000-square-foot addition and reconfigure these spaces in the re-installed permanent collection.

03/17/2000 to 05/14/2000   NOTHING BUT NUDES: SELECTIONS FROM THE PERMANENT COLLECTION
The changing role and meaning of the nude in art from ancient times to the present will be reflected in various media, from painting and sculpture to works on paper, photographs, plus decorative and folk art.

Patrick & Beatrice Haggerty Museum of Art

Affiliate Institution: Marquette University
13th & Clybourn, Milwaukee, WI 53233-1881
☎: 414-288-1669   ◙ www.mu.edu/haggerty
Open: 10-4:30 Mo-Sa, 12-5 Su, 10-8 Th   **Closed:** 1/1, EASTER, THGV, 12/25
&   **Museum Shop   Group Tours**: 414-288-5915   **Sculpture Garden**
Permanent Collection: PTGS, DRWG, GR, SCULP, PHOT, DEC/ART 16-20; ASIAN, TRIBAL

Selections from the Old Master and modern collections are on exhibition continuously.

ON EXHIBIT 2000

ONGOING   MODERN GALLERY
20th century art from the collections including work by Dali, Lawrence, Man Ray and Nam June Paik.

ONGOING   THE GREEN ROOM:
Salon-style gallery hung with art from 16th-19th centuries by European Old Masters.

11/07/1999 to 01/02/2000   WISCONSIN ARTISTS BIENNIAL

UWM Art Museum

3253 N. Downer Avenue, Milwaukee, WI 53211
☎: 414-226-6509
Open: 10-4 Tu-Fr, 12-8 We, 1-5 Sa-Su   **Closed:** LEG/HOL!
&   ℗ Meters in front of building.
Permanent Collection: AM & EU: works on paper, gr; RUSS: icons; REG: 20

The museum works to provide its audience with an artistic cultural and historical experience unlike that offered by other art institutions in Milwaukee. It's three spaces on the campus provide the flexibility of interrelated programming.

WISCONSIN

Villa Terrace Decorative Arts Museum
2220 North Terrace Ave, Milwaukee, WI 53202
☏: 414-271-3656
Open: 12-5 We-Su **Closed:** LEG/HOL!
ADM: Adult: $2.00 **Children:** Free under 12 **Students:** $2.00 **Seniors:** $2.00
♿ &#9физ; **Historic Building**
Permanent Collection: DEC/ART; PTGS, SCULP, GR 15-20

Villa Terrace Decorative Arts Museum with its excellent and varied collections is located in a historic landmark building.

Paine Art Center and Arboretum
1410 Algoma Blvd, Oshkosh, WI 54901
☏: 920-235-6903
Open: 11-4 Tu-Su, 11-7 Fr extended hours apply Mem/Day-Lab/Day **Closed:** Mo, LEG/HOL!
ADM: Adult: $5.00 **Children:** Free under 12 **Students:** $2.00 **Seniors:** $2.50
♿ &#9физ; On-street parking **Museum Shop**
Group Tours: ext 21 **Drop-In Tours:** by appt **Historic Building Sculpture Garden**
Permanent Collection: FR & AM: ptgs, sculp, gr 19,20; OR: silk rugs, dec/art

Collections of paintings, sculpture and decorative objects in period room settings are featured in this historic 1920's Tudor Revival home surrounded by botanic gardens. **NOT TO BE MISSED:** 'The Bronco Buster', sculpture by Frederic Remington

Charles A. Wustum Museum of Fine Arts
2519 Northwestern Ave, Racine, WI 53404
☏: 424-636-9177
Open: 1-5 Tu, We, Fr-Su, 1-9 Mo, Th **Closed:** LEG/HOL!, 12/19/94-1/7/95
♿ &#9физ; Free **Museum Shop Group Tours Historic Building Sculpture Garden**
Permanent Collection: SCULP; WPA works on paper; Crafts

In an 1856 Italianate style building on acres of landscaped sculpture gardens you will find Racine's only fine arts museum. It primarily supports active, regional living artists.

John Michael Kohler Arts Center
608 New York Avenue, PO Box 489, Sheboygan, WI 53082-0489
☏: 920-458-6144 ◉ www.kohlerartscenter.org
Open: 10-5 Mo-We, Fr, 10-9 Tu, Th, 12-5 Sa, Su **Closed:** 12/31, 1/1, EASTER, MEM/DAY, THGV, 12/24, 12/25
♿ &#9физ; **Museum Shop** ⍕ **Group Tours:** ext 109 **Drop-In Tours:** ! **Historic Building Sculpture Garden**
Permanent Collection: CONT: cer; DEC/ART

This multicultural center is located in the 1860's villa of John Michael Kohler, founder of the plumbing manufacturing company. Special exhibitions at the Center offer unique perspectives on art forms, artists, and various artistic concepts that have received little exposure elsewhere. The facility expansion will add 69,000 square feet with nine New Arts Galleries, a theatre and studio performance space.

Leigh Yawkey Woodson Art Museum
700 North Twelfth Street, Wausau, WI 54403-5007

☎: 715-845-7010 ◉ www.lywam.org
Open: 9-4 Tu-Fr, 12-5 Sa-Su **Closed:** Mo, LEG/HOL!
🚻 Ⓟ Free
Group Tours Drop-In Tours: ! 9am-4pm **Sculpture Garden**
Permanent Collection: GLASS 19,20; STUDIO GLASS; PORCELAIN; WILDLIFE; ptgs, sculp

An English style residence surrounded by gracious lawns and gardens. A new sculpture garden features permanent installations and annually the garden will exhibit 10-15 temporary pieces.

ON EXHIBIT 2000
11/13/1999 to 02/20/2000 BUSHFIRE: AUSTRALIAN ABORIGINAL ART FROM THE KLUGE RUHE COLLECTION
A common farming technique to ensure that land will be cleared for hunting and new growth. This is a significant part of Aboriginal culture.

02/26/2000 to 04/16/2000 ALL-STARS: AMERICAN SPORTING PRINTS FROM THE COLLECTION OF REBA AND DAVE WILLIAMS
A selection of prints by more than 50 artists looking for colorful subject matter.

04/22/2000 to 06/25/2000 WATER
Water nourishes and refreshes us. Some artists look at the utilitarian functions of water white others consider the terror that it can sometimes elicit.

06/2000 to 05/2001 ART/NATURE/NURTURE
12 contemporary sculptors respond to the natural world through use of natural materials.

07/01/2000 to 08/27/2000 BATS AND BOWLS: CONTEMPORARY TURNED OBJECTS
24 North American wood turners take a "crack at the bat".- Baseball while simultaneously paying homage to artists whose tool of choice is the lathe.

07/01/2000 to 08/27/2000 TEMPE TEA PARTY
31 artworks by 28 artists showcasing the Teapot.

09/09/2000 to 11/12/2000 BIRDS IN ART
An annual autumn exhibition which brings together international artists whose work celebrates the beauty and bounty of the avian kingdom.

11/18/2000 to 01/14/2001 FROM EARTH AND SOUL: THE EVANS COLLECTION OF ASIAN CERAMICS
Examples from the major ceramic centers of east Asia including Thailand, Vietnam, the Philippines, Cambodia, Korea and China spanning the 6th to the 19th C.

WEST BEND

West Bend Art Museum
300 South 6th Ave, West Bend, WI 53095

☎: 414-334-9638 ◉ www.hnet.net/~artmuseum
Open: 10-4:30 We-Sa, 1-4:30 Su **Closed:** Mo, Tu, LEG/HOL!
🚻 Ⓟ
Group Tours Drop-In Tours: 8am-4:30pm **Sculpture Garden**
Permanent Collection: ACADEMIC ART WORK; REG: 1850-1950

WISCONSIN

West Bend Art Museum - continued
This community art center and museum is dedicated to the work of Wisconsin's leading artists from Euro-American settlement to the present and features changing exhibitions of regional, national and international art. **NOT TO BE MISSED:** The colossal 1889 painting "The Flagellants" measuring approximately 14' x 26' first exhibited in the US at the 1893 Chicago Worlds Fair, The Columbian Exposition.

ON EXHIBIT 2000

03/08/2000 to 04/16/2000	THE INTIMATE COLLABORATION: PRINTS FROM THE TEABERRY PRESS
04/19/2000 to 05/28/2000	500O YEARS OF CHINESE HISTORY
05/21/2000 to 07/23/2000	150 YEARS OF WISCONSIN PRINTMAKING
07/26/2000 to 09/03/2000	NATIONAL WATERCOLOR SOCIETY
09/06/2000 to 10/15/2000	RENDERING SYMBOLS AND CODES
10/18/2000 to 11/26/2000	WISCONSIN PAINTERS AND SCULPTURS: 100TH ANNIVERSARY EXHIBITION
11/29/2000 to 01/07/2001	WEST BEND ART MUSEUM FRIENDS EXHIBITION

Bradford Brinton Memorial Museum
239 Brinton Road, Big Horn, WY 82833
✆: 307-672-3173
Open: 9:30-5 daily May 15-LAB/DAY, other months by appt
ADM: Adult: $3.00   Children: Free under 12   Students: $2.00   Seniors: $2.00
♿ ⓟ   **Museum Shop   Historic Building**
Permanent Collection: WESTERN ART; DEC/ART; NAT/AM: beadwork

Important paintings by the best known Western artists are shown in a fully furnished 20 room ranch house built in 1892 and situated at the foot of the Big Horn Mountain. **NOT TO BE MISSED:** 'Custer's Fight on the Little Big Horn', by Frederic Remington

Nicolaysen Art Museum
400 East Collins Drive, Casper, WY 82601-2815
✆: 307-235-5247
Open: 10-5 Tu-Su, 10-8 Th   **Closed:** 1/1; THGV; 12/24; 12/25
Free Day: 4-8 1st & 3rd Th   **ADM:** Adult: $2.00   Children: $1.00 under 12   Students: $1.00   Seniors: $2.00
♿ ⓟ   **Museum Shop   Group Tours   Drop-In Tours: !   Historic Building**
Permanent Collection: CARL LINK ILLUSTRATIONS; REG

The roots of this Museum reside in the commitment of Wyoming people to the importance of having art and culture as an integral part life. **NOT TO BE MISSED:** The Discovery Center, an integral part of the museum, complements the educational potential of the exhibitions

Wyoming State Museum
Barrett Building, 2301 Central Ave., Cheyenne, WY 82002
✆: 307-777-7022 (◙ www.commerce.state.wy.us/cr/wsm/index.htm
Open: 9-4:30 Tu-Sa   **Closed:** Su, Mo, LEG/HOL!
♿ ⓟ Free in lot north of Barrett bldg . Metered parking nearby streets   **Museum Shop   Group Tours   Sculpture Garden**
Permanent Collection: 100,000 artifacts relating to Wyoming's heritage in all media

10 galleries which tell the story of Wyoming's human and natural history. **NOT TO BE MISSED:** Hands on history room with interactive exhibits.

Buffalo Bill Historical Center
720 Sheridan Ave., Cody, WY 82414
✆: 307-587-4771 ◙ www.bbhc.org
Open: 7am-8pm daily June-Sep,19, 8-8 daily May-8-5 daily Nov-Mar,!   **Closed:** THGV, 1/1, 12/25
Free Day: 1st Sa May   **ADM:** Adult: $10.00   Children: 6-17 $4.00   Students: $8.00   Seniors: $6.00
♿ ⓟ   **Museum Shop** ⏏ "Great Entertainer Eatery"   **Group Tours   Sculpture Garden**
Permanent Collection: WESTERN/ART: 19,20; AM: firearms; CULTURAL HISTORY OF THE PLAINS INDIANS

WYOMING

Buffalo Bill Historical Center - continued

The complex includes the Buffalo Bill, Plains Indian, and Cody Firearms museums as well as the Whitney Gallery which contains outstanding paintings of the American West by such artists as George Catlin, Albert Bierstadt, Frederic Remington and contemporary artists including Harry Jackson and Fritz Scholder. **NOT TO BE MISSED:** The Whitney Gallery of Western Art

ON EXHIBIT 2000
06/22/2000 to 09/17/2000   JOHN JAMES AUDUBON IN THE WEST: EXPLORING FOR THE QUADRUPEDS

COLTER BAY

Grand Teton National Park, Colter Bay Indian Arts Museum
Colter Bay, WY 83012

☎: 307-739-3594

Open: 8-5 daily 5/13-6/1 & Sept, 8-8 daily 6/1-LAB/DAY, closed 10/1-5/13   **Closed:** Closed 10/1-5/13

& Ⓟ   **Museum Shop**

Permanent Collection: NAT/AM: artifacts, beadwork, basketry, pottery, musical instruments

Organized into categories and themes, the Davis I. Vernon collection of Indian art housed in this museum is a spectacular assembly of many art forms including porcupine quillwork, beadwork, basketry, pottery, masks, and musical instruments. **NOT TO BE MISSED:** Sitting Bull's beaded blanket strip,(Sioux, South Dakota, ca. 1875

JACKSON HOLE

National Museum of Wildlife Art
P O Box 6825, Jackson Hole, WY 83002

☎: 307-733-5771   ◉   www.wqildlifeart.org

Open: 9-5 daily   **Closed:** 1/1, THGV, 12/25

ADM: Adult: $6.00   **Children:** Free under 6   **Students:** $5.00   **Seniors:** $5.00

& Ⓟ Free   **Museum Shop** ‖ café   **Group Tours   Drop-In Tours:** daily 11 am

Permanent Collection: WILDLIFE ART AND ARTIFACTS

One of the few museums in the country to feature wildlife, the collection is styled to sensitize visitors to Native American wildlife and the habitat necessary to sustain this priceless natural heritage. It is exhibited in a new facility. PLEASE NOTE: The museum offers special admission rates for families. **NOT TO BE MISSED:** Works by Carl Rungius

ON EXHIBIT 2000
Spring/2000 to 08/2000   JAPANESE WILDLIFE PHOTOGRAPHY

Spring/2000 to 09/2000   WORKS BY CHARLES LIVINGSTON BULL

08/18/2000 to 12/26/2000   POWERFUL IMAGES: PORTRAYALS OF NATIVE AMERICA
A consortium of ten museums dedicated to history, art and cultures of the West. The material offered is both Native and non-Native American perspectives.

11/12/2000 to Spring/2000   UNBROKEN SPIRIT: THE WILD HORSE IN THE AMERICAN LANDSCAPE
Original artwork, film footage, music and interactive media, painting a compelling picture of an animal which has captured the imagination of Americans for the past 4 centuries.

ROCK SPRINGS

Community Fine Arts Center
Affiliate Institution: Rock Springs Library
400 "C" Street, Rock Springs, WY 82901
☎: 307-362-6212
Open: 9-12 & 1-5 Mo - Fr ; We 6-9; 10-12 & 6-9 Sa   **Closed:** Su, LEG/HOL !
 ♿ Ⓟ
Drop-In Tours
Permanent Collection: AM: 19, 20

The art gallery houses the nationally acclaimed Rock Springs High School Collection, and is owned by the students. **NOT TO BE MISSED:** Loren McIver's "Fireplace", the first American women to exhibit at the Venice Biennial (1962).

Selected Listing of Traveling Exhibitions

2000 BC: THE BRUCE CONNER STORY PART II
10/10/1999 to 01/02/2000   Walker Art Center, Minneapolis, MN
02/06/2000 to 04/23/2000   Modern Art Museum of Fort Worth, Fort Worth, TX
05/21/2000 to 07/30/2000   Fine Arts Museums of San Francisco, San Francisco, CA

A CERAMIC CONTINUUM: FIFTY YEARS OF THE ARCHIE BRAY INFLUENCE
08/25/2000 to 10/28/2001   Boise Art Museum, Boise, ID
02/17/2002 to 04/14/2002   Dahl Fine Arts Center, Rapid City, SD

A MILLION AND ONE NIGHTS: ORIENTALISM AND AMERICAN CULTURE 1870-1930
02/03/2000 to 04/22/2000   Mint Museum of Art, Charlotte, NC
// to //2000   Sterling and Francine Clark Art Institute, Williamstown, MA

AMERICAN IMPRESSIONISM
06/17/2000 to 07/30/2000   Guild Hall Museum, East Hampton, NY
08/20/2000 to 10/29/2000   Minneapolis Institute of Arts, Minneapolis, MN
11/18/2000 to 02/04/2001   Munson-Williams Proctor Institute Museum of Art, Utica, NY

BARBARA KRUGER
10/17/1999 to 02/13/2000   Museum of Contemporary Art, Los Angeles, Los Angeles, CA
07/2000 to 10/2000   Whitney Museum of American Art, New York, NY

BEN SHAHN'S NEW YORK: THE PHOTOGRAPHY OF SOCIAL CONSCIENCE
02/05/2000 to 04/30/2000   Arthur M. Sackler Museum, Cambridge, MA
12/10/2000 to 02/25/2001   Wichita Art Museum, Wichita, KS

BERLIN METROPOLIS: JEWS AND THE NEW CULTURE, 1890-1918
11/14/1999 to 04/25/2000   Jewish Museum, New York, NY
04/01/2000 to 06/11/2000   Norton Museum of Art, West Palm Beach, FL

BIRDS IN ART
01/29/2000 to 03/26/2000   Saginaw Art Museum, Saginaw, MI
09/09/2000 to 11/12/2000   Leigh Yawkey Woodson Art Museum, Wausau, WI

BLURRING THE BOUNDARIES: INSTALLATION ART FROM THE SAN DIEGO MUSEUM OF
CONTEMPORARY ART
02/19/2000 to 04/09/2000   Jack S. Blanton Museum of Art, Austin, TX
05/20/2000 to 08/13/2000   San Jose Museum of Art, San Jose, CA

CELEBRATING THE CREATIVE SPIRIT: CONTEMPORARY SOUTHEASTERN FURNITURE
11/20/1999 to 01/02/2000   Montgomery Museum of Fine Arts, Montgomery, AL
01/15/2000 to 04/30/2000   Art Museum of Western Virginia, Roanoke, VA
05/28/2000 to 08/20/2000   Columbus Museum, Columbus, GA

CRAFTING A JEWISH STYLE : THE ART OF BEZALEL
01/15/2000 to 07/23/2000   Columbus Art Museum, Columbus,OH
08/26/2000 to 10/29/2000   Montgomery Museum of Fine Arts, Montgomery, AL

CROSSING THE THRESHOLD
11/13/1999 to 02/06/2000   Mississippi Museum of Art, Jackson, MS
03/31/2001 to 05/27/2001   Sioux City Art Center, Sioux City, IA

CUT FROM THE CLOTH OF LIFE: FABRIC COLLAGES OF ELIZABETH B NOYCE
09/22/1999 to 01/07/2000   Portland Museum of Art, Portland, ME
02/10/2000 to 04/30/2000   Farnsworth Art Museum and Wyeth Center, Rockland, ME

DALE CHIHULY: INSTALLATIONS
07/24/1999 to 01/16/2000   Mint Museum of Art, Charlotte, NC
02/12/2000 to 06/04/2000   Joslyn Art Museum, Omaha, NE

392

Selected Listing of Traveling Exhibitions

DALE CHIHULY: SEAFORMS
10/10/1999 to 01/02/2000   Indianapolis Museum of Art - Columbus Gallery, Columbus, IN
09/08/2000 to 11/12/2000   Fayetteville Museum of Art, Fayetteville, NC

DANCING AT THE LOUVRE: FAITH RINGGOLD'S STORY COLLECTION AND OTHER STORY QUILTS
11/26/1999 to 01/09/2000   Contemporary Art Center of Virginia, Virginia Beach, VA
01/23/2000 to 04/02/2000   Wichita Art Museum, Wichita, KS

DEGAS TO PICASSO: THE PAINTER, THE SCULPTOR AND THE CAMERA
10/02/1999 to 01/04/2000   San Francisco Museum of Modern Art, San Francisco, CA
01/30/2000 to 04/30/2000   Dallas Museum of Art, Dallas, TX

DO IT
01/14/2000 to 04/30/2000   Museum of Art, Fort Lauderdale, Ft. Lauderdale, FL
06/30/2000 to 08/26/2000   Scottsdale Museum of Contemporary Arts, Scottsdale, AZ

DREAMINGS: ABORIGINAL ART OF THE WESTERN DESERT FROM THE DONALD KAHN COLLECTION
12/11/1999 to 02/06/2000   Nevada Museum of Art/E. L. Weigand Gallery, Reno, NV
06/07/2000 to 08/13/2000   Museum of Fine Arts, Springfield, MA
06/19/2000 to 08/11/2000   Museum of Fine Arts, Missoula, MT

EARTH, FIRE AND WATER: CONTEMPORARY FORGED METAL
12/15/1999 to 03/10/2000   Dubuque Museum of Art, Dubuque, IA
07/05/1999 to 08/16/2000   Masur Museum of Art, Monroe, LA

EASTMAN JOHNSON: PAINTING AMERICA
10/29/1999 to 02/06/2000   Brooklyn Museum of Art, Brooklyn, NY
06/08/2000 to 09/10/2000   Seattle Art Museum, Seattle, WA

EDWARD HOPPER: THE WATERCOLORS
10/22/1999 to 01/03/2000   National Museum of American Art-Renwick Gallery -, Washington, DC
01/29/2000 to 03/26/2000   Montgomery Museum of Fine Arts, Montgomery, AL

FACES OF IMPRESSIONISM: PORTRAITS FROM AMERICAN COLLECTIONS
10/10/1999 to 01/30/2000   Baltimore Museum of Art, Baltimore, MD
03/25/2000 to 05/07/2000   Museum of Fine Arts, Houston, Houston, TX
05/28/2000 to 07/30/2000   Cleveland Museum of Art, Cleveland, OH

FACING DEATH: PORTRAITS FROM CAMBODIA'S KILLING FIELDS
01/02/2000 to 02/28/2000   Snite Museum of Art, Notre Dame, IN
04/01/2000 to 05/28/2000   Columbus Museum, Columbus, GA

FOUR OBJECTS; FOUR ARTISTS; TEN YEARS
11/12/1999 to 01/23/2000   Philip and Muriel Berman Museum of Art at Ursinus College, Collegeville, PA
02/2000 to 05/2000   Ogelthorpe University Museum, Atlanta, GA
06/24/2000 to 09/27/2000   Colorado Springs Fine Arts Center, Colorado Springs, CO
09/18/2000 to 12/15/2000   Hofstra Museum, Hempstead, NY

FROM SHIP TO SHORE : MARINE PAINTINGS
03/12/2000 to 05/07/2000   Mobile Museum of Art, Mobile, AL
01/08/2000 to 03/05/2000   Montgomery Museum of Fine Arts, Montgomery, AL
09/2000 to 10/2000   Mitchell Gallery, Annapolis, MD
11/05/2000 to 12/31/2000   Muskegon Museum of Art, Muskegon, MI

GEORGIA O'KEEFFE: THE POETRY OF THINGS
11/07/1999 to 01/30/2000   Dallas Museum of Art, Dallas, TX
02/19/2000 to 05/14/2000   Fine Arts Museums of San Francisco, San Francisco, CA

GIFTS OF PRIDE AND LOVE: THE CULTURAL SIGNIFICANCE OF KIOWA AND COMANCHE LATTICE
CRADLES
12/03/1999 to 02/27/2000   Gilcrease Museum, Tulsa, OK
04/2000 to 07/2000   Heard Museum, Phoenix, AZ

Selected Listing of Traveling Exhibitions

GIRLFRIEND! THE BARBIE SESSIONS BY DAVID LEVINTHAL
11/13/1999 to 01/16/2000   Norton Museum of Art, West Palm Beach, FL
07/09/2000 to 09/02/2000   Salina Art Center, Salina, KS
09/24/2000 to 12/31/2000   Birmingham Museum of Art, Birmingham, AL

GRANT WOOD AND MARVIN COHN: THE ORIGINS OF REGIONALISM
03/14/2000 to 07/02/2000   Dubuque Museum of Art, Dubuque, IA
07/22/2000 to 09/10/2000   Center for the Arts, Inc., Vero Beach, FL
02/03/2002 to 03/24/2002   Muskegon Museum of Art, Muskegon, MI

GREAT DESIGN: 100 MASTERPIECES FROM THE VITRA DESIGN MUSEUM COLLECTION
01/16/2000 to 04/09/2000   Allentown Art Museum, Allentown, PA
10/03/2000 to 03/04/2001   Cooper-Hewitt, National Design Museum, Smithsonian Institution, New York, NY

HALF PAST AUTUMN: THE ART OF GORDON PARKS
10/28/1999 to 01/02/2000   Norton Museum of Art, West Palm Beach, FL
02/05/2000 to 04/09/2000   Michael C. Carlos Museum, Atlanta, GA

HOT AND COOL CONTEMPORARY GLASS WORKS
11/21/1999 to 01/21/2000   Tyler Museum of Art, Tyler, TX
02/11/2000 to 04/06/2000   Washington Pavilion of Arts and Sciences, Sioux Falls, SD
04/27/2000 to 06/01/2000   Zanesville Art Center, Zanesville, OH

HOWARD BEN TRE: INTERIOR/EXTERIOR
12/15/1999 to 03/12/2000   Palm Springs Desert Museum, Palm Springs, CA
04/07/2000 to 06/11/2000   Scottsdale Museum of Contemporary Arts, Scottsdale, AZ

IN PRAISE OF NATURE: ANSEL ADAMS AND PHOTOGRAPHERS OF THE AMERICAN WEST
10/30/1999 to 10/02/2000   Dayton Art Institute, Dayton, OH
06/02/2000 to 08/11/2000   Orlando Museum of Art, Orlando, FL
10/08/2000 to 01/07/2000   North Carolina Museum of Art, Raleigh, NC

INNER EYE: CONTEMPORARY ART FROM THE MARK AND LIVIA STRAUS COLLECTION
10/22/1999 to 01/09/2000   Chrysler Museum of Art, Norfolk, VA
01/29/2000 to 04/14/2000   Neuberger Museum of Art, Purchase, NY

INNUENDO NON TROPPO: THE WORK OF GREGORY BARSAMIAN
12/10/1999 to 02/13/2000   Boise Art Museum, Boise, ID
04/16/1999 to 06/25/2000   San Jose Museum of Art, San Jose, CA

INSIDE OUT: NEW CHINESE ART
11/18/1999 to 03/05/2000   Henry Art Gallery, Seattle, WA
11/20/1999 to 05/03/2000   Tacoma Art Museum, Tacoma, WA

INVERTED ODYSSEYS: CLAUDE CAHUN, MAYA DEREN, CINDY SHERMAN
11/16/1999 to 01/29/2000   Grey Art Gallery, New York, NY
03/31/2000 to 05/28/2000   Joan Lehman Museum of Contemporary Art, North Miami, FL

JOHN SINGER SARGENT: THE WERTHEIMER PORTRAITS
11/07/1999 to 02/06/2000   Jewish Museum, New York, NY
03/03/2000 to 04/18/2000   New Orleans Museum of Art, New Orleans, LA
09/2000 to 11/2000   Ackland Art Museum, Chapel Hill, NC

JONATHAN LASKER: SELECTIVE IDENTITY, PAINTINGS FROM THE 1990'S
03/30/2000 to 05/28/2000   Rose Art Museum, Waltham, MA
06/25/2000 to 09/24/2000   Birmingham Museum of Art, Birmingham, AL

JULIE TAYMOR: PLAYING WITH FIRE
09/18/1999 to 01/02/2000   Wexner Center for the Arts, Columbus, OH
Spring 2000   Museum of Art, Fort Lauderdale, Ft. Lauderdale, FL

Selected Listing of Traveling Exhibitions

KENNETH TYLER: THIRTY YEARS OF PAINTING
11/05/1999 to 01/09/2000   Cornell Fine Arts Museum, Winter Park, FL
09/29/2000 to 11/26/2000   Lyman Allyn Museum at Connecticut College, New London, CT

KERRY JAMES MARSHALL
12/17/1999 to 02/27/2000   Santa Monica Museum of Art Bergamot Arts Center, Santa Monica, CA
05/20/2000 to 07/30/2000   Boise Art Museum, Boise, ID

LAND OF THE WINGED HORSEMEN: ART IN POLAND, 1571-1764
12/18/1999 to 02/27/2000   San Diego Museum of Art, San Diego, CA
03/26/2000 to 06/18/2000   Philbrook Museum of Art Inc, Tulsa, OK

LATINO ART: TREASURES FROM THE SMITHSONIAN'S MUSEUM OF AMERICAN ART
05/2000 to 07/2000   Saginaw Art Museum, Saginaw, MI
09/09/2000 to 11/14/2000   Wichita Art Museum, Wichita, KS
12/23/2000 to 02/25/2001   Orlando Museum of Art, Orlando, FL

LEWIS WICKES HINE: THE FINAL YEARS
12/04/1999 to 02/06/2000   New Orleans Museum of Art, New Orleans, LA
04/07/2000 to 06/04/2000   Greenville County Museum of Art, Greenville, SC

LIBERATED VOICES: CONTEMPORARY SOUTH AFRICAN ART SINCE MANDELA
09/15/1999 to 01/03/2000   Museum for African Art, New York, NY
05/11/2000 to 08/20/2000   Austin Museum of Art-Downtown, Austin, TX

MARTIN JOHNSON HEADE
02/13/2000 to 05/07/2000   Boston Museum of Fine Arts, Boston, MA
02/13/2000 to 05/07/2000   National Gallery of Art, Washington, DC
05/28/2000 to 08/14/2000   Los Angeles Country Museum of Art, Los Angeles, CA

MAXFIELD PARRISH, 1870-1966
11/26/1999 to 01/23/2000   Currier Gallery of Art, Manchester, NH
02/18/2000 to 04/20/2000   Memorial Art Gallery, Rochester, NY
05/26/2000 to 08/06/2000   Brooklyn Museum of Art, Brooklyn, NY

MIRIAM SHAPIRO: A RETROSPECTIVE
12/11/1999 to 03/05/2000   Polk Museum of Art, Lakeland, FL
03/11/2000 to 05/07/2000   Museum of Art and Science/Brevard, Melbourne, FL
12/02/2000 to 02/11/2001   Hunter Museum of American Art, Chattanooga, TN

MONET TO MOORE: THE MILLENNIUM GIFT OF THE SARA LEE CORPORATION
11/19/1999 to 01/23/2000   Portland Art Museum, Portland, OR
03/2000 to 05/2000   Art Institute of Chicago, Chicago, IL

NARRATIVES OF AFRICAN AMERICAN ART AND IDENTITY: THE DAVID C. DRISKELL COLLECTION
03/19/2000 to 05/14/2000   Cincinnati Art Museum, Cincinnati, OH
07/21/2000 to 10/17/2000   Colby College Museum of Art, Waterville, ME

NO ORDINARY LAND: ENCOUNTERS IN A CHANGING ENVIRONMENT
03/11/2000 to 06/04/2000   James A. Michener Art Museum, Doylestown, PA
10/08/2000 to 12/31/2000   Columbus Museum, Columbus, GA

OLD MASTER DRAWINGS FROM THE COLLECTION OF ALFRED MOIR
11/06/1999 to 01/09/2000   Wiregrass Museum of Art, Dothan, AL
10/10/2000 to 12/10/2000   Palmer Museum of Art, University Park, PA

ON THE ROAD WITH THOMAS HART BENTON: IMAGES OF A CHANGING AMERICA
11/14/1999 to 01/09/2000   George Walter Vincent Smith Art Museum, Springfield, MA
04/29/2000 to 06/25/2000   Frye Art Museum, Seattle., WA
10/08/2000 to 12/03/2000   Gilcrease Museum, Tulsa, OK

Selected Listing of Traveling Exhibitions

PARIS 1900: THE "AMERICAN SCHOOL" AT THE UNIVERSAL EXPOSITION
09/28/1999 to 1/16/2000   Montclair Art Museum, Montclair, NJ
02/12/2000 to 04/14/2000   Museum of American Art of the Pennsylvania Academy of the Fine Arts, Philadelphia, PA
05/19/2000 to 08/13/2000   Columbus Museum, Columbus, GA
09/16/2000 to 12/03/2000   Elvehjem Museum of Art, Madison, WI

PICASSO CERAMIC EDITION FROM THE EDWARD WESTON COLLECTION
03/2000 to 04/2000   Mitchell Gallery, Annapolis, MD
06/17/2000 to 08/13/2000   Montgomery Museum of Fine Arts, Montgomery, AL

POWERFUL IMAGES: PORTRAYALS OF NATIVE AMERICA
11/13/1999 to 03/19/2000   Heard Museum, Phoenix, AZ
05/06/2000 to 07/16/2000   Gilcrease Museum, Tulsa, OK
08/18/2000 to 12/26/2000   National Museum of Wildlife Art, Jackson Hole, WY

PURE VISION: AMERICAN BEAD ARTISTS
11/04/1999 to 01/28/2000   Islip Art Museum, East Islip, NY
01/28/2000 to 03/16/2000   Fuller Museum of Art, Brockton, MA

REFLECTIONS IN THE LOOKING GLASS: A CENTENARY LEWIS CARROLL EXHIBITION
04/22/2000 to 06/04/2000   Dayton Art Institute, Dayton, OH
09/20/2000 to 10/29/2000   Ackland Art Museum, Chapel Hill, NC

ROBERT GWATHMEY:1903-88
06/18/2000 to 08/13/2000   Museum of American Art of the Pennsylvania Academy of the Fine Arts, Philadelphia, PA
03/12/2000 to 05/28/2000   Telfair Museum of Art, Savannah, GA

RODIN: SCULPTURE FROM THE IRIS AND B. GERALD CANTOR COLLECTION
01/22/2000 to 03/26/2000   Dayton Art Institute, Dayton, OH
04/16/2000 to 08/13/2000   North Carolina Museum of Art, Raleigh, NC
09/21/2000 to 12/31/2000   Chrysler Museum of Art, Norfolk, VA

SALVADOR DALI'S OPTICAL ILLUSIONS
01/21/2000 to 03/26/2000   Wadsworth Atheneum, Hartford, CT
04/20/2000 to 06/25/2000   Hirshhorn Museum and Sculpture Garden, Washington, DC

SEARCHING FOR ANCIENT EGYPT: ART, ARCHITECTURE, AND ARTIFACTS FROM THE UNIV. OF PA...
10/03/1999 to 01/16/2000   Birmingham Museum of Art, Birmingham, AL
03/16/2000 to 07/30/2000   Honolulu Academy of Arts, Honolulu, HI

SHEER REALITIES: POWER AND CLOTHING IN THE NINETEENTH CENTURY PHILIPPINES
02/16/2000 to 04/22/2000   Grey Art Gallery, New York, NY
07/01/2000 to 01/01/2001   Seattle Asian Art Museum, Seattle, WA

STROGANOFF: THE PALACE AND COLLECTIONS OF A RUSSIAN NOBLE FAMILY
02/19/2000 to 05/31/2000   Portland Art Museum, Portland, OR
07/02/2000 to 10/01/2000   Kimbell Art Museum, Fort Worth, TX

SUNLIGHT AND SHADOW: AMERICAN IMPRESSIONISM
12/11/1999 to 01/30/2000   Museum of Art and Science/Brevard, Melbourne, FL
02/19/2000 to 04/12/2000   Tucson Museum of Art, Tucson, AZ
07/09/2000 to 08/20/2000   Rahr-West Art Museum, Manitowoc, WI

THE ART OF 20TH CENTURY ZEN: PAINTINGS AND CALLIGRAPHY BY JAPANESE MASTERS
10/29/1999 to 01/02/2000   Los Angeles County Museum of Art, Los Angeles, CA
01/29/2000 to 03/11/2000   Spencer Museum of Art, Lawrence, KS

THE ART OF NELLIE MAE ROWE: NINETY NINE AND A HALF WON'T DO
11/20/1999 to 02/26/2000   High Museum of Art, Atlanta, GA
03/18/2000 to 05/14/2000   African American Museum, Dallas, TX

THE GILDED AGE: TREASURES FROM THE SMITHSONIAN'S NATIONAL MUSEUM OF AMERICAN ART
06/27/2000 to 08/27/2000   Hunter Museum of American Art, Chattanooga, TN
09/24/2000 to 11/19/2000   Wichita Art Museum, Wichita, KS

Selected Listing of Traveling Exhibitions

THE GREAT AMERICAN POP ART STORE: MULTIPLES OF THE SIXTIES
11/23/1999 to 01/02/2000   Joslyn Art Museum, Omaha, NE
02/10/2000 to 04/02/2000   Lowe Art Museum, Coral Gables, FL

THE HUMAN FACTOR: FIGURATION IN AMERICAN ART, 1950-1995
02/2000 to 03/2000   Philharmonic Center for the Arts, Naples, FL
12/03/2000 to 02/04/2001   Albany Museum of Art, Albany, GA

THE JOHN A. AND MARGERET HILL COLLECTION OF AMERICAN WESTERN ART
09/03/2000 to 10/15/2000   Rahr-West Art Museum, Manitowoc, WI
11/05/2000 to 12/21/2000   Sioux City Art Center, Sioux City, IA

THE KINGDOMS OF EDWARD HICKS
10/10/1999 to 01/02/2000   Philadelphia Museum of Art, Philadelphia, PA
02/12/2000 to 04/30/2000   Denver Art Museum, Denver, CO
09/24/2000 to 01/07/2001   Fine Arts Museums of San Francisco, San Francisco, CA

THE MYSTICAL ARTS OF TIBET
02/03/2000 to 04/30/2000   Museum of Fine Arts, Springfield, MA
11/18/2000 to 01/14/2001   Bayly Art Museum of the University of Virginia, Charlottesville, VA

THE POTTERS OF MATA ORTIZ: TRANSFORMING A TRADITION
06/09/2000 to 08/11/2000   Plains Art Museum, Fargo, ND
11/04/2000 to 01/07/2001   Lakeview Museum of Arts and Sciences, Peoria, IL

THE ROYAL ACADEMY IN THE AGE OF QUEEN VICTORIA (1837-1901): 19TH CENTURY PAINTINGS
01/15/2000 to 03/12/2000   Norton Museum of Art, West Palm Beach, FL
07/16/2000 to 09/24/2000   Cincinnati Art Museum, Cincinnati, OH

THE WORK OF CHARLES AND RAY EAMES: A LEGACY OF INVENTION
10/12/1999 to 1/09/2000   Cooper-Hewitt, National Design Museum, Smithsonian Institution, New York, NY
02/19/2000 to 05/14/2000   Saint Louis Art Museum, St. Louis, MO

TO CONSERVE A LEGACY: AMERICAN ART FROM HISTORICALLY BLACK COLLEGES AND UNIVERSITIES
11/20/1999 to 01/31/2000   Corcoran Gallery of Art, Washington, DC
02/19/2000 to 04/30/2000   Art Institute of Chicago, Chicago, IL
6/29/2000 to 09/24/2000   High Museum of Art, Atlanta, GA
10/15/2000 to 12/01/2000   Duke University Museum of Art, Durham, NC

TO HAVE AND TO HOLD: 115 YEARS OF WEDDING FASHIONS
01/29/2000 to 08/06/2000   Flint Institute of Arts, Flint, MI
05/06/2000 to 08/12/2000   Mint Museum of Art, Charlotte, NC

TRASHFORMATIONS: RECYCLED MATERIALS IN CONTEMPORARY AMERICAN ART AND DESIGN
11/07/1999 to 01/02/2000   Anchorage Museum of History and Art, Anchorage, AK
04/29/2000 to 07/25/2000   Yellowstone Art Museum, Billings, MT

TWENTIETH- CENTURY STILL LIFE PAINTINGS FROM THE PHILLIPS COLLECTION
03/11/2000 to 05/21/2000   Orlando Museum of Art, Orlando, FL
06/11/2000 to 08/20/2000   Memorial Art Gallery, Rochester, NY

WILLIAM KENTRIDGE: WEIGHING... AND WANTING
01/21/2000 to 03/18/2000   Forum For Contemporary Art, St. Louis, MO
04/09/2000 to 06/25/2000   Salina Art Center, Salina, KS

WRAPPED IN PRIDE: GHANIAN KENTE AND AFRICAN AMERICAN IDENTITY
09/12/1999 to 01/02/2000   National Museum of African Art, Washington, DC
11/19/2000 to 02/25/2001   Anchorage Museum of History and Art, Anchorage, AK

YOUNG AMERICA: TREASURES FROM THE SMITHSONIAN'S MUSEUM OF AMERICAN ART
03/01/2000 to 05/21/2000   Greenville County Museum of Art, Greenville, SC
06/21/2000 to 08/13/2000   Delaware Art Museum, Wilmington, DE
09/10/2000 to 11/05/2000   Columbus Museum, Columbus, GA

WORLDWIDE

Discount Coupon

Present this coupon at the Acoustiguide Counter
and receive $1.00 off on an Acoustiguide Tour

Discount Coupon

Selected Listing of Acoustiguide Exhibitions

Acoustiguide Special Exhibition Audio Programs – 2000
(list in progress)

The Museum of Modern Art – MoMA 2000 (all three cycles)

The Southwest Museum – Down from the Shimmering Sky

Museum of Contemporary Art, Chicago – At the End of the Century: 100 Years of Architecture

Portland Art Museum – Stroganoff

Walters Art Gallery – Gold of the Nomads

Mingei Folk Museum – Georgia Show

Detroit Institute of Arts – Van Gogh Face to Face

Asian Art Museum of San Francisco – Golden Age of Chinese Archeology

San Diego Museum of Art – The Topkapi Palace: Jewels and Treasures of the Sultans

Acoustiguide Permanent Collection Audio Programs (U.S. Only)

Allentown Art Museum
Bruce Museum
Detroit Institute of Art
Isabella Stewart Gardner Museum
Mercer Museum
Mid-Atlantic Center for the Arts
Mingei International Museum
Museum of Contemporary Art, Chicago
Museum of Contemporary Art, San Diego
Norton Museum of Art
Pennsylvania Academy of Fine Arts
Santa Barbara Museum of Art
Solomon R. Guggenheim Museum
The Chrysler Museum
The Fine Arts Museum of San Francisco, The Palace of the Legion of Honor
The Frick Collection
The Museum of Modern Art
The National Gallery of Art
The Nelson-Atkins Museum of Art
The Philadelphia Museum of Art
The Portland Art Museum
The Toledo Museum of Art
Virginia Museum of Fine Arts
Walker Art Center

Alphabetical Listing of Museums

Alphabetical Listing of Museums

Alphabetical Listing of Museums

Alphabetical Listing of Museums

Alphabetical Listing of Museums

Alphabetical Listing of Museums

Alphabetical Listing of Museums

410

411

Alphabetical Listing of Museums

412

Alphabetical Listing of Museums

ABOUT THE AUTHOR

Judith Swirsky has been associated with the arts in Brooklyn as both staff and volunteer for more than forty years. The recipient of many awards, she has held both curatorial and volunteer administration positions at The Brooklyn Museum. While Executive Director of the Grand Central Art Galleries Educational Association she coordinated the 1989 Moscow Conference. She is now an independent curator and artists' representative. She is listed in *Who's Who of American Women.*